Listen

Third Edition

Listen

Third Edition

Joseph Kerman

University of California
at Berkeley

with Vivian Kerman

Worth Publishers, Inc.

Listen

Third Edition

Printed in the United States of America
Library of Congress Catalog Card No. 79-56787
ISBN: 0-87901-127-0
Designed by Malcolm Grear Designers

Type set by Progressive Typographers
Music set by Melvin Wildberger, Inc.
Picture Editors: Anne Feldman and June Lundborg
Printed and bound by R. R. Donnelley & Sons Co.
Third printing: November 1985

Cover: (Detail) and Frontispiece:
Mexican Musicians
Raoul Dufy
Oil, 39⅜″ × 31½″
Le Musée des Beaux Arts Jules Chéret
Nice, France

Worth Publishers, Inc.
444 Park Avenue South
New York, New York 10016

Preface

The third, expanded edition of LISTEN differs from its predecessors in one significant respect. The early editions concentrated on music from Bach to the present (with a dip back to the late sixteenth century). The more comprehensive third edition covers the whole span of Western music history, starting with Gregorian chant and continuing through late medieval, Renaissance, and early baroque music. Also included are two new chapters on popular music, the first viewing this topic in a broad historical perspective, and the second focusing on twentieth-century America.

A certain amount of revision has taken place, too, notably in the introductory *Vocabulary for Music* chapters (see below). But the present edition is best regarded as an expansion. None of the salient features of the original LISTEN has been abandoned or diluted.

In all of its metamorphoses, the main strengths of the book (we are now sure) have been three. First, the emphasis is on music, not on history, theory, or listening techniques in the abstract. As far as possible, theoretical and historical data are introduced, not for their own sake and not for the sake of "memorization," but in order to help convey the aesthetic qualities of actual pieces of music to which students *listen.* Second, each of the main chapters begins with a general stylistic overview of the historical period in question; this serves as a conceptual focus for understanding and teaching the music that follows. And third, short picture essays or inserts, set aside from the main text, present aspects of cultural history that can stir students' interest and perhaps also stimulate their musical response.

These features were at the heart of our original conception, and it has been gratifying to find them mentioned repeatedly when we have received positive (and sometimes enthusiastic) responses from teachers and students. The particular compositions treated have been carefully reconsidered, and a number of substitutions have been made for those that proved less successful for teaching purposes. But apart from this, teachers accustomed to the second edition of LISTEN will find little change in the central chapters, those covering music from the late baroque period to the present.

The entire text, however, has been repunctuated: that is to say, many new subheads have been introduced within the chapters—and the original chapters (some of which ran up to seventy-five pages) have been subdivided. All this necessitated a new design, one that is no less lucid and handsome, we think, than the original LISTEN. It is amazing how much structural changes of this kind can do to make a book easier to read—and easier to assign. The prose looks less forbidding, patterns of organization seem clearer, and the main points stand out as such with new emphasis.

The *Vocabulary for Music* section, which begins the book, is now organized as two chapters. We start with a very basic chapter and follow it with a more advanced one (including some topics we conceive of as optional). Chapter 1 deals with rhythm, dynamics, tone color, pitch, and melody. This chapter has, as an appendix, a much expanded, step-by-step explanation of musical notation—which students with musical background can skip, but which most other students will appreciate. Then, in Chapter 2, come those "fundamentals" which, for all their fundamentality, present greater conceptual problems: polyphonic textures, harmony, tonality and modality (for those teachers who wish to introduce these topics), musical form, and style. We think this two-chapter unit provides a logical, simple, graded approach to material that most of us agree is vitally important to get across to our students, and yet is also perhaps the hardest of all to present effectively in a book.

Early editions of LISTEN included a students' vinyl record with short examples attempting to demonstrate points made in the *Vocabulary for Music* section. Somewhat reluctantly, we have decided to drop this feature because, although the principle it represents still seems good in theory, we have come to see that the little record was not very practical. Logistics worked against it. While most teachers went along with the idea behind it, rather few found it to be of much use in their actual teaching.

Some teachers, especially those involved in shorter courses, will not wish to stress notation. They will find it easy enough to skip the occasional "line scores" in this book. Our discussion is quite complete without these scores—it does *not* proceed on the assumption that all students will actually be able to read music! But, as many teachers have discovered, simplified scores and listening guides are an added help to students who can follow along in a general way—and need not frighten the others. Indeed, to meet a real demand for such aids we have provided more line scores and numerous listening guides in the *Instructor's Resource Book*. This Resource Book also includes discussions of alternate selections and composers that some teachers may prefer to use, as well as suggested test questions. The tear-out format should make all this material easy to use.

Also expanded is the record set accompanying this book. Seventy-five percent of the compositions discussed are represented in whole or in part on the ten-record album available for student purchase. The supplementary record, which is distributed gratis to teachers and which students can also purchase, brings this figure up to eighty-five percent. The supplementary record contains extra examples from the Middle Ages, the Renaissance, the early baroque period, and the twentieth century, periods that are likely to be covered less extensively in some courses. Especially for these periods, the recordings have been selected with great care; indeed, very often the choice of music to discuss was determined by the availability of a striking, attractive recording.

Though the main emphasis of this book is not on history, its coverage is now such that some teachers may find it well suited to music history courses. If others might hesitate about using a larger LISTEN in short courses, we remind them that a larger book means more flexibility at no great increase in price. As just remarked, the chapters on early and twentieth-century music are the most likely to be bypassed, so we have made sure that the text is complete without them. In particular, teachers who wish to begin with the late baroque period will find it a natural starting place, after the *Vocabulary for Music.*

In conclusion, there is a thought that did not strike us particularly when we started to work on LISTEN ten years ago, but which seems worth making in today's textbook market. This is a coherent book. Each aspect of it has proceeded, if not from a single mind, at least from two minds that have been blending (or grinding) together over quite a long time. A single point of view, sensibility, and writing style inform all sixteen of the chapters; we ourselves decided on the material, wrote the prose, found the pictures, selected the performances of the album, and even juggled bands to assure at least a full twenty-six minutes on every side. The abrupt changes of attitude and expression sometimes encountered in other books, when different "experts" deal with different topics, will not disorient or divert readers of LISTEN.

And what is most important, perhaps, is that in expanding the scope of the book we have granted older music and popular music the same integrity, as aesthetic experience, that we previously accorded to the more traditional repertory. There is no tokenism here. Introductory courses should emphasize listening to music, the experience of music, not merely facts about it: everyone seems agreed on this point. The focus must be on aesthetic experience. This has always been my (JK) impetus as a teacher and writer on music for thirty years, and it has always been our guiding principle in writing, and rewriting, this textbook.

ACKNOWLEDGMENTS

Harry N. Abrams, Inc., cordially granted permission to reprint some sentences by the second author of *A History of Art and Music,* by H. W. Janson and Joseph Kerman (Harry N. Abrams and Prentice-Hall, 1968). Professor and Mrs. Janson also provided us with some of our original illustrations, as did H. H. Arnason (the superb Houdon photographs) and Alfred Frankenstein. Juanita Newland, Peter Kerman, and Joel Selvin contributed precious details to the book in the areas of musical instruments, jazz, and rock, respectively.

For their advice about improvements for the third edition, we are beholden to a small symphony of musicians and teachers. Professors Mark Gridley, George Hill, Ken Kennemer, James Mason, Joanne Hickey Prolo, Joan Ringerwole, and Martha Wurtz have sent us criticisms and suggestions—some of them extremely shrewd, thoughtful, and detailed—which have been literally invaluable. Several of our friends have done the same: Jane Bernstein, Josh Berrett, Jon Elkus, Dominic Intili, Owen Jander, and Robert Trotter. To Peter Gano, Robert Davis, and particularly another old friend, Marvin Tartak, we are especially grateful for their extensive work on the *Instructor's Resource Book.*

Finally, Worth Publishers—who exasperate us by forbidding mention in this space of individual members of the company. Otherwise they continue to amaze and inspire us. There is no one like them to work with. Humane values and inhuman work schedules are their stock in trade.

JOSEPH AND VIVIAN KERMAN
Berkeley, California
January 1980

Contents

CHAPTER 1 | A Vocabulary for Music   I

A Vocabulary for Music   I

Music appeals to the ear and the mind, to the senses and the intelligence, to emotion and intellect. We cannot generalize very far about these components of music's appeal, if only because the musical experience seems to differ so much with different listeners. Some people are physically excited by listening to music; some are exhilarated by following its intricate patterns. Other people will tell you that it gives them a sense of solace and serenity, and still others derive from it an almost mystical insight into the order of life, feeling, the cosmos. Everybody likes music of some kind, to some degree, and people's responses to it are various indeed.

But there is nearly always some combination of feeling and thinking in our responses to music, some combination of emotional and intellectual elements. This is the case with popular music, just as much as it is with the more self-consciously "artistic" music of the concert hall. It is true that many music lovers claim to enjoy music only for its emotional side, not for its intellectual side. Sometimes they proclaim this quite belligerently. But these people might ask themselves—for a start—whether the third or thirtieth time they listen to a song, a rock number, or a symphony, they have the same "gut reaction" they had the first time, in just the same way. Is not memory now a consideration, and is not memory an intellectual process?

However this may be, listening to particular pieces of music again and again is clearly an activity of major importance. It is *the* basic activity that contributes to the love of music and to its understanding; such, at least, is the belief underlying the present book, which consists mostly of accounts of musical compositions—symphonies, concertos, songs, and operas—that are well worth listening to many times. The accounts are designed to clarify the contents of these works and their aesthetic quality: what goes on in the music and how this affects us. Some material is also provided on the historical and cultural backgrounds of the various pieces, but the main emphasis falls on the music itself.

If a text is going to be of any real aid in the listening process, obviously it must be written in a language that fits the job at hand. We have to use a set of terms by which features in music can be referred to and described. A first task, then, is to develop a vocabulary for music—a special vocabulary that will allow the authors of this book to talk sensibly to the readers, and that will form the basis for clear discussion between teachers and students.

This vocabulary will not be entirely new to anyone. Its terms and concepts are, of course, the ones used by professional musicians. Some readers will have met them before at their music lessons, at choir practice, or while playing with a group. However, there is a basic difference in the use we wish to make of these terms. The idea is not to probe "the elements of music" for their own sake, however important this may be to the specialist. Certainly the idea is not to learn how to make music, which is the musician's real province. What we need is a way of talking *about* music, not a way of making it: a vocabulary *for* music, not a vocabulary *of* music.

Our stake in musical notation also differs from the professional musician's. Again, the idea is not to convey how to write down music or read it accurately, but merely how to follow it and gain a general sense of its patterns. Short music examples and simplified full-length "line scores" are not hard to learn to use, and, once this is accomplished, the music becomes clearer. Following with the eye helps us to focus on the things we need to catch with the ear—helps us, that is, to listen.

TECHNICAL AND NONTECHNICAL LANGUAGE

The prospect of learning a vocabulary for music often meets with some resistance on the ground that the terminology is unduly "technical." Some people seem to get really upset at the thought of associating dry, precise language with something as beautiful as music. But if we want to talk with any degree of precision about any special field, we have to use its own special, technical language. Music is no different from any other field in this respect. It is useful to understand what *shortstop* and *double play* mean even if we are not actually playing baseball, just watching it on television. Those are among baseball's technical terms.

One other point. Technical fields often assign meanings to certain words that differ somewhat from their everyday, nontechnical meanings. *Rhythmical* is one such word (and one of the first we shall consider); *sequence* is another. We are familiar with the problem from other fields, such as physics, which requires specialized definitions of such concepts as force, energy, and acceleration. In ordinary conversation, of course, such terms can always be used more loosely. Even after taking a physics course, no one is likely to shrink from saying, "She is a forceful character," or "He doesn't seem to have much energy tonight." But, for the purpose of understanding a special field, it is necessary to keep a clear idea of the limited meanings that field assigns to technical concepts: force and energy in physics, or rhythm, harmony, and melody in music.

Our order of topics is as follows. First we take up a number of concepts having to do with music in time: rhythm, meter, and tempo. Then we move on to the various properties of sound—dynamics, tone color, pitch. And from there we go to melody, musical texture, form, and, finally, musical style.

Rhythm

Music exists in time, just as painting exists on a flat surface, and sculpture and architecture exist in the three-dimensional world. Sounds mark off spans of time, as lines and brush strokes mark off areas on a canvas. Arranging sounds in time, then, is the composer's basic task—or at least this is one way of looking at that task. Some modern composers have chosen to do this in a random way. But for others (and they are the great majority) the art of composing comes in determining the length and weight of every sound or note* in their compositions. Music becomes a complex web of sound relationships in time.

rhythm

Rhythm, in the most general sense, is the term referring to the whole time aspect of music.

ACCENT

duration

accent

The term *rhythm* can also be used in a less general sense—and usually is. Before coming to this, we need to introduce the concepts of *duration* and *accent*. Duration is simply the length of notes. It can be compared to the length of lines in a drawing, for we speak of a "length of time" as well as length in space. A composer not only fixes the duration of his notes but also emphasizes some of them, just as an artist emphasizes some of his lines by such means as heavy shading. In music, emphasis of this sort is called accent. No single feature of music, not even melody, determines the effect of music more crucially than the timing and weighting of notes: duration and accent.

dynamic accent

There are many ways of accenting a note. A simple way—the way we think of first—is to have it played louder than its neighbors. This is called a dynamic accent (the word *dynamics* is used in music for loudness: see page 11). An even simpler way is to make the note relatively long and surround it by shorter neighbors. It will not be necessary to play the long note louder; it will sound accented and stand out from the others just because of its duration. Using a note that is higher than its neighbors is another way of providing it with a subtle accent.

In the most general sense, as we have said, the term *rhythm* refers to the whole time aspect of music. In a more specific sense, *a rhythm* or *the rhythm of a certain passage* refers to the particular arrangement of long and short notes in that passage and their accents.

Musical notation has developed its own system of signs to indicate the relative lengths of notes and to indicate accents. Some readers will already know this system, but those who are not familiar with it should refer to pages 23–33.

---

* The word *note,* common as it is, can prove to be slightly tricky in usage. It can mean either (1) a sound of a certain definite, single pitch and duration, (2) the written or printed sign for such a sound in musical notation, or even (3) one of the keys pressed with the finger on a piano or organ (as in "the white notes" of the piano).

The rhythm of *My country 'tis of thee* is notated thus:

My coun-try 'tis of thee, Sweet land of lib - er - ty, Of thee I sing

The sign > indicates a dynamic accent, called *sforzato* or *sforzando* from the Italian word meaning forced. You will sometimes hear musicians call it a *sforz.* An especially strong accent is sometimes indicated by the abbreviation **sf** or **sfz.**

The rhythm is changed if the same note durations are provided with different dynamic accents. At Christmas time *Jingle bells* is usually accented as follows:

Jin - gle bells, jin - gle bells, jin - gle all the way - (ay) —

The sleighbells jingle happily and provide accents thick and fast, including two on the single word "way." Fewer accents would produce a slightly different rhythm and a more relaxed feeling:

Jin - gle bells, jin - gle bells, jin - gle all the way —

Here is an alternative accentuation that forces us to read the words in an interesting way:

Jin - gle bells, jin - gle bells, jin - gle all the way —

And here is a hypothetical accentuation producing yet another rhythm—one that turns the words into nonsense, for it contradicts the natural accents of speech:

Jin - gle bells, jin - gle bells, jin - gle all the way —

METER

With most music, our minds do not experience rhythms strictly in their own terms. Back of the rhythms, we instinctively hear a regular pulse of beats in a simple recurring pattern. So long as the music is not too complicated, we find the beat almost automatically by beating it out with a hand or a foot. If we try this with *My country 'tis of thee,* it seems natural to tap once on each of the first three notes, "My country." Then we keep going at the same rate, though the beats do not quite fit the notes at " 'tis of," and three beats are required for the single note at "sing." This seems intuitively right to most people.

What is more, we tend to group these beats into a simple pattern, consisting of one accented beat and one or more unaccented ones. This repeating pattern of beats is called the <u>meter</u>. While listening to a rhythm, then, we organize it in our minds according to the regular pattern of the meter:

meter

My coun-try 'tis   of thee, Sweet land of   lib - er-ty,   Of thee I   sing
1   2   3 | 1   2   3 | 1   2   3 | 1   2   3 | 1   2   3 | 1   2   3

Another similar example:

Oh what a   beau-ti-ful morn - in',   Oh what a   beau-ti-ful   day,_____
1   2   3 | 1   2   3 | 1   2   3 | 1   2   3 | 1   2   3 | 1   2   3 | 1   2   3 |

The process of beating time consists of marking out the strong (accented) beats and the weak (unaccented) beats that make up the meter. In the above two examples, we beat: ONE two three ONE two three ONE two three, etc. Meter is a way of organizing time into simple units, the simplest units beyond the basic level of the beat itself.

The organization or division of time is made by the steady repetition of the accented beats, as we have said. The resulting unit, composed of a principal strong beat and one or more weaker ones, is called a <u>measure</u>, or *bar*. Measures are indicated by vertical lines in the above diagram. In a score, these verticals are called *bar lines.*

measure

There are only two basic kinds of meter, plus a third that amounts to a combination of the other two: duple meter, triple meter, and compound meter.

Duple Meter   In this meter, the beats are grouped in twos (ONE two ONE two ONE two). Duple meter is probably most familiar from marches, which almost always use it in deference to the human anatomy—LEFT right LEFT right LEFT right. "Almost always," because at least one composer, Robert Schumann, amused himself by ending his piano composition *Carnaval* with a three-legged march in triple meter. He had a special reason for this, as we shall see.

Triple Meter   In triple meter the beats are grouped in threes (ONE two three ONE two three). Triple meter is the characteristic meter of waltzes, such as *The blue Danube, Take me out to the ballgame,* and *Oh what a beautiful mornin'.* It also happens to be the meter of our national songs *My country 'tis of thee* and *The star-spangled banner.* In the early Middle Ages almost all music was in triple meter, but in later times duple meter became more common. Triple meter is especially rare in jazz.

Experiments with more complicated meters, going into five beats, seven beats, and so on, can be found as early as the sixteenth century, but they have never entered into general use. Also important, however, is the combination of duple and triple meter known as *compound meter.*

Compound Meter In this meter, each *main* beat is subdivided into three subsidiary beats. The most common type of compound meter has six beats, subdivided into two subgroups (ONE two three *four* five six). On the highest level it amounts to a kind of duple meter, but it is classified as compound meter when each of the two main beats is broken down into three smaller ones.

Good examples of compound meter are afforded by those two favorite rounds, *Three blind mice* and *Row, row, row your boat.* In each of these, we start out counting a moderately slow ONE two ("Three blind" and "Row, row"). But by the time we get to "cut off their tails with a" and "merrily, merrily," we see that the basic two beats are each subdivided into three faster ones, for a total of six. The notes are three times as fast. This is compound meter.

What is the difference between one measure of this kind of compound meter (ONE two three *four* five six) and two measures of triple meter (ONE two three ONE two three)? Not much, usually. The composer wants the *four* beat accented more strongly than the five and six but does not want it accented as strongly as a ONE. It is always possible to beat compound meter measures as two measures each of triple meter, but the result is likely to be too heavy and fussy or, if the music is fast, frantic.

In nearly all the music we hear, duple, triple, or compound meter serves as the regular background against which the more complicated course of the rhythm is measured or heard. As the rhythm momentarily coincides with the meter, then goes its own way, and then perhaps even contradicts or obscures the meter, all kinds of variety, tension, and excitement can result. It is the interaction of rhythm and meter that supplies much of the real vitality to music.

One way of contradicting the meter is to displace the accents away from

syncopation their normal places. This is called syncopation. An example of simple syncopation is the displacing of accents in duple meter so that the accents go one TWO one TWO instead of the normal ONE two ONE two. A certain amount of syncopation occurs in nearly all music, but it becomes especially important in jazz. We shall look more closely at syncopation in chapter 16, when we discuss American popular music.

METRICAL MUSIC AND NONMETRICAL MUSIC

Marches and dances, which exist in order to stimulate body movements, always emphasize the meter in a strong, obvious way. Most popular music has a heavy beat, too, because meter gives rise to a very basic (and therefore "popular") emotional response. All this we would call strongly metrical music.

Other kinds of music are less strongly metrical. The metrical underpinning is not always emphasized, or even explicitly beaten out at all, in back of the rhythm. It does not need to be, for the listener can almost always feel it under the surface. People will even imagine they hear a simple duple or triple meter in the steady dripping of a faucet or the click of a motor. The psychological reason for this probably lies in the fact that simple repetitive patterns of stress/unstress underlie so many of our basic life functions: the heartbeat, breathing, walking, as well as more obvious activities such as dancing and marching.

We observed a moment ago that the interaction of rhythm and meter is characteristic of most music. However, there are certain kinds of music that do without meter. Listening to them may help focus our understanding of both meter and rhythm. For example, if you have access to the record set accompanying this book, play a portion of John Cage's *Aria* and *Fontana Mix* on side 19. The various astonishing sounds and noises appear to follow one another in an entirely random time sequence—which is not surprising, since in fact they were produced, and were intended to be produced, by chance. Obviously there is no metrical basis here. Efforts to beat time to *Aria* and *Fontana Mix* are doomed to failure.

Another example of music without meter is the Gregorian introit on side 1, sung by a choir of Catholic monks. Composed in medieval times, music of this general style constituted the daily church music of Europe for many centuries. There is melody of a kind here—a kind that we are not accustomed to —but the rhythm strikes us as halting and indefinite, constantly fluctuating and devoid of bold accents. Once again, it is impossible to beat out a recurring metrical pattern behind this music. Perhaps, indeed, this was the point. As religious music of the Catholic Church, Gregorian chant had to be kept separate from the more physical manifestations of the world, such as dancing.

These are instances of nonmetrical music. But to think of them as unrhythmical is not correct. Like all other kinds of music, these pieces consist of sounds in time, and the time relation of sounds creates rhythm. "Unrhythmical music" is really a contradiction in terms, and "rhythmical music" is a redundant phrase. Granted, when we are not speaking technically, we often call music "rhythmical" when its rhythmic qualities impress us particularly. People even tend to call music "rhythmical" whenever the *meter* is strongly emphasized, as it is in dance music of all kinds, jazz, and rock. But in correct, technical language this should be called *strongly metrical* music, not rhythmical.

TEMPO

tempo

In our discussion so far, we have referred in passing to the *relative* duration of notes—some three times as fast as others, and so on—but we have said nothing about their *absolute* duration in fractions of a second. Tempo takes account of this. It is the term for the speed of music, fast or slow. All music has tempo, of course. In metrical music, the tempo is the rate at which the basic, regular beats of the meter follow one another.

metronome marks

Tempo can be expressed quantitatively by such indications as $\quarternote$ = 126, meaning 126 quarter notes per minute. Such indications are metronome marks, named after the metronome, a mechanical or electrical device that ticks out beats at a wide variety of tempos. Metronome 100 is an average easy march tempo; 42 is very slow, and 156 is very fast.

When composers give directions for tempo, however, they generally prefer qualitative language. Rather than freezing the speed, they prefer to leave some latitude for different performers, different acoustical conditions in concert halls, and the like. Italian terms for tempo have become conventional, because in the period when these terms began to be used regularly, Italy dominated the musical scene in Europe:

COMMON TEMPO INDICATIONS		LESS COMMON TEMPO INDICATIONS	
adagio	slow	*lento, largo, grave*	slow, very slow
andante	on the slow side, but not too slow	*larghetto*	somewhat faster than largo
moderato	moderate tempo	*andantino*	somewhat faster than andante
allegretto	on the fast side, but not too fast	*vivace, vivo*	lively
allegro	fast	*prestissimo*	very fast indeed
presto	very fast		

Not all of these Italian words refer in their original meaning to speed itself. Most of them are terms for a certain character or mood, which is associated in a very general way with a range of speed. In the last analysis, composers are less interested in speed for its own sake than in the character that a certain speed can give their music, and they feel safer in giving performers indications along these lines. *Vivace* is close to our "vivacious" and *allegro* actually means "cheerful." *Grave* is our word "grave" and *largo* means "wide" or "spacious." *Andante,* derived from the common Italian word for "to go," might be translated as "going along steadily."

Looking at musical scores, you may come across some of these other terms that are used to indicate irregularities of tempo and tempo changes:

accelerando (*accel.*)	gradually getting faster
ritardando (*rit.*), *rallentando* (*rall.*)	gradually getting slower
più lento, più allegro	slower, faster
fermata (⌢)	a hold of indefinite length on a certain note
rubato	a short temporary change in tempo (see also page 331)

The most important terms to remember are those listed under "common tempo indications" above. When they appear at the top of a symphony movement or the like, they usually constitute its only heading or title. People refer to the Andante of Beethoven's Fifth Symphony, meaning a certain movement (the second), which is to be played at an andante tempo.

Dynamics and Tone Color

Music is sound in time. The time aspect of music has been discussed over the last few pages, and now we come to sound itself.

Sound may be said to have three distinct properties: pitch, tone color, and dynamics (for their scientific basis, see the picture insert on pages 14–15). We shall take them up in order of increasing difficulty, starting with dynamics and tone color in the present section. Pitch and important matters that grow out of pitch—scale, melody, and harmony—will be discussed at some length in the following sections of this chapter and in the next.

DYNAMICS

dynamics

The general name for the volume of sound, the loudness or softness of a musical passage, is dynamics. Scientists measure it quantitatively in units called decibels; the movement to ban supersonic passenger planes was based on the fact that their decibel count was over the excruciating level of 110 decibels. Musicians use qualitative language to describe dynamics (as they do to give directions of tempo). Again, Italian terms have long been conventional:

pianissimo (***pp***) . . very soft	*forte* (***f***) . . . . loud
mezzo piano (***mp***) . medium soft	*mezzo forte* (***mf***) . . . . medium loud
piano (***p***) . . . . . . soft	*fortissimo* (***ff***) . . . . . very loud

Sometimes changes in dynamics are sudden. A stretch of very loud music may be followed all at once by a hush. But often the changes are gradual; we hear a quiet passage swell into a loud one, or a powerful blare fade into quietness. Terms for changing dynamics are:

crescendo (*cresc.*, $\diagup$) . . . . gradually getting louder
diminuendo (*dim.*, $\diagdown$) . . . . gradually getting softer

TONE COLOR (TIMBRE)

tone color

The notes that we hear in music, loud or soft, differ in general *quality* of sound, depending on the instruments or voices that produce them. Tone color and *timbre* are terms for this quality. Tone colors are almost impossible to describe, let alone notate; about the best one can do is use imprecise adjectives such as bright, warm, harsh, hollow, or brassy. Yet tone color is one of the most immediate and easily recognized musical elements.

Many people know and can distinguish the sounds of various different instruments, even though they cannot carry a tune or follow rhythms. And even without recognizing particular instruments, we can all hear the difference between the smooth, rich sound of violins and the bright sound of trumpets or the thump of drums. The most distinctive tone color of all belongs to the first, most beautiful, and most widely used of all musical instruments, the human voice.

For an introduction to the world of musical instruments, see the picture inserts on pages 55–65. It is amazing how many different devices have been invented in all societies to produce the different tone colors that people have wanted for their music. And the search goes on in the new spheres of sound opened up by electronic technology (see pages 460–62).

Pitch and Scales (I)

pitch

Some sounds seem high, others low. This we hear instinctively—though we might be hard-pressed to say just how the adjectives high and low match up with our experience of the sounds in question. But the quality of "highness" or "lowness," which is called pitch, obviously figures centrally in the whole notion of music. If sound lacked this quality, music would be truly impoverished, a matter of rhythm, dynamics, and tone color alone. Without pitch, there would be no melody or tune, and a roar and a shriek would sound much the same.

Of course, roars and shrieks are not the normal material of music. This is not because they are too loud or too horrible, but because they are too indefinite. For sounds which are to be used in music, it is important that the pitch be focused, rather than blurred or indefinite as it is in low or high noises. There are some musical instruments with indefinite pitch—think of the bass drum and cymbals—but they can't carry the tune.

Our experience of pitch is formed very early from the outside world. Birds sing and pet mice squeak in the upper pitch range, while thunder and motorcycles without mufflers make low-pitched noises. Men generally speak and sing lower than women do—and no doubt our first, most intimate acquaintance with pitch differences comes from the voices we hear during infancy.

Shown below are the average vocal ranges of the common types of men's and women's singing voices as used in a chorus. (For those who are not familiar with musical notation for pitch, it is explained on pages 28–31.)

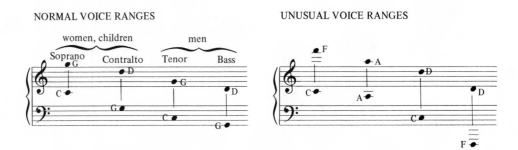

Trained singers, especially those trained for opera, often have astonishing vocal ranges, far beyond these averages. There are several choice opera roles that require sopranos who can hit the high F above the normal soprano high G. Tenors—French tenors, in particular—sometimes go up to D above the normal tenors' high G. And the Russians specially cultivate the low range of the bass voice in their choruses. Russian basses growl their way far down below the normal range as shown above.

OCTAVES

In addition to this quality of "highness" and "lowness," there is another important aspect of pitch that everyone recognizes instinctively. (Or nearly everyone: tone deafness, like color blindess, afflicts only a small proportion of humanity.) If someone plays a series of higher and higher pitches—say an upward run on a piano—there comes a point at which the pitch seems in some sense to "duplicate" an earlier pitch. The new pitch does not sound identical to the old one, but somehow the two sounds are very similar in their different ranges or levels. They blend extremely well. They may almost seem to melt into one another.

octave   This auditory "duplication" is known as the phenomenon of <u>octaves</u>, a term whose origin will be explained in a moment. The scientific explanation for the phenomenon (see page 15) matters less to us than does the fact that people perceive it so generally and so easily. For instance, when men and women sing together, they instinctively sing in octaves, duplicating each other's song an octave or two apart. This fits their vocal ranges (see the above example). If you asked them, they would all say they are singing "the same tune," and only the most sophisticated of them would even think of adding "at different octave levels."

Some writers have referred appreciatively to "the miracle of octaves." Without the miracle of pitch, music would be sadly impoverished, as we have already remarked. Without the phenomenon of octaves it would be rather poor (and not very sociable). Only by developing this fundamental resource has Western music progressed to the rich state in which we know it.

SCALES

As a result of the phenomenon of octaves, the full continuous range of pitches that exists in nature (and that is covered, for example, by a siren starting very low and going up higher and higher until we can no longer hear it) falls into a series of "duplicating" segments. About ten of these octave segments are audible to us. A large pipe organ covers all ten. A piano covers about seven. Two segments are shown in the diagram on page 16.

It is interesting to consider the difference between these similar segments of pitch materials and the range of colors available to the painter. (Like pitches, colors also result from vibrations—light waves of different frequencies.) One difference is that the painter's palette extends all the way from red through orange, yellow, green, blue, and indigo to violet without any kind of duplication effect. There is no phenomenon in the visual world that can be compared to octaves.

Another difference is that the painter mixes pigments at will and uses all the subtle shades between one primary color and the next. The musician, on the other hand, generally uses only a small, limited number of fixed pitches in each octave segment. Which exact pitches and how many differ from culture to culture. Twelve pitches have been fixed for most of the music we know. But five were traditionally used in Japan, as many as seventeen have been used in Arab countries, and Western Europe originally used seven.

The Science of Sound

This "picture insert," like others later in the book, contains material that is supplementary to the main discussion. The inserts can be read along with the main material, or later, or not at all, as you wish. At the present point in this chapter, we can develop the concepts of pitch, dynamics, and tone color without going into the science of acoustics. However, this may be of interest to some readers, and for others it may tie the discussion in with information they already know.

Musical pitch was one of the first natural phenomena to be investigated scientifically in the Western world. Only astronomy goes back as far—and astronomy does not allow for direct experimentation, as the study of pitch does. Only later were light, mechanics, chemistry, and even medicine studied in a truly scientific way.

The pathbreaking investigations are credited to the Greek mathematician-philosopher Pythagoras, who lived before 500 B.C., before the time of Socrates, Plato, or Euclid. He is also famous for his theorem about right-angled triangles $(a^2 + b^2 = c^2)$. Pythagoras discovered or codified numerical facts about the sounds produced by plucking strings. If we pluck a taut string, it gives out a certain pitch. Then if we pinch the string exactly in the middle and pluck the half-length string, the new pitch is exactly an octave (see page 13) higher. Another way of saying this is that string lengths in the ratio 2:1 produce notes that sound at the octave. Strings in other simple numerical ratios—such as 2:3, 3:4, 4:5, 8:9—produce all the other notes of the diatonic scale (see page 16).

To the Greeks, this seemed fascinating and extremely significant. It showed that physical phenomena that can be detected by the senses (in this case, the sense of hearing) relate directly to mathematical abstractions that can be understood by reason. They did not know that falling bodies, light waves, electrons orbiting the nucleus of the atom, and so on, obey mathematical laws too. Nonetheless, Pythagoras went ahead and proposed the hypothesis that all nature is governed by number. This was quite an insight—though today we would put it a little differently, and say that natural phenomena can be described in terms of mathematics.

Pythagoras's experiments were repeated and discussed with great admiration and interest for more than two thousand years after his death. In the Middle Ages, they formed the basis of the university music curriculum. Shown here are woodcuts from a fifteenth-century music theory book. Pythagoras is represented as a professor of the time demonstrating his musical theories using tuned bells, glasses of water, strings under different tension (with different weights attached), and pipes of different lengths. Perhaps, after all, there is something to the popular view that musical and mathematical talents go together.

What Pythagoras did not know—what was not grasped until the sixteenth century—was how sound is actually produced. Sound results from very small but very rapid vibrations that are set up in certain objects or bodies; in taut strings, plates, gongs, bells, and columns of air enclosed in tubes of one kind or another. One complete vibration is called a *cycle*.

The human ear can detect a considerable range of these vibrations, from around 16 cycles per second up to around 20,000. What sounds to us like an "average" musical sound—for instance, the A that is used to tune up at the beginning of a symphony concert—has a frequency of 440 cycles per second.

The three properties of sound are pitch, tone color, and dynamics:

1. *Pitch*, the "highness" or "lowness" of sound, depends on the speed or rate of the vibrations. The smaller the vibrating body, the faster the vibrations and the higher the sound (a piccolo encloses a smaller length tube of vibrating air than does a trombone). If you blow across the top of a beer bottle as you fill it up with water, the sound becomes higher as the vibrating column of air above the water becomes shorter.

The phenomenon of octaves has to do with the remarkable fact that strings and other sound-producing bodies tend to vibrate not only along their full length but also simultaneously in halves, quarters, etc. Scientists call these fractional vibrations *partials*; musicians call them *overtones*. The sound of the overtones is very, very much softer than that of the fundamental note. But when a second string, half the length of the first, vibrates it also reinforces an overtone of the first (full-length) string. The ear receives this as a kind of "duplication."

2. *Tone color*—that indescribable quality of sound—depends on the amount and proportion of the overtones. In a flute the air column happens to vibrate largely along its total length and not much in halves or quarters, whereas violin strings vibrate simultaneously in many subsegments. This is what seems to account for the "white" tone color of the flute and the "rich" tone color of the violin.

3. *Dynamics* or loudness depends on the amplitude of the vibration, on how far or hard the string or air column vibrates. For example, in a guitar, loudness depends on how many sixteenths or thirty-seconds of an inch the string flares out when you pluck it. The harder you pluck, the louder the sound. Players of wind instruments control dynamics by the wind pressure that they produce by blowing. It is no accident that loudness in music is associated with force and exertion.

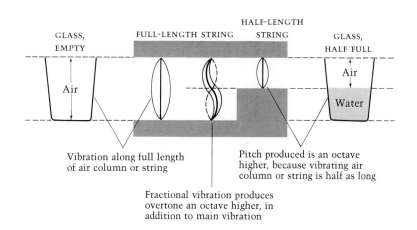

GLASS, EMPTY

FULL-LENGTH STRING

HALF-LENGTH STRING

GLASS, HALF FULL

Air

Air

Water

Vibration along full length of air column or string

Fractional vibration produces overtone an octave higher, in addition to main vibration

Pitch produced is an octave higher, because vibrating air column or string is half as long

diatonic scale

This set of seven pitches is called the <u>diatonic scale</u>. When the first of them is repeated at a higher duplicating pitch, the total is eight. Hence the name *octave,* meaning "eight span." Anyone who knows the series "do re mi fa sol la ti do" is familiar with the diatonic scale. You can count out the octave for yourself, starting with the first "do" as *one* and ending with the second "do" as *eight.*

scale

<u>Scale</u> is a term for the total pitch material that is considered, by convention, to be available for making music in any particular culture. Although students are taught to "play scales" as though they were simple melodies, a scale does not imply a melody. Nor does it really imply any particular order of the constituent notes, even though the word comes from the Latin for "ladder," and when people describe scales they conventionally start at the bottom and work their way up the rungs. But they might just as well work their way down from the top. The scale should be thought of simply as the store of notes available—seven per octave, in the diatonic scale—carried up and down through the octaves. The set of white notes on the piano constitutes this scale:

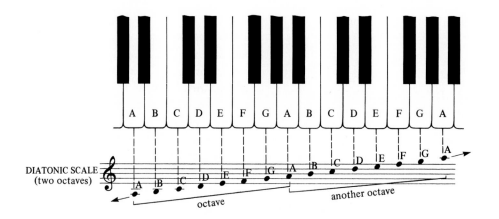

The earliest European keyboards (they were on organs) had only the white notes, because music was written for only seven pitches in each octave, the pitches of the diatonic scale, as shown above. At a later point in history, five further pitch subdivisions were settled on between some of the others. The point was that the original seven pitches had not been equidistant, as we shall explain in the next subsection of this chapter; some of them were farther apart than others, so it was possible to fill in the gaps. This is what the new pitches accomplished. Soon black keys were inserted into the keyboard to allow the five new pitches to be played. The total now stood at twelve equidistant pitches.

chromatic scale

These twelve pitches constitute the <u>chromatic scale</u>, the aggregate of all the white and black notes of the keyboard or all the fretted notes on the guitar:

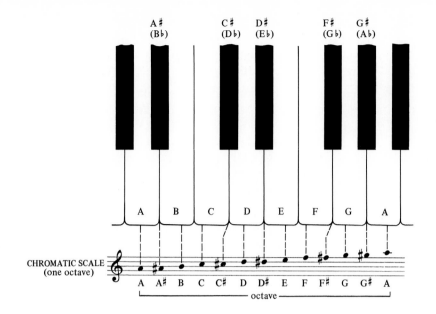

Until very recently, Western music used these twelve pitches, duplicated through all the octaves, and in principle no other pitches. Features of many instruments are designed to produce these particular pitches exactly: frets on guitars, carefully measured holes in flutes, and the tuned sets of strings of harps and pianos.

Other instruments, such as the violin and the slide trombone, have a more continuous range of pitches available to them (as does a police siren or the human voice). In mastering these instruments, one of the first tasks is learning to pick out exactly the right pitches. We call this *playing in tune;* singing in tune is a matter of constant concern for vocalists, too. It is true that many instrumentalists and all singers regularly perform certain notes *slightly* off tune for an important and legitimate artistic effect. "Blue notes" in jazz are an example. The fact remains that these "off" pitches are only small, temporary deviations from the main notes of the scale—the same twelve notes that, on instruments such as the piano, are absolutely fixed.

INTERVALS

interval The space or distance between any two pitches is called the <u>interval</u> between them. Consider the chromatic scale shown in the above example, and pick any single note in that scale. You will see that the interval between this note and each of the others is different in each specific case. We already know the name of the interval between a note and its "duplicating" note: from C to the next C, from C♯ to C♯, from D to D, etc. For all these duplicating pairs, the interval is the octave. There are also eleven other intervals between our particular note and the other eleven notes of the chromatic scale.

half step

whole step

All these intervals have their technical names, which can be found tabulated on page 439. But for the purposes of the present discussion, apart from the octave we need to know only two more. The smallest interval is the *semitone* or half step, the distance between any two successive notes of the chromatic scale. (*Step* is a name for small intervals.) The distance from C to C♯ (or D♭) is a half step, as is C♯ to D, D to D♯, D♯ to E, and E to F. The *whole tone* or whole step is equivalent to two half steps: C to D, D to E, E to F♯, F♯ to G♯, etc.

The chromatic scale consists exclusively of half steps. Therefore this scale is symmetrical, in the sense that you can start on any one of its notes and move up the scale (or down) with exactly the same result as if you started anywhere else. The diatonic scale is *not* symmetrical in this sense. Between B and C and between E and F, the interval is a half step, but between the other pairs of adjacent notes the interval is twice as big—a whole step. In the diagram below, the two scales are lined up in order to show their differences in interval structure:

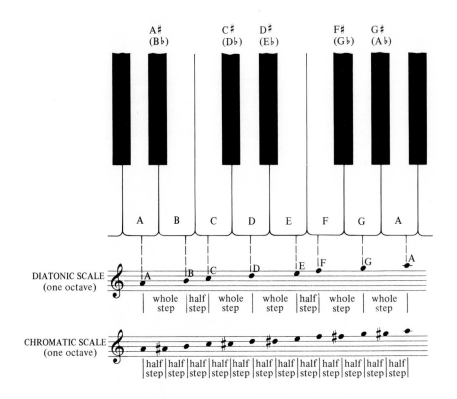

The asymmetry of the diatonic scale—apparent in this example—has important consequences for melody and harmony, as we will point out later. The symmetry of the chromatic scale has different, equally important, consequences. (See pages 42–48, which can be taken up at this point of the chapter if desired.)

The Two Main Dimensions of Music

This is a good stopping place for a moment of review. Proposing to develop a working vocabulary for music, we started with aspects of music in time: rhythm, meter, and tempo. Then we moved on to the properties of sound: dynamics, tone color, and finally pitch. We are now ready to put time and sound together, as it were, to consider melody and tunes, and then, in the next chapter, harmony and counterpoint.

For this purpose, it often helps to think of pitch and time as the two main dimensions or "coordinates" of music. Just as a graph with food prices and time as coordinates can help the public visualize the change in grocery bills from month to month, so a graph with pitch and time dimensions can help us to visualize music. In fact, musical notation comes quite close to this concept:

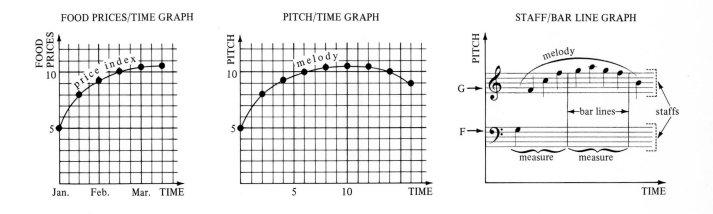

Low and high notes are positioned on a sort of grid, made up of rows of horizontal lines crossed with verticals. The horizontals mark off pitch, from low to high; they are grouped into *staffs* of five lines each (see page 28). In a score, a number of staffs can be lined up so that the whole range of usable pitches is represented (see pages 32–33).

The vertical lines of the graph are *bar lines*. They mark off time (in fractions of a minute, rather than months or weeks, as on the price index). Measures are the basic time units of music, as explained on page 7.

To see how this concept can be put to use, consider a melody—that is, a series of notes of various pitches following one another in time. They can be plotted on the pitch/time graph with dots, as in the middle diagram above. The pitch of each note (its "highness" or "lowness") is indicated by its placement up or down, and its position in time is indicated by its placement from left to right. In an actual score, the big dots or note-heads are "plotted" on the staff/barline grid in much the same way (see the right-hand diagram).

Melody

The pitches that make up music occur simultaneously or successively in time —usually both. As we have just seen, successive pitches can be plotted on the pitch/time graph as a rising and falling line. A coherent succession of pitches is called a melody, and indeed musicians very commonly speak of "melodic line" or simply "line" in this connection. The importance of melody in the musical experience hardly needs to be stressed. This is an article of faith with musicians and music lovers of all descriptions.

melody

Just as a line in a drawing can possess character and strike us as bold, firm, graceful, or delicate, so a melody can gain character from the succession of pitches in time from high to low, low to intermediate, and so on. A melody is a "line in time," with the direction and shape of the line given by the pattern of pitches. As the notes follow one another, each higher than the last, the melody seems to climb. A low note or a low passage acts as a setback; a long series of repeated notes on the same pitch may seem to wait ominously—we develop an interest in how the melody is going to come out. In a satisfactory melody, we feel that the succession of notes holds together as some sort of meaningful unit.

On page 9 we made the point that it is not correct to speak of "unrhythmical" music, since rhythm refers to the relationship of sounds in time, and all music has such relationships. There is unmetrical music; there is music that downplays its rhythmic aspects; but "unrhythmical" music is a contradiction in terms. Does such a thing exist as music without melody, that is, "unmelodic" music? In drum solos, perhaps—though even here, remember that certain drums do have clearly focused pitch (timpani and bongo drums are examples) and, if several such drums are used, they will produce a rudimentary melody. As long as music involves a succession of pitches and the mind can detect some kind of rationale in them, it has melody.

Such music should not be thought of as "unmelodic" or "unmelodious," then, any more than music should be considered "unrhythmical." You may not like the melody or you may not be able to follow it—but that is quite another matter, a matter of your preferences and capabilities, not an inherent quality of the music.

TUNES

tune

When people call music "unmelodious," they generally mean that it does not strike them as having a tune—a simple, easily singable, "catchy" melody such as a folk song or a dance. In this book the word *tune* will be reserved for this use. A tune is a special kind of melody. *Melody* is a term that includes tunes, but also much else.

Several general characteristics of tunes can be enumerated. As you read the following, keep singing *The star-spangled banner* to yourself to furnish illustrations of the various points.

phrase

Division into Phrases Tunes naturally fall into smaller sections, called phrases. This is really true of almost all melodies, but with tunes the division into phrases is especially clear and sharp.

In tunes with words (that is, songs), the musical phrases typically coincide with the poetic lines. And since most lines in a song lyric end with a punctuation mark and a rhyming word, these features also serve to emphasize the musical phrase divisions:

> And the rockets' red *glare,*
> The bombs bursting in *air* . . .

Singing a song, you have to breathe—and you tend to breathe at the ends of phrases. You may not need to breathe after the first phrase of *The star-spangled banner,* but you are well advised not to wait any longer than the second:

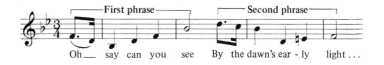

Balance between Phrases In many tunes, all the phrases are two, four, or eight measures long. (Measures are the basic time units of music. See page 7.) Blues tunes, for example, typically consist of three four-measure phrases; hence the term *twelve-bar blues*—*bar* is another term for measure. Almost all the phrases of *The star-spangled banner* are two measures long, as you will discover if you count them all the way through. But one phrase broadens out to four measures, with a fine effect: "Oh say, does that star-spangled banner yet wave. . . ."

Other phrase lengths, besides two, four, and eight measures, can certainly occur in a tune and make for a welcome contrast. The main requirement is that there be a sense of "balance" between the phrases of a good tune, in terms of phrase lengths, and in other terms, too. Taken together, the phrases of a tune add up to a well-proportioned whole.

Parallelism and Contrast Balance between phrases of a tune can be strengthened by means of melodic and/or rhythmic parallelism. Sometimes two phrases are identical in both melody and rhythm, differing only in the words ("Oh say, can you see," "Whose broad stripes and bright stars"). Sometimes they have the same rhythm but different pitches ("Oh say, can you see," "By the dawn's early light"). The other possibility—same pitches, different rhythms—is less frequently exploited as an artistic device.

Sometimes phrases have the same general *pattern* of pitches, but one phrase is slightly higher or lower than the other ("And the rockets' red glare," "The bombs bursting in air"). Sequence is the technical name for this device. Duplication of a phrase at two or more different pitch levels occurs frequently in music, and nearly always to good effect.

sequence

Composers also take care to make certain phrases contrast with their neighbors. One phrase is short, another long, one phrase low, another high (perhaps even *too* high, at "O'er the land of the free"!). A tune containing some parallel phrases and some contrasting ones will seem to have logic, or coherence, and yet will avoid monotony. "Unity in variety" is a good slogan for artistic success of all kinds.

Climax and Cadence A tune has *form.* It has a clear, purposeful beginning, a feeling of action in the middle, and a firm sense of winding down and concluding at the end. There will probably be a distinct high point, either a single high note or a high passage, which the earlier part of the tune seems to be heading toward. This is usually referred to as the <u>climax</u>. The climax of our national anthem highlights the all-important word "free."

climax

Then the later part of the tune relaxes from this climax ("And the home of the brave"), until it reaches a very conclusive stopping place at the end. In a less conclusive way, the music also stops at earlier points in the tune—or, if it does not fully stop, at least it seems to pause or settle. Which points are these in *The star-spangled banner?* "That our flag was still there" is an obvious one, and there are several others.

cadence

The term for these stopping places or settling places is <u>cadences</u>. Cadences can be made with all possible shades of finality about them. The art of making cadences, indeed, is one of the most subtle and basic in all of musical composition.

Take any song you know and sing it through; all or nearly all of these features will hold true, just as they do in *The star-spangled banner.* Why do people like to sing one particular tune rather than another? Because of the words, perhaps. But also because there is a pleasure in going through again and again a good, shapely melodic pattern—a pleasure involving an appreciation of its comfortably balanced phrases, an anticipation of working up to its climax, and a feeling of accomplishment and relaxation at rounding it all off with a decisive final cadence.

MOTIVES

Other music exists that does not consist of tunes—music that people probably do not sing much but that they seem to enjoy anyhow. Neither the longer, more ambitious rock numbers nor symphonies and other concert pieces consist exclusively of tunes, though they generally have tunes or fragments of tunes embedded in them, along with much other material.

motive

Such musical fragments are called <u>motives</u>. A motive can be as short as two or three notes—just long enough so that its rhythmic and/or melodic character is easily recognized and easily remembered when it comes back again. We do not listen the same way to music built out of motives as we do to tunes. The experience is less direct and immediate, but it is more diverse and broad-ranging and has potential for more powerful emotional expression.

In listening to music of this kind, we first recognize a motive and then lose it, as something else is played. We wait for it to come back; when it does, it may be presented in such a way as to heighten its effect. There may be several such motives, coming back in order or out of order, in combination or in other new ways. Indeed, interest is likely to center not on the fragments themselves but on what happens to them. We listen not to the unfolding of phrases, one directly after another in a relatively short span of time, as in a tune, but rather to the way things are "worked out" over a much longer span.

THEMES

theme   Another term used to refer to musical material is <u>theme</u>. This is the most general term that can be used for the basic subject matter of a piece of music. The themes of a political speech are the main points that the politician elaborates, enlarges, and develops. The composer of a symphony or a fugue treats themes in somewhat the same way.

Themes vary in length and characteristics, depending on the type of music. For the themes of fast symphony movements, composers tend to use short motives of the type just described above. However, in a form such as the theme and variations (see page 283), it is traditional to use full tunes as themes, often taken from actual songs or dances. For still other types of music, the basic elements of themes can be harmony or tone color (see page 366).

Musical Notation

We end this chapter with a section on the notation of rhythm, meter, and pitch. Many of the readers of this book will skip these pages, or at most skim them for review purposes. But others will come to this material new. We are going to go slowly for the benefit of these readers. Musical notation is quite a complicated (and, truth to tell, not always a logical) system, which is something that musicians who have grown up with it are apt to forget.

NOTE VALUES

The longest note in common use today is called a whole note. (There is a kind of inflation at work in music history. Money gets cheaper, notes get slower. Would you believe that our whole note was once one of the fastest? If you run into English writings on music, you will still find the whole note referred to as a *semibreve*—that is, a half of a "brief" note! There used to be "briefs" and "longs" and even "double longs.") But to return: A half note lasts for half the time of a whole note. A quarter note lasts for a quarter of the time of a whole note, and so on. The notation for the various notes is:

whole note   half note   quarter note   eighth note   sixteenth note

The eighth note is distinguished from the quarter by a little curl on the top that is supposed to look like a pennant flying in the wind—it is called a *flag.* The sixteenth note has two flags.

To make rhythms, composers use not just sounds but also short silences called *rests* (because the players rest—or at least, catch their breath). The following diagram shows, at the left, the relation between note values and, at the right, the relation between rests, which are equivalent in duration to their corresponding notes.

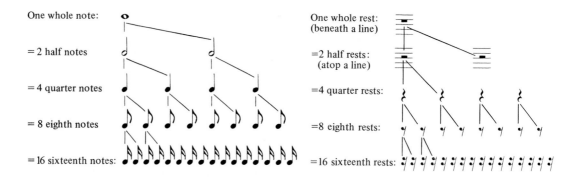

As you see, the eighth rests and sixteenth rests have their own sort of curls or flags. More flags can be added to notes and to rests, with each flag cutting the time value in half. Three flags on a note (♪) would make it a thirty-second note, and four flags (♪) would make it a sixty-fourth. The same thing applies to rests: ♪ , ♪ .

There is another way of writing the eighth and sixteenth notes:

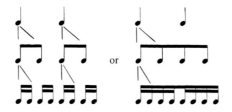

or

In this example, the flags have been starched up and joined together to form thick straight lines called *beams*. This makes them a good deal easier to read; this notational change is purely cosmetic, it does not change the time value of any of the notes. Added beams have the same effect as added flags. These are thirty-second notes: ▭ , and these are sixty-fourth notes: ▭ .

Here is a simple music example showing how these rhythmic equivalents work. A *measure* (or *bar*) is the basic time unit chosen for a piece of music (see page 7)—in this case, a whole note. Measures are marked off by vertical *bar lines*. Each measure in the example covers the same time span, one whole note, which is equivalent to *two* half notes (measure 1) or *four* quarter notes (measure 2) or *eight* eighth notes (measures 3, 4, 5, and 6):

DOTTED NOTES AND DOTTED RHYTHMS

A dot placed after a note lengthens its time value by 50 percent. Thus putting a dot after a quarter note makes it equal to a quarter plus an eighth: ♩. = ♩ + ♪. In a similar way, a dotted eighth rest equals an eighth plus a sixteenth: 𝄾. = 𝄾 + 𝄿 . Even the simplest of tunes, such as *My country 'tis of thee*, make use of the dot convention (see page 7).

A dotted rhythm is one consisting of dotted (long) notes alternating with short ones: ♫ ♫ or ♩. ♫ ♩. ♫. The lively, lilting quality of dotted rhythm is characteristic of the folk music of certain nations, such as Scotland:

TIES

Two notes of the same pitch can be connected by means of a curved line called a *tie*. This means they are played continuously, as though they were one note. Any number of notes of the same pitch can be tied together, so that this notational device can serve to indicate a pitch of very long duration.

Here is a case of the confusing nature of musical notation, for the same sort of curved line connecting notes that are *not* of the same pitch means simply that they are to be played smoothly. These curved lines are called *slurs*.

TRIPLETS

Three notes bracketed or slurred together and marked with a 3 thus: ♩ ♩ ♩ are called a *triplet*. This indicates that they are to be played a little faster than usual—just enough so that the three take exactly the same time that would normally be taken by two notes. A quarter note triplet takes the same time as two ordinary quarter notes: ♩ ♩ ♩ = ♩ ♩; an eighth note triplet equals two eighth notes: ♫♫ = ♫; and so on.

The convention can be extended to groups of five notes, seven notes, etc., but this does not happen very often. For an example, see page 335.

Notice that this whole system of rhythmic notation deals only with the *relative* length of the notes; it says nothing about their *absolute* duration. Hence the rhythmic notation alone does not tell us how fast or slowly a piece is to be played (see our discussion of tempo, page 9). What is more, the rhythm of a piece can be indicated quite correctly in several different ways, depending on which note is chosen for the basic beat:

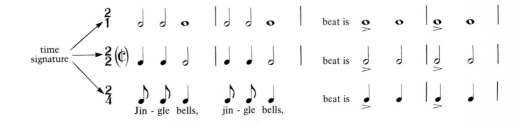

patris. A men.
Sanctus. Sanctus. Sanctus. dominus
deus sabaoth. Pleni sunt celi et terra gloria
tua osanna in excelsis. Benedictus qui ve
nit in nomine domini o sanna in ex
qui tollis peccata mun celsis
di miserere nobis. Agnus dei qui tollis
peccata mundi: miserere nobis. Agnus de
i qui tollis peccata mundi dona nobis pa
cem. Ite missa est.
In festis sim plicibus.

Musical Notation Then and Now

Our modern musical notation is a refinement of the notation that was developed for Gregorian chant (see page 74) in the Middle Ages. Shown here is an illuminated manuscript of Catholic Mass music dating from the fourteenth century, now in the library of Cambridge University, England.

Instead of our staff, consisting of five lines, the music of the Middle Ages used four—drawn in red, which makes the black notes stand out beautifully. The notes are mostly square or lozenge-shaped, not oval as in musical notation today. The three-dot mark at the beginning of each of the staffs (save the first) is the ancestor of our bass or F clef, which also consists of three elements (𝄢). The two dots straddling the top line of the first staff on this page are not notes, though they look like the other notes. They are the precursors of a C clef, indicating that the top line of the four-line staff represents middle C. The modern C clef can be seen in the score on page 33, on the second line from the bottom. Violas, and sometimes cellos and bassoons, use the C clef today.

Staffs and notes are present in this ancient notation, but there is no indication of rhythm and meter. That is because Gregorian chant has no meter and is vague and floating in rhythm. Though some notes are stemmed and others are not, this has nothing to do with their time values, all of which can vary considerably, within certain limits, according to the taste of the singers. And there are no bar lines. The small vertical strokes are put in only to mark the ends of phrases, not measures.

The first complete chart on this page, with the elegant capital S, is a Sanctus, one of the items of the Ordinary of the Mass (see page 78). The preferred way of transcribing this notation, so that it can be read today, is without a time signature (or meter indication), without bar lines, and in notes that are to be understood schematically, that is, as not having strict rhythmic values:

San - ctus, san - ctus, san - ctus.

This page of the manuscript also includes some other Gregorian chants besides the Sanctus. The top staff has the very end of a Gloria, with the words "[In gloria De]i patris. amen." The sixth staff begins an Agnus Dei. After the elaborately decorated, long-tailed initial letter A, the next few letters have faded out over the centuries, but the rest of the text (see page 119) is clear.

At the very end, with its initial I looking like a J, comes an Ite missa est (see page 78).

METER

time signature

The meter of a piece is indicated by means of a <u>time signature</u>. This is usually a sign consisting of two numbers, one printed on top of the other, like a fraction (but it is not a fraction). Time signatures are printed on the staffs at the beginning of all pieces of music:

If the meter changes later in the piece, a new time signature has to be put in at that point (see the music example on page 386).

The top digit shows *how many beats* come in each measure. If there are to be two beats in the measure, the top digit will be 2; if there are to be three beats, it will be 3; etc. The bottom digit shows *what kind of note* represents a beat. If the bottom digit is 2, the beat is a half note long; if it is 4, the beat lasts for a quarter note; if it is 8, this shows that each beat equals an eighth note.

In the example above, the 3 indicates three beats to each measure (triple meter), and the 4 indicates that the beats are quarter note beats. This $\frac{3}{4}$ time signature is the most common for triple meter. *Two hearts in three-quarter time* was someone's idea of a cute title for a waltz song. The most common time signatures for duple meter are $\frac{4}{4}$, sometimes indicated by the sign **c**, and $\frac{2}{2}$, frequently indicated by the sign **¢**.

PITCH

staff

For the notation of pitch, notes are placed on a set of five parallel lines called a <u>staff</u>. The notes can be put on the lines of the staff, in the spaces between them, or (yes) right at the top or bottom of the staff:

In addition, more notes can be added by extending the staff above or below with additional short lines called *ledger lines.* Ledger lines are used just like ordinary staff lines; they simply extend the staff up or down when necessary. A staff with two ledger lines below it and two above it can include enough notes for two octaves and more, which is enough for almost any melody:

What we have said so far does not tell us which pitch each position on the staff represents. We need more. To begin with, letter names are assigned to the original seven pitches of the diatonic scale, as is well known: A B C D E F G. Then the letters are used over and over again for pitches in the duplicating octaves. The octaves can be distinguished by prime marks such as A', A'', and so on. (This is a fine system if the conventions are agreed on, but unfortunately there are several conflicting systems in operation.)

Another, rougher, system designates the C in one octave "high C," that in another "low C," and the one in the octave in between "middle C." Middle C is the comfortable note that nearly any man, woman, or child can sing and that can be played by the great majority of instruments. It lies in the middle of the piano, right under the maker's name:

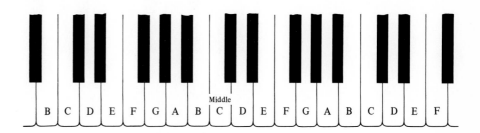

To clue us in to precise pitches, signs called *clefs* (French for "key") are placed at the beginning of each staff. What the clef does is to peg one of the five lines of the staff to a specific pitch. Then the other lines and spaces of the staff are read in reference to this fixed point.

Thus in the treble clef, or G clef (𝄞), the spiral in the middle of the antique capital G converges on the second line up. This second line is the line for the pitch G:

In the bass clef or F clef (𝄢), the two dots straddle the fourth line up. The pitch F goes on this line.

Adjacent lines and spaces on the staff have adjacent letter names. So all the other pitches find their places on the staff in relation to the fixed points marked by the clefs. With G as the fixed point, here is how the pitches are placed on the treble clef:

And with F as the fixed point, here is how the pitches are placed on the bass clef:

Why use two clefs? (Actually, there are even more.) Though the pitches occupy different positions on the staffs, it may look as though on the whole they are merely being duplicated. But no, the two clefs accommodate different octaves. The treble and bass clef staffs fit together like this:

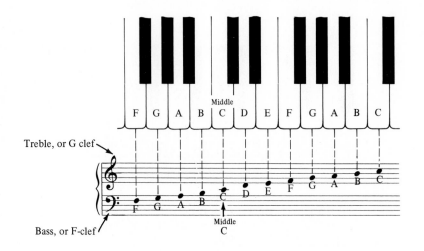

One handy thing is that middle C lies on a ledger line between the two staffs. Remember that even when just one staff is used, middle C is always to be found on one ledger line below the treble clef staff or one ledger line above the bass clef staff.

Here, finally, is the notation for the pitch A in six different octaves, requiring the two staffs and a good number of ledger lines.

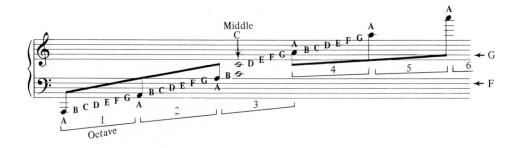

SHARPS AND FLATS

The pitches produced by the black keys on the piano are not given letter names of their own. (This is a consequence of the way they arose in history: see page 16.) Nor do they get their own individual lines or spaces on the staffs. The pitch in between A and B is called either A sharp (A♯, meaning higher than A) or B flat (B♭, meaning lower than B).

The name used depends partly on convenience, partly on convention, and partly on theoretical considerations of some importance but of no interest to us here. If our note is regarded as A♯, it appears in the same position on the staff as A, but with a sharp sign in front of it. If it is thought of as B♭, it will be placed on the staff in the B position with a flat sign in front of it:

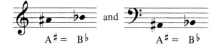

In either case, understand that it represents the same pitch. The other black notes are notated in the same two ways: for instance, the note between C and D is called either C♯ or D♭.

The original pitches of the diatonic scale, played on the white keys of the piano, are called "natural." Sometimes it is necessary to cancel a sharp or a flat and to indicate that the "natural" note should be played instead. The natural sign is used before a note (♮•) or after a letter (A♮, B♮ = A natural, B natural) to show this. Here is an example in music notation:

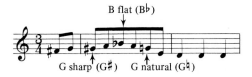

Notated music does not always have to be referred to the piano, of course. Here is how the keyboard notes correspond to the notes on the guitar:

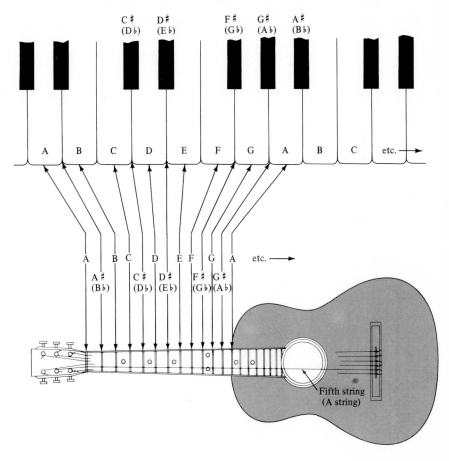

Scores

Here we show a page from Mozart's original score for his *Jupiter* Symphony, and, across the page, a modern printing of this, with arrows pointing out the various elements of notation that were explained on the preceding few pages.

In scores, each instrument and voice that has its own independent music gets one staff (the piano or harpsichord gets two—one for each hand). Simultaneously sounding notes and measure lines are lined up vertically. A song for solo voice and piano requires only three staffs, one for the voice and two for the piano, but band and orchestra scores may have up to forty or fifty staffs (see page 468).

In the page from the Mozart symphony, notice that many of the instruments do not come in at the beginning of the movement; their parts are full of rests (whole rests) until measure 9. At this point, some of the instruments are playing the same notes (French horns and trumpets) or notes an octave apart (first and second violins).

It is interesting that Mozart himself separated the string

choir (see page 62) in writing his scores. He wrote the parts for the violins and violas on the top and those for the cellos and double basses at the bottom, separated by the rest of the orchestra. In measure 5 of the viola part (the third staff down in Mozart's original), he saved himself some work by scrawling *coVc*, meaning *con violoncello*, "with the cello." A music copyist was using Mozart's score to prepare individual instrumental parts, and this told the copyist to write the same music for the violas as for the cellos, an octave higher.

To follow music with a full score takes considerable experience and agility—the eye has to keep scanning up and down and across like a television camera. For the sake of simplicity, the longer music examples in this book have been reduced to "line scores," in which the main musical events are shown measure by measure on a single staff. It is not hard to follow music on two staffs, such as piano scores (page 335, etc.), or on three (page 187).

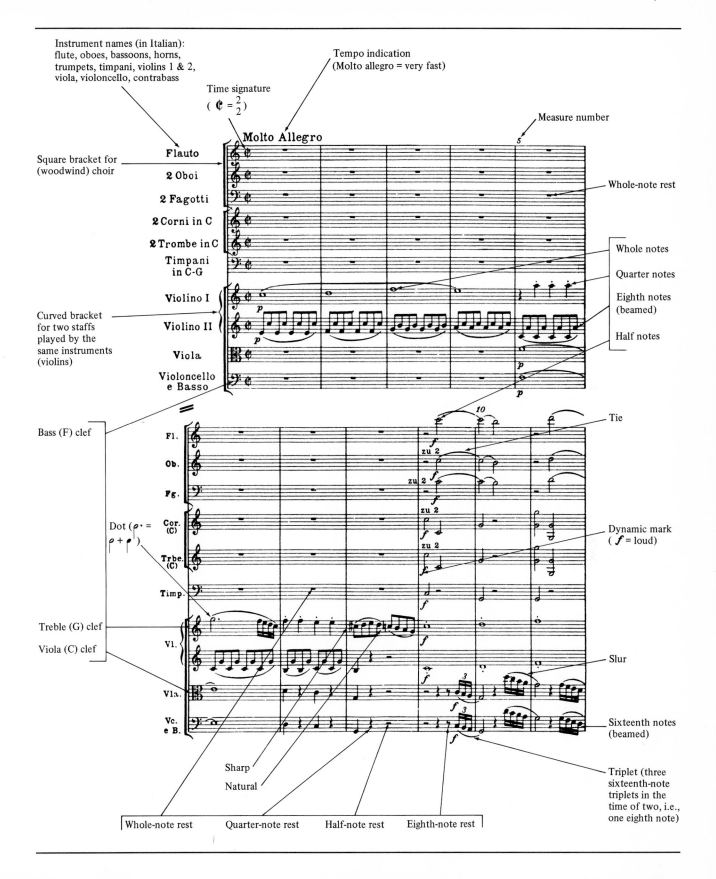

CHAPTER 2   A Vocabulary for Music   II

A Vocabulary for Music   II

So far, we have been discussing music as though at any moment only a single note is heard—as though in a span of time a single melody, rhythm, and tone color is experienced without accompaniment of any kind. This is, of course, rarely the case. It happens only in some special situations: when people sing by themselves, in archaic types of music such as Gregorian chant, or momentarily within larger pieces, for special effects of contrast.

Most music is more dense and complicated, deriving much of its effect from simultaneous sound factors, from what musicians call the "vertical" dimension of music as well as from the "horizontal." Look back at the pitch/time graph that we discussed on page 19, and you will see that it is quite possible to plot more than one melody on it.

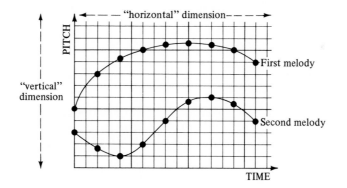

Melody exists in the "horizontal dimension" of music. The relationship between simultaneous melodies or other sounds is perceived in the "vertical dimension."

texture   Texture is the term used to refer to the blend of the various sounds and melodic lines occurring simultaneously in a piece of music. The word is adopted from textiles, where it refers to the weave of the various threads— loose or tight, even or mixed. A cloth such as tweed, for instance, by design leaves the different threads clearly visible. In fine silk or percale, the weave is so tight and smooth that the individual constituent threads are hard to detect.

Texture: Polyphony

monophony

The term for the simplest texture of all, a single unaccompanied melody, is monophony. Monophony may be compared to a single thread, spun out in a line and bending up and down. Simple as this texture is, some very sophisticated music has been written in monophony, just as artists such as Pablo Picasso and Saul Steinberg have done wonderful things with line drawings.

polyphony

When two or more melodies are played or sung simultaneously, the texture is described as *polyphonic*. In polyphony, the melodies are felt to be independent and of approximately equal interest. The whole is more than the sum of the parts, however; the play of the melodies against one another makes for greater richness and interest than they could have had singly.

counterpoint

Another term frequently applied to polyphonic texture is *contrapuntal*. It comes from counterpoint, which means the technique of working the melodies together in a satisfactory way. The actual derivation of the word *counterpoint* is the Latin *punctum contra punctum*, point against point, that is, note against note.

IMITATIVE AND NONIMITATIVE POLYPHONY

Two types of polyphony or counterpoint should be distinguished. (People tend to use the two terms interchangeably, though strictly speaking, polyphony refers to the texture itself and counterpoint to the technique of producing the texture.) Imitative polyphony, or *imitation*, occurs when the various lines sounding together use the same or quite similar melodies, but at staggered time intervals, with one coming in shortly after another, as in a round. Anyone who has ever sung *Three blind mice* or *Row, row, row your boat* has taken part in imitative polyphony.

imitative polyphony

Imitation reached the height of its importance as a musical technique during the Renaissance and baroque periods. In the motet *Veni sponsa Christi* by Tomás Luis de Victoria (side 2), each of the five short lines of the Latin text consists of imitations on a short motive designed to fit the line. Fugues get a different sort of effect by using a single motive treated in imitative polyphony all the way through, in principle (see page 185).

nonimitative polyphony

Nonimitative polyphony occurs when the melodies are essentially different from one another. In popular music, a familiar case of nonimitative polyphony occurs in traditional jazz when the trumpet, clarinet, trombone, and other instruments are each improvising on their own simultaneously. Each instrument has its own interest and its own melodic integrity; each has its own kind of melody suited to the nature of the particular instrument; each seems to be trying to sound more brilliant and imaginative than the others. Listening to contrapuntal music of this kind, our attention shunts rapidly (and happily) back and forth from one instrument to another.

For a good example in classical music, play the third number, *Zion hört die Wächter singen,* from Johann Sebastian Bach's Church Cantata No. 140 (side

7). A steady melody is introduced by the violins, joined after a while by a quite different tune sung by the chorus tenors; these two nonimitative contrapuntal lines are heard working in and around one another all through this composition. For another example, take Guillaume de Machaut's motet *Quant en moy* (side 1). Or, for another, listen to the sensational place in the last movement of Hector Berlioz's *Fantastic Symphony* (side 12) where the composer actually contrives to combine two preexisting tunes, his own *"idée fixe"* and the Gregorian *Dies irae* (see page 349). Make your own nonimitative polyphony by combining *Swanee river* with *Humoresque.*

Using the musicians' concept of "melodic line," we can draw the following graphs to represent imitative and nonimitative polyphony, respectively. Below each graph is the same polyphony in standard musical notation:

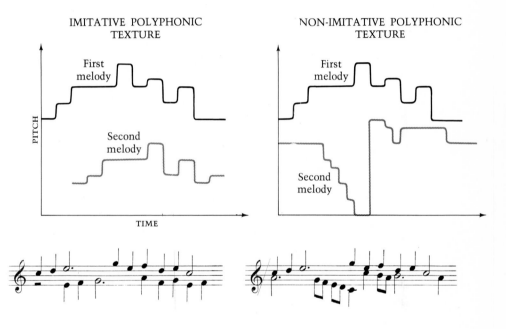

Texture: Homophony

homophony

When there is only one melody of real interest and it is combined with other sounds that are markedly subsidiary, the texture is called <u>homophonic</u> or (more loosely) *harmonic.* The subsidiary sounds form "the accompaniment." A folksinger accompanying himself on a guitar or a dulcimer is spinning a simple homophonic texture.

chord

Very likely the folksinger uses a number of standard groupings of simultaneous pitches that practice has shown will work well in combination. Any grouping of simultaneous pitches is called a <u>chord</u>. An imaginative guitar player will also discover nonstandard chords and unexpected successions of chords in order to enrich his accompaniment.

harmonization

We say that the folk song is <u>harmonized</u> when it is provided with subsidiary chords in this manner. Hymns offer another example of music in a simple homophonic texture: each note of the melody is underpinned by a single chord. Such harmonizing can be done either by the organist or by the choir, with the various different voices contributing the notes that make up the chords. The soprano sings the hymn tune.

Represented below is a simple homophonic texture, in which the accompanying instruments or voices generally move simultaneously with the main melody. Each move creates a chord. Compare this graph with the one on the previous page.

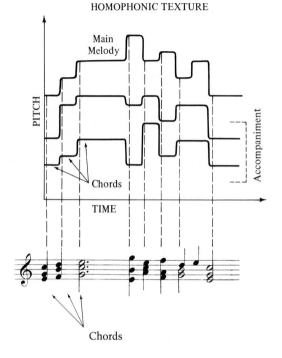

An important means of obtaining variety and contrast in music is to change the texture. A composer can insert polyphonic passages in an otherwise homophonic piece or, conversely, he can create a special effect by bringing homophonic phrases into polyphony. When a jazz soloist takes over from the group and plays a solo, while most of the others drop out, that also is a change in texture.

harmony

Different chords can be used in the harmonization of any melody, and the overall effect of the music depends to a great extent on the nature of these chords, or the <u>harmony</u> in general. This is especially true of music of the last 250 years, which is the most familiar to us. We instinctively sense the difference in harmony between Mozart and Mahler or between New Orleans jazz and rock—though how to describe such differences is a problem. Qualities of harmony (in this general sense) are exceptionally difficult to characterize, except in highly technical language.

CONSONANCE AND DISSONANCE

consonance
dissonance

A pair of terms often used in discussions of musical texture is <u>consonance</u> and <u>dissonance</u>, meaning (roughly speaking) chords that sound at rest and those that sound tense, respectively. These qualities depend on the kind of intervals (see page 17) that make up these chords; octaves, for example, are consonant. A dissonant chord leaves the listener with a feeling of expectation. It takes a consonant chord to complete the gesture, as it were, and to make the music come to a point of stability.

Here again is a case where we should distinguish carefully between the technical and nontechnical uses of a word. In ordinary speech, "dissonance" implies something unpleasant; dissonant human relationships are ones we avoid. But even if they wanted to, musicians could not avoid dissonance in its technical meaning, for it supplies the subtle tensions that are essential to make music what it is. Without dissonance, music would be like food without salt, like bread pudding made out of sandwich white bread and powdered milk. To mention only the most obvious situation, the ends of pieces of music—the cadences—are almost always helped by the use of dissonance, so that the sequence from tension (dissonance) to rest (consonance) can contribute to the sense of finality and satisfaction.

The real point about dissonant harmony is that we instinctively expect its feeling of tension to relax into the calm of consonant harmony. (The technical verb used by musicians is *to resolve.*) Composers use dissonance and consonance in conjunction, deriving artistic effects from the contrast or alternation between the two. It is very much a relative matter, and in modern music, where the overall harmony is quite dissonant, a mildly dissonant chord can actually sound restful. When it is necessary to distinguish between degrees of dissonant tension, the terms *high-level* and *low-level dissonance* can be used (see page 413).

Although it is simplest to think of consonance and dissonance in reference to the chords of homophonic music, the terms apply to polyphonic music, too. As several "horizontal" melodic lines are arranged to go together in counterpoint, the "vertical" result at any individual moment is likely to be a standard chord. (At least, this is true for a good deal of polyphonic music.) Besides following the progress of the various lines, we cannot help hearing a succession of chords formed in this manner. And these chords will be consonant or dissonant, depending on the way the composer fits the individual melodic lines together.

HOMOPHONY VERSUS POLYPHONY

Indeed, you may have sensed that in some situations the distinction between homophony (a single melody with accompaniment) and polyphony (several simultaneous melodies) is hard to maintain. From the point of view of the choir singing a hymn, don't the altos, tenors, and basses all have melodic lines of their own? Who is to say that the guitar accompaniment to a folk song doesn't have a modest melody, too?

In a way, then, homophony and polyphony are two ways of viewing or hearing the same set of simultaneous sounds. Homophony is the "vertical" view, polyphony the "horizontal" view. The distinction can sometimes come down to a matter of degree.

It is good to keep this in mind, but it is also important to keep a sense of perspective about the distinction. Generally there is a clear enough emphasis in music on one texture or the other, homophonic or polyphonic. We should politely but firmly reject the claims of the chorus tenor and the guitar accompanist, for while they may feel quite pleased with the melodic lines they are producing, probably the listener hardly notices them at all. Similarly, in a finely spun cloth, individual threads are there, but no one discerns them individually (except the weaver). If only one melody stands out, the texture is called homophonic. As soon as another begins to attract attention too, the texture deserves to be called polyphonic.

Scales (II): Key and Mode

The simplified treatment of scales on pages 13–17 is adequate as a grounding for basic concepts of melody and texture, but as we now approach the topics of musical form and style, a more advanced understanding of scales and melody formation will be useful. The material in this section follows logically from the discussion of pitch and scales on pages 12–18.

The concept of a *scale,* as we developed it in chapter 1, is obviously an abstraction. A scale was defined as the store of pitches considered by convention to be available for music making: the twelve notes of the chromatic scale into which the octave is divided for Western music, or the five notes into which it is divided for Japanese music, or whatever. But how is music actually made from these scales? Are all the notes treated equally? The discussion begins to get less abstract when we inquire into the actual mechanics of melody building.

TONALITY

The fundamental fact about melody building is really quite a simple one: Melodies nearly always exhibit the sense of a *center.* There is one particular pitch that sounds fundamental, on which the melody seems to come to rest most naturally. And in a sense, all the other notes in the melody are heard in relation to this center. They all sound high or low, dissonant or consonant, in reference to it, and some may actually seem to "tend" or "lead" toward it. That is, when we sing or play one of these "leading" notes, we feel an instinctive urge to go next to the central note itself.

The easy way to identify the central note of a melody is to sing the whole thing though. The ending note is almost invariably *it.* Take *The star-spangled banner,* for example: this tune ends on its central note; it also has this note as its first accent (on the word "say"). In fact, can you think of any traditional tune that does *not* end on its central note? There are some, but not many.

tonality
tonal

This feeling that a single pitch is central to a melody, and to whole pieces of music, can be referred to as <u>tonality</u>, and the music in question can be described as <u>tonal</u>. (These terms are, however, often restricted to strongly tonal music of a specific type: see the discussion of functional tonality, page 156.) Music in which the feeling of centrality is compelling can be called *strongly tonal music; atonal* music, meaning not tonal, lacks centrality. The central note itself is called the *tonic note,* or simply the <u>tonic</u>. An equivalent term used in the days of Gregorian chant was the *final.*

tonic

THE MAJOR AND MINOR MODES

Which note of the scale, then, is the central one? The scale in question is the diatonic scale, which was the basis of Western music until relatively recent times (and still is, for much music composed today). And as we pointed out on page 18, the diatonic scale is asymmetrical: if you start on one of its seven notes and sing up (or down), you will find yourself singing one series of intervals, but if you start on any other note, the series of intervals will be different. This is a consequence of the fact that in the diatonic scale some of the intervals are half steps and some are whole steps, and they come in an irregular order.

Using the diatonic scale, it was and is theoretically possible to use any one of the seven notes as a center. In the Middle Ages and the Renaissance, most of them were so used (see page 75). Each center resulted in what we might describe as a unique perspective on the diatonic scale, as viewed from that center. For instance, if the center is B, the first move up is a half step up to C, and the first move down is a whole step down to A. How do the corresponding moves look, however, if the center is F?

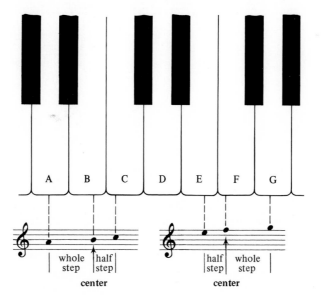

Because each center has a unique arrangement of steps between it and the other notes of the scale, all melodies written around one center resemble each other in character and coloration, and they differ subtly from melodies built

modality
modes

around a different center. The term for these varying aspects of the diatonic scale is modality. The different centers are said to determine the different modes of music.

The two modes that survived past the Middle Ages and the Renaissance are called *major* and *minor*. The major mode was originally an orientation of the diatonic scale around C. The minor mode was an orientation around A. The diagram below shows how the modes were derived from the diatonic scale, and the orientation of the intervals:

major mode
minor mode

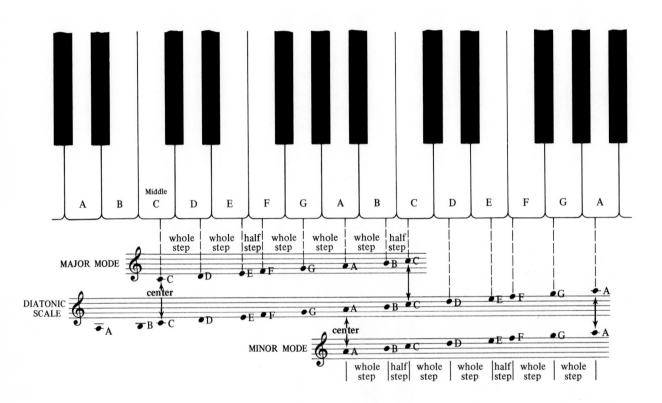

It should be mentioned that music in both modes can, under certain conditions, include some notes—sharps and flats—other than those shown above. But the ones shown are the basic components of the modes.

Once again: the real point about the modes is that the intervals are arranged differently around the center. Composers learned to use these different arrangements as artistic resources, from which they could derive a broad range of aesthetic effects. The major and minor modes diverge from one another mainly in their third and sixth steps above the center. In the minor mode, step 3 is a total of three half steps higher than the center, and step 6 is eight half steps higher. In the major mode, step 3 is four half steps from the center and step 6 is nine. Check out this arithmetic on the above diagram, and you will be able to see how these modes are dissimilar and why one is called major (larger) and the other minor (smaller).

Scales

A scale is the store of pitches considered by convention to be available for the making of melodies. We tend to take our diatonic and chromatic scales for granted, but other cultures use quite different scales, with the result that their music sounds strange and different. Scales used by non-Western cultures may include our half steps and whole steps, but they may also include certain intervals smaller than the half step and bigger than the whole step.

To determine the scale used for ancient Egyptian music, musicologists have studied paintings such as the one shown below. The girl in the middle is playing a lute-like instrument whose frets are carefully represented. A fret is a small cross-piece on the fingerboard of a lute or a guitar which determines the exact length of the sounding part of the string when the string is pressed down just above the fret. The length of the string determines the pitch, and each pitch produced by each fret was an element of the Egyptian scale.

Our inferences about this scale can be supported by measurements of the lengths between the holes of ancient flutes, some of which have been found in archeological excavations.

You may have more trouble actually *hearing* modality, that is, recognizing the distinction between music in the major and minor modes. This is something that comes easily to some people, less easily to others. As a consequence of the difference in intervals described in the last paragraph, music in the minor mode tends to sound more subdued than music in the major. It seems clouded, by comparison with the major. It is often said that the major mode sounds cheerful, and the minor sounds sad, and this is true enough in a general way. But people have legitimate differences about what constitutes "sadness" and "cheerfulness" in pieces of music. To learn to distinguish the modes requires attentive comparative listening. The following well-known tunes are in the minor mode: *We three kings of Orient are, Joshua fit the battle of Jericho, Summertime,* and *When Johnny comes marching home again.* Sing them through, and see if you can catch the characteristic minor-mode inflection involving the third step at the final cadence:

And compare this with the third step in typical major-mode songs such as *Happy birthday to you, Row, row, row your boat, The star-spangled banner,* and many others:

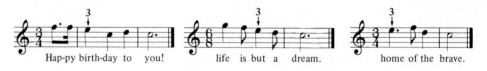

KEYS

Mode and key are concepts that are often confused. Let us see if we can keep them clear.

We have discussed the derivation of the major and minor modes from the original seven-note *diatonic* scale. Within this scale, these two modes are centered on C and A respectively. If you try the experiment of using any of the other notes as center—D, E, F, G, or B—you will find that in each case the arrangement of intervals is different from that of either the major or the minor mode.

Using the whole *chromatic* scale, however, it is possible to construct both modes around any of the twelve notes in the octave. Whichever point we choose as center, starting from there we can pick out the correct series of half steps and whole steps. (This is because the chromatic scale includes all possible half steps, and therefore all possible whole steps.) The piano keyboard, you remember, is color-coded so that the diatonic scale comes out on the white notes, with the extra notes needed to complete the chromatic scale on the black. Therefore if we start from C, the major mode comes out all on the white notes. But if we start the same mode from E, two black notes are required right away. And starting the major mode from one of the black notes—say G♯— we find that our third note is white, our fourth and fifth black again, and so on. You can work out the right intervals for each mode starting on every one of the twelve chromatic notes.

Some examples are given below. Next to the major mode centered on C and the minor mode on A, the diagram shows the *minor* mode centered on C, and the *major* mode centered on A:

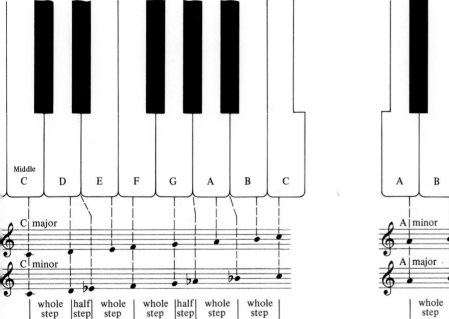

Thanks to the chromatic scale, then, many positions are possible for the major and minor modes. These different positions are called <u>keys</u>. If the major mode is positioned on C, the music is said to be "in the key of C major," or just "in C major." If it is positioned on D, the key is D major, and so on. Likewise we have the keys of C minor, C♯ minor, D minor, and —since there are twelve notes in the chromatic scale—no fewer than nine others.

keys

This already hints at the tremendous artistic resource that composers discovered in the possibility of changing from one key to another. Changing keys during a composition is called <u>modulation</u>. There is no corresponding term for a simple change of mode without a change of key, as from C major to C minor. But a modulation may be accompanied by a change of mode at the same time —for example, a modulation from C major to B minor.

modulation

Between the modes, the difference can be described as internal; in each mode the notes form their own special set of intervals with one another and with the center. Compare the half steps on the above diagram for C major and C minor, and you will see where they differ. Between the keys, on the other hand, the difference amounts only to the positioning of the whole set of notes, taken as a group. The half steps on the diagram for C major and A major are all the same.

As for actually *hearing* tonality, that is, recognizing the different keys and the modulations between them: to some people this presents an even greater problem than hearing modality, though to others it comes more easily. The latter are the fortunate ones born with absolute pitch or perfect pitch, the innate faculty of identifying pitches the way most of us can identify colors. However, this is not the great boon of nature that it is sometimes believed to be. The essential thing is not to identify keys in themselves but rather to be able to tell when keys change, that is, to identify *relative* tonality. Modulation is the resource that composers have made so much of, in respect to tonality. And this relative hearing of tonality can be developed whether or not you are born with absolute pitch.

Form

form   Form is a general word with a long list of dictionary definitions. As applied to the arts, it is an important concept referring to the shape, arrangement, relationship, or organization of the various elements—of the words, phrases, meters, rhymes, and stanzas, to take poetry as an example. In painting, the elements of form are lines, colors, shapes, and so on.

In music, the elements are those we have already discussed: rhythm, tone color, melody, and texture. In a musical piece of some length, the organization is carried out by means of repetitions of themes, rhythms, tone colors, and textures, and by extended contrasts and balances among these elements.

In this book we shall be speaking about musical form a good deal. The fact is that over the years Western music has been very largely concerned with constructing long or relatively long pieces of music, such as masses, fugues, symphonies, and operas. Everyone knows that music can easily make a nice effect for a minute or two. But how does it extend itself (and justify itself) for a time span of ten minutes, half an hour, or two full hours?

This is the problem of musical form. Rarely have composers thought of music as a continuous stream, like Muzak or airline earphone music, which listeners can hook into absentmindedly at will, enjoying what they hear for as long as they happen to be paying attention. Rather, composers have designed music as a specific sound experience in a definite time span, with a beginning, middle, and end, and often with subtle routes between. Musical form is the relationship of these beginnings, middles, and ends.

It is a striking fact that non-Western music has not developed this emphatic concept of musical form. The special richness of Western music depends on form, and we should certainly regard this as a positive value. The distinction between non-Western and Western music is perhaps clarified by thinking of the difference between a continuous decorative frieze around a wall and a wall painting, or mural. The frieze can be understood even when only a part of it is seen. But we can understand the mural only by seeing the whole thing.

However, analogies between musical form and other artistic phenomena can become deceptive if they are pushed too hard. Musical form is very much its own thing, as is equally true of form in any of the other arts. The special factor with music is the crucial importance of memory—and of anticipation, the reverse of memory. (The main talent involved in an "ear for music," in fact, is memory.) In grasping musical form, we are continuously putting together in our minds what we are hearing at the present moment, what we heard earlier in the piece, and what we feel we have been led to expect to hear later.

This is not as forbidding as it may sound. Our discussion of tune (see page 20) exemplifies musical form perfectly, and no one has any trouble exerting memory and anticipation in order to appreciate musical form on this level, at least. In the various phrases of a tune, with their parallel features or contrasts, in the climax, the cadences, and so on, we have a microcosm of musical form in larger pieces.

For a symphony is, in a way, a tune "writ large" or blown up, and the mental process necessary to grasp its form is of the same kind. To be sure, a symphony requires more concentration for its comprehension than a tune does. Composers are aware of the potential difficulty here, and they exaggerate their musical effects accordingly. In other words, the larger the piece, the more strongly the composer is likely to emphasize the features of repetition and contrast that determine the musical form.

FORM AND "FORMS"

Like the words *rhythm* and *melody,* the word *form* has its general meaning and its more specific one. *Rhythm* refers to the whole time aspect of music, but "a rhythm" refers to the particular time and accent pattern of a specific musical passage. *Form* in general refers to the organization of elements in a work of art or music, but "a form" refers to one of the many standardized patterns or arrangements that have been used by composers over the centuries. Some of the implications of the distinction between these two uses of the word are discussed in the picture insert on pages 50–51.

Musical forms, in this second sense, are expressed by letter diagrams. The two essential factors that create musical form, as we have said, are *repetition* and *contrast.* In a form that is diagramed A B A, the element of *repetition* is A and the element of *contrast* B. Some sort of theme or other musical section is presented at the beginning (A); then another section is presented that contrasts with the first (B); then the first one returns (A). We can speak of a simple *balance* in a form of this kind. If A returns with some significant modifications or variations, this can be indicated on the diagram by a device such as a prime mark: A B A'—a "weighted" balance.

"Outer Form" and "Inner Form"

In most periods, artists have tended to employ certain standardized patterns of form, which we can speak of as "outer forms." These patterns have their fixed elements, but they are always general enough to allow for many possibilities of organization on the detailed level. Hence the quality and feeling of works in a single outer form can vary greatly—or, to put it another way, works adhering to a common outer form also have an individual "inner form" of their own. Indeed, the interplay of the two can be an important factor in the aesthetic effect.

In literature, a familiar example of an outer form is the sonnet, with its fourteen five-stress lines, its standardized rhyme schemes, its tendency to pause after eight lines and to reach a "point" or climax at the very end. Within this framework, in their inner form, sonnets can be as different as night and day:

Shall I compare thee to a summer's day?
Thou art more lovely and more temperate. |
Rough winds do shake the darling buds of May,
And summer's lease hath all too short a date. |
Sometime too hot the eye of heaven shines,
And often is his gold complexion dimm'd;
And every fair from fair sometime declines,

By chance, or nature's changing course, untrimm'd; |
But thy eternal summer shall not fade
Nor lose possession of that fair thou ow'st,
Nor shall Death brag thou wand'rest in his shade
When in eternal lines to time thou grow'st. |
So long as men can breathe or eyes can see,
So long lives this, and this gives life to thee.
—Shakespeare

A shilling life will give you all the facts: |
How Father beat him, | how he ran away, |
What were the struggles of his youth, | what acts
Made him the greatest figure of his day: |
Of how he fought, fished, hunted, worked all night, |
Though giddy, climbed new mountains; | named a sea: |
Some of the last researchers even write
Love made him weep his pints like you and me. |
With all his honours on, he sighed for one
Who, say astonished critics, lived at home; |
Did little jobs about the house with skill
And nothing else; | could whistle; | would sit still
Or potter round the garden; | answered some
Of his long marvelous letters but kept none.
—W. H. Auden*

Salisbury Cathedral, 1220–1284

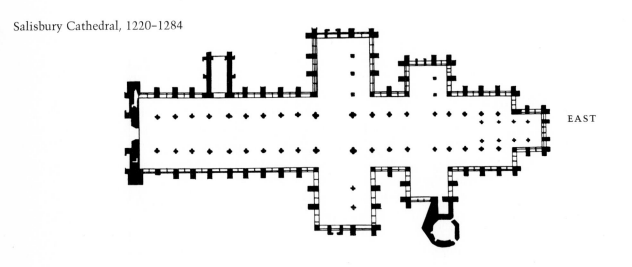

EAST

It is not only the subject and the language that are so different, it is the way the thought develops. Vertical lines on the poems show how they divide up into thought units. Shakespeare announces his "theme" in the first two lines and then discusses it in beautifully balanced two- or four-line units. In the modern sonnet by W. H. Auden, the thought proceeds vividly by fits and starts, with brief, irregular units cutting across the lines. Shakespeare moves steadily up and up to a climax in his very intricate final line. Auden stops in the middle, digresses, and jabs his way to a climax (or anticlimax?) of three simple, devastating words.

These diagrams are architectural ground plans of churches from various periods in history. Thin walls are indicated by lines, and heavy masonry columns, etc., by black areas. Christian churches traditionally follow the same "outer form," in that they are built in the shape of a cross and face in the direction of Jerusalem (east, for us). But the ground plans show how widely the architectural "inner forms" have ranged. One can imagine how different these cruciform churches would seem if one were actually in them.

* Copyright 1945 by W. H. Auden. Reprinted from *Collected Shorter Poems 1927–1957.* by W. H. Auden, by permission of Random House, Inc.

San Vitale, Ravenna, ca. 530–548

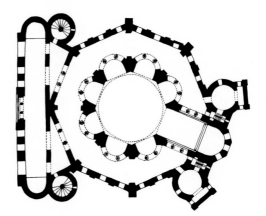

San Lorenzo, Florence, 1418–1446

Christ Church, London, 1677

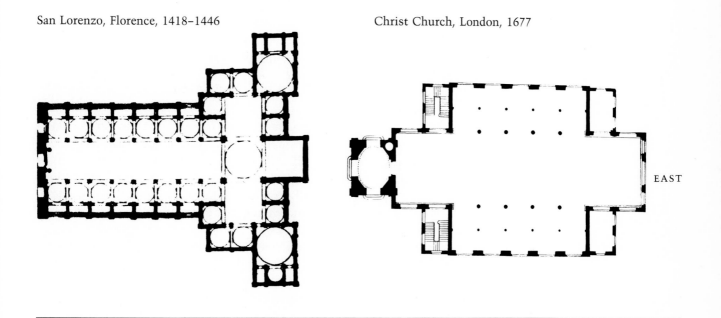

EAST

Diagrams are mainly useful for indicating repetitions and "returns"; they are less helpful with the contrasts. For the letter leaves us in the dark as to the nature of the contrast set up by section B. Is it in a different mode? In a different key? Does it present material radically different in rhythm, melody, texture, tone color, any or all of the above? These are all resources of contrast.

The form that is diagramed A B A is a straightforward one, involving the basic idea of a return in a relatively simple way. We shall meet it again and again in music of all kinds and of all centuries. There are many other possibilities. At this point we will do no more than sketch out the range of these possibilities in the broadest terms, leaving the details for later, when specific forms can be studied together with actual music.

For example, an even simpler form is A A B, which we find in the songs of the medieval troubadors and trouvères. Sometimes called *bar form,* it is considered simpler because there is no return.

On the other hand, the idea of return can be allowed to snowball as follows: A B A C A D A E A, etc. Here A keeps returning. This is the basis of such forms as *ritornello form* and the *fugue* of the baroque period and the *rondo* of the Viennese period.

A different type of form does without any basic contrast, so there is no need for the letters B and C. Instead, A is repeated in different varied states, with revised harmonies, perhaps, or melodic decorations, or changes in tempo, mode, or key. This is diagramed A A^1 A^2 A^3 A^4 A^5, etc. The *passacaglia* and the *theme and variations* follow this scheme. Another whole set of possibilities results from expanding the elements of a simple pattern (such as A B A) and subdividing them:

A   B   A

a a b a′ b a′   (etc.) (etc.)

Here the diagram grows complicated, as small letters trace out the formal subdivisions within the larger elements, still indicated by capital letters. *Minuet and trio form* and *sonata form* are examples of such expansive forms.

GENRES

People sometimes refer to symphonies, quintets, operas, oratorios, and so on as "musical forms." But this is an example of loose terminology that it is best to avoid in the interests of clarity. All of these categories or types of music can be composed in different forms—that is, their internal orders or organizations can be of different kinds. We shall see that the last movement of a symphony by Haydn (No. 88) is in rondo form, whereas the last movement of a symphony by Brahms (No. 4) is in passacaglia form.

genre

The best term for these general categories of music is a borrowed French one, genre (zhahn′r). A genre is usually determined in part by the instrumental or vocal combination involved; a cantata is always sung, a symphony is for orchestra, a quartet is for four singers or instrumentalists. The main genres treated in this book, all of which will be defined when we come to them, are the following:

Style

style — Style, like form, is another of those broad, general, and rather vague words—general, but very necessary. The style of a tennis player is the particular way he or she reaches up for the serve, swings, follows through on the forehand, hits the ball deep or short, and so on. A life-style means the whole combination of things one does and doesn't do, the food one eats, the way one dresses and talks, one's habits of thought and feeling. The style of a work of art, similarly, is the combination of qualities that makes it distinctive.

In this book musical styles will be discussed in terms of the various qualities that have already been described in this chapter. One style may favor jagged rhythms, simple harmonies, and tunes to the exclusion of all other types of melody, while it pays little attention to tone color. Another may exhibit a highly refined preference for certain kinds of tone color. Another may concentrate on a special type of form. We shall not always be able to develop a clear, definitive list of such characteristics for each musical style, but we should at least be able to make a start. We can define intelligently some of the features that make styles different from one another and viable in their own terms.

It is possible to speak of the life-style of a generation as well as the life-style of a particular person. Similarly, in music a distinction can be made between the style of a historical period and the style of a particular composer. To a large extent Handel's manner of writing, for example, falls within the broader limits of his day. But there are some features that make his style unique. And perhaps this constitutes the measure of his musical genius.

In any historical period or place, the musical style must bear some relation to the life-style in general; this seems self-evident. A soul number by Stevie Wonder or Aretha Franklin summons up instantly the emerging urban black consciousness of the 1960s and 1970s. A country-music record would suggest something different, and so would a hard rock record. Indeed, is there anything that expresses today's life-styles so strongly—even so passionately—as does popular music?

With older styles of music, although everybody recognizes in a general way that they relate to total cultural situations, the relationships have rarely been demonstrated in a detailed and convincing way. Nevertheless, we shall try to suggest some of these relationships as we go on to study the music of various historical periods. For each period, an attempt will be made to sketch some aspects of the culture, history, and life-style of the time. We shall briefly out-line the musical style and wherever possible suggest correlations. Then the musical style will be examined in more detail through individual composers and individual pieces of music.

These individual pieces are our main concern, of course, not history or culture or any general concepts of musical style. This point may be worth stressing as we come to the end of our discussion of a "vocabulary for music," a section designed to focus and sharpen the listening process. This book is called *Listen,* and it rests on the belief that the love of music depends first and foremost on careful listening to particular pieces. These pieces are experienced for their own sake. We are not primarily interested in how they can be seen as "good examples" or as "typical" of some musical style or historical period.

But we *are* interested the other way around, in what history and style can tell us that illuminates music. If a glimpse into the cultural history or the life-style of a period can shed light on the musical style, fine—for the more background we can obtain for the appreciation of art, the better. Certainly understanding the musical style in general can contribute to an appreciation of particular pieces of music written in that style. The general reflects upon the particular. It may seem paradoxical, then, but in that indirect way, history too can help us to *listen.*

Musical Instruments of the World (1) Indonesia

Different tone colors or timbres are produced by different voices and different instruments. Over the course of history and over the entire world, an enormous number of devices have been invented for making music, and the range of tone colors they can produce is almost endless.

In Indonesia (Java and Bali) elaborate court orchestras called *gamelans* are made up chiefly of large groups of instruments of the "chime" type, which consist of sets of tuned blocks, tubes, disks, etc., generally played with hammers. The result is a fascinating blend of multicolored tinkles and delicate gong sounds unlike anything known in Western music. Indonesian chime instruments employ wood blocks (*gambang*), bronze slabs (*gendèr*), bamboo pipes (*angklung*), or metal disks or vases (*bonang*). In our illustration of a Balinese gamelan, performing music for a ceremonial occasion, several sizes of bonangs (more precisely *réong*) are seen at the left, gendèrs at the right, as well as drums and cymbals (called *rinchik*).

"Chimes" are a subgroup of the broad instrument category known as percussion, one of five main groups into which instruments are sometimes classified. These five groups are:

String instruments, whose strings are either played with a bow (violin, cello), or plucked (guitar, harp, the Indian sitar, the Japanese koto), or hammered (dulcimer).

Woodwind instruments, including hollow pipes in which air vibrates to produce the sound (flute, recorder) and pipes containing reeds that do the vibrating while the air in the pipe acts as a resonator (oboe, clarinet, the ancient Greek aulos). These instruments all used to be made of wood—hence the name—though today flutes are made of metal.

Brass instruments—wind instruments played with a special kind of small cup- or funnel-shaped mouthpiece. When this is blown into, the player's lips actually vibrate to produce the sound (trumpet, trombone, French horn). Again, the air in the tube acts as a resonator.

Percussion instruments, in which something is struck or rattled to produce the sound (drum, cymbal, tambourine, castanets, xylophone, and the various members of the gamelan).

Keyboard instruments—piano, harpsichord, pipe organ, piano accordion.

Musical Instruments of the World (2) India

The main instruments of India are "plucking" instruments, for which a generic name is *lutes,* after the main early European variety. (The main modern variety, of course, is the *guitar.*) Lutes are a subgroup of the broad instrument category of *strings,* which includes instruments whose strings are plucked as well as those which are played with a bow, such as the violin.

In India, lute-type instruments come in marvelous shapes and with extraordinarily beautiful decorations. On the facing page, from left to right, are a *sitara,* a *long-necked lute,* and two *vinas.* Below, the famous Indian virtuoso Ravi Shankar playing the best-known of Indian instruments, the *sitar.*

In recent years many Westerners have fallen under the spell of the Indian *ragas.* This term is often misunderstood; it does not refer to a musical genre like a sonata. The concept of a raga is (to us) a difficult one, combining aspects of a special scale, a mode, a mood, and a set of melodic formulas used as the basis for composition and, especially, improvisation.

There are very many different ragas, associated with different sentiments, seasons, and even times of day ("Morning Raga," "Evening Raga"). Artistry is shown by choosing just the right raga for the particular occasion and by using it to build lengthy, intricate compositions expressing the musician's own personality and mood of the moment. The player's personality is reflected by the particular instrument, too, for sitars and other Indian instruments are much less standardized in size, shape, etc., than their Western counterparts. An artist's unique propensities determine the selection of one instrument to play on rather than another.

Musical Instruments of the World (3) South America

The second instrument category, *woodwinds,* includes air pipes which vibrate by themselves and also those activated by reeds. Flutes—hollow pipes—are the most characteristic instruments of South America. Our pictures show flute-like instruments from the Andean highlands, covering Peru, Bolivia, and parts of Ecuador. This area was once the center of the powerful Inca Empire, which lasted until the Spanish conquest in the sixteenth century.

The vertical flute shown on page 59 is a *pinkillo,* played by a highlands Peruvian Indian. We know that at the time of the Inca Empire groups of up to a hundred pinkillo players performed melodies to drum accompaniment for ceremonial dances.

The very long flutes shown below are called *mosenos.* Both men seem to be expending great amounts of energy to produce a sound, which is understandable considering the prodigious size of their instruments. The sound of the moseno, naturally, is much deeper than that of the pinkillo.

At the right is another pre-Columbian instrument, the panpipe or *zampoña.* The zampona consists of a set of pipes of varying lengths, one for each pitch, which are tied together to resemble a miniature raft. The number of pipes can vary from three to fourteen—seven are visible in our picture, which shows a Bolivian in ceremonial dress.

There is a South American fable that shows the importance of flute playing to the Andean Indians. Music historian Robert Stevenson tells the story: "In the remote past, Pariacaca lived in one of five big egg-shaped mounds on the coast. He instructed his hero son Huathiacuri how to cure a local chieftain by killing a pair of serpents in his roof and a two-headed toad under his grinding-stone. In payment, the chieftain had to give Huathiacuri (who traveled in poor and shabby disguise) his beautiful daughter in marriage.

"Family connection with such an upstart medicine-man so annoyed the brother-in-law of the daughter that he challenged Huathiacuri to a musical contest. . . . Pariacaca told Huathiacuri how to find a magic zampoña and drum. When he met a fox and a skunk who had stopped to feast on a dead guanaco, they would run away, the fox leaving his zampoña, the skunk her drum. With these he would be sure to conquer.

"The brother-in-law assembled two hundred women to shake their small drums and numerous men to help him play the zampoña, but Huathiacuri defeated them all. Moreover, he drank as much chica beer as two hundred guests. . . ."

Musical Instruments of the World (4) Africa

In music, Africa is famous above all for its drums and for its unparalleled cultivation of the art of drumming. Drums are the most important member of the *percussion* category of instruments, which includes all those that are struck or rattled to produce the sound.

Drums in a bewildering variety of shapes and sizes are found throughout the various parts of Africa. Besides accompanying other performers, drums are played by themselves, singly or in groups. They can convey messages in "tone language," represent deities, and express the majesty of kings. The rhythms that African drummers can tap out and comprehend are so subtle and complex that Western observers simply could not discern them until very recent times.

The rhythms of African drumming differ from those of jazz (and even from those of jazz drumming). But clearly it was the African heritage of black Americans that led to the evolution of jazz, a musical style that depends on intricate rhythmic effects of its own. Slaves brought with them the highly developed rhythmic sense of the African tribes. Preserved and modified on the plantations and in the black urban ghettos, this finally emerged in a new form to in-spire the most vital form of twentieth-century popular music (see pages 504–24).

Below (to the right) we see a variety of drums from the Ivory Coast, and on the facing page, yet another type of drum played by a young initiated man of the Senuoto tribe. The remarkable carved drum also shown on the facing page has as its base a man who seems to be teaching a boy the mysteries of African drumming. But why is he sitting on a leopard? The secret meaning of this wonderful artifact of the Vili people, in the Congo, is not known.

Finally, the picture below left shows one African example of the last musical instrument category, *brass instruments*—even though these trumpets from Ghana are made of elephant tusks, not metal. What characterizes instruments of this category is not the substance of which they are made but the manner in which the sound is produced, by means of cup- or funnel-shape mouthpieces. The wooden *alphorn,* up to ten feet in length, blasts over the Swiss mountainside to call in flocks. The rams-horn *shofar* has been employed since Biblical times in Jewish ceremonials. Bronze trumpets calls *lurs* have survived from Scandinavia, perhaps from as early as 3000 B.C.

Instruments of the Orchestra (1)

The double spread on the next four pages shows the instruments of the standard symphony orchestra. On pages 64–65 the main instruments are illustrated (with all the pictures reduced by the same scale, 15:1). On this page and the facing page, the same instruments are categorized and described. As far as possible, instruments are described and illustrated in the same areas on the pages, so that you can flip back and forth from one to another.

Instruments are made in *families,* which consist of items of the same basic construction but of different sizes and therefore with different ranges of pitch. Violins and cellos are examples of instruments belonging to the violin

family; alto and tenor saxophones belong to the saxophone family, and so on. By including whole families of instruments, bands and orchestras can get a full pitch-range of sound in every tone color, and they can also use the family members together, to make a group that blends particularly well.

For the general categories in use for Western instruments, see page 55. The capsule descriptions below are arranged so that instruments having a relatively *high* range are on the left, those with *low* range on the right.

Finally, on page 63 are shown two seating plans for orchestras that are popular today.

STRING INSTRUMENTS

VIOLIN	VIOLA	VIOLONCELLO	DOUBLE BASS
The violin family, in four sizes, covers almost any pitch needed in symphonic music.	The "tenor" instrument, two or three inches longer than the violin.	Usually abbreviated to *cello;* the bass instrument, played between the knees.	Also called *string bass* and *bass viol;* the deep bass instrument, up to six feet tall.

HARP The orchestra harp is a large instrument covering six and a half octaves.

←--high range ---------------------------- middle range ------------------------- low range----→

BRASS INSTRUMENTS

TRUMPET   BASS TRUMPET

A long *cylindrical* tube (except for the very end, which flares out). The player blows into a small cup-shaped mouthpiece; the lips themselves actually vibrate, like a double reed. Mouthpieces of this kind, sometimes called *loose-lip mouthpieces,* are used with all the brass instruments.

The player controls pitch by *overblowing* (blowing in a way that produces overtones: see page 15) or by pressing valves that open or shut extra pipes linked to the main tube.

TENOR TROMBONE   BASS TROMBONE

Low-range instruments essentially similar to the trumpet, except for the fact that pitch is controlled by a sliding mechanism (the *slide*) instead of by valves. Less bright and martial than the trumpet, the trombone can produce a variety of sounds, ranging from an almost vocal quality in the higher register to a hard, low, blaring tone in the lower.

FRENCH HORN

A long *conical* tube wound into a handsome spiral shape. The funnel-shaped loose-lip mouthpiece and conical tube produce a beautiful mellow tone. Pitch is controlled as on the trumpet.

TENOR TUBA   BASS TUBA

Low-range instruments similar to the French horn, but with conical tubes of somewhat different proportions. The tone is "fatter" and less focused than that of the French horn.

WOODWIND INSTRUMENTS

PICCOLO
Short for *flauto piccolo*, Italian for "small flute." Higher in pitch than the flute.

FLUTE
Basically a cylinder with a side hole for blowing. The player holds it horizontally, blows down through the hole, and to control pitch covers or uncovers other holes in the cylinder (as on all woodwinds). The flute is the highest and gentlest of the woodwinds.

E♭ CLARINET
A small, high clarinet.

CLARINET
An elastic reed made of cane is fitted against a mouthpiece (*beak*). When held in the mouth and blown through, the reed vibrates against the beak. The clarinet is more mellow and flexible than the other woodwinds.

BASS CLARINET
This rather long instrument is bent twice, like a saxophone.

OBOE
A double reed (two reeds clamped together with an air space in between) is held in the mouth and blown through. The reeds vibrate against one another; this gives the oboe its bright and pungent tone.

ENGLISH HORN
Hopelessly named, this is *not* English and *not* a horn but just a "tenor" oboe.

BASSOON

CONTRABASSOON
(or double bassoon)

The bass members of the oboe family are so long that they have to be bent back on themselves several times. Of all bass instruments, bassoons have the clearest, most penetrating tone.

PERCUSSION INSTRUMENTS

XYLOPHONE
Tuned wood blocks played with hammers.

TIMPANI Also called *kettledrums*; large drums tuned to a definite pitch, used in sets of two or three. *Pedal timpani* are provided with a device to change pitch instantaneously.

TRIANGLE
A bent metal bar, struck with a metal beater; produces a bright tinkling sound.

CYMBALS
Two brass plates clapped together, producing a shattering crash.

GONG
(Not illustrated.) A rich, bell-like roaring sound.

BASS DRUM
(Not illustrated.) The lowest, heaviest sound in the orchestra.

ORCHESTRAL SEATING PLANS

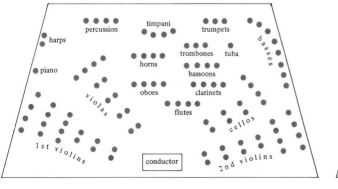

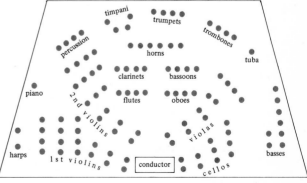

Instruments of the Orchestra (2)

STRING INSTRUMENTS

Violin

Viola

Cello

Double bass

Harp

The Metropolitan Museum of Art, Crosby Brown Collection of Musical Instruments, 1889

BRASS INSTRUMENTS

Trumpet

French horn

Trombone

Tuba

WOODWIND INSTRUMENTS

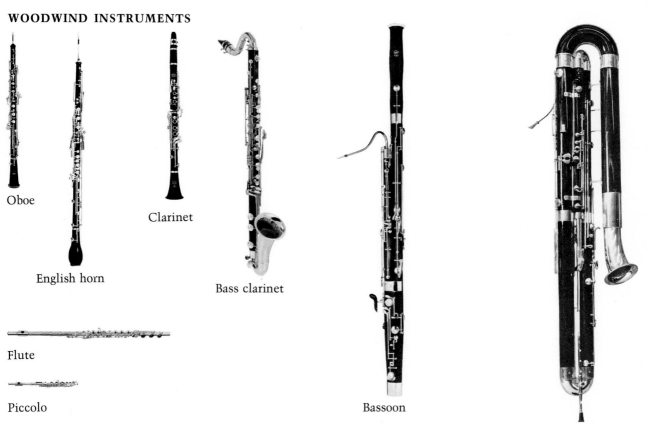

Oboe

English horn

Clarinet

Bass clarinet

Flute

Piccolo

Bassoon

Contrabassoon
(Double bassoon)

PERCUSSION INSTRUMENTS

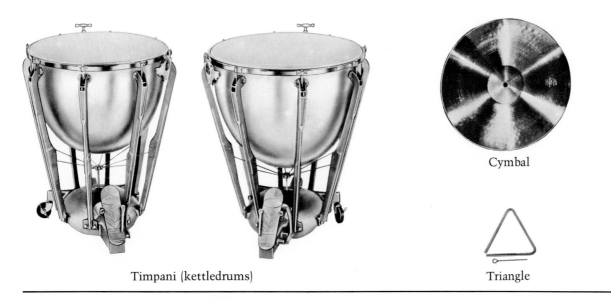

Timpani (kettledrums)

Cymbal

Triangle

CHAPTER 3 | The Middle Ages I

The Middle Ages   I

We take it as a matter of course that music and the other arts are available to all. Time, patience, a little money, incentive—incentive is the main thing—if we only care enough, we can all come to enjoy painting, architecture, poetry, or music. But this was not always the case. It is only in our century that art has become more or less "democratic" and that a major new art form, the movies, has grown up on a mass basis. In the past, the arts belonged to a small elite.

Before the invention of printing in the fifteenth century, books were few and jealously guarded; access to written literature was considered a rare privilege. Though architecture—exterior architecture—was always visible to those in the neighborhood, easel paintings were not, until the institution of public art galleries in the nineteenth century. The beautiful ceramics, gold work, and statuary we see in museums were purchased by the rich. Music, too, or at least the most highly developed music, used to be heard and cherished by only a small fraction of the population.

Two major forces led to its democratization—a sociological development in the eighteenth century, and a technological advance in the twentieth. The latter we know well: it is the invention of sound recording. Today millions of people who rarely attend actual musical performances hear music every day, thanks to cassettes, records, and broadcasts. Popular music is geared to the tastes of this mass audience—and to the packaging and promotional routines of today's music industry.

The sociological development was the institution of concerts. Occasions on which music was presented to the general public, at a price, did not always exist. They came into being during the eighteenth century in great cities such as London, Paris, and Vienna. Concerts served the rising bourgeois or commercial classes of Europe—not what we would call a mass audience, but nevertheless one that was much wider than before. These people paid their money and expected a concert to be something of an occasion. They demanded (and got) music of a certain substance and dignity: symphonies, concertos, and the like, which they could think of as impressive "masterpieces."

What were music making and listening like in the days before concerts and records? We should give a moment's thought to this before starting our examination of old music, for the music of early times was designed by and for people whose view of music was very different from our own. If we come to it with modern expectations, we risk misunderstandings and disappointments.

Music and the Church

The paramount influence of the Christian Church on the history of Western music is not easy for us to conceive today (see the picture insert on page 72). For hundreds of years from the beginning of the Middle Ages, the Church was the only source of intellectual and artistic life, and for hundreds of years after that it was the main source, if no longer the exclusive one. The Church cultivated music as it did art, architecture, poetry, and learning. The great monasteries were the first great centers of music, joined later by the cathedrals and court chapels. All composers were churchmen, and all musicians got their training as church choirboys. (Exception must always be made for popular musicians, minstrels, and jongleurs, whom we shall discuss briefly later. As a class they already had the reputation of vagabonds. Alas, we know next to nothing about their music, because the only people who wrote music down were monks and other clerics.)

As a result, the study of music of the Middle Ages is concerned largely with church music, and the study of music of the Dark Ages—the early Middle Ages from the fifth to about the tenth centuries—is concerned exclusively with church music. In our own secular age, this may strain the patience of some readers. Perhaps the strain may be eased by the thought that these readers themselves would almost certainly have been in the Church if they had been living in the early Middle Ages. Almost anyone who could *read* was in the Church. Anyone with an education in any way analogous to a college education today would have obtained it from the Church and would have expected to enter the Church. Business, engineering, medicine, law, advertising—such careers were almost nonexistent. Those who were lucky enough to be barons feasted and hunted and warred and wenched as they pleased. The awfulness of a peasant's life defies the modern imagination, and soldiering was not for everybody. The only other careers were those of the Church.

In any case, medieval church music deserves study, not only for its intrinsic beauties, but also for historical reasons. As will become clear from the next few chapters of this book, the music of the medieval Church was fundamental to that of the several succeeding eras of music history. It still resonated in the time of Mozart and the time of Stravinsky. If we wish to have a comprehensive understanding of Western music, we cannot afford to hurry past it.

MUSIC AND LITURGY

liturgy Central to the Christian Church, as to most others, is a highly organized system of services of worship, or a liturgy. Music was deeply involved with this system, down to its smallest detail. If we could say that the services were at the heart of Christianity, we could also say that music was its heartbeat.

For it was the role of music to smooth the progress of the services and also to make them more impressive and solemn. Music ornamented the services.

What the architects of the great abbey churches and cathedrals did for the places where worship was held, and what the illuminators of manuscripts did for the books used in worship, musicians did for the actual performance of worship itself.

The "worship" we are talking about here was that conducted in monasteries and cathedrals. It was, essentially, private devotions for a community of monks or nuns or for the members of cathedral chapter (which is the name for the clergy attached to a bishop—an ecclesiastical district administrator centered at a cathedral). There was no outside congregation. What happened in the parish churches attended by the peasants is not known, but it is highly unlikely that much music was ever heard in them. Parish priests, who were overworked and not overeducated, probably spoke or mumbled their way through the services. Their congregations did not understand Latin anyway, except perhaps in the early Middle Ages in Italy. And these parishioners spent most of their time working in the fields, not praying.

Members of monastic communities, however, spent an amazing amount of their time in communal prayer. Besides the Mass—a lengthy ceremony that might take place more than once every day—there were no fewer than eight other services distributed throughout the day (and night). These are called the Office Services, or Canonical Hours. The modern evensong service is derived from the Office Service called vespers. Though each of the nine services had its standard form, many details changed daily according to a fixed schedule. Thus on December 25, reference was made to the birth of Jesus, on the 26th (St. Stephen's Day) to the martyrdom of that saint, on the 27th (St. John's) to the truth of the Gospel of John—and so on, day by day throughout the year. As a result, there were literally thousands of texts specified for the Mass and the Office Services on the various days of the Church calendar. And the majority of these texts had to be set to music and sung.

Why sung? The answer to this question is not unique to the Christian Church. Nearly all religions (the Quakers are an exception) have built their services around the communal repetition of sacred texts—not silent repetition (few could read in those early days) but *sounded* repetition, through which the holy words could be heard, mouthed, and absorbed by all. And for such "sounded repetition," singing has always seemed more natural than speaking. Apart from the tediousness and sheer ugliness of communal speaking, the rhythm of song (even when it is comparatively free) keeps everyone together and allows for audibility. And the melody of song helps people remember the words.

In the early Middle Ages, the actual composing of church music was less a matter of free invention than of making small additions and adjustments to a traditional and sanctified prototype. For example, if a new Mass or Office was needed for a new saint, the composer might do no more than shuffle around some pieces that already belonged to the service of a similar saint or, at most, compose music rather similar to such pieces. Listening to church music was not so much listening as worshiping, while allowing music to expand the devotional experience.

Light in the Dark Ages

The term *Middle Ages* covers a historical period of almost a thousand years, from around 450 A.D. to 1400—which is clearly too much for comfort. Perhaps the main orientation points to bear in mind, when scanning this huge historical panorama, are the fall of the Roman Empire in the fifth century, the rise of towns in the eleventh century, and the rise of universities in the twelfth. The eleventh and twelfth centuries are also the ages of the great Romanesque and early Gothic cathedrals, respectively (see page 82).

The graphic term *Dark Ages* is sometimes used for the early part of this long period. In political terms, Europe spent the Dark Ages groping for some kind of political order to replace the Roman Empire. In religious terms, it was preoccupied with the conversion of one barbarian nation after another to Christianity and with the various schisms and heresies that Christianity had to weather for hundreds of years after its inception. With honorable exceptions at certain places in certain periods, the state of culture and learning was low.

However, there was one light that could be said to have burned continuously throughout the Dark Ages. This was the monastic side of Christianity. Founded as early as the sixth century, the monasteries brought together men (and later women) committed to the religious life. Monks were not recluses; they were the main instruments in the spread of Christianity throughout Northern Europe. Their monasteries were hospitals, dispensers of charity, agricultural estates, and centers of such primitive technology as existed in those times. They were also Europe's centers of meditation, literacy, and the arts.

A remarkable document exists at the Abbey of St. Gall in Switzerland, a detailed architectural plan for a ninth-century monastery. Evidently it was a master plan, perhaps never executed exactly, but intended to be followed as closely as local conditions would admit. Thanks to its extensive annotations (which have not, however, been carried over into our much-reduced reproduction), this St. Gall Plan provides a vivid record of a self-contained medieval community living under an elaborate system of

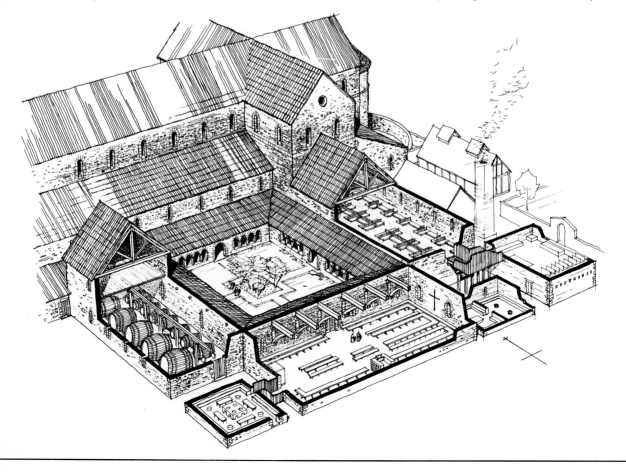

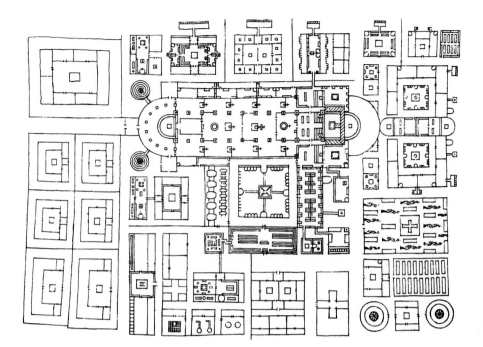

rules. It has attracted much attention recently among planners and sociologists. Today we know how to split the atom, but the ancient art of community organization eludes us.

Look first at an artist's reconstruction of one part of the Plan. Nestling up against the church, as though seeking sustenance or protection from it, we see the monks' quarters. In the center is the cloister, a garden with a well in the middle and an enclosed walkway around it, where the monks could take exercise even in the rain and the snow. In the front is their dining hall, with the adjoining kitchen and the cellar at the left. The pantry was above the cellar. At the right, under the gable, is the dormitory, and to the far right, the privy.

On the Plan itself, you can perhaps make out the same features (including the wine and beer barrels, whose size and number were specified exactly). Three large buildings are shown above the church: the guest house, the school, and the abbot's house. Since the abbot was an administrator who had to deal with the outside world, his house was placed outside the monks' compound—but with a direct entrance to the church. Stables, chicken coops, water mills, a cemetery (marked with a cross), an herb garden to grow medicinal herbs: every detail of life is accounted for in this amazing record of community organization.

The systematic frame of mind that spelled out the rules by which the monks lived as precisely as this also planned the center of their lives—the services—with the same precision. Notice that there is not even a space in front of this church, let alone an imposing front or façade to it, as there is in the city or even the village churches we know. An abbey church was not designed to welcome (or impress) an outside congregation, but rather to receive the monks, insiders whose whole lives were conducted within its shadows. They observed eight services a day (the Office Services) as well as Mass, and these were all worked out in minute detail according to the Church year. Music decorated these services, and the music, too, was worked out in similar detail to fit the services. Gregorian chants called introits, at the beginning of Mass, had a different musical style from later chants called graduals, and so on.

Just as this Plan was intended to be followed in the building of all monasteries, books of Gregorian chant were circulated to specify all the chants to be sung at every monastery, at every service on every day of the Church year. Depending on local conditions, one could vary the architectural plan somewhat. Similarly, latitude was allowed for local conditions in the type of chant known as tropes, additions to the fixed, traditional Gregorian repertory (see page 81).

It is therefore not surprising that this music should strike us very differently from later music. It was conceived in an entirely different sociological context. It was designed not for an audience but for the performers—the worshipers—themselves. Hearing Gregorian chant or later church music of the Middle Ages, we feel less like listeners in the modern sense than like privileged eavesdroppers, who have been allowed to sit in at a select occasion that is partly musical but mainly spiritual. The experience is an intimate and tranquil one, cool and satisfying in a unique way.

Gregorian Chant

Gregorian chant

The official music of the Catholic Church in the Middle Ages (and far beyond the Middle Ages) was a great repertory of plainchant or plainsong known as Gregorian chant. It is called "plain" because it is unaccompanied, monophonic (one-line) music for voices without fixed rhythm. It is called "Gregorian" after Pope Gregory I (circa 540–607). Tradition gives Gregory credit for assembling and standardizing the hundreds of chants required for all the services on all the days of the Church year. He resolved questions and confusions about which chant went where, and he seems to have tried to establish rules about performance.

Gregory codified the chant; he did not compose it. Much had been written earlier, and a great deal was added later to the so-called Gregorian repertory. But the importance of his work should not be underestimated. The popes sought to establish the central authority of the Church over all its far-flung branches, and a major part of this program involved standardizing the services. They wanted a single body of "official" music, sung not only in Rome but throughout Christendom, by Africans and Norsemen, by the Eastern Franks and by the Welsh and the Irish. Singers were sent from Rome to ecclesiastical centers all over Europe to assure that the right notes were sung in the right manner.

There are very many categories of Gregorian music, of which we shall take up just a few. They range widely in their melodic styles—from simple chanting on a monotone, with only slight deviations from a single pitch, to extremely long and complicated songs ranging well over an octave in pitch, reminiscent of the ecstatic, improvised singing still to be heard in the Middle East. What determined the melodic style of any particular chant was not its words but its role in the services. At the high points of major services on major feast days—at Midnight Mass on Christmas, for example—the melodic style is at its most elaborate. At the daily round of Office Services, the music is much simpler.

THE MEDIEVAL MODES

In chapter 1, when first discussing scales (page 16), we pointed out that the original scale of Western music was the diatonic scale, the "white note" scale on the piano. The chromatic scale was only introduced later. Then on pages

42–6, discussing the concepts of tonality and modality, we remarked that most of the music familiar today employs the note C or A as the central one within the diatonic scale. Centered on C, the music is said to be in the major mode; centered on A, it is in the minor. The major and minor modes, too, like the chromatic scale, are of relatively recent origin.

The early Middle Ages was a time when the diatonic scale was the only one, and when the two modern modes, major and minor, were not yet in use. It is an interesting fact that, whereas Gregorian chant uses more than two modes —four, in fact—these four are all different from our modern two.

Reduced to its simplest terms, the modality of Gregorian chant is based on one of the four notes D, E, F, or G as centers within the diatonic scale. The modes were referred to by numbers or by Greek names, since medieval musical scholars traced them back to the modes of ancient Greek music. (Not that they had heard any Greek music, but they were able to read some writings about it that had somehow been preserved in the Dark Ages. The joke is that we now know they got things mixed up: the medieval Dorian is actually what the Greeks had called Phrygian, etc.) Here are the medieval modes:

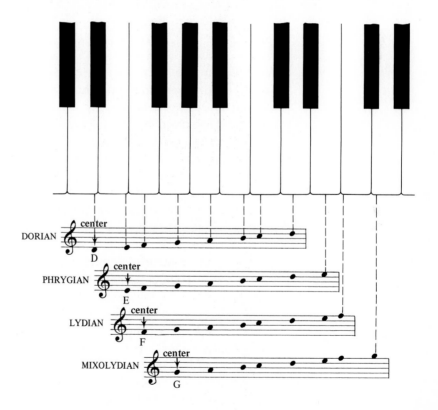

The essential distinction between the major and minor modes comes in their different arrangements of intervals—half steps and whole steps—around the centers. The medieval modes provide four other arrangements. (Compare the above diagram with the one on page 44.) In this respect, then, medieval chant is richer than modern music. If it sounds puzzling at first, that is partly because we are not sensitive to the subtleties available to this richer modal system.

The modal system of Gregorian chant continued, with some modifications, throughout the Middle Ages. It also continued during the Renaissance. This is an impressive record of longevity; what is more, later composers have not infrequently employed "modal" (that is, medieval modal) sounds for special effects of one kind or another. We are familiar with such modal sounds from folk songs, some of which may go all the way back to the Middle Ages or the Renaissance, and others of which have been composed later in the same modal style. *Greensleeves* is a Dorian melody (with a modification at its cadences). Bob Dylan's *Tomorrow is a long time* is Mixolydian.

The surge of popularity of folk songs in the 1950s—some old, some new—brought these modal sounds into the forefront of people's awareness. What is more, harmonies based on modal scales became increasingly characteristic of rock music—partly as a result of the folk movement, which was one of the influences on rock. So perhaps we are now coming to the point where medieval modal melodies sound more familiar to us than pieces in the major-minor system. Perhaps, if we could bring a medieval musician back in a time machine, he would feel more at home with a rock number than with a Beethoven symphony.

HYMNS

hymn

A simple category of Gregorian music is the <u>hymn</u>, a regular item of the Office Services. (There are no hymns in the Mass.) Hymns can serve as a good introduction to the world of Gregorian chant, even though they stand somewhat apart from the main repertory; of all the Gregorian categories, this is probably the one that seems least mysterious to modern listeners.

Gregorian hymns consist of straightforward tunes that are not very long, with clear phrases, sung over and over again, to poems of many stanzas. At the end comes a brief Amen. In fact, Gregorian hymns are in principle exactly like the modern hymns we are familiar with; a few of these venerable tunes even appear with translations in current Protestant hymnbooks. You may remember that in chapter 1, when we discussed melody for the first time, we specifically made the point that a typical plainchant is *not* a tune. Very true—and the point will be clearer by the end of this chapter. But Gregorian hymns form an exception.

Is it that the hymns come from a later, more modern period than the rest of Gregorian chant? Yes and no: for while the actual tunes we have may be relatively late, we know that the concept goes back several centuries before the time of Gregory. The idea of taking popular songs and writing spiritual words to them, as a way of bringing religion to the people, is attributed to St. Ambrose (circa 340–397), one of the four great doctors—that is, scholars or teachers—of the early Church. (St. Gregory was one of the others, along with St. Jerome, who translated the Bible into Latin, and of course St. Augustine.) But shortly after the death of Ambrose, edicts were passed prohibiting hymns, on the ground that popular music was having a deleterious effect on the purity of the Church. In any case, by the time hymns were regularized in the liturgy, they were no longer a popular, evangelical device but an element of the daily round of monastic services.

HYMN *Ave Maris Stella* (Hail, Star of the Oceans)

The charming hymn *Ave maris stella* is sung on all feasts honoring the Blessed Virgin Mary and celebrating the various events of her life. The ecstatic rising line in the first of the four phrases seems to fit nicely the words "stella" (star) and "Ave" (hail) in the first two stanzas:

Stz. 1 A - ve ma - ris stel-la,_____ De - i ma - ter al - ma, At-que sem-per Vir-go,_____ Fe-lix coe-li por-ta.
Stz. 2 Su - mens il - lud A - ve_____ *etc.*

Ave maris stella,	Hail, thou star of ocean,
Dei mater alma,	Gentle mother of God,
Atque semper virgo,	And also always virgin,
Felix caeli porta.	Joyous portal of the sky.
Sumens illud Ave	Taking that *Ave* [hail]
Gabrielis ore,	Uttered by Gabriel,
Funda nos in pace,	You establish us in peace
Mutans Hevae nomen	By reversing the name of "Eva" . . . .

(Five more stanzas)

Highlighting important words in this way is something familiar to us from more recent music. What is *not* familiar about this hymn is the freely flowing rhythm, which refuses to fit into a regular meter. Notice, too, characteristic modal sounds in the melody in phrases 1 (the note B) and 3 (the note C). If you find that they do bother you a little, after all, you can try the experiment of "correcting" or modernizing *Ave maris stella*; you will find that changing the Dorian mode to the modern minor by substituting B♭ and C♯ doesn't help. On our record, five of the hymn's seven stanzas are heard. After listening to the tune five times, you will very probably find yourself looking forward with more pleasure to these modal features than to any others in the hymn. They seem in the end absolutely right, natural, and lovely.

CHANTS OF THE MASS

More complex (and more characteristic) Gregorian chants belong to the Mass. This most important of the Catholic services will require a word or two of explanation.

The importance of the Mass lies in the fact that, for the participants, it is a daily reaffirmation of their association with Christ, of their essential Christianity. In the symbolic ritual of Communion, they reenact the Lord's Last Supper with the twelve apostles, and become one with Him by partaking of His body and blood through the consecrated bread and wine. There are various preparations for and ramifications of this central rite—for example, two solemn New Testament readings, drawn from the Gospels of Matthew, Mark,

Luke, or John and the Epistles of St. Paul to the Romans, Corinthians, etc. Many texts have to be set to music. Incense, the ringing of bells, rich ecclesiastical garments, and stylized action all contribute to the solemnity of this impressive service.

Ordinary of the Mass

The best known chants of the Mass are those that make up the so-called Ordinary of the Mass, whose texts are invariable: the Kyrie, Gloria, and Credo near the beginning of the service, and the Sanctus and Agnus Dei toward the end. These chants appear with the same words in every Mass. We shall have much to say about the Ordinary later in this book. Starting with the French poet-composer Guillaume de Machaut in the fourteenth century (see page 101), composers through the ages have set these Ordinary texts to music, making them into a unified artistic whole. Among later Mass composers are Josquin Des Prez, Palestrina, Monteverdi, Bach, Beethoven, Schubert, Liszt, and Stravinsky.

Proper of the Mass

No less important than the Ordinary, and much more numerous, are the chants of the Proper of the Mass. The word *proper* in this context means appropriate—the words of these chants vary from day to day, so that they are appropriate to the season of the Church year, the saint of the day, or the particular occasion. Consequently there are many more Proper chants than Ordinary ones. They fall into six categories: introits, graduals, tracts, alleluias, offertories, and communions.

The way the Ordinary and Proper items fit together in the Mass is shown by the following diagram:

PROPER CHANTS	ORDINARY CHANTS	ELEMENTS OF THE SERVICE
Introit (*introduction to the Mass*)		
	Kyrie	
	Gloria	
		Reading of the Epistle
Gradual (*or, during the Easter season, a second* Alleluia)		
Alleluia (*or, during Lent, a* Tract)		
		Reading of the Gospel
	Credo	
Offertory		
	Sanctus———	⌈The central ⊦ceremony of ⌊the bread and wine
	Agnus Dei	
Communion		
	Ite missa est (*conclusion of the Mass*)	

For the Ite missa est, see page 101. On page 26, a page from a medieval manuscript service book shows a Gloria, a Sanctus, and an Ite missa est.

Each category of chant has its own special characteristics. We shall examine only two of these categories: the introit, one of the simpler chants, and the gradual, one of the richest and most complicated. By choosing our examples of an introit and a gradual from the same Mass, we shall be able to suggest something of the total context of Gregorian music, as well as discussing the chant categories.

On the day of a person's death or funeral an extra Mass is celebrated, the Mass for the Dead, one of the most solemn and impressive of all Catholic services. The same Mass is also celebrated on days when the death is commemorated and on All Souls' Day, November 2, which is set aside for the remembrance of all the dead. Our examples are taken from that Mass.

INTROIT   *Requiem Aeternam* (Eternal Rest)   SIDE 1

The introit, from the word meaning *introduction,* is the first proper chant of the Mass. As such, it immediately sets the tone by stating the "proper" theme that is to be held in mind, along with all the "ordinary" themes of masses in general. In the case of the Mass for the Dead, the introit *Requiem aeternam* (Eternal rest) proposes a prayer for the souls of all the departed: "Grant them rest eternal, O Lord, and may the light of your blessing shine upon them forever."

The same words will be repeated and developed in several other of the Proper chants of this Mass. Indeed, the Mass takes its alternate name, the Requiem Mass, from the first word of the introit. (And from the first word of the introductory Gregorian chant to the Office Service for the Dead, "Dirige Domine," we derive our word *dirge.*)

Introits always fall into an A B A form, with A and B sections that differ in style. (On the use of letters for musical forms, see page 49.) A is more melodic, B simpler and more repetitious. This is because B consists of the recitation of a

reciting formula   psalm verse, "Te decet hymnus . . . ," according to a <u>reciting formula</u>. The music consists largely of a single repeated note, the note A, as shown by asterisks on the music example on page 80. This *reciting note* is generally approached by a sort of standardized melodic launching figure F–G–A (as at the words "et tibi" and "exaudi"; an expansion of the same figure comes at the words "Te decet"). Such reciting formulas are used very commonly, not only in introits but also in other Gregorian categories.

Gregorian chant, as we have emphasized, lacks fixed rhythm, and it seems only natural to speed up the tempo somewhat during these repetitious passages sung to reciting formulas. In the A section of the introit, furthermore, notice how the singers stretch out certain notes and hurry over others, in order to "mold" the flexible melodic line into as graceful and coherent an entity as possible.

The introit's A section is much more melodic than the B section (though neither could possibly be called a tune). Considering how few notes are used—no more than five in all—it is amazing how free and buoyant the climax points sound (on the note C, marked by an arrow):

The melody is balanced by careful parallels between its phrases. Phrase 4 is a slightly abbreviated version of phrase 2, and phrases 1, 2, and 4 all end with approximately the same group of notes (marked with a bracket). Despite its genuinely melodic character, this A section will, on careful listening, reveal its origin in recitation—recitation on the same note (A) as in the verse, with the same launching figure (F–G–A).

GRADUAL *Requiem Aeternam* (Eternal Rest)   SIDE S–1

responsial chant

To get to the full scope and richness of Gregorian chant, we have to turn to the general type of chant known as <u>responsorial chant</u>. Here one or two trained soloists "respond" to, or sing in alternation with, the main choir of monks. Two categories of responsorial chant from the Proper of the Mass are the gradual and the alleluia (see the table on page 78). They form a musical interlude between the two New Testament readings, the Epistle and the Gospel.

Gradual may seem an odd name for a chant; actually, it comes from the Latin *gradus,* meaning a step, since graduals were originally sung at the altar steps. It may also seem odd that in the Mass for the Dead, the words of the gradual *Requiem aeternam* are identical with those of the introit (throughout their A sections). But, since the gradual *Requiem aeternam* occupies a more important place in the service than the introit *Requiem aeternam,* the same words are now sung to much more elaborate music.

melisma

The main means of achieving elaboration is the use of <u>melismas</u>, groups of many notes for a single syllable of text. This is an important stylistic feature of Gregorian chant. Listening to this gradual, we can easily understand that the melismatic style was too taxing for ordinary monks. It required trained soloists: hence the development of the responsorial style.

Even in the introit (look at the example on page 80) there is a modest melisma of eight notes on the syllables "e*is*" and "luce*at*." In the gradual, however, the emphasized syllables in the text below have melismas with from fourteen to thirty-seven notes:

SOLOISTS: *Requiem . . .*
Rest . . .

CHOIR: *. . . aeternam dona eis Domi**ne**: et lux perpetu**a** luceat **eis**.*
. . . eternal be granted to them, O Lord: and let eternal light shine upon them.

SOLOISTS: *In memoria ae**ter**na erit iu**s**tus: ab auditione **mala** . . .*
The just man shall be remembered eternally: ill tidings . . .

CHORUS: *. . . non time**bit**.*
. . . he shall not fear.

Those who know some Latin will see at once that the melismas do not usually highlight the words by stressing the most important syllables, as we might expect; when those words are spoken, the accents do not fall on "Do-mi*ne*," "perpetu*a*," "e*is*," "ma*la*," or "time*bit*." The melismas come at the ends of phrases because the composers found that this gave them the greatest scope for their art of spinning out melodies into long, infinitely subtle strands. These melodic strands seem to oscillate unpredictably, yet somehow always purposefully—floating, hovering, meditating, all in a remarkable mood of quiet controlled ecstasy.

Tropes

An important category of later plainchant that is not considered "Gregorian" is that of the *tropes*. Tropes were composed from the ninth to the fifteenth centuries. In the musical style and form of the tropes, some scholars see the first influences of the kind of melodic thinking that characterizes modern music.

The basic principle of troping is to add to the traditional service music. That "official" repertory had now been more or less fixed forever by Pope Gregory; but the Middle Ages developed a mania for adding words and music to the beginnings and ends of standard chants, and even to the middles. Here, for example, is what happened to the simplest item of the Ordinary of the Mass, the Kyrie:

ORIGINAL CHANT: *Kyrie eleison. Christe eleison. Kyrie eleison.*
Lord have mercy on us. Christ have mercy on us. Lord have mercy on us.

ORIGINAL CHANT WITH TROPE: *Eia omnigenis vocibus domino, reddentes odas debitas. Kyrie eleison. Invocantum nomen tuum, rex sabaoth, audi preces supplicum. Christe eleison. Kyrie eleison.*
Yea, with multifarious voices let us return the praises that are due to the Lord. Lord have mercy on us. As we invoke thy name, O King of Hosts, harken to the prayer of thy supplicants. Christ have mercy on us. Lord have mercy on us.

Romanesque and Gothic

The use of the epithet "Dark Ages" for the early Middle Ages evokes images of hardship and ignorance. As far as it goes, the picture is certainly true. The common people of Europe endured the most meager existence, sustained by means of endless hard work. They lived in isolated, vulnerable communities, lacking acquaintance with the outside world. The knowledge that had been acquired in ancient times was largely forgotten.

But, even in the darkest period, new learning developed and spread. Where land was flat and fields were wide, the peasants learned to harness a plow to fast horses instead of the slow, plodding oxen of even earlier times. They learned how to rotate crops, which further increased the yield of their land. Others learned to use running water as a source of power, to turn the wheels of their mills. And eventually they learned to use the power of the wind. The European landscape was soon dotted with windmills.

The outcome of all the slow learning of the Dark Ages was in the end momentous. Better methods of farming provided a greater abundance of food for a larger population. New sources of power led to the beginning of manufacturing, especially of cloth. Towns such as Paris and London, Bruges in Belgium and Basel in Switzerland, were built up, and trade developed. By the year 1100, Europe had settled into the elaborately organized system of feudalism that typifies the High Middle Ages, and society had achieved a stability that was to last for several centuries. Confidence, a sense of permanence, and high technical skill inspired the work of the High Middle Ages and directed the energies of the period toward building instead of just surviving.

The wonderful churches of this period, solid, grave, and confident, are called *Romanesque,* because such features as their rounded arches were carryovers from Roman times. But the quality of a Romanesque church, such as this one at Toulouse in central France, is far removed from the classical spirit of Rome (see facing page). Its thick walls and strong geometric shapes are firmly tied to the earth. Its decorations are clearly and beautifully molded without being flamboyant. The building conveys strength and solemnity without vanity or self-consciousness.

No such impressive construction had yet been achieved in music. Nevertheless we can see the constructive spirit at work in this art, too. It is shown in the impulse to decorate a syllable with melismatic flourishes. It is shown even more in the elaboration of thought by means of the added commentary expressed in tropes. And it is shown especially in the invention of polyphony, the most original creation of medieval construction in music. We shall trace the early development of polyphony through several stages in chapter 4.

As the skills and the imagination of the Middle Ages mounted up, so did the aspirations of the time. The great medieval builders began to reach for a new radiance. Their cathedrals became more sinuous and intricate. Stone was given a marvelous lightness and delicacy in great columns that extended to astonishing heights. The high vaulted ceilings together with the carved decorations, stained glass, and fine pointed arches all mark the celebrated architectural style known as *Gothic.* The famous flying buttresses of Notre Dame Cathedral in Paris (see below), the outcome of an impressive technological advance of later Gothic architecture, can be compared to the airy intertwining voice lines of late medieval polyphony.

With music to match. And there were dozens of different Kyrie tropes of this kind, most of them much longer.

Although we might consider that nine services a day were quite enough, the monks and clerics of the time did not hesitate to extend them. Troping was the only way they could make an individual commentary on behalf of themselves or their local situation or, indeed, their era. They could not change the traditional services, but they could contribute something of their own to these rituals by a process of addition. Many tropes ran on for much longer than the original plainchants to which they were attached and that had provided the excuse for their existence.

In a later, less leisurely age, all but a very few favorite tropes were abolished from the services. Consequently this chant category is less known today, though it was a major outlet of artistic creativity in the later Middle Ages.

THOMAS OF CELANO *Dies Irae* (The Day of Wrath) SIDE 1

Tropes made use of the best modern poetry, though still in Latin, and a vigorous, tuneful, melodic style. The most famous of them, the *Dies irae* (Day of wrath), originated as an insert to a chant from the Office (not the Mass) for the Dead. But it was so popular it was transferred to the Mass, where it is still sung today, despite the demise of hundreds of other tropes. The *Dies irae* has a strong, terrifying poem by the poet Thomas of Celano about the rigors and the anguish of judgment day:

The day of wrath, that dreadful day,
Shall the whole world in ashes lay,
As David and the Sibyls say.

Oh, what fear shall it engender,
When the Judge shall come in splendor,
Strict to mark and just to render!

The last loud trumpet's wondrous sound
Shall through the rending tombs rebound,
And wake the nations under ground.

All aghast then Death shall shiver
And great Nature's frame shall quiver,
When the graves their dead deliver.

Then shall, with universal dread,
The sacred mystic Book be read,
To try the living and the dead.

The Judge ascends the awful throne,
He makes each secret sin be known,
And all with shame confess their own.

Wretched man, what can I plead?
Whom can I ask to intercede,
When even the just His mercy need?

Dreadful King, all power possessing,
Saving freely those confessing,
Save Thou me, O Fount of Blessing!

(Twelve more stanzas)

It has a melody which perhaps more than any other plainchant has seared itself onto the musical consciousness of later centuries. We shall hear this melody referred to in the works of more than one modern composer.

Typical of tropes is the series of different little tunes here, each consisting of only three phrases. (These match the poetic stanzas of three short lines each.) Also typical is the one-time repetition of the three tunes—each with three phrases—shown in the example below, making a chainlike form, A A B B C C, for stanzas 1–6:

tune A

Stz. 1. Di - es i - rae, di - es il - la, Sol - vet sae - clum in fa - vil - la: Tes - te Da - vid cum Sy - bi - la.
Stz. 2. Quan-tus tre-mor est fu-tu-rus, Quan-do Ju - dex est ven-tu-rus, Cun-cta stri-cte dis-cus-su-rus!

tune B

Stz. 3. Tu- ba mi- rum spar - gens so - num__ Per se-pul-cra re - gi - o -num, Co- get o - mnes an- te Thro-num.
Stz. 4. Mors stu-pe-bit et na-tu - ra,__ Cum re-sur-gat cre-a - tu - ra, Ju - di - can - ti re-spon-su - ra.

tune C

Stz. 5. Li- ber scri-ptus pro - fe-re - tur, In quo to-tum con-ti - ne - tur, Un-de mun-dus ju - di - ce - tur.__
Stz. 6. Ju - dex er - go cum se-de - bit, Quid-quid la-tet ap-pa-re - bit: Nil in - ul-tum re-ma-ne - bit.__

At this point the *Dies irae* goes back and starts the music over again for stanzas 7–12 and 13–17. Perhaps the composer did this to convey a gloomy, obsessive feeling; he certainly seems to have sought such an effect by repeating phrases between tunes A and B, which are not so different after all (see the brackets in the example). Over the whole span of the *Dies irae,* the music of phrases 1 and 2 is heard no fewer than twelve times.

So when at stanza 18 the music finally breaks out of its repetitive pattern, the effect is very moving. (The words are "Lacrimosa dies illa . . . ," "That will be a day for weeping.") Do you hear what the composer does here that is new? And after this he has yet another fresh effect at his disposal: the nearly hopeless, childlike, numb appeal of the final prayer "Blessed Lord Jesus, grant them peace." *Pie Iesu, Domine, Dona eis requiem:* this final sentence reiterates once again the cardinal words of the Mass for the Dead.

The Play of Daniel

Toward the end of the Dark Ages, the principle of troping (page 81) allowed poets and musicians to make their own contributions to or commentaries on the traditional, fixed Gregorian chant. Medieval artists expressed their individuality only in the shadow, as it were, of authority.

The most extraordinary tropes involved a dialogue between several singers and even some stylized action: they are the medieval *liturgical dramas.* In recent times *The Play of Daniel* and *The Play of Herod,* dating from the thirteenth century, have been revived with success. Performed in a church or a cathedral, with colorful costumes and lively accompaniment on medieval instruments, as in our illustrations, they make a delightful religious entertainment. They are, to all intents and purposes, little operas, sung in Latin and lasting for up to forty-five minutes.

Daniel started life as a trope to the *Te Deum,* an important chant that comes at the end of the Office Service called matins. Its musical style resembles that of the *Dies irae,* and its story tells how Daniel interpreted the mysterious words "Mene mene tekel upharsin" to mean that the Babylonian King Belshazzar would be overthrown by Darius, king of the Medes and Persians, and how God preserved Daniel from his troubles under the new king (Book of Daniel, v–vi). A narrator sets the scene. A chorus sings the praises of King Belshazzar, and later another chorus announces the arrival of the army of Darius. Daniel's enemies denounce him to Darius with a wheedling song. Daniel sings a prayer in the lions' den. The Angel leads him out, and the lions eat Daniel's enemies. Everybody joins in the *Te Deum,* which is the occasion for a solemn, triumphant procession around the church.

This liturgical drama grew up as an enormously extended trope to an innocent Gregorian melody. In fact, sung drama came before spoken drama. *Daniel* and *Herod* are the forerunners of all later European drama—the late medieval mystery plays, the morality plays like *Everyman,* Shakespeare, and beyond.

CHAPTER 4 | The Middle Ages   II

The Middle Ages   II

Two momentous developments in the history of Western music can serve to demarcate two broad periods within the huge span of the Middle Ages. The change from what is called the Dark Ages to the high Middle Ages was reflected as strongly in music as in art, technology, thought, and the organization of society.

The music of the early Middle Ages, plainchant, was monophonic music composed for the Church. Now came the development of music for more than one voice line, that is, polyphony (see page 38). And a little later, we have evidence of the serious cultivation of secular music—songs and dances stemming from the princely courts outside the Church. The first polyphonic pieces are found in a famous manuscript of around 1000 A.D., the Winchester Troper, but we have one or two monkish descriptions of the technique of polyphony from an earlier period. (How accurate they are, it is hard to say. The trouble with monks is that they tended to write about how things *ought* to go rather than how they actually *did* go.) The first surviving court music comes from after 1100.

The development of medieval polyphony is bound to capture the modern reader's special interest. We see in it, rightly, the distant origins of harmony and the music we know today. Yet it would be a mistake to think that polyphony immediately moved to the cutting edge of musical progress—if such a concept of progress can even be imagined for the Middle Ages. It took the cumulative experience of many generations before composers learned to master the art of combining the different voice lines that make up polyphony. Indeed, even as late as the thirteenth century, polyphony was not clearly "better" than the best monophonic music that was still being written, such as the *Dies irae* (page 84) and some of the court songs to be examined presently. It was clearly more intricate and ambitious, but complexity is not the same thing as artistic success. Ultimately, of course, composers perfected the art of polyphony, and the rest is history—the history of music traced in the succeeding chapters of this book.

The Development of Polyphony: Organum

As far as we can tell, polyphony did not arise simply because people liked the rich sound of two melodic lines in combination and the resulting harmony. Rather it arose as another way of enhancing the Church services. Polyphony was a way of embellishing the Gregorian chant; in fact, it was a parallel development to troping. It is no accident that the first polyphony is found in the Winchester Troper, which is primarily an anthology of tropes.

As we saw on page 81, the composer of tropes took the established Gregorian plainchant repertory as his point of departure. The way he found of adding his own contribution of words and music was by adding to the chants in the horizontal dimension. The composer of polyphony (who was often the same person) added to the same chants in the vertical dimension. Instead of cutting them up and interpolating his contribution, or adding it to the beginning or the end, he worked by a process of superimposition. His contribution was not added successively but simultaneously.

For obvious reasons, the composer of polyphony tended to work with the soloists' sections of plainchant—for it required trained soloists to sing this difficult new music. His favorite sections were the solo verses of responsorial chants such as responds and alleluias (see page 80). One of the soloists would still sing the traditional chant as required at the proper point in the service, but now another soloist would sing another, non-Gregorian, newly composed melody at the same time. The result is called organum (plural: *organa*). The difference between the *successive* addition of tropes and the *simultaneous* addition of organum can be shown in the diagram on the facing page.

organum

It would take us too far afield to illustrate all the stages through which organum developed, but we can mention a few of them briefly. Originally, it seems, if we can trust monkish testimony, each note of the chant was accompanied by one note of the added polyphonic voice. In principle, the two voices always moved along together with the same type of interval (see page 17) between them. This cannot have been very interesting.

Soon the added voice started to behave more independently—it would sometimes go up when the chant went down, and so on. Organum of this type was really "composed," not produced by formula. Its composer had to figure out a way of writing down what he had in mind, and singers of some skill were required to decode his notation and sing the organum.

Next, the added voice began to fit more than one note to each note of the underlying chant. What a complex step this must have seemed to medieval composers, and what a puzzling set of new problems it must have posed for the singers! Eventually there got to be so much activity above the chant that the latter had to be slowed down considerably to make performance possible.

By this time the chant melody could scarcely be recognized as such; it was slowed down into a series of drone notes like those on a bagpipe. The interest of medieval musicians was concentrated more and more on the polyphonic voice in organum. The fact that the basic chant was being distorted seems not to have bothered them.

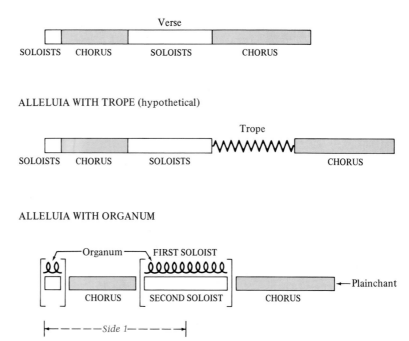

ORIGINAL GREGORIAN ALLELUIA

Verse

SOLOISTS   CHORUS   SOLOISTS   CHORUS

ALLELUIA WITH TROPE (hypothetical)

Trope

SOLOISTS   CHORUS   SOLOISTS   CHORUS

ALLELUIA WITH ORGANUM

Organum   FIRST SOLOIST
CHORUS   SECOND SOLOIST   CHORUS   ←Plainchant

|←————Side 1————→|

At a later point, definite rhythms were introduced into organum, no doubt at least partly because this made it much easier to keep the two (or, by now, three) simultaneous melodies in step. Organum flourished in the famous Cathedral of Notre Dame in Paris, which was built slowly over the period 1163–1220. We even know the names of some composers of the so-called Notre Dame School, Master Leonin and his follower Master Perotin. (The title *magister* was also the one accorded to the master masons and master sculptors of the great cathedral.) Perotin astonished the musical connoisseurs of thirteenth-century Paris by producing lengthy organa for as many as four polyphonic voice parts.

LEONIN   Organum on the Alleluia *Pascha Nostrum* (Our Passover)   SIDE 1

Easter Day at the great new cathedral-in-progress was the occasion for music of the most jubilant kind. Master Leonin composed highly ornate organa for the two responsorial chants specified on this day for the musical interlude between the Epistle and the Gospel readings at Mass (see the table on page 78). We shall look at only one of these, the alleluia *Pascha nostrum,* and only at the first portion of it. Our segment is indicated ("side 1") on the diagram above, which shows the general scheme of an organum based on a Gregorian alleluia.

In its original form without organum, this alleluia starts with the few notes shown at the left of line 1 of the music example below, sung by the soloists. But it would take several lines of music to show the organum based on this short solo beginning:

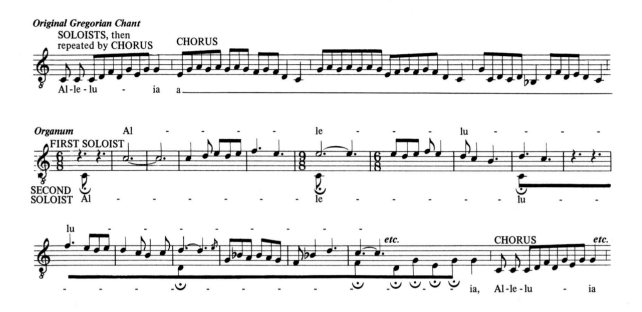

Original Gregorian Chant
SOLOISTS, then repeated by CHORUS — CHORUS

Al -le - lu - ia a ___

Organum
FIRST SOLOIST — Al le lu
SECOND SOLOIST — Al le lu

lu — *etc.* CHORUS *etc.*
ia, Al -le - lu - ia

The chant notes are slowed down, as though huge fermatas (page 10) were applied to them. Above these slow notes, the polyphonic voice glides along in the compound meters which, as we shall see, are characteristic of music of the early Middle Ages in general. The virtuoso singer strings out the individual syllables "al-," "-le-," "-lu-," etc., into elegantly shaped little phrases.

After the organum section on the opening solo, the chorus returns to sing the next portion of the Gregorian chant. Then, at the next solo section, organum starts up again. The chant is drawn out into a long series of solemn alternations of this kind.

Whether the organ support heard on our recording is historically authentic we do not know, but the patient singers of the slow notes probably needed *something* to remind them when to move on from one text to the next. Perhaps the organ helped them out. Perhaps that explains the word organum.

Some decades later, as Notre Dame Cathedral gradually assumed its present imposing form, Perotin composed a more imposing organum on this same Easter alleluia *Pascha nostrum,* in a more modern style. Perotin's most famous organum is the great Christmas gradual *Viderunt omnes* (They all saw), for four voices. This great work must have made an incredible sound as it echoed up and around the great towering nave and the new chancel. Above the rock-like sustained notes of the slowed-down Gregorian chant, the polyphonic voices are linked together and conducted through intricate patterns of compound-meter rhythms. We can almost hear the constructive power of this music, just as we can see a similar quality in the Gothic architecture for which and in which the music was designed. Perotin's *Viderunt omnes* lacks, however, the spontaneous, almost wayward charm of Leonin's more modest compositions.

Music at Court

It is only from around the year 1100 that anything very serious remains to us about music at the great courts of Europe. But over the long span of the Middle Ages, as the kings and barons gained political power at the expense of the Church, they also assumed leadership in artistic support. The princely courts became another major institution, besides the Church, that fostered music in the late Middle Ages.

TROUBADOURS, TROUVÈRES, MINNESINGERS

troubadours
trouvères
Minnesingers

The earliest court music is associated with chivalry—the ideal code of honor, courtesy, duty, consideration for the weak, and respect for the feminine that every knight was supposed to espouse. Chivalry was celebrated in poetry; indeed, knightly behavior probably shone more brightly in verse than in daily life. However this may be, a remarkable group of aristocratic poets flourished at the courts of France for nearly two hundred years, from around 1100 to 1275. They were known as troubadours in the south of France (Provence) and trouvères in the north, and their poetry was always set to music. Their German counterparts called themselves Minnesingers (*Minne* means not "diminutive" but "romantic").

These poets wrote crusaders' songs, songs of comradeship, laments for a dead prince, and especially love songs—songs praising a lady's beauty and/or complaining about her coldness. One striking poetic type was the *alba*, the "dawn song" of the knight's faithful companion, who has kept watch all night and now warns him to leave his lady's bed before the castle awakes. There were also highly regarded women poets, such as the troubadour Countess Beatrix of Die and the trouvère Gormonda of Montpellier.

Perhaps these nobles wrote only the words of their songs, leaving the music to be taken care of by their musician-servants. These attendants were called jongleurs. However, the music is simple enough so that it is not beyond the capabilities of a moderately musical knight—just a pleasant and not very long tune, in most cases, without any indication of accompaniment. Though once again, perhaps the jongleurs played the tune while their masters sang it, or they may even have provided simple polyphony.

Some of the songs have a haunting charm that still touches us today. Among the best known are *Kalenda Maya* (The first of May), a song about spring by the troubadour Rambault de Vaqueiras, *Robin m'aime* (Robin loves me) by the trouvère Adam de la Hale, and the *Palestine song* by the Minnesinger Walther von der Vogelweide. Another is *Ja nuns hons pris* (No captive, indeed) by King Richard I ("Richard the Lion-Hearted") of England, written in prison to shame his friends into paying his ransom—one of the most urgent of chivalric duties in those warlike and rapacious days.

The Rules of Chivalry

The thought of chivalry stirs up visions of romance: we think of knights and ladies, adventures and quests, heroic combat and devoted love. The ideal of chivalry was a powerful one in its own time, too. It stood for human conduct at its most noble, most faithful, most selfless. Great medieval poems recounted the sublime actions of chivalrous knights and celebrated their capacity for loyalty, for friendship, and for passionate love. Troubadours and trouvères (page 93) sang this same refrain.

Real knights did not live up to the ideal, of course. But chivalry did have a significant restraining influence on the actual conduct of men. And this was not just because the principle of chivalry recommended worthy behavior, but also because it embodied a system of rules. All ranks of society were united in their deep conviction that sets of rules had to be followed by everybody, or else society would break down. What they feared was what they had known only too well—unpredictable, arbitrary power, wielded by uncontrolled nature and uncontrolled men.

In the monasteries, as we have seen, people voluntarily placed themselves under a system of controls that determined the most minute aspects of their lives. Secular society was controlled by feudalism, which defined the rights and obligations of each member of society in relation to everybody else. The serfs, at the lowest rung, were tied to the land where they were born and were not free to move to any other place. Clearly, their obligations far outweighed their rights. But the rights of kings and princes, at the highest level of society, were also balanced by the most complex network of obligations and allegiances, which, in theory at least, determined and ruled their conduct.

All male members of the aristocracy (including kings and princes) were also knights, so they were bound by the rules both of feudalism and of chivalry. In battle, for example, a knight could allow himself to be taken prisoner, but it was forbidden for him to retreat. If captured, he could count on being treated very courteously; but his

captor had the right to demand a ransom and to set the amount of the ransom, however outrageous. No obligation was more important than the carrying out of an oath, whether it was an oath to fast for a stated time, or to pursue revenge against an enemy, or to undertake a journey to Jerusalem.

All societies regulate themselves through the use of laws and customs. But in the Middle Ages, a preoccupation with rules animated not just practical affairs but also the whole of intellectual life. Latin translations of the great Greek philosopher Aristotle had introduced the study of logic. It seemed to the medieval mind that Aristotle showed how everything in the universe, every fact, every manifestation of nature, humanity, or God could be understood by arranging all things into their proper categories and then subjecting them to the rules of logic. In this way a chaotic, frightening, unintelligible world could be reduced to rational order. It seems fitting, then, that the earliest trace of polyphony that has come down to us con-

sists of the *rules* of organum (page 90). They are found in a manuscript dating from the ninth century, earlier than any remaining piece of actual polyphony.

Our illustrations come from a medieval manuscript of German Minnesinger poetry, which contains a remarkable series of miniature portraits of the poets. Only one of them, Meister Heinrich Frauenlob (Sir Henry Praiselady), is depicted in a musical setting. The others are shown in more conventional knightly pursuits. Despite his musical name —"klingen" means to tinkle, ring, or sound—Herr Walther von Klingen appears at a tournament, jousting on behalf of his lady, who watches admiringly with her attendants from the castle above, while the other knight's party expresses dismay. The rules and regulations governing tournaments were particularly stylized and complex. Until recently, the game of tennis (which goes back to late medieval times) still preserved some of the aristocratic tone, etiquette, dress codes, and ritual quality of these ancient chivalresque contests.

CONON DE BÉTHUNE (DIED 1219) *Ahi! Amours, con Dure Departie* (Alas, Love, What a Hard Parting)   SIDE 1

This is a haunting song by a crusader-trouvère whose thoughts keep returning from visions of Christian glory to thoughts of the lady he must leave behind him:

Ahi! Amours, con dure departie	Alas, Love, what a hard parting
me convendra faire pour la meillour	Must I have from the best lady
ki onques fust amee ne servie!	Ever to be loved and served!
Deus me ramaint a li par sa douçour	May God in his goodness bring me back to her
si voirement que m'en part a dolour.	As surely as it is true I leave her with great pain.
las! qu'ai je dit? ja ne m'en part je mie:	Alas! what have I said? I am not leaving her:
ains va mes cors servir noste seignour,	Even if my body serves our Lord,
Mes cuers remaint del tout en sa baillie	My heart remains entirely at her side . . . .

(Two more stanzas)

The simple but graceful rhythms in compound meter are characteristic, as is the form of the stanza, A A B (sometimes called *bar form*). There are eight phrases in each stanza.

Ahi! Amours is a good example of the Mixolydian mode (see page 75). The song has three stanzas, all musically identical, except that the last is extended to A A B B. In our performance, someone has made an attractive guess at the sort of accompaniment Conon's jongleur might have been expected to provide.

THE ESTAMPIE

estampie

A genre of instrumental music at this time—probably a dance, though we are not sure—is the <u>estampie</u>. These lively pieces survive in manuscripts which say nothing about what instruments are supposed to play them; but modern performers can pick up some ideas about this by studying contemporary paintings and tapestries. The *Sixth Estampie Royale* is played on our record (side 1) by a rebec (a forerunner of the violin) and an early type of guitar called the citole.

Like *Ahi! Amours*, the *Sixth Estampie* features rather simple rhythms in compound meter, though the effect is certainly much less languid than in

Conon's love song. The form of this estampie is the same chain form we encounter in contemporary church music, A A B B C C D D, etc. No doubt the jongleurs could learn to improvise this kind of thing for as long as needed.

More precisely, the form of the *Sixth Estampie* is ax ax' bx bx' cx cx' dx dx', etc., where x and x' are two different forms of a cadence phrase. So, while the music gets more and more spirited as it goes along—the melody reaching higher, and the phrases growing longer—the repeated cadence phrases have the effect of unifying the whole composition and keeping it oriented around a clear center.

Secular Polyphony

The trouvère songs and the estampies were monophonic, as we have seen. Inevitably polyphony entered court music. During the thirteenth century, secular polyphony takes its place alongside sacred polyphony, and in the fourteenth century secular outstrips sacred.

The best-known of all medieval compositions, *Sumer is icumen in,* is a secular polyphonic piece, though it is not a courtly one. It was written down by a monk of Reading (an abbey not far from London) around 1300. This will serve to remind us that the monks were not entirely wrapped up in their religion, especially in the later Middle Ages, when attacks on their worldliness (not to say downright profligacy) became more and more frequent. *Sumer is icumen in* actually sets music to the first known secular poem in English— Old English:

Sumer is icumen in,
lhude sing cuccú!
Groweth sed and bloweth med [meadow]
and springeth the wude nu.
Sing cuccú!
Awe [ewe] bleteth after lomb,

lhouth after calve cu;
bulluc sterteth, bucke verteth,
murie sing cuccú!
Cúccu, cúccu,
wel singes thu, cuccú!
Ne swik [nor cease] thu naver nu.

The polyphony is ingeniously contrived as a round, like *Three blind mice* or *Row, row, row your boat,* for up to four singers. This makes the imitation of the cuckoo call at "sing cuccú" all the more delightful, as though cuckoos can be heard singing from all sides. On our record, the famous English words are preceded by a more solemn religous version in Latin, which was no doubt more appropriate for monastery use (side S–1).

All this is certainly fairly sophisticated, and shows how far polyphony had developed in the relatively short time since its beginnings. The only "elementary" aspect of the piece is its rhythm, consisting of simple patterns in compound meter like those of the contemporary trouvère songs and estampies. And rhythm is the aspect of music that was to be developed most fantastically in the next century.

The Dance of Death

Throughout the Middle Ages, the precariousness of human life was a reality that haunted daily experience. Death came from starvation or disease, or from the attacks of marauding brigands such as the Norsemen who raided England, or from the arbitrary brutality of local chieftains.

Gradually, as society became better organized, some of the random perils of existence were reduced. But along with the organization of society came better organization of armies, and inevitably new incitements to combat appeared. In the Crusades against the Moslems, and in local wars between rival barons, high-born knights died in battle alongside of their troops. Those who happened to be in the way, peasants working in the fields, villagers in their houses, died too. In the tormented melody of *Dies irae*, we hear a medieval composer's response to the calamity of death.

It was at the very end of the Middle Ages that an accident of history raised people's obsession with death to new heights. In the middle of the fourteenth century, the bubonic plague swept through the Middle East, North Africa, and all of Europe, killing a third of the population within a couple of years. It is estimated that around twenty million people perished. This terrible disease, called the Black Death on account of black swellings on the bodies of the victims, killed quickly, painfully, and indiscriminately.

People thought at the time that it was the end of the world. The world did not end, but the plague returned a number of times, and for two centuries afterward the awesome power of death permeated everyone's thoughts and imagination.

In art, one pervasive theme was the Dance of Death, which was depicted in many series of pictures and poems. The figure of Death, sometimes grim, sometimes mocking, steps his way through a ghastly dance as he comes for every person, man or woman, young or old, rich or poor, after long illness or suddenly in the middle of life. In these examples from a series of fifteenth-century woodcuts, we see Death dancing and playing instruments as he leads away a cardinal, a lady, and a beggar.

Guillaume de Machaut (circa 1300–1377)

The greatest fourteenth-century composer, Guillaume de Machaut, was also France's leading poet, admired by his great contemporaries Francesco Petrarch in Italy and Geoffrey Chaucer in England. Such a combination of musical and literary talent in one person has never occurred again in Western culture. (The Elizabethan poet Thomas Campion wrote attractive music for his verses, but Campion was no more than a minor composer. The great nineteenth-century opera composer Richard Wagner wrote both the words and the music for his works, but no one since Wagner has taken the words seriously as poetry.)

Guillaume served as secretary to the chivalrous and romantic (and very active) King John of Bohemia, Count of Luxemburg, who died fighting beside his friends the French at the Battle of Crécy in 1346. A sinecure at Rheims Cathedral was then given to Guillaume, but it seems his inclinations were never very spiritual. His best-known poem concerns a love affair with an aristocratic young girl, who attached herself to the then sixty-year-old poet-composer, insisted on playing the role of his muse, and pestered him by sending him sonnets. It is startling to read of this medieval groupie, and fascinating to reflect on the eternal glamor that seems to attach to artistic (and perhaps especially musical) creators.

Guillaume wrote numerous love songs not too different from those of the trouvères in both their poetry and their music. But he also wrote songs in a new kind of polyphony, polyphony that makes *Sumer is icumen in* seem innocent indeed. One of the techniques developed in fourteenth-century polyphony, isorhythm, is perhaps the most complex principle of composition that we shall encounter until the twelve-tone technique of the twentieth century.

isorhythm

ISORHYTHM

An isorhythmic piece is planned by the composer ahead of time in several equal-length sections. Depending on the length of the poem, these sections will last from, say, twenty or thirty seconds to one or two minutes. In the first section, each of the vocal or instrumental parts of the polyphony naturally has its own distinct rhythm; sometimes this is very simple and sometimes it is very complex, extending over dozens or even hundreds of notes. Then, after the first section, the composer writes the other sections using different pitches but in principle reproducing the original rhythms, however complex, exactly.

This certainly seems like an artificial and involved way of constructing a piece of music. We must not, however, dismiss it out of hand without seeing what this remarkable principle could lead to in the hands of the most skillful composers of the time.

MACHAUT *Quant en Moy* (When First to Me)   SIDE 1

This isorhythmic motet is for two solo voices and an accompanying instrument. We are likely to be struck first of all by the exceedingly complicated rhythms, the spikey harmony, and the nervous, elegant way the words are de-claimed. Every so often the voices suddenly stop and rest, and then suddenly start up again, creating a texture (see page 37) that it is not unfair to describe as moth-eaten. Then, if we can catch the words, we will be amazed to realize that the mezzo-soprano and the tenor are actually singing two different poems simultaneously (!), though Machaut wrote these poems to fit together in meaning, as appears from their opening stanzas. The four-line tenor stanza is stretched out so as to last as long as the eleven-line mezzo-soprano stanza, and also so as to coordinate the short, one-word lines contained in each stanza. These one-word lines are heard at the same time:

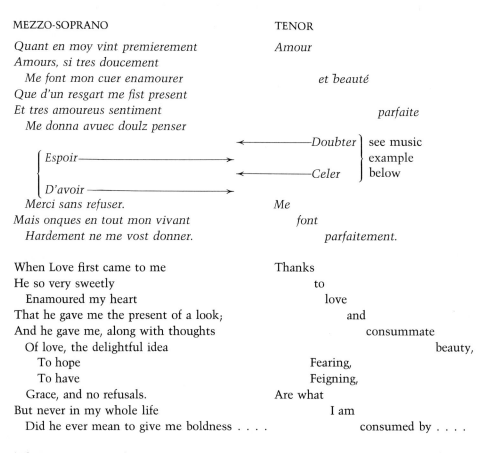

MEZZO-SOPRANO

Quant en moy vint premierement
Amours, si tres doucement
  Me font mon cuer enamourer
Que d'un resgart me fist present
Et tres amoureus sentiment
  Me donna avuec doulz penser

  Espoir
  D'avoir
  Merci sans refuser.
Mais onques en tout mon vivant
  Hardement ne me vost donner.

TENOR

Amour

  et beauté

          parfaite

Doubter
Celer } see music example below

Me
    font
        parfaitement.

When Love first came to me
He so very sweetly
  Enamoured my heart
That he gave me the present of a look;
And he gave me, along with thoughts
  Of love, the delightful idea
    To hope
    To have
  Grace, and no refusals.
But never in my whole life
  Did he ever mean to give me boldness . . . .

Thanks
    to
    love
        and
            consummate
                        beauty,
Fearing,
Feigning,
Are what
    I am
        consumed by . . . .

(Three more stanzas)

The isorhythm—the long-range repetition of a complex rhythmic pattern—is easiest to hear at the cadence points and at the curious points in the middle of the stanzas. Here the voices sing just a few quick notes and stop and start again, dovetailing their short lines with one another: in stanza 1, tenor: "Doubter," mezzo-soprano: "Espoir," he: "Celer," she: "D'avoir" (see above); in stanzas 2 and 3, he: "De vous," she: "Qu'amours," he: "Cuer doulz," she: "Secours," and he: "Merci," she: "Je scay," he: "Vous pri," she: "De vray" (see facing page).

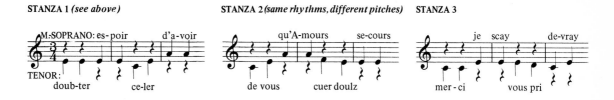

STANZA 1 *(see above)*   STANZA 2 *(same rhythms, different pitches)*   STANZA 3

hocket   This rather showy and amusing device is called <u>hocket</u>. Hocket flourished in this period, and only in this period, at least partly because it did help to clarify isorhythmic structure.

Meanwhile, as a support for all this intricate interplay between the two voices, a viol plays a fragment of Gregorian chant—even though the voices are singing (and acting out?) a love song. Just as well, perhaps, that the chant is slowed down and perforated so that it could not possibly be recognized in this distorted form. Distorted or not, the chant was still important to Machaut. Constructing more complicated music by starting from the traditional Gregorian chant, as in the tropes and organum of earlier times, was an idea that died hard.

MACHAUT   Mass of Notre Dame

It has been suggested that Guillaume de Machaut wrote his Mass of Notre Dame as a petition for peace during the ravages of the Hundred Years' War. The title presumably refers to Rheims Cathedral, where he was a canon, for this cathedral, like Notre Dame in Paris, was dedicated to Our Lady.

In this, his most famous work, Guillaume set to music all five sections of the Ordinary of the Mass (see page 78), a procedure that would become common only in the next century. He also included an extra section, not set by later composers, the Ite missa est, which comes at the very end of the service. The priest says: "Go forth, it is ended." From the word "missa" (dismissed, or ended) we get the word Mass (Latin: Missa).

It was only after Guillaume and other composers started setting the five sections of the Ordinary of the Mass together that the sections were thought of as a unit. People would not have associated them, perhaps, because they are so different in length, form, function, and even language (the Kyrie is in Greek, a relic of the earliest days of Christianity). The Kyrie and Agnus Dei are very short prayers. The Sanctus is a short song of praise to God the Father. The Gloria is a long, rambling prose hymn to the Trinity. The Credo is an even longer recital of the Christian's list of beliefs.

Composers have always had difficulty uniting these disparate items with their music for the Ordinary of the Mass. Guillaume set the Kyrie, Sanctus, Agnus Dei, and Ite missa est as isorhythmic pieces for four voice parts, with instruments, but for the long Gloria and Credo movements he adopted a simpler style, more like chordal recitation. The overall effect is craggy and monumental, as contrasted with Guillaume's love songs, in which he seems to have caught perfectly the unique mood—at once elegant and neurotic, playful and complicated—that marks the waning of the Middle Ages.

Mary and Her Angel Concert

In the late Middle Ages, an extraordinary amount of popular devotion centered on the figure of the Virgin Mary. A merciful mother untouched by impurity (that is, sexuality), sinless in a way no Christian could ever feel themselves to be, she seemed more gentle and approachable than Jesus. Although she had no ultimate power herself, it was devoutly hoped that at the last judgment she would intercede for humanity with her Son.

The most beautifully illuminated of the medieval Books of Hours are special prayer books to Mary. More churches and cathedrals were dedicated to her than to any other saint. The name "Notre Dame" means "our lady"; Notre Dame of Paris is the most famous of thousands of Notre Dame churches. They had special "Lady Chapels" attached to them to house services in her honor, and the chapels were often the most ornate and beautiful spots in the entire church or cathedral.

Large bodies of poetry were composed about the Virgin, and much of this was set to music, either as tropes (or other varieties of late plainsong) or as polyphonic motets. In many Lady Chapels "Marian" music was carefully specified throughout the Church year. Furthermore, the charming tradition grew up of making altar paintings of Mary surrounded by angels playing musical instruments and singing. They are making music to praise her, to beautify the scene, and to symbolize her own beauty. Dozens of these so-called Angel Concerts have survived from the fourteenth and fifteenth centuries.

"Peerless Mother, meek and mild," Mary was called by an anonymous English poet of the time; and across the page we see how a late medieval German painter, Stephan Lochner, envisioned her. No more than a child herself, she sits clothed in the coolest, most peaceful blue under a wispy rose bower, set in a lawn that is studded like a tapestry with violets and strawberries. Some angels are using her flower box as a pew to pray from while others are earnestly offering apples to the Christ child. God and the Holy Ghost (the Dove) bless her affectionately from above; He looks more like Santa Claus than the stern Father of the Old Testament. Mary seems conscious of none of this. The faraway look in her eyes tells us that she is wrapped in meditation of the Christian mystery. She is in perfect harmony with her role.

As for Mary's Angel Concerts, they are invaluable to music scholars as evidence of when musical instruments came into use, how they looked, and the way they were actually played. To be sure, the scholar needs to know the artist. Some medieval painters prided themselves on the most precise reproduction of the smallest details in everything they depicted. But others took the line that angels probably played on instruments such as were never seen on earth, and played them with a heavenly disdain for fingerings, bow-arm technique, and the like.

Some Angel Concerts include dozens of instruments and singers. Lochner paints a more intimate, chamber music scene, with four angel children playing gentle lutes, a harp, and a portable organ called a *portative*. These little organs were popular in the Middle Ages among those who could afford them, for they are not hard to play: only one hand plays on the keyboard, while the other works the air bellows. There is a rare contemporary portrait of a composer playing a portative: the blind Florentine organist Francesco Landini (1325–1397), who was, next to Guillaume de Machaut, the most famous composer of the time.

CHAPTER 5 | The Renaissance   I

The Renaissance   I

The concept of historical "periods" is a more complicated one than most people at first realize. This is true whether music is in question, or one of the other arts, or culture in general. Period terms such as "the Middle Ages" and "the Renaissance" imply something more than a chronological division: they imply a certain general shared quality of life or civilization that permeates and unifies the period—what the Germans call the *Zeitgeist,* or spirit of the age. It is hard to do without some such concept, if we are to deal with historical questions of any breadth. Yet we all know that the spirit of the age is an extremely nebulous thing, and never simple or straightforward to define.

We know, for example, that the quality of modern life is not quite the same in San Francisco, Salt Lake City, Omaha, and Memphis, to say nothing of Copenhagen, Moscow, and Teheran. And even in a single country or a single region, the modern spirit (or that region's version of it) seems always to be tempered by the spirit of an earlier age. How else can we account for the waves of nostalgia that sweep over us periodically, nostalgia for the fifties or the twenties, for "Victorian" houses and "Gothic" novels, for the old-fashioned moral world of the Western? Late Victorian operas, ragtime piano music, and 1920s jazz all owe some of their popularity to people's inclination to cling to some aspects of the past.

So a caution is necessary: in studying the effects of the Renaissance on music of the fifteenth century, no one should suppose that medieval habits died overnight. The fifteenth century was in fact a difficult, complicated time of transition, and manifestations of medieval culture continued to flourish. Gregorian chant continued to be sung daily at the Mass and at the Office Services. Chant and other monophonic music was no longer composed afresh, but people still heard more Gregorian chant than any other kind of music.

Still, things *did* change: not overnight, not over a decade, not even over several generations, certainly not at an even rate in the north and south of Europe—but music in 1500 was fundamentally different from what it was in 1400. Musicians at the time were quite articulate in recognizing this. Our aim in the following pages is to chart this change in concise general terms.

The Renaissance

We know the Renaissance best, perhaps, as the age of discoveries, the age of Magellan and Columbus. When Michelet coined his phrase about "the discovery of the world and of man," he meant to indicate that something of the spirit of the great explorers can be detected in almost every branch of intellectual life at the time. It was an age of discovery in science and technology, archaeology, and all the arts, including music.

The "discovery of the world" could not proceed very far as long as people still had the habit of accepting authority. Ancient doctrine said that the world was stable and our knowledge of it was fixed once and for all by God. People of the Middle Ages believed this without question. If Columbus and Copernicus had believed it, they would never have embarked on their epoch-making investigations. Columbus was not afraid of falling off the edge of the world.

Musicians did some investigating, too. Pythagoras and his authoritative experiments on sound were mentioned on page 14. In the sixteenth century people finally began to examine these experiments critically, and once they did so, they saw that it was necessary to revise them and supplement them. The discovery of vibrations as the source of sound was made by the Venetian G. B. Benedetti around 1560.

The painting, sculpture, and architecture of the Renaissance have probably been more admired than those of any other period. This is the age of Donatello, Brunelleschi, Botticelli, Leonardo da Vinci, Raphael, Michelangelo, Titian, and many other famous artists. The development of perspective is a manifestation of painters' new concern for the world around them (even if they still often painted the afterworld, too). Artists developed new and more sensuous techniques, such as oil painting on canvas, and they turned to more sensuous subjects. Renaissance sculptors and painters began depicting nudes—seldom encountered in the Middle Ages except in a moralistic context, such as scenes of Adam and Eve expelled in shame from Eden.

Here the Renaissance followed a new authority: not the Church, but classical antiquity. The ancient Greeks and Romans provided a powerful stimulus through their humanistic philosophy, their political structures, and their wonderfully rich languages and literatures. Classical art and artifacts were dug up and studied with great enthusiasm by scholars and connoisseurs of the time.

Not only this: strenuous efforts were also made to imitate classical styles, to bring them into contemporary life. Renaissance nude statues were imitations of classical ones. People scrutinized Greek writings about music to see what inspiration they might provide for sixteenth-century composers. True, no actual Greek music had survived. But Greek philosophers from Plato on had said some very interesting things about words and music, musical expression, and so on.

Our illustration shows a relief sculpture of the early Renaissance by Luca della Robbia. It comes from the *cantoria*, a large marble gallery or choir loft built for the singers of Florence Cathedral (the composer Guillaume Dufay certainly knew this *cantoria* and probably sang from it himself). Luca decorated it with sculptured panels showing musical scenes. We may imagine these choirboys singing Dufay's newly sonorous polyphony. Full of life, self-contained and self-confident, they are taking the same sensuous pleasure in their singing that Luca evidently experienced in sculpting their handsome bodies.

Rather less self-contained are the figures on one of the other panels, who are supposed to be illustrating these phrases from the Book of Psalms: "Praise Him with the timbrel and dance . . . praise Him upon the loud cymbals." But they certainly look more like ancient Romans than ancient Hebrews. Place Luca's sculpture next to a Roman marble sarcophagus—Luca is on the left—and the source of his classical inspiration is very clear.

Museo dell' Opera del Duomo.

The Renaissance and Music

Renaissance is the name given to a complex historical current that worked deep changes in Europe during the fifteenth and sixteenth centuries (see pages 108 and 109). By rediscovering and imitating the civilization of ancient Rome, Italians hoped they could bring about a rebirth of their glorious past; the word *renaissance* means rebirth. It was a somewhat confused dream, and one that came to nothing in political terms. Instead of turning into some new Roman Empire, Italy at the end of the Renaissance consisted of the same pack of warring city-states that had been at each other's throats all through the Middle Ages.

However, the revival of classical culture provided a powerful model for new values, which were coming to the fore both in Italy and in the rest of Europe. In the famous phrase of the historian Jules Michelet, the Renaissance involved "the discovery of the world and of man." Medieval society was essentially stable, conservative, authoritarian, oriented toward God. The Renaissance laid the groundwork for the world we know today, a dynamic society oriented toward humanity.

Man, rather than God, became the measure in philosophy, science, the arts, and even religion. In the arts, what this meant was that artists tried to make their work more directly relevant to people's needs and desires. They began to reinterpret the world around them—the architect's world of space and stone, the painter's world of images, the musician's world of sound—in new ways to meet these new ambitions.

THE NEW SONORITY

Music had always exhibited the power to delight people's senses, and this was something that Renaissance musicians now wanted to exploit. Sonority, the overall blend of sound, came to occupy the center of their interest. In order to cultivate the sensuous side of music, composers turned their attention increasingly to a dimension of music that had been neglected up to then, the dimension of harmony.

Let us remember that polyphonic music, such as that of Machaut and the other composers of the late Middle Ages, does not in itself preclude harmony. As we noted on page 41, almost all polyphony entails some chords, and hence harmony, as a product of its simultaneously sounding lines. But in Machaut's music it is more of a by-product. Machaut concentrates on the "horizontal" aspects of polyphony at the expense of the "vertical" ones; he delights in the separateness of his different voice lines; the chords seem to come about almost accidentally. Certainly we do not feel that Machaut labored to make chords sound ingratiating in themselves.

People now learned to listen for the "vertical" sounds produced by polyphony and to relish them for their sensuous quality. This was the Renaissance "reinterpretation of the world of sound." On their part, composers developed two important musical techniques to accommodate the growing interest in sonority.

The first is homophony (see page 39). Pure homophony simply amounts to a melody accompanied by a series of chords (the concept of a chord, incidentally, did not even exist before the Renaissance). One can also write music which is not strictly homophonic but sounds essentially chordal, all the same; this music gives the effect of homophony. The other technique is imitative polyphony (see page 38). Imitative polyphony, or imitation, occurs when the various melodic lines sounding together use the same or quite similar melodies (but at staggered time intervals, with one coming in shortly after another). Echoing, repeating, and answering one another, the voices blend in a way that the voices of medieval polyphony seldom did.

Homophony and imitative polyphony worked their way slowly but surely into music over the course of the fifteenth century. By the sixteenth century, as we shall see, these two techniques had become the main determinants of musical style.

MODERNIZING THE PLAINCHANT

We hear much more about secular and worldly pursuits in the Renaissance than in the Middle Ages. It would be a mistake, however, to think of the new era as "pagan" or irreligious. Nothing shows the profoundly religious temper of the time more vividly than the Reformation. When Martin Luther nailed his ninety-five theses on the Wittenberg church door in 1517, and when the twenty-six-year-old John Calvin penned his powerful *Institutes of the Christian Religion* in 1534, they did not do so in order to abandon or weaken Christianity. Their impetus was to purify what they saw as the corruptions of religion and to bring it closer to the individual. Thousands died for their faith, whether Protestant or Roman, in the terrible persecutions and Wars of Religion that followed on the Reformation.

So it should come as no surprise to find that the Renaissance was a golden age of church music (though secular music flourished as well). Ever since the sixteenth century, indeed, the masses and motets of Palestrina and his contemporaries have been recognized as the "classic" music of the Catholic Church. In addition, distinguished bodies of music were composed for the new Protestant churches of France, England, the Netherlands, and especially Germany.

In Catholic lands (Italy, Spain, most of France, and much of Germany), Gregorian chant continued to be sung as the basis of the services, as we have already remarked. But there was an interesting tendency to modernize it. In 1589, Pope Gregory IX resolved to revise the entire Gregorian repertory so as to bring it closer to modern ideals of melodic beauty. He appointed Palestrina, already recognized as the "official" composer of the Catholic Church, to supervise this project.

The fifteenth century did not go so far in tampering with the chant. But when those earlier composers incorporated Gregorian melodies into their polyphonic compositions, they took care to decorate them with extra notes, sing them in attractive rhythms, and smooth out passages that struck them as awkward and antiquated. This important procedure is known as paraphrase. Medieval composers had treated the chant much more casually. In their organa and motets the chant was often distorted, certain notes being lengthened, not

paraphrase

for their own sake, but merely in order to accommodate the new polyphonic lines that were being added (see pages 91 and 101). It almost seems as if late medieval composers had lost any feeling for the beauty of their Gregorian heritage.

Composers of the early Renaissance, in order to make their art more directly relevant and pleasing to people, transformed plainchant into melodies they felt had a much more sensuous aspect. For this they used paraphrase. What is more, paraphrased Gregorian melodies now appear typically in the highest voice, the soprano. In this position they are heard most clearly, and the soprano voice was probably considered the most beautiful.

We shall see the effect of these Renaissance tendencies on the Gregorian hymn *Ave maris stella,* which we studied on page 77. Later in this chapter we shall examine two pieces of fifteenth-century church music related to it: the version of *Ave maris stella* by Guillaume Dufay, and the Mass based on this hymn by Josquin Des Prez.

CHANGING ATTITUDES

Renaissance artists were sharply aware of the novelty of the art of their own time and its difference from that of the Middle Ages. Johannes Tinctoris, a minor composer and writer on music of the period, left one of the first historical commentaries of music that has come down to us. Singling out for admiration the music written by his friends and contemporaries, Tinctoris remarks that there is no music worth listening to that hasn't been composed in the last forty years! This was in 1476. Not a word about poor Guillaume de Machaut, whose poetry, too, was now badly out of fashion.

Tinctoris names names; composers were now being taken seriously as "artists," rather than as more or less anonymous craftsmen. To be sure, Machaut had been famous in his day—but primarily as a poet, who happened also to write music. The great fifteenth-century composers, such as Guillaume Dufay and Josquin Des Prez, gained international fame on the basis of their music alone.

New respect from the world was accompanied by new self-respect. Toward the end of his long life, Dufay wrote a motet (*Ave regina coelorum*) in which the standard liturgical words were extended by a brief prayer to the Virgin Mary "for thy servant, Guillaume Dufay." This might strike us as an act of piety, but a medieval musician would have considered it very bold. Dufay was in effect signing his own composition.

As for Josquin Des Prez, forty years after his death in 1521 his music was still being sung, and so were his praises. Josquin signed one of his compositions without any pious pretext, by setting to music a religious poem that is an acrostic on his name (the first letters of the poem's lines spell out his name). And there exists an interesting letter about him from a recruiting agent to Duke Hercules I of Ferrara. The duke needed to hire a musician for his court chapel, and the agent says that Josquin is the best one available, but recommends against him because he commands a higher salary, has a reputation for being "difficult," and cannot be counted on to produce music on order. The duke engaged Josquin anyway.

The Musical Supply Route of the Renaissance

This map shows the supply route of musicians from northern France and Flanders (Belgium) to Italy, the home of the Renaissance and a great employer of foreign talent. At the top of the map, we have noted only a few places, associated with the composers discussed in this book: Guillaume Dufay, Josquin Des Prez, and Roland de Lassus in the next century (see page 134). The map would have to be dotted with dozens more locations if we tried to take into account all of the traveling Franco-Flemish musicians who established themselves away from home.

It was a long, hard journey, one that had to traverse the Alps. In the north of Italy, the two most important musical centers were Milan, then (as now) a major city, and Ferrara, a little court blessed with a long line of music-loving dukes. Josquin worked at both places. But the main center of Renaissance culture was Florence, in the center of Italy. Interest in classical antiquity grew up in Florence as early as the fourteenth century, and in the fifteenth the first great Renaissance artists, architects, and sculptors flourished there (see page 108). Florence imported Franco-Flemish musicians eagerly, starting with Dufay.

Second to Florence, the great Renaissance center was Rome, still further to the south. Both Dufay and Josquin served in the papal chapel there, with many of their countrymen. The greatest days for music in the papal chapel were during the papacy of Leo X (1513–1521), who is supposed to have said: "Since God has seen fit to present us with the papacy, let us enjoy it."

Guillaume Dufay (circa 1400–1474)

The greatest composer of the first part of the fifteenth century, Guillaume Dufay, was born and bred in the far north of France near Flanders (Belgium), a region that supplied the whole of Europe with musicians. Perhaps the most important fact about his biography is that he spent over twenty-five years working in Italy. Italy was the land of the Renaissance; there Dufay came in contact with the artists and the literary men who were leading the new movement and (equally important!) with the patrons who were supporting them. A signal event in the history of Renaissance Florence was the building of a magnificent "classical" dome for the cathedral there, designed by the great Renaissance architect Filippo Brunelleschi. Dufay, by age thirty-five the most admired composer of Europe, was commissioned to write an imposing Latin motet to celebrate its dedication.

DUFAY   *Helas Mon Dueil* (Alas My Woe)   SIDE 1

chanson

Dufay's beautiful *Helas mon dueil* will show us how a fifteenth-century composer of genius went about writing a love song. *Helas mon dueil* belongs to the genre called the chanson (French for "song"). As a genre title, a chanson is a Renaissance composition for voice or voices, with or without instruments, setting music to a secular poem in French.

    The form of the music follows that of the poem, A B B A, except that the second B is extended by a melisma (see page 80) in both voices:

(A)	*Helas mon dueil, a ce cop sui ie mort,*	Alas my woe, at this blow I am dead,
	Puisque Refus l'esragié si me mort.	Because insane Refusal kills me thus.
	Certes, c'est fait de ma dolente vye;	Indeed, all is over with my sad life;
	Tòut le monde ne me sauveroit mye,	The whole world could never rescue me,
	Puisque m'amour en a esté d'acort.	Because my love has let this happen.
(B)	*Il ne fault ia que ie voise a la mer*	No more need I go to the sea
	N'a Saint Hubert pour moy faire garir;	Nor to Saint Hubert to make me well;
(B)	*La morsure me donne tant d'amer*	The biting wound gives me such grief
	Que de ce mal il me fauldra morir.	That from this illness I must die.
(A)	*Helas mon dueil . . .* (etc.)	Alas my woe . . . (etc.)

Especially after hearing a work like Guillaume de Machaut's *Quant en moy*, we will be impressed by how perfectly Dufay's tenor and soprano voices are coordinated. At many points the polyphony seems to settle into homophonic "singing in thirds," or something like it. Even the third voice, played by a viol, seems to blend in. But there is one prominent passage of imitative polyphony, at line 5—which is exactly the line that makes the main point of this rather feeble poem. The use of the special technique, imitation, serves to underline the climax of the poet's thought.

Smoothness is perhaps the key characteristic of Dufay's style in works of this kind—smoothness of rhythm, melody, and harmony. As a result, the sonority is richer and more sensuous than ever before. The beginning of the B section is almost purely homophonic in style. Even the long melismas on "*d'a*cort" and "*mo*rir" are handled with a new quiet grace, untroubled by the charming little quirks that characterize melismas in fourteenth-century music.

Not all of Dufay's eighty chansons are as melancholy as *Helas mon dueil*. He wrote cheerful pieces about May Day, about New Year's Day, and about a drinking contest. And some of his love songs are parodistic, such as *Je ne suy plus tel que souloys* (I am no longer what I used to be), in which the aging lover complains that he can no longer satisfy the ladies—or at least that is the story he puts about when striking up new acquaintances. In the next century, bawdy chansons become quite common.

The Motet

motet   Like some other important musical terms, the term <u>motet</u> is troublesome to define, because it was used over many centuries and its meaning changed with the times.

In the twelfth century, a motet was a short piece rather like a fragment of an organum, but with words—Latin or French, sacred or secular—other than those of the original plainchant. The name itself comes from the French *mot* meaning "word." In the fourteenth century, motets became large-scale isorhythmic compositions, often written for some important occasion, such as a royal wedding ceremony or the signing of a peace treaty. But some of Machaut's isorhythmic motets are simply complicated love songs, as we have seen (pages 99–101).

Eventually the term *motet* came to be restricted to relatively short pieces with Latin texts, almost invariably of a religious nature. This is the main use of the term in relation to the Renaissance and later periods. Most familiar is the sixteenth-century *a cappella* motet of Palestrina and his contemporaries;

a cappella   <u>a cappella</u> means sung by unaccompanied voices. However, early Renaissance motets, such as those of Dufay and his contemporaries, sometimes require instrumental accompaniment.

DUFAY *Ave Maris Stella* (Hail, Star of the Oceans) SIDE S–1

This motet, one of Dufay's simpler works, is based on both the words and the music of the Gregorian hymn *Ave maris stella,* which we have already heard (see page 77). The hymn contains seven stanzas, but Dufay sets only the even-numbered ones to his own new music, leaving the others (and the concluding Amen) to be chanted Gregorian-style in alternation with them. This system is called alternatim setting.

alternatim setting

His music for stanzas 2, 4, and 6 is the same each time, and the style is quite homophonic and suave. The top voice presents the ancient Gregorian tune in a paraphrased version (see page 111), decorated with some extra notes, extensions, and so on, all in a relatively simple, fixed rhythm. It is interesting that Dufay tried to modernize the chant by providing the cadences of the various lines with melismas of much the same kind that he wrote in his chansons.

This motet would have been sung in the Office Services dedicated to the Blessed Virgin Mary, at the point where the Gregorian hymn was specified. Therefore it is classified as a liturgical motet, a motet designed to be used in the services (the liturgy) in place of the traditional chant for the text in question. Most fifteenth- and sixteenth-century motets were functional compositions in this sense. Thus *Alma redemptoris Mater,* another lovely liturgical motet by Dufay, was again destined for the Office of the Virgin and again makes use of the original plainchant—a much more complex plainchant, in this case. The piece opens with a striking soprano solo, in which the chant melody is paraphrased, and it ends with an equally striking slow section in pure polyphony.

liturgical motet

Josquin Des Prez (circa 1440–1521)

Like Dufay, Josquin Des Prez came from the north of France but spent many years of his long life working in Italy: at Rome in the papal chapel, and at Milan and Ferrara in the service of some of the most glamorous princes of the Italian Renaissance. Josquin was one of the most many-sided and inventive composers who ever lived. He excelled in monumental, constructive compositions as well as in simple semipopular ones, and he pioneered an amazing number of techniques for the composition of motets, masses, and chansons of new kinds. One can see almost all of sixteenth-century music growing out of Josquin's work, just as Beethoven's work seems to predict the music of the nineteenth century.

Josquin was one of the first composers whose music circulated widely thanks to the new technology of music printing (see page 122). When printing was introduced in 1501, his work was more highly regarded than that of any other master, and more eagerly sought out by publishers. It was still being published sixty years later.

Something of the range of Josquin's genius can be sensed from the two songs on side 1. *Petite camusette* is a chanson in the French love song tradition that we have traced from the troubadours and trouvères to Machaut and Dufay.

Petite camusette,	Little snub-nose,
A la mort m'avez mis.	You'll drive me to my death.
Robin et Marion	Robin Hood and Maid Marion
S'en vont au bois joly,	Have gone to greenwood fair,
Ilz s'en vont bras à bras,	They have gone arm in arm,
Ilz se sont endormis.	They have dropped off to sleep.
Petite camusette,	Little snub-nose,
A la mort m'avez mis.	You'll drive me to my death.

Josquin now uses six polyphonic voice parts, and the imitations between them come thick and fast, so thick and fast that the listener cannot (and is not expected to) grasp every one. The harmony is rich, the rhythm smooth and powerful, the texture very dense. The music exudes a feeling of complexity kept under wraps, as it were, so as not to overpower the gentle poem ("camusette" is a term of endearment). Actually, there is a popular tune at the basis of this chanson, and this relatively simple tune helps to organize the rich polyphony, that is, helps to guide it into musical phrases following one another in a logical sequence.

Next, in Italian, we have the well-known *Scaramella va alla guerra*—raucous, almost wholly homophonic, with lilting rhythms and catchy repetitions. Once south of the Alps, these northern musicians would sometimes unbend considerably. The nonsense poem is about a clown who goes to war, a sort of Renaissance Italian Yankee Doodle. The contrast, both musical and poetic, with *Petite camusette* could hardly be more extreme:

Scaramella va alla guerra	Scaramella goes off to war,
Colla lancia et la rotella,	With his lance and with his shield.
La zombero boro borombetta,	With a rum-tum-tum,
La zombero boro borombo.	(*Etc.*)
Scaramella fa la gala	Scaramella plays the gallant
Colla scarpa et la stivala.	With his fine shoes and his boots.
La zombero . . . (etc.)	With a rum-tum-tum, (etc.)

Both of these songs, incidentally, are performed on the record with actual voices on all the polyphonic voice parts (though in *Petite camusette* the voices are discreetly doubled by viols and recorders). Vocal performance now becomes the preferred way of presenting Renaissance music, for the simple reason that the voice parts are all carrying essentially similar music. It is no longer the case, as in Machaut and even in much of Dufay, that certain voice parts differ so much from the others in rhythm and melody that they practically cry out for differentiation by being assigned to different instruments. From the late fifteenth century on, *a cappella* performance (see page 115) becomes the ideal for the presentation of Renaissance music.

(This is not to say that musicians of the time did not perform motets and chansons with all conceivable combinations of instruments or instruments and voices. They did, and many modern recordings present Renaissance vocal music in this way; it often sounds enchanting. However, just because "*they* did it" doesn't mean they always did it in the best way. *A cappella* performance remains the ideal.)

The same expressive range exhibited by Josquin's *Petite camusette* and *Scaramella* is also to be seen in his many marvelous motets. His early *Ave Maria* conveys an unforgettable mood of bright, childlike innocence, whereas *Absalon fili mi,* a setting of King David's lament for his son Absalom, is deeply anguished. A more controlled, elegiac lament is Josquin's *Déploration sur la mort de Jehan Ockeghem.* Written in memory of the composer Johannes Ockeghem, who died in 1495, this is a highly original work, half chanson and half motet—for, while four of the five voices sing a funeral poem in French, the tenor sings the Gregorian introit *Requiem aeternam* of the Mass for the Dead (see page 79). There is a particularly moving place where the poet asks "Josquin, Brumel, Pierchon, Compère" to weep "great tears" for Ockeghem. These were all contemporary composers; notice Josquin signing his composition, once again. His own death in 1521 called forth three such musical elegies.

The Mass

mass

To experience Josquin's work at its most brilliant and monumental, we have to turn to his <u>masses</u>. Anticipated by Guillaume de Machaut in the fourteenth century, the composition of masses became a major feature in the fifteenth, and the works themselves became far and away the most impressive samples of their composers' art. What the symphony was to nineteenth-century composers and audiences, the mass was to their fifteenth-century counterparts.

The idea was to write music that would in some sense unify the five movements of the Ordinary of the Mass. These five liturgical items needed some unifying, too, for they vary greatly in length, serve different functions, and come at widely separated times in the actual service (see page 78).

So large a musical structure presented composers with a challenge, and they accepted this in a spirit of inventiveness and ambition that we recognize as characteristic of the Renaissance. To help unify the Mass, they developed various new technical devices. First and foremost, they would select a Gregorian melody and work it into each of the five movements. The melody was typically sung by the tenor voice in long, drawn-out notes, thus forming a sort of scaffolding for polyphony moving at a more normal pace in the other voices.

tenor mass

Hence the terms *tenor construction* and <u>tenor mass</u>. (A third term is *cantus firmus mass; cantus firmus* means "fixed song.")

canon

Another technical device was <u>canon.</u> In a canon, a single voice is composed in such a way that one, two, or more entire voices in the polyphony can be derived from it exactly. They sing the same music all the way through, a few beats later, either at the same pitch (in which case the canon resembles a round) or at some other or others. Canons of a more esoteric type might have the later voices doubling the tempo of the first, reversing all its intervals, reading it backwards, etc. Composers did not necessarily expect all canons to be heard as such, but they seem to have felt that canons helped provide compositions of unprecedented length with an element of coherence.

Canons and tenor construction certainly reveal a technical preoccupation on the part of these Renaissance composers. This preoccupation does not seem to have much to do with the devotional mood one might think appropriate to the composition of a mass. Composers moved even further from devotion when they started basing their masses not on Gregorian chant melodies but on secular songs. Dufay wrote a Mass based on one of his love songs (!), the chanson *Se la face est pale* ("If my face be pale, lady, the reason must be love . . ."), and also one on a popular song called *L'homme armé* (The man of arms).

The latter set off an extraordinary musical rivalry. Composers over several generations wrote masses using this same song as a basis, competing with their forerunners and their contemporaries by means of canons and technical feats of all descriptions. It was like Josquin to write *two* Masses on *L'homme armé*. For the first, he had the ingenious notion of changing the mode of the original tune in each of the movements. In the second, called *L'homme armé sexti toni*, he included, among other refinements, a particularly brilliant fast canon in the final section (Agnus Dei III)—while simultaneously the *L'homme armé* tune is sung slowly by the tenor and is also sung backwards by the bass. Technical bravado apart, this makes an immensely powerful, exhilarating musical conclusion to the lengthy Mass service.

JOSQUIN DES PREZ *Ave Maris Stella* Mass: Agnus Dei   SIDE 2

To fully appreciate the accomplishment of fifteenth-century musicians in the writing of masses, it is necessary to listen to one of these long compositions all the way through. Josquin's *Ave maris stella* Mass, for four voices, is one of the most attractive.

The Osanna (Hosanna) section of the Sanctus movement provides an example of tenor construction. Here the tune that is basic to this Mass—the same Gregorian hymn that Dufay turned into a simple motet (see pages 77 and 116)—is intoned solemnly by the tenor in long notes, while the others sing more animated polyphony.

Further evidence of Josquin's concern for construction is provided by the Agnus Dei movement, the last of the five. The text is in three parallel parts:

(I) *Agnus Dei, qui tollis peccata mundi, miserere nobis.*   Lamb of God, who taketh away the sins of the earth, have mercy on us.

(II) *Agnus Dei, qui tollis peccata mundi, miserere nobis.*   Lamb of God, who taketh away the sins of the earth, have mercy on us.

(III) *Agnus Dei, qui tollis peccata mundi, dona nobis pacem.*   Lamb of God, who taketh away the sins of the earth, grant us peace.

Josquin therefore laid out all three sections of the movement at precisely the same length, sixty-six beats. He introduced the *Ave maris stella* tune symmetrically into Agnus I and Agnus III, but omitted it from Agnus II. Furthermore, in each of the sections he wrote two of the voices in canon, selecting two different voices each time.

The canon can be heard and followed easily in Agnus II. In the absence of the hymn tune, the two canonic voices are the only ones involved, and the soprano faithfully follows the alto's intricate, winding lines, two beats later and at a higher pitch. This creates an effect of considerable charm. In the alto line itself, notice how many phrases are repeated in sequence (see page 21); Josquin was very fond of sequence as a way of spinning out his melodies. Here many phrases are heard at a first and second pitch level in the alto (as a result of the sequences) and then at a third and fourth pitch level in the soprano (as a result of the canon).

Agnus I, scored for the full choir of four voices, incorporates the *Ave maris stella* tune, paraphrased, as a canon between the bass and the tenor. This canon you will probably have more difficulty hearing, for the soprano and alto obscure it by presenting noncanonic material of their own. At the very beginning, however, before the low-voice canon comes in, these two high voices lead off with a graceful little passage of just a few measures that is both canonic and sequential: a forecast of their action in Agnus II.

Agnus III nicely balances Agnus I, after the rather gentle two-voice interlude of Agnus II. Agnus III returns to the full texture of four voices, and it again features the *Ave maris stella* tune in a paraphrased version—now paraphrased differently, for Josquin could invent endless ways of decorating the same plainchant. This time he puts the canon between the tenor and the soprano. If we have listened to the entire Mass, and listened attentively, we are now rewarded by the special bonus of hearing the tune sung radiantly for the first time by the highest voice, the soprano.

This lovely soprano melody can be followed on the "line score" on page 121. This is a simplified, full-length score of Agnus III, which leaves out the lower voices where they are hardest to hear. Asterisks mark the notes derived from the plainchant, as can be seen by comparing the line score with the music of the hymn *Ave maris stella* (observe that on page 77 the tune is written out four notes lower). The notes without asterisks were added by Josquin as part of his paraphrase process.

Several other fine points emerge from careful listening to Agnus III while following the line score:

(1) Since Josquin begins Agnus III with all four voices singing the music at staggered time intervals, we are at first not sure where the canon comes. Only after about half a dozen bars do we realize that it comes in the tenor followed by the soprano. In retrospect, the alto and bass are understood to have taken part in a preliminary imitation, not a canon. Voices in imitation follow one another temporarily and freely. Voices in canon stick like glue.

(2) At measure 18, the soprano paraphrase reaches that distinctively "modal" place that we noted on page 77. As though recognizing this modal quality and wishing to underline it, Josquin brings in the tenor here with a change of meter (indicated in the line score by the double time signature in parentheses). What is involved is more of a delicate metrical ambiguity than a forthright change. There is an analogous effect in the last two measures of the piece, and this effect helps to brake the movement in preparation for the final cadence.

(3) In the final two measures, after the main voices (the canonic tenor and soprano) have come to rest on their cadence note G, the others keep moving for a time in such a way as to make the cadence sound even more solid. Especially at the end of long pieces such as Masses, this kind of cadential "prolongation" becomes characteristic of Josquin's music and that of the sixteenth century.

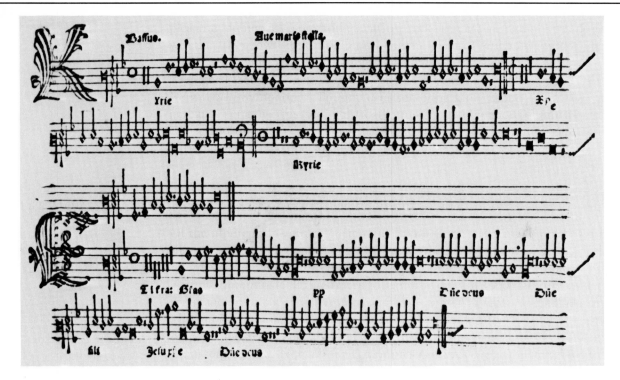

Music Printing

The circulation of music gained immensely from the invention of printing, certainly one of the most significant and far-reaching innovations of the Renaissance. While printing had been known in China since at least the ninth century, Europe had to reach its own "age of discovery" in order to reinvent this powerful technology. From its beginning with Johann Gutenberg in Germany, around 1450, printing spread rapidly all over Europe.

With it spread literacy, knowledge, and the inclination to independent thought. People with a modest amount of wealth could now own their own Bibles and prayer books, or Books of Hours. The classical authors that so interested intellectuals of the Renaissance were made available in good scholarly editions. Newspapers were to come some time in the future, but pamphlets were printed giving people's opinions on topical events. We have even seen a sort of grim printed comic strip, the Dance of Death (page 98).

Music printing was begun in 1501 by a Venetian printer named Ottaviano Petrucci. So popular was Franco-Flemish music in fifteenth-century Italy that Petrucci actually started with anthologies of French chansons, even including a few old classics by Guillaume Dufay. He then moved on to masses and motets and many books of popular Italian songs called *frottole*. The work of Josquin Des

Prez, who was then the most famous composer of the time, appeared in about ten editions as well as many anthologies. By the time we come to Roland de Lassus in the late sixteenth century (see page 134), we find more than 275 known editions of his music from all over Europe.

Shown here is page 1 of the bass (*Bassus*—the old *s* looks like an *f*) voice part of Josquin's *Ave maris stella* Mass, from one of Petrucci's earliest publications (1505). We recognize the opening tune. Although the notes are lozenge-shaped, they can be seen to follow modern principles of rhythmic notation, by and large. No bar lines are used, however, because the meter was not considered something to be emphasized. Bar lines are mainly useful when various voice parts are lined up in scores, and early printers never put out scores, only voice parts for the use of individual singers. The diagonal mark at the end of the staffs is a *direct*, a handy cue showing the singer what the next note will be on the next line. There is even a direct to the next section of the Mass, on another page.

Petrucci's workmanship is greatly admired by printing specialists. However, he had a technical problem in getting both words and music on the same page. He managed the words "Kyrie," "Xρε" (abbreviation for "Christe"), and a second "Kyrie" on the first two lines, but no "eleison" as required by the Mass text (see page 81).

CHAPTER 6 | The Renaissance II

The Renaissance   II

By the time of Josquin's death in 1521, the style of Renaissance music had reached a distinct plateau. Composers tired of the feats of technical virtuosity so characteristic of the late fifteenth-century Mass—or, to put it more accurately, they moved past the stage where such things were necessary. They had mastered the art of large-scale musical construction, and with it the basic techniques of homophony and imitative polyphony. These techniques were now cultivated intensively and brought into an ideal equilibrium. The result was a remarkably cohesive style, which we shall call the musical style of the High Renaissance. It held sway, allowing for refinements and ripenings, for the better part of a century.

Music of the sixteenth century was not all the same, of course. The better composers of the time naturally employed the normative High Renaissance style in subtle individual ways, and this style had to be applied somewhat differently to different musical genres, in any case. Nevertheless, the century was dominated by a single idiom to an extent that has not often been matched in music history. A sign of this is the fact that the style was soon codified into "rules" for the teaching of musical composition. Counterpoint "in the Palestrina style" formed the basis of the music curriculum almost everywhere until quite recently. It still does, in some places.

Closely linked with this normalization of style was an important new impetus that can be discerned around the same time: the desire to make music expressive. It is on the basis of this motivation, indeed, that we can divide Renaissance music broadly into a first and a second phase, as reflected by the chapters of this book. Musical expressiveness is one of the great cultural legacies of the Renaissance. In this feature, perhaps more than in any other, we can recognize the Renaissance as the starting point of modern music, as it was of other fields of modern human endeavor.

Music and Expression

We have discussed the "new sonority" of early Renaissance music in the work of Dufay and his contemporaries (see pages 110 and 115). Seeking to bring music closer to people's needs and desires, composers in the first part of the fifteenth century developed the sensuous side of music, in effect "reinterpreting the world of sound" in their chansons, motets, and masses, in ways we have examined. But to charm the ear is one thing, to stir the feelings another. As the century drew to a close, some composers began also to investigate the possibilities of linking music and emotion. They turned their attention more and more to working out means of making music expressive.

Bringing up this subject means broaching a famous problem that has given rise to lengthy philosophical controversies (and to many lengthy student bull sessions). Everyone agrees that music has something to do with emotion, and many people are also convinced that music can be said to "express" emotion. But how does it do this? And just what are the feelings involved?

People of the Renaissance thought they had the answers to both these questions. The feelings involved were those described or implied by the words, phrases, and sentences of vocal music. And the way music "expressed" those feelings was by supporting the words, by making what the words said more vivid and convincing. It was through the interplay of music and words that the Renaissance composers sought to infuse their work with fresh human relevance.

Hence the continuing prestige of vocal music in the sixteenth century. The major composers concentrated on vocal music, mainly music for small groups of singers and for choirs. They worked constantly to refine the relationship between words and music. In common with the architects, painters, and poets of the time, they were able to take encouragement for their interests from classical antiquity. Although no ancient Greek music had survived, there were many impressive accounts of it that stressed its extraordinary ability to stir the emotions. Only music with words did this, according to the Greek writers, and the Renaissance tended to treat anything the ancient Greeks or Romans did or said as gospel.

MUSIC AND WORDS

declamation

Concern for the relationship between words and music took two forms. First, composers tried to assure that the words could be clearly understood. They employed what is called accurate <u>declamation</u>; that is, they had words sung to rhythms and melodies that approximated normal speech patterns. This may seem elementary and obvious, but listen again to the Gregorian introit and gradual on sides 1, S–1: how little the early Middle Ages cared about the audibility and comprehensibility of the words! The same is true for the intricate music of the late Middle Ages, for the isorhythmic motets of Guillaume de Machaut. The Renaissance was the first era in which words were set to music naturally and clearly, vividly and beautifully.

Second, composers tried to match their music to the *meaning* of the words. In a trouvère song, the words are easy enough to hear, but as one stanza follows another (and another, and another) exactly the same music turns up with different words, whether angry or amorous, ecstatic or depressed. Composers now tended to match gloomy texts with long drawn-out notes, a low range, and dissonant harmonies. Lively rhythms they reserved for texts or portions of texts with a joyful character.

On a more detailed level, single words such as "run" and "fly" were set to rapid notes, and phrases such as "He ascended into heaven" (from the Credo of the Mass) were always set to brilliant high ones. Often this is apparent on the page, even without the sound, as in this Elizabethan madrigal of 1597, in which the word "Fly" can be seen to flutter in a fast eighth-note melisma, and "aloft" and "heaven" jump up to successive high notes:

Fly,   Love, a - loft   to heav'n to seek out for - tune . . .

word painting

The term word painting is used for this practice—the strategy of making vocal music illustrate the meanings of the words being sung. Word painting could become mechanical and silly—for example, when in Italian music of the time the word *occhi* (eyes) was set to two whole notes (oo). But when skillfully used, it could intensify the emotion inherent in words in a striking way, as Renaissance doctrine demanded. Developed in the sixteenth century, word painting has remained an important expressive resource in all later music.

The High Renaissance Style in Music

The High Renaissance style concentrated on the two techniques that had been gaining ground in the fifteenth century: homophony and imitative polyphony. Both techniques help make the words audible. This is obvious with homophony, less obvious with imitative polyphony. But consider that in writing imitative polyphony, the composer invents a melodic fragment or motive that declaims a verbal phrase clearly, and perhaps also "paints" the words; then the motive (with the words) is repeated many times in the many voices of the composition. If the words are obscured the first time by other voices singing other words, they will nonetheless be heard by the time *all* the motive entries have been accomplished, and the next set of words has started.

Imitative polyphony also reflects the ideals of simplicity, moderation, and balance that characterize the visual arts of the High Renaissance (see pages 128 and 129). By its very nature, imitative texture depends on a perfect balance between multiple voice parts. First one voice begins with a motive specifically designed for the words in question; soon another voice enters, singing the same motive at a higher or lower pitch level, then a third, then a fourth, and so on.

Raphael

Balance, order, moderation, dignity, and gravity were especially prized in the Renaissance. The classical ideal of the "golden mean" was held up as a model for human behavior—though it cannot be said that this ideal was always attained at the murderous courts of the Sforza, Medici, and Borgia princes. Today's (or yesterday's) ideas about etiquette go back to the Renaissance. Gentlemen were counseled to do everything in moderation, to walk, dance, and ride gracefully without abrupt movements, and never to seem overeager, boastful, or aggressive.

The Shakespeare sonnet on page 50 shows how Renaissance poetry achieved effects of moderation and gravity through its balanced proportions.

The same spirit infused the visual arts in what is called

the High Renaissance, the great age of Leonardo da Vinci, Michelangelo, and Raphael, around the beginning of the sixteenth century. Leonardo's *Mona Lisa* and *The Last Supper* are familiar to all, and exemplify the ideal of the age in both their composition and their mood. The simple, weighty pose of Mona Lisa, without any other figures, objects, or even ornaments to distract attention from her, is characteristic. The same is true of the smooth, echoing curves of her face, breast, hands, and clothing and the timeless dignity of her mysterious look. *The Last Supper* is an almost evenly balanced picture, with its inevitable yet undramatic focus on Christ sitting quietly at dead center. Around Him all the Apostles are gesturing actively, yet the whole effect is curiously grave and beautiful.

Consider also our two *Madonna and Child* pictures by Raphael. (Raphael painted many variants of this scene, all of them great favorites.) The Virgin in the first picture looks as unruffled as Mona Lisa—her face just as symmetrical, her clothing just as sober and smooth. From her central position she seems to control the picture; since the children play on the left side, she turns slightly as though inviting us to consider the other side, too. Her extended bare foot serves as a horizontal counterpoise to the boys' bare flesh. For vertical balance, the landscape rises more steeply and thickly on the boys' side.

The second picture is even more impressive in terms of balance. Raphael has contrived to bring two more figures into a design he had developed for only three. Yet he has maintained the same equilateral triangle enclosing the group, the same central figure that turns, the same foot, the same landscape—and the same calm, dignified repose emanating from all the figures and faces.

At the risk of becoming overfanciful, a musician might compare the first Madonna to a piece of perfectly balanced polyphony for three voices, which Raphael then rescored for five voices in the second Madonna. In sixteenth-century music, too, this general ideal of balance and simple dignity came strongly to the fore.

Raphael Sanzio (1483–1520) was a younger contemporary of Josquin Des Prez, whose *Ave maris stella* Mass is discussed on pages 119–20. Both men were favorites of the famous art-loving Pope Leo X in Renaissance Rome.

Meanwhile the earlier voices continue with new melodies artfully contrived to fit in with the later voices without swamping them. Each voice has its own shapely melody drawn from a single source. None is a mere accompaniment or "filler," and none stands out for very long over any of the others. The whole texture is alive and even, a web of similar gestures all beautifully coordinated.

The ideals of calm and balance permeate the High Renaissance style in other ways. In tone color, the *a cappella* ideal (see page 115) became established at this time, and with it our standard four-part choir of soprano, alto, tenor, and bass. Tempo and dynamics are relatively constant factors. Or, at least, composers never gave specifications for them; we must assume that in most cases a "golden mean" was applied.

Such basic musical elements as rhythm and melody are very restrained in character. The rhythm of sixteenth-century music is fluid, devoid of sharp accents, and quietly shifting all the time, so much so that the meter is often obscured. It is a significant fact that this music was still—like Gregorian chant and like earlier polyphonic music—written without bar lines. Bar lines mark the meter. This music has a definite meter (unlike Gregorian chant), but composers did not think of stressing it.

The melody is fluid, too; it never goes very high or very low, and the ups and downs are carefully balanced. It often reminds us of the smooth, oscillating flow of Gregorian chant. These rhythms and melodies almost recall the Renaissance ideal of good breeding: calm, controlled, considerate of others, shunning all obvious gestures. Except in actual dance music, the music of the sixteenth century rarely settles into the easy swing of a dance rhythm or into the clear patterns of an actual tune.

Detailed analysis reveals that these rhythms were put together from a surprisingly limited stock of different note values, and the melodies from an equally limited stock of intervals. The point, however, lies not in the analytical data but in the special feeling that such limitation engenders. This music can sometimes strike modern listeners as vague, but if we listen more closely—and always listen to the words as well as the music—we may catch something of its flexibility, sensitivity, and quiet expressive potential. Does it perhaps remind us of a wonderfully musical and subtle speaking voice? The sixteenth century would have been pleased to think so.

Mass and Motet in the Sixteenth Century

These two genres can be taken up together, for in the sixteenth century the Mass and the motet were very similar in style and in general effect. They differ in extent and in form: the Mass is much longer, of course, and the various movements fall into well-defined sections according to their texts. In style, however, there was little distinction. The composer first divided up the given text into short, manageable fragments. Then he set each one either to a section of imitative polyphony or to a section of homophony. The characteristic sound of a sixteenth-century motet or Mass is a smooth succession of such sections.

THE RENAISSANCE II | 131

The general mood of the music is always a reflection of the text as a whole (or, in the case of the Mass, the text of the section). Christmas motets sound very different from funeral motets. In the Sanctus of the Mass, listeners can always look forward to a contrast between the serene Benedictus section ("Blessed is he that cometh in the name of the Lord") and the following triumphant Osanna ("Hosanna in the highest").

Individual words are declaimed carefully and sometimes "painted," in ways we have described (see page 127). Where the text fragments follow one another directly in their sense, the music flows right on between them; typically a new imitative section, with its new motive, starts up before the previous one has quite finished. The beginning of the new section can be said to overlap the cadence of the old one. Really decisive breaks in the musical flow are reserved for major punctuation marks—colons, periods, paragraphs—in the text.

VICTORIA *Veni Sponsa Christi* (1576)   SIDE 2

The career of the great Spanish composer Tomás Luis de Victoria is outlined on page 135. The serene motet *Veni sponsa Christi* is one of Victoria's early works, written while he was still under the spell of Palestrina. It is a liturgical motet (see page 116), designed for one of the Office Services in honor of holy women who have devoted themselves to the life in Christ.

(1) *Veni, sponsa Christi,*	Come, Bride of Christ,
(2) *accipe coronam*	accept the crown
(3) *quam tibi Dominus*	which for you the Lord
(4) *praeparavit in aeternum.*	has prepared for eternity.
(5) *Veni, sponsa Christi!*	Come, Bride of Christ!

This motet employs the classic four-part choir, consisting of sopranos, altos, tenors, and basses; in early times the soprano parts in church music were always sung by choirboys, not women. Its five text fragments are all set in imitative polyphony. (As it happens, this motet has no sections in homophony.)

point of imitation

The term point of imitation is used for a section of music in imitative polyphony with all voice parts using the same motive, or sometimes two motives simultaneously. The next point of imitation uses another motive. Besides the main motive for the words "Veni sponsa Christi" in the first point of imitation, Victoria writes a second motive that always accompanies the first and that is imitated at the same time (see page 132).

The main motive, thanks to its long notes, shines through the polyphony at each of its appearances (three are shown in the example). Remarkably little of the music is "free," that is, not derived from either the main or the subsidiary motive. One free fragment, the little upward scale in the soprano in measures 6–7, is repeated a moment later and contributes greatly to the floating, devotional quality of this music.

Points of imitation 2, 3, and 4 are all introduced quietly by the bass and tenor voices. None of these points has a second, subsidiary theme, as point 1 does. In each case the new point overlaps the previous point. There is more of a break (though still not a very strong one) at the end of the fourth line of the motet's text, where the sentence ends, with a period, and where the composer then repeats the first words in a fifth point of imitation.

Point 5 briefly resumes the music of point 1, with a faster version of the main motive in the tenor voice that is as beautiful as it is ingenious. Can you hear that the subsidiary motive of point 1 is also revived in this luminous conclusion?

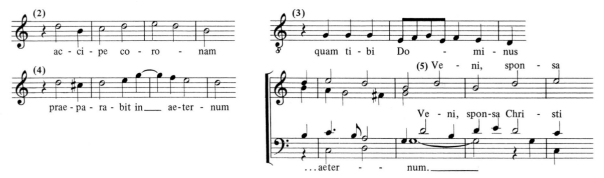

How delicate the word painting is in this motet: a melisma (see page 80) on the word "coronam" suggests the Virgin's ornamental crown, perhaps, and the sound grows fuller and almost triumphant at the climactic thought "in ae-ternum" (for all eternity). Its most beautiful feature, the return of the music of point 1 in point 5, is not typical. However, motets often contrive some special effect for their final sections. In Victoria's well-known Christmas motet *O magnum misterium* (O great mystery), for example, the final words, "alleluia, alleluia," move in pure homophony in a distinct and lively triple meter. Victoria might have been shocked to think that this would remind us of a dance, but in any case he has conveyed to perfection the sense of worshipers breaking into jubilation, almost in spite of themselves, as they contemplate the mystery of Christ's birth in the manger.

PALESTRINA *Pope Marcellus* Mass (1567)   SIDE 2

Presented to Pope Marcellus and named after him, this Mass is Palestrina's most famous work and his response to the dictates of the Council of Trent for the "purification" of Catholic church music (see page 134).

Composed for a choir of six voice parts, comprising soprano, alto, two tenors, and two basses, the *Pope Marcellus* Mass produces a much richer effect than a modest four-part motet such as Victoria's *Veni sponsa Christi*. In the first section, the Kyrie, each of the three subsections is handled with two separate points of imitation. But it seems clear that Palestrina was less interested in bringing these out distinctly than in piling up imitative entries so that they would intertwine in an ecstatic fashion:

(1) *Kyrie eleison.*   Lord have mercy on us.

(2) *Christe eleison.*   Christ have mercy on us.

(3) *Kyrie eleison.*   Lord have mercy on us.

Each subsection comes to a solid cadence and a stop. The first and last of these cadences are prolonged in the way Josquin used for the Agnus Dei in his *Ave maris stella* Mass (see page 120).

The next section, the Gloria, has a lot more text to get through, and it is more important that the many words be plainly understood. After the first line of text, "Gloria in excelsis Deo" (Glory to God in the highest), which is traditionally left in Gregorian chant, Palestrina turns to homophony. He shifts from one semichoir, or segment of his six-part choir, to another, thus:

		SOPRANO	ALTO	TENOR 1	TENOR 2	BASS 1	BASS 2
Et in terra	And on earth,	X	X		X		X
pax hominibus	Peace to men						
bonae voluntatis;	of good will;	X	X	X		X	
laudamus te,	we praise thee,	X	X		X		X
benedicimus te,	we bless thee,	X	X	X		X	
adoramus te	we adore thee,			X	X		X
glorificamus te . . .	we glorify thee . . .	X	X		X	X	

The idea of using homophony for sections of a Mass or a motet in which the words needed maximum comprehensibility was not new with Palestrina. What was new in the *Pope Marcellus* Mass, and in other works written to meet the demands of the Council of Trent, was the way this style was allowed to take over certain pieces completely. The long Gloria and Credo sections of this Mass, almost entirely homophonic, make their effect by brilliant alternation of homophonic semichoirs.

Four Renaissance Careers

In its broad essentials, the High Renaissance style was established by Josquin Des Prez in his late works, around and after 1500. After his time, the style was cultivated by composers over several generations, working at diverse musical tasks. It was a truly international phenomenon. The four most famous sixteenth-century masters were active in widely distant corners of Europe, and their careers differed very widely from one another.

In the sixteenth century we at last have a reasonable amount of biographical information about many composers, information that can provide some important insights into their music as well as "human interest." But composers' portraits, as we shall see, are still very rare.

Lassus Roland de Lassus (1532–1594), also known as Orlando di Lasso, came from Josquin's and Dufay's part of the world. More than a hundred years after the birth of Dufay, the region of Flanders and northern France still served as the great exporter of musical talent to the rest of Europe. In those days, boys with beautiful soprano voices stood in danger of being kidnapped to serve in the chapels of music-loving princes; Lassus was exported in this way more than once. He worked in the Netherlands, Italy, and even briefly in England, before settling at the great court of the Bavarian Elector at Munich. Here he composed prodigiously and was heaped with honors. He became an intimate of princes, the writer of amusing letters, and, on at least one occasion, an actor in *commedia dell'arte* plays. He died, however, in a state of acute "melancholia" in 1594.

Lassus completed a staggering 2,000 or more compositions—masses, motets, French chansons, Italian madrigals, German songs, even some pieces in Flemish. He stands out among his contemporaries in the flair and variety of his writing. Lassus was famous not only for his *Seven Penitential Psalms*—seven lengthy essays in pure dejection—but also for his bawdy madrigals, not only for his avant garde experimental works but also for chanson "hits" that were sung and played in countless arrangements all over Europe.

Before his melancholy days Lassus was a dashing figure, to judge from the elegant portrait shown to the right. There also exists a fascinating group picture of Lassus surrounded by the singers and instrumentalists of the Bavarian court chapel.

Palestrina A less colorful figure, Giovanni Pierluigi da Palestrina (circa 1525–1594) moved from his home (Pales-

trina, near Rome) to the Holy City as a young man, and stayed there for the rest of his life. He served in one after another of the most famous musical establishments of Rome, including the Papal Chapel. It is not clear that his was a particularly spiritual nature: when he married his first wife he had to quit the Papal Chapel, and when he married his second he came into a lucrative fur business. But he was certainly a faithful servant of the Church who did not hesitate to modify his singularly pure musical style according to its dictates. The Council of Trent, convened from 1545 to 1563 to mount a Catholic counterattack against the Reformation, determined among other things that Catholic church music should be reformed so that the words could be heard more clearly. Palestrina's most famous composition, the *Pope Marcellus* Mass, admirably fills this prescription.

He wrote mostly church music, including over a hundred masses (an extraordinary number—one wonders how he could respond to the same words over and over again). In his early days he wrote some secular music, including one or two madrigals that became widely popular, but later he made a public apology for them. In the atmosphere of the Council of Trent, it was not seemly for Rome's official composer to write music to love poems.

The best known portrait of Palestrina is the indifferent one reproduced on facing page, left.

Victoria Born in Avila, Spain, Tomás Luis de Victoria (circa 1549–1611) came to Rome at the age of sixteen to prepare for the priesthood. He admired Palestrina—it is said he cut his beard like Palestrina's—and may have studied with him. Before returning to Madrid in 1594, Victoria was for a time in charge of music at the Collegium Germanicum, founded by St. Ignatius Loyola to train Jesuits for their missionary work.

Father Tomás was a composer who wrote only church music. His personality has been compared to those of his fellow Spaniards: St. Ignatius, the painter El Greco, and even the mystical and ecstatic St. Theresa, comparisons that are not always easy to follow. But there is no doubt that of all the great Renaissance masters, Victoria in his music evokes the greatest sense of spirituality, devotional intensity, and mysticism.

No undisputed portrait of Victoria has survived.

Byrd The career of William Byrd (1543–1621) is perhaps the most interesting of all. At the time of his birth, England was still a Catholic country, even though Henry VIII had broken with Rome. Byrd continued to adhere to the religion of his birth after the Reformation, when Mass was illegal in England and Catholics suffered persecution. This composer must have been a thoroughly practical man and a shrewd politician, for, in spite of associating with Jesuits

and writing music to some suspiciously Catholic texts, he held on to his important position in Queen Elizabeth's Chapel Royal and was honored as the "Father of English Music." He accumulated enough of a fortune to retire to a good-sized farm away from London, where he could attend secret masses that were conducted in barns and in the attics of great country houses, with spies posted down the road to warn against discovery.

Byrd wrote numerous Catholic motets and three beautiful masses, still often sung in Anglican churches. But, under the circumstances, music of this kind could not occupy the whole of his activity, as it did for Victoria. Byrd wrote English songs, anthems, and services for the Anglican religion, as well as extremely fine instrumental music, for strings and for harpsichord.

The one surviving portrait of Byrd (see above) comes from a Dutch history of music written in the eighteenth century. Presumably the artist was copying an earlier portrait that is now lost, but . . .

In the present chapter, we are studying the main genres of the High Renaissance style through the compositions of these four men, picking a motet by Victoria, a Mass by Palestrina, an English anthem by Byrd, and a French chanson (but one very strongly influenced by the Italian madrigal) by the cosmopolitan Lassus.

Italy and the Madrigal

madrigal

The most notable new genre of the sixteenth century was the Italian madrigal. This was also the genre that absorbed most fully the new impetus toward musical expression. Developed in the early part of the century, mainly by northern composers working in Italy, the madrigal soon became the most imaginative and vital music of its day.

A madrigal in many ways resembles a motet—a short composition in which the various text fragments are set in imitative polyphony or in homophony. However, with secular words came a decisive change in emphasis. The imitations are handled more concisely and informally, and there is more and more concern for the words.

In fact, the words become the one and only rationale of the madrigal. In this respect, Italy pulled further and further away from France. In a typical French chanson—Josquin's *Petite camusette* (side 1) is a representative early sixteenth-century example—the music matches the general mood of the poem but does not illustrate individual words or phrases. A French chanson often feels like a somewhat attenuated tune. A madrigal is more of a musical commentary on its poem.

And the better madrigalists strove not merely to illustrate or comment on individual words and phrases but also more generally to reflect all the subtleties of verbal expression. Hence they tended to use the finest poetry they could lay their hands on. The century of Shakespeare was also a century of great poetry in Italy; the Italians honor Ludovico Ariosto (1474–1533), author of the epic poem *Orlando furioso*, and Torquato Tasso (1544–1595), author of *La Gerusalemme liberata*, along with their fourteenth-century giants Dante and Petrarch. Indeed, more madrigal texts were drawn from Petrarch's book of sonnets than from any other source, even two hundred years after his death.

ANDREA GABRIELI (CIRCA 1510–1586) *Ecco l'Aurora* (Behold the Dawn) (1566)   SIDE 2

Andrea Gabrieli is a composer who tends to be overshadowed by his nephew Giovanni; both played important roles in the history of music in Venice. We shall hear some of Giovanni's music later (see pages 157–59). Andrea was largely responsible for the typical light madrigal quality we recognize in *Ecco l'aurora.*

Listen to this madrigal through first without thinking about the words. It is all so wonderfully light, transparent, playful—so *secular,* after the grave *a cappella* church music of Palestrina or Victoria. The imitations are crisp and easy to hear. The imitative motives seem almost to have been chiseled out of the music, and the singers seem to be having great fun throwing the chips back and forth between them. Madrigals are a form of vocal chamber music, performed ideally by a single singer on each part, rather than by a small choir, as in church music; like all forms of chamber music, this genre exists in the first place for the pleasure of its performers. That is why madrigal groups are still popular today and why sixteenth-century madrigals still form a major part of their repertories. Madrigal singing also makes a good spectator sport, however; it is not only for insiders.

Now listen to *Ecco l'aurora* again, this time trying to follow the Italian words simultaneously with their English translation (see below). At first this may take a little doing, especially for those who do not know Italian. Few Americans learn Italian in school or college. But you can pick up the knack of following music sung in a foreign language while looking at the text and at the same time reading an English translation. This facility is important for the appreciation of vocal music of the later sixteenth century, for at this period music begins to reflect its words, as we have stressed—so if the music is to be enjoyed fully the words obviously have to be understood. Madrigal composers help by declaiming the words nicely.

Thus the word "l'aurora" (the dawn) in line 1 provided the general inspiration for Gabrieli's cheerful music. (We do not yet know that the poet is actually weeping at this traditionally upbeat time of day.) At line 2, however, Gabrieli slows the music down to match the words "a passo a passo" (step by step, or slowly). "La notte" (night) is set to low notes, and the singers sing them quietly; the word "monte" (mountain) gets a high note, as it always does in madrigals. More impressive is the series of rich, at least slightly mournful harmonies that Gabrieli provides for the reference to weeping in line 7. But it seems neither he nor the poet takes this mood too seriously, and, at the observation that dawn brightens everything, the prevailing lively character of the music is restored.

All this can be represented in a tabular form, as follows:

Ecco l'aurora con l'aurata fronte,	LIVELY, CHEERFUL RHYTHMS	Behold the dawn with its gilded brow
Ch' a passo a passo ci rimena il giorno;		Slowly bringing back the day;
Ecco che spunta sopra l'orizzonte	SUSTAINED MUSIC	Behold how it breaks over the horizon,
Con volto suo di bianca neve adorno;	LOW, "DARK" NOTES	Its face adorned with whitest snow;
Ecco la notte nell'avverso monte	HIGH NOTE	Behold the night over those other mountains
Che va fuggendo al suo antico soggiorno:		Fleeing to its ancient home.
Ed io pur piango all'apparir dell'alba,	RICH, EXPRESSIVE HARMONIES	And I still weep at the coming of dawn
Ch'omai d'intorno l'aere tutto inalba.	BRIGHT, LIVELY IMITATIONS	Which now in the air brightens everything.

LASSUS *La Nuit Froide et Sombre* (Night, Cold and Sombre) (1576) SIDE S–1

Now for another song about daybreak, very different in mood, by an even finer composer than Andrea Gabrieli—Roland de Lassus, "the divine Orlando," as he was called, perhaps the greatest composer of the sixteenth century.

We have stressed the cosmopolitan nature of Lassus's genius (see page 134). Technically, *La nuit froide et sombre* counts as a French chanson, since it has French words. But Lassus composed it in a completely Italian fashion; if it were sung without the words, even an expert would guess that it was an Italian madrigal. Since more readers of this book will know some French than will know Italian, *La nuit froide et sombre* will serve as a good example of a madrigal, even though it has French words. In the next section of this chapter an English composition will provide us with another example, even though it has English words.

Like his Italian colleagues in their more serious moments, Lassus avails himself here of a distinguished poem. In a calm progression from the first six-line stanza to the second, darkness and sleep yield to light and labor, in preparation for a powerful and rather solemn image of the universe at work, "composing" its iridescent tapestry. This thought, incidentally, betrays the Renaissance orientation of the poet, Joachim Du Bellay, a member of the premier French group of poets called the Pléiade. In the medieval scheme of things, the universe did not compose tapestries, God composed the universe.

Lassus rises to the artistic challenge presented by such poetry. Composers had now developed an extensive vocabulary of chords to make homophony effective, and with such means Lassus can "paint" a richly atmospheric picture of night—somber but peaceful, and not really *very* cold. Another wonderfully rich chord sequence comes at the words "Aussi doux que miel" (as sweetly as honey):

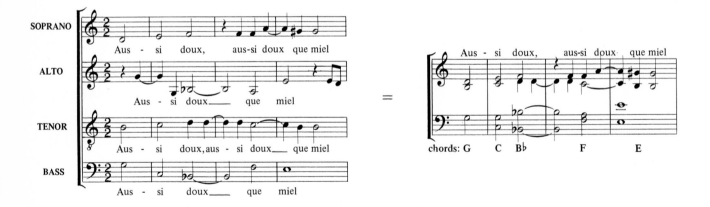

The intimate way in which his music reflects other words and phrases of the poem, line by line, can be summarized in another table (see page 139).

But over and above details, what Lassus catches so well is the poem's progression from dreaminess to activity. This he symbolizes by the broad progression from slow homophony at the beginning of the compositon to imitative polyphony at the end. Throughout the poem his response to the ideas—not only the words—is thoughtful, alert, and serious. In his attention to the details of the world and his quiet enjoyment of them, and in his ability to weave the many hues into a coherent musical tapestry, this composer shows himself to be as much a man of the Renaissance as his poet.

	QUIET, SOMBRE RHYTHMS AND HARMONIES	
La nuit froide et sombre		Night, cold and sombre,
Couvrant d'obscure ombre	LOW NOTES, THEN HIGH	Wraps a dark shadow round
La terre et les cieux,	RICH HARMONY	The earth and the skies,
Aussi doux que miel		As sweetly as honey
Faict couler du ciel	FASTER-MOVING, DESCENDING FIGURE	Night draws down from heaven
Le sommeil aux yeux.	"DRAGGING" EFFECT	Sleep into our eyes.
Puis le jour luisant	HIGHER, FASTER, BRIGHTER	Then shining Day,
Au labeur duisant		To match our labors,
Sa lueur expose;		Reveals its brightness;
Et d'un tien diverse	FULL CHOIR SOUND	And with multicolored strands
Ce grand univers		This great universe
Tapisse et compose.	WEAVING (?) EFFECT OF IMITATIVE POLYPHONY	Designs its tapestry.

The most familiar madrigals are lighter and more cheerful in sentiment than *La nuit froide et sombre.* But it is important to understand that the reason the madrigal captivated the sixteenth century was because of its extraordinary range of expression—somber as well as light, pathetic as well as mocking, delicate as well as brilliant, thoroughly serious as well as thoroughly trivial.

Music in Elizabethan England

England did not feel the full impact of the Renaissance until the reign of Queen Elizabeth (1558–1603). Shakespeare has given his name to this Golden Age, which also produced the scientist-philosopher Sir Francis Bacon, the architect Inigo Jones, and the "Renaissance man" Sir Philip Sidney—poet, literary arbiter, courtier, lover, and gallant soldier. Sir Walter Raleigh brought back tobacco from Virginia (named after the Virgin Queen), and Sir Francis Drake dropped anchor near San Francisco as he plundered his way around the world. Music, too, flourished more vigorously in England at this time than at any other, before or after.

A Renaissance Lady and Her Archlute

She is Lady Mary Sidney, Countess of Pembroke, sister of Sir Philip Sidney, and, like him, one of the main ornaments of cultural life in Queen Elizabeth's time. Mary was an excellent poet and translator, like her brother, and a great patron of literature and music. Both Sir Philip and the poet Edmund Spenser wrote important works for her, and the first book of English madrigals, by Thomas Morley (see page 142), was dedicated to her in 1593.

In earlier centuries, aristocrats liked to have their portraits included at the sides of pictures of the Virgin Mary, with prayer books in their hands, as a way of stressing their piety. Later portraits of the English nobility show them in their splendid gardens with their dogs and horses. Lady Mary, however, had herself painted indoors, grasping her enormous archlute—for music was an important fashionable accomplishment for ladies and gentlemen of the Renaissance. *The Courtier*, by Baldassare Castiglione, a sort of superior etiquette book of Renaissance court life, stresses that all truly civilized people should play the lute, just as they should know how to dance and ride horseback. Castiglione was translated and read all over Europe. It was thanks to attitudes such as those inculcated by his book that madrigals and other elegant secular musical genres were supported and enjoyed by the sixteenth century aristocracy.

The same Thomas Morley reports that, after dinner, society people would pass out madrigal part books and expect the guests to be able to join in by sight-reading. A guest would probably take a few quick music lessons before going to dine with the formidable Lady Mary.

Her archlute is the ancestor of our bass guitar, without amplification. You may be able to observe that it has two peg-boxes, carrying two sets of strings, so that it covers a range of four octaves, starting from the F three octaves below middle C.

THE ENGLISH MADRIGAL

Elizabethans were delighted by that most interesting and fashionable of late Renaissance musical genres, the Italian madrigal. They went so far as to have Italian madrigals published in London, but with word-by-word translations under the notes, so that the relationship between the music and the original words could be appreciated. At the same time, native composers tried their hand at composing madrigals to English words.

THOMAS WEELKES (CIRCA 1575–1621) *As Vesta Was from Latmos Hill Descending* (1601)   SIDE 2

Thomas Weelkes was an excellent minor composer who never rose beyond the position of a provincial Anglican cathedral choirmaster, probably because of a drinking problem. His well-known *As Vesta was from Latmos hill descending* is a fine example of a madrigal of the lighter, more brilliant kind.

Weelkes wrote *Vesta* for a patriotic anthology called *The Triumphs of Oriana*. Twenty-three English composers contributed madrigals set to different poems all ending with the same refrain:

> Then sang the shepherds and nymphs of Diana:
> Long live fair Oriana!

Oriana was a mythological name for Queen Elizabeth, and the nymphs and shepherds of Diana—the goddess of virginity—were her subjects. In this particular poem, another goddess, Vesta, is pictured strolling down her hill in Rome accompanied by Diana's "darlings," the Vestal Virgins, who nevertheless desert her when they see Elizabeth (and her shepherds) coming up it.

The word-painting can be shown in a tabular form, once again. It is very high-spirited and often amusing:

HIGH NOTES		FAST DOWNWARD SCALE
	As Vesta was from Latmos hill descending	FAST UPWARD SCALES
	She spied a maiden Queen the same ascending,	
	Attended on by all the shepherds' swain;	FAST DOWNWARD SCALE AGAIN
TWO VOICES, THEN THREE VOICES	To whom Diana's darlings came running down amain	FULL CHOIR
SOPRANO SOLO	First two by two, then three by three together	
	Leaving their Goddess all alone, hasted thither;	
	And mingling with the shepherds of her train,	
	With mirthful tunes her presence did entertain.	
LONGA IN THE BASS VOICE	Then sang the shepherds and nymphs of Diana: Long live fair Oriana!	EFFECT OF SPONTANEOUS, IRREGULAR CHEERING

This madrigal uses an even more brilliant choir than that chosen by Palestrina for the *Pope Marcellus* Mass: two sopranos, alto, two tenors, and bass.

Weelkes makes particularly good use of the six voices in his lengthy setting of the poem's last line. Here we can easily imagine many more than six loyal voices cheering the queen again and again in a spontaneous, irregular way, one after another:

In this last line, Weelkes also allowed himself a word-painting pun. He has the word "Long" sung by the bass voice on a note four times as long as a whole note, a note-value whose Latin name was *longa*.

THE BALLETT OR FA-LA

ballett   Though usually classified with the madrigal, the ballett is really a sophisticated dance-song, as its name indicates clearly enough. Most balletts consist of clear, simple tunes sung through several times to different poetic stanzas, with little if any word painting. After each part of the tune, however, comes a lively refrain to the nonsense syllables "fa la la." Hence the alternate name for the fa-la   ballett used by composers at the time, the fa-la.

Weelkes wrote balletts or fa-las that display the same irresistible verve as *Vesta*. More familiar, though, are examples by a slightly older Elizabethan composer, Thomas Morley (1557–1602), the man responsible for introducing both the ballett and the madrigal from Italy into England. Morley's *Sing we and chant it, Now is the month of Maying,* and *My bonny lass she smileth* remain perennial favorites with choirs and madrigal groups.

And simple as they are, balletts still manifest the characteristic features of the High Renaissance style. The "verse" parts of *My bonny lass* consist of pure homophony, while the "fa la" sections consist of light imitations. Even in this simple dialect, the general language of sixteenth-century music shows its admirable viability.

BYRD *Bow Thine Ear O Lord* (1580)   SIDE S–1

anthem   The term <u>anthem</u> was given to motetlike compositions in English. William Byrd, the greatest of the Elizabethan composers (see page 135), set the five lines of *Bow thine ear* symmetrically. He reserved homophony for the middle line, using imitative polyphony for the first two and the last two:

(1) Bow thine ear, O Lord, and hear us:

(2) let thine anger cease from us.

(3) Zion is wasted, wasted and brought low:

(4) Jerusalem, Jerusalem

(5) desolate and void.

Compared with Victoria's motet *Veni sponsa Christi* (see page 131), *Bow thine ear* is much more drawn out and grave in spirit. It also shows the influence of the madrigal in its attention to the words. In the homophonic middle section, the mournful chord on the second "wasted" (phrase 3) is made even more intense the second time around (Byrd here shifts among segments of his choir, like Palestrina in the Gloria of the *Pope Marcellus* Mass: see page 133). The motive for "Bow thine ear" (phrase 1) droops gently:

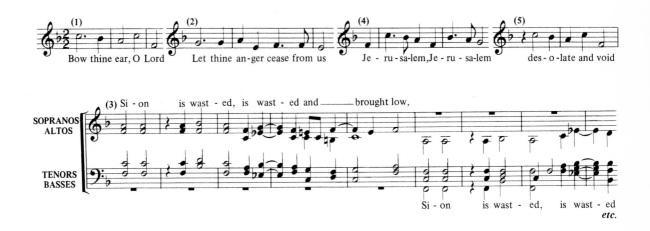

Modern listeners are often struck or puzzled by the way words are reiterated so many times in sixteenth-century motets and anthems—words such as "desolate and void" in this one, for example (phrase 5). But we must try to remember that the intended audience was not listeners but worshipers. Byrd wanted to be sure they got the religious message and meditated on it for a while. His ploy is more pleasurable, doubtless, than having the words said over and over again by the minister. In any case, there is a compensation here in the great climax that finally erupts (on our record, the organ supports this climax) and then in the breathtakingly lovely passage leading to the concluding cadence.

Instrumental Music of the Sixteenth Century

The continuing high prestige of vocal music in the sixteenth century militated against the development of purely instrumental music. The main composers concentrated their best efforts on refining the expressive relationship between words and music; with the exception of Byrd, none of them paid any appreciable attention to music without words. Nevertheless, important strides were taken at this time. The basis was laid for the great development of instrumental music, which is one of the glories of the baroque age.

At the beginning of the century, hardly any music existed that was designed first and foremost for instruments. Instrumentalists sometimes played along with the singers in vocal music, and sometimes they played vocal music by themselves. For example, Benvenuto Cellini boasts of how beautifully he and some friends played a motet on wind instruments for Pope Clement VII around 1525. (Cellini was a leading sculptor and goldsmith, who also wrote a famous racy and vainglorious autobiography.) Later in the century he would have played balletts (see page 142) and other new genres. The main genre of the second part of the century, however, the madrigal, would not have made much sense without its words.

But by this time there were also new genres specifically for instruments. Of these, dances were the most widespread. It will hardly come as a surprise to learn that dancing made prodigious advances in the Renaissance, in view of the new respect for human feelings and human nature that characterized the era. People moved freely again, and suggestions of sensuousness, even of eroticism, were not squelched by churchly disapproval. Contemporary books by dancing masters teach us the steps for many of the new dances, especially in the sixteenth century, and much music has survived that can be coordinated with this choreography.

PAVANE AND GALLIARD

Of the many dances that were popular in the sixteenth century, two that were particularly well developed in music were the pavane and the galliard. The

pavane

galliard

pavane was a solemn dance in duple meter—more like a sort of glamorous procession, with the dancers stepping and stopping in a very formal fashion. The galliard moved faster, in a triple meter, and featured leaps that over the years grew higher and (we are told) more and more obscene. Often a pavane and a galliard were written to go together as a pair. Pavanes and galliards usually consisted of three simple phrases each, which were played twice in succession to produce an A A B B C C form.

Side 2 of our record has two representative examples, the pavane *Bergerette* and the galliard *Au Joly Bois.* Probably they were written by instrumentalists who entertained no ambitions as composers; in any case, their names have not been recorded. The titles of the dances show that they were arranged from popular chansons of the period. The rather slow, stately pavane is played by a little Renaissance dance band consisting of recorder, viols, and a small drum called a *tambourin* (illustrated on page 489). Notice the heavy cadences at the end of the A, B, C phrases. It would have been easy to remember your steps, dancing to this pavane.

For the faster dance, the galliard, the wind player changes from the recorder to an oboe. Dancers might have a little more trouble with this charming piece, for the A phrase is ten measures long, rather than eight as in the B and C sections, and as in all the sections of the pavane. Was some dancing master trying out a new step, or was some composer seeing if he could make the almost invariable eight-measure phrases of dances of this time more interesting?

We see in this first phrase of the galliard *Au Joly Bois* a tendency that will assume more importance in the baroque period, a tendency to elaborate dance music and provide it with elements of more strictly musical interest. Irregular phrase lengths, tricky rhythms, complicated harmony, and polyphony are all introduced into certain dances. The next stage is "stylized" dance music that evokes dancing but is not intended for the actual dance floor. When a great jazz player starts improvising, people stop dancing and turn to listen. The principle of the stylized dance is of great importance, as we shall see, for both popular and "classical" music of the last few centuries.

CHAPTER 7

The Baroque Period   I

The Baroque Period   I

Music in the period from around 1600 to 1750 is referred to as *baroque,* a designation adopted by musicologists from the field of art history. The derivation of the word itself is both curious and revealing. Apparently it comes from a term used by seventeenth-century jewelers for large pearls of irregular shape. Baroque pearls, then, were imperfect or at best eccentric; but, with changing taste over the centuries, what was originally a negative implication was turned around into a positive one—for it is safe to say that nobody today describes art or music as "baroque" in a spirit of criticism. There is another, even better-known term for an artistic style that also reminds us of such changing attitudes. Gothic architecture, which we admire today, was originally found guilty by association with the barbarian Goths, wreckers of the Roman Empire.

Like the term *Renaissance,* the term *baroque* covers a great deal of territory, and it is best to think of the baroque period in two (or even more) subperiods. The chapters of this book reflect such a subdivision. We shall undoubtedly be sensitive to the striking differences that exist between the music of such masters as Claudio Monteverdi in the early baroque period, and Johann Sebastian Bach in the later baroque period. (This is also true of the early and late Renaissance: think of Dufay and Palestrina.) Nevertheless, certain underlying principles bring Monteverdi and Bach together, and these principles make the work of composers of the broad period 1600–1750 stand out from music written earlier and written later. We shall try to focus on some of the principles in the introductory sections of our chapters.

Both early and late baroque compositions are widely performed and appreciated nowadays, more so than at any time since the seventeenth and early eighteenth centuries. The history of the revival of this music has an interest of its own. After around 1750, the year when Bach died, baroque music went out of fashion with a vengeance. Even the works of so great a composer as Bach went underground, as it were, surviving in copies written out by some of his students, which were passed on from one generation to the next. Bach was "rediscovered" in the nineteenth century, and most of baroque music waited until the twentieth—after the First World War and particularly after the Second. Why this was so is not altogether easy to say. But whether we find it strange or not, many music lovers today seem to feel closer to this music, written some 250 to 350 years ago, than to certain more recent styles.

From Renaissance to Baroque

Around the end of the sixteenth century, explosive tendencies began to be felt at the sophisticated musical establishments of northern Italy—at the princely courts of Florence, Ferrara, and Mantua, and in the Republic of Venice. The new ideas caught on instantly and were soon transforming music all over Italy and in most of the rest of Europe too.

The main musical genres of the time were the motet and the Italian madrigal. In the motet, the most sensational developments took place at Venice (see page 160). From the Gloria movement of Palestrina's *Pope Marcellus* Mass (page 133), and elsewhere, we remember how sixteenth-century composers had often subdivided their choirs of, say, six voice parts into semichoirs of three or four, and then had these semichoirs answering one another. This technique was now expanded enormously, as Venetian composers started out with two or more separate choirs of four, five, or six voice parts each. These whole choirs—or semichoirs drawn from them—would answer and contend with one another throughout whole compositions, coming together only for climactic sections of glorious massed sound.

To the resources of this multiple-choir style, Giovanni Gabrieli, the greatest of the Venetian composers, added further refinements. (He was the nephew of Andrea Gabrieli, whose madrigal *Ecco l'aurora* we examined in the last chapter.) As we shall see, some of Giovanni's "choirs" were designated for singers on some of the voice lines and instruments on others, or else whole choirs would consist of instruments. As Gabrieli's motets grew more and more extravagant, the stately decorum of the sixteenth-century "classic" style was forgotten. Composers from other regions scrambled to imitate Gabrieli's new sounds, until in 1628 the Roman composer Orazio Benevoli, writing a particularly important Mass to consecrate a new cathedral, boggled minds with a combination of seven different choirs for a total of fifty-two separate voice lines. Plus organ.

In the madrigal, leadership was assumed by the music-loving courts of Ferrara and Mantua. As we have stressed, madrigalists from the outset of the genre in the early sixteenth century concentrated on one thing with a passion, the musical illustration of words, or word painting. Now the thirst for "expression" grew more and more esoteric and exaggerated. The most remarkable figure of the late madrigal development was a noble amateur, Prince Carlo Gesualdo, ruler of a minor principality called Venosa, whose madrigals (though still ostensibly for five voices *a cappella*) use dissonances and chord progressions so extreme that they are not matched in music until the later nineteenth century. (Gesualdo was no stranger to extremity in his personal life, either. In 1590 he had his wife murdered in bed with her lover, and later he had himself whipped by his servants as a daily routine.)

Florence, meanwhile, was nurturing a reaction *against* madrigals, no matter how extreme. The Florentines dismissed the madrigalists' word painting as an artificial, childish game. They pointed out, with some show of logic, that the many voices of a madrigal ensemble tended not to focus emotion and express it strongly, as the madrigalists claimed, but rather to fritter it away in counterpoint. For true emotionality, Florentine critics asserted, one had to use a single human voice—or, rather, a single individual delivering words in a style modeled on that of a great actor, someone who can move an audience to laughter or anger or tears. They developed a passionate style of individual recitation that was half music and half elocution, oratory, or rhetoric. This led inevitably to the stage: and *opera*, invented around 1600 in Florence, became one of the most important and characteristic products of the baroque imagination.

All in all, knowledgeable travelers to Italy around 1600 would have obtained the impression that music was bursting out all over. But, if they were not only knowledgeable but also thoughtful, they might have been a little puzzled to notice a tendency in the other direction as well. Musical form was becoming more rigorously controlled and systematic. Later in this chapter we shall trace this countertendency in all the musical genres touched on so far— the Venetian motet, the late madrigal, opera—but for now we shall mention only the most graphic example of it, the important baroque form called *fugue.*

Fugue (for a full discussion, see page 185) was descended from the sixteenth-century motet, as cultivated by Palestrina, Lassus, Victoria, and Byrd. What is the essential difference between the parent genre and the offspring? As we have seen, a motet consists of a series of musical sections, some (perhaps most) of them employing imitative polyphony, others homophony, and all having different themes. Like a motet, a fugue employs imitation—but much more single-mindedly: in the first place homophony is excluded, and in the second place *only one theme* is used all the way through. The baroque fugue, then, takes one element of the "classic" Renaissance style and works it out exhaustively. This is what we meant when we said that musical form was more rigorous and systematic in the baroque period than in the Renaissance.

It may be puzzling for us, too, as well as for our hypothetical observers of 1600, to hear the baroque period described in terms of opposite currents—a "free" one exemplified by opera, and a "strict" one exemplified by fugue. It would undoubtedly be simpler if the music of the time were all a matter of uncontrolled effusion, or if it were all system and control. It would be simpler, but it would also be less interesting and less alive. The tension between the two is what gives the greatest baroque music its unique quality. Consciously or unconsciously, composers seem to have realized that, as they sought to make music more untrammeled in one respect, they had to organize it more tightly in another, so that listeners would not lose track of what was happening. The control exercised by baroque form, in other words, was an appropriate response to all that baroque extravagance, exaggeration, and emotionality. We shall see rather similar forces and counterforces at other points in musical history later in this book.

Style Characteristics of Early Baroque Music

Given the diverse, extravagant, experimental quality of early baroque music, we could scarcely hope to be able to draw up a long list of stylistic earmarks that would hold for all of it. We shall find this easier to achieve with later baroque music, composed after the dust had settled (see chapter 8). However, two important features do mark the early style uniformly, or almost uniformly. One is a new attitude toward rhythm and meter, and the other is a new musical texture. In each of these stylistic areas, we shall see signs of the systematic spirit we noted in the previous section as a characteristic of baroque musical form.

RHYTHM AND METER

Rhythm is the basic element of music, and perhaps the most obvious way in which baroque music makes a radical departure from the characteristic style of the Renaissance is in this basic area. Rhythms become more definite and regular; a single rhythm or closely similar rhythms may be heard throughout a piece or a major segment of a piece. This is very different from Renaissance music, with its subtle, floating rhythms changing section by section as the themes change. (Renaissance dance music is an exception, of course—and in the area of dance music there is a direct line from the Renaissance to the much more vigorous baroque development.)

Related to this is a new acceptance of meter. One small technical feature tells the story: bar lines begin to be used for the first time in music history. This means that the meter of music is systematically in evidence, over the whole range of music, rather than being downplayed as it was in the Renaissance. The strong beats are emphasized by certain instruments, playing in a clear, decisive way. To be accurate, we should note that, when singers were delivering the more passionate passages in early opera, the meter was still obscured and rhythms were still free—or, rather, free in a new way. Yet other sections of these same operas are sharply metrical, almost as if to compensate.

walking bass

One device that comes up in many (though by no means all) baroque pieces shows the new attitude toward rhythm and meter with special clarity and neatness. This is the so-called walking bass, a bass part that keeps going rigorously in the same note values—all quarter notes, or eighths, or halves— throughout an entire composition or long segment. The walking bass provides a steady support for the meter; over this steady (and even monotonous) foundation, other voice parts in the composition can weave their more varied rhythms. Here is an example that we shall see from the music of Monteverdi:

Just looking at it on the page, this seems like a simple enough device. But, once again, we would never encounter such a bass part in music of the sixteenth century. To a Renaissance musician, the walking bass would have seemed impossibly crude and elementary. Composers now had a fresh insight into how such simplicities could be turned to new aesthetic ends.

TEXTURE: THE CONTINUO

basso continuo

Some baroque music is homophonic in texture, and some is polyphonic—but these textures are both of a special kind. Baroque homophony and polyphony alike are complicated by a factor unique to the period, the basso continuo or *figured bass*. Indeed the continuo—to adopt the shortened term that has become customary—is one of the main features that unifies the lengthy baroque period and marks it off from those around it.

In a composition of the baroque period (as of every other) the lowest line is performed by a bass voice and/or low instruments such as bassoons or cellos. What is different about baroque texture is that, in addition, the same bass is always played also by a chord instrument such as a harpsichord, an organ, or a lute. And the player does not merely reinforce the bass line, but also, more importantly, systematically fills in chords above it. "Fills in," because the chords are not actually written out in the score but left for the player to improvise. As a guide, the *general* form of the chords is indicated by a numerical shorthand above or below the bass notes, but the *specific* form is left to the player. The individual musician determines, for example, whether to put the chords in a low or a high octave, whether to supply little connections between chords, and whether to sustain the chords or keep repeating them.

All this is called the art of *realizing* the continuo. The term *figured bass* comes from the numerical shorthand mentioned above, which can be viewed on the scores on pages 176 and 187. The term *continuo* (continuous) reminds us that the chords run on systematically throughout the composition. One other term that is sometimes encountered is *thorough-bass*, an old English translation of basso continuo (thorough = through = throughout).

As a result of this improvised practice, baroque homophony and polyphony both have a special quality. The main musical outlines are surrounded by a sort of harmonic haze. Depending on the performers at any particular occasion, the haze may turn into a blur or it may be so light that the listener scarcely notices it at all (and some modern performances of baroque music incorrectly leave out the continuo chord instrument entirely). At the time, the continuo was probably more prominent than it is in most modern situations, for baroque musicians seem to have preferred to fill up musical "space" in this way, and they apparently did not worry much about linear clarity.

It is not hard to understand how the continuo came into being. It answered a practical need felt by early baroque musicians. In the previous section of this chapter, we mentioned the organ continuo in the fifty-two-voice Mass by Orazio Benevoli; without that continuo, his colossal forces would never have stayed together. Gesualdo's madrigals are scored for a traditional *a cappella* choir—but, if modern experience is any guide, when those madrigals were performed they were accompanied by a harpsichord or a lute in order to help the singers thread their way through the fantastically difficult passages the prince had dreamt up for them. And to give a third example, once opera singers were encouraged to sing in a highly emotional, free manner, complicated polyphonic accompaniments for such singing would have led to rhythmic chaos. But the single harpsichord and cello of the continuo could follow the singer's slowdowns and speedups, all determined on the spur of the moment to bring out the emotional quality of the text in the most spontaneous manner.

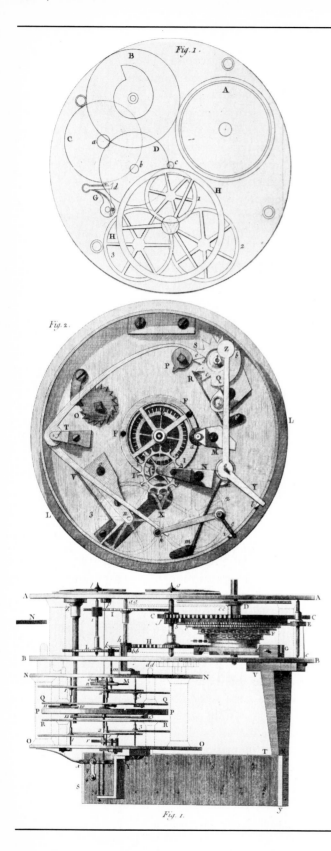

Fig. 1.

Fig. 2.

Fig. 1.

The Scientific Temper

That human reason, coupled with accurate observation, could gain control over natural phenomena was an exciting idea that became more and more pervasive during the baroque period. Emerging from the spirit of inquiry that had developed in the sixteenth century, the idea took support from a veritable flood of scientific discoveries in the seventeenth. Galileo, Kepler, and Newton laid the foundations of modern astronomy, mechanics, and physics. Harvey discovered the circulation of the blood, Boyle produced a vacuum, Leeuwenhoek observed protozoans. And Newton and Leibniz, in independently inventing calculus, found the mathematical tool to make sense out of all this new observation and discovery.

One symptom of the new confidence in human knowledge was the undertaking of great comprehensive encyclopedias—the famous one prepared by the French Encyclopedists and the more modest *Encyclopaedia Britannica.* The first true dictionary of music dates from this period, too: Sébastian Brossard's *Dictionaire de la Musique* (1703). Another symptom was the extensive development of scientific instruments of all kinds. Since music is the art of sounds in time, perhaps the best symbols for baroque music are time-measuring instruments: clocks, watches, and chronometers, which baroque craftsmen brought to a fantastic level of accuracy.

Among the philosophers, Locke and Hume transferred the habit of scientific observation into a cold, hard look at human nature and thought processes. Others, such as Leibniz, actually tried to investigate God by the quasi-mathematical methods that had worked so well in other areas. They came up with the notion of God as the "Great Watchmaker," a sort of supertechnocrat regulating humanity and the world by the application of scientific laws.

Musicians, too, responded to the new intellectual climate, though less directly and no doubt less consciously. Late baroque composers favored intricate melodies, dense polyphonic textures, regular, methodical rhythms, and formal plans that let them pursue a single musical idea rigorously in repetitions of all kinds (see pages 194–96). We can detect in all this an ambition to stake out the field of music, as it were, and fill it in systematically—an ambition based on the conviction that all the elements of music could be investigated, encompassed, and controlled at will. A similar conviction underlay the bold efforts of scientists, philosophers, technicians, and craftsmen of the time.

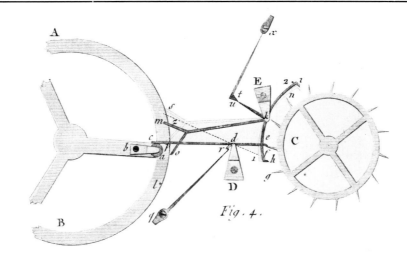

Fig. 4.

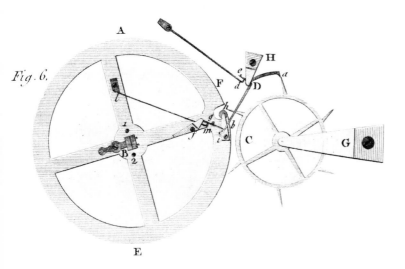

Fig. 6.

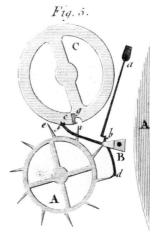

Fig. 5.

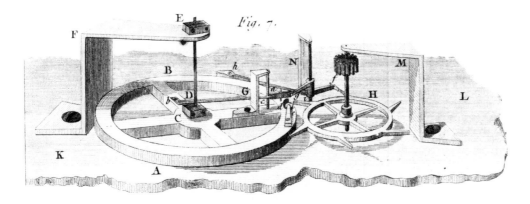

Fig. 7.

FUNCTIONAL HARMONY

What the continuo also demonstrates—and dramatically enough—is the growing dependence of baroque music on harmony. The opera style was frankly homophonic, consisting as it did of one voice accompanied by chords. But by means of the continuo, a homophonic (or harmonic) concept also invaded other types of baroque music that remained densely polyphonic. For the polyphony and the continuo fitted together. At the beginning of the period the continuo may appear to be merely following the polyphonic voice lines, but as the baroque style congeals we get the impression that things are beginning to work the other way around. The harmonic framework established by the continuo comes first, and the contrapuntal lines are then adjusted to it. Baroque polyphony, in short, has a systematic harmonic underpinning.

As a result of this pervasive use of the continuo, the art of harmony during the baroque period developed prodigiously. (Or did the pervasive use of the continuo arise from a growing fascination with harmony? A chicken-and-egg situation.) Whereas Renaissance music had still used the medieval modes (see page 75), albeit with important modifications, baroque musicians developed the major-minor modal system that is familiar to us. We mentioned in passing on page 111 that the concept of a chord was first introduced in the Renaissance, when chordal sonorities began to be appreciated for their own sake. The first important and profound book on harmony dates from the baroque period: it is the *Treatise on Harmony* written by the great French composer Jean-Philippe Rameau in 1722.

Related to the development of the major-minor system was a new way of handling chords so that their interrelation was more logical. Each chord that could be formed from the notes of the major and minor modes now had its special place or role to play in reference to the tonic, or central, note (or chord). Thus when one chord followed another in baroque music, it did so in a newly satisfactory and purposeful way. On page 43, *tonality* was defined as the feeling of centrality around a single note that comes up naturally in melodies, in whatever modes they are cast. The term functional tonality is used for this more sensitive, systematic, and highly developed sort of centrality that emerged in the baroque period, by which each note and chord had its well-defined "function" in relation to the tonic.

Functional tonality and the functional treatment of harmony that makes it possible are somewhat difficult concepts. But they are qualities that we hear easily, instantly, and instinctively. What makes baroque music sound so *familiar*, compared to that of the sixteenth century, is essentially the use of functional harmony. The chords seem to be "going" where we expect them to—and with them goes the sense of the music. No longer does the music seem to wander, detour, hesitate, or evaporate. So ingrained is our instinct for functional harmony, in fact, that however well we come to know music earlier than that of the baroque period, it will probably always sound strange to us. It is an attractive strangeness, perhaps—to some listeners, an irresistibly attractive strangeness; but it is strange all the same, because of the lack of functional tonality. With the introduction of this important musical resource, baroque music brings us firmly to the familiar, to the threshold of modern music as we know it.

(margin note) functional tonality

Music in Venice

The rather amazing development of music in late sixteenth-century Venice has been attributed to a number of factors. First, there is the well-known enthusiasm of the Venetians for bright colors and brilliant pageantry (see page 160). Second, the architecture of St. Mark's Cathedral, which was the sociopolitical as well as the religious center of the city's life, lent itself to sonic experimentation. A wide, round basilica with two bulging choir lofts, St. Mark's encouraged composers to supply each loft with a separate choir (and a separate organ, and a separate band of instruments) and have them perform back and forth stereophonically.

A third factor is political. Music was consciously exploited by the State of Venice to glorify itself, with the most elaborate pageants slated for days of both religious and political significance. Such were the feast of the patron saint, St. Mark, for example, and the Feast of the Annunciation of the Blessed Virgin Mary, when tradition said the city had been founded. Every year there were fourteen great occasions of this kind. Elsewhere in Europe music sounded to the glory of princes, but Venice was a genuine republic; composers did not write motets in praise of the doge—an elected, temporary head of state, like a glorified mayor—but rather in praise of the "Serene Republic" itself. Perhaps composers and audiences, too, could enter into this with more than the usual enthusiasm.

In any case, tourists in Venice around 1600 (Venice was Europe's first great tourist center) responded to the major civic feast-day services at St. Mark's the way modern tourists do to big shows at Las Vegas. The difference is that they came home full of admiration not only for the art and entertainment in Venice, but also for the civic virtue and power that this was seen to symbolize.

GIOVANNI GABRIELI (CIRCA 1555–1612) *In Ecclesiis* (In the Congregation) (circa 1610)   SIDE 2

Giovanni Gabrieli's extraordinary motet *In ecclesiis* is a work for three "choirs," but only choir 2 is treated in the standard way. The voices in choir 1 sing singly or in pairs, accompanied by the organ continuo, until near the end, while choir 3 consists exclusively of instruments.

After the first solo, performed by the sopranos of choir 1, the famous Venetian double-choir effect is heard in a richly resonant alleluia (choir 1 versus choir 2). Even more sumptuous, after another solo, is the effect when the brass choir (choir 3) comes crashing in. Remember this one stroke if you want to savor a typical baroque gesture: stupendous, astonishing, dazzlingly brilliant, and also more than a little pompous.

Similar in effect is the organ *intonation* played prior to *In ecclesiis* on our record. Intonations were used to give the singers the pitch—and with typical baroque exaggeration, Gabrieli inflated these simple, functional pieces so as to give the organist *his* moment of magnificent display. Gabrieli's official position at St. Mark's was Second Organist.

We have mentioned the more controlled aspect of baroque musical form, a seeming counterforce to the flamboyance and drama. In *In ecclesiis* this appears in the returns of the alleluia, which is heard five times in all, getting louder (because usually more heavily scored) at each appearance:

(A)	*In ecclesiis benedicite Domino.*	Praise the Lord in the congregation.
(B)	*Alleluia*	Alleluia
(C)	*In omni loco dominationis benedic anima mea Dominum*	In every place of worship my soul blesses the Lord.
(B)	*Alleluia*	Alleluia
(D)	(Interlude)	Interlude
(E)	*In Deo salutari meo et gloria mea. Deus auxilium meum et spes mea in Deo est.*	In God is my salvation and glory. God is my help, and my hope is in God.
(B)	*Alleluia*	Alleluia
(F)	*Deus meus, te invocamus, te adoramus. Libera nos, salva nos, vivifica nos*	My God, we invoke thee, we worship thee. Deliver us, save us, revive us.
(B)	*Alleluia*	Alleluia
(G)	*Deus adiutor noster in aeternum.*	God is our advocate unto eternity.
(B)	*Alleluia*	Alleluia

In the total musical form, which can be diagramed A B C B D E B F B G B, the alleluia (B) holds the long work together. It also, incidentally, provides a simple demonstration of the psychology of musical form. The returns may be systematic, but there is nothing dry or merely "formal" about them. We begin to wait for the alleluias, and we take a special satisfaction at hearing them again and again, louder and louder. That satisfaction is a central part of the exciting aesthetic experience provided by music such as Gabrieli's.

GABRIELI *Sonata Pian' e Forte* (circa 1610) SIDE S–2

Only a composer who loved instrumental music and had written a good deal of it could have thought up the vocal-instrumental contrasts of *In ecclesiis*. Gabrieli was the first major composer after the Elizabethan William Byrd to devote himself seriously to instrumental music, music without words. In some of his pieces he specified the instruments exactly, as he did in *In ecclesiis*, though it must be said that he usually followed Renaissance practice and left the choice of instruments to the performers. In recent years Gabrieli's *canzonas* (a late Renaissance instrumental genre) have achieved popularity scored for the brilliant-sounding modern brass choir.

In one famous work, Gabrieli took another important step by again specifying a musical element that had traditionally been left to the performers' discretion: dynamics. His *Sonata Pian' e Forte* is written for two instrumental choirs of carefully differentiated tone color. Choir 1 is a low group, consisting of three trombones and a viola, and choir 2 is a high group, consisting of three trombones and a *cornetto:* not a cornet, but an archaic instrument resembling a curved recorder that is played with a type of trumpet mouthpiece. The two groups alternate and echo one another, playing now softly, now loudly—hence the title of the composition—and coming together for occasional massive climaxes. With the whole texture enlivened by darting rhythms and rich harmonies, the iridescent play of instrumental tone colors makes a dazzling effect.

What Gabrieli does not indicate is any kind of gradation between "piano" and "forte." In terms of dynamics, his sonata alternates between two more-or-less fixed levels. This is called terraced dynamics, and is characteristic of music until the end of the baroque period. We may reflect that in a work like *In ecclesiis,* too, each choir has its own natural dynamic level, and so the composer obtains an effect of terraced dynamics simply by skillful deployment of his forces, without needing to write "piano" or "forte" at all.

terraced dynamics

Do not imagine, however, that baroque music was performed at an absolutely dead level of dynamics, or at several such levels "terraced" rigidly. Instrumentalists certainly made small changes in dynamics to bring out rhythmic accents, and singers allowed themselves to sing louder on high notes than on low ones (it is unnatural and quite hard not to do so). But natural variations of this kind were minimized, and gradual swellings from soft to loud, and the reverse, were not used. This musical resource remained to be exploited by the Viennese composers of the late eighteenth century.

Claudio Monteverdi (1567–1643)

Claudio Monteverdi was born in Cremona, a town located not far from Milan and revered by musicians as the home of the great violin maker Stradivarius. A child prodigy, Claudio published a whole book of little motets at the age of fifteen. His first position was as a viola player and singer at the nearby court of Mantua, where madrigals were cultivated with a passion, and he soon became the greatest madrigalist of his time (though his madrigals, as we shall see, refused to lie still and sometimes turned into miniature opera scenes and the like). His early operas, too, were written for important court festivities at Mantua.

In 1613 Monteverdi received the call from Venice; to be chapelmaster there was the most prestigious musical position in Europe. After taking that post, he composed much festive church music in the Venetian manner. At the age of fifty-five Monteverdi took holy orders, out of gratitude for escaping the plague, and God granted him another twenty-one years of life and labor. These were capped by his completion of two magnificent operas, which helped initiate the triumphant course of Venetian public opera: *The Return of Ulysses* (1641) and *The Coronation of Poppaea* (1642). (Poppaea was the scheming mistress of the Roman Emperor Nero.)

Venice

Venice, the island city of canals, lies on a tidal lagoon of the Adriatic Sea near the northeast corner of Italy. This location was ideal for trading with the Near East and northern Europe and for resisting attacks from the mainland. Wealthy, liberal, and cosmopolitan, Venice developed a more representative form of government than any of its rivals. In the sixteenth century it became a showplace, one of the most brilliant and powerful of the Italian Renaissance city-states.

The glorious topography of Venice, highlighted by the Italian sun and the blue Adriatic, seems to have enlivened the spirt of its inhabitants. They built their city in flamboyant, varied architectural styles using building materials of many colors, collected from their trading routes. The great Venetian painters—the Bellinis, Titian, Tintoretto, Veronese—specialized in warm, rich colors. Parades and pageantry, on land and on water, were a special feature of life in the "Serene Republic." They still are today, as our picture of the Grand Canal shows.

Perhaps, then, it is more than a play on words to describe Venetian music of the sixteenth century as "colorful." In vocal music, Venetian composers added more and more voices to the polyphonic texture, reaching as many as twelve or sixteen. They divided these big choirs into two, three, or more sections singing "stereophonically," from different locations. Musical forces like this demand a conductor, and this institution seems to have been invented by the Venetians.

Instrumental music, too, was particularly developed in sixteenth-century Venice. Giovanni Gabrieli, organist of St. Mark's Cathedral, the greatest church in Venice, was the first composer who systematically indicated exactly what instruments were to play some of his canzonas, motets, and sonatas. St. Mark's itself is a huge circular church with two choir lofts on opposite sides—an ideal location for multichoir music of the kind written by Gabrieli. The walls were hung with Oriental carpets (supplied by Venice's trading partners), which reduced the echo.

MONTEVERDI *Lamento della Ninfa* (Lament of the Nymph) (1638)

Because there is no single word for a beautiful young woman in Italian (or English), poets have had to fall back on the mythological term from the Greek. Monteverdi's *Lament of the nymph* was published in *Warlike and Amorous Madrigals,* his eighth and last book of works ostensibly in this genre, and it begins like a traditional madrigal.

A choir of men's voices presents the first part of the text (see page 163) in sections, some of them homophonic and some polyphonic. The continuo is present but adds nothing of importance. There is the usual word painting, too—busy counterpoint for "errava hor qua, hor là" (she went back and forth), mournful chords on "dolor" and "piangendo" (grief, weeping), and little gasps of air before and after "sospir" (sigh). The latter was one of those madrigalists' clichés denounced by the Florentine intellectuals as especially artificial and inexpressive.

But the Florentines would have had no quarrel with the rest of Monteverdi's "madrigal." For when the young woman speaks, Monteverdi beckons her to the center of the stage and turns the spotlight on her. Her passionate and somewhat erotic lament is sung by a single soprano; the individual emerges from the anonymity of the group even more clearly here than in Gabrieli's *In ecclesiis.* And the emotional poignancy that Monteverdi can obtain with this solo line goes far to justify the whole aesthetic of the early baroque.

You can probably tell that much of the excruciating effect of the lament comes from the bold dissonances between the soprano's notes and those of the accompaniment (of which more below). Monteverdi was hauled over the coals for this sort of thing by contemporary critics. He replied coolly that, while such dissonances would certainly be wrong for traditional music, he was writing a new kind of music—what he called "the second practice"—and for this any dissonances, any means at all, were right as long as they brought out the passions of the text. His revolutionary stance was entirely conscious.

Monteverdi might also have added that all the contortions and distortions of the soprano line are held in check by the unusual rigidity of the bass line in the accompaniment. It is a "walking bass," moving entirely in the same note value (dotted quarter). But in addition to this, the cello and harpsichord (or lute) of the continuo play the same simple figure over and over and over again:

ground bass
ostinato

A repeating bass figure of this kind is called a <u>ground bass</u>, or, in Italian, a *basso ostinato*. (The vivid term <u>ostinato</u>, meaning "obstinate," is applied to any repeating figure in music, whether in the bass or elsewhere. Ostinato technique becomes important in the twentieth century, as we shall see.) The ground bass in Monteverdi's *Lament of the nymph* provides another excellent example of the baroque dualism between untrammeled emotion on the one hand, and strict formal control on the other.

Best of all, perhaps, in this remarkable composition, is the role of the men while the soprano is singing. Though they opened the work by setting the scene in a neutral fashion, they are now gradually drawn into the dramatic action. Overwhelmed by the young woman's outpouring of anguish, jealousy, and sheer amorous energy, they murmur broken phrases of consolation and distress—in the background, quietly, so she does not hear. Sympathetic voyeurs, they express what we in the audience are feeling. Once she stops, they pull themselves together and pronounce a dry commentary to conclude. But of course it is not this, but rather the soprano lament that sears itself into the memory. Many a later opera composer would envy Monteverdi's power to express raw emotion, as shown in this piece.

Lamento della Ninfa

Non havea Febo ancora	The sun had not yet
Recato al mondo il dì,	Brought day to the world,
Ch'una donzella fuora	When a maiden
Del proprio albergo uscì.	Stepped forth from her lodging.
Sul pallidetto volto	On her pale face
Scorgeasi il suo dolor;	Was inscribed her sorrow,
Spesso gli venia sciolto	And often from her grief
Un gran sospir dal cor.	Issued a great sigh.
Si calpestando fiori	Aimlessly over the flowers
Errava hor qua, hor là,	She wandered here and there,
I suoi perduti amori	Her lost love
Così piangendo va:	Lamenting, in these words:
"Amor," dicea, il ciel	"God of Love," she said,
Mirando, il piè fermò,	Stopping and gazing up at the sky,
"Amor, dov'è la fè,	"Love, where is that faith
Che'l traditor giurò?	That the traitor swore to me?
"Fa che ritorni il mio	"Make my love return
Amor com'ei pur fu,	To me as he was,
O tu m'ancidi ch'io	Or else kill me, so that I
Non mi tormenti più."	No longer torment myself."
(Miserella, ah, più, no, no—	(Unhappy girl, no more:
Tanto gel soffrir non può.)	She cannot suffer such scorn.)
"Non vo' più ch'ei sospiri	"I do not want him to sigh,
Se non lontan da me,	Unless he is far from me,
No, no che i martiri	No, nor to tell me
Più non dirammi, affè."	Of his sorrows—no indeed!"
(Miserella, etc.)	(Unhappy girl, etc.)

"Perchè di lui mi struggo,	"Since I long for him,
Tutt'orgoglioso sta,	He haughtily ignores me;
Che sì, che sì se'l fuggo	But if I were to leave him,
Ancor mi pregherà!"	Would he beg me again to stay?"
(Miserella, etc.)	(Unhappy girl, etc.)
"Se ciglio ha più sereno	"If my rival has
Colei che'l mio non è,	A fairer face than mine,
Già non rinchiude in seno	She does not have in her heart
Amor si bella fè."	So true a devotion."
(Miserella, etc.)	(Unhappy girl, etc.)
"Nè mai si dolci baci	"Nor shall he ever from her lips
Da quella bocca havrà,	Taste such sweet kisses,
Nè più soave—ah taci,	Nor such exquisite—but enough:
Taci che troppo il sa."	He knows this only too well."
(Miserella, etc.)	(Unhappy girl, etc.)
Si tra sdegnosi pianti	Thus with indignant complaints
Spargea le voci al ciel,	Her voice rose to the heavens;
Così ne' cori amanti	Thus in the hearts of lovers
Mesce Amor fiamme e giel.	The God of Love mixes fire and ice.

MONTEVERDI *Zefiro Torna* (The Spring Breeze Returns) (1638) SIDE S–2

In this famous "madrigal," Monteverdi chose a cheerful ground bass to match the (initially) cheerful poem, an elegant Italian sonnet:

This ground bass (not a walking bass, this time) will remind some listeners of the so-called Pachelbel Canon (which is *not* a canon—see page 118—but another ground-bass piece, composed later in the century). Above Monteverdi's bass, two voices take up the text, one phrase—or one word—at a time, with charming, sometimes amusing, echoes and sinuous, sometimes brilliant, duets.

The poem begins with the phrase "Zephyr (i.e., the west wind, the spring breeze) returns," but the Italian word for "return," *torna,* is the same as that for "turn," and this seems to have given Monteverdi the genial idea of having the two tenors twist and turn playfully, while the ground bass is repeated again and again. If we follow the words carefully, we shall see that not only is a general feeling of springtime burgeoning created by the tenor warbling and the lively bass, but also many individual words are illustrated:

Zefiro torna, e di soavi accenti	The spring breeze returns, and its sweet breath
L'aer fa grato, e'l piè discioglie a l'onde,	Freshens the air, and ruffles the waves,
E mormorando tra le verde fronde	And murmuring through the green branches
Al bel suon fa danzar su'l prato i fiori.	Makes for dancing, with its music, among the meadow flowers.
Inghirlandato il crin, Fillide e Clori	Garlands in their hair, Philida and Cloris
Note temprando amor care e gioconde,	Sound ravishing and joyous notes,
E da monti e da valli ime e profonde	And from mountains and valleys, low and deep,
Raddopian l'armonia gli antri canori.	The harmony re-echoes in sonorous caves.
Sorge più vaga in ciel l'aurora, el sole	The dawn is lovelier in the sky, and the sun
Sparge più luci d'or; più puro argento	Scatters its gold more brightly; a purer silver
Fregia di Teti il bel ceruleo manto.	Tints the Sea Queen's beautiful blue robe.
Sol io, per selve abbandonate e sole,	Only I am abandoned and alone in the woods;
L'ardor di due begli occhi el mio tormento,	The light of two fair eyes and my torment
Come vuol mia ventura, hor piango, hor canto.	Constitute my destiny: which now I lament, now I sing.

There is rapid movement for "discoglie a l'onde" (ruffles the waves), smooth movement for "mormorando" (murmuring), high and low notes for "da monti e da valle" (from mountains and valleys), and so on. So perhaps, with all this word painting, the composer had some justification for calling this brilliant tenor duet a madrigal, after all.

The words also explain the extraordinary event after fifty-four (!) appearances of the ground bass, where there is an abrupt change in harmony, rhythm, tempo, melodic style—everything. The effect is as extravagant as anything in Gabrieli's *In ecclesiis,* if we allow for the different scopes of the two compositions. Here the poet says that *in spite of* all the fifty-fold varied joys of spring, *he* is miserable—and this quite unanticipated reversal of mood is mirrored by the music, all in the best traditional madrigal spirit. But not in the traditional madrigal style: the exaggerated way in which lines 12, 13, and 14 are declaimed, with certain words on very long notes and others on fast ones, shows the influence of the kind of dramatic recitation developed by the Florentines. The passage brings us, indeed, to the very brink of opera.

Baroque Opera

opera   Opera—drama presented in music, with the characters singing instead of speaking—is often called the most characteristic art of the baroque period. This is because it combines so many different arts: not only music, drama, and poetry, but also dancing and scene design—indeed, scene design of the most elaborate kind. The artists and architects attached to baroque opera theaters developed ingenious machines to work amazing transformation scenes, aerial entries and exits, shipwrecks, volcanos, and the like; these men often received the top billing, ahead of the composers! Opera provided the sort of extravagant melange that especially delighted the baroque imagination.

From a more strictly musical point of view, opera was an ideal answer to the general desire for individual emotionalism. This genre provided a stage on which the single individual could express his or her feelings in the most direct and powerful fashion. Monteverdi's nymph need only slip on a costume and she will find herself a new career (she already has a built-in audience). At the same time, composers of full-length operas—as opposed to short "scenes," like the *Lament of the nymph*—felt an urgent need to relieve the constant emotional pressure exerted on their characters by the ever-changing dramatic action. They had to contrive moments of relaxation. This led to a standard dualism between two basic operatic elements, called *recitative* and *aria.* And this dualism, as we shall see, reflects that other baroque dualism, between "free" emotionalism and "strict" control.

recitative

Recitative, from the Italian word for "recite," is the technique of reciting words to music in a natural, expressive way. It was developed in Florence around 1600. The voice brings out the words clearly and vividly, following the free rhythm of language carefully; it mirrors the natural ups and downs that occur as we raise our voices at a question, lower them in "asides," or cry out in distress. The accompaniment is kept to a minimum—the continuo only—so that the singer-actor can interpret the dialogue or the action in the most spontaneous fashion. Recitative was used for the main dramatic scenes in baroque opera. Simple recitative was also used for giving directions, information, and all the other necessary but prosy lines that go into theatrical writing.

aria

An aria is a "set piece" for solo singer that has much more musical elaboration and coherence than a passage of recitative. Typically the accompaniment includes the orchestra, not just the continuo. In an aria, the single-actor mulls over emotions at some leisure, instead of reacting moment by moment, as in recitative. The aria is a soliloquy, meditation, or tirade during which the character can "get out feelings." For this, the composer needs the various resources of musical form on all levels: clear melodies, first of all, and probably also repeated motives, thematic returns, ground basses, and so on. Later in the baroque period, arias, unlike recitatives, tend to repeat their words many times, to music that is often related though not identical to that of the initial words. All this has the effect of developing and so fixing the emotion.

The combination of recitatives and arias has proved a highly serviceable framework for opera over the nearly four hundred years of its existence. While in style and form both have changed radically over the years, the basic principles they embody—music for action and music for reflection—can be traced throughout opera's history. Some operas also include choruses, delivering communal sentiments, and we shall meet with other special features in particular cases. But recitative and aria remain the staples.

A word, before we go any further, about listening to operas. Some people like them, while others seem to nurture a constitutional aversion to the genre. But even those who like or might come to like them experience more problems of comprehension in connection with operas than with other types of music.

The reasons are obvious. Operas are stage works, so, unless you witness actual performances or telecasts, you miss a vital component of the aesthetic effect. And operas are as long as stage plays: yet, because they are dramatic works, it is imperative to get a sense of the beginning, the middle, and the end. It is no use trying to understand opera by listening only to small snippets such as favorite arias. You might as well try to understand *Hamlet* by reading "To be or not to be" and "O that this too too solid flesh would melt," leaving out Hamlet's denunciation of his mother, his murder of Polonius, the play within the play, the ghost, and poor Yorick.

Opera has been exceedingly important to the art of music since its invention around 1600. We cannot skimp on this genre and deal responsibly with our subject. Techniques of central importance were pioneered in opera before they inspired purely instrumental music, and major composers have devoted some of their principal efforts to opera. We shall try always to look at opera scenes of some length—consisting, for example, of a section in recitative, an aria, and a chorus—for only in this way can we begin to get a sense of the total picture. Ideally, you should try to listen to an entire opera all the way through, following the text. This can be done with recordings and radio broadcasts. Better yet, you should see a performance. In recent years, fortunately, operas have been televised much more frequently, and numerous videotapes are now available.

MONTEVERDI *Orfeo*, Act IV, Scene ii (1607)   SIDE 3

The early Florentine operas were court entertainments, put on to celebrate royal weddings and the like. This was true also of Monteverdi's first opera, *La Favola d'Orfeo* (The Fable of Orpheus), produced at Mantua in 1607. But an important step was taken in 1637 with the opening of the first public opera house in Venice. Spurred on by Monteverdi's late operas and those of his student Francesco Cavalli, opera soon became the leading form of entertainment in Italy. By the end of the century there were seven opera houses in Venice, fulfilling much the same function as movie theaters in modern cities of the same size (about 145,000 people).

Monteverdi's subject was a beautiful Greek legend about music, about a great singer who could soften stones and tame wild beasts with his song—

> Orpheus with his lute made trees
> And the mountain-tops that freeze
> Bow themselves when he did sing,

as Shakespeare puts it in *Henry VIII*. When his wife Euridice dies, Orpheus is even able to charm his way into Hades and persuade Pluto to let him bring her back to the earth. But he lacks the self-control to meet Pluto's shrewd condition that he not turn and look at her before they reach the upper regions; overcome by emotion, he looks and she dies again. Orpheus then renounces women and is torn to pieces by a mob of intoxicated nymphs celebrating the rites of Dionysus. (But this does not happen in the opera.)

Orpheus

Opera arose out of Renaissance intellectuals' admiration for the culture of classical antiquity and their desire to emulate it. At Florence, the greatest center of classical studies, some musicians and musically-minded poets reasoned that by reintroducing the Greek ideal of poetry recited by a single singer-actor to the accompaniment of a lyre, they could recapture the extraordinarily moving effects that Greek writers said resulted from their music. The Florentines did not reintroduce Greek music, but they did invent a new musical genre that has moved millions of people in the centuries following.

It is not surprising, in view of opera's origins, that the first examples took their subjects from Greek mythology. Nor is it surprising that so many early opera heroes were mythological musicians and singers, such as Apollo, the god of music, and the musician Arion, who was thrown overboard (like Jonah) but rescued by music-loving dolphins. For if the characters are musicians, singing a play rather than speaking it seems more natural.

Our illustration shows Arion, as portrayed in a semi-operatic stage entertainment of 1589 by Jacopo Peri, a Florentine singer and composer who wrote the first operas a few years later. One was based on the legend of Orpheus; Monteverdi studied Peri's work before producing his version of the story. Orpheus, the Thracian singer whose music was powerful enough to soften the heart of Pluto and regain his wife from Hades, and who then lost her again because of his own lack of self-discipline, had a special fascination for opera composers. Its symbolic aspects are clear enough. Early baroque composers were trying to invent music of a new emotional power, but at the same time they understood the need for controls to hold this music together and make it sound coherent. This resulted in the characteristic baroque dualism that we have spoken of already (page 151).

The figure of Orpheus has haunted musicians through the centuries. In the eighteenth century he turns up as the subject of a very important "reform" opera by Christoph Willibald von Gluck, a contemporary of Haydn and Mozart, in the nineteenth as the title of a symphonic poem by Franz Liszt (see page 350), and in the twentieth as the subject of perhaps the most beautiful ballet by Igor Stravinsky (see page 441). In the early days of operetta (see page 496), Jacques Offenbach wrote an amusing parody of the legend, called *Orpheus in the Underworld* (1858). Here Orpheus is a drudge of a music teacher who drives his wife crazy by playing lugubrious violin solos, including the main theme of Gluck's famous opera. On his part, he is only too glad to see her go to Hades since he is interested in a shepherdess.

ACTS I–IV

Orfeo consists of five short acts, after Music's prologue; the whole opera lasts only about an hour and a half. Act I shows Orpheus, Euridice, and their mythological friends celebrating their betrothal (this went over well at the ducal wedding in Mantua). In act II, Orpheus learns from a messenger that Euridice has been killed by a snake bite, and he resolves at once to go down to Hades and get her back. In act III, on the banks of the River Acheron, he sings a very elaborate aria that lulls Charon, the ferryman, to sleep. This is how Orpheus gets across, even though he is still alive.

He does not appear at the beginning of act IV, but his presence is known; Proserpina, the Queen of Hades, pleads with Pluto to release Euridice for the sake of their own love, as well as that of Orpheus and Euridice. Pluto agrees. We take up the action with act IV, scene ii.

ACT IV, SCENE ii

A short chorus by the Dead Spirits hails Pluto's action. The spirits are accompanied by trombones, which characterize the infernal regions all through the opera; the upper world is expressed instead by violins and recorders. Different characters have the continuo "realized" (see page 153) by different chord instruments, too: Orpheus speaks to the accompaniment of the organ, Euridice to a harp or lute, and a hostile Dead Spirit to a harsh reed organ (called a *regale*). In his enthusiasm for varied tone colors, Monteverdi yielded nothing to Gabrieli and the other Venetians.

Orpheus's first reaction to the chorus's announcement is to sing a joyous aria in praise of his art, which has regained him Euridice. It is a simple, lively song with violin interludes, built over the "walking bass" illustrated on page 152. After fully expressing his joyful feelings in this aria—there are three stanzas of nearly the same melody—Orpheus suddenly stops to think, and then begins to spell out his thoughts in recitative.

Recitative depends utterly on the words, and it is no use pretending that one can get much out of even the most beautiful recitative in Italian unless one knows the language. For this reason, our main discussion of recitative will wait until we come to an opera in English, later in this chapter. We can, however, appreciate in a general sort of way the depiction of Orpheus's growing excitement as anxious questions surge up in his mind (in part 1 of his recitative below). He sighs realistically and emotionally: "ohime" (ah me!—pronounced *oy-may*—a word without which baroque opera would collapse). In part 2, his imagination begins to run away with him, in faster and faster rhythms. In part 3, the rhythm becomes firmer as he proclaims vaingloriously his decision to obey the dictates of love.

A fatal moment. How tenderly he turns to his beloved Euridice (part 4), and how frantically he reacts when he turns and sees nobody, but hears instead the ominous rattle of the harpsichord continuo. Harshly and contemptuously, a Dead Spirit dashes all his hopes. In Euridice's touching recitative, we recognize the harmonic underpinning of her words "dolce" and "amara" (sweet, bitter): these are the same sort of bittersweet chords Monteverdi used to depict sorrow in the *Lament of the nymph* and in lines 12–14 of *Zefiro torna*.

Orfeo, Act IV, Scene ii

CHORUS OF
SPIRITS:
*Pietade oggi e Amore
Trionfan nel' inferno.*

Pity, today, and Love
Triumph in Hades.

SPIRIT:
*Ecco il gentil cantore
Che sua sposa conduce al ciel superno.*

Behold the gentle singer
Who leads his wife to the heavenly sky.

(Orpheus enters playing his lyre; Euridice follows him.)

ARIA

ORPHEUS:
*Qual onor di te sia degno,
Mia cetra onnipotente,
S'hai nel tartareo regno
Piegar potuto ogni indurata mente?*

What honor shall you deserve,
My lyre omnipotent,
Since in Hades's realm
You have been able to sway every hardened spirit?

*Luogo avrai fra le più belle
Imagini celesti,
Ond' al tuo suon le stelle
Danzeranno in gir', hor tard', hor presti.*

You shall have a place in the fairest
Images of heaven,
Where, to your sound, stars
Will dance in a ring, now slowly, now fast.

*Io per te felice a pieno
Vedro l'amato volto
E nel candido seno
De la mia donna oggi sarò raccolto.*

I, thanks to you all-happy,
Shall see that beloved visage,
And in her white breast
My lady will today enfold me.

RECITATIVE

(1) *Ma mentre io canto, ohime! chi m'assicura
Ch'ella mi segua? ohime! chi me
nasconde
De l'amate pupille il dolce lume?*

But while I sing, ah me! who can assure me
That she is following me? Ah me! who
is it denies me
The sweet light of those beloved eyes?

(2) *Forse d'invidia punte
Le deità d'averno
Per ch'io non sià quaggiù felice appieno
Mi tolgono il mirarvi,
Luci beati e lieti,
Che sol col sguardo altrui bear potete!*

Perhaps, stung by envy,
The deities of Hades—
Lest I become all-happy in this world—
Are taking from me the vision of you,
Your bright eyes, blessed with light,
Which could bless others merely with a glance!

(3) *Ma che temi, mio core?
Ciò che vieta Pluton, commanda Amore!* . . .

But what do you fear, my heart?
Pluto forbids, but Love commands! . . .

(He turns and looks at Euridice.)

(4) *O dolcissimi lumi, io pur vi veggio;
Io pur . . . ma qual eclissi, ohime!
v'oscura?*

O sweetest of eyes, now I see you:
Now . . . but what new eclipse, alas!, is
hiding you?

VOICE OF
A SPIRIT:
*Rotto hai la legge, e se' di grazia
indegno!*

You have broken the compact; you are
unworthy of mercy.

EURIDICE:	*Ahi, vista troppo dolce e troppo amara:*	Ah, your look is at once too sweet and too bitter:
(dying)	*Così per troppo amor, dunque mi perdi?*	Is this how you have lost me—by loving
		me too much?
	Ed io, misera, perdo	And I, wretched, am losing
	Il poter più godere	The power to enjoy henceforth
	E di luce e di vita, e perdo insieme	Both light and life; and at the same time I lose
	Te, d'ogni ben più caro, o mio consorte.	You, dearest of all, my husband.

Another Dead Spirit summons Euridice away, and Orpheus breaks down in a paroxysm of grief. We can practically hear his hysterical cries and sobs. The act ends with another chorus of Spirits, still resplendent with their dark, burnished, trombone accompaniment, flanked by purely instrumental sections. This sounds like a particularly solemn Venetian madrigal. "Orpheus conquered hell, but was conquered by his own emotions. Worthy is only he who can claim victory over himself."

ACT V

Back on earth, Orpheus gives himself over to lamentation, until he is reproved by Apollo, the god of music, who is also his father. Apollo leads Orpheus up to heaven as a demigod so that he can contemplate Euridice forever in tranquillity. Then there is a final dance, in which, at the original performance, the cast was joined by the Mantuan wedding guests; the entertainment was first presented not in a theater but in a great hall in the ducal palace.

When this distinctly anticlimactic last act is forgotten, listeners to *Orfeo* will remember two things. One is the almost incredible emotional punch of Monteverdi's recitatives. The composer of the nymph's lament was more than equal to the laments of Orpheus and Euridice. The other is the opulent variety of Monteverdi's score. There are profoundly moving recitatives, but there are also numerous simple, catchy arias of the kind we have seen in act IV, scene ii: the "free" and "strict" sides of baroque music. Rich, Venetian-sounding choruses of Dead Spirits are contrasted with airy choruses of Nymphs and Shepherds reminiscent of the ballett or fa-la (see page 142). Orpheus's fantastic virtuoso aria which charms Hades is placed next to a half-comic song by

Charon, the none-too-smart boatman, who has been tricked before and is determined not to be this time. Monteverdi in his madrigals could project unforgettably both the fun of *Zefiro torna* and the pathos of the *Lament of the nymph;* in his operas he wove multicolored tapestries with all the variety, brilliance, and exuberance that characterize the early baroque period.

Henry Purcell (circa 1659–1695)

At a time when sons generally entered their fathers' occupations, there were families of musicians just as there were families of notaries, grooms, and candle makers. Fathers passed on the tricks of the trade to their sons and were well situated to find them positions. Presumably musical talent ran in the family, too, and every once in a while this would blossom into genius. The Bachs in Germany were the most famous of these musical families; the Purcells in England were another. Henry Purcell's father and uncle (it is not certain which was which) were both musicians in the Chapel Royal of Charles II, and his younger brother Daniel was something of a composer also.

Toward the end of his short life, Henry composed a great deal for the London theater—for Shakespeare potpourris and original plays by John Dryden and William Congreve, among many others. However, English theatrical conventions called for plays with only a few songs and other musical numbers, so none of Purcell's theater scores can really be called operas. His one true opera was composed not for professional singers and musicians but for amateurs. Commissioned for a girls' school, *Dido and Aeneas* does without any virtuoso singing roles, and it contains many short choruses and dances. The whole opera lasts less than an hour. *Dido and Aeneas* is an exceptional work, then, and a miniature, but it is also a work of rare beauty and (rarer still) a great opera in English written prior to the twentieth century.

PURCELL *Dido and Aeneas,* Act III (1689)   SIDE 3

Purcell's opera is derived freely from Virgil's *Aeneid,* the noblest of all Latin epic poems, well known to every seventeenth-century schoolgirl. Written to celebrate the glory of Rome and the Roman Empire, the *Aeneid* tells the story of the city's foundation by the Trojan Prince Aeneas, who escapes from Troy when the Greeks capture it with their wooden horse. After many adventures and travels (including a journey to Hades, incidentally, where he sees Orpheus and Euridice and has the usual troubles with Charon), Aeneas finally reaches Italy, guided by the firm hand of Jove, king of the gods.

At the seaport of Carthage, on the North African coast, Aeneas and the widowed Queen Dido fall deeply in love. But Jove appears in a vision and tells the prince to stop dallying and get on with his important journey. Regretfully he leaves, and Dido kills herself out of grief. According to the "official" interpretation, this episode shows Aeneas putting aside personal considerations so as to fulfill his glorious destiny, but even in Virgil, Dido comes out looking much better than Aeneas. The changes in the story as Purcell set it make Aeneas seem even shabbier.

ACTS I AND II

In act I, Dido already expresses apprehension about her feelings for Aeneas, even though he makes amorous speeches to her, and all her courtiers keep encouraging the match in chorus after chorus. Next we see the plotting of some highly un-Virgilian Witches. For malicious reasons of their own, they decide to dress up a goblin as a Messenger from Jupiter (Jove), who will send Aeneas off. Ever since Shakespeare's *Macbeth*, witches had been popular with English theatergoers, and they were perhaps especially enjoyed, like horror movies today, by schoolgirls.

In act II, Dido and Aeneas are shown on a hunt, which is dispersed by a storm conjured up by the Witches. Then their "trusty elf, in form of Jupiter himself" tells Aeneas he must leave. The unhappy prince accedes, in a long recitative derived from laments such as those of Monteverdi's Orpheus and Euridice.

ACT III

In Monteverdi's *Orfeo*, we noted the presence of simple, attractive tunes in early opera, alongside the recitatives. Here is an example from Purcell: a sort of hornpipe, sung by a Sailor and then repeated by the chorus. The Sailor cheerfully bids his mates to prepare to weigh anchor and to console their "nymphs on the shore" with hypocritical promises, while "never—no, never—intending to visit them more." The beauty of this song is that we cannot help applying it to the situation of Dido and Aeneas. Certainly, as far as she is concerned, he is as heartless as his departing sailors.

There is a sailors' dance, and then a final cackling scene of triumph for the Witches, who do a grotesque dance of their own. We are now ready for the great final scene and the final tragedy.

This begins with a furious recitative for Dido and Aeneas, when he comes in to make his excuses. The text can be divided into four parts, each consisting of a single exchange (see page 178). In part 1, Aeneas is thoroughly downcast. His low notes inch upward slowly and rather deviously, only to collapse again at the end; rests inserted between several of his words and phrases show how hard it is for him to complete his unpleasant sentence. Dido pounces on him with high notes and fast rhythms. In her anger she rushes past some words, and she pauses for emphasis, her voice rising, on others—such as the word "weeps," when she accuses him of weeping crocodile tears. Scorn drips from this word, the way she sings it.

Opera of the Baroque

We have spoken of opera as the most characteristic art of the baroque age (see page 165). The theater flourished and a grand theatrical quality often characterized the visual arts as well. Consummately in the spirit of the time, opera, which had been invented around the beginning of the seventeenth century in Italy, soon spread all over Europe. Then, as now, stage display was an extremely important factor in opera. Music, poetry, costume, stage architecture and painting, action, ballet—this dazzling blend of artistic elements gratified the baroque passion for comprehensiveness. Of all the art forms, opera is perhaps the one that best sums up the spirit of the period.

This fascinating picture was painted to celebrate the opening of the Royal Theater in Turin, Italy, at the end of the baroque era, in 1740. The leading scene designer of the time, Giuseppe Galli Bibiena, produced a characteristic set (one of many for this single opera): a grandiose representation of a baroque palace interior, loaded with elaborate ornamentation. Notice how extremely symmetrical and mathematical it is. Notice also the special emphasis on vast spaces, both at the back of the set and also, thanks to some ingenious illusion, at the top. The set suits to a

tee the royal characters of the opera, whose larger-than-life emotions can be read clearly enough from their stage attitudes. One hand on his hip and the other extended in a grand gesture, the prince is performing an act of impossibly noble forgiveness while the princess, in remorse, turns and shudders in her handkerchief.

Also characteristic is the deliberate blurring of distinctions between architecture and painting and between the stage set and the theater itself. The columns, proscenium arch, painted ceiling, and painted drapery of the theater all blend together with the set—part of which is solid, while the rest is painted on backdrops. Even the boxes are pressed into decorative service, like the organ pipes in the baroque church on page 199.

Besides its accurate representation of the opera orchestra, the picture offers much else of sociological interest. The best box seats were actually over the stage, so that we could say that the audience and the actors blend together, too. But clearly many of the audience were less interested in the opera than in conversation or looking around at society. Boys are selling oranges and sherbet, and there is even what looks like a security guard.

Pietro Domenico Olivero, Interior of the Royal Theater, Turin, 1740: Museo Civico, Turin

In part 2 of the recitative, Aeneas, stung, begins a feeble oath, but Dido takes the words right out of his mouth:

Entering before his beat has had time to end, she cuts him short and mimics his voice, singing the same music in her woman's range, an octave higher. Even more devastating is the next measure, where she repeats the same words in the same tone of voice, while the continuo changes the harmony in a sarcastic way. Her disdain bristles in the clipped rhythms on "promised" and "fly," and (dare we say?) a touch of royal self-pity echoes in her "forsaken." Notice the very emphatic rhythm at the cadence of Dido's line, on the words "forsaken Dido die." All Dido's cadences use this same decisive rhythm, a habitual speech tic that characterizes her vividly. A warm, yielding person Dido is not; she is every inch a queen.

Even more stung, Aeneas says he will stay (part 3), but this exasperates Dido even more. When he tries again (part 4), she cuts him off contemptuously and will not let him get a word in. They sing together in a style known as arioso, a loose term for a style in between that of recitative and that of aria (or, here, duet). A magnificent "Away, away!" from Dido drives Aeneas off, never to be heard from again. Also magnificent is her final phrase, spoken not to him but to herself: "But death, alas, I cannot shun . . . ." This majestic calm after the storm is as baroque as is the high fury of the altercation itself.

arioso

Hushed and shocked, the chorus utters a few pensive words, as Dido moves to the canopied bed where she intends to stab herself. She has hardly had time to think during the recitative with Aeneas, but now she pulls her thoughts and feelings together. After another brief recitative addressed to her confidante, Belinda, she sings her famous dying aria, usually known as "Dido's lament."

This is built over a ground bass, one that is more mournful than any of Monteverdi's (see pages 162 and 164) because of the slow descending line with its chromatic semitones. (You will notice this line imitated by the upper string parts of the orchestra while Dido is singing, and especially after she has stopped.) As often happens in arias, the words are repeated a number of times; Dido has little to say but much to feel, and the music needs time to convey the emotional message. Recitative makes little sense unless the listener understands the exact words, but with arias a general impression of them may be enough—indeed, even that is unnecessary when the music is as poignant as Purcell's here. The most heartbreaking place comes (twice) on the exclamation "ah," where the major-mode harmony that has been heard over the bass note D during the first six appearances of the ground bass is altered to the minor mode.

The last notes of this great aria run into a wonderful final chorus, which transmutes Dido's intense personal grief into a communal sense of mourning. If you have listened to the whole opera, this chorus seems even more wonderful, because the courtiers who sing it have matured so much since the time when they thoughtlessly and cheerfully urged Dido to give in to her love. We are to imagine a slow dance, as groups of sorrowful cupids (first graders, perhaps) file past her bier. The general style of the music is that of the madrigal— imitative polyphony, with some word painting for the first three lines, then homophony.

But more clearly than with Monteverdi's choruses, Purcell's style shows the inroads of functional harmony and of the sort of definite, unified rhythms that had been developing in the seventeenth century. We could not mistake this touching chorus for an actual Renaissance madrigal. And its function in the drama, in revealing how the personal tragedy of Dido affects her nation, could not have been achieved within the framework of sixteenth-century music.

Dido and Aeneas, Act III, Scene ii

RECITATIVE

AENEAS: (1) What shall lost Aeneas do?
How, Royal Fair, shall I impart
The god's decree, and tell you we must part?

DIDO: Thus, on the fatal banks of Nile
Weeps the deceitful crocodile!
Thus hypocrites, that murder act,
Make heav'n and gods the authors of the fact!

AENEAS: (2) By all that's good—

DIDO: By all that's good, no more:
All that's good you have forswore.
To your promised empire fly,
And let forsaken Dido die!

AENEAS: (3) In spite of Jove's commands, I'll stay—
Offend the gods, and love obey . . .

DIDO: No, faithless man, thy course pursue:
I'm now resolved as well as you!
No repentance shall reclaim
The injured Dido's slighted flame:
For 'tis enough, whate'er you now decree,
That you had once a thought of leaving me.

AENEAS: (4) Let Jove say what he will, I'll stay—

DIDO: Away!
To death I'll fly if longer you delay.

(*Exit Aeneas.*)

But death, alas, I cannot shun;
Death must come when he is gone.

CHORUS OF DIDO'S
COURTIERS: Great minds against themselves conspire
And shun the cure they most desire.

RECITATIVE

DIDO: Thy hand, Belinda! darkness shades me;
On thy bosom let me rest.
More I would—but death invades me:
Death is now a welcome guest.

ARIA

When I am laid in earth
May my wrongs create
No trouble in thy breast;
Remember me, but ah, forget my fate.

(*Stabs herself.*)

CHORUS: With drooping wings, ye cupids, come
And scatter roses on her tomb.
Soft and gentle as her heart
Keep here your watch, and never part.

Instrumental Music

The development of instrumental music—music that does not depend on words for its rationale, or part of its rationale—counts as one of the most far-reaching contributions made by composers of the early baroque period. One strand of instrumental music evolved smoothly from a genre we have seen in the sixteenth century, dance music (see page 144). But baroque dance music received a special impetus from opera, the genre that most fascinated people at the time.

While we have seen dances in Monteverdi's *Orfeo* and Purcell's *Dido and Aeneas,* it was especially in French opera that dances were introduced most lavishly. The French were then the ballet masters of Europe, as the Russians are today, and the dances of Jean-Baptiste Lully, court composer to Louis XIV and the dominant figure of French opera and ballet, were universally admired and copied. Musicians would put together sets of dances selected from operas or ballets, called suites of dances. These could then be played and enjoyed apart from an actual performance, as a pleasing memento of it.

suites

Composers also wrote dances and suites for harpsichord—an instrument whose light tone scarcely qualifies it as an effective support for dancers. We can speak of these as "stylized dances" or "idealized dances," pieces written in the style of dance music but intended for listening rather than actual dancing, for mental rather than physical action.

The Suite

In the seventeenth century, Renaissance dances such as the pavane and the galliard went out of fashion, and they were succeeded by many others. Each type has its own steps and its own characteristic music to match them—a characteristic meter, tempo, and set of rhythmic idiosyncrasies. For example, certain dances always kick off with an upbeat, a weak beat or fraction of a weak beat preceding the first strong beat (or *downbeat*) of the first full measure. These characteristics are most easily listed in a table:

upbeat

	METER	TEMPO	SOME RHYTHMIC CHARACTERISTICS
Minuet	$\frac{3}{4}$	Moderate	Rather plain in rhythm
Gavotte	$\frac{4}{4}$	Moderate	Upbeat of two quarter notes (*true only of later gavottes—not of all early examples*)
Bourrée	$\frac{4}{8}$	Quite fast	Short upbeat
Passepied	$\frac{3}{8}$	Quite fast	—

While the number, type, and arrangement of dances in a suite varied considerably, at least in the early baroque period, the *form* of all dances was more standardized than in the sixteenth century. A baroque dance generally has two sections, each of which is repeated immediately. The diagram for this is a a b b or ‖: a :‖: b :‖ (the signs ‖: and :‖ indicate that everything between them is to be repeated). An important difference between Renaissance and baroque dances concerns the length of the a's and b's. In baroque dances more variety occurs—there may be 4, 6, 8, 10, 12, 14, and more measures—and there is also more contrast between the lengths of sections in a single dance. Lully manipulated such contrasts with considerable charm.

trio

On another level of form, dances tended to be grouped in pairs of the same type, with the first coming back again after the second—an A B A form. The B dance in such a pair was called the trio, because it was often scored for only three instruments (plus continuo chord instrument). Next to the full scoring of the A section, this creates a simple and agreeable contrast of terraced dynamics (see page 159). Thus a baroque minuet and trio consists of one minuet followed by a second, quieter minuet, after which the first is heard again. But this last time the repeats are omitted:

	Minuet	*Trio*	*Minuet*
	A	B	A
	‖: a :‖: b :‖	‖: c :‖: d :‖	a b
(*same as:*	a a b b	c c d d	a b)

JEAN-BAPTISTE LULLY (1632–1687) Suite from the Opera-Ballet *Le Temple de la Paix* (The Temple of Peace) (1685) SIDES 3, 4

An "opera-ballet" is what the name suggests—an opera with an inordinate amount of dancing, or a ballet with characters who sing, depending on the point of view. Such entertainments thrived at the court of Louis XIV, where Lully ruled musical life with an iron hand. *The Temple of Peace* was one of his latest works, but he had been writing dance music of the same general kind since the beginning of his career in the 1650s. Our suite from this opera-ballet includes an overture, four different dances, two of which have trios, and a rondeau.

French overture

Overture A suite does not usually begin with one of the dances, but with a special preparatory number called a French overture. *Overture* is a general term for any substantial piece of music introducing a play, opera, or ballet. What was later called the *French overture* (in the seventeenth century there was no other kind) consists of a slow, majestic-sounding section followed by a faster one. The latter makes use of imitative or fugal texture. The slow section features dotted rhythms (see page 25), which give the French overture its easily recognizable pompous gait:

If you listen carefully, you will notice that in many cases the performers exaggerate the "dotting" effect—that is, they make the dotted note a little longer than its written value, and the following short note(s) shorter. This observes contemporary performance rules, as explained by writers of the time, and gives the music more bite.

The overture to *The Temple of Peace* has its slow section repeated, and then brought back freely after the fast section (‖: A :‖ B A'). These are common but not invariable characteristics of French overtures.

Minuet and Trio   The basis of Lully's orchestra is a rather rich five-part string group: three violins, viola, and cello. (The cellos, with double basses playing their same music an octave lower, and with a harpsichord playing chords, constitute the continuo.) Strings and continuo play the stately minuet. The two oboes and bassoon of the trio contrast effectively with this, while the 6-measure phrases contrast with the steady 8-measure phrases of the minuet.

On our recording and others, some of the repeated sections are played more loudly or softly than the originals. Though not indicated by the composer, this use of terraced dynamics makes good sense in connection with dance form.

Entry of the Shepherds and Shepherdesses: Gavotte   This gavotte, in moderate duple meter, is musically more subtle than the minuet.

rondeau   *Rondeau*   Though Lully liked to put rondeaus in his suites, the <u>rondeau</u> is not a dance (with a fixed meter etc.) but a simple musical form based on the idea of thematic return (see page 52). It consists of an alternating pattern such as A B A C A or A B A C A B A, and so on. The B and C sections in this rondeau contrast with A in dynamics, length, and mode.

Entry of the Basques: Bourrée   This is a livelier dance than the other "entry" piece—but Lully makes no effort to provide any Spanish coloration, leaving that to the costumer and the scene designer. Notice the little echo in the B section (another example of terraced dynamics).

Entry of the Bretons: Passepied and Trio   Particularly delightful here is the effect of having phrase c (the first phrase of the trio) only 4 measures long, whereas the other sections are 8, 12, and 16.

Almost all of Lully's compositions, including *The Temple of Peace*, were presented with great pomp before Louis XIV at the great baroque palace of

The Harpsichord

The harpsichord: for the baroque period, the universal keyboard instrument, and for us today, the source of the most characteristic "baroque sound": the crisp bright sonority of metal strings rapidly plucked by mechanized quills.

The great rise in popularity of baroque music over the last twenty years has caused a resurgence of interest in this ancient "historical" instrument. For a brilliant late baroque harpsichord solo, listen to the end of the first movement of Bach's *Brandenburg* Concerto No. 5 (side 5).

Baroque opera and orchestral music is generally heard today with the clear rhythmic sound of the harpsichord aerating it—a welcome change from the customary thick, dreary performances of half a century ago. And nowadays Bach's keyboard suites and fugues are generally performed on the harpsichord, as he intended, rather than on the modern grand piano, which was not developed until after his death and which distorts the quality of his music.

This revival has been made possible by a new wave of harpsichord building. A new handmade instrument can be bought for less than the price of a grand piano. There are also firms that make kits from which you can construct your own harpsichord! One is illustrated here. While we can hardly describe home harpsichord building as a major leisure industry, tens of thousands of instruments have been made from these kits. This surely represents a very respectable number of Americans who are engaged in an activity of devoted historical restoration.

In their own way, the harpsichord kit builders are going back to the craft spirit of old in trying to fashion their instruments from raw (or relatively raw) materials. Baroque harpsichords were beautifully crafted, in terms of both the sound produced and the cabinetwork. Sometimes they were also elaborately decorated with paintings, designs, or wood inlay. A seventeenth-century instrument decorated in this way is shown on the facing page.

A harpsichord looks something like a small piano, and its basic "works," a set of tuned strings activated from a keyboard, are essentially those of the piano. The difference comes in the way the sound is generated. On the piano, sound is produced by striking the strings with soft, felt-covered hammers. These are controlled by a rather complicated mechanism (the *action*). The complication is required to permit slight changes of finger pressure to achieve all possible dynamic shadings, from very soft to very loud, and then to have the sound stopped, or damped, when the fingers are lifted off.

On the harpsichord, sound is produced by plucking the strings with small hard quills, one per string, activated from the keyboard. Hence the sharp, brittle sound. Harpsi-

chord action and damping are simple and direct (which is fortunate for the kit builders).

It follows from the brief discussion above that the harpsichord does not allow for changes in dynamics. (It was to meet this situation that the hammer instrument was developed in the eighteenth century—and at once entitled the *pianoforte* or *fortepiano*, "loud/soft.") The best that harpsichord builders could do to allow for dynamics was to add another set of slightly different strings with slightly different quills, controlled from a second keyboard. A player could then obtain terraced dynamics, as on the organ, though the range was not so great.

Italian harpsichord: The Metropolitan Museum of Art, Gift of Susan Dwight Bliss, 1945

Versailles. This opera-ballet has another half dozen dances, including an Entry of Native Americans ("We have crossed the great sea To pay homage to thee, Greatest of Kings . . . ."), plus numerous dance-songs, choruses, and short recitatives.

The Trio Sonata

chamber music

Chamber music is a general term for music to be played (or, more rarely, sung) by small groups—in practice, groups of from two to nine musicians. The main genre of baroque chamber music was the trio sonata.

trio sonata

This is not an easy term to define. Originally the word *sonata* simply meant "sounded," "something sounded," or "a piece that is sounded," as distinct from *cantata*, "a piece that is sung" (page 188). The trouble is that musicians have used these terms over many centuries for compositions of vastly different styles and forms. When Giovanni Gabrieli wrote his *Sonata Pian' e Forte,* the term was new and could cover almost anything, including the one-movement orchestra piece in echo style that we examined on page 158. (The term *movement* is discussed below.) In the baroque period, the sonata was a chamber music piece for from one to half a dozen instruments, consisting of several short movements—the number was not fixed—in a variety of different forms. Later the term *sonata* was used in a more limited sense, as we shall see.

The adjective *trio* is also, alas, open to misunderstanding. The word itself means "three"; the trio sonata is written for three *main* instruments, usually two violins and a cello (or two flutes and a cello, or two oboes and a bassoon). But in addition a continuo player fills in harmonies at the harpsichord or organ, performing a subsidiary, supporting role to the others. A trio sonata, then, is a baroque sonata for three main players plus a subsidiary player—four in all.

movement

A movement is a coherent section of music that is part of a larger piece. Ordinarily, the boundaries of a movement are clear enough; it ends with a strong cadence and a full stop. (Yet there are exceptions: within some larger pieces, one movement runs into another after an expectant pause, a special transitional passage, or some such device.) The several movements in a single work often have different meters, and they always have different tempos, fast and slow. They nearly always have different themes.

PURCELL Trio Sonata No. 10 in A (1683)   SIDE 4

The trio sonata was an Italian genre; Purcell at the age of twenty-four introduced it into England with the fine set of twelve sonatas from which ours is taken. At the end of his preface to this book, Purcell thought the reader should

be enform'd, that he will find a few terms of Art perhaps unusual to him, the chief of which are these following: ADAGIO and GRAVE, which import nothing but a very slow movement: PRESTO LARGO, POCO LARGO, or LARGO by it self, a middle movement: ALLEGRO, and VIVACE, a very brisk, swift, or fast movement: PIANO, soft. The Author has no more to add, but his hearty wishes, that his Book may fall into no other hands but theirs who carry Musical Souls about them . . . .

Compare page 10; today we would not define *largo* as "a middle movement" but as a rather slow one. Terraced dynamics specified by a composer were still "perhaps unusual" enough so that Purcell felt he had to explain the term *piano*, and he does not risk the abbreviation **p** but writes the word out in full the one time he indicates it on the score (see the very end of page 187).

Sonata No. 10 has four movements, of which the third runs into the fourth. Notice the varied tempos and meters.

Movement	I	II	III	IV
Tempo indication	—	Largo	Grave → Presto	
Tempo	fast	moderate	slow	very fast
Meter	$\frac{2}{2}$	$\frac{3}{2}$	$\frac{4}{4}$	$\frac{4}{4}$

(A more common arrangement is slow - fast - slow - fast, but there is really no standard plan for the movements of a trio sonata, or even a fixed number of them.) Purcell's *first* movement is a vigorous piece in imitative polyphony, with a very individual harmonic quality about it. The *second* movement, in a graceful triple meter, has the two violins moving in smooth parallel motion almost throughout. The brief *third* movement, with its slow dotted rhythms and its solemn harmonies, may remind us of the first part of a French overture (see page 180). If so, we will not be surprised that the *fourth* movement, which emerges from it, is a vigorous fugue.

FUGUE

fugue   Fugue is one of the most important musical forms perfected by the baroque, and it counts as one of the most impressive cultural products of the entire age. Bach is the recognized master of the form, and Bach was able to build on a long tradition. Impressive fugues were written for organ and harpsichord in the seventeenth century, and most trio sonatas contain movements that are simple fugues, like Purcell's fourth movement.

As we have pointed out before (see page 151), fugue can be seen as a logical outcome of Renaissance imitative polyphony. The Renaissance invented this technique; the baroque, characteristically, systematized it. A typical Renaissance work consists of a series of "points of imitation" (see page 131), short sections of music in which a motive is imitated once or twice through all the voices, before the composer moves on to the next motive. In a motet or Mass the motives are associated with successive fragments of the text, but there are also Renaissance instrumental genres in which the points of imitation follow one another without text.

If we can now conceive of a single point of imitation extended to last for an entire coherent piece, the result is a fugue. Or, to define it another way: a fugue is a polyphonic composition for a fixed number of voices or instruments, built fugue subject   on a single theme, called the fugue subject, which enters systematically in all the voices.

A fugue begins with the subject in one voice alone, followed by the subject in another voice, then another, then another, until all the voices are sounding together. Thereafter, at frequent intervals throughout the fugue, the subject will appear again in one voice or another: at the top of the texture, at the bottom (the bass), or else in the middle surrounded by other polyphonic lines. The subject appears in different keys, too. Although the modulations (see page 47) in a fugue are not too obvious, without modulations the music would get badly bogged down.

episodes The entries of the fugue subject are spaced off by passages called <u>episodes</u>. Episodes are sections in which the subject is not presented in its entirety. They are made up of melodic fragments, motives, sequences, etc., that may be derived from the subject but do not follow it exactly. Episodes present nothing strikingly new; the idea is not to make a truly arresting contrast. In its attitude toward the aesthetic maxim "unity in variety," the fugue leans to the side of unity.

The Purcell fugue begins with each of the main instruments—second violin, first violin, and cello—playing the subject in turn. Thereafter subject entries follow thick and fast, for this fugue is unusually short on episodes—in fact, there is only one, lasting for no more than three of the total thirty-six measures. The subject is being played by one instrument or another all through the other thirty-three. A systematic structure, certainly; as we have suggested before, fugue exemplifies particularly well the "strict" side of the basic strict-free dualism underlying baroque music.

stretto At several points, a subject entry follows the previous one not at the usual time interval (two measures) but at a shorter one—a common device in fugues, called <u>stretto</u>. In other words, the second voice enters with the subject before the first has finished it. Stretto automatically produces tension and excitement. The subject entries overlap, as it were—with a dizzying effect, when more complicated fugues pile up four, five, or six entries in this way.

augmentation Another device used by some fugues is <u>augmentation</u>: the subject is played in longer note values. This happens toward the end of Purcell's piece. A violin entry in double-time augmentation makes an exhilarating climax, helped along by a specially emphatic line in the bass.

Musical Souls who listen carefully to this fugue two or three times will probably be able to detect the episode, the augmentation, and some of the strettos. They are shown on the diagram below and marked on the line score across the page.

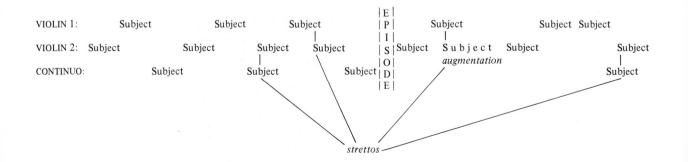

Try following the fugue on the line score on page 187. Only the main musical lines—the most important ones to follow—have been filled in on this score. Each of the three main instruments has its own staff of music, while the continuo chord instrument (organ) reads from the same staff as the cello. With the left hand the organist plays exactly what the cello is playing, and with the right hand he or she fills in chords according to the numerical shorthand below the staff (figured bass: see page 153).

An important factor in the effect of all trio sonatas is the sense of contest between the two high instruments—here, the two violins. Although in some passages they complement one another—in the second movement of this Purcell sonata, for example—these occasions seem to be temporary truces. Ordinarily the two violins play against one another, taking each other's measure, clashing, crossing, and competing for top position. Obviously fugue fits in very well with this sense of contest, for every time one violin plays the fugue subject that instrument stands out over the other—only to give up its place a moment later.

To make an interesting contest, the contestants should be fairly evenly matched, as is the case here. A count of the line score shows that, in about fourteen of the thirty-six measures of Purcell's fugue, the second violin tops the first. And the second violin gets that big augmentation.

The Cantata

The seventeenth century was fascinated by opera, and we must pay one last visit to the genre before closing the present chapter. The word *cantata,* parallel to *sonata,* originally meant simply "a piece that is sung." Today the term is most familiar as applied to a sacred cantata, or church cantata. We shall examine a church cantata by Bach on pages 231–37. But a baroque musician would have thought first of the secular variety, and a secular cantata was, in effect, an imitation opera scene.

cantata   A <u>cantata</u> consists of several recitatives and arias; it is not acted or staged, but the singer assumes a character who goes through a rather artificial thought-sequence in recitative. In the course of this, he or she stops and sings arias of different moods, expressing different emotions. (Some cantatas include more than one singer, in which case they can react to one another.) The genre was ideally suited to show off a singer's skill in both recitative and aria, and in arias of different kinds.

That is the key feature. Virtuosity, both vocal and instrumental, assumed more and more importance as the century progressed. We have already sensed this from the brilliant violin writing in the fast movements of Purcell's trio sonata. The violin became the most popular instrument of the time because it could play so fast and so high, so richly and so flexibly, but other instruments, such as the flute and the trumpet, also had their possibilities exploited. In

Italy, vocal virtuosity reached fantastic levels. Sopranos and male castrato singers, who sang in the soprano and contralto ranges, were the most extravagantly admired (and highest paid) of all musicians. Cantatas and opera roles were written specially for these great *prima donnas* and *primi uomini* (leading ladies, leading men). When such stars were joined by virtuoso instrumentalists, as sometimes happened, the result was a truly baroque riot of brilliance and display.

ALESSANDRO SCARLATTI (1660–1725) *Su le Sponde del Tebro*
(On the Banks of the Tiber) (circa 1695)   SIDE S–2

This virtuoso cantata from the end of the century shows us something of the rich combinations of voices and instruments that were becoming possible. In an early opera such as Monteverdi's *Orfeo,* the instruments (except for the continuo) generally played in alternation with the voices. Even in Purcell's *Dido and Aeneas,* eighty years later, the strings accompany Dido's Lament in a simple and restrained (if highly expressive) manner. But as instrumental writing grew more assured, in suites and trio sonatas, composers began combining voices and instruments in more complex and interesting ways; sometimes the instruments accompany the voices, sometimes they echo them, sometimes they echo one another. Doubtless such techniques can be traced back to the experiments of Gabrieli and the other Venetians, but things are now infinitely more subtle.

Su le sponde del Tebro opens with an instrumental number, a dialogue for solo trumpet and string orchestra. On the banks of the Tiber, the shepherd Aminta complains in recitative that he has been deserted. A male soprano, he next sings a forceful aria whose text bristles with exaggerated military metaphors: he is a general being attacked by troops of sorrow, his sighs are like fanfares, etc. (at least we see where Scarlatti got the idea of using a trumpet in this particular cantata). Aminta's second, more subdued recitative runs into a remarkably beautiful and quite long passage of arioso (see page 176). This leads in turn to a rather depressed aria accompanied by the string instruments only. Finally, having resolved in a third recitative to put his shepherdess out of mind, he cheers up considerably in another vigorous trumpet aria. It is all very absurd, but it provides the occasion for some exciting music making.

da capo aria

The final aria, "Tralascia pur di piangere" (Put aside, then, your weeping), falls into a form that became standard in Italian operas and cantatas, A B A. Arias in this form are called da capo arias; *da capo* (from the beginning) is a direction placed on the score after the B section, telling the musicians to go back and perform A all over again. The point was to allow the singer (and instrumentalists) to improvise fancy ornaments the second time around. Since Scarlatti provided two whole stanzas for "Tralascia pur di piangere," to the same music, these virtuosos had no fewer than three opportunities to show their stuff (A B A A B A). You can hear on our record how some imaginative modern musicians rise to the challenge.

Su le Sponde del Tebro, final aria

STANZA 1: (A) *Tralascia pur di piangere,*   Put aside, then, your weeping,
                Povero afflito cor—   My poor afflicted heart—

          (B) *Chè sprezzato del tuo fato*   For, spurned by your fate,
                Non ti resta che compiangere   Nought remains but to bewail
                D'un infida il suo rigor.   The faithless one's severity.

  da capo: (A) *Tralascia pur di piangere,*   Put aside, then, your weeping,
                Povero afflito cor!   My poor afflicted heart!

STANZA 2: (A) *Non ti curar di vivere*   Reconcile yourself to living
                Misero nel mio sen—   Miserably within my breast—

          (B) *Chè spietata Clori ingrata*   For cruel and pitiless Clori
                Ha pur uso il saper fingere,   Knows from practice how to deceive
                E negl'occhi il ben seren.   While never batting an eyelash.

  da capo: (A) *Non ti curar di vivere,*   Reconcile yourself to living
                Misero nel mio sen!   Miserably within my breast!

CHAPTER 8 | The Baroque Period   II

The Baroque Period   II

Discussing music of the early baroque period, on page 151, we introduced the idea of an underlying dualism between freedom and control, a dualism from which baroque music derives much of its vitality. Emotionalism and extravagance are evident everywhere in the early seventeenth century, but so is an urge for increased rigidity of musical form. Later in the period, a process of broad settling can be discerned. There are now further developments on the "strict" side of the dualism, and on the "free" side, if not a falling off, at least a marked change of emphasis can be detected.

Recitative is the characteristic expression of baroque emotionalism, as we have seen, and fugue the characteristic expression of musical control. In the operas and related genres of the later baroque period, recitative loses much of its power; arias grow more and more extended and important. We have perhaps already sensed this with the recitatives in Scarlatti's cantata *Su le Sponde del Tebro,* composed near the end of the seventeenth century. Fugue, on the other hand, reaches its climax in the work of Johann Sebastian Bach, the most famous of the late baroque composers and the one who is famous for fugues above all else. Bach's fugues remain models for composition students to this very day, just as Palestrina's masses and motets remain models for counterpoint more generally. There were excellent fugue writers before Bach, and not all his contemporaries excelled in the form; still, his mastery stands out as a symbol of the general tendency of late baroque musical style. We shall also see many other instances of the development of the "strict" side of the baroque dualism.

As for the "free" side, while recitative itself declined from the great days of Monteverdi, late baroque music did not tame down completely. Stupendous, astonishing, extravagant, grandiose effects—these were still very much in demand, and were still supplied by willing composers. But, since the taste for this sort of thing continued unquenched, and since composers had used up one emotional effect after another, they were compelled (or, rather, inspired) to find more and more ways of getting such effects. In place of the spontaneity of their predecessors, they substituted cunning, ingenuity, and impressive craft. So the emotional current of early baroque music was not so much slowed as channeled. Things are now less unpredictable, perhaps, but they lack for nothing in sheer smooth power.

Metaphors drawn from nature, such as "maturing" or "aging," seem to fit the process we have outlined between the early and late baroque periods. Indeed, in thinking about the greatest composers of these periods, Monteverdi and Bach, it is tempting to speak of adolescent vitality, fire, and turmoil on the one hand, mature wisdom and serenity on the other. It is perhaps questionable to compare something as abstract and nebulous as a musical style to the human condition. Yet it is a very human thing to do—it grasps at a way of bringing highly complex general concepts down to a level where we can all comprehend them. To be sure, such comparisons must not be applied indiscriminately. Other major stylistic periods cannot be said to "age" in this way. They end not in maturation but in stagnation, explosion, or (another metaphor from nature!) metamorphosis.

In any case, the task of determining the characteristics of late baroque music is less a matter of defining new style characteristics than of reviewing and sometimes extending features already known from early baroque music. In the coming section, we shall follow the general order of musical categories established in chapters 1 and 2 on the vocabulary of music.

The Style of Late Baroque Music

After listening to a late baroque piece carefully all the way through, we may be surprised to realize how soon all the basic material is set forth and then how regular and repetitious the music is. It often seems as though the composers had set about with some enthusiasm to wring their material dry, spin it out methodically to the maximum extent, and in general exhaust its possibilities. Once these composers get hold of a musical idea, they seem very reluctant to let go.

It is probably *rhythm,* more than any other element, that contributes to this quality in baroque music. A single rhythm or closely similar rhythms may continue to be heard throughout a whole piece or a major section of a piece. The meter nearly always stands out, emphasized by certain instruments playing in a clear, decisive way. Late baroque music is brimming with energy, and the energy is channeled into a highly regular, determined sort of motion.

Dynamics are another very steady feature of baroque music. Even at the end of the period, composers still employed loud and soft indications (p and f) sparingly. Once a dynamic was chosen, it generally continued for the whole section—sometimes even for the whole composition. Or perhaps two different dynamic levels would be set up in alternation, according to the principle of terraced dynamics (see page 159).

The matter of *tone color* presents something of a contradiction. A feature of the early baroque period was a new sensitivity to the quality of individual instrumental sounds. With this came a more careful specification of the particular sounds that the composer had in mind. No one who has heard Gabrieli's motet *In ecclesiis* will forget the brass choir there, and no one who has heard Monteverdi's *Orfeo* will forget his dramatic use of trombones, flutes, organ, and harpsichord to characterize different people in the opera. Later in the period, Scarlatti knew just what he was doing when he wrote for the trumpet, Bach composed especially beautifully for the flute, and a whole school of harpsichord composers in France developed the sonorous possibilities of that instrument in a very elegant way. There are characteristic "baroque sounds" that delight us and that we do not meet elsewhere: the virtuoso recorder, the bright baroque organ, the ever-present harpsichord, and the "festive" orchestra featuring high trumpets and drums.

Nevertheless, a significant amount of music was written in such a way that it could be shifted from one instrument or vocal group to another. It was a regular practice to designate music for harpsichord *or* organ. Bach rewrote a trio sonata for two flutes and continuo as a sonata for viol da gamba (a cello-like instrument) and harpsichord. Handel in his oratorio *Messiah* rewrote solo arias and duets as choruses. In the last analysis, then, it seems the original tone color as such was not critical. If it had been, the composers would not have sanctioned changing it, let alone made such changes themselves.

In *melody*, later baroque music tends toward complexity. Composers liked to push melodies to the very limits of ornateness and density. We may grasp and enjoy these long, intricate melodies, with a wealth of "decorations" added to the main direction of the line, but if we try to sing them we find ourselves getting lost—they rarely fall into anything as simple as a tune. Even their appearance on the page seems to tell the story:

The sign ～ in the first measure directs the performer to add yet another extra detail of melodic decoration. Compare also the score copied out by Bach shown on page 232.

An easily recognized feature of baroque melodies is their frequent use of sequence (see page 21). They repeatedly seem to be catching hold of a motive or some other feature and working it methodically through several pitch levels. Sequences provided baroque music with one of its most effective means of forward movement.

The *texture* of baroque music, as we have emphasized (see page 153), is ruled by the continuo. Whether the music is homophonic or polyphonic— whether there is just one important line, as in an opera recitative, or many, as in a four-part fugue for orchestra—a chord instrument plays chords continuously, as a support or background for those main lines. (Understandably, one exception to the rule is a work, such as a fugue, for a chord instrument alone—for organ or harpsichord solo.) We shall hear the continuo played by cellos (and sometimes double basses) plus a harpsichord in concertos by Bach and Vivaldi. In the more massive religious music of Bach and Handel, we shall hear the chords played by the organ and the bass line bodied out by cellos, double basses, bassoons, and the deep organ pedal notes.

Remember that in every case only the general form of the chords is indicated, by a numerical shorthand, in much the same sort of way that chords are indicated by abbreviations on a modern song sheet. The exact form of the chords is improvised by the harpsichordist or organist of the hour. In a way, this individual discretion exemplifies nicely the baroque dualism of "free" and "strict" elements that we have discussed above. The chord player improvises, while, thanks to that harmonic support, the other players are free to pursue lines of fantastic brilliance and complication. Yet at the same time they are constrained by the relentless, continuous definition (by the chords) of the harmonic territory in which they are able to operate. In baroque music, the continuo is the ultimate control.

MUSICAL FORM

Relentless, too, was the later baroque concept of musical form. In some favorite musical forms of the time, a single musical idea, or theme, continues throughout the piece with scarcely a moment's letup. Two clear examples are the ground bass and the fugue. And, just as composers tended to minimize sharp contrasts in rhythm or dynamics, so they also preferred not to incorporate many sharply contrasting themes in their pieces and play them off against one another. Now, to be sure, contrast is a relative matter; all music has some contrast, or it would amount to a single unvarying note. But music of this period employs less contrast than music of later ones. In extending their music through time, singlemindedness was the basic attitude of late baroque composers.

Where they did work to achieve contrast was *between* musical pieces, not *within* them. We shall observe very extreme contrasts in technique and feeling between the successive movements of the concerto grosso, for example, or between the two pieces that make up the Agnus Dei of Bach's Mass in B Minor. The impression is always that of a massive confrontation and a standoff. Only later did the Viennese composers bring serious contrast into a single movement, as though to show that there are several sides to every question and that the answer has to reconcile them all. The treatment of contrast is a central aspect of the Viennese style, as we shall see in chapter 9.

THE EMOTIONAL WORLD OF THE BAROQUE

Composers at the time were much concerned with music's expressive powers. They had no doubt that music could mirror a wide range of human feelings, and they attacked the problem of bringing this about with their usual relentless drive. The result can be very powerful and yet, in a curious way, also impersonal. For it is hard to feel that these men were trying to mirror their own emotions in music. Rather, they seem to have tried to isolate emotions in the abstract and then depict them as single-mindedly as possible.

The exhaustiveness of their musical technique made for a similar exhaustiveness of emotional effect. As the rhythms and themes are repeated over and over again, the music hammers away at a single feeling, intensifying it and magnifying it to a remarkable extent. Sadness in baroque music is presented as the deepest gloom, gentleness as sentimentality, cheerfulness as pomp and splendor, joy as wild jubilation.

These are exaggerated sentiments; the people who experience them seem to be larger than life. This may prove puzzling until we remember an important fact about the baroque age: its fascination with the theater. Both the spoken theater and the opera took great strides in the seventeenth century, and their impact on people's minds can be compared to that of the movies and television in the twentieth.

The baroque theater concentrated on grandiose gesture and high passion, on ideal emotions expressed by ideal human beings. Kings and queens were shown performing noble actions or vile ones, experiencing intense feelings, reciting thunderous tirades, and taking part in lavish stage displays. How these personages looked and acted can be seen in the picture on page 175, which also shows them in a typically extravagant setting.

Theatricality is a key to the emotional world of baroque art, whether in music, the visual arts, or poetry. In baroque paintings people tend to be posed in stagelike attitudes. Architectural interiors, and even the formal gardens of the time, look like stage sets. Or take a characteristically high-pitched passage from a poem of 1717 by Alexander Pope, in which Heloise is dreaming of her lover Abelard:

> Oh curst, dear horrors of all-conscious night!
> How glowing guilt exalts the keen delight!
> Provoking demons all restraints remove,
> And stir within me every source of love!
> I hear thee, view thee, gaze o'er all thy charms,
> And round thy phantom glue my clasping arms . . .
> I shriek, start up, the same sad prospect find,
> And wake to all the griefs I left behind.

The exaggerated words for the intense emotions, the grandiloquent phrases, and even the gestures that are suggested—clasping, gazing, starting up—all seem to have come straight from the theater.

There is nothing necessarily "false" about theatrical emotion, as we know from the strong effect it has on us in the theater or at the movies. It has the virtues of great intensity, clarity, and focus; it has to have, or it would not reach its audience. The actors analyze the emotion they are required to depict, shape it and probably exaggerate it, and then methodically project it by means of their acting technique and craft. It is not their personal emotion, though for the moment they make it their own. We may come to feel that baroque composers proceeded in much the same manner, not only when they composed operas—actual stage works set to music—but also oratorios, church cantatas, and even instrumental music.

The Organ

The baroque period witnessed the perfection of many musical instruments—the violin of Stradivarius, the harpsichord, the guitar—but none went through a more impressive development than the organ. Especially in Germany, the craft of organ building and design reached a level that has never been matched, though in recent years some builders have recaptured the sound of the "baroque organ." Organ technology supported whole schools of organ composing, culminating in the great fugues and chorale preludes of Johann Sebastian Bach.

The organ is one of the most venerable, as well as the most powerful, of Western instruments. The great monastic musical center at Winchester in England—we mentioned its tropes and organa on page 89—had in 956 A.D. an instrument with four hundred pipes and twenty-six bellows. The basic principle—a tuned set of pipes, fed by air from a bellows and controlled from a keyboard—goes back to those early times. Medieval musicians soon saw the advantage of having several sets of pipes of different acoustical properties, with alternate air-feeding channels. This allowed the use of different tone colors and dynamic levels.

But early organs rarely went beyond a dozen such sets of pipes, or *stops*, as they are called. It remained for the baroque to systematize and extend this principle enormously. Important organs of Bach's time had up to eighty stops, methodically deployed to cover all pitch ranges, to include a great variety of tone colors, and to provide a wealth of possibilities for the blending of sounds.

Stops with a soft, fluty quality, nasal-sounding "reeds," and so-called "strings"; very high stops and very low ones; "solo" stops and stops designed to fill combination sounds—organs grew so complex that the pipes had to be divided into several sections. Each section, in an enclosed case of its own, could be played separately or coupled with others. Among names for these sections were the *great organ, choir, positive,* and *pedal.* The last of these, containing the lowest and some of the noisiest pipes, was of course the one played by the feet on a special bulky keyboard, the pedal board.

The subtle blending of the tone colors of the various stops was a great art among baroque organ builders. Their practical knowledge of acoustical science appears from their development of an ancient type of stop called a *mixture,* which actually gives each note *several* pipes tuned to several different partials (see page 15). Played alone, mixtures sound blurred or even out of tune, but in combination with other stops they add just the topping required to give the tone color special brilliance.

It is as though the organ builders set about to cover the whole of "musical space" as they could conceive it in the mind or discern it by the ear. And they sought to dominate another kind of space—the kind they could see—by means of the physical design of their instruments. The organ of Wilhering Abbey, Austria, built in 1733, shows how organ design fitted in with baroque church architecture. If the organ pipes did not catch the light pouring in from the great recessed window, we might mistake them for just one more decorative element in this busy, exciting space. These pipes look like serrated columns reaching up to the ceiling and holding it up, one level above the sculptured columns at the sides. The intricate wood carving of the chambers enclosing the pipes runs into the sculptured figures, which seem to be on the point of soaring across to meet their opposite numbers on the ceiling painting and the bas reliefs.

The main pipes in the photograph constitute the so-called great organ and the pedal. The smaller set in the middle makes up the positive. The console, where the organist sits, is hidden behind the positive.

Johann Sebastian Bach (1685–1750)

The baroque period was a great age for the theater; it was also a great age for the crafts. Furniture making, metalworking, wood carving, and musical instrument making were all highly developed (see page 198). Musical performance was regarded as another such craft, and so, in much the same way, was musical composition.

It may be hard for us to grasp this, perhaps, since the romantic idea of the composer is so firmly ingrained: the lonely genius working over each masterpiece as a long labor of love expressing his own individual personality. But earlier the composer thought of himself as a servant with a master to satisfy, a craftsman with a job, turning out music on demand (and on schedule) to fill a particular requirement. This is why many pieces of early music seem relatively anonymous, as it were. They strike us less as unique masterpieces than as excellent examples of their type—their style—of which there are many other equally excellent examples.

Crafts are the products of long family traditions. Over the generations the Bachs supplied a relatively small area of central Germany with dozens of musicians. All the surviving male members of Johann Sebastian's huge family became musicians, too, some of them major composers in their own right. One feels that from the start Bach was conditioned (if not always happy) to accept his "place." He served first as church organist in several sleepy towns, then as a musician at the petty courts of Weimar and Cöthen. He never attained a major court position, settling instead as cantor of the Thomaskirche at Leipzig, which was a large and important town but no great artistic center.

Outside of Leipzig, Bach's music was little known. As for the position of cantor, that was the highest one within the hierarchy of the Lutheran Church, but it was hedged in by bureaucratic restrictions that would have exasperated even a less independent spirit than Bach's. He had to compose music and manage the choirs for the big churches in town, every Sunday of the year, to say nothing of the many church holidays. He was supposed to teach music and Latin in the choir school (the Thomasschule). And he was forbidden to play the organ in the church services, since that was the prerogative of other officials.

Bach gained an awesome control over all the craft aspects of music. He also exhibited an unusually systematic and encyclopedic turn of mind. It is not that he had studied the scientific discoveries that so interested his time (see page 154), but he seems to have absorbed the scientists' confidence in reason and calculation as guides for all human activities, including music. Thus, within many of his compositions, there is a decided element of calculation in the layout of the musical form, as we shall see. Bach also developed a mania for collecting his music together in orderly sets following some clear plan. Among these are *The Well-tempered Clavier,* two sets of twenty-four preludes and fugues written in all the possible keys, to show how all were usable. The last thing he wrote, *The Art of Fugue,* is another "demonstration" work, containing seventeen different canons and fugues composed from the same brief theme.

Saying all this about Bach could give rise to the idea that his music must be remote and merely intellectual. This is far from the case. One or two pieces in *The Art of Fugue* may be on the dry side, but the others are profound, brilliant, powerful, highly expressive. They are among the most miraculous pieces written in the whole baroque period. Bach's unmatched control over musical materials and processes—his unmatched sense of craft—allowed him to probe deeper into emotional states than any of his contemporaries. Whether in bold jubilation or in quiet meditation, he constantly amazes us by the variety of feeling he is able to convey in music.

BACH Passacaglia and Fugue for Organ (circa 1715)   SIDE 4

In the Passacaglia and Fugue for Organ, Bach built a very interesting large-scale piece of music from a single short theme. It is hard to think of many more rigorous, single-minded pieces in the whole musical repertory. Yet there is nothing pedantic about it; this brilliant essay in organ virtuosity is a tribute to the high level of organ technology, organ playing, and composition for the instrument in eighteenth-century Germany (see page 198). What is especially clear in this piece is the way in which musical form contributes to a musical effect—in this case, an effect of massive, exhaustive cumulation.

THE PASSACAGLIA

passacaglia

A passacaglia is an extended piece built over a ground bass, such as we have seen in the music of Monteverdi and Purcell. A single short figure, or theme, is repeated over and over again in the bass, while other instruments weave ever-new lines above it.

In Bach's organ passacaglia, the theme itself is just that much longer than the earlier examples (compare pages 162, 164, 177), and what happens above it is differentiated more clearly. Each appearance of the theme (after the first) is called a variation, because in each one the theme seems to be varied in a different way—the upper lines do something distinct each time that makes the unit of theme-plus-upper-lines stand out clearly from the others. As we shall see later, the passacaglia can be thought of as a special case of another form, the *theme and variations* (see page 283).

variation

First, Bach's passacaglia theme is heard quietly, without accompaniment of any kind. It is played on the organ pedals:

There follow twenty variations, in which this theme appears in different guises or with different accompaniments above it. Often it appears exactly as shown in the example, the variations consisting simply of fresh contrapuntal lines above or below it. At other times the theme is somewhat obscured, though never so far that the listener loses it entirely. Through it all, Bach pours forth an inexhaustible supply of fascinating musical ideas, which seem to spring up under the organist's fingers like an inspired improvisation.

We develop a sort of "double listening" for a piece like this, listening at one and the same time to the theme (which hardly ever changes) and to the material presented with it (which changes constantly, variation by variation). This is not hard to do, no harder than it is to take in a distant view while also admiring someone in the foreground. Our interest and pleasure in the piece depend on our double awareness of the fixed element—the regular, stately recurrence of the eight-measure theme—and the versatile, temporary additions to it.

Bach has imposed a master plan on the twenty variations. At first the variations hold to the original form of the theme, by and large, while building up methodically from the quiet beginning to a level of considerable vigor. Then, suddenly changing this procedure, Bach starts to manipulate the theme in miscellaneous freer fashions. Finally a third group of variations returns to the original form of the theme, in the organ pedals—very loud, emphatic, and triumphant in spirit. Bach plans his passacaglia in a three-part form, then, with the general pattern *buildup—digression—climactic return.* In detail, the work proceeds as follows:

Variations 1 and 2   Quiet, mainly homophonic

Variation 3   Contrapuntal, with flowing rhythms

Variations 4 and 5   Contrapuntal, with faster rhythms—the same in each case (♩♪), but variation 5 is more intense.

Variations 6–8   A still faster rhythm (♪) is introduced, developing into scales: first upward, then downward, and then upward and downward together, for an obvious climactic effect.

Variation 9   At this point, Bach digresses from this orderly scheme and directs his attention to alterations of one kind or another within the theme itself. The digression begins as the upper imitative figure (marked with a bracket) infects the theme in the bass rhythmically, as it were:

Original form of the theme:

The pedals play what may be described as a decorated version of the theme.

Variation 10   Played in a detached fashion with chords, the theme in the bass now sounds like mere accompaniment to the scales above it. This is a surprise in view of the contrapuntal texture of the music up to this point.

Variations 11–13   The theme moves away from the bass and into the higher regions, with an effect of brightness and liberation.

Variations 14 and 15   The theme disappears entirely, though we sense its background presence from the pattern of harmonies associated with it.

Variations 16–20   This is the last group of variations, the climactic return. With the theme back in the organ pedals, sounding loud and solemn, each of the new accompaniments above it seems more impressive than the last.

THE FUGUE

After twenty variations, Bach has exhausted the possibilities of this way of treating his theme. But he has not exhausted the theme itself. In the second part of the Passacaglia and Fugue he treats it in a new way, as a fugue. This is sufficiently different from the passacaglia form, he believes, to lend fresh interest to what is by now a very old story.

As we have seen on page 185, at the heart of a fugue is a series of subject entries, in the various contrapuntal parts, spaced by freer sections called episodes. This is true here, just as in the fugue from Purcell's Trio Sonata in A. Purcell also employed two fugal "devices," *stretto* and *augmentation,* which Bach does not use in the present fugue, even though it is much richer and more complex than Purcell's piece (and even though Bach used these devices masterfully in other fugues). Instead he relies on another such device, the use countersubject of a countersubject or countersubjects. These are distinctive contrapuntal lines that accompany the subject regularly and that tend to stand out from it because of their particular melodic and rhythmic profiles. Countersubjects are introduced for the first time either at the first statement of a fugue subject, or (usually) at subsequent statements.

The episodes of a fugue often make use of fragments of the fugue subject; likewise they often use fragments of the countersubjects. The fugue in Bach's Passacaglia and Fugue has two countersubjects, heard again and again in conjunction with the now-familiar subject. In the music example on page 204, notice how systematically the rhythms are arranged—the subject moving in half and quarter notes, countersubject 1 in eighths, countersubject 2 in continuous sixteenths. As for the melodies: that of countersubject 1 is actually derived from the passacaglia theme (measures 4 and 5), while countersubject 2 owes its dull melodic shape to the fact that it is intended to be played on the organ pedals. Playing fast passages with two feet is not easy unless the notes are mostly close together.

Why does Bach judge that treating his passacaglia theme as a fugue will give it renewed life, after he has already wrung it dry through the twenty variations? First, the theme is reduced from eight measures to four, which makes things sound brisker and more urgent; furthermore, there are many episodes of different lengths, so that the regular, stately eight-measure pattern is ruptured. Second, the fugue subject *modulates:* it comes in a new key at its second appearance, as is obligatory with fugues. After hearing the theme twenty-two times in the same key, to hear it somewhere else is a true breath of fresh air. It is also quite a revelation to hear the minor-mode theme in several major keys, a little later.

Third, new interest is added by the countersubjects. And in relation to these, Bach develops a plan that could almost be called mathematical. Three contrapuntal lines—high, middle, and low—can be changed around the octaves in six different arrangements (cs = countersubject):

HIGH:	subject	subject	cs 1	cs 1	cs 2	cs 2
MIDDLE:	cs 1	cs 2	subject	cs 2	subject	cs 1
LOW:	cs 2	cs 1	cs 2	subject	cs 1	subject

Bach uses five out of the six possibilities, so that the same three-part combination is heard in five distinct ways. Sometimes the second countersubject rattles away in the pedals; at other times it fades into the middle of the texture.

Sometimes the main subject sounds out like a tune at the top of the texture; at other times it serves as a rocklike support in the bass. In its different way, this fugue is as rigorous a musical structure as the passacaglia, and again the structure is in the service of the musical effect.

Through the repetitions of the theme in the passacaglia and the subject in the fugue, the music has built up great cumulative momentum, like some gigantic flywheel. Bach's final task is to apply the brake, which he does with the help of a particularly flamboyant stop on a very unexpected chord. Then the piece grinds to a halt with a long majestic cadence. The organist must pull out all the stops at this point. There is something highly theatrical about this conclusion, which may make us think of the sweeping gestures of the larger-than-life saints and angels on a baroque painted ceiling (see pages 222–23).

For other baroque fugues, which differ enormously from this one in emotional effect, see the discussion of Purcell's Trio Sonata in A, with a line score (pages 186–88), the "Amen" chorus from Handel's *Messiah* (page 229), and the "Dona nobis pacem" of Bach's Mass in B Minor (page 241). As we have already stated, fugue was one of the great art forms perfected in the baroque period. But it did not die out afterward. It was still considered a richly expressive medium by Viennese, romantic, and early twentieth-century composers.

The Concerto Grosso

The concerto grosso is the most important orchestral genre of the baroque period. Basic to this genre is confrontation between a group of soloists and the total orchestra. Indeed, the word "concerto" comes from the Latin *concertare,* which means "to strive together"—a rather vivid derivation that accurately indicates a joint contest between soloists and orchestra.

The concerto grosso involves more contrast than do most other baroque genres, then. But the contrast is still not as marked as it is in later types of music. For a distinctive fact about the concerto grosso is that the several soloists play as a group. This means that individually they cannot lose themselves in brilliant virtuoso fireworks (as happens in later solo concertos); extreme contrasts between soloists and orchestra are ruled out. Furthermore, the soloists were usually not special "artists" hired at a high fee when they were on tour, but simply the best regular members of the orchestra. When the solo parts had rests in the score, these "first-desk men" (as we would call them) played right along with the orchestra parts. The whole system was not conducive to the star psychology.

In Bach's *Brandenburg* Concerto No. 5, as we shall learn in a moment, an interesting development takes place before our very ears. One of the solo instruments, the harpsichord, breaks free for a time and, while the other instruments watch silently, launches into a long, brilliant, almost improvisational passage of personal display. This *cadenza* gives us a clear glimpse into the future: the virtuoso solo concerto for a single instrument, already present in the baroque period, will later become the norm (see pages 298 and 302).

In Bach's time, the concerto and the concerto grosso most often consisted of three movements, though the number was flexible—much more so than in later forms, such as the symphony. Generally, the first movement of a concerto grosso is an extroverted piece in fast tempo. The second movement is slow and quiet. The third movement is fast again—if anything, faster than the first. (For the term *movement,* see page 184.)

ritornello form

The first movement typically employs <u>ritornello form</u>, another favorite baroque means of musical architecture. This form depends on the alternation of two musical ideas or groups of ideas, one of which belongs to the orchestra and

ritornello

the other to the solo group. <u>Ritornello</u> is the name for the orchestra material, which tends to be shorter and more homophonic. *Ritorno* is the Italian word for "return"; the function of the ritornello is to come back again and again within the movement as a key element of the form.

BACH *Brandenburg* Concerto No. 5, for Flute, Violin, Harpsichord, and Orchestra (1721)

SIDE 5

Bach wrote his set of six *Brandenburg* Concertos in 1721 for the Margrave of Brandenburg, a minor nobleman with a paper title: Brandenburg had recently been merged into Prussia, the fastest-rising state in Europe. Probably the composer expected some preferment, but he received none. Let us hope that he at least got a good fee, for these works are now regarded as the finest examples of the concerto grosso written in the late baroque period. Bach, with his encyclopedic turn of mind, decided to write each concerto for a different combination of instruments, some of them never used before or after. *Brandenburg* Concerto No. 5 uses a solo group consisting of flute, violin, and harpsichord, with a small orchestra of string instruments plus harpsichord.

FIRST MOVEMENT

A concerto grosso begins with the ritornello. The present ritornello is loud, vigorous, and straightforward in quality, and basically homophonic in texture. (Every once in a while, though, the bass takes on an independent melodic character and begins to sound like a real polyphonic line.) The melody itself is agreeable and easily recognized but, like so many baroque melodies, becomes more complicated as it proceeds:

(For simplicity's sake, this music example omits the note repetitions on the eighth notes.) We can probably learn to sing the first phrase, a, after a couple of tries, but after that things get difficult. There is no clear stop between phrases b and c, as the melody begins to wind around itself in an intricate, decorative manner. Yet undoubtedly it is just these features that give the melody its strength and its flair.

Once the ritornello ends, with a very solid cadence, the three solo instruments enter with rapid imitative counterpoint. They tend to dominate the rest of the movement, introducing new themes and exchanging fragments in all kinds of artful ways. Occasionally the orchestra breaks in again with parts of its ritornello (phrase a, phrase b, or phrases a + b), in various different keys. For the rest, the orchestra sometimes plays accompaniment to the soloists as they spin out their contrapuntal web. Gradually the harpsichord outpaces the flute and the violin, until at last it seizes the stage and plays its lengthy virtuoso passage. (As we have already said, the virtuoso harpsichord passage in this concerto grosso is an unusual feature.) Finally the orchestra returns with a full-length statement of the ritornello, verbatim—the first time all of it has been heard since the piece began.

If we were to count the ritornello fragments between the full statements at the beginning and end of this long movement, we should arrive at about seven. A diagram of the movement could be prepared as follows (R = the whole ritornello and [R] = a fragment of it):

R	solo	[R]	solo	[R]	solo	[R]	solo	[R]	long	[R]	solo	[R]	solo	[R]		long	R
abc		a		b		b		b	solo		a		ab		b	harpsichord solo	abc

However, the point is not the number of ritornello fragments or the details of the diagram but the general sense we have of the ritornello acting as a sturdy, reliable support for the rapid and sometimes fantastic flight of the solo instruments. The instruments may sometimes forget themselves, as the harpsichord in particular seems to do, but the ritornello is always there, ready to bring them back down to earth and to remind the listener of the original point of departure. This is the real feeling behind ritornello form. The ritornello may be compared to the solid metal setting for the more brilliant jewels in a crown or, better, to the piers of a bridge holding up the soaring spans:

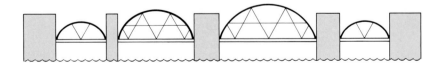

These slightly fanciful similes are correct to the extent that the ritornello, the setting, and the piers serve as supporters for the solo passages, jewels, and spans that in each case occupy the centers of interest and importance.

An Early Eighteenth-Century Park

View of a baroque park. The seventeenth-century idea that reason and calculation could control natural phenomena shows up very clearly in the planning of parks and gardens. In a baroque formal garden and its surrounding park, everything was rigorously patterned according to geometrical plans. Lawns and flowerbeds were planted in neat shapes, and walks were laid out straight beside them. Bushes were clipped down, even carved into shapes, and shrubs were planted at regular distances. Waters were run into channels and fountains.

It was also very characteristic to have the whole garden prominently furnished with classical statues, which seem to stand guard lest the poor plants try to be bushes and trees and flowers rather than elements in the master plan created by human reason.

Formal gardens were not new to the baroque period, but one new feature was the emphasis on long vistas reaching far into space, guided by long lines of shrubbery, lawn, or water. Past the lawn in our photograph, which already extends for a great distance, there is an endless straight canal bounded on either side by high trees. The baroque landscape architect shared a fascination with space with the contemporary stage designer and ceiling painter, some of whose work is illustrated on pages 175 and 222–23.

This view is of a German park, designed in 1722, at the castle of Nymphenburg near Munich. The park has been considerably simplified since the eighteenth century—as we can see from the old print below—but the general formal layout remains the same.

SECOND MOVEMENT

After the forceful first movement of a concerto grosso, a movement that is relatively quiet is needed as a relief. Working in a world of terraced dynamics (see page 159), the baroque composer had a very simple way of achieving this: leave half the instruments out. Thus in the *Brandenburg* Concerto No. 5 the slow movement employs only the three solo instruments—flute, violin, and harpsichord—plus a cello to reinforce the harpsichord left hand, playing the continuo bass (see page 153). This movement, and many another concerto grosso slow movement, would be entirely at home in a baroque chamber music piece, such as a trio sonata (see pages 184–85 and 218–19).

Bach makes a rather subtle movement of considerable length out of two main motives:

inversion — These motives are also heard in <u>inversion</u>, meaning that all their melodic intervals are reversed; wherever the original motive goes up, the inversion goes down, and vice versa. Conceived in the abstract, inversion may seem like a merely mathematical device, but here it sounds perfectly elegant and natural:

THIRD MOVEMENT

The full orchestra returns in the last movement, which is probably the finest of the three. The fast, dancing compound meter (see page 8), with its triple component (ONE two three *four* five six), provides a welcome change after the duple meter of the two earlier movements.

The ways Bach finds of playing off the soloists against the orchestra are more varied and interesting in this third movement than in the first. On the other hand, the orchestra and soloists do not have contrasting material. The whole piece grows out of a single darting theme, introduced at the very beginning by the soloists:

Sometimes this seems to be treated as a fugue, but at other times it is developed more freely than the fugue form usually allows. You may be able to hear a lively stretto, used to prepare for an important interior cadence.

One imaginative detail is a rather songlike melody that emerges from the theme after a time:

Tempo and meter remain the same, but the rhythm feels markedly slower, as indicated by the dotted half notes in every other measure. When the rhythms marked a and b were first heard within the main theme itself, they were indistinguishable from the body of that theme, but now they sound strikingly different: they seem to be no more than little decorations to the dotted half notes that are slowing down the rhythm.

The structure of this movement is as complex and ingenious as the mood is high-spirited and airy. You may notice that a large section of the music—nearly eighty measures—at the beginning of the movement returns verbatim at the end, like a huge ritornello.

ANTONIO VIVALDI (1678–1740) Concerto Grosso in A Minor for Two Violins and Orchestra, Op. 3* No. 8 (1715)   SIDE 6

The Venetian composer Antonio Vivaldi, one of the most important international musical figures of his day, has come to the fore in the baroque music revival of the last twenty years. While Vivaldi wrote quantities of church

---

* *Opus* (abbreviated Op.) is Latin for "work." Opus numbers are assigned by composers or publishers when musical pieces are printed, as a means of distinguishing them—a pressing necessity when a composer writes as many concertos, for instance, as Vivaldi did. Twelve Vivaldi concertos were published together as Op. 3. Our particular concerto was the eighth of the set.

Sometimes pieces are distinguished not by opus numbers but by numbers assigned in a musicologist's catalog of the composer's music. Most familiar are the K numbers used for Mozart's music, after the catalog by a certain Ludwig von Köchel (see page 281).

music and operas, he was especially industrious as a composer of concertos, of which over 450 (!) are known. The Concerto Grosso in A Minor for Two Violins and Orchestra appeared in 1715 as one of a group with the charming title *L'Estro Armonico* (Harmonic Fancy).

This work shares a number of the general features that have been pointed out in Bach's *Brandenburg* Concerto. First there is the emphatic orchestral ritornello in the opening movement:

Then there is the busywork of the solo sections, making extensive use of sequences:

And, like Bach's concerto grosso, Vivaldi's has a quiet slow movement for a reduced orchestra and a lively last movement. At the same time, we shall probably also sense that the whole piece has been conceived from a simpler point of view. The texture is thinner, and the melody is less subtle, especially in the solo passages. Technique relates to expression; Vivaldi's expressive range is relatively limited and also externalized, lacking the depths that seem to be lurking even in Bach's simpler compositions.

FIRST MOVEMENT

The first movement of the Vivaldi concerto appears on pages 214–15, in a simplified, full-length line score. If you follow the piece through with this score, it should help you hear the rigorous structure underlying a typical late baroque concerto grosso movement. Follow the music line by line without stopping at the ends of lines (which have sometimes been made to come out at different lengths in order to isolate and thus distinguish the ritornellos, solos, etc.). A line score shows only the most important melodic lines in the music.

The fairly long opening ritornello actually falls into four separate subsections, here labeled "main theme," "sequence," "cadence-phrase 1," and "cadence-phrase 2." (We have mentioned the baroque love of sequence within long melodies.) After the solo violins enter, the orchestra interrupts with one or another of these subsections, or several in a row, until all are well represented by the time the movement comes to a close. It is as though the composer had laid out the ritornello on a drawing board, snipped it into sections, and then methodically shifted these into place. The solo sections, too, have many similarities among them, as is indicated on the line score.

However, several of the ritornellos and solo sections do come in different keys, which gives the piece interest and drive. And, in spite of the almost mathematical structure, there are some unpredictable elements (see the circled numbers on the line score):

1.   The new figure introduced by the solo violins at the end of solo 2, which the orchestra violins can hardly wait to pick up in ritornello 3 (page 214, lines 10 and 11)

2.   The forceful repetition of the special new cadence at this same ritornello, a repetition in a different key (page 214, last line)

3.   The energetic new upbeat figures that launch ritornellos 4 and 6 (page 215, lines 2 and 7)

Perhaps we especially appreciate these more spontaneous elements; perhaps we appreciate them all the more because they appear within an otherwise formal structure.

At the beginning of solo 3, a motive derived from the opening ritornello grows more and more important. In the ritornello, it appeared directly after the main theme. In solo 1 it was referred to briefly and rather freely, but now it dominates the solos, developed into sequences of various kinds.

A diagram for this movement, on the pattern of the one given for Bach's *Brandenburg* Concerto No. 5 (page 207), runs as follows:

R *solo* [R] *solo*   [R]   *solo* [R] *solo* [R] *solo* [R] *solo* [R] *solo* [R]
abcd   d   b, etc.   a   c   a   bd   d

SECOND MOVEMENT

The second movement of the Vivaldi concerto begins with a passacaglia theme:

First presented alone by the orchestra, like a ritornello, this theme later serves to conclude the movement. Between these appearances, the solo violins weave contrapuntal lines that are gentle and wistful. Meanwhile, the orchestra plays the passacaglia theme quietly or makes new phrases out of the theme's two motives. The treatment is much freer than that of Bach's Passacaglia and Fugue for Organ.

Vivaldi, Concerto Grosso, Op. 3 No. 8: First Movement

THIRD MOVEMENT

The last movement is a strong, brilliant piece of the same general nature as the first. The ritornello is shorter, and comes back less often than the first movement ritornello does. Furthermore, the orchestra here is not restricted to its opening ritornello material. Instead, it introduces some definite new ideas—they are rather fantastic in quality—during the later course of the movement. And, rather surprisingly, a warm, songlike solo theme appears among the customary rapid figures for the two violins. This theme seems to move more slowly than the rest of the movement, and its expressive quality, too, recalls the slow movement rather than the first or third.

Was Bach also struck by this theme, and could he have had this very piece in mind when he wrote the songlike passage we discussed in the last movement of the *Brandenburg* Concerto No. 5 (see page 211)? Baroque music was often rearranged for different instruments, with a resulting change in the original tone colors, as we pointed out before. This concerto of Vivaldi's was one of several that Bach arranged for organ or harpsichord—evidence of his admiration for Vivaldi and his interest in keeping abreast of modern developments in Italian music.

In fact, Bach's organ arrangement is just as likely to be heard nowadays as Vivaldi's original. The organist plays the orchestral passages on the pipes of the "great organ," which is the heaviest of the various sections into which organs are divided (see page 198), and plays the solo passages on the "positive," a smaller and more delicate section. In this way the terraced dynamics of Vivaldi's piece are maintained exactly, and the form is just as clear. Neither composers nor audiences at the time would have been much bothered by the change in tone color between the two versions. Listen to them both and see if you agree.

Georg Philipp Telemann (1681–1767)

Telemann was another excellent and enormously prolific composer who, like Vivaldi, is enjoying new popularity in the revival of baroque music in our time. His career, like Bach's, progressed through a series of church, court, and civic positions in Germany; the two men worked at some of the same places. Although today he is not ranked with Bach, Telemann was more famous in his own day and was one of the first composers to think of writing an autobiography. He was the first choice for cantor of the Leipzig Thomaskirche when the position fell vacant in 1721, but he decided not to move from Hamburg, which was a much more important musical center. The position was then offered to Bach, and Bach took it.

Vivaldi is remembered today mainly for his concertos. Telemann is remembered, not for his forty operas, his six hundred overtures, and his endless church cantatas and motets, but mainly for his chamber music. Examination of a trio sonata by Telemann will give us a good idea of the state of chamber music in the later baroque period.

An Early Concert

Pictured here is a concert in London's Vauxhall Gardens, the famous "pleasure garden" of the middle and upper classes. Laid out as a formal garden, Vauxhall received its smart bandstand in 1732. In it, Handel's *Fireworks Music* was rehearsed before an admiring crowd of 12,000 people. Music was a regular attraction, together with good food, pleasant walks, and blazing lights at night—all for a shilling's admission. Music was one of the pleasures that the middle class came to enjoy and was ready to support. The concert shown here actually took place later, in 1785.

On the introduction of concerts, and their impact on music making and music listening, see page 69. Indoor concert series were also established in the eighteenth century, such as the *Concert spirituel* in Paris, the *Tonkünstler Societät* concerts in Vienna, and the "Academy of Antient Music" in London. The first actual concert hall opened in 1748 in a university town, Oxford.

The orchestra, well furnished with Handelian "festive" trumpets, has not been depicted too gently by the painter, Thomas Rowlandson, one of the best of early cartoon satirists. But none of Rowlandson's subjects has been spared. In the alcove at the left, leading literary lights of the day, including Dr. Samuel Johnson and James Boswell, are seen attacking a large meal. The amorous youth at the right is the Prince of Wales, later King George IV, here shown at the start of a career which was to be marked by unusual debauchery.

Indeed, what is most interesting about this picture is the leveling of royalty, nobility, middle class, and even artisans such as the musicians. "Democracy" as we think of it was still some time off, in England and elsewhere, but the rigid class boundaries of old were beginning to break down, at least in certain situations, such as that of the "pleasure garden."

TELEMANN Trio Sonata for Recorder and Violin in D Minor

The essential characteristics of the baroque trio sonata had not changed from the time of the Purcell sonata we examined on pages 184–88. Two high instruments (such as violins or flutes) tended to compete with one another over the basic support of the continuo, played by a bass instrument (such as a cello) and a chord instrument (such as an organ or harpsichord). So a trio sonata has three main musical lines—see the line score on page 187—but always requires four players. A sonata consists of several movements; the number, character, and order of these is not standardized. However, a common plan for the movements is slow - fast - slow - fast, and some of the movements are likely to be fugal.

Unlike Purcell, who wrote only relatively few trio sonatas, Telemann, who wrote hundreds, experimented with many different instrumental combinations. Our Trio Sonata in D Minor was written for recorder and violin on the upper lines. Compared to the flute, which we had a good opportunity to hear in Bach's *Brandenburg* Concerto No. 5, the recorder has its own intriguing tone quality—thin, airy, precarious, naïve. Notice, too, that Telemann writes several themes featuring rather fast repeated notes, which are especially appropriate to this instrument and certainly make the music tingle.

On our recording, the problem of balance with the relatively frail recorder is helped by the gentle, sensitive, and slightly nasal quality of an old violin—a baroque violin in its original form. Everyone knows that the greatest of all violins are those of Stradivarius, made in the baroque period. But it is not widely known that those "Strads" that are still around to command astronomical prices at auctions have all been altered appreciably. They sound considerably different (though perhaps not less beautiful) than they did in the days of Stradivarius and Telemann.

The continuo bass instrument is not a cello but a viol da gamba, which has a more throaty quality than a cello, though this may not be too obvious on the recording.

The plan of movements in Telemann's Trio Sonata in D Minor is as follows (compare Purcell's plan, on page 185):

Movement	I	II	III	IV
Tempo indication	Andante	Vivace	Adagio→	Allegro
Tempo	slow	fast	slow	fast
Meter	$\frac{2}{2}$	$\frac{3}{8}$	$\frac{2}{2}$	$\frac{4}{4}$

Telemann's *first* movement is a songlike, imitative piece in free da capo form (A B A'); A' differs from A mainly in the charming little stops that come shortly before the ends of these sections. The *second* movement is an informal fugue—informal because the bass (continuo) never has the subject:

First entry:
RECORDER

(Violin rests)

tr

VIOLIN

Second entry:

etc.

Unlike the fugue in Purcell's sonata, which consists almost entirely of subject entries and only one episode, Telemann's fugue has only six subject entries interspersed with generous episodes.

The *third* movement is built for the most part on a walking bass (see page 152). It runs directly into the *fourth* movement, which is a visitor from another baroque genre, the suite. This movement is a rondeau of the kind we have seen in the work of Lully (see page 181), in the form A B A C A D A. Section A is itself a little a a′ form, and traces of the a occur in both the B and C sections; the D section is a special delight. As in so much baroque music, the composer would have expected the players to improvise melodic decorations, and some deft examples are provided by the musicians on our recording.

George Frideric Handel (1685–1759)

Handel was a very different type of personality from Bach. He counts as an exception among composers of the time in not stemming from a family of musicians. Indeed, a little story used to be told about how he had to brave his father's displeasure to become a musician, and used to practice secretly at night by candlelight. Perhaps because he lacked musical roots, he traveled widely from his native Germany and gravitated to the glamorous and lucrative world of the theater—a world far removed in spirit from Bach's organ lofts. After apprenticeship in the opera houses of Germany and Italy, Handel came to England, where he seems to have sensed perfectly the national mood and character. In London, which was rapidly becoming the world capital, he made a career for himself as an opera composer, impresario, and musical entrepreneur.

His career had its ups and downs, but Handel enjoyed quite unusual fame and fortune for a musician. At his death in 1759, an admiring nation had him buried in Westminster Abbey under a grandiose baroque monument.

Like Bach, Handel was a formidable organ virtuoso and a phenomenal worker. His famous oratorio *Messiah*, which lasts for more than two hours, is said to have been written in twenty-four days. And like all composers of his day, only more so, Handel was constantly rearranging his old music for new occasions. This is another reflection of the craft spirit in baroque music; when Handel or Bach was required to provide music for some one-time ceremony at court, he tried to rewrite it later with new words as an opera or a church cantata, which could then be performed again. These composers would no more put it on a shelf to gather dust than a silversmith would abandon a candelabrum that was for some reason no longer salable.

Handel even extended this economical practice to other men's music: an appreciable number of his pieces were "borrowed" from other composers, sometimes with an ingenious new addition by Handel and sometimes without. The interesting point is that late baroque musical style is so uniform that he could do this without exciting comment. We can scarcely imagine anyone getting away with this in the individualistic art world of today.

Though Handel was primarily an opera and oratorio composer, he by no means neglected the instrumental forms of his day, such as the concerto grosso. He produced a superb set of twelve (op. 6) for two violins and orchestra, the same solo combination used by Vivaldi in the piece we discussed above. His best-known instrumental works preserve the memory of great outdoor festivities in London. The *Water Music* was composed for an aquatic fête on the River Thames in 1717, and the *Fireworks Music* was composed to celebrate the end of the War of the Austrian Succession (sometimes known as King George's War) in 1749.

These works and these occasions remind us of the role Handel took for himself as musical spokesman for eighteenth-century England, expressing its satisfactions, its values, and its aspirations. The popular tone that he achieved on such occasions, and for which he had to bend his normal style only slightly, still has a very strong appeal today.

HANDEL *Royal Fireworks Music* (1749)

Outdoor music needs to be simple in form as well as popular in tone. Both the *Water Music* and the *Fireworks Music* are suites. This genre consists basically of a set of different dances, either drawn from a popular opera or ballet or composed afresh (as Handel's are), and usually preceded by a more weighty introductory number called the overture. The suite developed in France in the seventeenth century, as we noted (see page 179).

In the later baroque period, the makeup of a suite, like everything else, became more systematic, and all of Bach's examples are built around the same nucleus of four dances (allemande, courante, sarabande, and gigue). Handel, however, still preferred to vary his choice of dances. For the *Water Music* and the *Fireworks Music,* we may as well say that Handel used the suite as a kind of grab bag, into which he threw an informal array of lively ideas. It is not even necessary to hear all the dances in order; for modern performances, conductors sometimes pick and choose among them.

The *Fireworks Music* was written for a big band: a total of sixty trumpets, French horns, oboes, bassoons, and drums. Later Handel arranged it to include string instruments, and today it is usually heard in this version.

The long preliminary movement defies formal classification, like much of Handel's music. In the first section, the grand pompous tone and the dotted rhythms recall the first part of a French overture (see page 180), but in the second section, the alternation of "solo" sections for trumpets and horns recalls the concerto grosso. However, the main point about music of this kind is not its form but its verve and forcefulness. Few composers have been as successful at creating this effect as Handel. The rhythms in the second section keep changing, over the steady triple meter, until they reach this splendidly energetic rhythmic and melodic climax (note the use of sequence, at the end):

Following this opening number comes a group of different dances. The first is a sprightly item in duple meter which we have seen in Lully, a *bourrée* (see page 179). Next comes a slow-swinging *siciliana*, in compound meter ($\frac{12}{8}$), featuring the French horns; this is entitled "La paix," which is French for "Peace." (Why should a German composer working in England put a French name on a piece of music written to celebrate the end of a war against France? Probably because at this time it was a French habit to provide dances in suites with special titles of one kind or another, and the French were admired as specialists in dance music.)

The next piece is called "La réjouissance," meaning "Rejoicing"—military rather than peaceful rejoicing, to judge from the brisk martial tone. This would have made a perfect quick march for the redcoats, whose baroque military pomp fared so poorly thirty years later in the American colonies.

A majestic *minuet* in triple meter, the simplest of all the dances, concludes the suite. It alternates with another, quieter minuet, the trio (see page 180); an A B A form results. In both minuets, it is easy to hear the repetitions of the two internal sections, a and b in the first and c and d in the second (see page 180; the sections are all eight measures long). Outdoor band music needs plenty of repeats, and Handel left directions for repeating several movements of the *Fireworks Music* with varying instrumentations.

The rehearsal of the *Fireworks Music* at Vauxhall Gardens, the famous pleasure garden of the London middle and upper classes (see page 217), was attended with great approval by 12,000 persons. At the celebration itself, which was led off by a hundred brass cannons, everything went wrong: the great set piece caught fire, the crowd stampeded, two spectators died, and the man in charge of the fireworks had a mad fit. Music should stay indoors.

Opera in the Late Baroque Period

If Handel was first and foremost an opera composer, the reason was that for an ambitious musician of his time, opera was at the center of the action. Opera was the favorite genre of music lovers in the eighteenth century, fascinated as they were by things theatrical. Its influence was pervasive, so that the Bach church cantatas, to mention one significant nonoperatic form, can scarcely be understood without some knowledge of opera.

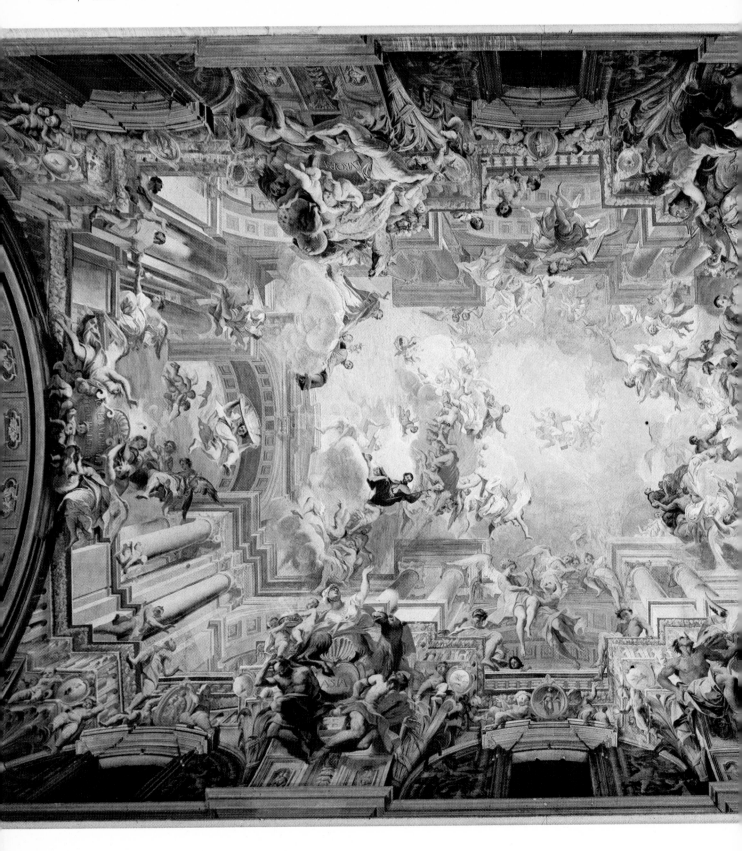

Baroque Ceiling Painting

Ceiling paintings are perhaps the most astonishing products of the baroque artistic imagination. Sometimes covering the entire ceiling of a church or a hall in a palace, they give the impression that the roof has suddenly been thrown open to reveal a miraculous vision of the dome of heaven. Angels, cherubs, saints, and mortals spin around in the clouds, lose themselves in the sun's rays, or spill back into the church itself. Great winds are all but visible in the swirling drapery. Vast spaces and ecstatic, violent motion—or, rather, vast spaces in violent motion—this was the essential illusion cultivated by the ceiling painters. Shown on these two pages is the apotheosis, or ascent to heaven, of St. Ignatius Loyola, founder of the Jesuit Order, on the ceiling of the church dedicated to him in Rome.

The twin illusions of space and motion are created by the most sophisticated application of the laws of mathematical perspective. In our illustration, for example, all the "architecture" is painted on the flat ceiling (compare the theater set on page 175).

There are some points of contact between ceiling painting and dense baroque polyphony, such as that found in the Sanctus of Bach's Mass in B Minor (see page 240). This, too, gives a sense of powerful, complex movement filling all the reaches of "musical space" from the lowest notes on the organ pedals to the highest of flute and trumpet tones. And only Bach's very impressive control over the craft of counterpoint enabled him to gear all this musical movement into the total breathtaking effect.

St. Ignatius himself would have been happier with the music of his own sixteenth century, music by Palestrina or Victoria. But if this baroque depiction of his apotheosis calls for music—and who can doubt that it does?—it is music such as that of Bach's Sanctus.

Furthermore, the emotional world of the arts of the time, music as well as painting and sculpture, seems to have revolved around the stage. We pointed out above that the grand gesture and high passion of the baroque theater encouraged composers to think of feelings in extreme, intense forms. The majestic theatricality of a baroque opera scene finds its emotional analogue in concerto grosso movements, virtuoso organ pieces, and other instrumental music of the period.

Opera depended on brilliant singing, and, since the most glamorous singers were Italians, Handel's operas for London were in Italian. A strange, unnatural situation—and after a while London audiences rebelled and deserted Handel, as we shall see (page 491). Opera also depended on extravagant spectacle. Handel's first London success, *Rinaldo* (1711), contains two of his most popular arias, but people were just as excited by the production's amazing stage effects: the great pitched battle at the end, the flocks of sparrows that were released to fly around the sorceress's magic garden, and the machinery by which "a black cloud descended, all filled with dreadful monsters spitting fire and smoke on every side."

Handel also left an example of a simpler type of opera, in English, one that is shorter and less spectacular than *Rinaldo*. It was written not for the London theater but for the country mansion of a music-loving nobleman, the Duke of Chandos. Appropriately, it has a pastoral subject.

HANDEL *Acis and Galatea* (1724)   SIDE 6

The shepherd Acis loves the water nymph Galatea, and she returns his love. She rejects the suit of Polyphemus, an ugly one-eyed monster (who also plays a "heavy" role in Homer's *Odyssey* and Virgil's *Aeneid*). Overcome by jealousy, Polyphemus kills Acis, and the grieving Galatea turns Acis into a river so that they can always be together.

libretto
This exceedingly simple story provided Handel with the occasion for some of his loveliest music. The words of an opera are called the <u>libretto</u> ("little book" in Italian), and the task of the author or *librettist* was to recast the story in verses suitable for musical setting. Handel's librettists were not as good poets as he was a composer; some of the language in *Acis and Galatea* is unfortunate (for example, Polyphemus addresses the boulder with which he will crush Acis as "thou massy ruin"). Nonetheless, the librettist was a necessary link in the chain, and he supplied Handel with a workable series of recitatives and arias, which he could set to beautiful music.

We have put together a composite scene from *Acis and Galatea* consisting of three recitatives, an aria, and a trio.

Coming to Handel's recitatives after those of Purcell and Monteverdi, we cannot fail to be disappointed. The elements are basically the same as in the example from *Dido and Aeneas* on page 176—the voice following the natural word accents rather than singing tunes, and the continuo (only) providing discreet support rather than "accompaniment" in any functional sense. But Handel's heart does not seem to be in it. Acis has little to say and he does not say it in a very interesting way. Late baroque opera composers tended to skimp on recitative and devote more and more of their attention to the arias.

RECITATIVE: Acis	Acis, whose "melancholy air" has been noted by his fellow shepherds, comes upon Galatea and throws himself at her feet.
ARIA: Acis, "Love in her eyes sits playing"	He sings elaborate compliments to her, in faintly erotic language.
RECITATIVE: Galatea	She encourages him.
TRIO: Acis, Galatea, Polyphemus, "The flocks shall leave the mountains"	They sing happily together of their love. Polyphemus enters, observes them, and grows angrier and angrier, till he finally heaves a great rock at Acis and kills him.
RECITATIVE: Acis	Acis gives a short, pathetic dying speech.

"Love in her eyes sits playing" is a da capo aria (see page 189) in Handel's most ingratiating melodic style. The tenor melody in smoothly flowing compound meter is occasionally intertwined with exquisite imitative lines in the orchestra—but not too often, not often enough to deflect attention from the voice. A purely orchestral ritornello appears at the beginning of the aria, previewing the tenor melody. This ritornello returns at several points in the middle, and then returns again at the end. Its function is like that of a concerto grosso ritornello: it provides a series of firm anchor points to which the freer flow of the soloist (here a singer) can be tied.

Handel achieves an admirable balance of unity and variety in this aria. The B section maintains the same melodic and rhythmic style as the A section, but the orchestra drops out, save for the continuo, and the harmony moves predominantly to the minor mode. Then, when the singer returns to the A section and improvises just a very few graceful ornaments on the original melodic line, the seemingly repetitious A B A form comes to life as something flexible and interesting. "Love in her eyes" could not be called a musical representation of deep passion, though the composer could handle that, too, when necessary. As a depiction of youthful infatuation in the never-never land of nymphs and shepherds, however, it could hardly be bettered.

After another brief recitative, for Galatea this time, there follows the trio "The flocks shall leave the mountains," the most original and probably the finest number in the whole of *Acis and Galatea.* An opera *trio* is simply a number for three singers (a *duet* is a number for two, a *quartet* for four, and so on). This trio begins like a duet, with the lovers and the orchestra joining in a graceful, calm theme in imitative counterpoint. Acis sings of his flocks, with an oboe (a shepherd's pipe?) accompanying him, and Galatea sings of her fountains. Meanwhile in the orchestra, a walking bass (see page 152) contributes to the serene atmosphere by its placid, unvarying movement.

After sixteen measures, however, Polyphemus, a bass, enters unobserved. He sings quite different music to express his quite different sentiments. Muffled cries of "Torture! fury! rage! despair!" shatter the rhythmic pattern of the walking bass, but Acis and Galatea are too preoccupied to hear him. The music all fits together marvelously, of course. The conflicting feelings of the dramatic figures are represented simultaneously:

In the second half of the trio, the lovers sing new themes, but they continue to blend with one another in smooth, amorous counterpoint. Polyphemus gets angrier and angrier, and when he urges his massy ruin to "fly swift," a vivid flash of word painting on the word "fly" emphasizes his action. Most vigorous of all is his music for "die, presumptuous Acis" at the end. While this trio ends with an orchestral ritornello, just as "Love in her eyes" did, it is not the same ritornello as at the start but a new, agitated one. For the situation has changed. The drama has progressed, and it has progressed in and through the music.

In this trio, the repetition of words does not seem at all as tiresome as in Acis's (and many another) aria. Text repetition is undoubtedly an artificial feature of the late baroque da capo aria, redeemed in the case of "Love in her eyes" only by the sheer inspiration of Handel's melodic writing. But in "The flocks shall leave" it is natural enough for lovers to repeat their endearments, and Polyphemus's obsessive mutterings paint an apt picture of his rising fury. Excellent, too, is the way Handel has him shout "die, die, die!" three times just before the end: the ultimate in spite.

The dying speech of Acis, which now follows, is a great advance over the two previous examples of recitative. Expressive chords underpin his exclamations of "help," and after a few words he slips into arioso, a style in between recitative and aria (see page 176). Very quiet, mournful harmonies are heard in the orchestra. His last gasps, realistically punctuated by rests, sound genuinely affecting. This is baroque theater at its most majestic.

Counterparts of Acis's dying speech, set in expressive recitative and arioso, can be found in many operas of the time. But the trio preceding it, during which Acis is struck down, is not a usual piece. Most late baroque operas consist of a string of static da capo arias, like "Love in her eyes," spaced out by recitatives and not much else. But Handel was not a usual composer. He was a genius, and he thought about drama as well as about beautiful singing. The reason his operas are still remembered and recorded, while those of his contemporaries are not, is that he was always ready to break with conventions and take imaginative risks, as in the remarkable trio of *Acis and Galatea*.

From *Acis and Galatea*

RECITATIVE

ACIS: Lo! here my love!
Turn Galatea, hither turn thine eyes,
See, at thy feet the longing Acis lies.

ARIA

(A) Love in her eyes sits playing,
And sheds delicious death;
Love in her lips is straying,
And warbling in her breath.

(B) Love on her breast sits panting,
And swells with soft desire;
No grace, no charm is wanting
To set the heart on fire.

(A) Love in her eyes (etc.)

RECITATIVE

GALATEA: Cease, O cease, thou gentle youth!
Trust my constancy and truth;
Trust my truth, and pow'rs above,
The powers propitious to love.

TRIO

ACIS, GALATEA: The flocks shall leave the mountains,
The woods the turtle-dove,
The nymphs forsake the fountains
Ere I forsake my love!
POLYPHEMUS: (Torture! fury! rage! despair!
I cannot, cannot, cannot bear.)

ACIS, GALATEA: Not show'rs to larks so pleasing,
Not sunshine to the bee,
Not sleep to toil so easing
As these dear smiles to me.
POLYPHEMUS: Fly swift, thou massy ruin, fly!
Die, presumptuous Acis, die!

(Throws rock and exits.)

RECITATIVE

ACIS: Help, Galatea! help, ye parent gods!
And take me dying to your deep abodes.

The Oratorio

dramatic oratorio

Handel's most famous compositions, his oratorios, are thoroughly operatic in form and spirit. The great majority of them can be referred to as "dramatic oratorios." The dramatic oratorio is a long religious piece in English, cast in semi-dramatic form, with characters, dialogue, plot, action, and even division into separate acts—all this, even though Handel was not planning actual stage performances. Oratorios were intended to be performed in the concert hall, not in the theater or in church. But their audience was the opera audience, and it is not surprising that many oratorios take very well to stage production, as experience in recent years has shown.

Typically, Handel would start from an Old Testament story. Among his subjects were Esther, the prophetess Deborah, Samson, and King Solomon. Then the rudimentary skeleton of a story line in the Bible would be fleshed out by the librettist (see page 224), who would supply subplots and even add new characters in order to make the whole thing more like a play. He would also fit in extensive passages for Handel to set as choruses.

The chorus assumed a central role in the dramatic oratorio, modeled ultimately on the role of the chorus in classical Greek drama. While the characters act out their story, the chorus speaks for the people of Israel or for the heathen tribes with whom the Israelites were always warring. The chorus comments on the action, shows how the fate of the individuals reflects on the fate of nations as a whole, and draws the final moral.

HANDEL *Messiah* (1742) SIDE 6

Composed in 1742, *Messiah* (not *The Messiah*) is the most famous and beloved of Handel's oratorios. It is exceptional among them in several respects. The subject comes from the New Testament rather than the Old, the words are taken directly from the Bible rather than from a newly written libretto, and there are no characters or plot line. Perhaps it is just as well that we do not have to listen to the story of Jesus expressed in the eighteenth-century verse of Handel's librettists.

Nevertheless, *Messiah* employs the same operatic form as do the dramatic oratorios: a series of recitatives, arias, and choruses. The difference is that the solo singers of recitatives and arias do not represent particular Bible characters, but instead generalized voices from the Christian community, just like the chorus. They tell the story of Christ's birth, suffering, and resurrection with more emphasis on ideas than on actual Bible incidents.

Messiah opens with a French overture (see page 180). Not only that, but Handel also wrote a sort of choral version of the characteristic first part of a French overture to launch act II of the oratorio. This is the splendid chorus "Behold the Lamb of God":

For listeners of the time, the solemn, pompous dotted rhythms and the slow changes of harmony meant a beginning, a new beginning—even though this is not a strictly orchestral number, but an orchestrally accompanied chorus.

   Almost every one of the fifty-odd numbers in *Messiah* is a gem, and we can only pick and choose among them for brief comment. The celebrated "Hallelujah" chorus, which serves to conclude act II in unparalleled triumph, is largely homophonic in texture. It uses the "festive" baroque orchestra featuring trumpets and drums with special brilliance. It may remind us of the *Fireworks Music,* and indeed, all baroque composers tended to praise the works of God in much the same spirit as they celebrated the exploits of great princes.

   The "Amen" chorus—actually the third part of a longer chorus, "Worthy is the Lamb"—is, on the contrary, polyphonic. A fugue with a clear countersubject (see page 203), it concludes the oratorio with solemnity and magnificence:

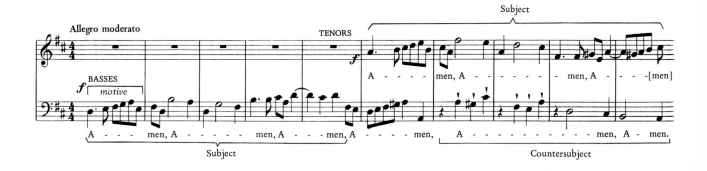

The grand subject is intoned first by the bass voices, then by tenors, altos, and sopranos, followed by the two violin sections of the orchestra. The basses have the subject twice more, and eight measures later the altos have it. But then Handel abandons the subject as a whole, concentrating instead on contrapuntal treatments of a short motive from the very beginning of the subject. He also uses the motive upside down (inversion: see page 210):

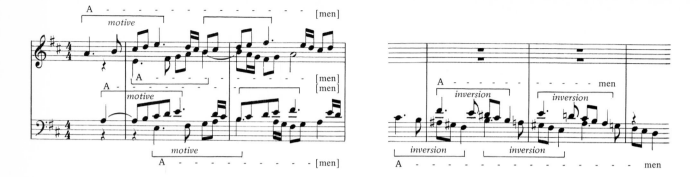

The arias in *Messiah* range in mood from the rousing vigor of "The trumpet shall sound" (bass) to the pastoral gentleness of "He shall feed his flock" (contralto and soprano) and from the pathos of "He was despised" (contralto) to the serenity of "I know that my Redeemer liveth" (soprano). The last is an especially fine testimony to Handel's skill as a melodist—the hauntingly tuneful first phrase, for example:

This aria does not fall into the usual da capo (A B A) form, no doubt because the biblical text in prose does not easily return on itself in sense:

> I know that my Redeemer liveth, and that he shall stand at the latter day upon the earth. And though worms destroy this body, yet in my flesh I shall see God. For now is Christ risen from the dead, the first fruits of them that sleep.

Although the words change considerably as the piece proceeds ("though worms destroy this body," "for now is Christ risen," etc.), Handel avoids any really striking new musical ideas. He prefers to have the orchestra return from time to time with the main fragment of tune, and also with a second figure:

In arias, as in other kinds of music, baroque composers tended to emphasize a single sentiment rather than to deal in contrasts.

The Church Cantata

Always remember that Handel wrote his oratorios (even *Messiah*) to be performed in a concert hall for an audience that was accustomed to opera. Bach wrote his religious music for particular church services and, what is more, tailored it closely to the specific content of those services.

In the Lutheran Church of Bach's time, there were prescribed Bible readings and prescribed hymns for every Sunday of the year, as well as for the feasts of Christmas, Easter, Ascension, and so on. The readings set the tone of the service and provided the basis for the sermon. For every Sunday and feast day, church cantata   Bach had to reflect the religious content of the service in a church cantata written specifically for that day. Another way of saying this is that the church cantata was "proper" to the service (see page 78).

A cantata is a general name for a piece of moderate length for voices and instruments—one singer and orchestra in Scarlatti's secular cantata *Su le sponde del Tebro* (see page 189), several solo singers, orchestra, and chorus in a typical Bach church cantata. As cantor of the Thomaskirche in Leipzig, Bach was required to provide church cantatas for the full year—a stupendous task that must have kept him composing constantly for some time after he was appointed. Over two hundred Bach cantatas have survived, including some secular ones written for court or civic celebrations.

BACH   Cantata No. 140, *Wachet auf, Ruft Uns die Stimme*
(Awake, the Voice Calls to Us) (1731)   SIDE 7

The way in which a cantata could reflect its service was through the words of the libretto, of course. The words would refer to the readings of the day and enlarge upon them. Thus Bach's Cantata No. 140, *Wachet auf, ruft uns die Stimme*, composed for a certain Sunday in autumn, refers to the prescribed reading for that day (Matthew 25:1–13):

> There were ten girls, who took their lamps and went out to meet the bridegroom. Five of them were foolish, and five prudent; when the foolish ones took their lamps, they took no oil with them. . . . As the bridegroom was late in coming they all dozed off to sleep. But at midnight a cry was heard: "Here is the bridegroom! Come out to meet him." With that the girls all got up and trimmed their lamps. The foolish said to the prudent, "Our lamps are going out; give us some of your oil." "No," they said; "there will never be enough for all of us. You had better go to the shop and buy some for yourselves." While they were away the bridegroom arrived; those who were ready went in with him to the wedding. . . . Keep awake, then; for you do not know on what day your Lord is to come.

Whether Bach and his librettist cared for this rather stern parable we have no way of knowing. It was there, and they had to use it. But it may be significant that the librettist says nothing about the discomfiture of the foolish girls, and dwells only on the joys accorded to the wise.

Bach's Musical Handwriting

A score copied by Johann Sebastian Bach. To judge from this score, Bach would not have minded our speaking of "winding lines" in reference to baroque melodies; his handwriting seems unconsciously to have mirrored the quality of his melodic style. And his impressive powers in weaving together five different contrapuntal melodies are mirrored by the really ingenious way in which he manages to write them all down on two staffs. This is an organ prelude and fugue; nowadays we make things easier and always put organ music on three staffs, one for each hand plus one for the pedal (see pages 202 and 204).

In decorative terms, this intricately crowded, fluid-looking score shares some of the characteristics of the visual art of the time. We spoke of the baroque composers' urge to fill up "musical space." Here we see Bach actually filling the tiny space that was left at the end of the third line, even though this meant breaking the measure in two—a rare occurrence in music writing.

THE CHORALE

An even more intimate way in which a cantata could reflect its service was through one of the chorales (the German word for "hymn") that were specified for the service. To the congregation, the words of the chorale would probably be even more familiar and vivid than the Bible words themselves. Those were churchgoing days, and everybody learned their hymns by heart in early childhood, the words right along with the tunes. What is more, the congregation would be singing the same chorale at the same service. Thus, composers who used that chorale tune in the cantata gave the congregation a sense of immediacy and participation. This could only make the service a more meaningful religious experience.

And so Bach incorporated into Cantata No. 140 all three verses of the chorale of the day, *Wachet auf, ruft uns die Stimme.* In fact, the cantata libretto is built around (or within) the three hymn verses in a symmetrical way, as the following table shows:

(1)	CHORALE (verse 1): Christians, *"Wachet auf, ruft uns die Stimme"*	As though by a watchman at midnight, the prudent girls are exhorted to awake and prepare for the coming of the Bridegroom.
	RECITATIVE	The daughters of Zion are told that the Bridegroom is coming at once.
(2)	DUET: The Soul and Jesus, *"Wann kommst du, mein Heil?"*	"Savior, I await Thee; when wilt Thou come?" "I come; I open the door to heaven."
(3)	CHORALE (verse 2): Christians, *"Zion hört die Wächter singen"*	Zion rejoices at the coming of Jesus, the Son of God.
	RECITATIVE	Jesus promises to support and cherish the Soul.
(4)	DUET: The Soul and Jesus, *"Mein Freund ist mein"*	"My Friend is mine; nothing will separate us." "I am thine; you will come with Me to joy."
(5)	CHORALE (verse 3): Christians, *"Gloria sei dir gesungen"*	Glory to God.

In this cantata, only verse 3 of the chorale is presented in a straightforward way, that is, in a way that might fall within the range of actual congregational singing. This verse 3 (No. 5 in the cantata) is a simple but masterly four-part harmonization of the chorale, with all voices and instruments joining together to provide solid chords. In the other two verses, Bach changed the chorale in tempo, meter, rhythm, and accents—though not in pure melody—as indicated on the next page.

CHORALE, VERSE 1 (CANTATA, NO. 1)

Wa - chet auf, ruft uns die stim - - me,___ der Wächter sehr hoch auf der Zin - - ne___
Wake, awake! now strikes the hour,_____ the watchmen call high on the to - - wer___

VERSE 2 (CANTATA, NO. 3)

Zion hört die Wächter sin - gen, das Herz tut ihr vor Freuden sprin - - - gen
Zion hears the watchmen call - ing the faithful hark with joy en - thrall - - - ing

VERSE 3 (CANTATA, NO. 5)

Glo - ri - a sei dir ge - sun - gen mit Menschen und mit eng - li - schen Zun - gen,
"Glor - i - a" sing all our voi - ces, with angels all man - kind re - joi - - - ces,
Von zwölf Per - len sind die Pfor - ten an deiner Stadt; wir sind Kon - sor - - ten
Of twelve pearls are made Thy por - tals where Thou hast ga - thered Thy im - mor - - tals

mit Harfen und mit Cymbeln schon. Kein Aug' hat je ge - spürt, kein Ohr hat je ge - hört
with harp and joyous cymbal tone. No eye has ev - er seen, no ear has ev - er heard
der Engel hoch um deiner Thron.
as Angels high a - round Thy throne.

sol - che Freu - de. Des wir sind froh, i - o! i - o! e - wig in dul - ci ju - bi - lo.
the joy we know. Our prai - ses flow, i - o! i - o! to God in dul - ci ju - bi - lo.

The entire chorale tune is printed above only at verse 3. It is a grand tune, by the way, and much of the popularity of this cantata comes from our pleasure in hearing the tune with Bach's various additions and decorations. (We might stop for a moment to sing the chorale and to analyze it along the lines suggested on page 21. Notice the symmetrical phrase repetitions, the fine high climaxes, and the excitement provided by the successive shortening of the phrase lengths up to the very end, when a return of the sturdy third phrase makes a very satisfying cadence.)

In verses 1 and 2 of the chorale (Nos. 1 and 3 in the cantata), Bach does not present the whole tune consecutively but in a "gapped" form. The lines are separated by rests (as indicated in the example above) and embedded within a much longer and more complex musical structure. Such a movement has the aspect of a meditation on the chorale verse, or an interpretation of it from a musical point of view. On a larger scale, indeed, we could think of the entire cantata as a meditation on the entire three-verse chorale.

No. 1: Chorale, Wachet auf, Ruft Uns die Stimme (*Awake, the Voice Calls to Us*) This is the most complex movement in the cantata and an impressive testimony to Bach's structural powers. The chorale itself is sung by the sopranos so slowly that it seems like a solemn framework, as though it were sounding impassively on great bells. There is more activity in the material sung by the lower voices of the chorus (the altos, tenors, and basses) and much more in the orchestra, which consists of strings, three oboes, and organ playing the continuo.

The orchestra begins with a long ritornello full of different motives, alternating between violins and oboes, while the bass keeps up a steady marchlike pace. For long stretches it is a walking bass (see page 152). Perhaps Bach meant this ritornello to suggest the approach of the wedding procession:

After the chorale begins in the sopranos, fragments of the ritornello continue to weave their way in and out of the chorus parts. And when the chorus stops for short periods between the lines of the chorale, the march can still be heard following its vigorous course.

There is an impressive place where the lower voices seem to forget themselves in joy at the word "alleluia," and the soprano has to wait with the chorale while they spin out jubilant imitations:

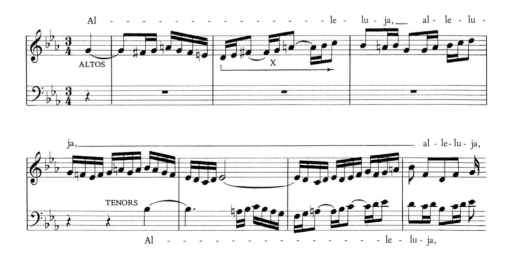

These imitations take up the most vigorous of all the motives in the original ritornello (marked x on the first musical example above). After the chorale is over, the lower voices stop, too. The orchestra concludes with a repetition of the whole ritornello. Thus the chorale is actually enclosed and solidified by a ritornello form.

No. 2: Duet, Wann Kommst Du, Mein Heil? (*When Will You Come, My Savior?*) A rather emotional recitative for tenor announces that the Bridegroom is at hand and that the girls should make ready. This really repeats the message of the previous chorale verse, No. 1, but brings it onto a more personal plane.

The duet that follows is like a tiny opera scene. The bass voice, representing the Savior, or Bridegroom, answers worried questions from the soprano, representing the Christian Soul, or one of the girls who is not quite ready yet. Bach is at his most baroque in the melodies of this duet. As we listen to the skittering solo violin of the ritornello (see the example on page 195) and the two intertwining vocal lines, we may well see winding lines before our eyes, lines swirling like the arms and legs and drapery of the baroque ceiling on pages 222–23. But a characteristically steady rhythm in the bass and continuo seems to hold rein on all the ornament and all the anxiety.

This duet is in a free type of da capo form (page 189), free in that the second A section, with the original words and music, is not exactly the same as the first (A B A′). The other duet, No. 4, is in strict da capo form (A B A).

No. 3: Chorale, Zion Hört die Wächter Singen (*Zion Hears the Watchmen Singing*) Another "gapped" chorale with ritornello, this piece uses the same general form as that of the opening movement, although it is simpler in style and texture. The ritornello consists of only one melodic line plus continuo; the chorale itself is sung by the chorus tenors only. The rest of the choir is silent. The well-known ritornello melody is both firm and gentle, and it sounds so self-sufficient that we are pleasantly surprised when it fits in with the chorale tune—a particularly clear example of how nonimitative counterpoint can make an interesting effect.

We have mentioned a number of times the tendency of baroque composers to rearrange their music for different instruments. Bach arranged this cantata movement also for organ. In this version, the ritornello is played on one set of pipes, the chorale tune on another, the continuo bass on another (the pedals).

chorale prelude

This was an economical way of making pieces of the type known as the chorale prelude, a composition for organ based on a chorale tune. Such works were a staple with the Lutheran organists of the baroque period. The congregations knew the tunes and the words so well that a wealth of religious associations would be set up simply by the organ music, even without any singing.

Bach composed dozens of chorale preludes afresh, using almost all the familiar hymns of his day. Together with his organ fugues, these pieces make up a body of organ music that by common consent far surpasses that of any other composer, of any time. Listen to Bach's organ chorale prelude *Wachet auf* after listening to the cantata movement, and see which of the two tone colors you prefer.

No. 4: Duet, Mein Freund Ist Mein (*My Friend Is Mine*) In another recitative, the bass voice reassures the Soul in an even more personal and warm tone than was used in the tenor recitative preceding the earlier duet, No. 2. And in the duet No. 4 itself, all anxiety has passed, as the voices blend happily together beneath the smiling tunes and curlicues of the solo oboe. More than one commentator has observed that as far as the music is concerned, this duet could be representing the billing and cooing of a newly married peasant couple as well as a colloquy between Soul and Savior. Perhaps that is why the piece sounds convincing.

No. 5: Chorale, Gloria Sei Dir Gesungen (*Glory Be Sung to You*) The third and last verse of the chorale is sung in a simply harmonized, homophonic version, making a very solid conclusion. This forthright statement has the effect of resolving all the doubts, tensions, and complexities noted earlier in the cantata.

Indeed, if we think back—or "listen back" in memory—we realize that Bach has arranged a deliberate succession of moods in this cantata. He has isolated a series of emotional moments and then exaggerated each emotion in a musical number. He moves from considerable tension (No. 1) to anxiety and apprehension (No. 2) to calm solidity (No. 3) to simple joy (No. 4) to exultation (No. 5). In religious terms, the Christian Soul prepares in several psychological stages for the coming of God and, after some qualms, accepts Him. It is not incorrect to speak of a dramatic progression in the cantata as a whole and to say that this has been achieved by a semioperatic form.

Bach, as we mentioned, wrote a great many church cantatas, of which about two hundred have survived. Almost all of them incorporate chorales, though some entail no more than a single, simply harmonized verse at the very end of the cantata. Others use chorales more extensively, including the well-known Cantata No. 4, *Christ lag in Todesbanden* (Christ lay in death's bonds). There are no recitatives in this cantata. The six numbers all use the words and music of the six verses of a sturdy old Easter hymn written by Martin Luther himself.

Bach's famous Passions are settings of the story of Christ's last days and His crucifixion, designed for Good Friday services. The story for each was taken word for word from one of the Gospels: hence the titles *Passion According to St. Matthew* and *Passion According to St. John.* The librettist, however, interspersed this biblical material with many recitatives, arias, choruses, and chorales. Basically, then, passions are like oratorios, except that they include chorale numbers, as church cantatas do. In the *Matthew* Passion, the sad and gentle so-called passion chorale, "O haupt voll blut und wunden" (O sacred head sore wounded), returns many times with different simple harmonizations: a wonderfully expressive devotional effect.

Finally, a favorite secular cantata by Bach, the *Coffee Cantata,* finds him in a rare unbuttoned mood. The burgher Schlendrian will let his daughter get married only if she promises to break her terrible coffee habit. Lieschen agrees, in the aria "Heute noch" ("Today, today! Dear father can I have a man Without delay?"), but somehow manages to end up with both her man and her coffee.

Cantata No. 40, Wachet auf

(1) CHORALE

Wachet auf, ruft uns die Stimme	"Awake," the voice of watchmen
Der Wächter sehr hoch auf der Zinne,	Calls us from high on the tower,
Wach auf, du Stadt Jerusalem!	"Awake, you town Jerusalem!"
Mitternacht heisst diese Stunde;	This is the very midnight hour;
Sie rufen uns mit hellem Munde:	They call to us with bright voices:
Wo seid ihr klugen Jungfrauen?	"Where are you, wise virgins?
Wohl auf, der Bräutgam kommt,	Take cheer, the Bridegroom comes,
Steht auf, die Lampen nehmt!	Arise, take up your lamps!
Alleluja!	Alleluja!
Macht euch bereit zu der Hochzeit,	Prepare yourselves for the wedding,
Ihr müsset ihm entgegengehn!	You must go forth to meet him."

RECITATIVE

Er kommt, er kommt, der Bräutgam kommt!	He comes, he comes, the Bridegroom comes!
Ihr Töchter Zions kommt heraus,	Daughters of Zion, come forth,
Sein Ausgang eilet aus der Höhe	He is hurrying from on high
In euer Mutter Haus.	Into your mother's house.
Der Bräutgam kommt, der einem Rehe	The Bridegroom comes, who like a roe
Und jungen Hirsche gleich	And a young hart
Auf denen Hügeln springt	Leaping upon the hills,
Und euch das Mahl der Hochzeit bringt.	Brings you the wedding meal.
Wacht auf, ermuntert euch!	Wake up, bestir yourselves
Den Bräutgam zu empfangen;	To receive the Bridegroom;
Dort, sehet, kommt er hergegangen.	There, look, he comes along.

(2) DUET

Soul:	(A) *Wann kommst du, mein Heil?*	When will you come, my Savior?
Jesus:	*Ich komme, dein Teil.*	I am coming, your own.
Soul:	*Ich warte mit brennendem Öle.*	I am waiting with burning oil.
	(B) *Eröffne den Saal*	Throw open the hall
	Zum himmlischen Mahl!	To the heavenly banquet!
Jesus:	*Ich öffne den Saal*	I open the hall
	Zum himmlischen Mahl.	To the heavenly banquet.
Soul:	*Komm, Jesu!*	Come, Jesus!
Jesus:	*Komm, liebliche Seele!*	Come, beloved Soul!
Soul:	(A') *Wann kommst du, (etc.)*	When will you come, (etc.)

(3) CHORALE

Zion hört die Wächter singen,	Zion hears the watchmen singing,
Das Herz tut ihr vor Freuden springen,	For joy her very heart is springing,
Sie wachet und steht eilend auf.	She wakes and rises hastily.
Ihr Freund kommt vom Himmel prächtig,	From heaven comes her Friend resplendent,
Von Gnaden stark, von Wahrheit mächtig,	Sturdy in grace, mighty in truth,

Ihr Licht wird hell, ihr Stern geht auf.　　Her light shines bright, her star ascends.
Nun komm, du werte Kron,　　Now come, you worthy crown,
Herr Jesu, Gottes Sohn,　　Lord Jesus, God's own Son,
Hosianna!　　Hosanna!
Wir folgen all zum Freudensaal　　We follow all to the joyful hall
Und halten mit das Abendmahl.　　And share in the Lord's supper.

RECITATIVE

So geh herein zu mir,　　Come enter in with me,
Du mir erwählte Braut!　　My chosen bride!
Ich habe mich mit dir　　I have pledged my troth
Von Ewigkeit vertraut!　　To you in eternity!
Dich will ich auf mein Herz,　　I will set you as a seal upon my heart,
Auf meinen Arm gleich wie ein Stiegel setzen　　And as a seal upon my arm
Und dein betrübtes Aug ergötzen.　　And restore delight to your sorrowful eye.
Vergiss, o Seele, nun die Angst, den Schmerz,　　Forget now, o Soul, the anguish, the pain,
Den du erdulden müssen;　　Which you had to suffer;
Auf meiner Linken sollst du ruhn,　　On my left you shall rest,
Und meine Rechte soll dich küssen.　　And my right shall kiss you.

(4) DUET

Soul: (A) *Mein Freund ist mein!*　　My Friend is mine!
Jesus: 　　*Und ich bin sein!*　　　　And I am thine!
Both: 　*Die Liebe soll nichts scheiden!*　　Nothing shall separate love

Soul: (B) *Ich will mit dir* ⎫ *in Himmels*　　I will with you ⎫ graze upon
　　　　　　　　　⎬ *Rosen weiden,*　　　　　　　⎬ heaven's roses,
Jesus: 　*Du sollst mit mir* ⎭　　You shall with me ⎭
Both: 　*Da Freude die Fülle, da*　　There shall be fullness of joy, there rapture!
　　　　Wonne wird sein!
Soul: (A) *Mein Freund ist mein,* (etc.)　　My Friend is mine, (etc.)

(5) CHORALE

Gloria sei dir gesungen　　*Gloria* be sung to you
Mit Menschen und englischen Zungen,　　With men's and angels' tongues,
Mit Harfen und mit Zimbeln schon.　　With harps and cymbals.
Von zwölf Perlen sind die Pforten　　Of twelve pearls are the gates
An deiner Stadt; wir sind Konsorten　　At your city; we are consorts
Der Engel hoch um deinen Thron.　　Of the angels high about your throne.
Kein Aug hat je gespürt,　　No eye has ever sensed,
Kein Ohr hat je gehört　　No ear has ever heard
Solche Freude.　　Such a delight.
Des sind wir froh, Io, io,　　Of this we rejoice, io, io,
Ewig in dulci jubilo.　　Forever *in dulci jubilo.*

The Baroque Mass

Although Bach was a Lutheran, the most immense composition he ever wrote was a Roman Catholic Mass. He began it in the hope of impressing a Catholic prince and gaining an important court position; the maneuver failed. Even masses at this time were written in a semi-operatic form—without recitatives, to be sure, but with a succession of arias, duets, and choruses. Each one expresses the emotional quality of the successive fragments of the Mass text in the usual baroque fashion.

It can be revealing to consider the differences among settings of the same text, such as the immemorial Mass text, by composers of different eras. In the Renaissance, the Mass was regarded as a coherent experience; Josquin's *Ave maris stella* Mass is level, cool, and unified in style, in spite of all its effective small-scale contrasts. The same is true of the masses of Palestrina. But the more dynamic and theatrical atmosphere of the baroque turned the Mass into a vivid series of emotional tableaus. Bach seems to be constantly shifting back and forth from agonized repentance in certain numbers to ecstatic jubilation in others. Where Josquin stands back from the Mass text and sets it to music with a sense of decorum and balance, Bach plunges in, stressing all the contrasts, paradoxes, and elements of wonder inherent in it.

BACH   Mass in B Minor: Agnus Dei (1735)

From Bach's Mass in B Minor, like Handel's *Messiah*, we can choose at random among many superb pieces on which to comment. The Sanctus is superlative: a six-voice chorus (two soprano parts, two altos, tenor, bass) with a "festive" orchestra, consisting of strings, flutes, oboes, trumpets, and drums. As the voices and instruments pursue their contrapuntal lines—some of them ornate, others emphatic, but all intricately bound together—the musical space almost seems to sway with the change of the framework harmonies determined by the continuo. We can visualize numberless angels singing praises to God ("Holy, holy, holy, Lord God of Hosts!") as they swirl around in the clouds and drapery of a great baroque ceiling—under which, indeed, this music would have been performed (see pages 222–23). As the Mass text moves on to the phrases "Heaven and earth are full of Thy glory" and "Hosanna!" Bach provides new musical ideas of similar brilliance from a seemingly inexhaustible supply.

Turning to the final part of the Mass, the Agnus Dei, we see that Bach has read the text thoughtfully and decided to emphasize the contrasts within it. The first section encompasses the words "Agnus Dei, qui tollis peccata mundi, miserere nobis" (Lamb of God, who taketh away the sins of the world, have mercy upon us). This Bach sets as a personal utterance, a grief-stricken aria for alto voice with a ritornello in the strings that seems to stumble and halt. Here it is easy to picture—indeed, it is hard not to picture—some deeply suffering sinner, prostrate in prayer, out of a baroque dramatic oratorio: Mary Magdalene, perhaps. Bach sets the second section, "Dona nobis pacem" (Give us peace), more impersonally, as a fugal chorus that expresses confidence in the glory of God and the inner peace that he will provide. The two sentiments in the two sections are never reconciled, only placed in dramatic contrast with one another.

The "Dona nobis pacem" fugue that concludes the Agnus Dei is one of the densest ever composed by Bach or anyone else. It has a tight subject imitating itself at very close time intervals:

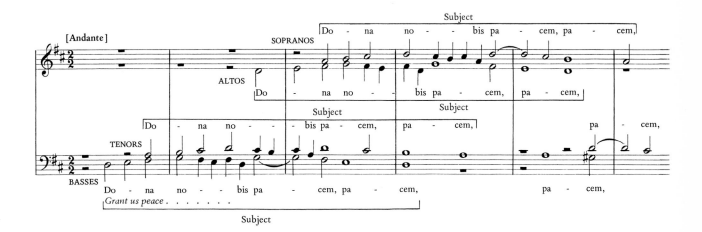

In other words, the fugue subject is presented immediately in stretto (see page 186). Usually composers reserved stretto for points of climax later in their fugues.

A fugue with words brings out those words very strongly, of course. The words are repeated over and over again with the fugue subject. In this chorus, the impression is that all the nations of the world are trooping in, one by one, with the demand for peace—and all the trumpets of the world as well: halfway through the fugue, the piled-up subject entries in the voices soar up to the roof of heaven as the trumpets add brilliant new entries of their own. This fugue has a second subject, or motive, that moves in relatively fast notes, but it has hardly any episodes. All emphasis is on the clamor for peace, endlessly repeated by the subject.

For those who like statistics, Bach's fugue brings in the subject twenty-eight times in its total of forty-six measures! This certainly counts as a rigorous structure, which would doubtless have delighted any of the eighteenth-century systematic thinkers and scientists who knew about music. Yet the effect is not one of dry calculation but rather of overwhelming glory. Think back at this point to the fugal "Amen" chorus that concludes Handel's oratorio *Messiah.* Whether you prefer Handel's more casual, bold, and loose-jointed fugue style or Bach's marvelously tight construction is largely a matter of taste. Each in his own way, these two great composers end their large works in the grandiose, exhaustive fashion that is typical of the baroque period. Each fugue makes a personal statement within the dual baroque conditions—system and structure on the one hand and grand theatrical gesture on the other.

CHAPTER 9 | The Viennese Period   I

The Viennese Period   I

In the second half of the eighteenth century, a new musical style was developed by several great composers active in Vienna, the capital of Austria. Geographically, Austria stands at the crossroads of four other musical nations: Germany, Czechoslovakia, Hungary, and Italy. In political terms, too, Vienna at the time was central. As the capital of the powerful Hapsburg Empire, covering parts of Hungary, Czechoslovakia, Yugoslavia, and Italy, it was plunged into every European conflict of the time and was exposed to all the new cultural currents and shades of opinion. During the years in question, Vienna lived through the absolutist monarchy of Empress Maria Theresa, enjoyed the liberal, "enlightened" rule of Joseph II, and was overrun by the revolutionary French armies of Napoleon. After 1815, Vienna submitted to Europe's first modern police state, the counterrevolutionary regime of Prince Metternich.

Through all this, a remarkable group of composers worked in an environment that buzzed with music. Often they worked in close personal contact with one another. Gluck, Haydn, Mozart, Beethoven, Schubert—musicians can point with pride to this galaxy of great composers, and compare the accomplishments of Viennese music with those of other such rich cultural flowerings: art in Renaissance Florence and Venice, for example, or literature in Elizabethan England.

A "CLASSICAL" STYLE?

The new musical style developed by the Viennese composers is traditionally referred to as *classical.* Recently, however, musicians and musicologists have been objecting to this term even more strongly than to the term *baroque,* and in this book we shall take the plunge and eliminate it entirely. Unlike the term *baroque,* the term *classical* can lead to real misconceptions. The word has live implications that can inhibit our appreciation of the music.

The notion that Viennese music takes its inspiration from classical times is only the first of these misconceptions. It is true that in the visual arts and literature of the time there was much interest in Greek and Roman models, and this interest extended to such areas as furniture and dress design. But even in the visual arts "neoclassicism" was only one trend among others and was part of a larger tendency, as is suggested by our illustration on page 274. In music, the influence of classical antiquity counts for so little that it can safely be ignored.

A second misconception is that a "classical" style has to be entirely serene and unemotional. But we shall see that it was exactly the Viennese composers —first Haydn and Mozart, then Beethoven and Schubert—who pioneered a new degree of personal involvement and expression in their music. Music in this period reaches a new subtlety, a new depth in its depiction of emotion. Furthermore, romantic (or at least preromantic) stirrings are already felt in the music of the late eighteenth century, as in the other arts (compare pages 329, 344, 356). Later we shall discuss briefly the "Storm and Stress" movement of the 1770s, the strongest of several early warnings of the turmoils and passions conventionally associated with the nineteenth century.

Certainly events of the time did nothing to promote serenity. Rarely has civilization been so shaken as by the revolutions of this age. Perhaps the American Revolution of 1776 was far enough away to be ignored somewhat, and perhaps the ominous effects of the Industrial Revolution were not yet apparent. But the French Revolution of 1789 traumatized the whole of Europe. As the proudest of all monarchies fell to an uneasy coalition of the middle and lower classes, the whole basis for the class structure and governance of Europe was thrown in doubt. Anarchy, atheism, socialism, the guillotining of kings, a general reign of terror—these were the specters of the time. There followed a quarter of a century of Napoleonic wars, during which Europe wondered whether revolution might overrun the world. Deep passions and ugly forces had arisen that shook human faith in reason. The arts in this period could not and did not remain calm, stable, and above the fray.

In discussing the general features of the Viennese musical style, we shall find ourselves contrasting it directly with the baroque style. Every rising generation reacts against the older generation to some extent, and this tendency is particularly clear with the music that grew up in this time of revolutions. We shall also need to bear in mind the difference, or at least the change in emphasis, between the early Viennese style of Haydn and Mozart in the 1770s and 1780s and the late Viennese style of Beethoven's music after 1800, shared from around 1815 on by Schubert.

The Character of the Viennese Style

Thoroughness, single-mindedness, and massive power are qualities that come to mind in considering late baroque music. With Viennese music, the key qualities are flexibility, variety, and contrast. These qualities can be discerned in all the elements of musical technique—rhythm, dynamics, tone color, texture, melody, and form. And a new sensitivity of feeling developed in this music as a result of its new technique.

RHYTHM

We have said before, and it bears repeating, that of all the elements of music, rhythm and motion are the ones that contribute most centrally to its effect. Viennese music is highly flexible in rhythm. Throughout a single movement or large section, the meter and tempo remain constant, but the rhythms of the various themes or of the subsections tend to contrast sharply. The first theme may move in half notes and quarters, followed abruptly by the second theme moving in eighth notes and sixteenths, and so on. (See, for example, the first music example from Mozart's Clarinet Quintet, on page 281.) Within themes, too, rhythmic surprises are frequent. The music slows down and speeds up, stops suddenly, presses forward by fits and starts, or glides by as though on ball bearings.

All this gives a sense that the music is moving in a less predictable, more exciting way than baroque music does. We shall hear evidence of this in all compositions by the Viennese composers: in Beethoven's Fifth Symphony, with its driving first theme and its gentle second one, in Mozart's vivid opera ensembles from *Don Giovanni*, and in dramatic songs such as Schubert's *Erlkönig*.

DYNAMICS

Instead of using the steady dynamics or the terraced dynamics (see page 159) of the earlier period, composers now worked extensively with gradations of volume. The words for "growing louder" (*crescendo*) and "growing softer" (*diminuendo*) first came into general use at this time. Orchestras of the mid-eighteenth century were the first to practice long crescendos—which, we are told, caused audiences to rise up from their seats in excitement. Doubtless these passages were subtly managed in terms of rhythm, too.

The clearest sign of the new flexibility in dynamics was the rise in popularity of the piano. The foremost distinction between the piano and the omnipresent harpsichord of the baroque era was in dynamics. The harpsichord could manage only one sound level, or at best a few slightly different terraced dynamics. The new *pianoforte* or *fortepiano* (loud/soft) could produce a continuous range of dynamics from soft to loud (see pages 182–83). It attracted composers because they wished their keyboard instruments to have the same flexibility in dynamics that they were teaching to their orchestras at this same period.

Even the organ, whose different sets of pipes could produce terraced dynamics most directly, depending on whether the player connected them in or left them out, was now fitted with a device to allow for crescendos and diminuendos. The mechanism was a type of Venetian blind, controlled by the player, that either muffled the sound or allowed it to come forth full blast. This *swell mechanism* was a fixture in all nineteenth- and early twentieth-century organs.

TONE COLOR: THE ORCHESTRA

The Viennese composers also devoted increasing attention to tone color. The clearest sign of this is the development of the symphony orchestra. The orchestra standardized in this period forms the basis of the orchestra of later times.

For the first time, orchestral music was distinguished clearly from chamber music. Instrumental resources could no longer be changed around so easily for any particular piece, and an orchestral piece could no longer look like a chamber music piece (remember the slow movement of Bach's *Brandenburg Concerto No. 5*). The orchestra was made more forceful and various in tone color, while chamber music groups were made more intimate and flexible.

THE VIENNESE ORCHESTRA
(As in Mozart's Overture to *Don Giovanni*)

Strings:	first violins, second violins, violas, cellos, double basses
Woodwinds:	2 flutes
	2 oboes
	2 clarinets
	2 bassoons
Brass:	2 French horns
	2 trumpets
Percussion:	2 timpani

The foundation of the Viennese orchestra was a group of *string instruments:* about twelve violins, divided into two separate groups ("first violins" and "second violins"), about four violas, and about three cellos, and a few double basses playing the same music as the cellos an octave lower.* With the strings as a framework, *woodwind instruments* were added on the outside, generally in the highest range. More or less in the spirit of decorative frosting, pairs of flutes, oboes, clarinets, and bassoons provided variety in certain melodic passages as well as strengthening the string sounds in loud passages. And *brass instruments* were added on the inside, as it were, in the middle range. Pairs of horns and trumpets gave solid support for the main harmonies, generally limiting their activity to occasions such as cadences (see page 22) when the harmonies needed to be made particularly clear. The only regular *percussion* instrument was the timpani, which played along with the brass.

Learning to identify the various instruments of the orchestra by name is not important in itself, but it does help you to distinguish the various sounds —and this certainly *is* important if you are to appreciate the increasingly sensitive use that composers made of tone color in their total musical effects. For brief descriptions of the main orchestral instruments, see pages 62–65.

---

* Today's symphony orchestras include about three times as many string instruments in each category, without a proportional increase in the winds. To play Mozart and Haydn properly, modern orchestras have to cut down on their forces sharply.

TEXTURE

The predominant texture of Viennese music is homophonic. Again and again in Viennese compositions, a single melody with a simple chordal accompaniment is heard, something that comes up much less frequently in baroque music. The new texture arose partly as a reaction against baroque polyphony. Polyphony struck the new age as heavy, pedantic, and unnecessarily complex.

But the new texture was not merely a negative reaction. It was also a positive move in the direction of flexibility, for music with many contrapuntal lines that have to fit in with one another simply cannot be fast on its feet. As a result of this simplification of texture, harmony could receive more subtle treatment than before. The reasons are of the same order: when composers did not have to find places for all notes of their chords in individual contrapuntal lines, they could more easily refine chords for their own sake.

Along with the preference for homophonic textures went an interest in rendering them more precisely. There is a great difference, obviously, between homophony made up of chords held steadily on one set of organ pipes and the same chords played in rapid, light repetition by string instruments. In their desire to calculate carefully the precise tone color given to accompaniment chords, the Viennese composers jettisoned the continuo (see page 153), which had spread its thick chord patterns over nearly all baroque music. They no longer took the easy way out, relying on the continuo player to fill in the harmony according to personal preference. Composers now wanted it filled in exactly to their own specifications.

Yet it is important to realize that Viennese composers used counterpoint, too. They used a more delicate type of counterpoint than that of the baroque, but they were not ready to give up the richness and variety of effect achieved by polyphonic textures. In fact, they gained a sharper awareness of the expressive possibilities of polyphony. For polyphony was now generally used to give the impression of tension, of one line rubbing against another. The more intense, complex texture stood out by contrast with the predominant homophonic style. The development section in Viennese sonata form, a section whose principal quality is tension, typically involves some contrapuntal textures; and sonata form was the most important musical form of the time.

MELODY: TUNES

In the melodic writing of this period, a significant feature is the emphasis on tunes. The Viennese composers stood much closer to popular and folk music than did their predecessors of the baroque. In the music of Joseph Haydn—the real founder of the new style—there is an unquenchable popular lilt that people have often traced to the folk music of his native Serbo-Croatia. Beethoven arranged dozens of folk songs for various instrumental and instrumental-vocal combinations, including Scottish, English, and Irish numbers such as *Auld lang syne, There was a jolly miller once,* and *Paddy O'Rafferty.*

It is therefore not surprising that many of the short themes in Viennese symphonies strike us as tuneful. Their phrases might, in another context, have gone on to make excellent songs. By comparison with a baroque concerto, a

Viennese symphony leaves us with a good deal more to hum or whistle as we leave the concert.

Often entire tunes were worked into larger compositions. For example, the theme and variations form (see page 283) grew popular, both for separate pieces and for movements within larger pieces. As the "theme" in this form, the Viennese composers took a regular tune (not a bass, as Bach did in his Passacaglia for Organ, discussed on pages 201–5). Sometimes they even took actual popular songs or folk songs. Beethoven wrote variations on *God save the king* and *Rule Britannia.* Mozart wrote variations on *Twinkle, twinkle little star,* or *Baa baa black sheep,* which he knew as the French song *Ah, vous dirai-je, maman.* All composers of the time wrote variations on current hits from the opera.

Another form that grew more important was the rondo (see page 277). It, too, takes its point of departure from a full-fledged tune, which comes back many times during the movement in a more or less constant form. A descendant of the baroque *rondeau* form (see page 181), the rondo falls into A B A C A D A or A B A C A B A etc. form. Rondo tunes are usually rather lighthearted.

Finally, there is a special convention established by Viennese composers for symphonies, sonatas, and chamber music pieces: the inclusion of a dance movement in nearly every one. Music lovers tend to take this convention for granted, but we ought to notice that it represents a real change from the baroque. Baroque composers had also written dances, as we have seen, but they had segregated them into dance suites, in which whole sets of complex and simple dances stand side by side. Other important baroque genres, such as the concerto grosso and the trio sonata, do not necessarily include any dances.

The one dance that figured in the earlier Viennese symphonies and sonatas was the *minuet.* This dance began as one of the simplest baroque types (Handel used one to end the *Fireworks Music:* see page 221). Some Viennese minuets are simple and genuinely tuneful; others are less so, and Beethoven transformed the minuet into an explosive kind of movement that he christened *scherzo* (joke). But even with these reservations, the omnipresent minuets and scherzos of the Viennese period presented a clear mandate for tunefulness and simple melodic structure.

MUSICAL FORM

Composers whose ideals were flexibility and variety found themselves facing a special problem: How was all the variety to be held together as a coherent whole? This was a matter of musical form, which is the aspect of music that concerns its total extension in time.

Viennese composers worked with contrasts of themes, rhythms, tone color, dynamics, tonality, and all the rest. By the use of certain principles and certain formal schemes, they managed to make all these contrasts live together harmoniously in the same universe. These two principles—contrast and coherence—can be seen as a large-scale application of the aesthetic maxim "unity in variety."

The main formal scheme developed in this period is the *sonata-allegro form,* or *sonata form.* We shall examine it in detail later. At this point, we need only observe that although sonata form and other Viennese forms might appear at first to be rigid and constraining, at least on the conceptual level, they did not actually work out that way. In fact these forms accommodated or made possible a quite amazing variety of music. There are sonata-form movements that sound elegant and fluid, and others that sound forceful and driven by fate; there are playful theme-and-variation movements and melancholy ones. There are even tragic-sounding minuets.

Sonata form, in particular, seems not to have inhibited the Viennese composers at all, but rather to have served them as a stimulus to endless possibilities. Like the sonnet in literature and the cross-shaped plan in church architecture, mentioned on pages 50–51, the sonata form has an "outer form" flexible enough to encompass a great range of different "inner forms."

Working to achieve coherence, after having used so much contrast, the Viennese composers saw the value of including long passages of repetition in their music. This, too, might strike some people as unnecessarily formal. But to produce a satisfying effect, a generous amount of repetition is required here, just as it is in the architecture of a Greek temple or a Cape Cod cottage. Without these large-scale repetitions, the music would really lack stability and a sense of coherence.

Of course, this is hard to prove, since the composers didn't write any music that does, in fact, lack coherence. A test can be suggested, however. If you listen carefully to about half of a Viennese symphony or sonata movement and then take the stylus off the phonograph, the effect will be distinctly frustrating. Some connection will be missing; you want to know how the music "comes out"; the composer's real point has not yet been driven home. But although it may be unconventional to say so, you can listen to half of a baroque piece and still get a fair enough idea of the composer's meaning without staying to the end.

EXPRESSIVE QUALITY

On first hearing a variety of Viennese music, it is not uncommon for listeners to be impressed as much by the differences between the earlier and the later styles as by the similarities. The music of Haydn and Mozart may seem light and neat, possibly charming, and possibly (though mistakenly!) somewhat superficial. Beethoven is likely to seem forceful and dramatic. But on listening further, we discover works by Mozart, too, that are passionate, intense, forceful, and dramatic—some of his greatest works, in fact: the Symphony in G Minor and the opera *Don Giovanni* are famous examples. Whereas some of Beethoven's greatest compositions emanate deep serenity and gentleness. One that will be discussed later is the Piano Sonata in E Major, Op. 109.

Variety, once again, is a central fact about the expressive quality of the music by the Viennese composers. Moreover, after getting to know one of their pieces well—really well—we may become disenchanted with any easy label that critics attach to it. Music that seems "passionate" at one moment can easily become "serene" at the next. The music changes—that was the point of our discussion of Viennese musical form—and it changes in a way that indeed seems to mirror emotional experience. For if we attempt to analyze such experience within ourselves, we will have to acknowledge that it is constantly changing, complex, and fluid. Feeling is never static.

The Enlightenment

The Enlightenment is the name given to an important current of thought in eighteenth-century Europe and America. It developed out of the faith in reason that had led to the great scientific discoveries of the baroque period. Now, however, the emphasis veered away from the purely intellectual and scientific toward the social sphere. Less intent on controlling natural forces than on turning them to universal benefit, people tried to use their reason to solve questions of public morality, education, sociology, and especially political science.

The American Constitution and the Federalist Papers constitute the Enlightenment's most tangible and impressive products. This period also saw the beginning of several social science subjects: economics (Adam Smith) and demography (Malthus). Meanwhile scientific research moved in the direction of technology, which put science to a social use. By 1800, the Industrial Revolution was well underway.

Social injustice came under strong fire in the eighteenth century. So did entrenched religion—and not only from intellectuals. Many people turned to Methodism, the new popular religion concentrating on salvation, evangelism, and the Christian life. This met their needs more closely than did the rituals and doctrinal subtleties that dogged both Catholic and traditional Protestant worship, each in its own way.

Meanwhile, philosophers expressed skepticism about miracles, hellfire, the sacraments, and so on, such as had never been voiced before. There were currents of agnosticism and even outright atheism.

> Mock on, Mock on, Voltaire, Rousseau:
> Mock on, Mock on: 'tis all in vain!
> You throw the sand against the wind,
> And the wind blows it back again. . . .

wrote William Blake, incensed by Enlightenment attacks and satires on religion. The names of these two French thinkers are always mentioned in connection with the Enlightenment: Voltaire (pictured to the left) the older and

more far-ranging, Rousseau (pictured here) the younger and more equivocal.

An amazingly diverse and influential man of letters, Voltaire produced a stream of philosophical, scientific, and legal essays, satires, stories (*Candide*), plays, poems, tracts, and slanted history, all in the service of a tireless crusade for tolerance and humanity. Judicial torture, for example, was repealed in France owing to Voltaire's attacks.

The activities of Rousseau were more focused: whatever his subject, this passionate man always came around to blasting the social institutions of his day as forces stifling the individual. He was Europe's first self-announced "alienated" intellectual; perhaps no other has ever impressed his contemporaries more. Rousseau was something of a composer, too, and a widely-read music critic. Predictably, he favored simple music, close to the heart of the "natural man" and far from what he considered the repressive formalism of late baroque music. If Rousseau had been born in our time, he would be turning up as an aging, argumentative fan at pop-music events.

After the middle of the eighteenth century, concert music, too, moved closer to the "natural man." One thinks of the dances in Viennese symphonies, and the simple, moving, hymnlike melodies in many Haydn and Beethoven slow movements (see pages 276, 296, 302, and 306). Beethoven's Ninth (*Choral*) Symphony includes a famous hymn to universal brotherhood, the "Ode to Joy." One could also say that the more precise psychological depiction of Mozart's operas reflects the new respect for individual human nature.

This is not to say that Mozart, Haydn, and Beethoven were directly influenced by Rousseau. If they had read his criticism, they would have sniffed, and if they had heard his music, they would have laughed. Yet Rousseau, Voltaire, and other thinkers of the time radically changed the intellectual climate, and this was something composers and their audiences reacted to, whether they knew it or not.

With baroque music, perhaps, static words such as "mournful" and "jubilant" will do, more or less. The baroque composer distills emotion and projects it with relative simplicity—with something of the same single-minded intensity as is employed by a great actor, as we have suggested (see page 197). In presenting shifting feelings, equivocations, conflicts, and resolutions, the Viennese composer is the more sensitive psychologist.

Looking at the vivid portrait busts by the sculptor Houdon on pages 252, 253, 286, and 287, anyone might despair of guessing his "secret" and yet feel sure that in addition to his technical skill, he possessed unusual powers of discernment into human personality and feeling. With his contemporaries, the great Viennese composers, the secret certainly begins with their exciting new flexibility of musical technique. But over and above technique, each in his own way drew upon remarkable stores of human insight. For many listeners, the music of these composers rings truer in emotional terms than almost any other music written before or since.

Wolfgang Amadeus Mozart (1756–1791)

As is well known, Mozart displayed extraordinary musical talent at an early age and was taken around Europe as a child prodigy. He played, improvised, and composed special music for Vienna, Munich, Amsterdam, Venice, and Rome. He charmed Queen Marie Antoinette, and he delighted the English so much that his London concert tour was extended for longer than a year. Without knowing it, young Mozart was placed in the position of being the harbinger of a whole new concept of the musician, the concept of "artist" rather than "artisan." Yet he came from a solid, lower-middle-class musical family, and his father's intention was always to have Wolfgang follow in his footsteps as court musician to the Archbishop of Salzburg, in central Austria.

In London, Mozart was the subject of a learned essay on infant psychology by an eccentric scholar of the time named Daines Barrington. Alas, while people were much intrigued by unusual talent in the child, they were not yet ready to respond to genius in the adult. Mozart's adult life was one long disappointment. He himself contributed to this by giving up his court position and going to Vienna, the center of the musical universe, where he tried to make a career for himself as an independent musician.

By this action, Mozart seemed to be saying that it was impossible for the artist to continue in a servant role and that genius must work untrammeled. Even Handel had not cut himself off entirely from the traditional bonds, and Handel, a bachelor, was much better able to take care of himself than was Mozart, who was impractical, sensitive, "difficult" in personal relationships, and married to a woman who was less than effective at money management. Despite some moments of success, Mozart lived in poverty and illness, dying after only ten years in Vienna at the age of thirty-five.

Of all the great composers, Mozart is the hardest to characterize and the hardest to get to know. Perhaps there has to be one great composer who wears a

Mona Lisa smile. But behind the smile—underneath the light and formal sur-face of much of his music—there is a fantastic intelligence at work, and the more one listens, the more one marvels at the shades of subtle feeling that Mo-zart is able to convey. What is more, there is a considerable body of his music that is not light at all—dark, intense compositions that demolish the old-time view of Mozart as the composer of frivolous charm and nothing else.

Mozart wrote many letters that have been preserved, and in them he ap-pears sharp and sensitive, good-humored and self-aware, shrewd and sympa-thetic about people and events—enormously likable, in fact, even today, though he stands so far away from us in time. It is no accident that he was a special master of opera. Mozart could depict psychological character in music with a skill that has never been exceeded. We may come to feel that his activi-ties as an opera composer spilled over into his instrumental compositions, giv-ing them, too, a vivid sense of personality in spite of exteriors that may appear formal and restrained.

MOZART Overture to *Don Giovanni* (1786) SIDE 7

The opera *Don Giovanni* contains some of Mozart's most serious and even tragic music, as we might guess at once from the impressively solemn slow music that begins the overture. We mentioned on page 180 that operas and oratorios in all periods begin with an orchestral number, the overture; *Don Giovanni* is no exception. The solemn slow section of this overture leads into a longer section in fast tempo.

This introduces us immediately to the vivacity and high contrast that mark the Viennese style. The delicate, yet very alert-sounding opening theme ends with a little wind-instrument fanfare that contrasts abruptly:

We can almost hear one set of characters mocking another. As the music rushes ahead, there are sharp changes in dynamics and decided stops in the rhythm, stops that announce the arrival of new themes. After one of these stops, another theme, bristling with internal contrast, appears:

The gruff beginning and the twittering continuation give the effect of speedy repartee. Thus there is actually sharp contrast *within* these themes, short as they are, as well as contrast *between* one theme and the next. "Tuneful" is not a word we would apply to this overture, perhaps, except for one small idea:

This might have turned into a pleasant tune, like a folk song, if Mozart had not been more interested in a total effect of helter-skelter activity.

All the themes are presented in a homophonic texture, accompanied by the simplest of chordal backgrounds. But, as the music proceeds, the gruff part in the second example also figures in extended contrapuntal passages. As for tone color, the orchestral sound glitters constantly, whether in loud passages or in soft. Better yet, tone color is used in an integral way to bring out the character of the musical material. The fanfare in the first example would sound pale if it were not played by the wind instruments, in contrast to the strings earlier in the theme. The contrapuntal treatments of the second example would lack bite if the imitations were not staggered between strings and winds.

Sonata Form

sonata form

The fast part of Mozart's Overture to *Don Giovanni* is also an example of sonata form. This will require discussion at some length, for sonata form is the most important form developed by the Viennese composers. It was pioneered by Haydn, treated by Mozart with his own elegant simplicity, and transformed by Beethoven and Schubert. We shall see examples by all of these masters; Mozart's are the easiest to begin with.

Characteristically, sonata form is the form that most exploited the interest of the Viennese composers in contrast. In particular, sonata form uses contrast of thematic material and contrast of tonality, or key (see pages 46–48).

There is no problem in understanding what is meant by contrast of thematic material. A Viennese composer may start a piece with a theme consisting of no more than a few memorable rhythms, and then directly afterward go into a long suave tune. He achieves an effect of contrast simply by means of the juxtaposition.

Key contrast, however, is a more difficult concept. It is a familiar fact that melodies can be played in different keys, which sound different in some sense. (You can verify this by picking out a tune at the piano—*My country 'tis of thee*, for instance—starting first with the note C and then with the note F♯.) But contrast means more than mere difference: it implies a feeling of opposition, even confrontation. How does a composer obtain such a feeling between two keys and use it for aesthetic purposes?

EXPOSITION

exposition

A movement in sonata form begins with a large section of music called the exposition, because its basic material is presented or "exposed" here. First, a main theme is presented in the first key, which is that of the piece as a whole (for example, in Mozart's Symphony in G Minor, the first key is G minor).

first theme

This first theme may be a tune or a group of small phrases that sound as though they want to grow into a tune. Or the theme may consist of nothing more than a few small motives (see page 22) of a memorable rhythmic character.

Soon after the first theme is well established, there is a change of key, or *modulation,* as it is called, which gives a sense of dynamic forward movement.

bridge

The subsection of the exposition that accomplishes this is called the bridge or *transition.* The composer tries not to make the modulation too smooth, at least in rhythm, so that there will be some tension in the way the new themes, now to be introduced, will "set" in the new key. To contribute to this tension, the new themes generally contrast with the first theme in melody and rhythm, as well as in key.

second group
second theme
cadence theme

The group of themes in the new key is called the second group. The most striking of them is usually called the second theme. The last one, which is always constructed so that it makes a very solid ending, is the cadence theme or *closing theme.* The end of the exposition is typically marked by a loud series of repeated cadences. The composer wants listeners to know exactly where they are at this point.

DEVELOPMENT

development

The following section, the development, works with, or "develops," earlier themes and motives. These are broken up, recombined, extended, and in general shown in unexpected and often exciting new contexts. There is likely to be much use made of counterpoint. In tonality, the development section moves around restlessly; there are continual modulations, changes of key. We have the impression of a purposeful search for the right position for the music.

After a time—usually after the tension has been built up considerably—the last modulation of the development section returns to the first key, in preparation for the recapitulation. The passage that accomplishes this is called the

retransition

retransition. The crucial function of the retransition is to discharge the tension and prepare for the recapitulation to come. It is amazing how many ways the Viennese composers found to make this important juncture of the form seem fresh and exciting.

RECAPITULATION

With a real sense of relief or resolution, we next hear the themes and other elements of the exposition come back in their original order (or something that is close to their original order). Hence the name for this third section, the

recapitulation

recapitulation.

There is an important difference, however: everything now remains in the same key (the first key). Stability of key is very welcome after the instability of the development section—and what is more, the old material now has a slightly new look. Thus the strong feeling of balance between the exposition and the recapitulation (A B A′) is a weighted balance, because the second A section (A′) has achieved a new solidity.

coda   If even more solidity seems to be needed, another section is added at the end, as though to deliver concluding remarks on the subject matter of the movement. This coda (meaning "tailpiece"; a general term, not restricted to sonata form) is generally subsidiary and quite brief in Mozart's work, but Beethoven and Schubert expanded it greatly.

Diagrams of various sorts have been devised to try to clarify sonata form. Here is one, in which the changes of key are indicated by different vertical levels of a continuous line or band:

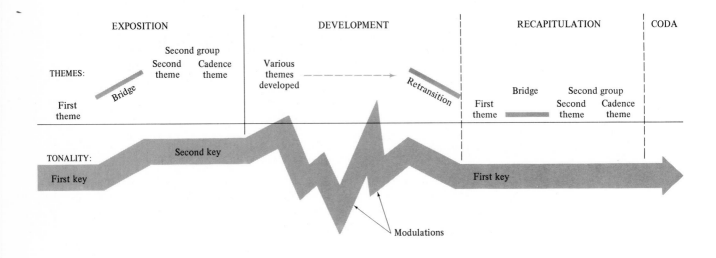

It is surely no accident that the terminology of sonata form—exposition, development, recapitulation—resembles the terminology of the drama. Sir Donald Tovey, one of the most perceptive writers about music, observes that Viennese music has a "dramatic" quality, compared to the "architectural" quality of baroque music. In a complex Viennese sonata, the themes seem almost like people to whom things are happening. They seem to change, grow, have adventures, and react in relation to other themes.

Listening again to the Overture to *Don Giovanni*, we can hear how the fast section of this falls into sonata form and how this form holds the dizzy contrasts of the piece together as a convincing and interesting whole. It may help to follow the line score on pages 260–61. Read each line across the double-page spread.

Exposition The main theme appears twice, but the second time, instead of being mocked by the wind instrument fanfares, it shoots off purposefully in a new direction. After a firm stop, the *bridge* commences with an especially busy rhythm, forecasting its role in making the modulation. Note also the abrupt changes in dynamics.

Another firm stop, and the *second theme* makes its sharp contrast to everything that has gone before, in terms of both melody and key. (This is the "gruff" and "twittering" passage illustrated by the second music example on page 255.) After a brief dialogue between flute and oboe comes the loud *cadence theme* (a part of the second group). It sounds conclusive, and a high-spirited, amusing passage of fanfares makes it sound doubly so.

Development This begins directly with the second theme. At the very second playing of the gruff part of this theme (line 5, measure 5), an interesting melodic change occurs—a "development." Soon a contrapuntal treatment of this gruff part begins to modulate repeatedly. Underneath the polyphony in the winds, we may be able to hear the other part of the second theme twittering away in the strings simultaneously. (By the way, this part of the second theme sounds suspiciously like a part of the main theme; see line 1, measures 6 and 7.) The modulations land in a tentative-sounding key.

Here the main theme is played, complete with fanfares (line 6). Then another modulation prepares for a series of modulating sequences (see page 21) on the second theme. These add an unexpectedly serious note—a real "development" in mood, we might say (line 7). After all this activity, a *retransition* high in the strings leads us with a sense of relief back to the original key and the main theme, in its original form once again, at the recapitulation.

Recapitulation As is often the case with Mozart, the recapitulation in this overture follows the exposition closely. Mozart makes the minimum number of changes to achieve the all-important sense of stability by keeping all themes and sections in the original key. Can you hear where these changes come, without looking at the line score?

Only one is really obvious, and this change is of a kind that would never occur in a symphony. It is conceivable only in an opera overture. After the cadence theme at the end of the recapitulation, suddenly the second theme appears and modulates once again, rather slyly, leading to a mysterious halt that breathes expectancy. The point is that the curtain goes up at this very moment, to reveal a mysteriously darkened stage. The mood of the first scene is going to be very different from the brightness of the overture. Mozart carries off a dramatic stroke even before the curtain goes up, by running the overture directly into the action rather than coming to a formal stop.*

---

* One is irresistibly drawn into the opera at this point! However, for class purposes some may prefer to postpone the subject of opera and now examine some other movements in sonata form and in other Viennese forms, beginning on page 271.

Mozart, Overture to Don Giovanni: Fast Section

read across page

TRANSITION TO ACT I INTRODUCTION:

* Same music as the previous measure

Vienna

The Austrian Empire in 1786, showing the importance and centrality of Vienna. Also shown are sites associated with the great Viennese composers:

Salzburg, the beautiful city where Mozart was born, which is today a favorite tourist attraction largely on account of that fact. Although Salzburg is really a part of Austria, it used to be an independent state ruled by an archbishop, and so was not included within the Austrian Empire.

Eisenstadt, the location of the country palace of the Esterházy family outside Vienna, where Haydn worked for so many years of his life. For a painting of an opera performance in the Esterházy palace theater, with Haydn at the harpsichord, see pages 268–69.

Bonn, Beethoven's birthplace, at that time a center of liberal Enlightenment thought. Today it is the capital of West Germany.

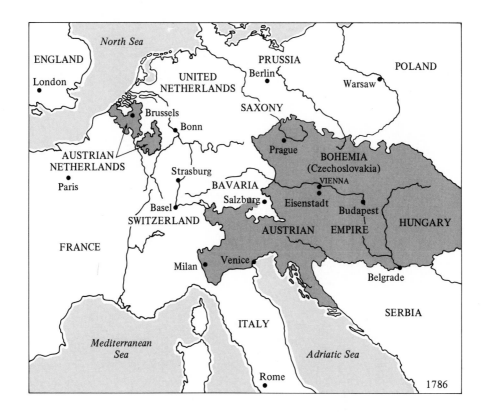

Opera Buffa

In the late eighteenth century, comic opera grew to equal in importance the serious opera that had monopolized the grandiose theaters of the baroque. The new flexibility of style was well suited to the casual, swift, and lifelike effects that are the essence of comedy. Mozart wrote some German comic operas; he also composed Italian comic operas for Vienna, just as Handel—another German—had once written Italian serious operas for London.

opera buffa

Serious Italian opera was called *opera seria;* comic Italian opera was called opera buffa. The techniques employed in Mozart's *Don Giovanni* are the techniques of *opera buffa,* techniques that could have been made possible only by the new style.

MOZART *Don Giovanni* (1786)

SIDES 7,8

Mozart wrote *Don Giovanni* in 1786 for Prague, a city where, for the moment, his music was more popular than it was in Vienna. It is a very unusual work. Neither wholly a comic opera nor wholly a tragic one, it is a thought-provoking mixture of both—what might be called today a "dark comedy." It seems to represent Mozart's opinion that events have both an element of farce and an element of tragedy, and that life's experiences cannot be safely pigeonholed. We have already seen evidence of this ambivalence in the overture, with its two sharply contrasted sections, and we shall see more evidence in other numbers of the opera.

The story gave Mozart his cue. Don Giovanni is the Italian name for Don Juan, the semi-legendary Spanish lover. The rambling tale of his endless escapades and conquests is meant to stir up incredulous laughter, often with a bawdy undertone; certainly the subject belongs in *opera buffa.* But in his compulsive, utterly selfish pursuit of women, Don Juan ignores the rules of society, morality, and God. He commits crimes and sins—and not only against the women he seduces. In one instance, he kills the father of one of these women.

This action—the killing of the Commandant—is taken as the symbol of his generally evil life. As the legend goes, Don Juan, when hiding in a graveyard, is reproached by the marble statue that has been erected over the Commandant's grave. He arrogantly invites the statue to dinner; the statue comes and drags him off to hell. On the literal level we may find this hard to take, but below the surface there is a serious allegory, indeed a profound one, which is stressed by Mozart's music.

INTRODUCTION TO ACT I

ensemble

After the curtain rises during the last measures of the overture (see page 259), the opera's first number, or introduction, is an ensemble. This is a general name for musical numbers in opera sung by two or more people, in which some sort of action is incorporated. We saw an example in Handel's *Acis and Galatea,* the unusual trio which indeed foreshadows the spirit if not the technique of the Viennese *opera buffa* ensemble.

An ensemble depicts different sentiments of the various characters simultaneously (in *Acis*, the gentle endearments of the lovers versus the rage of Polyphemus). The music also depicts these sentiments changing, for, in the course of an ensemble, the action proceeds and the situation changes. Almost always this involves musical changes—in key, in themes, and even in tempo. One of the most potent forms developed by the Viennese composers, the *opera buffa* ensemble extended the range of musical drama immeasurably.

The darkened stage reveals a single character. From his grumbles, we can tell that he is a servant, the traditional comic servant in the drama of all ages. Always work, never a word of thanks, no sleep, bad food—a marvelous musical figure depicts his complaints:

The nagging quality achieved by the sudden fortes and sforzatos and the jerky rhythm would be impossible without the flexibility of the Viennese style. (The actor could invent some action to synchronize with these sforzatos; for instance, he could use his cane to slash away spitefully at an innocent tree.)

This music is over in a moment, and a fragment of real tune shows what is really eating our man. "Voglio far il gentiluomo!" he sings: "I want to play the gentleman"—the gentleman who, he goes on to tell us, is in the house with the lady while he, Leporello, has to stand guard outside. In a stroke we have Leporello's character, the clue to all his actions in the opera: he wants to be Don Giovanni. Later, when he comes to sing his big aria, Leporello cannot even talk about himself, but instead spins a fantasy about his master's amorous adventures.

But for all his intensely human features, Leporello is also a bit of a clown, as we can tell from the "no, no, no's" injected into his complaining. Hearing a noise, he goes into hiding. There is a vigorous modulation and change of theme as Don Giovanni runs onto the stage, trying to shake himself free from the grasp of Donna Anna, the latest of his interests. Just how far Don Giovanni has gotten with Donna Anna is a famous unanswered question, but in any case she is determined to unmask him in order to identify him and put in motion the customary Spanish revenge. There is a new dark urgency to the music as they argue in angry, short musical phrases, sometimes singing separately, sometimes together.

DONNA ANNA:
Come fu - ria dis - pe - ra - ta, dispe - ra - ta ti sa - prò per - se - gui - tar.
Like a desperate avenging fury I shall seek you out!

DON GIOVANNI:
Questa fu - ria dis - pe - ra - ta mi vuol far pre - ci - - pi - tar.
This desperate creature means to ruin me.

LEPORELLO:
Stà a veder che il liber - tino mi farà precipi - tar, stà a veder che il liber - tino mi farà precipi - tar.
We'll see how the villain is going to ruin me...

Meanwhile, Leporello chatters away simultaneously in a faster rhythm, as shows up clearly in the example above. He is half enjoying the scene, though he knows it may spell trouble. This juxtaposition of different sentiments—the two principals on the one hand, Leporello on the other—shows how vividly *opera buffa* ensembles can point up dramatic situations.

Another modulation and another deepening change of mood: Donna Anna's father, the Commandant, has been awakened by her shouts. He enters with sword drawn. When Don Giovanni refuses to fight an old man, the Commandant calls him a coward, an insult that cannot be borne. As the two Spanish grandees square off, Leporello's background remarks (words and music) take on a significant new tone: he is now genuinely frightened. The music tells us that the duel is somber and formal, fought according to the rules of swordsmanship. A loud dissonant chord is held for a moment in the orchestra, and we know that the Commandant has been mortally wounded.

The last section of the introduction, a trio (Donna Anna has run off), allows the three men to stop and think and express their individual reactions. Tempo and mood change completely. The Commandant groans his last; Leporello mumbles in horror; Don Giovanni muses with a strange mixture of grimness and sympathy on the incredible course of events. Since all of these three male roles are assigned to the bass voice, or to the slightly higher bass-baritone, the tone color is especially dark and strange. Though this trio lasts only a short time, it stays in the memory as one of the most haunting parts of the opera. One feels that Mozart has made his characters equal to the emotional demands of a sudden, meaningless death.

The overture, we remember, had not really stopped but had merged into the beginning of the introduction. Now the introduction itself trails off without a true cadence into a passage of recitative, as Don Giovanni and Leporello try to collect themselves in the darkness. Plain recitative, accompanied only by cello and harpsichord, makes a wonderful contrast with the preceding tragic intensity as the two men get back to the glum realities—enlivened by some bad jokes from Leporello, which are not appreciated by Don Giovanni. This abruptly restores the mood of comedy in which Leporello's grumbling had begun the opera. As the opera continues, there are constant abrupt changes of this kind.

DUET, "LÀ CI DAREM LA MANO"

Operas depend on memorable tunes, as well as on musical drama. The greatest opera composers are able to write melodies that are not only beautiful in themselves but also further the drama at the same time.

Perhaps the most famous tune in *Don Giovanni*, "Là ci darem la mano" (There you'll give me your hand), comes in a duet (another ensemble) in which Don Giovanni attempts to seduce another woman, Zerlina. The simple, almost childlike quality of this tune gives us an insight into the Don's "line," for he adopts this tone for Zerlina because she is a simple peasant girl (though not, it turns out, as simple as he thinks). And the way the melody is divided up between the two singers shows us how gently and yet irresistibly Don Giovanni is able to apply his amorous pressure.

In the recitative preceding the duet, Don Giovanni invites Zerlina to his castle and promises (of course) to marry her and make her into a lady. Then he sings his first stanza, to the simple tune that manages to combine ardor and seductiveness with a delicate sense of banter. He knows that what she wants out of an affair is fun, not deep passion. When Zerlina sings the same tune, we know she is hooked; but she hesitates. This is expressed by tiny rhythmic changes, and by her reluctance to finish up the tune in eight measures; she hesitates for two more. Giovanni grows more insistant and romantic in his second stanza, and Zerlina hastily checks him with little interruptions. When she says she is worried about Masetto, her peasant lover, the woodwinds comment ironically.

So the duet continues: Giovanni presses more and more ardently, Zerlina keeps drawing back, or at least pretending to do so. How sorry for herself she sounds when she at last says, "non son più forte, non son più forte, non son più forte" (I'm not strong enough any more)! A second later she falls happily into Giovanni's arms, echoing his "andiam" (let us go). The innocent love that they say they will now celebrate is depicted by a charming rustic melody in a faster tempo. But this too has a delicious sensuous undertone, expressed by the orchestra after the singers' first phrase in the new tempo.

No need to worry about Zerlina. She is never made into a lady, but she does not lose her Masetto, either. After Masetto has been beaten up by Don Giovanni, she wins him over with a seductive aria of her own that Giovanni would have admired.

GIOVANNI:	*Là ci darem la mano,*	There [*in the castle*] you'll give me your hand,
	Là mi dirai di sì!	There you'll tell me yes!
	Vedi, non è lontano;	Look, it isn't far—
	Partiam, ben mio, da quì!	Let's go there, my dear!
ZERLINA:	*Vorrei, e non vorrei;*	I want to, yet I don't want to;
	Mi trema un poco il cor;	My heart is trembling a little;
	Felice, è ver, sarei,	It's true, I would be happy—
	Ma può burlarmi ancor.	But he could be joking with me.
GIOVANNI:	*Vieni, mio bel diletto!*	Come, my darling!
ZERLINA:	*Mi fa pietà Masetto . . .*	I feel sorry for Masetto . . .

GIOVANNI:	*Io cangerò tua sorte.*	I shall change your lot!
ZERLINA:	*Presto non son più forte.*	Suddenly I'm not strong enough any more!
BOTH:	*Andiam, andiam, mio bene,*	Let us go, my dear,
	A ristorar le pene	And relieve the pains
	D'un innocente amor.	Of an innocent love.

FINALE TO ACT II

Let us not attempt to recount the whole complicated plot of *Don Giovanni*. The hero pursues several more women, but ultimately things close in on him. In numerous ensembles and arias, some serious, some comic, the personalities of the characters are all made marvelously clear through the music. At last comes the scene in which the Commandant's statue arrives to dine with Don Giovanni and Leporello, in the finale of act II, the last act.

finale   The word finale is used in music with two similar meanings. It can refer to the last movement of a work with several movements, such as a concerto grosso or a symphony. Or it can refer to the ensemble that concludes an act in an *opera buffa* (or any opera of later times). *Opera buffa* finales are the longest and most complex of ensembles, usually involving everyone in the cast and encompassing an entire lengthy scene of dramatic action.

    Only after the act II finale has been going on for some time, in a spirit of slapstick comedy, does the statue finally arrive, on a loud dissonant chord held in the orchestra. This chord is especially chilling if we remember it as the same one we heard when the Commandant was killed, in the act I introduction. We certainly remember the music he now sings as the same solemn music we first heard at the beginning of the overture:

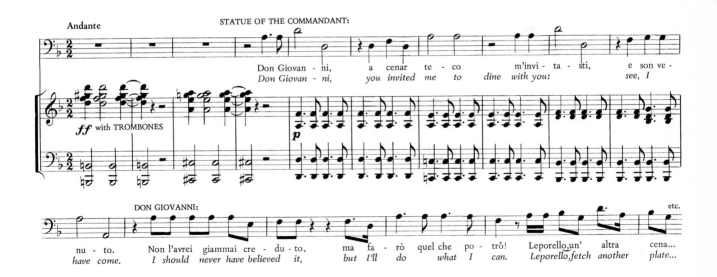

Like a recapitulation in sonata form, the return of this earlier music helps make the opera into a coherent whole, with a consistent message.

Opera Buffa

A performance of an *opera buffa* at the Esterházy castle near Vienna, probably a work by Joseph Haydn, and probably in 1775. Haydn worked for the Esterházy family for most of his life. The composer himself is shown playing the harpsichord.

Light and flexible, comic opera (*opera buffa*) typified the operatic world of the late eighteenth century, just as heroic opera (*opera seria*) characterized the baroque. If we place this picture next to the illustration of the baroque opera on page 175, everything in the comparison seems to stress the difference. Instead of the grandiose, architectural set designed for great princes and princesses, we have here an intimate and unassuming country scene, well stocked with painted animals. The people are grouped on the stage lightheartedly, in contrast to the self-serious poses of the baroque actors. The young Italian ladies are clearing up some comic complications with the visiting Turks.

The colors show a new lightness of spirit, too. Instead of the deep, rich tints of the baroque picture, this one employs light blues, greens, and yellows, with the charming brick-colored coats of the orchestra men making a bright contrast, which we might be tempted to compare with a musical contrast in the Viennese style. Even the architecture of the theater seems to be on the light side. The big columns are flattened out and marbled so that they do not attract much attention to themselves.

In the gripping scene that follows, each character sings quite different music. The statue delivers slow rhythms that are truly marble-encased. Don Giovanni speaks in vigorous, manly accents. Meanwhile, Leporello, from underneath the dinner table, chatters in terror and even makes compulsive jokes. When the statue invites Don Giovanni to dinner with him, Leporello babbles, "Oibò! oibò! tempo non ha, scusate!" (Too bad! too bad! he hasn't the time, please excuse him!)

As the statue demands repeatedly that Don Giovanni repent ("Pentiti! pentiti!"), the orchestra plays again the somber music accompanying the duel in the act I introduction. Don Giovanni proudly refuses. The music gets faster and more furious. A chorus is heard from the underworld, flames burst out, and Don Giovanni sinks screaming into hell. His final cry is parodied by a shriek from Leporello—terrified, but quite safe—and, after this grisly scene ends, there is another sudden switch to the world of comedy as the various characters return to sing (among other things) a cheerful moral: "That's the way all sinners end up."

The trouble is, we are still shaken by the statue. The musical pressure he applies is terribly impressive, and Don Giovanni's bravery in resisting this reveals itself in every musical phrase he utters. Sinner or not, he has a consistency and integrity that we cannot help admiring. Don Giovanni is an "existential man," who refuses to live by the "absurd" standards of society and follows his own course—here, frank self-gratification—to the end, even if it dooms him. The "absurdity" has been made very clear by the comedy. Don Giovanni simply could not repent his ways and never engage with another woman.

Is this something that we in the twentieth century are reading into this old *opera buffa?* We would never do so if Mozart's music were not so sensitive and so convincing. The music is so "intelligent" that we cannot help thinking closely and sympathetically about all the people in Mozart's operas—not only Don Giovanni but also Leporello and all the others.

Joseph Haydn (1732–1809)

Haydn was a member of yet another musical family. His brother Michael also became an important composer, who, as it happens, worked beside Mozart's father at the court of the Archbishop of Salzburg. Joseph for most of his life served a noble family of Hungarian music lovers, the Esterházys, whose estate was situated forty miles outside of Vienna. An unusual painting of an opera performance at this estate is reproduced on pages 268–69; Haydn is conducting from the harpsichord.

The Esterházy family also had palaces in the city, and Haydn was the most famous composer around Vienna when Mozart arrived there in 1781 and became his friend. A year after Mozart's death, in 1792, young Beethoven came to Vienna to study with the sixty-year-old master, then at the very crest of his fame. Thus Haydn formed a personal link among the main members of the Viennese school.

It is an ironic fact that if Haydn had died at the age of thirty-five, as Mozart did, he would hardly be remembered today. All his great music—and there are huge quantities of it—was written after he had passed that age. There are around sixty symphonies (out of a grand total of over a hundred) and a like number of string quartets, as well as piano sonatas, piano trios, masses, and two celebrated oratorios. These last are *The Creation* and *The Seasons,* written to words translated from the English nature-poet James Thomson. *The Seasons* consists of descriptions of the four seasons (a strange subject for an oratorio!), and *The Creation,* too, though its real subject is God's creation of the world according to Genesis, spends much loving care in portraying His created natural objects. These works reflect the new respect for nature that developed in this period, a respect that is very evident in contemporary landscape architecture such as that illustrated on page 274.

Perhaps the earthy tone that is often apparent in Haydn's music is another reflection of this intellectual current. Or perhaps it resulted from Haydn's own humble background. The latter does not, however, explain the sophistication, subtlety, and even musical "wit" that Haydn achieved in symphony after symphony and string quartet after string quartet. It was Haydn who pioneered the Viennese style, and he handled it with a mastery that was not exceeded by any of the other composers.

It is gratifying to read that, after his retirement from the service of the Esterházys, Haydn was invited on two occasions to visit London, then the world capital. He was wined and dined by society, even royalty, and presented with an honorary degree by Oxford University. He was applauded for his magnificent set of twelve *London* symphonies, and even drawn into a discreet autumnal flirtation with a widow (memorialized in the dedication of some of his best piano trios). Probably no other great composer has ever been so handsomely lionized abroad—though plenty of instances can be cited of performers who were, from the sopranos of the eighteenth and nineteenth centuries to the rock stars of the twentieth.

The Symphony

slow introduction

The symphony—a large, impressive concert piece for orchestra—is the most famous genre developed by the Viennese composers, and probably also the most important. It is not for nothing that we commonly speak of the *symphony* orchestra or *symphony* concerts. The standard symphony consists of four good-sized movements. First comes a fast movement, which may be preceded by a relatively short passage of slow music, called the slow introduction. Then there is a slow movement, a minuet movement, and last another fast movement. Occasionally the order of the middle two movements is reversed.

In nearly all of their first movements, Viennese composers employed sonata form. Let us trace this through in the first movement of Haydn's Symphony No. 88, again in some detail. This will supplement our discussion of sonata form in Mozart's Overture to *Don Giovanni,* for the treatment of form by the two composers, and hence the effect of their pieces, is very different.

HAYDN Symphony No. 88 in G (1787)

The Symphony No. 88 is scored for a rather small orchestra, without clarinets (compare page 248)—and, oddly enough, the trumpets and drums do not play at all during the first movement.

FIRST MOVEMENT

The slow introduction to this movement is short and rather routine—at least by comparison with that of the Overture to *Don Giovanni.* Later, Haydn took a cue from Mozart and made his symphony introductions longer and more involved than this.

Exposition   The fast part of the movement begins with a lively little tune with a folklike swing about it:

It soon dawns on us that in this movement Haydn is not going to wait till the development section to start developing his main theme. Part of this theme, a motive (r) marked mainly by its rhythm, is heard repeatedly. In one of its manifestations, it serves as a bridge, changing the key:

This reaches a strong cadence (though there is no complete stop), and the dynamics drop to a hush for the second group. Even the second theme has rhythmic connections with the original main theme:

Still another version of motive r is present in the cadence theme, which is initially played by the wind instruments alone:

After a firm but brief concluding passage, the exposition finally comes to an expectant halt.

In symphonies and sonatas (but not in overtures), composers often allow the performers of sonata-form movements the option of repeating the exposition—and even the development plus recapitulation, too. Since this particular symphony movement is quite brief, conductors often do repeat the whole exposition at this point. Such repeats do not include the slow introductions.

Development   The development begins by quietly working over fragments of the main theme. There are many modulations, going through keys that sound very tentative. The rhythms, too, sound tentative, until a new phase of development is initiated by a sudden forte. This phase is highly contrapuntal, a riot of confusion in which the bridge, second theme, and cadence theme are all heard in and around the reigning rhythm r. But each has a new quality. The second theme is no longer quiet, the bridge no longer points in any clear direction, and the cadence theme no longer makes a firm cadence.

Another expectant stop, and we realize with a real sense of relief that the recapitulation is about to restore order.

Recapitulation   The first theme returns, safely in the original key but with a delightful new feature: a cool counterpoint is added high above it by a flute. Then the bridge is completely rewritten, the second group is abbreviated, and a short coda reminds us yet again (as if we need reminding!) of the first theme. The very last bars bring up an amusing new echo version of motive r:

Although this symphony movement uses sonata form as clearly as the Overture to *Don Giovanni* does, the two pieces hardly sound similar at all. Haydn treads the fine line between providing just enough contrast among his various themes to keep the interest up and making the themes similar enough in rhythm to create confusion and fun. We should be ready to laugh with Haydn (or at any rate, smile inwardly with him) as he runs the modest, even rustic theme through all those improbable developments. His ingenuity in finding new ways of making the familiar rhythm of motive r sparkle—down to a new idea in the very last bars—seems unlimited. It is qualities of this kind that make people speak of wit in Viennese music, and especially in music by Haydn.

Haydn's control of sonata form ensures that the piece does not sound rambling or arbitrary. He may loosen the reins pretty far in the recapitulation, but while we are enjoying the relaxed sense of freedom in the presentation, we can tell that the exposition material is all arriving in the original key. Imaginative treatment of form adds to the sense of exhilaration and high spirits.

A Late Eighteenth-Century Park

Between this park and the baroque park shown on page 208, the change in concept is striking indeed. Nature is no longer sternly controlled but is allowed to run free and delight us with its rich and rather mysterious random arrangements. Whereas the early eighteenth-century park seems cool and serene, the late eighteenth-century one seems soft, gentle, inviting.

Yet it is important to understand that this landscape is every bit as artificial, and just as precisely calculated, as the other. It has all been laid out and planted to create the impression of "wild" vegetation in an especially engaging manifestation. The paths were planned to seem to wander aimlessly, wild flowers were transplanted, and the lake was dug with carefully irregular outlines.

Both parks employ "classical" features: rows of statues and urns in one case, a little imitation Greek temple in the other. But whereas in the baroque park the classical element emphasizes the park's regularity and constructed quality, the temple here seems to peep out accidentally from under the great trees. The work of the architect exists in the friendly embrace of nature—which almost obscures it. If we refer to the visual arts of this period as "classical" or "neoclassical," then, we should realize that classical elements were used not for their own sake but for their associations.

The view is from the beautiful garden at Stourhead, England, which was designed between 1750 and 1780. Today it looks much the same as it did in those times, as shown by the old engraving.

SECOND MOVEMENT

The second movement of Symphony No. 88 is a glorious example of the Viennese composers' affection for tunes. A better way to put it might be *intoxication* with tunes, for in this case the movement contains scarcely any music besides the main melody—a remarkable circumstance, especially since the melody is really quite short:

Notice how many dynamic marks Haydn has put in to gain an expressive effect. Does this tune, lovely as it is, overstay its welcome? It appears no fewer than seven times. Haydn means to lend it fresh interest by presenting it in different keys and by adding little counterpoints above it, but he cannot bear to have them disturb the tune too much. This warm, direct, and somewhat hymnlike tune shows another side of Haydn, one that is just as typical as the "wit" in the earlier movement.

THIRD MOVEMENT

minuet and trio

The third movement of a typical Viennese symphony is a minuet and trio, as we said above. Let us review the points about dance form made during our discussion of the Lully suite on page 180. They need to be extended at this point.

Baroque dances usually consist of two parts, roughly equal in length. Each part is repeated, that is, played twice in succession before the music goes on. So a dance can be diagrammed as a a b b or ‖: a :‖: b :‖ . The signs ‖: and :‖ tell the player to make an exact repeat of the music between them.

Furthermore, baroque dances tend to come in pairs, alternating in an A B A pattern. The second dance in such a pair is called the *trio*, a name that lingers on even though the scoring for three instruments has become obsolete. Thus a minuet and trio simply amount to a minuet plus another minuet—probably contrasting in mood—after which the original minuet is played a second time. However, on this second occasion the internal sections of the original minuet are each played only once, rather than twice, as in the first playing. A baroque minuet movement can be charted as follows:

Minuet	*Trio*	*Minuet*
A	B	A
‖: a :‖: b :‖	‖: c :‖: d :‖	a b

The a's, b's, c's, and d's stand for the internal parts of the minuets.

The Viennese composers generally extended the internal form of their minuets. They brought the music of the first part, a or c, back again (either exactly or with some alterations) at the end of the second part, b or d. In other words, their minuets developed internal a b a structures, and as a result the two parts of the dance were no longer roughly equal in length. Most Viennese minuet movements fall into one of the following schemes:

Minuet	Trio	Minuet
A	B	A
‖:a:‖:b a:‖	‖:c:‖:d c:‖	a b a
OR ‖:a:‖:b a′:‖	‖:c:‖:d c′:‖	a b a′

Just to clarify, the diagram ‖:a:‖:b a:‖ is equivalent to a a ba ba. The a′ and c′ symbolize parts that include significant extensions or alterations of the original a and c.

The third movement of Haydn's Symphony No. 88, like many of Haydn's minuets, has a rollicking country-dance feeling about it. The trio contrasts by its quiet dynamics, but here, too, a rustic element is introduced by the low drone notes held by the violas and bassoons; they seem to evoke peasant instruments such as bagpipes or a hurdy-gurdy (see page 321). This "popular" tone did not prevent Haydn from putting in many ingenious details, such as the disguised return of c′ in the trio.

FOURTH MOVEMENT

rondo Haydn's last movement in this and many other symphonies is a <u>rondo</u>. This form is basically the same as the French rondeau, which we found in the dance suites of Lully's time (see page 181). *Rondo* is the same word in Italian. One main tune alternates with other tunes or with other sections of music in a relatively simple pattern, such as A B A C A D A or A B A C A B A, etc. However, the tunes and contrasting sections of the Viennese rondo are a good deal more complex than those of the baroque, so perhaps it is just as well to keep the French and Italian forms of the word distinct.

The Viennese composers, always more self-conscious than their predecessors, were very aware of the fact that the high points of a rondo come with the many returns of the main theme, A. So they took care to make A memorable and interesting—the listener must be made to enjoy hearing it again and again! B, C, and D did not need to be defined so clearly.

The main tune here (A) is a cheerful, busy item (see page 278). There is an element of tease in this tune because it sounds suspiciously like the main theme of the first movement. Certainly it relies on a single motive (the first ten notes) almost as consistently—and twice as comically. The tune falls into an ‖:a:‖:b a′:‖ scheme, with a "witty" touch at the end of section b, in the first half of measure 24. The last two notes of b (two Ds) run right into a′, the return of a, which begins with an upbeat consisting of the same two Ds.

As we have said, the high points in a rondo come with the returns of the main tune, A. Haydn makes these returns as interesting and amusing as possible by playing around with two upbeat Ds ahead of time in a deceptive fashion:

Do you hear how this return to A enlarges on the passage at measure 24 within the theme itself where it runs into a'? As we indicate in the example, Haydn makes some effective changes of tone color in the returns of A, in spite of his relatively small orchestra. The dynamics are also neatly controlled.

This particular rondo can be charted as A B A' C A Coda. (In A', the little a' within the tune is much changed.) Just as in the first movement of the symphony, fragments of A are constantly poking their heads into the other sections. The result is again a high-spirited and rather brainy piece with a strong sense of unity. The combination of these qualities with strong rhythms and good-humored, folklike melodies is Haydn's special hallmark.

MOZART Symphony No. 40 in G Minor, K. 550 (1788)

Written a year later than Haydn's Symphony No. 88, Mozart's Symphony in
G Minor is one of his most famous works. It is a deeper and a darker work than
the Haydn. It is also a simpler one in its treatment of sonata form, which Mozart uses for three out of the four movements—all except the minuet and trio.
There is a sharper contrast between themes, and in general a clearer distinction
between sections and subsections.

This symphony has no slow introduction. The first theme is presented
with a strictly homophonic accompaniment, which starts up one measure
ahead of time. In popular music, such ahead-of-time accompaniment figures
(which are often improvised) are called *vamps:*

The subdued nervous tension of this theme, a blend of refinement and
great agitation, stamps the first movement unforgettably. The theme contains
motives that will go through extensive alterations in the course of the development section. The second theme is divided between the strings and woodwinds:

This is repeated at once with the role of the instruments reversed, the strings
taking the notes originally played by the winds, and vice versa. The instrumental alternations contribute something absolutely essential to the character of
the theme and show Mozart's fine ear for tone color.

In this movement, the key contrast between the first theme (in the minor
mode) and the second (in the major) is particularly clear. So is the feeling of
their both being held to the same tonality in the recapitulation. Mozart gives
the recapitulated second theme a wonderful new quality of pathos, and he provides the cadence theme with unexpected emotional depths.

The second movement, also in sonata form, is a calm and very beautiful
interlude. The minuet and trio fall into the usual A B A form. The minuet itself, however, has been transformed in spirit from the usual easygoing dance; it
is as though the mood of the first movement had been made more gloomy and
intense. Mozart employs the minor mode, and makes use of a good deal of

counterpoint, especially in the second part (b). As we have said, counterpoint usually means tension to a Viennese composer, whereas a baroque composer takes it as a normal and neutral stylistic element.

A serious symphony requires a serious, dramatic last movement. Mozart would not have ended this symphony with a rondo, as Haydn did with his Symphony No. 88; rondos tend to emphasize good-natured tunes and witty returns rather than contrast and forward movement. Mozart turned once again to sonata form, beginning with this tense, explosive theme:

A particularly angry transformation of this agitated theme opens the development section:

This modulates furiously and sets up a mood of conflict that the recapitulation brings under control only with difficulty. Here, as in the first movement, the quiet second theme sounds much more emotional when it is recapitulated than it did before. There is no coda. The brusque conclusion leaves the listener considerably shaken, disturbed as well as moved by Mozart's unaccustomed display of passion.

Viennese Chamber Music

The Viennese composers wrote chamber music (see page 184) for all kinds of instrumental combinations. Beethoven wrote a popular septet for clarinet, bassoon, French horn, violin, viola, cello, and double bass. Haydn wrote numerous trios for an archaic instrument called the baryton—not a baritone horn, not a baritone singer, but a peculiar sort of bass viol with additional strings to pluck. His patron, Prince Esterházy, fancied this instrument.

piano trio
string quartet The main chamber music combinations of the time were the piano trio (piano, violin, cello) and, most important of all, the string quartet (violin, violin, viola, cello). Mention should also be made of the five wonderful string quintets by Mozart, written for the string quartet combination plus a second viola.

String quartets have a reputation for being esoteric, and many listeners have the feeling that they must be dull. This is not the case; Haydn and Mozart wrote as many beautiful quartets as symphonies, and Beethoven's sixteen examples include some of his very greatest music. But it is true, of course, that in tone color and dynamics, the string quartet medium is more restrained than (say) the symphony orchestra. You have to listen carefully enough to get past the level of tone color to the real muscle of the music—the rhythm, melody, and texture. As an introduction to Viennese chamber music, we shall take Mozart's Clarinet Quintet, a work that adds the more colorful clarinet to the four standard string quartet instruments.

MOZART Quintet for Clarinet and Strings, K. 581 (1789) SIDE 9

Mozart's Clarinet Quintet (he wrote only one) was composed not long before his death. It shares a mood common to much of his late music, a mood rather different from the busy, brilliant confidence of the fast section of the Overture to *Don Giovanni.* Some of the same brightness is present, but there is also a quality of serenity and a tinge of passivity and regret.

This Clarinet Quintet is a fine example of the new interest in tone color among the Viennese composers—especially fine, perhaps, because it is so unflashy and restrained. How well Mozart understood the clarinet, and how fully he exploited its possibilities! He let it perform brilliant runs and hold mellow long notes (which sound much more effective than long notes on a violin); he had it play sensuous tunes and carry hard, driving rhythms; and he used the vibrant low register with special imagination, as though scooping up cups of water from a dark well. If today the clarinet is recognized as the richest and most flexible of all woodwind instruments, that is because Mozart showed composers how to capitalize on all its resources of tone color. Certainly we cannot conceive of the Clarinet Quintet transposed for some other solo instrument, as we might with a baroque concerto grosso.

FIRST MOVEMENT

The first movement of the Clarinet Quintet counts as a quiet one by the standards of other music of the time, such as Haydn's Symphony No. 88 or Mozart's Overture to *Don Giovanni.* It is nevertheless considerably more varied and dynamic than a baroque piece would be. The four string instruments, without the clarinet, play the peaceful main theme:

But the vivid interruption by the clarinet marks this instrument at once as a source of energy within the group. The clarinet introduces the next figure, too. This begins by sounding like a fluid continuation of the main theme, but it soon shows signs of pressing forward into new territory, and we recognize it as the bridge.

After an abrupt stop, the second group makes a definite contrast by its tone of muted agitation:

Agitation increases when the clarinet takes up the theme in an expressive new version in the minor mode. Then another theme, the final-sounding cadence theme, starts to wind up the exposition—

—though at the very end it is the main theme that returns in the violin to make the big cadence.

To begin the development section, the clarinet emerges slowly from the depths to play the main theme once again. But this statement sounds really fresh, and therefore counts as "development," for at least two reasons. First, we hear at last the theme with the rich, "liquid" tone quality of the clarinet. Second, we hear it suddenly in a new key, which provides a gorgeous new glow.

The interruption following the theme now has to be played by the violin, and the rest of the development consists of vigorous treatment of this interruption. The key changes repeatedly. Finally things calm down into a little retransition passage, which is clearly preparing for the return of something familiar to stabilize all the previous action.

As is usual with Mozart, the recapitulation by and large parallels the exposition, though of course all the music remains in the same key. Consequently the section sounds settled and essentially at rest, even though in the second group the clarinet grows more and more emotional. The clarinet also takes the lead in a very lovely extension of the cadence theme. It introduces some transitory new figures, after which a brief restatement of the first theme concludes the recapitulation, just as it concluded the exposition.

SECOND MOVEMENT

The second movement of Mozart's Clarinet Quintet centers around a long slow melody for the leading instrument. The two violins are directed to put on mutes to muffle the tone.* If we respond to this melody, and its glorification of the sound of the clarinet, the movement will stand out as a tranquil oasis in the middle of the other, more active movements. None of the other Viennese composers, not even Schubert, wrote such beautiful slow movements.

The clarinet plays the long melody twice, at full length, in just the same way. The material in between the two clarinet statements includes sequential passages graced by exquisite upward scales, first on the muted first violin, then on the clarinet.

THIRD MOVEMENT

The minuet movement of the Clarinet Quintet happens to be furnished with two trios, a rather rare occurrence that results in an A B A C A arrangement. It can be thought of as a simple type of rondo (see page 277). The internal dance parts are repeated only in the first A, in B, and in C.

The minuets of chamber music pieces, especially those by Mozart, naturally tend to be more elegant than the more robust minuets of symphonies. Here the first trio, B, scored for the string instruments alone, recaptures the disturbed tone of the second group of the first movement. The second trio, C, is an accompanied clarinet solo, displaying a peculiarly Mozartian grace, though obviously he meant it to sound countrified. Perhaps he even meant it as a tribute or a compliment to his friend Joseph Haydn, who made a specialty of rustic-sounding minuets (see page 277).

FOURTH MOVEMENT

theme and variations

Another relatively simple form was used by Mozart for the last movement of the Clarinet Quintet, the theme and variations. This form goes back to the Renaissance, and we have already seen an example from the baroque period in Bach's Passacaglia and Fugue for Organ (pages 201–5). In the Viennese period this form grows more important.

A theme and variations starts with a clear presentation of a theme—always a tune, for the Viennese composers. (In Bach's Passacaglia, the theme was a bass figure.) Then there follow a number of "variations," sections in which the composer runs through the theme again and again, measure by measure, varying certain aspects of it while keeping other aspects constant.

---

* A violin mute is a small clamp-like device that fits on the *bridge*—the part of the instrument that holds the strings up from the body (see diagram on page 460)—and thus inhibits resonance. The violin bridge is not to be confused with the bridge section of sonata form. Mutes for French horns, trumpets, trombones, and tubas are large conical wedges that fit into the open ends of these instruments.

Rhythm, meter, mode, tempo, tone color, and so on can all be varied, but it is hard to generalize further about theme-and-variations form, since the elements that composers vary and keep fixed differ from period to period.

Here is Mozart's tune—a lively and somewhat innocent-sounding one in aa' ba' form:

In the example below, the first few measures of the theme are lined up with the corresponding measures of the five variations. Scan the page vertically, and you will see some of the notes of the theme turning up in some of the variations, others not:

Variations in the Viennese style maintain the dimensions of the theme in measures, the phrase structure of the theme (including the position of the cadences), and the main outlines of its harmony. The melody itself tends to change from variation to variation, though sometimes Mozart keeps the original melody, too (see the beginnings of variations 1 and 4—though the melody gets lost again at the ends of these variations). In variation 4, it is the rapid passage-work played by the clarinet simultaneously with the tune on the violin that counts as the "variation."

The point of the variations is to obtain many contrasting moods out of the same theme, which is transformed but always discernible. Variation 2 seems rather nervous, and variation 4 brilliant. Variation 3 changes to the minor mode in order to capture again that note of agitation that briefly clouded all the earlier movements of the quintet. Indeed, "agitation" may be too heartless a word for the subdued sobbing of these rhythms. Variation 5 reminds us of the tranquil slow movement, for here Mozart changes tempo for the first time, to an adagio (slow).

After this meditative, nostalgic slow variation, part of the theme returns in its original form, but at an appreciably faster tempo. (Since only part of the theme occurs, this does not count as another "variation.") The movement concludes with some new continuations and repeated cadences in the Viennese manner.

Jean-Antoine Houdon

One of the most impressive artists of the late eighteenth century was the French sculptor Jean-Antoine Houdon (1740–1828). His work deserves to be better known, especially in the United States, where he voyaged in 1785 in the company of Benjamin Franklin. He did portrait busts of Washington, Jefferson, Franklin, John Paul Jones, Robert Fulton, and that other, more famous French visitor to our shores, Lafayette.

It is said that a sitting for Houdon was often a battle, with the sitter trying for days to hide his true personality and Houdon inevitably catching it in the end. His psychological penetration was remarkable, enabling him to portray exactly the personalities of the most diverse types. The emergence of this quality in Houdon can be linked with similar qualities in Jane Austen's novels (*Pride and Prejudice* was written in 1796) and in Mozart's supreme operas (*Don Giovanni* is discussed on pages 263–70). Many musicians feel they can sense the same sort of psychological subtlety and accuracy in Mozart's instrumental music, too. For thanks to its new flexibility of style, the music of the Viennese masters is constantly changing in

a way that seems to be modeled on our actual emotional experience.

Houdon's bust of Voltaire (see page 252), one of his most famous, shows us not only a man of extraordinary sharpness and humor—that we would know from reading the great philosopher's works—but also one of deep humanity, warmth, and charm. We are instantly drawn to this old gentleman. Rousseau, in bronze rather than marble (see page 253), is another proposition: complex, intense, resolute, and dangerously ironic. And Franklin: he has a far-away look, the look of someone who is coolly sizing you up and figuring out how you can best be used to advantage.

Houdon is also famous for his busts of women and exceedingly pretty little girls. A certain Madame de Sérilly, above, has been caught with an indescribable look—devious, even furtive, and yet possibly also coquettish. Will some cunning scheme succeed in getting her out of a compromising situation, or will she have to rely once again on her beauty? This complicated and intriguing court lady could almost be a countess in some *opera buffa* by Mozart.

CHAPTER 10 | The Viennese Period   II

The Viennese Period   II

Vivacity and serenity, perhaps, are the typical moods explored by the early Viennese composers. Within this broad general description, they found an inexhaustible fund of variety, as is shown by the movements of Mozart's Clarinet Quintet and Haydn's Symphony No. 88—to look no further. We also know, from Mozart's Symphony in G Minor and from *Don Giovanni,* that these composers sometimes probed the darker emotional regions. They did not do this very often, but when they did it was nearly always with a very powerful effect. Their first efforts in this vein come in the 1770s, and they seem to reflect a turbulent current in the arts of the time known as *Sturm und Drang* in German (Storm and Stress).

This short-lived but intense movement deserves a brief backward look. We can now see it as a preview of romanticism. The German theater was rocked by a number of furious revolutionary plays (one of them entitled *Sturm und Drang*). German literature saw its first great novel, which remains to this day the most famous of all novels of unrequited love and suicide: *The Sorrows of Young Werther* by Johann Wolfgang von Goethe. Several actual suicides of the time were attributed to the reading of *Werther,* just as street violence today is attributed to the watching of violence on television. Some painters, too, reached for more somber subject matter. Storm scenes became very popular, and the strange Swiss-English artist Henry Fuseli began setting down such macabre visions as *The Nightmare* (see page 344).

Haydn responded to the mood of the times with his first really impressive group of compositions. He wrote a number of symphonies in the years around 1770 that are much more moody and intense than No. 88 (more so, indeed, than almost any of his later symphonies). He also wrote some influential string quartets of the same character. Mozart, then a teenager in Salzburg, had just "discovered" Haydn and eagerly copied these dramatic, passionate works, along with others. Ten years later, they appealed just as strongly to another teenager, who was to put his stamp on the second phase of Viennese music as strongly as Haydn had put his on the first: the young Ludwig van Beethoven.

It sometimes comes as a surprise to realize that Beethoven was only fifteen years younger than Mozart. The difference in the generations was decisive, however. When the Parisian crowd stormed the Bastille in 1789, Haydn at fifty-five was well set in his ways, and Mozart at thirty-three was preoccupied with the losing battle for survival in Vienna. But Beethoven was nineteen; he had grown up in an environment famous for its liberal ideas; many of his friends cheered the French Revolution and Beethoven must have joined them, to judge from the libertarian ideas he professed in later years. In 1792, when he set off to make his career in Vienna, the coach he was riding in had to dodge the invading armies of Napoleon.

A more dramatic, robust, adventurous quality marks the second phase of Viennese music, under the influence of Beethoven. We shall not be surprised to encounter a good deal that is new in the upcoming generation. Novelties, however, should not be allowed to obscure the very real continuity among all the Viennese composers, as determined first and foremost by the flexibility of their musical technique and second by the breadth and subtlety of emotional expression that this made possible. The new expressivity was pioneered by Haydn and Mozart, then extended by Beethoven and Schubert. To this common factor may be added the personal contacts between these men and the dependence of all of them on such forms and genres as sonata form, theme and variations, symphony, and string quartet.

Ludwig van Beethoven (1770–1827)

Probably no figure in any of the arts meets with such a strong universal response as Beethoven. People may respect Michelangelo and Shakespeare, they may admire Leonardo da Vinci and pity Van Gogh, but Beethoven instantly summons up a powerful, positive image: that of the tough, ugly, angry genius forcing out one deeply expressive masterpiece after another in the teeth of adversity. His music has enjoyed broad-based, uninterrupted popularity from its own day to the present; today its place is equally secure with unsophisticated listeners and with the most learned of musicians. The bicentennial of his birth in 1970 produced, among other things, a commercial edition on records of his complete output, a package running to seventy-five LPs. His themes have been turned into pop songs. His beetling brows have been emblazoned on T-shirts. He has been immortalized by a comic strip.

While the popular Beethoven image has been much romanticized over the years, it has a solid basis in fact. His life was not very interesting in terms of outer events, but there was one shattering inner event: at the age of thirty he began to lose his hearing. The effect of this calamity could be compared with that of a craftsman having both hands amputated. Even if he could continue to compose with the "inner ear," no musician had ever before existed purely as a composer, but had also played, conducted, run musical establishments.

But thanks to his genius and to his uncompromising personality, Beethoven made himself into a pure composer, and he forced the aristocracy of Vienna to support him at it, more or less on his own terms. Whereas Mozart had starved in Vienna, Beethoven made a living and even amassed some stocks and shares.

His capital, we might say, was a new concept of artistic genius, which society was now ready to support. Beethoven did not create this concept, but he exemplified it powerfully for his own age, and he still exemplifies it today. No longer a mere craftsman, the artist suffers and creates; endowed not just with greater talent but also with a greater soul, he suffers and creates for humanity. Music was no longer held down to bodily implements such as the ear or the fingers. It existed in the highest reaches of the artist's spirit.

As we have already mentioned, Beethoven belonged to a generation that more than any other responded to the French Revolution. The outer connections between the Revolution and his music are slight, although he did, from a distance, dedicate one of his greatest works, the *Eroica* (Heroic) Symphony, to Napoleon, only to scratch out the dedication in a rage when he learned that the liberator had turned tyrant (see page 301). The inner connections are more significant. To Beethoven's generation, the French Revolution represented an ideal of perfectibility, not so much of society (as Beethoven himself acknowledged in his scrapped dedication) as of human aspiration. That is what the triumph over deafness meant to Beethoven, and also to those of his contemporaries who were swept away by his music and watched his accomplishments with awe.

That is what generations since have cherished in Beethoven's music. As we listen to the *Eroica* Symphony, we surely suspect that it had less to do with Napoleon than with the composer's own self-image. The sense of heroic striving and inner conquest is what emerges so magnificently in Beethoven's most famous compositions.

His output has been categorized as belonging to three periods. The first of these reminds us of his close connections with the earlier Viennese composers, for in his first hundred works or so, Beethoven followed in the footsteps of Mozart and Haydn. There is certainly a highly individual flavor in the first-period works—witness, for example, the well-known *Pathétique* and *Moonlight* Sonatas. But Beethoven was not one of those composers who step forward with something dazzlingly new at a very tender age. After a slow development, he arrived at the second period, the characteristically "heroic" period of the *Eroica* Symphony, the Fifth and Seventh Symphonies, the Overture to *Egmont,* the *Appassionata* Sonata, and most of his other best-known works. Then at the end of his life he evolved a new style that is now regarded as his greatest. We shall return to the third-period compositions later.

BEETHOVEN   Symphony No. 5 in C Minor (1807–1808)   SIDE 10

The tag "Fate knocking at the door," which is always associated with Beethoven's Fifth Symphony, sounds as if it were a romantic invention, but apparently it originated with the composer himself. Over the course of the four movements, the listener seems to experience not just the conquest of fate but a complete demolition of it. The first movement—the actual "fate" movement—is one of Beethoven's greatest sonata-form pieces, and the scherzo is an amazingly imaginative creation. As an introduction to Beethoven's strengths, as well as his excesses, we can hardly do better than this most famous of all symphonies.

FIRST MOVEMENT

Coming to the first movement of Beethoven's Fifth Symphony after the music of Haydn and Mozart, we are likely to be struck most forcibly by the differences. Beethoven was always a conspicuously "unpretty" composer even in his first-period pieces, which stay closest to the older masters. In second-period pieces such as the Fifth Symphony, the tremendous energy and sheer power seem a far cry from the elegance and wit of the earlier Viennese style.

But we discover something interesting if we try to pinpoint the actual stylistic features that make us think so. One such feature is the thorough saturation of the music by a single motive ♩ ♪♪♪ ♩ which occurs constantly and seems to grow in endless versions. Others are the breathless sense of development, the many emphatic cadences preceded by extended preparatory material, the short sections of music in sharp contrast, and the long passages of balanced repetition. All these features we know from Haydn and Mozart. Haydn's Symphony No. 88 even carries a single motive through the entire first movement with something of the same consistency and sense of growth.

What is the real difference, then? Not the basic style itself, but the way it is being used—or, rather, the expressive purpose it is being used for. The Viennese style was flexible enough so that a composer with a certain frame of mind could take it in deadly earnest. The difference is one of attitude more than of purely musical technique.

Beethoven insisted on treating musical contrast not as a source of humor, as Haydn had, but rather as a source of conflict, a confrontation. In the development process, he saw not merely a stimulating exploration, as Mozart often did, but also a struggle—sometimes a struggle to the death. A recapitulation is more than an occasion of relief and stability; to Beethoven it is a moment of exultation, rescue, triumph, consummation. As we study Beethoven pieces, we shall find ourselves using the same terms as we did for earlier Viennese music; but the adjectives will be very different.

Exposition ("Confrontation") The example below shows how the famous motive ♩ ♪♪♪ ♩ begins to saturate this movement. First it forms the rhythmic substance of the main theme. Then it begins the bridge. And then it even mutters away underneath the quiet, songlike second theme, which in other ways contrasts so obviously with everything else:

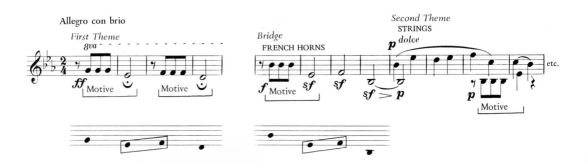

The bold horn call, which serves as the bridge, behaves like an unusual example of the type in many ways, but it does one essential thing very clearly: it really cements the new key and with power and authority clears the terrain for the second theme.

The example also shows how the first theme and the bridge both consist of a similar aggregate of four pitches (never mind the rhythm, for the moment). The bridge can be regarded as a kind of broadening out of the first theme, hinging on the two middle pitches. Does this seem like an artificial way of thinking of these two themes? Any doubts on this score will be dispelled by Beethoven's own actions in the development section and coda.

Remember that it was the Viennese convention to allow an optional repetition of the exposition in sonata form (see page 273). Generally, conductors do indeed repeat the present exposition, after a stormy passage (featuring the main motive once again) has led from the second theme to a strong cadence.

Development ("Struggle")   As is often the case, the beginning notes of this development section make an immediate modulation, the first of many restless changes in key that electrify the section. The present modulation sounds like the crack of doom, thanks in part to Beethoven's orchestration, simple as it is (the effect is created mainly by two French horns).

For a time Beethoven develops the first theme, leading to an earsplitting climax; then he turns to the bridge. In the following passage, he extracts the two middle pitches of the bridge, which we mentioned above, and echoes them between high wind instruments and lower strings:

Then, at the end of the example, he actually breaks them in two and starts echoing just a single note! This kind of development process is called *fragmentation*. It may seem fanciful, or worse, to point to a single half note in the middle of a score and say that it was "derived" from the middle of some particular theme. Yet because of the way in which Beethoven has led up to this point, each of these single half notes is heard as a logical and enormously tense outcome of the fragmentation of the bridge theme.

Beethoven is famous for the tension he builds up in sonata-form movements prior to the recapitulation. In the Fifth Symphony, the hush at this point becomes almost unbearable. Finally, in the retransition, the whole orchestra seems to grab the listener by the lapels and shake him back and forth, shouting the motive again and again until finally the first theme settles out, safe and sound in the original key. Now, this is much the same technique that Haydn used in preparing the humorous returns of his rondo theme in Symphony No. 88 and elsewhere. The opening motive of a theme is played over and over again until it serves as the kickoff of the theme itself. But in place of Haydn's wit, Beethoven gives a sense of tremendous achievement.

Recapitulation (*"Consummation"*)   The recapitulation sticks very closely to the exposition, except for an expressive slow solo for the oboe—an extremely original and affecting moment. Everything stays in the original key.

Coda   Long, action-packed codas are a feature of Beethoven's movements in sonata form. The stormy passage at the end of the recapitulation does not come to a cadence, as it did in the exposition, but instead plunges headlong into a violent climax reminiscent of one in the development section. Then this powerful concluding idea appears:

Compare the bottom line of this with the example on page 294. Here the *pitches* of the main theme are played in the *rhythm* of the bridge, and then those two middle notes—the common ground between the themes—are emphasized by a long downward sequence. This does not strike us as an abstract demonstration of ingenious theme-building. It adds something important to the loudness and rhythmic drive of this passage: a sense of tightness and wonder, wonder that the basic themes of the movement can be expanded into ever-new emotional gestures. The triumph over fate is the triumph over musical raw materials.

SECOND MOVEMENT

After so tense and urgent a beginning, Beethoven deliberately made the second movement of the Fifth Symphony relatively gentle in tone and relaxed in form. Like the second movement of Haydn's Symphony No. 88, this piece centers on a single short tune, which appears seven times in relatively simple variations:

The tune reaches a climax at the end, a climax with something of the character of a fanfare.

We have stressed the Viennese composers' affection for tunes. Beethoven's melody may not be as beautiful as Haydn's, but perhaps the movement makes up for this by its interesting form. A second theme, not altogether unrelated to the first, appears after a rich and unusually clear modulation. Played by the brass, it sounds even more like a fanfare:

Variations of both themes follow. This songlike movement has its moments of mystery and more than one hint of not-so-distant military music. It ends firmly with the first fanfare.

THIRD MOVEMENT

scherzo
The very interesting third movement is a free _scherzo_. Beethoven developed this type of movement out of the Viennese minuet and trio, and used it as a substitute. The meter is triple, as in the minuet, but the tempo is faster. As for the mood, while Beethoven calls it a "joke" (_scherzo,_ in Italian), we may think instead of an impatient and sometimes explosive rush.

Beethoven's earliest scherzos took over the form of the minuet and trio:

Scherzo	_Trio_	_Scherzo_
A	B	A
‖:a:‖:b a′:‖	‖:c:‖:d c′:‖	a b a′

Later he often expanded the form to A B A B A Coda, and ignored some or all of the internal ‖:a:‖:b a′:‖ and ‖:c:‖:d c′:‖ plans. The present scherzo runs as follows:

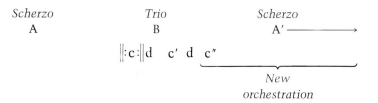

There are striking differences of tone color in this piece. In the scherzo part (A), contrast between two themes—a quiet, somewhat ominous one and a raging, loud one, both in the minor mode—is heightened by the instrumentation. Cellos and double basses answered by woodwinds play the first theme, whereas French horns play the second. The trio (B) begins with the double basses alone—an unusual, gruff sound that does perhaps constitute a "joke."

pizzicato
Then, in the final section of the trio, c″, and in the whole of A′, the orchestration changes radically. Pizzicato strings (plucked with the finger instead of being played with the bow) and a brittle-sounding oboe replace the smooth and raging sounds heard before. Everything is transformed into a quite unexpected mood, a mood approximating mystery, numbness, even terror.

FOURTH MOVEMENT

The point of this change in tone color appears in the sequel, the most unusual idea in this symphony. Beethoven runs the ghostly scherzo right into the blaring last movement. Thus the final movement has the very literal effect of a triumph over some sort of adversity. The transitional passage between the movements features another famous tone color in its ominous drumbeats on the timpani (the rhythm is that of the second scherzo theme). Then, after a huge crescendo, the last movement introduces trombones and a piccolo for the first time, over and above the normal forces of the Viennese symphony orchestra (see page 248).

Again in sonata form, this last movement adopts the accents of a military march to create a steady mood of rejoicing. It is almost entirely in the major mode. Perhaps in mood it is a bit exaggerated, though in making such a judgment we should give due weight to its role in balancing the grim struggle of the earlier movements. The coda of this movement is one of the most emphatic in all music.

But whether we find the movement as a whole exhilarating or merely exhausting, we should be able to appreciate another highly original stroke of musical form at the retransition, the passage leading from the development section to the recapitulation. The second theme of the scherzo reappears for just a moment, a complete surprise (and even a change in tempo and meter, from $\frac{2}{2}$ back to $\frac{3}{4}$). This theme now sounds neither raging nor ghostly, but rather like a dim memory. It has come to remind us of the battle that has been won. Fate and terror alike have yielded to Beethoven's forceful, optimistic, major-mode vision.

The Concerto

On page 205 we discussed the baroque concerto grosso at the time of Vivaldi and Bach in terms of the basic concerto idea: the contest or contrast between a group of soloists and an orchestra. This basic idea was refined and sharpened as the eighteenth century progressed. The norm became the solo concerto, with a single soloist, who was that much freer than a solo group and could be treated as a formidable virtuoso. Both Mozart and Beethoven (before his deafness) were famous as concerto soloists.

At the same time, the orchestra was growing. With its well-coordinated string, woodwind, and brass choirs, the Viennese orchestra was much more flexible and powerful than the baroque concerto orchestra. So the balance between two such forces presented a real problem—but it was the sort of problem that brought out the best in the great composers of the time. Mozart was particularly fascinated by it, and worked it out in a series of about a dozen superb concertos for piano written during his years in Vienna. Beethoven's Fourth and Fifth Concertos for piano date from his second period, as does his single Concerto for Violin.

Listening to one of these concertos, we find ourselves following a constant give and take between two opposing forces. It is a fascinating contest, in which neither side can ever emerge definitely as the winner. To put it in general terms, the art of the Viennese concerto was to pit the soloist's greater mobility, brilliance, and expressive ability against the orchestra's increased power and variety of tone color.

BEETHOVEN Piano Concerto No. 5 in E♭ (*Emperor*) (1809)

Written soon after the Fifth Symphony, Beethoven's Fifth (and last) Piano Concerto is another work in the characteristically heroic, optimistic vein of his second period. Unlike the symphony, however, the concerto does not seem to depict an inner struggle over which ascendancy is attained. We might say that its mood is less one of triumph than of sheer power and magnificence. Others seem to have felt this when they gave the concerto its nickname, the *Emperor* Concerto, some time after Beethoven's death.

FIRST MOVEMENT

The opening passage of this movement presents the basic concerto idea—namely the contest between sharply differing forces—in a nutshell. The orchestra thunders out a series of three simple chords like a blind giant, and the piano runs or rather stomps all over them in rapid, brilliant displays of agility. The last display grows expressive; and then ends with a rush, as the soloist dusts off his hands and leaves the menial business of exposition to the orchestra. Here is the first theme:

double exposition form
orchestral exposition
solo exposition

For the first movements of concertos, the Viennese composers used sonata form in an extended version called the double exposition form. This is adapted to the concerto medium by having two expositions: an orchestral exposition, followed by a solo exposition (soloist plus orchestra) in which most of the same material is "exposed" a second time. Then come the usual *development, recapitulation,* and *coda.* This is a lengthy and somewhat complicated form, and we shall not attempt a point-by-point analysis, but only mention a few of the highlights.

You may be able to tell that the entire *orchestral exposition* remains in the same key, without the modulation that is basic to the ordinary sonata-form exposition. The quiet second theme, played staccato by the strings, is in the minor mode of the basic key (E♭ minor), but even this deviation is soon canceled by a very rich, legato version of this same theme in the major, played by the French horns. Do not forget this horn theme; it returns with a stunning effect later in the movement.

Engrav'd Printed & Sold by PAUL REVERE BOSTON

The Age of Revolutions

Revolutions are never the work of the oppressed masses alone. Financial interests come into play, intellectuals argue the case, and artists plead the cause. None of these people can foresee the end of the course of events once it is put in motion. The American Revolution led to a stable, rational political order that was the admiration of the liberal world for years after the Enlightenment. The French Revolution backfired in political terms, though it left an unforgettable legacy to romanticism and the European consciousness.

Our first picture is of the Boston Massacre of 1770—which some historians say was a case of justified self-defense on the part of British soldiers provoked by an ugly mob. However that may be, this propaganda picture was widely promulgated, and by none other than Paul Revere.

Some think the amateur artist was Revere, too. An inflammatory poem was added:

Unhappy Boston! see thy sons deplore
Thy hallow'd walks besmear'd with guiltless gore,
While faithless PRESTON and his savage Bands
With murd'rous Rancour stretch their bloody Hands;
Like fierce Barbarians grinning o'er their Prey
Approve the Carnage and enjoy the Day. . . .

Thus stoked, the memory of the Boston Massacre smoldered for five years until the American Revolution broke out.

The second picture illustrates a bitter irony of the kind revolutions breed. Napoleon was first hailed by liberals as the savior of the French Revolution, but they discerned an

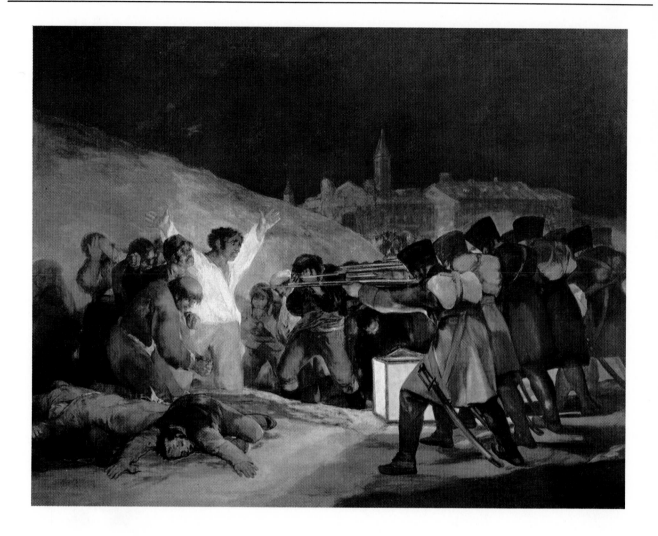

ominous new turn when he had himself crowned Emperor in 1804. Beethoven, who was about to call his latest symphony *Bonaparte* in admiration, hastily scratched out the dedication and substituted the neutral title *Sinfonia Eroica* (Heroic Symphony). Indeed, Napoleon's imperialistic policies led France into calamitous campaigns in Spain and Russia. With a ferocity that had scarcely been matched in all of Europe's endless wars of the previous century, the Spanish people rose up against oppression by a country that had only recently overthrown its own oppressors. France lost 300,000 troops in Spain alone, a number about equal to the total population of Paris in those days.

The French atrocities in Spain found a great painter to record them, Francisco Goya. Besides the famous painting shown above, *The Third of May, 1808,* Goya did a series of etchings called *The Disasters of War,* some of which are too ghastly to be reproduced in an ordinary book.

It was no news in 1808 that war was disastrous. What was new was the passion with which some artists were now identifying with popular causes and using their art to plead those causes. There was a very new sense of the artist's importance and authority. Goya and even Beethoven are cases in point. Only sixteen years later, Byron died in Greece, where he had gone to fight and write for that nation's independence.

Whatever historians might tell us, can we believe that the executions of May 3 were "justified"? Or do we believe the artist?

At the end of the orchestral exposition, the (motive) b from the first theme (see the example, above) is heard insistently, an anxiously repeated cue for the entrance of an actor who has been away much too long. At last the pianist arrives, with a long upward chromatic scale (see page 16) covering more than three octaves. This scale is neither very fast nor very loud nor particularly brilliant. It just happens to be one thing no orchestral instrument can play without sounding ridiculous.

Having made its point, the piano offers its own expressive version of the military-sounding first theme (beginning of the *solo exposition*). When the orchestra comes in with the continuation of this theme, notice how swiftly the piano cuts in with new minor-mode material, which soon modulates to the new key; here the piano plays even more expressive variations on the second theme. The change of key that counts for so much in sonata-form compositions does not occur in the orchestral exposition, but is saved for the soloist. Modulation is a resource that demonstrates the soloist's superior range and mobility.

In the *development,* motives a and then b are worked over by the orchestra; the piano accompanies with arpeggios, which grow more and more power-

arpeggio

ful. An arpeggio is a chord played one note at a time up and down one or more octaves. There comes a very characteristic place where the orchestra and the pianist seem to square off and brandish motive b at one another—and it is the orchestra that backs off, as the piano marches ahead with grand scales moving steadily down and then up, each time reaching a new peak and a new key.

The *recapitulation* ends with the piano's chromatic scale, now sounding decidedly victorious. To begin the *coda,* the orchestra makes obvious—even pompous—gestures of preparation. Some exciting event seems to be at hand.

This is the traditional place in the Viennese concerto for the *cadenza.* The soloist was supposed to improvise at this point—to show his or her mettle both in making fascinating new thematic developments that the composer himself had not thought of, and also in carrying off brilliant feats of virtuosity. The orchestra stops, and the soloist has a moment of freedom—a long moment—to stake out a final claim for dominance.

But in the *Emperor* Concerto Beethoven specified the cadenza and wrote it out himself. He had a special effect in mind. This was to salvage, as it were, an element that had been squeezed out of the form—that memorable French horn passage from the opening exposition. Its appearance *during* the soloist's cadenza is completely unexpected, yet perfectly "right" and satisfying. A stroke of this kind shows Beethoven's imaginative mastery of musical form.

SECOND MOVEMENT

The second movement, striking a profound contrast with the extroverted mood of the first movement, opens with a slow hymnlike melody played reverentially by the muted strings. The piano's response is a meditative, somewhat vague series of new ideas, culminating in a long passage of trills that seems to pull the orchestra gently along with it, higher and higher. Only after this does the piano play the hymn, in a slightly varied form, and only after that do the woodwinds have their chance to present it. During this last statement, the piano plays very peaceful passage-work.

The sense of great calm deepens as the hymn comes to rest on a single low note. The note shifts mysteriously, in both pitch and tone color. Above it, the piano begins to pick out tentative-sounding motives. The music is obviously *waiting*, waiting for something new. It is as though Beethoven were sitting at the piano, warming up, before starting to improvise a new movement. Like the last movement of the Fifth Symphony, the third movement of this concerto is led into from the previous movement—but by means of a transition passage of a very different character.

THIRD MOVEMENT

The third movement turns out to be a rondo (see page 277). Based on a theme (A) in Beethoven's most triumphant manner, the form of this movement can be charted as A B A' C A B' A'' Coda.

The B section includes a new theme that is purposely given a low profile, so as not to divert too much attention from A. As for the C section, that does not introduce a new theme at all, but instead develops the motives of A. This is a good place to use for practice in hearing modulations, for the piano brings in the rondo theme, somewhat varied, in three sharply contrasted keys, one after another. Notice that although the orchestra sets up these keys by making the necessary modulations, the piano takes them over and makes them its own. There is no doubt as to who has the upper hand in this C section.

Beethoven abbreviates the second A (A') and extends the fourth A (A''). Here the piano, flushed by its success in the C section, presents the A theme in yet another new key, which the orchestra corrects as tactfully as it knows how —for, of course, by this time in the movement everything is supposed to remain solidly in the main key. The effect of this combined maneuver is to give the rondo theme, at its last appearance, even greater breadth and emphasis.

Toward the end of the coda, the piano plays an unusual little cadenza accompanied by the timpani and nothing else—a cadenza that gradually slows to a complete stop. This is even more unusual. As if suddenly waking up, the piano and then the orchestra end the movement with very forceful, concise gestures. Some of Beethoven's blunt humor is mixed in with the buoyancy and power of this splendid final movement.

The Sonata

The term *sonata* is a confusing one, with multiple meanings, as we remarked on page 184. We know its adjectival use in the term *sonata form,* the name for the scheme employed in the first movements of Viennese compositions— among them overtures, symphonies, quartets, and also (as it happens) sonatas. As a noun, *sonata* refers to a piece in several movements for a small number of instruments or a single one. The most important type of sonata in the baroque period was the trio sonata (see pages 184 and 218).

In reference to music of the Viennese period, the noun *sonata* is restricted to compositions for one or two instruments only. Sonatas were composed for violin and piano, cello and piano, and so on. Mozart wrote one for bassoon and cello. But most sonatas were designed as solo pieces for the favorite new instrument of the time, the piano.

Some piano sonatas adopted the general movement plan of the symphony: an opening fast movement (in sonata form, perhaps with a slow introduction), a slow movement, a minuet or scherzo, and another fast movement. However, there was also a tradition of forms in three or even in two movements. It was this more intimate tradition that Beethoven followed in composing his Piano Sonata in E, Op. 109.

BEETHOVEN   Piano Sonata in E, Op. 109 (1820)   SIDE 9

At the end of Beethoven's life, in his so-called third period, his style moved in a direction of greater serenity, subtlety, and introspection. The music loses some (though not all) of its earlier tone of heroism; it loses all of its earlier heroics. The control of contrast and musical flow becomes even more potent than before. A new freedom of form leads to a range of expression that can only be called miraculous, encompassing all the strength of Beethoven's earlier music together with a new gentleness and spirituality.

This freedom of form and corresponding expressive freedom is a harbinger of things to come in the later nineteenth century and in the twentieth. It is no accident that the great works of Beethoven's last years have impressed people more and more deeply with the passing of time. These works have remained influential on composers, up to the present day. Even Igor Stravinsky, a modern composer who consciously turned his back on the nineteenth century (and liked to shock people by disparaging the "heroic" Beethoven), nonetheless proclaimed his warm admiration for the music of the third period.

As we might expect, this music is not often cast in the "heroic" orchestral genres, such as the symphony and the concerto. Beethoven now preferred the string quartet and the piano sonata. As a young man, Beethoven had made his name in Vienna as a virtuoso pianist, and, although now he was stone-deaf and never played in public, he continued to be drawn to "his" instrument, the instrument that allowed him the greatest sense of intimacy and flexibility. Amazingly, his "inner ear" still enabled him to develop fascinating new piano tone colors.

FIRST MOVEMENT

The brief first movement of the Piano Sonata in E is the freest in form and the most subtle in mood. Two expressive themes contrast in every possible way, even in tempo and meter:

The first theme barely murmurs its way into our consciousness, whereas the second breathes considerable passion and draws on some brilliant piano effects. Both themes sound inconclusive, even fragmentary, and they follow one another so suddenly that the flow of the music does not sound like that of a sonata-form movement or a rondo. This is true even though these two themes return later in a sort of climactic recapitulation.

In the middle of the movement, the first theme does not undergo fragmentation (see page 295) or any of the usual development procedures. Instead it grows into long, smooth melodic lines:

At the end, after the "recapitulation," new ideas seem to emerge spontaneously, as though from a quiet well of melody. There is an air of flickering meditation about this movement, a strange combination of tenderness and fantasy.

SECOND MOVEMENT

The very fast (prestissimo) second movement is an ingenious hybrid. It conveys the brusque mood of the traditional scherzo that Beethoven regularly placed in the center of his large pieces. But being a piece in sonata form, it runs through the drama of confrontation, struggle, and consummation that he regularly placed at the beginning—for example, in the first movement of the Fifth Symphony. The difference in position makes all the difference in the effect. It is one thing to place a dramatic sonata-form movement at the beginning of a long piece, where it necessarily sets the tone for everything that follows. It is quite another thing to place it as an interlude between two quiet movements.

The line score on pages 308–9 shows how concisely and yet how strictly and lucidly Beethoven now used sonata form. Everything seems to be expressed with a minimum of fuss and a maximum of directness; there is not an ounce of fat. The development section focuses hard on an unexpected detail of thematic material, the bass line underneath the main theme (marked with a square bracket in the line score). It is treated in counterpoint, inverted, and fragmented.

Then, at the recapitulation, this bass line is twisted around and placed high *above* the theme when the theme is repeated. This touch, immensely strong and sinewy, shows Beethoven's ability in these years to derive the greatest effect out of the smallest details. Notice, too, the expressive extension of the bridge in the recapitulation, and the almost incredibly concise hammer strokes that constitute the coda.

In third-period works such as this, Beethoven seems almost able to match the impressive, forceful accomplishments of his second-period symphonic movements while taking only half the time.

THIRD MOVEMENT

The last movement, the longest and obviously the weightiest of the three, concludes the sonata on a note of quiet spirituality. This movement is a theme and variations. In form it is comparable to the last movement of Mozart's Clarinet Quintet (see page 283), though the mood and tempo are certainly very different.

Beethoven uses as his theme a serene, hymnlike tune, both halves of which are repeated (eight measures each). Some of the fine points of this tune are the wonderful "deep" harmony marked at X in our example below, the sequence (see page 21) at the beginning of the second half of the tune (Y), and the rich cadence in a new key at Z.

The variations depart much farther from the theme than those of Mozart's Clarinet Quintet or, indeed, those of any earlier piece by Beethoven. We have the feeling that extraordinary depths are being plumbed within the theme, that its inner nature and possibilities are being revealed. At first the variations may sound remote, but, as we listen closely and allow for changes in tempo, we hear that they follow strictly the eight-measure structure of the tune with its cadences. Listen especially for the points mentioned above—X, Y, and Z; they all turn up one way or another in the variations, often with a very unusual effect.

Variation 1   Beethoven has transformed his hymn almost into a romantic reverie. The treatment of the sequence Y is very striking.

double variation   *Variation 2 (Double)*   A so-called <u>double variation</u> is used, in which each half of the theme is varied in some different manner in the repetition. Thus if the theme is diagramed ‖:**a**:‖:**b**:‖ variation 1 will be ‖:**a'**:‖:**b'**:‖ and variation 2 will be **a''** **a'''** **b''** **b'''**. This variation seems to dissect the theme, display all its nerves and tendons, and then put everything back together again.

Variation 3 (Double)   This cheerful variation, with its country dance rhythms, may remind us of Haydn. Strictly speaking, this counts as a double variation, too, though the differences are less apparent than they are in variation 2.

Variation 4   A languorous, highly decorative variation. In the second part, at the sequence Y, a cloud of fury blows up and then passes as suddenly as it had begun.

Variation 5 (Double)   This fast, firm-sounding contrapuntal variation is based on a motive derived from the first notes of the theme. Extensive imitations of this motive (plus a new scalewise countersubject) are fitted into the eight-measure pattern, cadences, sequences, etc. After the usual thirty-two measures (8 + 8 + 8 + 8) have gone by at a steady forte, the last eight are repeated quietly as preparation for variation 6.

Variation 6 (Double)   In this remarkable double variation, the accompaniment speeds up under a broken version of the theme until violent trills and passage-work create an astonishing welter of piano sound. There is a feeling that we are on the verge of some enormously powerful and solemn revelation; then this feeling gradually subsides.

To conclude, the theme returns exactly as it was at the beginning but without the repeats. The effect is of a profound quietude. Far from seeming redundant or anticlimactic, the theme seems newly and unexpectedly rich as it harks back over all the vast resources that have been explored within the boundaries of its single melodic unit.

The simple—even innocent—device of bringing the theme back at this point shows once again Beethoven's masterful control over musical form. He achieves an almost mystical effect: the still voice after the hurricane.

Beethoven, Piano Sonata in E, Op. 109: Second Movement*

read across page

DEVELOPMENT ⟶

bass figure

Damper (left) pedal on etc.

pp

etc.

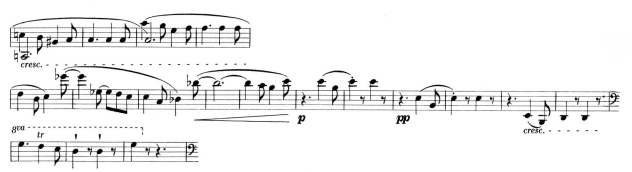

cresc.

cresc. - - - - -

* In piano music, curved brackets enclose staffs that are played by the right hand and left hand simultaneously. The left hand is not always shown in this line score, though of course it continues all the way through the piece.

Beethoven's Musical Handwriting

Beethoven was the first composer whom people viewed as a solitary genius struggling to produce masterpieces in the face of affliction. One fact that contributed to this image was his practice of working out his pieces very carefully and laboriously, sketching the themes, transitions, and so on, on music paper again and again until they finally came out right. Few earlier composers had had the time or the temperament for such perfectionism.

Beethoven never threw out his old sketches. He clung to them as though feeling unconsciously that their record of the creative process was a part of his real life. Though he was constantly moving from one apartment to another, and though he made no effort to preserve his finished scores, the pile of fifty-odd sketchbooks remained with him to the last.

A typical Beethoven sketch—our example is from the Ninth Symphony—is an all-but-indecipherable scrawl, in which the impatience and struggle of genius seem to be set down in graphic form. It is a loaded comparison to place this picture against the sample of Bach's handwriting shown on page 232, perhaps. For this is a rough sketch and that is a finished copy. Still, after making allowances, we can see in these two pictures the changeover from the old concept of the composer as "artisan" to the new view of the composer as "artist." Developed by the romantics, this concept is still with us, though many modern composers are fighting against it.

Franz Schubert (1797–1828)

Schubert was the only true native among the famous Viennese composers. Born in Vienna in 1797, he lived very unspectacularly and died of typhoid fever when he was only thirty-one, shortly after the death of Beethoven. It is said that Schubert was so shy he never even introduced himself to the formidable older master, whose music impressed him—and disturbed him—greatly.

Schubert did not achieve fame outside Vienna during his lifetime: hardly a surprise for one who was so young and so self-effacing. He took pleasure in the admiration his music received from his close circle of friends, the so-called Schubertianer (see page 316). And he lived to see nearly a hundred of his works published—piano pieces and sonatas, songs and choruses, some chamber music, and the most delightful waltzes imaginable. This number would exceed the wildest dreams of a thirty-one-year-old composer of our time, and it testifies to the rich musical culture that supported the Viennese composers. Even today, by the way, Austria devotes *one-fifth* of its total state income to music and the other arts.

SCHUBERT String Quartet in A Minor (1824) SIDE 11

Schubert is popularly known as an outstanding song composer. So he was; but in addition, he wrote symphonies, sonatas, and chamber music works in his last years that rank beside the masterpieces of Haydn, Mozart, and Beethoven. The general style and formal assumptions of the Viennese composers remain at the basis of these instrumental compositions of Schubert's, together with some new features of his own. The most striking of these, one that will hardly cause surprise coming from a song composer, is the increasing use of long song-like tunes in his instrumental pieces. The first movement of Schubert's Quartet in A Minor is a case in point.

FIRST MOVEMENT

Even before hearing the long tune, we are struck by a restless, haunting accompaniment figure which serves as a sort of introduction or vamp (see the example on page 312, measures 1–2).

When first mentioning the string quartet, on page 280, we made the obvious point that this medium is more restrained in tone color and dynamics than, say, the symphony orchestra. But it is also more intimate and subtle. The unique color of this introduction figure, combining the winding second violin with the throbbing viola and cello underneath, could only have been produced by a string quartet. The figure will be heard many times during the first movement, always with a moving effect.

Here at the beginning it leads into a long, melancholy tune, during which Schubert seems to forget that he is starting up a sonata-form movement, which is supposed to be dramatic, forward-looking, contrast-oriented, etc. True, in the recapitulation he pulls himself together and abbreviates the tune somewhat.

Notice the last measure of the example, which starts the bridge passage. The *ff* motive employed here has been forged out of the beginning of the tune itself—motive a, with a forceful alteration in rhythm and with an impatient trill added to the second note. This expert detail shows that Schubert knew very well the distinction between a typical sonata theme and a long tune. His innovation was unashamedly to incorporate long tunes into his sonata-form movements anyway.

The development section dwells on the main theme, or tune. It is treated in imitation, modulating. Then the motive marked b is fragmented out for especially vehement polyphony, and a particularly beautiful retransition follows. The coda, too, uses the main theme, which obviously occupied the center of Schubert's affections.

SECOND MOVEMENT

The form of this slow movement, and also that of the last movement, follows a sort of modified sonata form:

Sonata Form   Modified Sonata Form

EXPOSITION	DEVELOPMENT	RECAPITULATION	C O D A
first second theme group		first second theme group	

EXPOSITION	RECAP	BRIEF DEVELOPMENT	ITULATION	C O D A
first second theme group	first theme		second group	

This plan is fairly "strict" and not new with Schubert; his use of it stresses his traditional orientation. It must be admitted, though, that in listening to these two movements, we feel encouraged to lose ourselves in the many charming melodies rather than thinking too much about form and coherence. Here is the first theme of the second movement:

Schubert thought well enough of this tune to come back to it several times. He used it in an orchestral piece written to accompany a play called *Rosamunde* and as the basis for a theme and variations for piano, the Impromptu in B♭, Op. 142 No. 3. It is interesting to compare the treatment of the tune in the quartet with these others, especially the piano variations.

THIRD MOVEMENT

With its marvelous mood of hushed mystery, this movement certainly makes an original transformation of the usual straightforward, spirited minuet. Soon after the beginning, with its vague but unmistakable similarity to the beginning of the first movement, we hear a kind of dream waltz starting up and fading out again. This "minuet" actually uses a musical idea from one of Schubert's songs, *Die Götter Griechenlands* (The Gods of Greece), to words by the famous poet Friedrich von Schiller:

> Beautiful land of Greece! where art thou?
> Come back again, o age of Nature's flowering. . . .

So here (at last!) is a touch of "classical" antiquity in Viennese music. Yet the classical reference has much the same nostalgic quality as the little temple in the park shown on page 274. Schiller is lost in feelings of regret for times past, and with Schubert this nostalgia becomes almost romantic. Note especially the deep, throbbing modulation at a', the return of the a theme within the traditional ‖:a:‖:b a':‖ form.

FOURTH MOVEMENT

Again Schubert employed the modified sonata form shown in the diagram on page 312. Key contrast is especially clear between the first theme and the second group in the exposition—between the delicate, sprightly opening theme and the wary, mock-ominous theme in the second group. The "misplaced" development section, although short, works its way up to quite an aggressive climax.

But once again it is the tunes themselves that occupy the center of attention. They have an unmistakable popular-music lilt about them; this delightful movement is much lighter in tone than the three earlier ones. We are reminded of the fact that, before Johann Strauss, Schubert was the greatest of the Viennese waltz composers. However, since this movement is in duple time Schubert could not evoke the waltz, a triple-meter dance. His first and second themes recall two other popular dances of the time, the écossaise and the galop.

Schubert and the Lied

The German word for song is *Lied* (plural: *Lieder*—pronounced "lead" and "leader"). Besides its general use, the word *Lied* has a special application to an important genre of German song that evolved in the late eighteenth century and flourished mightily in the nineteenth. It is accompanied by the piano, which usually contributes a great deal to the total artistic effect; indeed, the pianist becomes more of a partner to the singer than an accompanist. And it is usually set to a poem of some literary distinction, or at least to one with ambitions in that direction. At its best, the *Lied* sets fine poetry to beautiful music and matches or enhances that poetry in a unique way.

Schubert was the first master of the *Lied*. He wrote over six hundred in his short lifetime, half of them before he was twenty. They differ very widely in form, scope, and sentiment. One type consists of lovely tunes repeated for each stanza of the poem; they may approach folk songs in their quality, or they may

strophic song be considerably more sophisticated. Songs of this type are said to be in strophic form (like almost all folk songs, hymns, etc.).

Another type of *Lied* provides new music for the later stanzas of the poem, in order to reflect the changing words. The usual term for this technique,

through-composed song *durchkomponiert* in German, translates into English as through-composed. Although there are exceptions, through-composed songs tend to be more dramatic than strophic ones.

Familiar examples of Schubert strophic songs are *Heidenröslein* (Hedge rose) and *An Silvia* (To Silvia), and of through-composed songs, *Gretchen am Spinnrade* (Gretchen at the spinning wheel) and *Erlkönig* (Elfking). The latter is set to a terse ballad by the famous poet Johann Wolfgang von Goethe. (A ballad is a poem or song that tells a story.) Though Schubert did not write many "story" songs, *Erlkönig* is probably his most famous composition.

SCHUBERT *Erlkönig* (Elfking) (1816)   SIDE 11

Goethe's poem tells of a father riding frantically through the night with a delirious child who thinks he hears the voice of the demon Elfking. The Elfking first invites the child to join him, then cajoles him, then threatens and assaults him. The father tries to quiet the child, but by the time they reach town the boy is dead.

Wer reitet so spät durch Nacht und Wind?	Who rides so late through the <u>night</u> and the <u>wind</u>?
Es ist der Vater mit seinem Kind;	It is the father with his child.
Er hat den Knaben wohl in dem Arm,	He holds the boy in his arm,
Er fasst ihn sicher, er hält ihn warm.	Grasps him securely, keeps him warm.
"Mein Sohn, was birgst du so bang dein Gesicht?"	"My son, why do you hide your face so anxiously?"
"Siehst, Vater, du den Erlkönig nicht?	"Father, do you see <u>the Elfking</u>?
Den Erlenkönig mit Kron und Schweif?"	The Elfking with his crown and tail?"
"Mein Sohn, es ist ein Nebelstreif."	"My son, it is only <u>a streak of mist</u>."
"Du liebes Kind, komm, geh mit mir!	"Darling child, come away with me!
Gar schöne Spiele spiel ich mit dir;	I will play fine games with you.
Manch bunte Blumen sind an dem Strand,	Many gay flowers grow by the shore;
Meine Mutter hat manch gülden Gewand."	My mother has many golden robes."
"Mein Vater, mein Vater, und hörest du nicht,	"Father, father, do you not hear
Was Erlenkönig mir leise verspricht?"	What the Elfking softly promises me?"
"Sei ruhig, bleibe ruhig, mein Kind:	"Be calm, my child, be calm—
In dürren Blättern säuselt der Wind."	The wind is rustling in the dry leaves."
"Willst, feiner Knabe, du mit mir gehn?	"You beautiful boy, will you come with me?
Meine Töchter sollen dich warten schön;	My daughters will wait upon you.
Meine Töchter führen den nächtlichen Reihn	My daughters lead the nightly round,
Und wiegen und tanzen und singen dich ein."	They will rock you, dance to you, sing you to sleep!"
"Mein Vater, mein Vater, und siehst du nicht dort	"Father, father, do you not see
Erlkönigs Töchter am dustern Ort?"	The Elfking's daughters there, <u>in that dark place</u>?"
"Mein Sohn, mein Sohn, ich seh es genau:	"My son, my son, I see it clearly:
Es scheinen die alten Weiden so grau."	It is the gray gleam of the old willow trees."
"Ich liebe dich, mich reizt deine schöne Gestalt;	"I love you, your beauty allures me,
Und bist du nicht willig, so brauch ich Gewalt."	And if you do not come willingly, I shall use force."
"Mein Vater, mein Vater, jetzt fasst er mich an!	"Father, father, now he is seizing me!
Erlkönig hat mir ein Leid's getan!"	The Elfking has hurt me!"
Dem Vater grauset's, er reitet geschwind,	Fear grips the father, he rides swiftly,
Er hält in den Armen das ächzende Kind,	Holding the moaning child in his arms;
Erreicht den Hof mit Müh und Not;	With effort and toil he reaches the house—
In seinen Armen das Kind war tot.	The child in his arms was dead.

Schubert writes different music for the three different voices. Each "voice" characterizes the speaker perfectly and differentiates him from the others. The father is low, stiff, and gruff, the Elfking sings ominously graceful tunes, and the boy sounds frantic—especially since, each time he sings, his voice goes higher and higher.

What, then, holds the song together as an artistic unity? The piano accompaniment has agitated repeated notes, suggesting the horse's hooves on this grim ride, and these keep going throughout, until just before the journey's end. During the Elfking's first and second stanzas, when the child hearing him is half asleep, the horse's hooves are muted. But they pound away distinctly in the king's third stanza; when the Elfking threatens him with force, the child is wide awake in terror. A wonderfully imaginative touch—and Schubert was only eighteen when he thought it up.

Schubert among His Friends

Although there is some reason to consider Schubert one of the early romantic composers, there is not much in his biography to make one think of a typical romantic career in the style of Byron, Chopin, or Edgar Allan Poe. For a time he worked as a low-level schoolteacher, like his father. Though he entertained ambitions as a theater composer, he lacked utterly the force and the wile necessary to succeed in that field. He did gain a few private pupils among young ladies of the aristocracy and upper middle classes, but old anecdotes suggest that he felt more comfortable in the company of the maids downstairs.

He was happiest of all in the small devoted circle of his friends, who called themselves the "Schubertianer" and provided him with friendship, admiration, and money for the better part of his brief composing life.

At a musicale among the Schubertianer, Schubert is at the piano, surrounded by a group of warm admirers. Most of them seem to be charming young people, except for the distinguished older gentleman sitting next to the composer—Michael Vogl, a retired opera singer, who was almost the only influential friend Schubert had. Vogl sang his songs in public and introduced them to publishers. His voice was a high baritone, and Schubert wrote directly for him. As a result, songs such as *Die Winterreise* sound best when sung by this kind of voice, though they are also often performed by sopranos, tenors, and basses.

The Schubertianer prided themselves on their universal artistic tastes, ranging from music to poetry and painting. The man who drew this pleasant picture, Moritz von Schwind, drifted into the Schubert circle at the age of seventeen. He later became a leading German painter, but he never forgot the musical enthusiasms of his youth. (Schwind himself is the second mustache to the right of Schubert.) In the 1860s, he painted a rather dreadful series of scenes from famous operas on the foyer walls of the Vienna Opera House, where they can still be seen today.

SCHUBERT Die Winterreise (The Winter Journey) (1828)

song cycle

Schubert's masterpiece of song composition, written near the end of his life, is a set of twenty-four songs collectively called *Die Winterreise* (The winter journey). This is a song cycle, a group of songs with some kind of loose unity—at the very least, a song cycle has a common idea connecting all the poems. Some or all of the songs may also be connected by musical means.

In the present case, we are to picture a young man disappointed in love, who takes to wandering through the countryside in wintertime. Everything he sees reminds him of his bitter experience and despair. Each sight forms the subject of one of the songs in the cycle, and in many songs the piano accompaniment illustrates some element in the nature scene. A carrion crow wheels in the winter sky, hounds rattle their chains at night, a last leaf is blown helter-skelter from a tree, and a beggar-musician plays his instrument with fingers numb from cold.

"Der Leiermann" (The Hurdy-Gurdy Man) The poet sees an old beggar-musician playing in the snow, with no one to listen or put a penny in his plate; this old man, he thinks, reflects his own condition.

Drüben hinterm Dorfe steht ein Leiermann,	Over there, beyond the village, stands a hurdy-gurdy man,
Und mit starren Fingern dreht er, was er kann.	With numbed fingers he grinds away as best he can.
Barfuss auf dem Eise wankt er hin und her,	He staggers barefoot on the ice
Und sein kleiner Teller bleibt ihm immer leer.	And his little plate remains ever empty.
Keiner mag ihn hören, keiner sieht ihn an,	No one wants to hear him, no one looks at him,
Und die Hunde knurren um den alten Mann.	And the dogs snarl about the old man.
Und er lässt es gehen, alles wie es will,	And he lets the world go by, whatever happens,
Dreht, und seine Leier steht ihm nimmer still.	He turns the handle, and his hurdy-gurdy is never still.
Wunderlicher Alter, soll ich mit dir gehn?	Strange old man, shall I go with you?
Willst zu meinen Liedern deine Leier drehn?	Will you grind your music to songs of mine?

What is famous about this song is the economy of means by which Schubert achieves his musical picture of hopelessness. Except for the question at the end, "Strange old man, shall I go with you? Will you play your music to songs of mine?," the song is strictly strophic, two stanzas with the same tune. What a numb tune it is, with its utterly regular rhythm and its monotonous phrase structure.

The piano accompaniment is frozen, too, with the same hollow left-hand chord droning away in every single measure to invoke the sound of the archaic peasant instrument (see page 321). Yet in mood this accompaniment recalls the figure that opens Schubert's String Quartet in A Minor: compare the example on page 312. Schubert has indeed contrived to make the hurdy-gurdy play "songs of mine"—songs of his own.

"Muth" (Courage) A more vigorous, rather abrupt song, this is the poet's response as he trudges on, brushing the snowflakes out of his eyes and taking a certain petulant satisfaction in defying snow and misery alike.

Fliegt der Schnee mir in's Gesicht,	If the snow flies in my face
Schüttl' ich ihn herunter.	I brush it off.
Wenn mein Herz im Busen spricht,	If my heart speaks in my bosom,
Sing ich hell und munter.	I sing brightly and cheerfully;
Höre nicht, was es mir sagt,	I do not hear what it tells me—
Habe keine Ohren,	I have no ears!
Fühle nicht, was es mir klagt,	I have no feeling for its complaints—
Klagen ist für Toren.	Complaining is for fools!
Lustig in die Welt hinein	Merrily through the world I go,
Gegen Wind und Wetter!	In the face of wind and weather!
Will kein Gott auf Erde sein	If there be no God on earth,
Sind wir selber Götter!	We'll make ourselves into gods!

Stanzas 1 and 2 have the same music, a short tune interspersed by piano passages. The singer's bursts of forced "courage" are depicted by sudden alternations between minor and major modes, and between three- and two-measure phrases. So far, the song is strophic.

For stanza 3, Schubert invented a second tune, related to the first; and when the words of this stanza are repeated, the tune gains a new little modulation that is very effective. This second tune stays in the major mode, since the words are "Merrily through the world I go." But at the very end, after the singer has stopped, there is a touch of grim humor as the piano counters all that major-mode music with its original minor-mode passage from stanzas 1 and 2. Merriment does not get the last word.

"Der Wegweiser" (The Signpost) Here the poet comes upon a country signpost, which makes him meditate gloomily on the directions his life has taken. There will be no return from the path he has to follow now!

Was vermeid ich denn die Wege,	Why do I avoid the roads
Wo die andern Wandrer gehn,	The other travelers use,
Suche mir versteckte Stege	And seek hidden paths
Durch verschneite Felsenhöhn?	Among the snowbound rocks?
Habe ja doch nichts begangen,	I have committed no crime
Dass ich Menschen sollte scheun,	That should make me shun mankind;
Welch ein törichtes Verlangen	What is this foolish desire
Treibt mich in die Wüstenein?	That drives me into the wilderness?
Weiser stehen auf den Wegen	Signposts stand on the roads,
Weisen auf die Städte zu,	Pointing toward the towns;
Und ich wandre sonder Massen,	And I wander beyond all reason—
Ohne Ruh, and suche Ruh.	Restless, yet seeking rest.
Einen Weiser seh ich stehen	I see a signpost that stands
Unverrückt vor meinem Blick;	Immovably before me;
Eine Strasse muss ich gehen,	I must travel a road
Die noch keiner ging zurück.	By which no one has ever returned.

As is Schubert's habit, the song begins with a piano introduction and a tune. But in the remaining stanzas of the poem, there are only suggestions of strophic form; the bleak tune never returns exactly. Schubert grows more and more obsessed with the chief motive:

Was vermeid ich denn die We - ge, wo die andern Wandrer gehn, suche mir versteck-te Stege durch verschneite Felsen - höhn?
Why do I avoid the roads *used by other travellers,* *and seek hidden paths* *among the snow-bound rocks?*

This is ultimately "developed" into a long series of repeated notes, the quiet tolling of a knell underlining the suggestion of death at the end of the poem. Although the feeling of this song is romantic, even sentimental, the treatment of motives shows Schubert's technical adherence to the Viennese style.

If we were to listen to the whole of *Die Winterreise,* we would be able to observe this motive coming back quietly in song after song. It provides a certain musical unity to the whole song cycle, in addition to the poetic unity.

The Hurdy-Gurdy

This curious and very ancient instrument consists of a set of strings in a sound box. The strings are not played by means of bowing or plucking; instead, a wooden wheel turned by the player rubs continuously against them to produce the sound. Rosin is a help, but the hurdy-gurdy can never have made a very refined sound. It was used almost exclusively for popular music in the streets or on the village green, although Haydn wrote some concertos for the instrument on the commission of a player who was none other than the King of Naples.

Like another famous popular musical instrument, the bagpipe, the hurdy-gurdy used many long drone notes. Composers often imitated this sound in their "art music," and it is possible to detect signs of a changing attitude toward the common people, under the influence of Enlightenment ideas, in the way they treated it. Baroque composers were interested only in creating a simple and piquant result. (For a familiar example, listen to the so-called Pastoral Symphony in Handel's oratorio *Messiah*.)

Haydn, in such works as the trio of the minuet in Symphony No. 88 (see page 277), is inclined to poke fun at the peasant musician, who does not seem to be quite sure when to shift his drone notes. He seems to lose count in the melody line, too. It is affectionate fun, though—and, if we listen closely, perhaps the peasant gets the last laugh, for these pieces are as artfully put together as any of Haydn's music, given their small scale.

As for Schubert, in his famous song *Der Leiermann* (The Hurdy-Gurdy Man) (see page 317), the simple countryman has now become a figure of pathos, from whom the poet can learn of life and suffering. Schubert, too, regards the "natural man" with awe, as a sort of model for artistic creation:

> Strange old man, shall I go with you?
> Will you grind your music to songs of mine?

This rather harrowing hurdy-gurdy man was painted by the seventeenth-century French artist Georges de La Tour.

CHAPTER 11 | Romanticism   I

Romanticism   I

Of all the terms used to describe style in the arts, *romantic* is no doubt the most familiar and the most evocative. Originally applied to literature of the early nineteenth century, the term conveyed attitudes that became so widespread that the word had to spill over into many other areas of life. The use of *romantic* to mean "amorous" dates from the nineteenth century and derives from the artistic movement—though love was only one of several important themes of romanticism.

In music, the term *romantic* is applied to music from near the beginning of the century to its end, a longer span than in any other art. Over this period, music shows rather more continuity of style than do literature and painting. At the basis of this musical continuity, perhaps, is a philosophical idea, a new concept of music and its role, that took a firm hold on the European consciousness.

Literary romanticism dwelt on a number of important themes, among them the glorification of romantic love, nostalgia for the past, and a new enthusiasm for nature (see pages 329 and 356). For poets and artists of the time, these were ways of getting to the real heart of romanticism: the insistence on spontaneous personal emotion. Men and women were determined to experience life to the full in defiance of the inhibiting conventions of society. And they were determined to express what they experienced just as fully.

Especially in Germany, romantics began to see that of all the arts, music could express inner experience most deeply and freely. Deeply, because music is closest of all to the subjective, instinctive springs of emotion—what we now call the unconscious. Freely, because the musician's imagination is not tied down to matter-of-fact words and statements (like the poet's) or to the representation of things (like the painter's.) Music seemed the perfect outlet for an age that insisted above all on the value of individual emotional expression.

This concept of music was widely held by musicians as well as other artists and thinkers. It found definitive formulation in the works of Arthur Schopenhauer, a much-read German philosopher who influenced the composer Richard Wagner at a critical period of his career. Wagner's opera *Tristan und*

Isolde, one of the most characteristic products of romantic music, practically spells out Schopenhauer's philosophy (see page 365). Music gained enormous prestige and status. "All art aspires to the condition of music," wrote a famous nineteenth-century critic, Walter Pater. Indeed, music was taken much more seriously in the nineteenth century than ever before—or after. Which may help to explain why nineteenth-century music continues to dominate the concert repertoire, and why Schopenhauer's views are shared in a general way by many people today who have never heard his name.

Emphasis on the importance of personal feeling naturally entailed new prestige for the artists themselves. Composers and performers no longer regarded themselves—and no longer allowed themselves to be regarded—as craftsmen serving society, but rather as free spirits expressing their own souls with a genius not granted to the common run of humanity. "My nobility is *here* and *here,*" Beethoven is supposed to have said, pointing to his heart and to his head. The pianist-composer Franz Liszt started his career playing in drawing rooms where a silk cord separated the "lowly" performer from the aristocratic listeners, but he lived to be sought out by these same people on terms of equality. Liszt's well-publicized liaisons with a countess and a princess may be taken as signs of the changing times. (Liszt surrounded by an admiring throng, including the countess, is pictured on page 351.)

The Style of Romantic Music

All of this individual expression will cause us something of a problem as we examine the features of romantic musical style. Since the main artistic value at the time was the interpretation of personal emotion, every artist labored to evolve a personal style. And since individuality was at a premium, we shall find talking about musical style in general terms considerably harder than spotting novelties and innovations. To be sure, all nineteenth-century composers shared some common interests, which we will discuss in the following pages. But one such common interest was to sound different from everybody else.

Another way of putting the problem is in terms of the distinction between "period styles" and "individual styles," a distinction that was made when the concept of musical style was first introduced (see page 53). The romantic period is the point in musical history when the balance shifted decisively in the direction of individual styles. If someone were suddenly to play us a piece of earlier music—by switching on a car radio, for instance—we might identify it at once as baroque and then puzzle over whether it was by Vivaldi, Bach, or Handel. With a romantic piece, our first reaction would probably be: "That sounds like Chopin" (or Berlioz or Wagner or Strauss). Whether or not we would also add dutifully that the piece sounded romantic, the center of our interest would be on its individualistic qualities. And certainly that is where the composer would have wanted it to be.

ROMANTIC MELODY AND HARMONY

It is not easy to characterize romantic melody and harmony. To a large extent, they go together. The melodic lines tend to have richness and intensity, and the harmony contributes to this by winding up great tensions and then providing great relief at points of relaxation. Each in an individual way, composers developed the knack of making their melodies passionate, dreamy, supercharged, intimate, or whatever shade of emotional coloring they sought to convey.

Sometimes these melodies grew so demonstrative and effusive that they may affect some listeners unpleasantly. This was a risk run by romantic artists in general, though it was overcome by the best of them. However, most listeners warm instinctively to romantic melody and to its typical harmonic underpinnings. It is familiar to us from its echoes in the more emotional popular music of the present and in what used to be called the "sweet" music of the jazz and swing eras.

Besides using harmony to support emotional melody, composers began to relish it for its own sake. Fascinating untried chords and juxtapositions of chords were explored, for it was found that harmony could contribute potently to those mysterious, ethereal, rapturous, or sultry moods that were so greatly enjoyed at the time. This was a true novelty, compared with the practice of earlier composers. Harmony began to encroach on the territory of tone color itself. There are even some themes in romantic music that gain their memorable character from harmony, rather than from melody or rhythm, as in earlier music (see the example on page 366 and the "magic sleep" theme in the line score on page 371).

THE EXPANSION OF TONE COLOR

Tone color had been treated with considerable subtlety by the Viennese composers, but the romantics seized on this aspect of music with particular enthusiasm and gave it special development. For the first time in Western music, the sheer sensuous quality of sound assumed major artistic importance, on a level with rhythm, melody, and form.

Bach and Beethoven wrote carefully for the various instruments, of course, but in one sense they seem to have applied their instrumental "colors" as a last touch, over and above the "drawing," that is, the real foundation of notes and structure. This is generally not so with the romantic composers, fascinated as they were by the emotional possibilities of pure sonority. For Chopin or Berlioz, piano sound or orchestral sound is primary. Their music can no longer be viewed in abstract terms apart from its particular tone color.

The romantic composers invented new musical instruments, greatly improved old ones, coaxed astonishing new sounds out of all instruments, and combined sounds in altogether unheard-of ways. The orchestra was expanded enormously. Compare the early romantic orchestra charted on page 330 with the typical Viennese orchestra on page 248. Indeed, the age was fascinated by the orchestra, both as an independent entity, in symphonies and the like,

Romantic Nostalgia for the Past

Two important preoccupations of early romanticism were fascination with nature and fascination with the past, especially the Middle Ages. Taste in fiction moved away from "contemporary" subjects (*Tom Jones, Robinson Crusoe*) to tales of historical adventure and romance (*Ivanhoe, The Hunchback of Notre Dame,* "The Cask of Amontillado"). Many early romantic poems were set in times of old: Sir Walter Scott's *Young Lochinvar,* John Keats's *La Belle Dame sans Merci,* Samuel Taylor Coleridge's *Kubla Khan* and *Christabel,* and Alfred Lord Tennyson's *The Lady of Shalott.*

Our picture illustrates a later and longer poem by Tennyson, *Idylls of the King,* which was begun in 1857 and became one of the great best sellers of Victorian England. The king is Arthur, the legendary ruler of sixth-century England, and the poem recounts the tales of the Knights of the Round Table and the Holy Grail in such a way that they seem vaguely relevant to the standards and ideals of the nineteenth century. Longfellow's *Hiawatha* is another example of this kind of work, a grandiose blend of romanticism, nostalgia, and middle-class patriotism.

The best example of all is Richard Wagner's four-night opera *The Nibelung's Ring,* based on the most famous of German medieval myths (see page 367). Incidentally, the Arthurian legends were also a rich source for Wagner, yielding him the subjects of his operas *Lohengrin, Parsifal* (Tennyson's Sir Percivale), and *Tristan und Isolde.*

Many other opera composers chose romantic subjects from the past, among them the stories of Joan of Arc, Ivanhoe, Francesca da Rimini, Mary Queen of Scots, and of course Faust—a great favorite. Composers also sometimes experimented with real or simulated old music to give their compositions an antique flavor. We shall see Berlioz and Liszt importing a Gregorian chant—the *Dies irae*—into their compositions (pages 349, 352). There was something of a cult at this time for the music of the famous sixteenth-century composer Giovanni Pierluigi da Palestrina (see page 134). Palestrina lived in the Renaissance, long after the Middle Ages, but he was about the earliest composer whose music was known to the nineteenth century.

Romantic interest in the past was less historical than nostalgic. Poets and their readers loved the past for the pleasant feelings it could stir up. Thus our artist (Gustave Doré, the most famous of nineteenth-century book illustrators) thought nothing of drawing King Arthur's costume and castle in a style that is fully six hundred years too late. The later period was, visually speaking, more "romantic"; compare the castle with the nineteenth-century fantasy castle of King Ludwig II shown on page 362. Other romantic features of this particular picture are the grisly skeletons, lit up by the moonlight, and the sentimental response to them conveyed by the droop of Arthur's head (and also his horse's!).

and also as a newly rich accompaniment to opera. On the whole, chamber music languished. If people today automatically think of the symphony orchestra whenever they think of "classical music," that is a holdover from the nineteenth century.

AN EARLY ROMANTIC ORCHESTRA
(As in Berlioz's *Fantastic Symphony*)

Strings: first violins, sometimes divided into 3 sections
second violins, sometimes in 3 sections
violas, sometimes in 2 sections
cellos, sometimes in 2 sections
double basses, sometimes in 4 sections
2 harps

Woodwinds: 2 flutes, one sometimes playing piccolo
2 oboes, one sometimes playing English horn
2 clarinets, one sometimes playing high clarinet (E♭ clarinet)
4 bassoons

Brass: 4 French horns
2 cornets
2 trumpets
3 trombones
2 bass tubas

Percussion: 4 timpani (two players)
bass drum, cymbals, side drum
chimes (tubular bells)

As though to symbolize all this, some of the main composers of the time wrote major textbooks on orchestration, the technique of writing most effectively for each orchestral instrument and combining them to produce the best blends. The texts by Hector Berlioz (1844, with important expansions by the late romantic composer Richard Strauss, 1905) and Nikolai Rimsky-Korsakov (1913) are still studied with profit, after all these years.

études   With a similar concern for tone color in mind, pianist-composers of the romantic period wrote studies for piano, or <u>études</u>, as they are called in French— a genre that had previously been left mainly to humble pedagogues. Needless to say, the études of Frédéric Chopin and Franz Liszt are a far cry from the mournful finger exercises of Czerny and Hanon, which afflict so many beginning pianists. Chopin and Liszt études train the fingers ingeniously for certain special technical problems, while at the same time they are marvelous pieces of music, among the finest written by their composers. One will be briefly discussed later (see page 336).

DYNAMICS AND RHYTHM

Dynamics were often controlled very closely by the romantic composers. As they sought greater contrasts for more and more expressive effects, they tried to mark dynamics on their melodies with a precision sometimes amounting to fussiness. Where the eighteenth century had been content with the signs, *ff*, *f*, *mf*, *p*, and *pp* (see page 11), the nineteenth century needed to go up to *ffff* and down to *ppppp*.

In rhythm, the romantic composers capitalized on and extended the flexibility that had been discovered by the Viennese composers. Not only did the romantics now want certain passages to be slowed down or speeded up, but they also expected performers to treat the meter freely all along, or at least in certain "expressive" passages. A style of playing was encouraged in which the meter is constantly "stretched" slightly and then compressed again—or, when the meter is handled strictly, the melody stretches so as to be slightly out of phase with it. Listen, for example, to the way the third beat of the triple meter tends to be played in a good performance of a Viennese waltz, such as *The Blue Danube.* This is called <u>rubato</u>, "robbed" time.

rubato

An artistic rubato can be sensuous and teasing, while the meter is always clear; indeed, rubato can make the meter seem more interesting and elegant. Excessive rubato is vulgar or spineless or both. It is up to the performer to tread the fine line, for composers have never tried to notate rubato precisely.

THE PROBLEM OF FORM IN ROMANTIC MUSIC

Spontaneity was an important goal of the romantic movement. (Though we may reflect that spontaneity was becoming harder all the time to achieve in such areas as harmony and orchestration, in which the composer now had to acquire more refined skills and learn more "rules" than earlier composers had needed.) And if there was any area in which the romantic composer wanted to be (or to seem) free and spontaneous, it was the area of musical form. The music should bubble out moment by moment, irrepressible and untrammeled, like churning emotion itself. Yet the music had to avoid real formlessness, lest the listener lose track of the musical thought and simply stop listening.

On page 50 we drew a distinction between "outer forms," such as the sonnet or sonata form, and the "inner form" of individual works of art. It was natural for romantic composers to stress inner form and pay less attention to outer forms. When they did use other forms such as sonata form, theme and variations, or rondo, they sometimes worked within the form so freely that it becomes a fine point whether the scheme is really there at all—a fine point, and usually a useless argument. More and more, composers found themselves creating a new inner form for every new composition.

This was hard to do, much harder than the task of the Viennese and baroque composers with their outer forms. It is not surprising, then, that not a few romantic pieces strike us as rambling and disorganized.

Thus we shall not be able to produce a list of "forms" for the romantic period to match those of, say, the baroque—ritornello form, passacaglia, fugue, da capo aria, and the rest. What we can do is make a two-sided point about the scope or size of romantic compositions. Also we can identify two general formal principles of the era: the *principle of the literary program* and the *principle of thematic unity.*

"Miniature" and "Grandiose" Compositions   The point about scope or size is this: romantic compositions show an interesting tendency to be either considerably shorter or else considerably longer than most earlier music. Some composers cultivated "miniatures," pieces lasting just a few minutes—in particular, short songs and piano pieces. This music conveys a brief but particularly intense whiff of emotion. The composer is able to commune with the listener in the most intimate possible way.

Short pieces were written in earlier times, of course, as movements within larger compositions—Viennese minuets in symphonies, baroque dances in suites—where their effect was balanced by other movements. But in the romantic era, short pieces often come singly and stand out more clearly as individuals in their own right.

Other composers (or sometimes the same ones) moved in the opposite direction, toward what we shall call grandiose pieces. They planned larger and larger symphonies, cantatas, and operas. The number of movements, the performing forces, and the total time span were all increased. Starting with the generously augmented romantic symphony orchestra, composers would then pull in all kinds of added performers: solo singers, a chorus or several choruses, and, in one famous instance, even four extra brass bands (the Requiem Mass by Hector Berlioz). With words added, the total effect was laced with poetry, philosophical or religious ideas, a loose story line, and/or dramatic action. The listener was to be impressed (even stupefied) by a combination of great thoughts, opulent sounds, grandiose emotions, and sheer length.

The "Principle of the Literary Program"   This principle emerged from the determination of the romantic composers to make music expressive. As we mentioned above, they believed that music came close to the basic sources of human emotion and therefore could express spontaneous feeling deeply and freely, even without further explanation. At the same time, the nineteenth century abounded in music associated with ideas, stories, evocative titles, and the like. One way or another, these were expressed in associative words—words that would indicate, and even in some sense "explain," the emotional content of the music.

Perhaps there is indeed a contradiction here. Romantic music needed no explanation, yet it was "explained" in words. But we must remember that the romantics were less interested in building consistent aesthetic theories than in pursuing all possible ways of maximizing emotional effect. In this spirit, they enthusiastically explored combinations of music with whatever literary elements they thought could enrich it.

The grandiose choral-orchestral compositions that we have just mentioned are a case in point, with their philosophical or narrative texts "expressed" in music. Opera flourished too (see page 354). As for the romantic miniatures, songs already had poetic texts, and the nineteenth century saw a wonderful outpouring of lyric poetry in all languages to supply the composers. Piano pieces, lacking the advantage of literary associations, were often fur-

miniatures *(margin note)*

grandiose compositions *(margin note)*

nished with atmospheric titles: either general ones such as *Songs without Words, Ballades, Woodland Sketches,* or else somewhat more specific ones— *Dream of Love, The Poet Speaks, Rustle of Spring.*

Finally, composers began to write large-scale instrumental pieces bearing not only titles but also literary "programs," actual stories or at least descriptions of emotional impressions arranged in some order. Step by step, the music follows the program, illustrates or reflects it, and even comments on it. The

program music   principle of program music looms large in nineteenth-century music.

Much ink has been spilled about this matter by aestheticians and amateur philosophers. How closely, if at all, does the music really illustrate the program? Does the program "explain" the music? If you are played the music without being told the program, could you tell it from the music? Does (or should) the music make complete sense on its own terms, even if perhaps we can see that the program does add another dimension to it?

But the point is that the romantics did not *want* to be without the program. They did not particularly *want* the music to "make sense on its own terms." They wanted the combination of dimensions provided by both. There are some people who instinctively tend to summon up "pictures" in their minds when listening to music. Perhaps this habit should be frowned upon as far as baroque, Viennese, or modern music is concerned, but it fits in perfectly with the spirit of romanticism.

The "Principle of Thematic Unity" This is the other broad principle that can be identified in romantic music. To put it simply, composers tended more and more to keep some of the same themes running through all the many movements in their large works. In the grandiose compositions mentioned above, this provided a measure of unity to pieces that otherwise might have seemed straggling and formless.

That puts it simply; but in practice things worked out in a rather more complicated way. We shall experience several different levels of thematic unity in nineteenth-century music. In some compositions, themes from one movement come back literally and obviously in subsequent movements. This

cyclic form   is called cyclic form ("cyclic" referring to the cycle of four or more movements in a symphony, etc.). Cyclic form is the least subtle manifestation of the principle of thematic unity.

In other compositions, free variations of a theme are used successively either in different parts of one movement, or in all the movements of a piece. This procedure differs from the theme-and-variations form of the baroque and Viennese periods (see page 283), in which the "theme" is usually an entire tune, the variations go all the way through the tune, and the variations follow one another directly, in an orderly series. It is best to use a special term,

thematic transformation   thematic transformation, for the variationlike procedure applied to relatively short themes, at relatively wide intervals of time, in romantic music.

In still other romantic pieces, we hear themes with even looser relationships among them. They bear a mysterious family resemblance, one that may be very hard to pin down. Clearly different, they nonetheless show vague similarities, though these similarities are too slight to count as variations by the standards of Viennese music (or even as transformations by the standards of romantic music).

This last phenomenon raises some fascinating questions: How is the line drawn between "variations," "transformations," and "vague similarities"? How about similarities so slight that some people (such as the composers) can hear them but other people cannot, at least not on the conscious level? Indeed —most fascinating of all—may there not be vague similarities that create the impression of unity subliminally, on a subconscious level, as though by some musical "hidden persuader"?

This notion would have delighted the romantics, with their view of music as the inner language of unconscious emotional experience. Vague similarity rather than precise recall, suggestion rather than outright statement, atmosphere rather than discourse, feeling rather than form: all these go to the heart of romanticism. We shall not be able to appreciate romantic music fully if we approach it in a literal frame of mind. In much of this music, the "inner form" is tied to the principle of thematic unity. Listening to this kind of form requires ears that are not only sharp but also imaginative, exploratory, and more than a little fanciful.

Romantic "Miniatures"

Romantic miniatures, for piano solo or voice and piano, are short pieces that convey a particularly intense, intimate whiff of emotion (see page 332). They are easy to listen to, because they are short and tend to concentrate on a single very striking musical idea. To be sure, this idea is usually so special, and of such limited applicability, that it could not keep up interest for too long. Obviously miniatures have less meat on them than bigger works. But no doubt there are people who relish these highly flavored snacks and do not care so much for heavy four- or five-course romantic symphonies and the like.

The later Viennese composers already reflected the fashion for miniatures. Beethoven wrote some piano pieces called *Bagatelles* (meaning "trifles"; one of them is only twelve measures long), and Schubert made a specialty of songs, as we have seen. The chief romantic composers of miniatures include Felix Mendelssohn (1809–1847) and the song composer Hugo Wolf (1860–1903), as well as Brahms, Chopin, Schumann, and Liszt.

Frédéric Chopin (1810–1849)

Chopin is remembered first, perhaps, for his wonderful feeling for tone color. Himself a superb pianist, he revolutionized the technique of playing the piano, so that it became an ideal medium for romanticism instead of the rather matter-of-fact instrument of earlier times. He created entire new sound areas of pianistic melancholy, languor, and delicacy; and, on the other side, he developed a range of power and brilliance that far outshone the barnstorming virtuoso pianists of his day. Besides his sensitivity to tone color, Chopin had an equally fine ear for melody and harmony and a great instinct for rhythm. Faint or bright, there is always a sparkle to his music, a rhythmic sparkle in addition to the exquisite piano sound.

With a fastidiousness that marked all his actions, Chopin limited the range of the music he wrote more sharply than any other important composer. Besides two early piano concertos and three sonatas, he wrote almost exclusively miniatures for piano solo. Their titles form a romantic gallery. The famous *nocturnes* are dreamy night pieces or serenades; the *impromptus* are supposed to sound like improvisations; the *études* have been mentioned above (see page 330). There are also *ballades,* which do not have specific ballad poems as programs but only mean to suggest the aura of some thrilling tale of yore. And there are *préludes*—preludes to nothing, which end expectantly and leave the listener dreaming of what might ensue.

More conventionally, Chopin wrote some scherzos (see page 297) and numerous dances for piano: waltzes, mazurkas, and polonaises. The latter two are Polish dance types; Chopin was a patriotic Pole even though his father was originally French and he himself lived in Paris. He wrote mazurkas and polonaises partly out of nostalgia for the land of his birth, partly to satisfy the Parisians' fascination with exotic foreign music, and most of all because these dances gave him the opportunity to experiment with novel melodic and harmonic effects inspired by Slavic folk sources.

CHOPIN Mazurka in A Minor, Op. 17 No. 4 (1830)   SIDE 11

The Mazurka in A Minor is said to have been sketched by Chopin when he was only fourteen. It opens with an atmospheric, floating introduction of four measures:

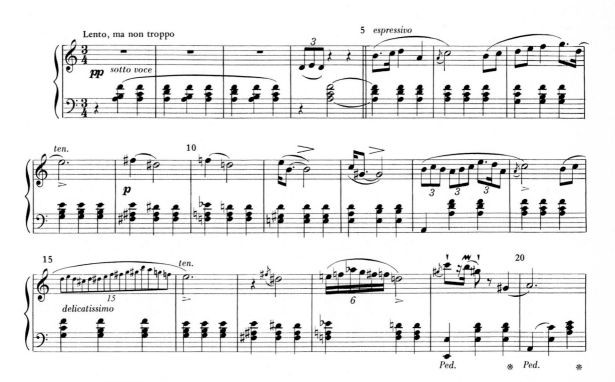

Unlike the usual purposeful introduction of a Viennese piece, this romantic introduction seems to grow up imperceptibly out of a great void, as though we have to bend an ear to catch its mysterious, delicate rustle. The identical four measures return at the end of the piece, leaving us suspended—for the piece does not come to a true cadence (see page 22) at all. As this music fades away, we should assume a pensive attitude, half musing upon the melancholy mazurka itself and half yearning for these delicate sounds to start up again in the silence. A truly romantic stance, this, if we achieve it.

The mood of melancholy is most unusual for a mazurka, for in real life this is a bright and rather hard dance. Chopin views it through his own special filter; only the characteristic dance rhythm (♪. ♪ ♩ ♩) slowed down greatly in tempo, refers hauntingly to the folk origins of the mazurka dance type. Chopin uses a short and simple, stripped-down dance form (a a b a c c′ c c″ a coda); compare the minuet form on page 277.

The delicious sliding harmonies in measures 9 and 10 are typically romantic and typically Chopinesque. So is the right-hand writing in measures 13, 18, and especially 15. Here a vague sensuous shimmer of sound, further blurred by the sustaining (right-foot) pedal, deliberately hides the rhythm, melody, and harmony in a wash of piano color, at least for a moment. We can draw an analogy between the obscuring of musical elements by tone color in Chopin's music and the obscuring of lines by actual color in romantic paintings such as those of Turner (see page 357).

In any good performance of Chopin, the pianist will apply some rubato (see page 331), slightly contracting and expanding the meter at many points. This adds even further to the emotional sheen.

CHOPIN Étude in C Minor, Op. 10 No. 12   (*Revolutionary Étude*) (1832)   SIDE 11

In another mood, Chopin's well-known Étude in C Minor makes its introduction (not shown) out of a torrent of fast piano runs. These continue in the left hand below a melody that catches the romantic spirit at its most hectic and its most magnificent:

Chopin marked this melody *appassionato* (impassioned). Just when it seems to have calmed down to an ominous hush, the fury bursts out again for a sudden loud conclusion. Whether or not this piece reflects the composer's patriotic in-dignation at the Russian capture of Warsaw in 1831, as has been said, the nick-name *Revolutionary Étude* seems fair enough.

Like the Mazurka in A Minor, the *Revolutionary* Étude is short and simple in form. It really consists of one long tune repeated with a new ending (A A').

CHOPIN Ballade No. 1 in G Minor, Op. 23 (1840) SIDE 12

A longer and more ambitious work is the Ballade No. 1 in G Minor. Though there is no real story to this "ballad," perhaps the solemn, almost "speaking" introduction does seem to say "once upon a time" before the main business begins. This takes the form of a tune with a brooding quality:

Notice that while the melody contains many eighth notes (indicated by the upward stems in the music), Chopin has directed that some of these melody notes be sustained (as indicated by the downward stems). This is another good, if quiet, example of Chopin's skill in manipulating piano tone color.

There are two further themes, embedded in a great variety of brilliant piano writing:

Although all three of these melodies are quiet when first heard, they return with different dynamics and in different moods. The first tune grows menacing from the point marked with the asterisk on, and the second tune rages in tri-umph. A form diagram for the piece must include a reference to the dynamics:

INTRODUCTION	MAIN SECTION								CODA
Largo	Moderato								Presto con fuoco
	A---→B	C	A		B	B	C	A	
p	*pp*	*pp*	*pp*<*ff*	*ff*		*ff*	*ff*	*pp*<*f*	*il più forte possibile*

Chopin and George Sand

The composer Frédéric Chopin and the novelist George Sand (Mme. Aurore Dudevant), painted by their friend Eugène Delacroix, the greatest of the French romantic artists. Delacroix's portrait of Chopin radiates a sense of agony and self-absorbed passion, qualities that probably would not have struck a Houdon so forcibly (see page 287). Here one romantic artist portrays another, consumed by the common fire of their genius.

When the romantics spoke of emotional freedom, what they generally meant first was "free love," and it is no coincidence that many artists of this time had intense and often irregular love affairs, which they made no effort to hide. Chopin, Berlioz, Liszt, Verdi, and Wagner can be mentioned among the musicians.

George Sand was a distinguished novelist, feminist, and

champion of sexual freedom who lived with Chopin after leaving the poet Alfred de Musset. After breaking up with Chopin, she wrote a rather unkind novel about their ten-year relationship. There had been literary ladies before in France (the "bluestockings") and elsewhere, but the romantic period was the first in which they began to preach and practice women's liberation. Besides adopting a male pen name, Sand sometimes wore men's clothing and was famous for her cigars.

From her photographs we know she was not beautiful, but evidently Delacroix was in no doubt as to her sensuousness and rich magnetism for the opposite sex. He has depicted these marvelously—the "romantic" woman behind the plain face. (The cigar is there, too, but notice how Delacroix has de-emphasized it.)

The Ballade in G Minor contains within itself something of the wide range of Chopin's sentiment. This extends from gentle to violent—most violent of all at the final cadence:

The markings for the coda of this ballade mean "very fast, with fire" and "as loudly as possible." But even in the most violent passages, Chopin never seems to lose his control or his sense of refinement.

Chopin was greatly admired for a hundred years after his death, during the great age of piano music. Doubtless this age is now passing. There are fewer great piano virtuosos and popular-music pianists; children are less docile about practicing their scales; young composers tend to use the new electronic composing machines rather than "work at the piano." It will be a pity if the popularity of Chopin's music suffers on this account. He was the most exquisite of the early romantic composers—the most poetic, some would say, of all the great composers.

Robert Schumann (1810–1856)

Another distinguished pianist-composer of the early romantic period was Robert Schumann. Like Chopin, he was happiest with miniatures, short piano compositions and songs. Unlike Chopin, Schumann always wanted to write music on a larger scale as well: symphonies, chamber music, cantatas, fugues, even an opera. He also tended to group his songs together in song cycles (see page 317) and to write piano pieces in big sets held together by some sort of program.

His style of writing for piano is just as individual as Chopin's but denser and less brilliant. One of Schumann's favorite notations to players of his music was the German word *innig,* meaning "inward," "introspective," "intimate"; he substituted a certain warmth and privacy for Chopin's more polished, refined style. These result as much from his harmony and melody as from his piano writing. But of course we cannot hope to find words to catch the musical character of these two composers, any more than we could really describe two of our close friends to someone who does not know them. Each composer emerges from his music as a fully rounded individual, and we can get to them only by immersing ourselves in their compositions.

SCHUMANN *Carnaval*, Op. 17 (1834)

Carnaval is a series of twenty relatively short piano pieces, linked both by means of similar themes and by a vague program. At a masked ball, the first piece, "Pierrot," arrives, followed by "Harlequin," "Coquette," Schumann himself in two separate manifestations, his friends "Estrella" and "Chiarina," and "Chopin"—the latter represented by a condensed little nocturne in which one romantic composer imitates another perfectly, and with perfect authority and affection. "Paganini" also arrives—Niccolò Paganini, the fabulous violinist of that time, who was said to be in league with the devil. Schumann does his best to translate Paganini's fiddle fireworks into pianistic terms.

For the last number (No. 20), they all join in a rollicking "March of the David League against the Philistines." This was a make-believe society of Schumann's, consisting of young spirits banded together against the Goliath of middle-class society and its conservative musical tastes. To show how unconservative he was, Schumann put his David March into triple meter. It includes a pompous old "Grandfather Dance" to stand for the Philistines, and a bit of Beethoven's *Emperor* Piano Concerto to cheer the David League along in their good fight.

Notice how many of the numbers in *Carnaval* feature the same three notes—Ab, C, and B—near the beginning of their melodies. This counts as a rather direct application of the principle of thematic unity that we mentioned on page 333. Can you hear the thematic similarity between some—any—all of these pieces, and does hearing it add anything to your enjoyment of *Carnaval?* What is even more fascinating, those three notes are derived from the name of the German town *Asch*—for the German names for Ab, C, and B happen to be *As, C,* and *H.* Asch was the home of Schumann's current girl friend, Ernestine von Fricken—"Estrella." (He later married "Chiarina"—the distinguished pianist and composer Clara Wieck.) To this day musicologists are puzzling about Schumann's use of private "codes" of this kind.

SCHUMANN Piano Concerto in A Minor (1841–1845)

Of Schumann's larger pieces, his single piano concerto is one of the best. He originally planned the first movement as a complete piece, adding the other movements later. While this first movement could hardly be described as a miniature, it is still true that, prior to the romantic period, composers would not have thought of writing a single concerto-like movement by itself. Nor would they (or could they) have written concertos on such an intimate scale—with such an intimate tone of voice—as that employed by Schumann in his first two movements.

FIRST MOVEMENT

The first movement is in sonata form, but handled very freely. (Schumann probably felt that the double exposition form—used by Mozart and Beethoven for their concerto first movements—was too unwieldly for the effects of intimacy that he was seeking.) An explosive little introduction (piano) is followed by the gentle main theme of the whole concerto (woodwind instruments, line 1):

But as soon as this theme is repeated by the piano, we know in a flash that the tone color of the piano suits it best.

The rest of the movement contains some very interesting versions of the main theme, in which tempo, mood, and other aspects are changed. These are not true variations, since they do not last all the way through the theme, but for one or two measures they act like variations. Schumann is giving us an instance of thematic transformation, one of the characteristic levels of thematic unity used by romantic composers (see page 333).

The version on line 2 of the example appears in the second group of the exposition (and also, of course, in the recapitulation). It is played by the orchestra with animated (*animato*) figures in the piano. The slower version of line 3 begins the development section, after a vigorous orchestral passage has modulated into a new dreamlike key. Here a dialogue—a sort of joint meditation—is set up between the piano and the orchestra clarinet.

Ultimately the marchlike version of line 4 arrives. It serves as a bright coda for the movement, directly after an introspective, richly expressive cadenza (see page 302). The cadenza was written out by Schumann; he did not trust the pianist to improvise.

SECOND MOVEMENT

Schumann calls the second movement *Intermezzo* (Interlude)—almost as if to apologize for its intimate, shadowy, almost casual quality. This movement is in a simple A B A′ form. The A section sounds like a tender whispered conversation between piano and orchestra. A nostalgic melody in the cello and some other instruments forms the B section.

At the end of A′, we are surprised to hear the orchestra playing a tentative fragment of the main theme of the first movement, while the piano makes puzzled comments (see line 5 of the example). These hints soon lead into a brisk theme—a decisive beginning for the last movement (line 6). Schumann borrowed the idea for this passage from the analogous place in Beethoven's *Emperor* Concerto (see page 303).

The asterisks on the example indicate how Schumann has tried to provide thematic unity between the themes of his different movements. The theme of the last movement is actually "derived" from the main theme of the opening movement, for the new theme centers on the most important notes in the first measures of the old one. Whether we can *hear* this, as well as *see* it, is another question; certainly this is an example of the "vague similarities" that we discussed on page 333. By means of the tentative little passage at the end of the second movement, Schumann has done his best to lead us by the hand (or by the ear) so that we do hear the themes in this way.

THIRD MOVEMENT

The last movement of this concerto is in sonata form, like the first. The second theme (another of Schumann's triple-meter marches) is intriguing because it seems to move twice as slowly as the rest of the movement; notice how ingeniously Schumann makes the two different tempos run into one another. The development section starts with a stiff contrapuntal passage, which we may feel to be out of place in a romantic work. The coda, after a firm final statement of the main theme, goes into a splendid spin with a new theme for the piano.

At one point within the second group, after the double-slow second theme, the piano passage-work sounds a little like Chopin. Evidently Schumann had picked up some pointers when doing his *Carnaval* portraits.

Romanticism and the Macabre

In their pursuit of all emotional sensation, the romantics did not neglect the netherworld of fantasy, dream, and nightmare. Like other romantic preoccupations, this can be traced back to the late eighteenth century. A weird picture by the Swiss-English painter-poet John Henry Fuseli, *The Nightmare* (1781), catches the combination of horror, irrationality, and sexuality that enters into romantic effusions in this vein.

We see something of the same combination in *The Sick Rose,* a powerful short poem by another painter-poet and a friend of Fuseli's, William Blake:

O Rose, thou art sick!	Has found out thy bed
The invisible worm,	Of crimson joy;
That flies in the night,	And his dark crimson love
In the howling storm,	Does thy life destroy.

Besides ordinary historical novels, this period also saw the rise of the Gothic novel, which spun elaborate tales of ghosts and tortures of old. Bloodthirsty old ballads were dug up and greatly relished. Fantastic stories became popular —among them Mary Shelley's *Frankenstein*—forerunners of our own science fiction.

Composers did their best to provide strange chords and terrifying orchestral sounds as their contribution to this aspect of romanticism. Giuseppe Verdi, in his opera *Macbeth,* composed such music for the witches and the visions they summon up for Macbeth's benefit. Richard Wagner's opera *The Flying Dutchman* depicted the legendary ghost ship and its spectral crew. Franz Liszt wrote a *Dance of Death.* And in the *Fantastic Symphony,* Hector Berlioz's "Dream of a Witches' Sabbath" bears comparison with Fuseli's *Nightmare.*

Hector Berlioz (1803–1869) and the Program Symphony

One of the most attractive and flamboyant figures of the early romantic period, the French composer Hector Berlioz moved firmly in the direction of "grandiose" compositions. He was an enthusiastic breaker of tradition, a shocker of the bourgeoisie, and a superb orchestrator, unmatched in some ways until the time of Gustav Mahler and Claude Debussy (see pages 399, 415). Berlioz could manage orchestral effects of breathtaking delicacy, but in his own time he was famous for effects that were so forceful that people have solemnly debated whether his decibel tolerance may have been greater than that of normal people. (He once planned to use thirty-two timpani in a piece.) One of the endless series of cartoons he inspired is shown on page 368.

Berlioz hit upon a plan, which is simplicity itself, for combining the two romantic principles discussed above: the principle of the literary program and the principle of thematic unity. Write a large symphony with a literary program concerning some person; then in each movement, have this person represented by a single tune, which can be treated to variation or transformation.
program symphony   The result is called a program symphony.

BERLIOZ *Symphonie Fantastique* (Fantastic Symphony) (1830)   SIDE 12

Produced in 1830, when Berlioz was only twenty-six years old, the *Fantastic Symphony* is certainly one of the most sensational pieces in the whole history of music. The written-out program consists of a general statement and then guidelines for the various movements:

> A young musician of morbid sensibility and ardent imagination is in love, and has poisoned himself with opium in a fit of desperation. Not having taken a fatal dose, he falls into a long sleep in which he has the strangest dreams, wherein his feelings, sentiments, and memories are transformed by his sick brain into musical ideas and figures. The beloved woman herself has become a melody which he finds and hears everywhere as an *idée fixe* [a "fixed
idée fixe   idea," an obsession; the *idée fixe* melody is usually heard in variation or transformation].

So the *Fantastic Symphony* counts as the first example of spaced-out music— or at least, so it seemed. Everybody knew, or soon came to know, that Berlioz was suffering from unrequited love for the Irish actress Harriet Smithson, who had taken Paris by storm with her Shakespearean roles. Was the program a piece of veiled autobiography, or was it merely a skillful advertising device?

In any case, audiences at the time may well have been bowled over by Berlioz's use of tone color, which was produced by an unprecedentedly large orchestra (see page 330) used in the most original ways. Also very original was the notion of having a single theme turn up in all the movements of the symphony (there are five, lasting fifty minutes in all) as a reminder of the musician's beloved. This *idée fixe* must be quoted in full;* Berlioz's long melodies are distinctive and much admired:

Like Schubert in the Quartet in A Minor (see page 311), Berlioz places this long tune in a sonata-form movement and breaks parts of it off to use as motives for the development section. The tune shows many typical features of romantic melody, such as the excited rising or surging movement in measures 1–2 and especially in measures 5–8. The whole of line 2 seems like a passionate struggle to inch higher and higher up the scale, gaining one note and then losing three. Measure 19, just before the cadence, provides a positive shudder of emotion.

Notice the profusion of dynamic marks in this tune, added by Berlioz to ensure just the right expressive quality. There are also many other marks; with the romantic composers, one has to become something of a linguist to follow all their directions. Compare this brief glossary for the *idée fixe* with the lists of more ordinary terms on pages 10–11:

canto espressivo	an expressive song
poco **sf**	accented, but not too strongly
dolce	sweetly
cresc. poco a poco	gradually getting louder
animato	animated
ritenuto	held back (in tempo)
a tempo	at the original tempo
poco **f**, *poco rit.*	somewhat loud, somewhat slowed down

To illustrate the shifting nature of the hallucination, Berlioz transformed the *idée fixe*—in rhythm, especially—for its appearances at other stages of the dream:

---

* In this example, note values have been halved and the odd measure lines omitted to facilitate reading. The *idée fixed* in its original notation appears on the first line of page 347.

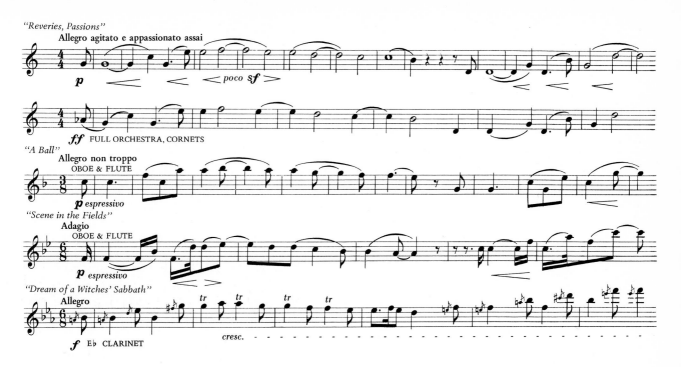

"Reveries, Passions"
Allegro agitato e appassionato assai

"A Ball"
Allegro non troppo

"Scene in the Fields"
Adagio

"Dream of a Witches' Sabbath"
Allegro

FIRST MOVEMENT: "REVERIES, PASSIONS"

> First he remembers the uneasiness of mind, the aimless passions, the baseless depression and elations which he felt before seeing her whom he loves. Then the volcanic love which she instantly inspired in him, his delirious agonies, his jealous furies, his fits of tenderness, his religious consolations.

His first memories are depicted not by the *idée fixe* but by another long tune— a halting, passionate melody which is perhaps even more striking. (It was taken from a love song written by Berlioz when he was eighteen.) The symphony does not even begin directly with this tune but opens with a short, quiet run-in; this typically romantic touch suggests that the music grows up imperceptibly out of silence. The early part of the movement hardly sounds like the introduction to something else, as did the slow openings of Mozart's Overture to *Don Giovanni* or Haydn's Symphony No. 88. It sounds more like a short movement in its own right.

After the appearance of the *idée fixe*, the movement picks up speed and follows sonata form—but very loosely. The *idée fixe* serves as the main theme. Some of the finest strokes run counter to the principles of the Viennese composers: for instance, the many striking slowdowns and the arresting up-and-down harmonized chromatic scale that crops up in the development section without any noticeable connection with anything else. Near the end, the *idée fixe* returns noisily at a faster tempo (see line 2 in the example above). And at the very end, the "religious consolations" mentioned in the program are clearly apparent in the music, still animated by fragments of the *idée fixe*.

SECOND MOVEMENT: "A BALL"

At a ball, in the midst of a noisy, brilliant fête, he finds his beloved again.

A symphony needs the simplicity and easy swing of a dance movement, and this ballroom episode in the opium dream conveniently provides one. It is a waltz rather than a minuet or scherzo; the *idée fixe,* in a lilting triple meter, appears in the position of a trio (see line 3 on page 347). However, the internal structure a b a, etc., that is usual in earlier dance movements does not occur: it might restrain the "spontaneity." Two prominent harp parts are featured in the score of this movement. Berlioz wanted each to be played by "at least two instruments."

THIRD MOVEMENT: "SCENE IN THE FIELDS"

A summer evening in the country; he hears two herders piping in dialogue. This pastoral duo, the location, the light rustling of trees stirred by the wind . . . gives him a feeling of unaccustomed calm. . . . But she appears again, his heart breaks. . . .

The "pastoral duo" at the beginning of this long country scene is played by an English horn (evidently the boy herder) and an oboe (the girl), backstage. At the end of the movement, the English horn returns to the accompaniment of distant thunder sounds, played with Berlioz's favorite sponge-tipped sticks on four differently tuned timpani. Alas, the girl oboe is no longer to be heard.

In between these pipings, the movement is built on another long tune, first played by violins and flute, later by violas, cellos, and four bassoons. When the *idée fixe* finally arrives (line 4 on page 347) it is interrupted by angry sounds, which swell to a surprisingly forceful climax.

FOURTH MOVEMENT: "MARCH TO THE SCAFFOLD"

He dreams that he has killed his loved one, that he is condemned to death and led to execution. A march . . . accompanies the procession . . . Finally the *idée fixe* appears for a moment . . . to be cut off by the fall of the axe.

This is perhaps the most impressive movement in the symphony, despite the grisly or ludicrous effect (depending on how you look at it) of the final guillotine chop and snare-drum roll. Besides the blaring march tune in the wind instruments—Berlioz wrote some highly impressive pieces for band—there is another theme, treated in counterpoint:

On two occasions, this appears at a higher octave in an extraordinary divided orchestration, a memorable instance of Berlioz's novel imagination in tone color:

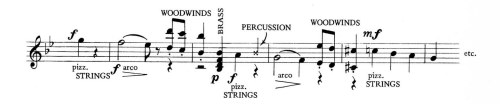

The direction *pizz.* (for *pizzicato*) means that the violin strings are to be plucked with the finger; *arco* means they are to be played with the bow.

FIFTH MOVEMENT: "DREAM OF A WITCHES' SABBATH"

> He sees himself at a Witches' Sabbath. . . . Unearthly sounds, groans, shrieks of laughter. . . . The melody of his beloved is heard, but it has lost its character of nobleness and timidity. . . . It is *she* who comes to the Sabbath! . . . She joins the diabolical orgy. The funeral knell, burlesque of the *Dies irae.* . . .

Berlioz really lets himself go in this movement, adding the element of parody to the sensational orchestral effects already pioneered in the earlier movements. As he himself points out, the "noble and timid" *idée fixe* theme loses its character and sounds cheap and raucous when played by the squeaky high E♭ clarinet, and when changed to a fast jig rhythm (line 5 on page 347).

A similar burlesque rhythm is applied to one of the most solemn and famous of all Gregorian chants, the *Dies irae,* which is introduced with church bell sounds:

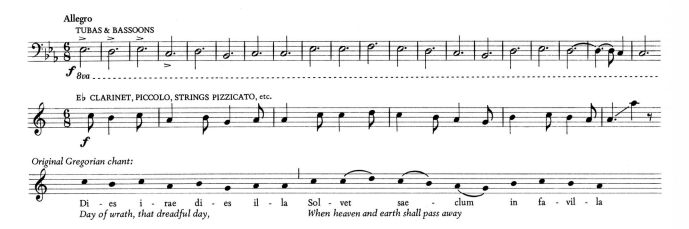

Below two of Berlioz's versions, we show the beginning of the original chant, which we have discussed and illustrated on pages 84–85.

The *Dies irae* is sung only at Masses for the Dead, or Requiem Masses. In a Catholic country such as France, an audience would have recognized it instantly. The effect of its burlesque treatment must have been shocking—and graphically illustrative of a Black Mass at the obscene witches' revels summoned up by Berlioz's drugged imagination. The early romantics enjoyed trafficking in the macabre and the diabolical (see page 344).

After taking revenge on Harriet Smithson by parodying her into an old hag, Berlioz does not, in fact, have her cavort much with the other revelers. The movement ends with a contrapuntal combination of the *Dies irae* and another dynamic theme illustrating the witches' dance.

Compared with works like Beethoven's Fifth Symphony and Schumann's Piano Concerto, the *Fantastic Symphony* may seem rather undisciplined in form. We cannot always sense the "logic" linking one musical event to the next. Later program symphonies by Berlioz do better in this respect; we should not forget that the *Fantastic Symphony* was his first major effort, an amazing production for a composer only twenty-six years old. Later he wrote symphonies entitled *Harold in Italy,* based on the once-famous epic poem by Lord Byron, and *Romeo and Juliet,* after Shakespeare. Shakespeare's plays greatly attracted the romantics because of their loose formal structure and their strong emotions. They attracted Berlioz also because of Miss Smithson, the Shakespearean actress, who by this time had become his wife.

In any case, formal "logic" was not the chief concern of Berlioz (or many another romantic composer). What we appreciate in his music is its flamboyance and imaginativeness, both in the extraordinary orchestral sounds and in the unpredictable sequence of novel musical ideas. Compared with the *Fantastic Symphony,* the Schumann Piano Concerto can seem rather tame.

Franz Liszt (1811–1886) and the Symphonic Poem

After Berlioz, the program symphony did not flourish widely. Composers who wanted to follow him in writing orchestral program music seem to have found the system too inflexible. They tended to write program music in one long movement, employing a great variety of forms: sonata form, rondo, theme and variations (all treated very freely), and most often, unique "inner forms" designed for the particular occasion, to match the particular program.

symphonic poem

The best general name for these pieces is <u>symphonic poem</u>, though the term *tone poem* and others are also used. A symphonic poem is an orchestral work in one movement with some kind of explicit extramusical association.

A key figure in the development of the symphonic poem was the Hungarian (but thoroughly cosmopolitan) composer Franz Liszt. A highly colorful figure, hardly less flamboyant in his own way than Berlioz, Liszt started his career as a sensational piano virtuoso, the greatest of his day. He produced brilliant or delicate piano miniatures, in which all of Chopin's innovations were extended and exaggerated. He then turned to conducting and writing orchestral music. In his two program symphonies and his many symphonic poems, Liszt made a specialty of thematic transformation (see page 333),

Liszt among His Friends

A popular sentimental picture of the nineteenth century, purporting to show the great pianist-composer Franz Liszt playing for a group of celebrities of his time. From left to right, the novelists Alexandre Dumas, Victor Hugo, and George Sand (see page 339), the violin virtuoso Niccolò Paganini, and the opera composer Gioacchino Rossini.

At Liszt's feet (!) is his first mistress, Countess Marie d'Agoult, who wrote novels under the pen name of Daniel Stern and wrote various articles that were published under Liszt's name. The painter wanted to get a cheap thrill by including this notorious lady, but he was too prudish to show her face. Compare Delacroix (page 339).

The expressions and attitudes of the listeners show that this painter, at least, believed that romantic music penetrates into the very souls of those who participate in it. If you compare this picture of music making with earlier ones you can see how romanticism changed attitudes toward music in the later nineteenth century. Music is no longer a casual entertainment (see page 217) or a pleasant, warm, social pastime (see page 316). For the nineteenth century, music is the occasion for communion—almost a seance.

Perhaps the most amusing detail in this picture is the somber bust of Beethoven on the piano, a bust that looms much larger than the heads of any of the people. Liszt gazes hungrily at it for inspiration.

extending Berlioz's concept of the *idée fixe* and its variations. A good friend of Berlioz's, and both friend and father-in-law to Richard Wagner, Liszt was the acknowledged leader of advanced new music in the third quarter of the nineteenth century.

LISZT *Totentanz* (Dance of Death) (1849, revised 1853–1859)

SIDE 13

Liszt's *Totentanz*, subtitled "Paraphrase on the *Dies irae*," is half symphonic poem and half piano concerto. It will give us an opportunity to observe the symphonic poem at an early, transitional stage, when Liszt's technique was still closer to that of theme and variations than thematic transformation. The piece will also show the direction that instrumental virtuosity was taking, after the relatively restrained days of Chopin and Schumann. There is undeniably a flashy, even a vulgar side to Liszt's musical personality.

His loose "program" for the *Totentanz* was a famous set of fifty-four Dance of Death woodcuts by the Renaissance artist Hans Holbein (whose name, by the way, means "hollow bone" in German). We discussed the Dance of Death in the late Middle Ages on page 98. People of the nineteenth century, fascinated by the macabre (see page 344), were naturally attracted to this grim manifestation of the "Gothic" world, a world that appealed to them so strongly.

Liszt must have thought at once of making use of the *Dies irae* tune, the Gregorian chant that more than any other was associated with the horrors of death. What is more, he knew perfectly well that it had made a sensational effect in the *Fantastic Symphony*. By writing a series of variations on the *Dies irae*, he could go one better than Berlioz and also give the impression of a whole series of different "characters" joining in the Dance. Over and above this, Liszt depicted with great gusto the "black humor" of the Dance as Holbein showed it, Death's sardonic brutality and—yes—vulgarity.

Perhaps it is the look of the piano keyboard as much as the instrument's actual sound that convinces people it can imitate the rattling of bones. A later composer of symphonic poems, Camille Saint-Saëns, wrote a *Danse Macabre* in which the xylophone is assigned this function. But it is doubtful that the xylophone tone color is any more realistic than the miraculous piano music that Liszt was able to provide for his *Totentanz*.

Liszt begins with fascinating low bell strokes, simulated by the piano playing in the low register with three timpani. Only two phrases of the *Dies irae* tune are blared out by the trombones and tuba before the piano cuts in with its first cadenza (see page 302), ignoring yelps of indignation from the orchestra. It seems Liszt borrowed this idea of an initial confrontation from another famous work for piano and orchestra, Beethoven's *Emperor* Concerto (see page 299). Here, too, the soloist easily dominates.

With the piano hammering away at a dissonant chord, the orchestra plays the *Dies irae* theme in this version:

A solo piano introduction presents phrases a and b of the *Dies irae;* then the first three variations are built on the theme furnished with repetitions, as though to make it resemble in form a traditional Viennese variation tune, ‖:**a b**:‖:**c**:‖ (compare the tunes shown on pages 284 and 306). The first variation sets the tone with a clattering bassoon melody in counterpoint with the *Dies irae,* which is played underneath by the double basses, *pizzicato:*

glissando   In the next variation, the piano plays rapid runs and <u>glissandos</u>. These are runs in which the pianist draws the back of the hand (the nails, actually) along the keyboard as fast as possible. Excitement mounts in the brass choir of the orchestra.

Six more variations follow, growing freer and freer. Several are for the piano alone, including a very informal fugue. Liszt sometimes makes the *Dies irae* sound like a love song, sometimes like a polka, sometimes like a parodistic jest—a true scherzo:

After a second cadenza for the soloist, there is a very striking series of horn calls, sounding like the crack of doom. They frame a second theme, which Liszt introduces at this point and then varies in its turn. This second theme resembles the *Dies irae* in some ways—in its first three notes, for example—and also has something of the character of a Lutheran chorale (compare *Wachet auf,* page 234):

Liszt now produces some variations on his new theme. Its first three variations feature the piano with various woodwind instruments and the triangle. Its fifth variation is another piano solo, featuring some wonderfully weird harmonies and pianistic effects. The sixth variation is interrupted by another cadenza—the soloist's third.

This cadenza reintroduces phrases a and b of the *Dies irae* theme in a final tenth variation of that first theme. When the orchestra rounds this off by playing phrase c, several times, the piano resumes the glissandos of variation 2. The piece comes to a rousing, garish conclusion with a return of music from the beginning, after the "bells" and before the first cadenza.

Early Romantic Opera

Romantic composers and their audiences alike were fascinated by the possibilities of combining music with literature and ideas in general. The atmosphere that produced the program symphony and the symphonic poem was also very conducive to the development of opera. It also meant that many (though not all) composers and librettists began thinking hard about the meaning and "message" of their operas. They came to view the genre as a sort of serious drama in music rather than simply as entertainment. Not surprisingly, opera flourished all over Europe in the nineteenth century even more brilliantly than before.

Many romantic novels supplied the subjects for romantic operas: for example, Sir Walter Scott's *Ivanhoe, Kenilworth, The Lady of the Lake,* and *The Bride of Lammermoor.* Shakespeare, the great "discovery" of the time, was also a very popular source for opera librettos; the tragedies *Romeo and Juliet, Macbeth, Othello,* and *Hamlet,* and even comedies such as *Much Ado About Nothing* and *The Merry Wives of Windsor* were used. Just as people today like seeing the movie or television version of a popular book, so people in those days enjoyed the "opera version." Remarkably few romantic operas have truly original stories, in fact. Most go back to novels, or stage plays, or (in the case of German romantic opera) to old legends and myths, even fairy tales.

Romantic opera made its serious start in the 1820s, the last decade of what we have called the Viennese period. It did not start in Vienna, however, although romantic stirrings had been known there since the *Sturm und Drang* movement of the 1770s. Both Beethoven and Schubert felt threatened by the popular rage for Rossini's operas, when they were imported into their home city. Of the main early romantic opera composers, three were Italians and one was a German.

Gioacchino Rossini (1792–1868) It may seem strange to count Rossini as a romantic, for he is most famous today for crisp, elegant opera buffas that are close enough to Mozart—the immortal *Barber of Seville* among them. (And these operas all have overtures written dutifully in sonata form.) But in his

bel canto opera

own day Rossini was admired equally for his serious operas, and these were extremely important in establishing the forms of Italian romantic opera, called bel canto opera because of its glorification of beautiful singing (*bel canto* means just that, beautiful singing). His operas also provided rich models of romantic expression: in Desdemona's Willow song from his Shakespearean opera *Otello,* in Matilde's aria from his last opera, *William Tell,* and even in the Count's serenade in *The Barber of Seville.* At the age of thirty-seven Rossini suddenly retired and spent the rest of his life as a bon vivant in Paris. No one has quite explained why. Perhaps it was because he sensed that he could not keep up with the new generation of romantic composers.

Gaetano Donizetti (1797–1848)   Five years younger than Rossini, Donizetti plunged further ahead into the simple, sentimental melodies and blood-and-thunder "action" music associated with *bel canto* opera. Enormously prolific, he wrote sixty-four operas in his relatively short lifetime, among them *Lucia di Lammermoor* and *Elisabetta al Castello di Kenilworth,* based on the Walter Scott novels mentioned above.

Vincenzo Bellini (1801–1835)   Bellini, the most romantic of the three great *bel canto* composers, died even younger than Donizetti. A writer of wonderfully refined, languid melodies, he was a significant influence on Chopin. Bellini first achieved fame with his early operas called *The Pirate* and *The Capulets and The Montagus* (derived from *Romeo and Juliet*). *Norma,* his greatest work, is the final testing ground for great sopranos.

Carl Maria von Weber (1786–1826)   The founder of German romantic opera belonged to an even earlier generation than Rossini. A man of many talents— conductor, pianist, writer, even lithographer—Weber wrote only eight operas and musical plays, a very small number for those times. Among them, *Der Freischütz* (The Magic Bullets) stands out. It has the quality of a German folk tale or a ballad: Max, a young huntsman, sells his soul to the devil for seven magic bullets, but he is redeemed by the sacrifice of his pure, blonde fiancée Agathe. Equally impressive are the two spiritual, yet highly romantic arias sung by Agathe and the famous scene of devilish conjuration in the Wolf's Glen, the effect of which depends largely on sensational orchestral writing.

Intense interest centered on Weber's work in Germany from the time of *Der Freischütz* (1821) until his premature death five years later, at the age of thirty-nine. Germans yearned to see the development of a national type of romantic opera that would end the dominance of Italian and French operas. Richard Wagner, who started his career in the 1830s as an opera composer in Weber's mold, succeeded in this beyond the wildest dreams of any of his compatriots—though only by transcending Weber's type of opera completely. Wagner's "music dramas," composed from the 1850s on, proved to be among the most impressive and, without exception, the most influential works of later nineteenth-century music. We shall begin the next chapter with an account of these remarkable operas as we go on to examine the later phase of romanticism in music.

Romanticism and Nature

An important facet of romanticism was a fascination with nature. William Wordsworth established a new tone of reverence and admiration for nature in English poetry, and he was followed in this by Keats, Shelley, Tennyson, and all the other great romantic poets. We may also recall the sentimental nature images of the poet of Schubert's *Die Winterreise* (see page 317).

The English also excelled in painting landscapes and seascapes. William Turner's *The Slave Ship* (1839), originally entitled *Slavers Throwing Overboard the Dead and the Dying—Typhoon Coming On,* shows a frail ship buffeted by the elemental forces of nature, including fantastic fishes (or are they, too, victims of the typhoon?). Turner's astonishingly bold use of color and free treatment of forms convey an unforgettable sense of the majesty, mystery, and menace of nature.

It may seem unfair to suggest comparing this highly imaginative painting with "real" nature as laid out in the parks illustrated on pages 208 and 274. But the point is that the romantics were less interested in "reality" than in imagination, less concerned with nature for its own sake than with the feelings that nature stirred within them. They were ready to heighten nature, even distort it, if this would increase the emotional effect. In Turner's picture, though the plight of the slaves is dire, viewers can enjoy the thrill of the mighty swirls of yellow water and the blood-red fog, while remaining safely outside the picture frame. Like historical novels, such pictures allowed the mind to roam over wild feelings that were safely distant from Victorian reality.

Composers shared in this romantic enthusiasm for nature by writing program music (see page 333). Felix Mendelssohn's *Hebrides* Overture (*Fingal's Cave*) has passages that sound a little like the orderly beating of waves, and even a romanticized foghorn; Mendelssohn himself was a talented watercolorist. The "Scene in the Fields" from Berlioz's *Fantastic Symphony* includes the sounds of shepherds piping and a thunderstorm (see page 348). Other musical landscapes of a somewhat later period include Bedřich Smetana's *Vltava* (a river, also known as the Moldau), Richard Strauss's *Alpine Symphony,* and Claude Debussy's *Clouds* (see page 416).

Courtesy of the Museum of Fine Arts, Boston, Henry Lillie Pierce Fund 99.22

CHAPTER 12   Romanticism   II

Romanticism   II

The gods were not kind to composers in the first half of the nineteenth century. Weber, Bellini, Donizetti, Mendelssohn, Chopin, Schumann—to say nothing of Schubert—all died young, some of them in their thirties. People may well have had the feeling that an era was passing in the years around 1850, which saw the deaths of Mendelssohn, Chopin, and Schumann. They were among the gentler spirits of musical romanticism. The music of the second half of the century was to become more monumental and dramatic than theirs, more powerful and sometimes more coarsely cut. While miniature and grandiose compositions continued to exist side by side, it is somehow now the grandiose ones that make the main impression.

The music of Liszt set the tone, though by no means everybody accepted it. His influential series of symphonic poems came out in the 1850s. These, however, were soon eclipsed by works in another genre that greatly appealed to the nineteenth century, opera: the "music dramas" of Richard Wagner.

Wagner, the composer of music dramas, dominates the second phase of romanticism just as Beethoven, the composer of symphonies, dominates the second phase of the Viennese period. Wagner was the greatest and most influential composer of his time and also, incidentally, a musician who had a profound impact on other artists—poets, novelists, even painters. Those who know the work of the important French symbolist poet Stéphane Mallarmé or that of the German novelist Thomas Mann, to mention only the most prominent examples, will know of their debt to "Wagnerism." Wagner's operas, which he insisted on treating as though they belonged to a special genre, "music drama," are indeed different from any other operas. The heated controversy that they occasioned at the time has scarcely cooled to the present day. To his admirers, Wagner's music dramas are the greatest operas ever written: what is more, they provide a unique and transcendent artistic experience.

They are also fatally easy to make fun of. The English singer Anna Russell, who delights audiences with her Wagnerian take-offs, is only the latest of a long tradition of Wagner parodists going back more than a hundred years. The uncommitted modern listener may well wonder at these pieces—why has such an enormous fuss been made about them. But there is no question about their importance or about the deep effect they have on the initiated, and it will be worth spending some time and effort to see if we can elucidate this.

Wagnerian Castles

Nineteenth-century German architecture: two sides of the coin. Shown below is Wagner's Festival Theater at Bayreuth. At the left, the castle of Neuschwanstein, built after 1867 by the extravagantly romantic young King Ludwig II of Bavaria. Bavaria was the largest state in Germany, though Prussia was the most powerful. Ludwig was later declared insane, on equivocal evidence, and deposed.

Neuschwanstein, perched on a lonely mountain, overlooking a dramatic gorge and waterfall, is a romantic fantasy in stone. Everything about it tells of the nineteenth century's yearning for the past, for the Middle Ages of fairy tale and myth: the picturesque turrets, the great keep, the minstrel's hall, the ancient-style furniture, the leaded-glass windows. Such yearning also made Ludwig, from his boyhood on, a deep admirer of Wagner and Wagner's operas celebrating medieval German myths. On his accession to the throne at the age of eighteen, he brought the composer to his court and for a time gave him unlimited support.

For Wagner, whose fortunes were then at a low ebb, this was indeed the action of a fairy godfather. It was the decisive turning point in his career.

What did Wagner do with the support? Besides maintaining himself on a scale of personal luxury that was the talk of the time, he built a special theater in the little Bavarian town of Bayreuth exclusively for the performances of his operas. There are very few frills on this building; it is a solid lump of nineteenth-century architecture, as functional as a factory. Today, while poor King Ludwig's castle is maintained by the state as a curiosity that tourists can visit for a small fee, the Bayreuth Theater is still putting on Wagner festivals and selling out every summer, at stiff prices, exactly as Wagner had planned a hundred years ago. The rest of the year the theater is dark.

It is hard to think of any other artist who ever carried off such an impressive act of entrepreneurship. Wagner's world was also that of the nineteenth-century robber barons.

Richard Wagner (1813–1883)

Wagner probably had the most fascinating career of all the great composers. We can hardly do justice to all its facets, but one aspect of it deserves to be brought out. This is Wagner's remarkable ability to play both sides of the nineteenth-century scene—not only the romantic, artistic side but also the materialistic. For, in spite of hardships over a great many years, Wagner finally emerged as a success symbol who might have been the envy of any nineteenth-century businessman.

He was an incredible sponger, living in a style of ostentatious luxury on borrowed money which he never paid back. His love life featured some sensational and widely discussed conquests. He treated people as ruthlessly as any robber baron. In his middle years he gained the support of royalty and started to dabble in power politics, a subject that, along with every other, he had written about in endless books and articles.

But perhaps his most impressive accomplishment of all was to build: not in sound, but in bricks and mortar. He designed a special theater in Bayreuth, Germany (see page 363), for the sole purpose of producing festival performances of his own operas. Starting in 1872, these events fairly hypnotized artists and intellectuals of the time. Bayreuth soon became a flourishing commercial venture, and a hundred years later, under the direction of Wagner's descendants, it is still doing very nicely with annual Wagner festivals.

All this was possible, of course, only because Wagner impressed the world so deeply as a romantic composer and, even more, as *the* ultimate romantic artist. He brought all the arts together into what he called the "combined art work" (*Gesamtkunstwerk*) to which he devoted virtually all his attention as a composer. This was his own special type of opera, "music drama."

music drama

In Wagner's music drama the music shares honors with the drama, the philosophy, the poetry—all provided by Wagner himself—and the stage design and acting. (No other opera composer has ever specified details of sets and acting so carefully; our line score on pages 370–72 reproduces only a fraction of Wagner's stage directions.) His operas are profoundly emotional, which suited the romantic temperament. They deal with weighty philosophical issues, or so at least Wagner and his admirers believed, and they do so under the symbolic cover of old medieval German legends. This was another romantic feature, one that anticipated Freud, with his emphasis on myths (for example, the myth of Oedipus) as embodiments of the deepest unconscious truths.

leitmotivs

Wagner was a great conductor and a superb orchestrator. He raised the orchestra to a new importance in opera, with the help of his famous system of leitmotivs, or leading motives. These are simply motives associated with some person, thing, or idea in the drama. By playing leitmotivs, the orchestra could "tell the story" and thus do what the program symphonists were doing, only better. Sometimes the leitmotivs grow very tiresome: whenever the hero draws his sword, for example, the orchestra obligingly comes up with the "sword motive." On the other hand, they could be used very subtly to show what was going on in the hero's mind even when he was saying something else.

Wagner also became extremely skillful at transforming leitmotivs so that they expressed unexpected shades of developing meaning.

The theory, in any case, was that leitmotivs, being music, could state ideas in *emotional* terms, over and above the intellectual terms provided by mere words. This was a logical end result of romantic doctrine. Furthermore, the complex web of leitmotivs provided the long music dramas with thematic unity of a particularly rich sort. On both counts, psychological and technical, leitmotivs were ideally calculated to impress the nineteenth century.

WAGNER *Tristan und Isolde:* Prelude and "Liebestod" (Love Death) (1859)   SIDE 15

Two persons helped to inspire Wagner's great secular hymn to love, *Tristan und Isolde.* One was the philosopher Arthur Schopenhauer, whose books Wagner had just discovered. The other was the wife of one of his patrons, Mathilde Wesendonck, with whom he was having a love affair.

Schopenhauer had made a particularly powerful formulation of the general romantic view of music's great importance in the scheme of things. According to his philosophy, life consists of "the Will," or inner feelings and drives, and "Appearances," or ideas, morals, reason, and everything else. He believed that the Will has complete power over Appearances, and that the only real outer manifestation of the Will is through music.

For Schopenhauer, the dominance of the Will was the source of life's misery. Wagner, less pessimistic, decided to write a music drama that would glorify the all-powerful Will through music—which, as Schopenhauer would have had to admit, was most appropriate. The aspect of Will would be sexual love, and the story would be taken (as usual) from an old legend. Wagner found it in a lengthy German poem of the twelfth century.

Tristan und Isolde, then, is not just a love story or even just a great love story; it is also more. It is a serious (and successful) effort to show passion as the ruling force, almost a religious principle, that transcends every other aspect of worldly Appearance. Thus when Tristan and Isolde fall in love, the Will first overpowers her fierce pride, which had previously branded Tristan as her blood enemy. It also dissolves Tristan's heretofore perfect chivalry, the *machismo* of the medieval knight, which had demanded that he escort Isolde safely to her marriage to King Mark, his uncle and liege lord. Love overcomes the marriage itself; they meet adulterously. All this can be applied to Wagner's own situation with the Wesendoncks.

The rest, fortunately, cannot. After the affair is discovered, Tristan receives a mortal sword wound—but Love negates this wound. Apparently he simply cannot or will not die until Isolde comes to him. Then, after he dies in a kind of ecstasy in her arms, she herself sinks down in like rapture and expires also.

At this point (if not earlier) the plot passes the bounds of reality—which was exactly Wagner's point. Once Tristan and Isolde have drunk the love potion of the original legend, they seem to move in a realm where conventional attitudes, the rules of the world, and even life and death have lost their powers.

They are guided and ruled only by their love, which overcomes everything. In fact, this opera's transcendental quality brings it very close to mystical experience. What the prudish, materialistic middle-class audiences of the time made of something that subverted their values so completely is hard to say. We can suspect that they accepted it as a kind of fantasy, one that they could enjoy while denying themselves (and others) such emotion in their actual lives.

In any case, the Prelude to *Tristan und Isolde* is one of the most impressive and justly celebrated of nineteenth-century compositions. (Prelude—*Vorspiel* —is Wagner's special name for "overture"; remember that he insisted on calling his operas music dramas to distinguish them from other people's mere operas.) It opens with a slow motive treated in a free threefold sequence (see page 21). The ending harmonies of the motive, in particular (measures 2–3, 6–7, 10–11), create a remarkably sultry, sensual, anxious feeling:

This is an example of a romantic theme that derives its essential character from harmony rather than from melody or rhythm. It becomes the chief leitmotiv of the long opera to come, associated with a rich compound of meaning, including passion, yearning, and release in death.

The motive is heard many, many times in the Prelude. After the huge climax in the middle of the piece, discharging tension that has built up to an almost unbearable pitch, the motive returns in an imaginative free variation of its original threefold sequence. Otherwise, the Prelude consists of a marvelous dark churning of emotion, produced partly by incessant sequences and partly by Wagner's very characteristic trick of avoiding cadences. The music constantly shifts in key (modulates); every time it seems ready to stop, it surges ahead, as though feeling cannot be satisfied. Love can be satisfied only by death, by the great cadence accompanying Isolde's death at the very end of the opera.

The long passage leading up to this great cadence is known as the "Liebestod" (Love death). An orchestral arrangement of this passage, leaving out Isolde's singing line, is often tacked onto the Prelude to make a sort of informal symphonic poem (though it is not labeled as such, for some reason). The sense of ecstasy and growing release is very powerful. The sequences continue; the motives now sound freer and less contorted than those of the Prelude. The orchestration, dense and very rich throughout, also grows lighter, though it is able to support an even more ecstatic climax than that of the Prelude. At the very last cadence of the "Liebestod," the main motive of the Prelude (measures 2–3, top line) returns once again, now radically transformed to suggest that love's yearning has reached its transcendent goal.

Except for this cadence, the music of the "Liebestod" is basically identical to a section that Tristan and Isolde sang at the height of their passionate love scene in act II of the opera. To the nineteenth century, at least, this music seemed dangerously sexual in its connotations. It may not strike us that way, but remember that there were no "adult" movies or frank novels in those days. The most suggestive elements in the arts, before *Tristan,* were the ankles and knees (*never* the thighs!) of female ballet dancers.

However this may be, there can be no doubt that *Tristan und Isolde* is made of stronger stuff, emotionally speaking, than other romantic pieces. Even our relatively brief orchestral excerpt shows this, and if we subject ourselves to the entire five hours of the uncut opera, the effect can be truly overpowering. By its successful expression of intense emotion, *Tristan und Isolde* approaches the ideal not only of Schopenhauer but also of the romantic nineteenth century as a whole.

WAGNER *Die Walküre:* Act III, Wotan's Farewell (1856)   SIDE 13

Wagner's *Der Ring des Nibelungen* (The Nibelung's Ring), an opera lasting for four separate evenings of three to five hours each, surely counts as the very limit of a romantic tendency we mentioned on page 332—the tendency toward the grandiose. Wagner required this length of time, perhaps, because of the extent of the material he wanted to cover. *The Ring* encompasses large portions of the most famous of all the old Germanic legends, involving gods and goddesses, giants and dwarfs, magical events and very human actions, all in a great variety of obscure and bloody incidents straggling over many decades.

Yet in back of all this tedious mythology, Wagner had a modern tale to tell. The basic theme is the corruption of the world through people's greed for money (gold) and the power it buys. In the guise of mythical gods, gnomes, and warriors, one group after another in modern society is shown destroying itself in the pursuit of gold. George Bernard Shaw accurately described *The Ring* as a devastating attack by a romantic artist on the capitalist middle-class values of his day. Wagner was a revolutionary activist in his youth and had been thrown out of Germany as a result (see page 381). This enormous work is one outcome of his early political passions.

DAS RHEINGOLD

The first opera of the four is *Das Rheingold* (The Rhine Gold). Here we see the gold in its original, "natural," and thus innocent, state in the possession of some mermaids in the River Rhine. (Wagner designed a stage machine to make these "Rhinemaidens" swim.) But the gold is stolen from them by a race of dwarfs and then by the gods themselves, who mortgage it to a race of giants.

"Noise"

As these Parisian cartoons of the mid-nineteenth century show, romantic music had to face a good deal of hostility from the conservatives of the day. They were offended by its overemotionalism, puzzled by its harmonies, and bored by its great lengths. But when people don't like new music and are not quite sure what it is that is bothering them, they usually complain about the *noise*.

The cartoon to the right is captioned "Field Marshal Berlioz." Cool, immaculate, his hair flying with correct romantic abandon, Berlioz leads an orchestra that includes a cannon, a rotating machine to strike the drum, and a tuba player with a sadistic glint in his eye. All this is having its effect on the critics, who cower among the coffins.

— Tu mènes ton oncle à l'Opéra, mais le pauvre homme est sourd !
— Justement, il a voulu profiter de l'occasion pour voir le *Tannhauser.*

The cartoon to the left refers to the first Wagner opera to be produced in Paris, *Tannhäuser.* "You're taking your uncle to the opera? But the poor old gentleman is deaf." "Precisely, my dear chap: and he wants to take advantage of it to see *Tannhäuser.*"

As a matter of fact, *Tannhäuser* did offer something for uncle to see: a voluptuous ballet at the Court of Venus, which Wagner, against his better judgment, had inserted into the opera to make it more palatable to Parisian taste. But the work was hooted off the stage, a famous fiasco that owed as much to political intrigues as to the undoubted novelty and "noise" of Wagner's musical style.

The dwarfs are called Nibelungs, and they forge the gold into a ring: hence the name of the total opera.

For Wagner, who was a notorious anti-Semite, the ugly dwarfs also served as a hint that the first race to be corrupted by gold was the Jews. But the "establishment" is shown moving in on them at once, as represented by the king of the Germanic gods of mythology, Wotan (from whom we get the name Wednesday, "Wotan's day"). The main message of the opera is the degeneration of Wotan's realm—that is, nineteenth-century Germany—as a result of his lust for gold, for power, for the Ring.

When one of the dwarfs, Alberich, steals the gold in the first place, he is really chasing the Rhinemaidens themselves. To get the gold, he consciously renounces love, that is, turns his heart forever from gentleness, affection, and charity. This was an ingenious way of turning the old myth into a commentary on the bias of the middle classes toward hard work and discipline and away from emotion. At the next stage, when Wotan steals the ring from Alberich, he doesn't give up anything, at least not right away. Everything is managed by guile and cruelty. *The Rhine Gold* shows gold corrupting all who touch it, including even the king of the gods.

DIE WALKÜRE

The next opera is *Die Walküre* (The Valkyrie). In Germanic mythology, amazon goddesses called Valkyries served the heroes of old in Valhalla with a pleasant combination of warlike companionship and feminine (if statuesque) charm. The Valkyrie in question is Brünnhilde, Wotan's favorite daughter. We can skip the involved details of the plot, important as they are for a full understanding of the opera, since we shall be concentrating on only a single scene.

Suffice it to say that Brünnhilde, disobeying orders, has intervened to save a mortal whom Wotan, with great reluctance, had agreed to kill in the course of his pursuit of the ring. Brünnhilde had understood Wotan's inner feelings and acted accordingly, but the law demands that Wotan punish her disobedience. Apparently, the mildest fate available for her is to be turned into a mere mortal woman and placed in a deep sleep on a mountain ringed with fire, where the first true hero who climbs through can claim her as his bride. Sleeping Beauty has many sisters in folktales and the world of mythology.

The last scene of the opera is usually called "Wotan's Farewell," his last farewell to Brünnhilde. We are likely to forget about punishment and gold and get caught up in Wotan's anguish. He feels this deeply, for not only is Brünnhilde his favorite daughter but she is also the only person with whom he has any real contact and mutual sympathy (his unsatisfactory married life has been displayed earlier in the evening). In other words, Wotan realizes that he, too, is going to have to renounce love—a fact that is made clear by a leitmotiv in the orchestra. Before the four-day opera ends, Wotan will also renounce his power (in one of Wagner's greatest scenes) and will see his entire world go up in flames.

Wagner, Die Walküre: Wotan's Farewell. Line Score*

PART 1 WOTAN, OVERCOME AND DEEPLY MOVED, TURNS EAGERLY TO BRÜNNHILDE, RAISES HER FROM HER KNEES, AND GAZES WITH EMOTION INTO HER EYES. HE SINGS:

Farewell, thou valiant, glorious child!
Leb' wohl, du kühnes, herrliches Kind!

Thou holiest pride of my heart, farewell, farewell, farewell!
Du meines Herzens heiligster Stolz! Leb' wohl, leb' wohl, leb' wohl!

If now I must leave thee and nevermore greet thee,
Muss ich dich meiden, und darf nicht minnig mein Gruss dich mehr grüssen,

if never again mayst ride beside me, nor bear me a cup of mead at banquet,
sollst du nun nicht mehr neben mir reiten, noch Meth beim Mahl mir reichen,

if I must abandon the child I love, thou laughing delight of my eyes—
muss ich verlieren dich, die ich liebe, du lachende Lust meines Auges—

such a bridal fire for thee shall be kindled as ne'er yet burned for a bride!
ein bräutliches Feuer soll dir nun brennen, wie nie einer Braut es gebrannt!

Threatening flames shall flare round the fell;
Flammende Gluth umglühe den Fels;

Let withering terrors daunt the craven! Let cowards fly from Brünnhilde's rock!
mit zehrenden Schrecken scheuch' es den Zagen; der Feige fliehe Brünnhilde's Fels!

For one alone shall win the bride, one freer than I, the god!
Denn Einer nur freie die Braut, der freier als ich, der Gott!

BRÜNNHILDE SINKS IN ECSTASY ON WOTAN'S BREAST; HE HOLDS HER IN A LONG EMBRACE AS THE ORCHESTRA PLAYS:

SHE THROWS HER HEAD BACK AGAIN AND, STILL EMBRACING WOTAN, GAZES WITH DEEP ENTHUSIASM INTO HIS EYES.

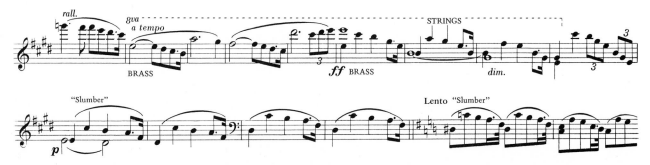

* In this line score, the language of the translation has not been modernized but retains Wagner's involuted and, as he thought, medieval-sounding quality.

PART 2 SMALL CAPS WOTAN RESUMES:

Thy brightly glittering eyes that smiling oft I caressed, when valor won them a kiss as reward,
Der Augen leuchtendes Paar, das oft ich lächelnd gekos't, wenn Kampfeslust ein Kuss dir lohnte,

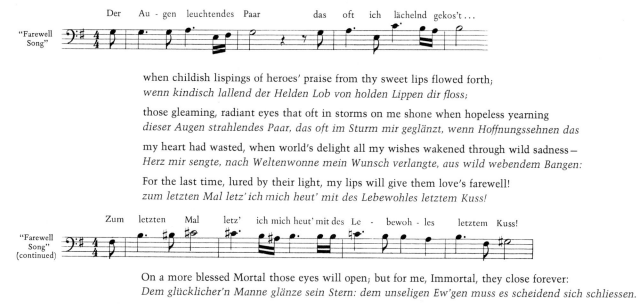

"Farewell Song"

when childish lispings of heroes' praise from thy sweet lips flowed forth;
wenn kindisch lallend der Helden Lob von holden Lippen dir floss;

those gleaming, radiant eyes that oft in storms on me shone when hopeless yearning
dieser Augen strahlendes Paar, das oft im Sturm mir geglänzt, wenn Hoffnungssehnen das

my heart had wasted, when world's delight all my wishes wakened through wild sadness—
Herz mir sengte, nach Weltenwonne mein Wunsch verlangte, aus wild webendem Bangen:

For the last time, lured by their light, my lips will give them love's farewell!
zum letzten Mal letz' ich mich heut' mit des Lebewohles letztem Kuss!

"Farewell Song" (continued)

On a more blessed Mortal those eyes will open; but for me, Immortal, they close forever:
Dem glücklicher'n Manne glänze sein Stern: dem unseligen Ew'gen muss es scheidend sich schliessen.

For thus I, the god, turn from thee; thus I kiss thy godhead away!
Denn so kehrt der Gott sich dir ab, so küsst er die Gottheit von dir!

HE CLASPS HER HEAD IN HIS HANDS.

HE KISSES HER LONG ON THE EYES. SHE SINKS BACK UNCONSCIOUS IN HIS ARMS. HE GENTLY BEARS HER TO A LOW MOSSY MOUND. .

HE TURNS SLOWLY AWAY, THEN AGAIN TURNS ROUND WITH A SORROWFUL LOOK.

PART 3 WOTAN STRIDES WITH SOLEMN DECISION TO THE MIDDLE OF THE STAGE AND DIRECTS THE POINT OF HIS SPEAR TOWARD A LARGE ROCK. HE CALLS UPON LOGE, THE GOD OF FIRE:

Loge, hear! attend!
Loge, hör'! Lausche hieher!

When first I found you, a flickering flame, you fled from me in a devious blaze;
wie zuerst ich dich fand, als feurige Gluth, wie dann einst du mir schwandest, als schweifende Lohe;

I caught you then; I release you now! Appear, and wind thee in flames round the fell!
wie ich dich band, bann' ich dich heut'! Herauf, wabernde Lohe, umlod're mir feurig den Fels!

Loge! Loge! attend!
Loge! Loge! hieher!

A FLASH OF FLAME ISSUES FROM THE ROCK, WHICH SWELLS TO AN EVER-BRIGHTENING FIERY GLOW.

WOTAN STRETCHES OUT HIS SPEAR AS IF CASTING A SPELL.

He who my spearpoint's sharpness feareth, ne'er cross the flaming fire!
Wer meines Speeres Spitze furchtet, durchschreite das Feuer nie!

HE LOOKS SORROWFULLY BACK AT BRÜNNHILDE.

HE LOOKS BACK AGAIN.   HE DISAPPEARS THROUGH THE FIRE.

(End of opera)

WOTAN'S FAREWELL

Wotan's Farewell consists of three parts, each beginning with a statement by Wotan (sung by a bass-baritone) and ending with a lengthy orchestral passage. If you follow Wotan's words with care on the combination libretto-line score on pages 370–72, you will see that Wagner the poet has inserted many complicated thoughts that Wagner the composer is able to bring out by means of nuances in the vocal melody and details of accompaniment. Both intellectually and emotionally, Wotan is a figure of great interest and stature. But as is Wagner's way, the emphatic orchestral passages at the end of his statements are almost more impressive than what Wotan actually sings.

Part 1 Wotan refers to some of the more superficial reasons why he will miss Brünnhilde, and he describes the ring of fire. The orchestral web, while he is doing this, is rich and complex. Thus at his mention of the fire, a striking leitmotiv dances and sparkles and modulates in the high strings and flutes. No one will have any trouble associating this leitmotiv with the *magic fire* that is going to surround the sleeping Valkyrie.

Brünnhilde can be wakened and won only be a mortal hero who is "freer than I, the god"—that is, by someone who has not been tainted by the gold and who is therefore morally freer than Wotan. Just before he says this, the most striking motive that has yet been heard in the scene swells up in the trombones. Wagner hopes that the audience will instantly accept this strong, bold music as a musical prophecy of the *hero-to-come.* [*]

The orchestral conclusion to part 1 continues with an emphatic passage depicting a great surge of love between Wotan and his daughter. After a heavy cadence in the brass, the instruments circle down with a short, repeated motive, which clearly has a lulling quality. This *slumber* leitmotiv has been heard before, and it comes again and again in the scene, blended into the other music with the greatest ingenuity and expressiveness.

Part 2 Wotan speaks more personally of his love for Brünnhilde before putting her to sleep with a kiss. His long, slow "Farewell song," the most tuneful part of the scene, gives us perhaps the most moving impression of his deep feelings. When at last he "kisses her godhead away," a sober motive is played by the English horn, a leitmotiv previously associated with *renunciation of love.* Is this Wagner's way of commenting for the benefit of the audience, or is it his way of showing Wotan's own awareness, in back of his actual words? Probably the latter, given the highly self-aware picture of Wotan that Wagner has built up during the opera—indeed, even during the earlier part of this scene.

The orchestral conclusion to part 2 begins with the famous leitmotiv of Brünnhilde's *magic sleep.* The harmonies are what are so magical—and tender. The still orchestration (first winds and harp, then strings) conveys an unforgettable effect. Thereafter, a long, slow, musing passage of rich music in-

---

[*] This music is traditionally called the "motive of Siegfried," for that is the name of the hero who, in fact, arrives next evening. But of course we do not know that yet; we have only a vague but portentous awareness that Brünnhilde will not be left sleeping forever.

corporates memories of Wotan's "Farewell song." Toward the end, a strikingly brief motive is heard twice in the lower brass instruments. It is not surprising to learn that this ominous leitmotiv has to do with the idea of *fate.*

Part 3 The last part of the scene begins with a blatant motive in the trombones; Wotan is a primitive warrior-king as well as a good father. This motive stands for the *law* which Wotan is bound to uphold—by force, it would appear. He summons the god of fire, Loge, and orders him to surround the sleeping Brünnhilde with a wall of flame.

The final tableau of the opera sounds as splendid as (we hope) it looks. The *magic fire* and *slumber* motives blend together into Wagner's most opulent orchestral sound. Thrice Wotan strikes flame from the rock with his great spear. Then he departs, after uttering a curse to protect Brünnhilde from all cowardly suitors; but, with his usual sixth sense, he finds himself singing his curse to the music of the *hero-to-come.* This impressive forecast prepares the way musically for the next opera, *Siegfried.*

The orchestral conclusion to part 3 includes a new recollection of Wotan's "Farewell song" and, as the ultimate determinant, the motive of *fate* (also heard at the end of part 2). Everything is wrapped up in gorgeous sound and flickering red lights. Wagner would have enjoyed the strobes in today's discotheques.

But for all his interest in decor and stage machinery, in poetry and philosophy, Wagner was first and foremost a musician. The principal element in his formidable "combined art work" was music. As we have seen, it is the music—the system of leitmotivs—that makes the essential point at every juncture of Wotan's Farewell. When Wotan realizes that he must renounce love, when Brünnhilde falls into her magic sleep, when the god of fire enters, even when Wotan prophesies the coming of Siegfried, the moment is invested with musical significance by means of an appropriate leitmotiv.

Giuseppe Verdi (1813–1901)

Giuseppe Verdi, the greatest of Italian opera composers, lived through almost the entire romantic era. His first sweeping success, *Nebuchadnezzar,* dates from around 1840, the time of Chopin's Ballade in G Minor and Schumann's Piano Concerto. His magnificent Shakespeare operas *Otello* and *Falstaff* date from around 1890, the time of Strauss's *Don Juan* and Brahms's Fourth Symphony. Throughout this long career, one that naturally encompassed many changes of style, Verdi worked steadily at the depiction of powerful emotion, like all his contemporaries. He strove for this with remarkable fidelity, and a case can be made that Verdi brought out the best of musical romanticism through all its changing phases.

People are inevitably drawn to compare and contrast Verdi and Wagner, the two masters of nineteenth-century opera. The heart of the contrast lies in Verdi's unswerving emphasis on the singing human voice. In this, he was a faithful follower of the *bel canto* principles of Rossini, Donizetti, and Bellini (see page 355). He never allowed the voice to be overshadowed for long by the orchestra, as Wagner often did with his leitmotivs, and he entertained no such grandiose ideas as that of Wagner's "combined art works" (see page 364). Opera was a singing art to Verdi, and generations of Italians before, during, and after his lifetime have enthusiastically agreed with him.

Verdi still used recitative and arias, though not exclusively. Of course, these forms had changed greatly since the time of Handel or Mozart. Many of Verdi's arias might be described as strophic songs (see page 314) with orchestra, in his own highly emotional, exuberant melodic style. Some of his most familiar music consists of timeless tunes such as "La donna è mobile" from the opera *Rigoletto*, the "Anvil Chorus" from *Il Trovatore*, "Celeste Aida" from *Aida*, and the duet from the Tomb Scene of the same opera, which we shall deal with presently.

But although people have always loved Verdi's tunes, in his own day the dramatic side of his operas was especially admired. First and foremost he was interested in people—people placed in dramatic situations where violent, exciting actions bring out equally violent emotions. Verdi sought out librettos full of breathtaking situations, and, to match these in music, he was able to turn his melodies to remarkable dramatic use.

Wagner, on the other hand, was principally interested in philosophical ideas, and he relied more on harmony and orchestration than on singing per se. The famous "Liebestod" of *Tristan und Isolde* (see page 366) still makes satisfactory music with the original voice part left out! Wagner was a fine psychologist in music, as we have seen, but at best his gods and heroes and Valkyries are "larger than life." They lack the immediacy of Verdi's vibrant and very human characters.

Verdi's *Aida* is perhaps the most frequently performed of all operas. Its last two scenes show the two sides of his art. The Judgment Scene is action-packed and intensely dramatic; none of the great "hit" tunes of *Aida* comes from this scene—there is no time for one—despite the powerful melodic lines sung by the mezzo-soprano and the chorus. The Tomb Scene moves much more calmly. While it is also dramatic, in the sense that it resolves perfectly the action that has been leading up to it all through the opera, this scene is much more lyrical. It centers on one of Verdi's most celebrated melodies. This melody continues to haunt us as we leave the theater, and it will not let us forget the drama we have witnessed.

VERDI *Aida*, Act IV: Judgment Scene (1871) SIDE 13

The plot of *Aida* is thoroughly romantic (in the sense of amorous). The young Egyptian general Radames and the beautiful Ethiopian slave girl Aida are in love, but Radames has aroused the passion of the Princess Amneris—a *femme fatale* in every sense of the word. Prodded on by the Egyptian priesthood, Amneris's father, the King of Egypt, is waging a holy war against Ethiopia. Aida, prodded on by *her* father, persuades Radames to reveal the secrets of his battle plan. But Amneris has eavesdropped on their tryst out of jealousy, and she turns him over to the all-powerful priests for justice.

At the beginning of act IV, the last act, Amneris proceeds with her plan. She offers to intercede and save Radames if he will return her love. To her astonishment, he refuses, saying he regrets his actions and would prefer to die rather than live without Aida. Amneris, whose nature is wildly passionate under the best of circumstances, rises to a perfect fever of rage, distress, and self-blame in this scene (scene i), but there is nothing she can do; Radames is led off by his guards. Now read on (and listen).

Act IV continues with the so-called Judgment Scene (scene ii). Wearing ominous white hoods, like members of the Ku Klux Klan, the priests march through the palace on their way to the crypt below, where Radames's trial will take place. Their tread is depicted by the sinister-sounding motive shown at the beginning of the following example:

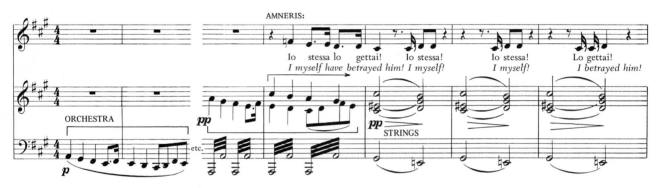

Though Verdi rarely used leitmotivs—they were very much Wagner's trademark (see page 364)—this motive does, in fact, occur many times in the course of *Aida* to signify the implacable priesthood. However, the motive is treated more simply and more melodically than it would have been in Wagner's hands.

When this brief march sets in motion the inexorable series of events leading to Radames's death, Princess Amneris has scarcely had time to collect herself and recover from her shock. She is almost too distracted to sing connected tunes, a rare condition indeed for ladies in nineteenth-century opera. Instead she utters broken phrases:

Oime! morir mi sento! Oh! chi lo salva?	Alas! death overcomes me! Oh, who will save him?
E in poter di costoro	And I have betrayed him into *those* hands,
io stessa lo gettai! Ora, a te impreco,	I, I myself! Curses on you,
atroce gelosia, che la sua morte	foul jealousy, which now prescribes his death
e il lutto eterno del mio cor segnasti!	and everlasting regret in my heart!
Ecco i fatali, gl'inessorati ministri di morte:	Here are the inevitable, inexorable ministers of death:
Oh! ch'io non vegga quelle bianche larve!	Ah! let me not see those white hoods!

As the march recedes into the depths, Amneris, in a passage with strangely beautiful harmonies (see the end of the example above), bleakly repeats over and over again that she is to blame. Verdi is usually praised for his melodies, but like most romantic composers he could also employ harmony in an individual and effective way. This passage is an example. Amneris may have spoken these words before, but only now does their true impact sink in on her.

With Amneris, the audience hears but does not see the trial in the crypt below. Since the court is an ecclesiastical one, the proceedings begin with a prayer, sung in a solemn, chantlike chorus, without orchestra. Amneris responds with a prayer of her own:

Numi, pietà del mio strazia - to core, Egli,è inno - cente, Lo salvate,o Nu - mi! Dispe - ra - to, tremendo,è il mio dolo - re.
Gods, have pity on my broken heart!   He is innocent;   save him, o gods!   Desperate, overwhelming is my sorrow.

This is the first of several magnificent phrases in which Amneris expresses her emotions, or to put it more accurately, hurls them across the footlights at the audience. Especially effective is the way in which Verdi aims unerringly for the high notes in the singer's range (Amneris is a mezzo-soprano, a voice type between soprano and contralto). These phrases never coalesce into full-scale tunes, though they could do so easily. For this highly dramatic scene, Verdi contents himself with single melodic phrases, which depict the unbearable grief of the unfortunate princess in a particularly intense, concise way.

The priests end their prayer on a note of naked force, as the motive of their march blasts out on the trombones. Now the hearing begins. The High Priest, Ramphis, puts the case for the prosecution:

Radamès! Radamès! Radamès! ⌈The name echoes thunder-⌉ *Tu rivelasti della patria i segreti allo straniero:*
Radames! Radames! Radames! |ously round the vault, on | You revealed your country's secrets to the foreigner:
⌊brass instruments. ⌋

Discolpati. ⌈ The priests ⌉ *Discolpati.* ⌈ But Radames does not; we hear ⌉ *Egli tace. Traditor!*
Defend yourself! ⌊ repeat ⌋ Defend yourself! ⌊ only a muffled drum roll. ⌋ He is silent. Traitor!

Amneris, hearing this from above, breaks into another tremendous sob of passion:

Ah pie - tà!   egli,è inno - cente, Nu - mi, pie - tà, Nu - mi, pie - tà!
Ah have pity!   he is innocent,   gods have pity,   gods have pity!

The High Priest intones two further accusations:

Radamès! Radamès! Radamès! ⌈ Echo: wind ⌉ *Tu disertasti dal campo   il dì che precedea la pugna. . .*
Radames! Radames! Radames! ⌊ instruments ⌋ You deserted the encampment on the day preceding the battle. . .

and

Radamès! Radamès! Radamès! ⌈ Echo: wind ⌉ *Tua fè violasti, alla patria spergiuro, al Re, all'onor. . .*
Radames! Radames! Radames! ⌊ instruments ⌋ You broke faith, your country perjured, your King, your honor. . .

At each new accusation, Radames remains silent, as before, and is greeted by the same shout of "Traitor!"

And at each new shout, Amneris delivers herself of another outburst. The music is essentially identical all three times, except that the second and third times are each one note higher. This seemingly minor alteration makes for a splendid intensification, for in voices a single note makes a remarkable difference in terms of excitement. Verdi arranges things so that, for her third outburst, Amneris is singing in the highest, most thrilling part of her vocal range.

After the third condemnation, the priests pronounce judgment without further ceremony. They do so in a coarse, marchlike tune, punctuated by harsh rhythmic explosions in the orchestra:

If they had sentenced Radames using the music of their original chant, there would at least have been the semblance of ecclesiastical dignity, but this particular tune reflects the savage relish with which they shout their fatal words. They are no longer priests but vengeful men.

Another cry from Amneris, and the priests emerge from the vault, marching to the same motive with which they had descended a few minutes before (in the example on page 376). Amneris confronts them on the way up, with yet another of her passionate phrases:

This melody is clearly related to the priests' sentencing song. Contemptuously, they merely address three words to her: "Traitor! he dies!" Amneris tries again and again with a new lament, but they pass swiftly off, leaving her alone on the stage. All but inarticulate with despair and humiliation, she hurls a wild curse at them:

Empia razza! anatema su voi!	Evil hierarchy! a curse on you!
la vendetta del ciel scenderà!	May the vengeance of heaven descend on you!
anatema su voi!	A curse on you!

All through this powerful dramatic scene the tension has been built up masterfully. A brutal onslaught of orchestral sound discharges it, and the curtain falls.

VERDI *Aida,* Act IV: Tomb Scene SIDE 14

Like the Judgment Scene, the Tomb Scene (scene iii) that follows includes action on two separate horizontal levels. This time we see both. Below, the large tomb in which Radames has been left to suffocate after the tomb has been bricked up. Above, the temple of Phtha, with the altar under which the priests have promised to bury him.

The mournful, hushed sounds that introduce the Tomb Scene represent a marked contrast to the intensity of the Judgment Scene. Yet we may notice that they are made up of a motive taken from the orchestral music accompanying Amneris's final curse in that scene.

Radames hardly has time to express the hope that Aida may live happily when he hears a sound in his tomb. Aida has secretly hidden in it, in order to die with him. After some accompanied recitative (see page 166), each sings a short aria-like section, consisting of several melodic phrases. Radames, a tenor, speaks very tenderly of the pathos of Aida's coming death. Aida, a soprano, already a little delirious from the thin air, speaks of the future joys of heaven.

Then Verdi mounts his impressive final tableau. The priests, now accompanied by priestesses, file into the temple above, singing a hymn with a near-Eastern flavor. It celebrates the great god Phtha (*Immenso Ftha*). Below, Radames and Aida begin their final duet, a farewell to the sorrows of earth and a welcome to eternity. It is a famous instance of Verdi's simple and yet highly effusive melodic style:

Notice how the melodic line is rooted around just a few notes: high and low G♭ and D♭. This feature gives the melody a unique ethereal quality, as befits a couple who are going to die from lack of oxygen a few minutes later.

Another feature that produces the same effect is the high accompanying haze of the strings which swells up ecstatically later.* We sense that the young people are already far out of this world, perfectly attuned to one another—they sing the same tune in octaves—in a love that transcends death itself. Was this Verdi's answer to Wagner's *Tristan und Isolde*? It is interesting to try to sense the difference in effect as these two composers portray a "love death" from very different standpoints.

Before the final curtain, a figure in mourning enters the temple above to pray. A broken woman, drained of all the emotion revealed in her desperate scene with the priests, Amneris can only whisper in a monotone: "Peace, peace, I implore!" (*Pace t'imploro!*). The different sentiments of the various characters are made more vivid by simultaneous contrast: we saw this principle already at work in the *opera buffa* ensemble (see page 263) of Mozart's day. Amneris's grief is set directly against the ecstatic, otherworldly togetherness of Radames and Aida.

Simultaneously, too, the priests continue their implacable chanting; in fact, they sing the last words in the scene (*Immenso Ftha*). One of the things Verdi wanted to show in this opera, below the level of the personal story, was the repressive effect of organized state religion. Like all Italian liberals, Verdi regarded the Papacy as a reactionary force; he was a "freethinker"—the characteristically romantic euphemism for "atheist"—and bitterly anticlerical. There is no question that in his very unsympathetic picture of these ancient Egyptian priests, in both the Tomb Scene and the Judgment Scene, Verdi was making a not-so-subtle political point for his own time.

Later Program Music

A generation or two ago, Piotr Ilyich Tchaikovsky (1840–1893) was everybody's favorite romantic composer. His long list of popular works includes six symphonies, which we shall discuss briefly later, brilliant concertos for piano and violin, and many operas and ballets, including the famous *Swan Lake* and the Christmas favorite *The Nutcracker.* The suites (see page 179) made up of music from these ballets are often heard in symphony concerts.

Tchaikovsky wrote several program music pieces based on Shakespeare: *Romeo and Juliet, Hamlet,* and *The Tempest.* Shakespeare was greatly admired in the romantic era, as we noted in discussing Berlioz. And there is *1812*, a patriotic number commemorating the Russian victory over Napoleon in that year, also the subject of Tolstoy's great novel *War and Peace.* Tchaikovsky introduces both the French national anthem (the *Marseillaise*) and a Russian hymn into this piece and has them battle with one another. It is program music with a vengeance.

---

* A third way in which Verdi achieves the ethereal quality of this passage is by specifying that the very highest note sung (B♭—see the asterisk in the example) be sung very quietly, rather than loudly, as it would ordinarily be sung—and as, in fact, it *is* sung in almost all performances, unfortunately. The romantic composers are particularly vulnerable to irresponsible performers. This whole duet is often performed with excessive rubato.

Viva Verdi!

An Italian political drawing of 1859. The agitators scrawling *"Viva Verdi!"* (Long live Verdi!) on the wall were the inventors of our modern-day acronyms: Verdi's name spelled out <u>V</u>ittorio <u>E</u>mmanuele, <u>R</u>e <u>D</u>' <u>I</u>talia: Victor Emmanuel, King of Italy, the symbolic leader of the Italian struggle for national unification.

It is interesting to compare Verdi and Wagner in the matter of their politics. In the Revolution of 1848, which broke out all over Europe, Wagner as a young radical (over thirty, at that) was associated with the famous anarchist Bakunin. Wagner even delivered speeches inciting revolutionary riots. The revolution was soon put down, however, and Wagner had to go into exile for many years. In later life, as he came close to the seats of power, he grew much more reactionary. He has been branded as an intellectual precursor of Nazism—a charge with a clear basis in fact, though it is one that requires a considerable amount of qualification.

Verdi, who never played the role of an active revolutionary, remained a staunch liberal to the end of his long life. And while Wagner's "music dramas" were élite pro-ductions, Verdi's operas were widely popular, the popular art of the Italian people in an age without television and movies. Again and again these operas show noble oppressed peoples suffering under tyrants, though of course in a disguised form to get around the censors. One Verdi melody, almost forgotten today, the song of the Israelite slaves in his biblical opera *Nebuchadnezzar,* became a semiofficial hymn in the Italian struggle for liberation—a parallel to the *Marseillaise* in revolutionary France or *We shall overcome* in the United States during the 1960s. A famous line in Verdi's opera *Attila* (Attila the Hun) shook the rafters every time it was sung in revolutionary Italy: "Give me Italy, and you can have the world!" (*Avrai tu l'universo, resti l'Italia a me!*).

Verdi's practical nationalism can make the musical nationalism of such composers as Moussorgsky seem rather trifling by comparison. When Garibaldi and Cavour between them ousted the Austrians, and a united Italy was established in 1861, Verdi was made an honorary deputy in the first Italian parliament. Probably no other composer has ever received so fine a tribute from his nation.

PIOTR ILYICH TCHAIKOVSKY (1840–1893) *Romeo and Juliet* (1867–1880)

Tchaikovsky's *Romeo and Juliet* treats Shakespeare's play more tactfully than *1812* treats the Napoleonic wars; the subject matter is followed only in rather general terms. Indeed, Tchaikovsky did not call it a symphonic poem but rather an "overture-fantasy." Still, once we know the title we easily identify the three main themes with elements in the drama. The high, surging melody must stand for the love of Romeo and Juliet. The very agitated theme suggests the deadly vendetta between their two families or, more generally, the fate that stands between these "star-cross'd lovers," as Shakespeare calls them. The religious-sounding theme stands for the kindly Friar Laurence, who devises a plot to help the lovers which goes fatally wrong.

Romeo and Juliet begins with a slow introduction, as low clarinets and bassoons play the Friar Laurence theme. Notice the solemn slow wind chords interspersed with strumming on the harp, an instrument that Berlioz had introduced into the orchestra (see page 348) and that Tchaikovsky liked particularly. Someone, we feel, is getting ready to narrate a serious, tragic tale. The slow introduction works up to a climax over a dramatic timpani roll.

The tempo changes to allegro and we hear the vendetta (or fate) theme. It is made up of a number of short rhythmic motives, which Tchaikovsky puts to use at once for development; this section too works up to a climax, when part of the theme is punctuated with sensational cymbal claps. The highly romantic love theme is played first of all by the English horn doubled by the violas—a mellow sound. It is followed by a curious but affecting passage constructed out of a little sighing figure:

This gradually turns into a contrapuntal accompaniment for the love theme, played by the French horn. The sigh is beginning to turn into a sob:

Tchaikovsky repeats these themes and develops them in various ways. He does not try to follow through the story step by step, any more than Berlioz does in the *Fantastic Symphony*. In the sections where the Friar Laurence theme and the vendetta theme are developed vigorously together, we may get the impression of a battle between the forces of good and evil; and at the end, we cannot miss a reference to the tragic outcome of the play. The tempo slows down again, and part of the love theme appears in a mutilated version over funeral drum taps in the timpani. The sighing theme, too, is now heard in a very mournful transformation.

However, the mood is not entirely gloomy; the storyteller (Friar Laurence, perhaps) seems to derive solace and inspiration from the tale. The harp strumming is resumed, and the love theme returns for the last time in a new cadential version, surging enthusiastically upward in a way that is very typical of Tchaikovsky. Does this not mean to suggest that, even though Romeo and Juliet are dead, their love is timeless—that their love transcends death? The influence of Wagner's "Liebestod" (see page 365) was felt everywhere in the later nineteenth century.

RICHARD STRAUSS (1864–1949) *Don Juan* (1887–1888)

The symphonic poems of Richard Strauss (which he preferred to call *tone poems*) are more complex than those of Tchaikovsky. *Don Juan* goes back to the subject of Mozart's opera *Don Giovanni:* the legendary Spanish lover who pursues women insatiably and is finally doomed for his sins. Strauss took his inspiration not from the old legend itself but from a long, extravagant version of it by the nineteenth-century German poet Nikolaus Lenau. The program consists of excerpts from the poem:

> Fain would I run the circle, immeasurably wide, of beautiful women's endless charms, in a full tempest of enjoyment, to die of a kiss at the mouth of the last one. O friends! would that I could fly through every region where beauty blossoms, fall on my knees before each one, and conquer. . . .
>
> I shun satiety and the exhaustion of pleasure; I keep myself fresh in the service of Beauty. . . . The breath of a woman that today is the odor of spring may perhaps oppress me tomorrow like the air of a dungeon. . . . Indeed, passion is always and only the *new* passion. . . . Away, then, to triumphs ever new, while youth's fiery pulses race!
>
> Beautiful was the fire that urged me on. It has spent its rage, and now silence remains . . . the fuel is all consumed, the hearth is cold and dark.

No doubt the lengthy opening theme refers to the hero:

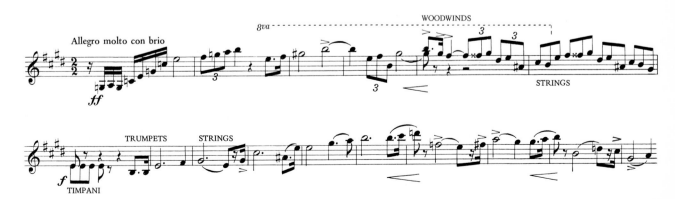

Do you detect some similarity to the *idée fixe* of Berlioz's *Fantastic Symphony*? The vehemence, ardor, and spontaneous flow of this music carry all before it, or so Strauss means to suggest. His own vaulting style of romantic melody is also used to very good advantage in the warm love scene that follows, at a slower tempo. It starts out like young love at first sight, but toward the end, we clearly hear Don Juan's impatience to get on to the next "tempest of enjoyment," as Lenau puts it. (We should not blame anyone for tiring of this particular lady, with her saccharine solo violin.)

Don Juan's original theme returns, and soon he launches into a new adventure—with a more mature woman, it appears, certainly someone more sensual and relaxed. But this second love scene also ends in disillusion. Note the wonderfully rich sound of the oboe in this scene; such orchestral opulence was one of the proudest accomplishments of the romantic composers.

Then a bold new theme blares out in the French horns, a revival of noble wanderlust in Don Juan:

For a moment, we can picture him chafing to leave while the lady wheedles him to remain. He gets away, and, in a long developmental section, this bold new theme is added to Don Juan's original musical material.

Suddenly there is a sharp break in the music. This place is usually explained as illustrating the death of Don Juan, which comes about in Lenau's poem through a duel; sensing that his youth has "spent its rage," our hero allows himself to be run through. Mournful memories of both women are heard in the orchestra, on various woodwind instruments and on the inevitable solo violin. However, before dying, Don Juan apparently remembers his whole career, in a passage that has the feeling of a sonata-form recapitulation. This passage includes both his original theme and the bold new one of the example above. Then the music sinks down, and the piece ends on an extended note of pathos.

The unique "inner form" of *Don Juan* may be diagramed as follows:

DON JUAN THEME	Love Scene No. 1 (*slower*)	DON JUAN THEME	Love Scene No. 2 (*slower*)	Developmental Passage		D U E L	Remembrance		D E A T H
				NEW THEME	DON JUAN THEME		DON JUAN THEME	NEW THEME	
					THEME				

To compare Strauss's *Don Juan* with Mozart's *Don Giovanni* (see pages 263–70) is to observe how romanticism transformed the half-scurrilous, half-moralistic old legend. If Strauss's hero strikes us as more immediately dashing and ardent, that may be because he tends to dramatize himself—both in the poem and in the music. Strauss furnishes him with generous helpings of brass and percussion, vigorous rhythms, and bold, overreaching melodic leaps. His women are sentimental, and he plays along.

Mozart's Don Giovanni, who is not in the least introspective, follows his nature unhesitatingly and faces the consequences when they happen to catch up with him. Strauss's Don Juan is always harping on the theme of his heroism, comparing his conquests, and worrying about the coming termination of his amorous career. He has no sense of humor at all about his adventures, as Mozart's Don Giovanni does. When Don Giovanni dies, he doesn't think of any of his women but only (as always) of himself. And he dies with a shriek of agony at the torments of hellfire, not with the sob or sniff that Strauss's Don Juan emits.

Nationalism

We have mentioned Giuseppe Verdi's participation in the Italian liberation movement (see page 381). Verdi was not the only nineteenth-century composer to place his art in the service of political nationalism, nor was Italy the only country engaged in a struggle for independence. The Czechs revolted against the Austrian Empire, the Poles rose up against Russia, and Norway broke free of Sweden. All over Europe, people were becoming more conscious of their history and destiny, their national character, and their artistic heritage.

nationalism   This gave rise to a musical movement, also called nationalism, which involved the incorporation of national folk music into concert pieces and operas. Generally, nationalist composers wrote program music or music with words, in which the programs and texts stress national themes of one kind or another. Add to these literary themes musical themes taken from folk songs, and the result is music that will stir strong emotions at home, and that may also make a very effective ambassador abroad.

Nationalism in fact involved a desire to make local music independent of Europe's traditional culture leaders: France, Italy, and the German countries. Composers working in those countries had the advantage of working within long-established, fully accepted traditions; they did not have to do anything especially "national" to gain attention and respect. Thus, although Verdi was definitely a *political* nationalist, we do not speak of him as a *musical* nationalist.

Nationalism flourished in outlying countries, then, among them Spain, Britain, Norway, Denmark, Czechoslovakia, Poland, and Russia. The origins of the movement go back to the polonaises and mazurkas of Chopin (see page 335), and it continued to be an important force in the early twentieth century. American nationalist composers first appear in this latter period (see pages 451–54).

Sometimes musical nationalism had no more profound impetus than the pleasure audiences got from hearing folk music at symphony concerts, whether their own folk music or someone else's. Frenchmen wrote Spanish music, Russians wrote Italian music, and Czechs wrote American music (Georges Bizet's *Carmen*, Tchaikovsky's *Capriccio Italien*, Antonín Dvořák's *New World* Symphony). These pieces serve the same function as travelogues, perhaps. Yet even this "nonpolitical" music had the effect of emphasizing the exotic and unique qualities of nations. Romantic individuality had become a national as well as a personal ideal.

MODEST MOUSSORGSKY (1839–1881) *Pictures at an Exhibition* (1874) SIDE 18

Of the nineteenth-century nationalist composers, the Russians were probably the most successful, and of the Russians, Modest Moussorgsky was probably the most original. *Pictures at an Exhibition* is an interesting sample of nationalist program music. It illustrates a memorial exhibition of pictures by a minor artist and architect called Victor Hartmann, who had recently died. Hartmann, a friend of the composer's, came from a Russian family (despite his German name) and cared deeply about getting Russian "motives" into his work, just as Moussorgsky did. Not all of Hartmann's pictures are unmistakably Russian (nor are all of Moussorgsky's musical pictures), but the most impressive ones are, such as his vision of the Great Gate of Kiev (see page 389).

Pictures at an Exhibition was written for piano solo, as a series of piano miniatures joined in a set, like Schumann's *Carnaval* (see page 341). In 1922 the set was orchestrated by the composer Maurice Ravel, and this is the form in which it has since become popular. Though Ravel's orchestration is more modern, light, and smooth than Moussorgsky's would have been, the general spirit is probably close enough to the original conception.

"Promenade" As a way of giving some overall musical unity to the set of different pictures, Moussorgsky hit on a plan that is as simple and effective as it is ingenious. The first number, "Promenade," does not refer to a picture but depicts the composer walking around the museum. Then the same music recurs several times in very free variations, to show the promenader's changes of mood. The promenade theme recalls a Russian folk song, since Moussorgsky, of course, thought of himself as typically Russian:

Ravel orchestrated the theme first for brass instruments, later for woodwinds and strings. Quintuple meter ($\frac{5}{4}$) is a distinct rarity, and having this meter alternate with $\frac{6}{4}$ is rarer yet. The metrical anomaly gives the impression of blunt, unsophisticated folk music—and perhaps also of walking back and forth without a clear destination, as one does in a museum.

1. "Gnomus" Moussorgsky's titles are sometimes fanciful and obscure; "Gnomus" refers to a drawing of a nutcracker carved like a gnome. The nut is cracked between his heavy jaws, the two handles form his long legs, and he has no body at all. A little child could be frightened by such an object, perhaps. Moussorgsky writes music that sounds suitably macabre, with a lurching rhythm to illustrate the gnome's clumsy walk on his handle-legs.

"Promenade" Quieter now, the promenade music suggests that the spectator is musing as he moves toward the next picture.

2. "Il Vecchio Castello" (Ye Olde Castle) Titled in Italian, this work must have been one of Hartmann's more conventionally romantic pictures. A troubadour sings a mournful tune outside a medieval castle. Ravel in 1922 used an alto saxophone for this tune, something Moussorgsky almost certainly would not have done back in 1874, when saxophones were still relatively new inventions and strangers to the symphony orchestra. Nonetheless, the tone color of the saxophone is highly evocative, and so are the bleak bassoons that Ravel puts underneath it.

Moussorgsky had created his own effect of bleakness by having a single note, G♯, sound constantly in the bass during every single measure—a simple type of ostinato (see page 163). Is the troubadour's song Italian, Russian, or neither?

"Promenade"; 3. "Tuileries: Children Quarreling after Play" First the boys are heard, then the girls, apparently; the rhythm is supposed to suggest their petulant squabbles. The Tuileries is a park in Paris. A few years before Moussorgsky wrote the *Pictures,* the neighboring palace of the same name was burned to the ground by revolutionaries.

4. "Bydlo" A ponderous Polish cattle cart, depicted with strong peasant accents in the music, is heard approaching, clattering by, and receding into the distance again. The tuba solo sounds excellently clumsy here.

"Promenade"; 5. "The Ballet of the Chicks in Their Shells" For this absurd work of Hartmann's—costume designs in the form of big eggs, intended for a ballet that in fact never materialized—Moussorgsky wrote appropriately comical and not particularly Russian-sounding music. He marked this piece *Scherzino* (little scherzo) *and Trio.* Notice the illustration of chicks clucking, on clarinets, flutes, and piccolo.

6. "Two Polish Jews, One Rich, One Poor" Once a composer is bitten by the nationalist idea, he is as glad to employ Polish or Jewish folk accents in his music as Russian. Here Moussorgsky draws a vivid contrast between two residents of the Polish ghetto, a pompous, rich Jew and a skinny, whining beggar.

Ravel uses rapidly repeated notes on the muted trumpet, another unusual orchestral sound. The total effect is that of a not-too-gentle parody.

First we hear one character, then the other, then both of them together; the technique recalls that of the *opera buffa* ensemble (see page 263). Indeed, Moussorgsky's illustrative and parodistic techniques were employed to best advantage in the field of opera. His operas have nationalistic subjects: *Khovanshtchina, The Fair at Sorotchinsk,* and, greatest of all, *Boris Godunov.* This last is based on a play about an early Russian czar, written by Alexander Pushkin, the famous Russian romantic poet.

"Promenade" The original piano piece includes another promenade here, but for some reason Ravel cut it out. He has Nos. 5, 6, 7, and 8 played consecutively, without pause.

7. *"The Marketplace, Limoges"* Another picture from Hartmann's wide travels. Limoges is in the south of France, but the music will do for busy marketplaces anywhere.

8. *"Catacombs: Sepulchrum Romanum"* Moussorgsky lapses into Latin to make these Paris catacombs, containing ancient Roman tombs, sound more mysterious. He made a specialty of the macabre, as we heard in "Gnomus." The harsh, weird harmonies he concocted for these slow chords create a very strange effect, and Ravel's orchestration adds to it: all brass and woodwinds, with no strings except double basses.

"Promenade: Con Mortuis in Lingua Mortua" Apparently the previous picture makes the promenader meditate upon the recent death of Hartmann as he walks slowly away. A halo of strings (a piano tremolo in the original) covers the promenade theme; this is Moussorgsky speaking "the language of the dead" (*lingua mortua*).

9. *"The Hut on Fowl's Legs (Baba-Yaga)"* In Russian folklore, the witch Baba-Yaga lives in a hut supported by chicken feet. She grinds up human bones to eat using a mortar and pestle, which also serves her as a broom for flying. In Moussorgsky's music, she is certainly a raunchy old lady with a strong Russian accent. This piece lasts longer than the preceding ones and falls into an obvious A B A' form, leading directly to No. 10.

10. *"The Great Gate of Kiev"* The longest number, and the climactic one, this illustrates a fabulous architectural design by Hartmann shown opposite. It was never executed. Moussorgsky summons up in the imagination a solemn procession with clashing cymbals, clanging bells, and chanting priests. In addition to the promenade theme, two Russian melodies appear, a forceful one and a quieter, hymnlike one. The ending is very grandiose, for grandiosity forms an integral part of the Russian national self-image—and, unfortunately, of many others.

The Great Gate of Kiev, by Victor Hartmann

The Late Romantic Symphony

As we have seen, the program symphony of Berlioz and Liszt was one of the exciting new genres of the early romantic period. However, ordinary, non-programmatic symphonies continued to flourish at this time, along with works in associated genres, such as concertos and sonatas. Schumann, for instance, wrote four symphonies and one concerto each for violin, cello, and piano.

If anything, later in the nineteenth century the production of non-programmatic symphonies was stepped up. Partly this was a matter of prestige; ever since Beethoven, composers had felt that somehow they were being judged on their ability to produce impressive symphonies. Some composers produced just nine symphonies, like Beethoven. Many of the great favorites on today's (or yesterday's) concert programs were written by symphony composers of the late romantic period:

Antonín Dvořák (1841–1904), a very prolific Czech composer whose warm, sunny melodies have caused people to compare him to Schubert. The best known of his nine symphonies is the last, confusingly numbered No. 5, *From the New World.* Some of the themes are said to reflect Negro spirituals, which Dvořák could have heard in 1892–1895 when he was directing the National Conservatory in New York, a predecessor of Juilliard.

Piotr Ilyich Tchaikovsky (1840–1893), whose symphonic poem *Romeo and Juliet* we have already studied. Like Moussorgsky and most Russian composers of the time, he was influenced by nationalism and put folk songs in his early Symphony No. 2 (*Little Russian*), No. 3 (*Polish*), and No. 4. The Symphony No. 5 contains a very famous French horn tune in the slow movement. The dance movement is a waltz, like that of Berlioz's *Symphonie Fantastique.* The fine *Pathétique* Symphony, No. 6, features some interesting innovations: a movement in $\frac{5}{4}$ time (compare Moussorgsky: page 386), and a slow movement placed at the very end of the piece, rather than in the middle. Characteristically, it is marked *Adagio lamentoso.*

Anton Bruckner (1824–1896), a distinguished Austrian cathedral organist —not the usual niche for a composer of symphonies, and one that may help explain the somewhat ponderous quality of his nine examples. As a symphony composer, Bruckner was unusual, too, in being deeply influenced by Wagner. His music has slowly grown in popularity since his death, first in Austria and now everywhere else.

Symphonies in the romantic tradition continued to be written at a great rate in the early twentieth century, too. Among the main composers are Jean Sibelius (1865–1957: 7 symphonies), Ralph Vaughan Williams (1872–1958: 9 symphonies), Roy Harris (1898–1979: 7 symphonies), and Dmitri Shostakovich (1906–1975: 15 symphonies). Many of these works continue to show some nationalistic features—Finnish, English, American, and Russian, respectively.

All of these symphonists were conservative for their time, to some degree. This was already true of Johannes Brahms, the greatest of all the late nineteenth-century composers of symphonies and associated genres.

Johannes Brahms (1833–1897)

Brahms is a strange case. Born in the dour industrial port city of Hamburg, he gravitated toward Vienna—once the city of Mozart and Beethoven, but by that time the city of Johann Strauss, the Waltz King. Here Brahms became, musically speaking, more Catholic than the Pope, soberly upholding the ancient Viennese style, while Vienna was drifting off in other directions. In his youth, Brahms even went so far as to sign a foolish manifesto condemning the "modernist" music of Liszt, Wagner, and others. He never wrote program music or operas but concentrated instead on straight symphonies, concertos, and many chamber music works.

In these, Brahms steadily cultivated sonata form, theme and variations, and all the other Viennese musical forms. Almost alone among the important composers of his time, he made no special effort to pioneer striking new harmonies or tone colors, in spite of his unquestioned mastery in these areas. He wrote many miniatures—songs and piano pieces—but he never ventured even as far as Beethoven into the grandiose possibilities of romanticism.

It might sound as though Brahms could be written off as a dull conservative, then—like some other composers of his and later generations. The fact is, though, that he had a good deal to add to the Viennese style: a grand sweep of romantic melody and harmony and an enormously impressive musical technique. Technique in music does not count for everything, but it can take a composer a long way, and Brahms cultivated the elements of musical craft with great sophistication and power. Even in his string quartets in sonata form, his music does not sound like imitation Haydn or Beethoven. What is similar —what is "traditional"—is the musical *flow*: the general rhythmic feeling and the way the themes are built, run into one another, contrast, and develop. The sentiment is very different, however, and here Brahms found as individual a voice as any of his contemporaries.

BRAHMS Symphony No. 4 in E Minor (1885) SIDE 15

Brahms's Fourth Symphony was his last (he had waited till the age of forty before feeling ready to undertake his first in the genre immortalized by Beethoven). He wrote all of the first three movements of it in sonata form. Then for the fourth movement, he chose a passacaglia—a form that had scarcely been used since the time of Bach. It could almost pass as another manifesto, proclaiming Brahms's traditional orientation to a new generation of modernists.

FIRST MOVEMENT

Traditionally, the first movement of a symphony is the richest and most complex of the four. Brahms's Fourth Symphony is no exception. To begin a sonata-form movement with a long gentle melody was a romantic practice that we found in Schubert and Berlioz (see pages 311 and 346). Brahms followed their example:

The little swells, up and down, on the half notes in measures 9–12 show the romantic composer's concern for expressive dynamics in his tunes.

Then the long theme actually starts to repeat itself, in a variation featuring woodwind scales. However, the pace of the exposition picks up skillfully, and a procession of contrasted themes follows—mostly stronger themes, including some stiff trumpet fanfares.

The development section opens with the main theme, which now starts to modulate at the point where motive X is marked on the example. Then, after many episodes, the retransition (end of the development) is based on the same motive X. This echoes back and forth among the various instruments as though they were groping their way through a fog toward the original tune and the original key. (The conductor must not neglect to bring out the little dynamic swells.) When the theme looms up at last, it is slowed down into deep, mysterious long notes. The original rhythm is resumed only at measures 4 and 5.

This effective moment shows something of what Brahms had to contribute to the Viennese style. He could create a sense of profound mystery at the recapitulation, a point that Mozart had generally treated as a release and Beethoven as a triumph. After measures 4 and 5 of the theme in the recapitulation, notice how strictly the music follows that of the exposition.

SECOND MOVEMENT

The second movement of the Fourth Symphony provided Brahms with an especially good opportunity to deploy his own variety of romantic melody. Though he cared mainly about the two mellow tunes, he found it most effective to hold them together in a modified sonata form, a plan that we have seen used by Schubert (page 312):

Sonata Form

EXPOSITION		DEVELOP-MENT	RECAPITULATION		C O D A
first theme	second group		first theme	second group	

Modified Sonata Form

EXPOSITION		RECAP	BRIEF DEVELOPMENT	ITULATION	C O D A
first theme	second group	first theme		second group	

The movement begins with a series of solemn introductory French horn calls, entirely unharmonized. They run into the first theme:

Andante moderato
CLARINET
pp
VIOLINS PIZZICATO

Though the orchestration may not sound strikingly brilliant or unusual here, it deserves a moment's pause. The clarinet (upward stems) plays the tune in one rhythm, while the strings play it pizzicato (see page 349) in a slightly different rhythm (downward stems). Which is the true rhythm of the tune? We cannot tell, but what we do hear is that the string rhythm reiterates the rhythm of the introductory horn calls. Thus by drawing a connection between two musical ideas, the orchestration makes a quiet point about musical form.

Clarinets and French horns, favorite components of Brahms's characteristic burnished tone colors, continue to dominate the tune as a whole. Its phrases are neatly balanced in the best Viennese fashion:

a	b	(a')	c	a	b'
4	4	2	7	4	4
measures	measures	measures	measures	measures	measures
clarinet------------------------→French			clarinet,	French	clarinet----------→
		horn	etc.	horn	

After this ends, the music swells into a forceful bridge passage. The lush second theme turns out to be a slower, smoother version of this very bridge:

Perhaps this ingenious detail of musical form makes the tune sound even more sensuous and relaxed, by comparison with its excited ancestor, the bridge.

In the recapitulation, which soon comes around, the clarinet no longer plays in the first theme (we shall appreciate the reason for this in a moment). Halfway through phrase c of the theme, a brief, angry development section intrudes, working with the horn-call rhythm, as is shown in the diagram on page 392.

Ultimately the bridge returns; so does the second theme, in a creamy new orchestration. What is more, it now appears loudly a second time, in variation. This, in turn, ends with a suave fragment of melody that was in danger of being forgotten: the cadential phase (b') of the first theme, further varied, and played by the long-lost clarinet, which celebrates by performing an extra little cadential flourish.

Brahms builds his coda out of the original horn calls. But now they are harmonized in a solemn, rich way; they have matured immeasurably as a result of all the development of the horn-call rhythm. The overall sense of growth in this movement—the special contribution of sonata form—is as impressive as the sheer beauty of the melodies themselves.

Brahms, Symphony No. 4: Fourth Movement

PART A

PART B

The Industrial Society

The age of romanticism was also the age of materialism. This was the era of robber barons, the twelve-hour factory shift, industrial disease, urban blight, and unregulated child labor, so vividly described by Dickens. The Industrial Revolution, based on the scientific discoveries of the seventeenth century and the technological advances of the eighteenth, was at its height. While artists concentrated on private emotion, others devoted themselves to the industrial and commercial development that made the nineteenth century a prototype of the industrial society we know today.

How did all this fit in with romantic ideals—and, indeed, accomplishments? It is hard to avoid the conclusion that the arts, especially in the later nineteenth century, served many people as a kind of fantasy world, a never-never land of feeling. The Victorians could enjoy this world while denying themselves and others such emotions in their real lives. We also notice that in the later part of the century the relationship between artist and society became significantly more ambivalent. People still respected artists, true, but the public was increasingly shocked by their actions and increasingly reluctant to accord them decent support.

Artists reacted in different ways. Some were content to become "bohemians"—forerunners of the nonconformists, expatriates, dropouts, and hippies of later times. Others were more aggressive. Wagner first pilloried nineteenth-century capitalism in his earlier *Ring* operas (see page 367) and then turned it to his own advantage by enlisting industrialists and bankers as supporters of his schemes. Still other composers could make no real accommodation in matter or in spirit. The resignation we sense in the music of Brahms and the half-nostalgic, half-desperate anxiety in Mahler both suggest that the uneasy quality of life in this era infected many of its finest artists.

As the nineteenth century drew to a close, philosophical and religious writings and the mood of music, art, and poetry increasingly reflected the tensions of society. These tensions, due in large part to unbridled industrialization and the new forces that rose to counter it, finally gave rise to the combination of political factors that exploded in the catastrophe of World War I.

THIRD MOVEMENT

In the third movement of this symphony, the relatively lively rhythm and a number of musical surprises make it safe to infer that Brahms was thinking of a Beethoven scherzo. But once again he wrote the piece in sonata form, with a slowed-down recapitulation providing an even more unusual effect than that of the first movement.

FOURTH MOVEMENT

The last movement, a passacaglia, holds to this archaic form as tenaciously as does Bach's Passacaglia for Organ, which we discussed on pages 201–3. The stern eight-measure theme is followed by no fewer than thirty strict variations, before the free (but not entirely free) coda. Unlike Bach, Brahms does not keep his theme in the bass most of the time. Like Bach, however, he divides his chain of variations into three groups, numbered A 1–11, B 1–4, and C 1–15 on our line score (pages 394–95).

Like baroque or Viennese variations, these variations reflect most clearly the phrase structure of the theme—here, a single eight-measure phrase—and also its harmonies. The melody itself appears in many guises. Sometimes its presence is more obvious (for example, in A 1, A 3, C 3, C 6, and C 9), at other times less so, particularly in group B. This was certainly by design, for Brahms obviously meant B to contrast with A and C, even slowing down the tempo for this reason. But, rather than marking a new tempo, he wrote each measure exactly twice as long as before. For those interested, asterisks have been placed over the telltale melody notes in some of the group B variations.

The group B variations place an unexpected island of tenderness and pathos in the flood of gloomy, vehement sentiment of groups A and C, a flood that abates only occasionally. Perhaps the piece as a whole conveys a sense of heroic striving against the limitations imposed by the relentless theme.

These thirty variations bear impressive testimony to Brahms's technique and to the great fertility of his imagination. (Yet we may also feel they lack something of the breathtaking unpredictability of the variations in Beethoven's Piano Sonata in E: see page 307.) The Brahms variations do not come in a random order. Group C acts as a "recapitulation," for C 1 sounds like the original theme, up to the cataclysmic new counterpoint in measures 4–8. Variations C 9–11 act as another "recapitulation"; they amount to a heightened version of A 1–3. Moreover, many pairs or larger groupings of variations go together with a sense of growth: A 4, 5, and 6; A 8 and 9; B 3 and 4; C 4 and 5; C 9 and 10; and C 12 and 13. And, although we described the coda as "free," above, the passacaglia theme can still be heard storming its way through to the very end of the movement.

The Fourth Symphony reveals Brahms in a very typical mood, a compound of earnestness, energy, and strong rich emotion. In the first movement, the earnestness has an aura of nobility about it, and, in the last movement, the nobility hints at an element of tragedy. There is a sense of iron control, too, which puts something of a crimp in Brahms's romanticism; this strenuous music can also strike us as velvety and world-weary by comparison with the enthusiastic accents of Chopin, Berlioz, or Wagner. Unlike the other romantic composers,

Brahms is rarely unpredictable. His music radiates the security and solidity that are provided only by a mature mastery of musical form.

Gustav Mahler (1860–1911)

The Viennese composer and conductor Gustav Mahler was, like Brahms, a late romantic symphonist, but his tendencies were more modern than those of Brahms. A brilliant but disturbed personality, Mahler suffered from the general malaise that infected late nineteenth-century Europe, from rising anti-Semitism (he was Jewish), and from other troubles; he once consulted his famous Viennese contemporary, Dr. Sigmund Freud. Despite this, Mahler was one of the most effective and sought-after conductors of his time—among the positions he held was director of the New York Philharmonic Orchestra—and he succeeded in carving out time to compose copiously during the summers. Controversial in its own day, Mahler's work is now regarded very highly, as one of the most important products of late romanticism.

MAHLER Symphony No. 4 (1901)   SIDE 16

Most of Mahler's symphonies are unusually long and represent yet another plateau in the grandiose tradition of romantic music. He wrote nine of them (plus one "unfinished symphony," the tenth). Apart from these, the only other music he wrote was a number of orchestral song cycles. Mahler and Richard Strauss were the last of the great line of German romantic *Lied* composers. Song crept into Mahler's symphonies, too; the Fourth Symphony requires a soprano to sing the last movement. This is only one of many features in his work that the more conservative Brahms would never have contemplated for a symphony.

FIRST MOVEMENT

Mahler begins with a few measures of what one commentator has called "farmyard noises" (besides the clucking sounds produced by flutes, clarinets, and sleigh bells, there is another reason for this appellation, as we shall see later). These measures serve as an unusual introduction to a sonata-form movement.

The main theme is a long, sunny melody (see the example on page 400). It is repeated at once, whereupon it starts to accumulate interesting new contrapuntal lines. It will do this more and more as the movement proceeds; indeed, an important general feature of Mahler's style is a renewed emphasis on counterpoint. This fits in closely with his highly original style of orchestration. He repeatedly picks individual instruments out of the orchestra to play momentary solos, which are heard in counterpoint with other lines played by other "solo" instruments. The changing combinations can create a fascinating kaleidoscopic effect, for the various bright strands are made not to blend but rather to stand out in sharp contrast to one another.

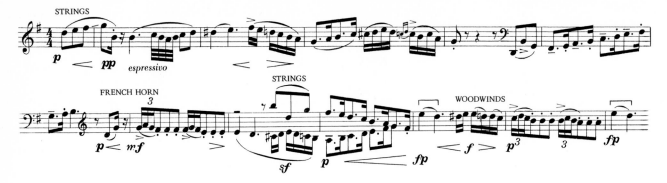

To facilitate this, Mahler often lightened his orchestration so far that it hardly sounds like the typical late romantic orchestra of Wagner or Strauss. At times it even sounds like Haydn. Or more exactly, it sounds like a full-scale romantic orchestra that has somehow been persuaded to behave like a huge chamber music group.

The highly sentimental second theme—a Mahler trademark—is appreciably slower than the first. Earlier we mentioned that the romantic composers tended to treat tempo more flexibly than their predecessors; with Mahler, the tempo changes many times within each movement. A rather rustic-sounding cadence theme appears in yet another tempo, after which the "farmyard noises" and the main theme return in their original keys.

Is this not the beginning of the standard exposition repeat, as sanctioned in most sonata-form movements (page 273)? No, for the main theme acquires a second set of new contrapuntal lines and leads off in a new direction. Instead of the bridge and the warm second theme, we hear a new cadence theme, one that emanates a deeply peaceful atmosphere. The movement could almost end right here.

Mahler does not hesitate to handle sonata form very freely, then. But from here on, he follows the orthodox plan. In an unusually long development section, motives from the exposition are worked over exhaustively. There are many quite obvious modulations, many strong changes in mood, and also this new theme:

Finally, out of the welter of sound the main theme turns up again—but at first it is distorted in key, orchestration, and even in rhythm (the longer notes of measures 1 and 2 in the example at the top of the page are extended almost beyond recognition). Only with measure 3 does the theme regain its original aplomb. Thus Mahler catches something of the humor of a typical Haydn recapitulation; and the feeling of returning to a long-lost original key (measure 3) is even clearer than is usual in Haydn.

The various exposition themes then return in their expected order. But the bridge is now sporting a new contrapuntal line: the theme shown above, which appeared first in the development section. Once again, the "farmyard noises" start off the last section, a long coda concentrating on the main theme and that peaceful second cadence theme. If anyone was wondering about measures 1 and 2 of the main theme, they are accounted for in this coda.

Our discussion has deliberately stressed the many formal features in this movement that recall Viennese practice. Yet we may get the impression that whereas a composer such as Brahms *uses* Viennese features, Mahler is *quoting* them in a self-conscious, even nostalgic spirit. We shall return to this point in a moment.

SECOND MOVEMENT

In this symphony, the dance movement comes second, rather than third, as is more often the case. It is a haunting waltz vision, with two slightly slower trios (A B A' B' A''). An oddly tuned gypsy violin sparkles its way through the A sections, sounding restless and faintly grotesque. In the two trios, moreover, there is a suggestion of sentimental German beer hall tunes that have somehow been spiritualized onto a higher plane. It is hard to pin down, but there is something disturbing about the "tone" of this movement.

THIRD MOVEMENT

The slow movement that follows is clearly the center of gravity of this symphony. In intensity and seriousness, to say nothing of sheer length, it overshadows the other movements in a way that rarely or never happens in earlier symphonies.

Two contrasting thematic ideas are used, A and B. Tranquil and spiritual in mood, A is a long, rambling melody played mainly by the string instruments. After sixteen measures, it starts to sprout new contrapuntal lines, like the main theme of the first movement. Notice the slow rhythmic bass below, which is heard with various modifications all through A and still beats away during the long-drawn-out cadence before the entrance of B. This bass continues to sound throughout the movement, serving as a device to unify all the sections except B' and the coda:

A	B	A'	B'	A''	INTERRUPTION	CODA
		Free variation;		In several		In the mood of A,
		faster		different tempos		but with thematic
		than A		and meters		touches of B

Section B is slower than A and much more disturbed and emotional. In particular, a great deal of anguish is extracted from the violin motive marked with the square bracket:

As the example shows, this motive surges up and up, becoming an insistent, excruciating cry of passion tinged with despair. The very last form of the motive illustrated, covering an octave, is also heard again and again in the wind instruments.

The tendency of romantic composers to unify their compositions thematically has been mentioned more than once (see pages 341 and 365). We ought to recognize this particular motive (with a thrill, Mahler hopes) as a climactic element of the main theme of the first movement: see example 1 on page 400. Consider also the moment when A'', the second free variation of A, has subsided to a huge quietistic plateau of sound, which surely seems like the end of the movement. Suddenly, without the least warning, there is a loud interruption, a vision of almost unsupportable ecstasy. The theme that blares out in the brass is the new theme from the development section of the first movement (example 2 on page 400).

Anyone who picks up these hints and listens closely for this kind of thing will soon discern an elaborate underground network connecting a great many of the themes and motives. Mahler has labored to make the entire symphony into a single thematic unit.

FOURTH MOVEMENT

The last movement is a quiet song for soprano, set to a curious, naive folk poem about the joys of heaven. In a note to the singer, Mahler insists that there must be no suspicion of parody, yet anyone might wonder about a composer of such world-weary sophistication treating poetry with such a strong peasant or childlike quality. Here is verse 1:

Wir geniessen die himmlischen Freuden	The pleasures of heaven make us joyous
D'rum tun wir das Irdische meiden,	And earthly ones we shun that annoy us.
Kein weltlich' Getrümmel hört man nicht im Himmel!	In heaven no rustle is heard of earth's bustle,
Lebt Alles in sanftester Ruh'!	Deep peace reigns all around.
Wir führen ein englisches Leben!	An angel's life we're living, yes,
Sind dennoch ganz lustig daneben!	But we're quite cheerful nonetheless:
Wir tanzen und springen, wir hupfen, wir singen!	We dance in a ring, we skip and we sing,
Sankt Peter im Himmel sieht zu!	Saint Peter in heaven looks down!

The last line is set off solemnly from the others, in a kind of imitation Gregorian chant:

Peasants of old rarely ate meat, except what they managed to poach, so their idea of heaven was startlingly carnivorous. Various saints who are associated with animals have them slaughtered and eaten in verse 2: St. John and his lamb, St. Luke and his ox. (The butcher is none other than Herod, though how he got into heaven is not explained.) And sure enough, the "farmyard noises" of the first movement return cheerfully at this point, introducing verse 2 and the remaining ones. The last line of verse 2 is "The angels bake the bread" (*Die Englein, die bakken das Brot*), set as in the example above.

Verse 3 talks about vegetables, fruit, fish—and more meat. The last line is "St. Martha must be the cook!" (*Sankt Martha die Kochin muss sein!*), set as in the example, again.

Verse 4 tells of the exquisite music in heaven. Our innocent poet pictures St. Cecilia, the patron saint of music, in a dazzling costume of the kind illustrated on pages 268–69:

Cäcilia mit ihren Verwandten	Cecilia and all her relations
Sind treffliche Hofmusikanten!	Are excellent court musicians!

The last words, "It wakes all things to joy" (*Dass Alles für Freuden erwacht*), are set to a melody similar to that used before, but now blended into the general flow. The whole verse is deeply serene and quiet; the ending fades away into nothing. The last sound of this symphony is the lowest note on the double basses alone, marked **ppp** and *morendo* (dying away).

This movement may amuse and delight us, but we must admit that it makes a most unusual ending for a great symphony. Indeed, as we think back, each of Mahler's movements seems decidedly ambivalent in mood. Despite some moments of intensity in the development section, the first movement is curiously neat, even cut-and-dried; its main gestures do not sound romantic at all but hark back to a more innocent, "objective" ideal. This movement is almost a parody—to be sure, an affectionate, sentimental parody—of a Viennese symphony.

The mood of nostalgia is particularly strong in the last movement, with its naive poem and its sophisticated-naive music to go with it. In the second movement, there is a disturbing air of distortion and pain. In the great slow movement, there is an exaggeration of emotion that slips past the bounds of "normalcy." For a piece to start as gently as this one does and then reach those half-hysterical, bittersweet throes of passion—all cannot be well in the composer's world. These are the first signs in music of a turn-of-the-century disillusion, a disillusion with the false confidence of the Victorian world that would soon turn to ashes.

Perhaps they are subtle signs; perhaps only listeners with some experience of romantic music will sense them at first. But compare Mahler with Brahms or Richard Strauss, composers who enter fully into the spirit of romanticism, expressing their individual emotions—whether gloomy (Brahms) or enthusiastic (Strauss)—to their heart's content and satisfaction. Mahler cannot accept romanticism, but neither can he shake it off. He is caught in ambivalence. The undertone of anguish in his music—or *Angst,* to use a German word combining the meanings of anguish, anxiety, dread, and malaise—has probably contributed to its significant revival in the last thirty or forty years and helps to explain its growing popularity.

CHAPTER 13 | The Twentieth Century   I

The Twentieth Century I

No convenient name has yet been given to the musical style of the twentieth century. For years people simply spoke of "modern music" or "contemporary music," until finally it became too embarrassing to be calling music written at the time of Wilbur and Orville Wright "modern," fifty years after the event. Airplanes continued to change after 1903, and so did musical styles. There came a point at which one could no longer ignore successive innovations following the 1900–1925 period.

After World War II, in particular, music and the arts experienced radical new developments—as radical as jet and rocket propulsion in the field of aeronautics. These developments will occupy us in chapter 14. Postwar music, which counts as "contemporary" at least for the period during which this book is written (and will be read), represents a sharper break with tradition than has been seen in a very long while. From the standpoint of the 1980s, the music of the early twentieth century can be seen as a final extension of romanticism. It is an extreme, even wild, offshoot of romanticism, perhaps, but an offshoot nonetheless.

As one indication of this, major composers around 1900 such as Gustav Mahler (see page 399) and Claude Debussy remained firmly bound to the past in one way or another, even while showing tendencies that mark the new style. Even the most "advanced" figures in early twentieth-century music preserved some ties with romanticism, though in their most mature music these ties were stretched pretty far. And this is not something that can be said of the important figures who led music in new paths after 1950, as will become apparent.

Early Twentieth-Century Style

Discussing romanticism on pages 325–26, we took account of the emphasis on individuality associated with this movement. "Individual" styles loom large, and the "period" style is not easy to pin down in terms of particular harmonic, melodic, textural, and rhythmic features. Composers responded to a common set of romantic attitudes, but each responded very much in a personal way.

This is even more true of music in the early twentieth century. Composers in this period showed an increasing tendency to go in different directions and to find themselves in different camps, "schools," or "isms." This tendency appears in the other arts as well, and some of the musicologists' names for these "isms" are borrowed from literature or painting. Impressionism, expressionism, serialism, and neoclassicism will all be discussed in the pages to come.

Antiromanticism, though it is not a label in standard use, accurately describes a primary impetus of many early twentieth-century composers. Especially in Paris, a reaction developed against the rich and, as it seemed, exaggerated emotionalism of such composers as Wagner, Tchaikovsky, Richard Strauss, and Mahler. Conservatism, too, became a striking feature of modern composition (as well as of listening habits). We have discussed a conservative figure of the late romantic era, Johannes Brahms (see page 390); for every one composer like Brahms in the nineteenth century, a dozen composers in the twentieth have turned decidedly toward the past. Usually they have been oriented to the late romantic period, though in some cases they have gone back to even earlier music.

Neoclassicism is a general term for the latter tendency (see page 445). Composers wrote fugues, the pre-eminent musical form of the baroque period, and sometimes searched for inspiration as far back as medieval music. Sonata form enjoyed a new lease on life. Compositions from the past were reorchestrated in a modern way, or even "recomposed" in a more modern style.

Neoclassicism and the rest of these labels should all be used with discretion, however. We should not imagine that they will answer all our questions about twentieth-century music. They can raise new questions of their own. Composers often complain that once they have been pigeonholed into some school, people will not listen to their music with open minds and accept it on its own terms, but instead think about how "typical" it is of the school. Still, these school names represent an honest (if not always adequate) attempt to puzzle out a complex musical situation. Music in the early twentieth century was enormously rich and diverse—or fragmented and confusing, depending on how you look at it. Popular music of various kinds, "advanced" music, conservative music, different schools: all these competed for the listener's attention.

"DISTORTION" IN TWENTIETH-CENTURY MUSIC

We might wonder whether there is anything that holds all this diversity together. Can we really speak of a coherent "early twentieth-century style" in music?

A cohesive style did not exist as it had in the baroque and Viennese periods, or even in the romantic period. Like it or not, this negative fact is part of the whole point: life in general has become incredibly more diverse and fragmented in our century, with results that we all perceive. Nevertheless, some generalizations can be offered, for certainly some common factors exist. Turn on the radio, and there is usually no question about whether or not we are listening to a twentieth-century piece, whatever "ism" it may adhere to.

Involved is what might be described as a massive stretching and straining at musical elements. They have not yet snapped, but it is astonishing how far they seem to give. Melody, for example, becomes so "sprung" that the tuneful quality sometimes is lost entirely. Changes in another important area, harmony, will be discussed on pages 412–15. Rhythm, tone color, musical form, even the physical capabilities of instruments—in all these areas, composers seemed bent on exploration, liberation, and the exploitation of extremes.

In fact, we could speak of a deliberate policy of distortion applied to all or nearly all the traditional elements of music. A number of works can be cited as examples, all written within a few years of one another (around the time of World War I) by composers of widely differing orientations and backgrounds. One that is close to home is *General William Booth enters into heaven*, a song by the American composer Charles Ives. In the course of this song, the gospel hymn *Cleansing fountain* is treated to a series of "unnatural" harmonies that make a none-too-gentle comment on the religious consolations offered by General Booth's Salvation Army. In this, Ives seems to have agreed with the bitter tone of his poet, Vachel Lindsay.

Or take *La Valse* (The Waltz), a symphonic poem of sorts by the French composer Maurice Ravel. Ravel's hatred for Germany, shared by most French people of the time, expressed itself as hatred of German and Austrian music. Although he never wrote out a program for *La Valse*, the piece suggests a grand society ball that starts out quietly, grows more and more frantic, and finally explodes into violence. Surely this was a metaphor for Europe in the decades prior to World War I. As the momentum increases, a popular waltz by Johann Strauss, *A Thousand and One Nights*, is torn apart, orchestrated in brutal ways, and made to seem a perfect symbol of everything ugly in German culture (from a patriotic Frenchman's point of view, that is). The final cadence comes on a screaming discord.

Yet another example is provided by one of the most famous of all twentieth-century compositions, the song cycle *Pierrot Lunaire* for soprano and five instrumentalists by the most "advanced" composer of the time, Arnold Schoenberg (see page 423). The songs were written to strange poems by a minor Belgian poet, Albert Girard; for a representative sample, look at song No. 19 on page 426. To match this, Schoenberg supplied equally strange music, which utterly lacks the tunes that one might fairly expect to find in a set of songs. The instruments often play sudden short spurts and surges, all seemingly dissociated. The voice does not exactly sing or exactly speak, but engages

Sprechstimme | in an in-between style invented by Schoenberg. This Sprechstimme (speech-song) ranges from a throaty whisper to a near-hysterical shriek. Not only were the elements of music distorted—or so it appeared to listeners of the time—but also the human voice, and what was worse, the female human voice.

Early in the century many people were outraged by painters, poets, and musicians who engaged in distortion of this emphatic kind. Over fifty years later, the same reactions are still sometimes met with. Why doesn't the painter just paint a face instead of double noses and inside-out ears? Why doesn't the composer just write tunes instead of strange combinations of seemingly arbitrary sounds?

Music and Painting: A Conjunction

For all the differences between the arts of music and painting, there are times when strikingly similar techniques can be observed in both. In postimpressionist and expressionist artworks (see pages 425 and 432), successive liberties were taken with visual reality. Then early in the twentieth century, some painters took the great step and abandoned the representation of visual reality altogether. These painters went "beyond distortion" in seeking to make an artistic language in abstract visual terms.

Their kind of abstraction is not the art language of today, to be sure, any more than Schoenberg and Stravinsky determine today's language in music. But the abstract art of the early twentieth century produced an impressive body of work that made today's art possible. Much the same thing can be said about early twentieth-century music.

Marcel Duchamp (page 419), Pablo Picasso, and the other cubists in Paris took one route to abstraction. The Germans took another. Artists Paul Klee and Wassily Kandinsky (a Swiss and a Russian who both worked in Germany) were associated with the composer Arnold Schoenberg in a group called "The Blue Rider" (after the title of a little magazine). They took their steps toward abstraction at the same time that Webern and Schoenberg were moving toward music without tonality and without themes, before World War I. In spirit, Klee reminds us of Webern, perhaps, and Kandinsky of Schoenberg or Berg.

Both Kandinsky and Klee were very closely involved with music. In these years Kandinsky provided many of his paintings with musical titles such as *Improvisation* and *Fugue*. Ours is entitled *Great Fugue*, the name of a celebrated string quartet piece by Beethoven. Klee actually hesitated between a career in music and one in art (Schoenberg painted, too, and even exhibited his pictures). Klee's half-whimsical, half-frantic *Drawing with Fermata* indicates that he was well acquainted with the musicians' slang term for a fermata, "bird's eye." (A fermata is a hold of indefinite length on a note, chord, or rest.)

Behind these questions lies an unspoken confusion between art and escapism. This, we have suggested (see page 397), was especially common in the late romantic era, and it is easy to understand the indignation of early twentieth-century listeners at the distortions they were confronted with. People do not like to have their established values twisted and then torn to shreds before their very eyes—or ears. But composers of the early twentieth century were followers of the romantics in at least this respect: they regarded music not as an escape from life's realities but as an essential comment upon them. And life in this century has not been so pretty—a circumstance for which artists and composers, after all, are not the ones responsible.

Artists tend to discern and express such things before other people do, however. Consequently they tend to get blamed, like the unfortunate messengers in Greek drama who are sacrificed for bringing bad news that they had no hand in creating.

If life is all that unpleasant, then, who needs art to reflect it with its own brand of unpleasantness? A reasonable question, to which two reasonable answers can be given. The first involves the psychological fact that art seems to fulfill deep and essential needs in the human consciousness. Human beings need to create art and need to consume it, almost as much as they need to work and play and make love. Crusaders against distortion in art always want artists to produce paintings, poems, music of a different kind. Very, very rarely do they advocate a total moratorium on art.

The other answer involves an aesthetic fact, or at any rate, an observation about art that has held up throughout history. Art has a miraculous way of renewing itself. After every great artistic revolution, unexpected new styles emerge that embody unexpected new kinds of beauty. What is interesting about twentieth-century music is what happened next, the evolution of a new musical language "beyond distortion."

Composers began to make something else out of the fascinating bent lines and sprung rhythms that their experiments in distortion had turned up. They searched for a new language to replace the language of the past. The various schools or "isms" of the early twentieth century are best regarded as individual gropings in this direction.

HARMONY: CONSONANCE AND DISSONANCE

Exploration of the extremes, distortion, the evolution of a new language beyond distortion: in the early twentieth century these three stages can be observed in almost all the elements of music.

They are most obvious with melody, perhaps. The eighteenth-century Viennese composers had brought tunes to the fore in their music, and the romantics had used tunes as the most emphatic means of conveying emotion. Advanced composers now wrote tunes that were, at best, distorted. Then they abandoned tunes altogether. This happened in *Pierrot lunaire* (1912); even in popular music, it finally happened in the modern jazz of the 1950s.

The same three stages are also apparent in early twentieth-century harmony. Harmony grew more and more dissonant, tense, and complex. At first, growing dissonance was the outcome of the exploration of new sounds. Then it was employed to distort the established order. Then it became the foundation of an entirely new language.

The concepts of dissonance and consonance were discussed on page 39. These concepts rest on the psychological fact that certain chords (consonant chords) sound stable and at rest, whereas others (dissonant chords) sound tense and need to "resolve" to consonant ones. Some dissonant chords are more tense than others, so that it becomes necessary to distinguish between "high-level" and "low-level" dissonances. When there is enough high-level dissonance around, low-level dissonance can sound relatively stable, i.e., relatively consonant.

If we haven't spoken much about these two qualities up to now, that is because for the listener they have been relatively unobtrusive. Dissonance might almost be described as the harmonic fuel necessary to keep music running. One thing that gives baroque music its characteristic springy quality is the alternation between low-level dissonance and consonance. One thing that gives romantic music its characteristic surging quality is the alternation (a different kind of alternation) between higher-level dissonance and consonance.

In the early twentieth century, harmonic exploration took two related steps. Composers first investigated higher and higher levels of dissonance. A traditional consonant chord has three different notes, and a traditional dissonant one has four or five. But here is an example of a dissonant chord (X) combining *seven* of the twelve possible notes from the chromatic scale:

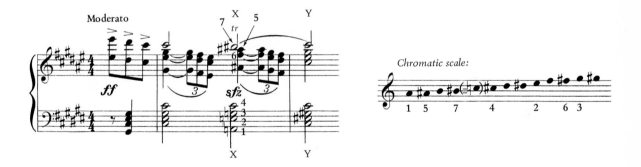

This dissonance was used to produce distortion, distortion for the sake of ugliness. It comes at the revolting climax of Richard Strauss's opera *Salome* (1907), as Salome kisses the mouth of John the Baptist's chopped-off head on the plate. But in the best orthodox manner, the dissonance resolves to a consonance (chord Y).

Composers took the second step when they started to tinker with the consonant harmonies. They still wanted the contrast between stable and tense sounds and then the effect of resolution. But, since the level of dissonance was now so high, they considered that the stable sounds could be made more complex and tense also. High-level dissonance resolved to low-level dissonance, rather than to consonance. Paradoxically, once a clear norm of consonance was lost, so was any clear sense of distortion.

Here is a (highly schematic) graph to help explain these developments:

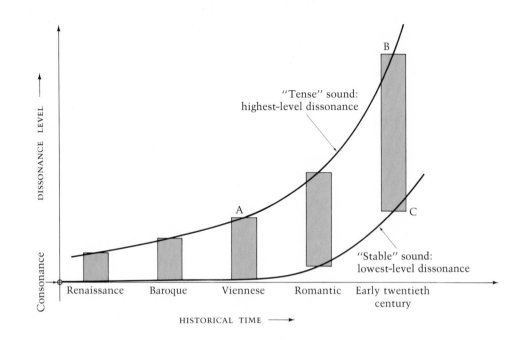

The range between stable sound and tense sound in early twentieth-century music (represented by the block *CB*) was at least as great as that in earlier periods. However, the level of the stable chords (represented by point *C*) might run as high as the highest-level dissonance used by composers in the Viennese period (point *A*). So no wonder this new music grated on the sensibilities of listeners who were still attuned to the music of Haydn and Beethoven.

TONALITY AND ATONALITY

Closely related to developments in harmony were developments in tonality. Tonality is the feeling of centrality, or focus around a single note, that we get from simple tunes and from much other music. We have also discussed the development of functional harmony in the baroque period, which made tonality clearer and more systematic than ever before (see page 156). As modern harmony grew more dissonant, tonality often grew more indistinct. Finally some music reached a point at which no clear center could be detected at all, a condition known as <u>atonality</u>.

atonality

Just as the term *dissonance* is ambiguous, or at any rate allows for different degrees (high-level and low-level), so tonality and atonality are not open-and-shut concepts. Some music sounds very firmly rooted in one place; other music gives only a tantalizing impression of focus around a general area. Many pieces that listeners early in this century called atonal—often as a term of abuse—can be heard on close listening to have a subtle sense of tonality after all. Really thoroughgoing atonality waited for electronic and chance music of the late 1950s.

We should not forget that tonality had already been weakened by earlier composers, at least in certain sections of their music. To take one familiar example, the Viennese composers weakened tonality every time they started up those continuous modulations in the development sections of sonata form (see page 257). The result was to strengthen the feeling of solidity at the return of the original key in the recapitulation. Could not the shifting tonality of a development section be used throughout the piece, without the effect of "resolution" achieved by the recapitulation?

Richard Wagner had done exactly this. The famous Prelude to *Tristan und Isolde* (see page 366) continuously shifts in tonality; this is just the feature that gives the piece its striking mood of sultry, never-to-be-satisfied yearning. The technique by which Wagner achieved this is called chromaticism, the very liberal use of all twelve notes of the chromatic scale (see page 16). Tonality depends on one note standing out from the rest in the ordinary (diatonic) scale: for example, C in the C major scale C D E F G A B. When all twelve chromatic notes appear so frequently, the centrality of any single note is automatically weakened.

chromaticism

Wagner's chromaticism was a significant forecast of the coming trend toward atonality. To be sure, *Tristan und Isolde* achieves resolution at the end—after several hours—in the closing notes (the cadence) of the famous "Liebestod" (see page 367). In advanced pieces, twentieth-century composers now weakened even a final, cadential feeling of tonal centrality.

Tune, harmony, tonality: all are closely related. The emancipation—or, as some would say, the cutting adrift—of melody, harmony, and tonality all went together. This joint emancipation counts as the central characteristic of early twentieth-century style.

It created difficulties for listeners and also for composers. The imminent danger of unregulated chaos spurred many of the latter into ingenious and imaginative new systems of aural logic; one of these, serialism, will be discussed later. But it also resulted in an enormous expansion of horizons for composers of all persuasions—not only members of the avant-garde but also relatively conservative composers, and popular musicians, too. It was only this emancipation that made possible the new ranges of expressiveness explored so brilliantly by Stravinsky, Webern, and Schoenberg in the first category; Bartók, Copland, and many others in the second; and George Gershwin, Duke Ellington, and Kurt Weill in the third.

The excitement these composers felt at the intoxicating wealth of new resources that had opened up for them almost seems to vibrate in their music. Some of the vibrations can still be caught by listeners today.

Impressionism: Claude Debussy (1862–1918)

Claude Debussy occupies the border area between the romantic and early twentieth-century styles. From the vantage point of the 1980s, his romantic allegiances are evident enough: in his investigation of marvelous new tone colors for orchestra and also for piano, in his rich harmonies, and in the unquestionably emotional quality of his music. Around 1900, the novelties of his style stood out more clearly. For instance, the tone colors, magical as they are, avoid the heavy sonorities that were usual at the time; instead they concentrate on blurring delicate shades of sound. His harmonies, rich as they are, are also strangely vague, seeming to float easily and naturally without ever finding a true focus or cadence place. And, while the total effect is certainly sensuous, it is also remarkably intimate and refined. Debussy shrank from the emphatic, broad emotion deployed by the other late romantic composers.

It might be said, in fact, that Debussy's passion was avoidance of the obvious, whether in emotional effect or in the technical features that help create that effect, such as tone color and harmony. This characteristic also extends to melody. Debussy's themes and motives (he hardly ever uses actual tunes) are nearly always fragmentary and tentative. There will be just a whiff of melody, a tantalizing suggestion of a tune, and then it will fade away into the shifting tone colors and sinuous harmonic flow. A little later, many composers abandoned tune, in the conventional sense, entirely. In light of this development, Debussy counts as a transitional figure of great significance.

There does seem to be something characteristically French about Debussy's music, with its almost exaggerated emphasis on subtlety and refined understatement. Debussy was proud to think so; he hated the German composers and their blatant overemotionality (as he might have put it—Debussy was a sharp-tongued music critic as well as a composer). His music may even make us think of elegant French cuisine, by comparison with the hearty sauerbraten being served up across the Rhine by Richard Strauss and Gustav Mahler.

impressionism

A more conventional (and less fanciful) comparison links Debussy with impressionism, the painting style evolved by French artists a few years earlier. Besides a similarity in feeling, there are also analogies in technique (see page 418). Debussy's musical style is often described as impressionistic.

DEBUSSY **Three Nocturnes** (*Clouds, Festivals, Sirens*) (1893–1899)   SIDE 17

Debussy's Three Nocturnes might be categorized as small symphonic poems (see page 350), though they have no literary programs. They are illustrative pieces—a nocturne is a piece that evokes a nighttime scene—and in this area it is probably safe to say that Debussy has never been matched, before or since. The first nocturne, *Clouds,* is a pure nature picture. The second, *Festivals,* evokes mysterious nighttime fairs or parades. The title of the third nocturne, *Sirens,* refers to the legendary seamaidens who tempt lonely sailors and pull them into the deep.

CLOUDS

The beginning of *Clouds* is shown below in a simplified score on the facing page. We may well find the theme of measure 1 a wonderfully atmospheric representation of great cumulus clouds, moving slowly, almost imperceptibly yet steadily, without any possibility of check or control. But at the same time we would also have to admit that as a theme, the chords of measure 1 circle around in a most inconclusive fashion. They make no strong declarations, and they lead nowhere definite. This is also true of the figure starting in measure 5 for the English horn. Yet even this muted gesture, with its vague rhythm and its fading conclusion, seems sufficient to exhaust the composition and bring it to a near halt in measures 7–10.

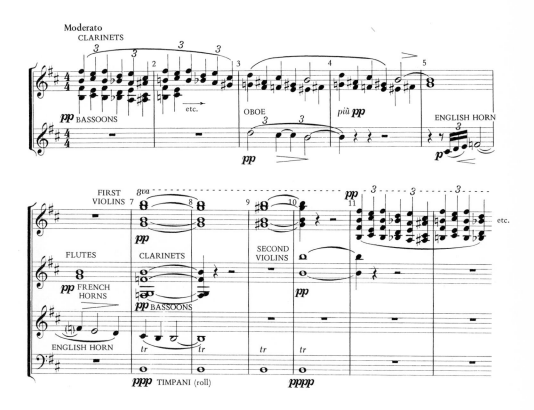

How different these themes are from the bold ranging theme beginning Richard Strauss's *Don Juan* (see page 383) or from the brief but taut and expectant theme beginning Wagner's *Tristan und Isolde* (see page 366). It is exactly this wispiness that gives Debussy's music its novelty and its particular expressive effect.

In terms of orchestration, too, Debussy's "sound" differs sharply from that of Gustav Mahler, another great innovator in orchestration of the same period (see page 399). Mahler treated the orchestra more and more contrapuntally. Each instrument tends to stand out against the others like a little romantic hero striving for his own say in the world. Debussy has some contrapuntal effects, but not many—a composer cannot have counterpoint without melodic lines, and this composer was much less interested in melody than in color and harmony. Thus, in contrast to Mahler's orchestra, Debussy's is a single, delicately pulsing entity to which the individual instruments contribute momentary gleams of color. An analogy can be drawn to the paint blobs of an impressionist picture, which fade into the overall lush effect.

Impressionism and Cubism

To exemplify the sheer sensuousness of impressionist painting and music, there is probably nothing better than an impressionist nude. The Renoir below could almost be an illustration for one of Debussy's seductive water sirens (see page 421). Impressionist painters did not try to depict shapes and objects so much as the *impression* shapes and objects give when they are bathed in actual light. To this end they evolved a painting technique involving iridescent patches of color. Notice how the technique softens the lines around the girl's body and renders the flesh as soft as the water and the clump of rushes in the background. The rushes and the water are painted in a particularly exaggerated impressionist way, with blue, green, red, and yellow patches of color.

An amusing contrast is Marcel Duchamp's *Nude Descending a Staircase* No. 2, one of the most famous (or notorious) of early twentieth-century paintings because of the scandal it caused at the New York Armory Exhibition of 1913. Seventy years later, we are probably not so appalled at the thorough destruction of the female form in this picture. Obviously, the painter was interested not in accurate representation but in abstract "composition," that is, in the arrangement of planes and shapes on the surface. It is pointless to criticize pictures of this kind for distortion; they have reached a stage "beyond distortion." Duchamp was investigating a new language in painting—cubism—that was also beginning to interest such artists as Juan Gris, Georges Braque, and Pablo Picasso.

NU DESCENDANT UN ESCALIER

The Louise and Walter Arensberg Collection, Philadelphia Museum of Art

Listen to the first few measures of *Clouds* and note especially the composite tone color at measure 7. As the English horn figure starts to fade, it is covered by a unique and magical sound blended together out of a low drum roll, a middle chord on the clarinets and bassoons, and an exquisitely high chord on the first violins. (They are actually divided into six groups in order to play this chord, though only four show in the example.) The sound grows even more strained as the G in the violins is replaced by G♯ (measure 9). Then both G and G♯ seem to dissolve, leaving a single octave B hanging in the second violins, as the drum roll fades to **pppp** (measure 10). When the first theme is resumed by the high violins (measure 11), it sounds somehow thinner and also more sensual, like a glint of moonlight at the corner of the clouds.

As for Debussy's celebrated harmony, a good example appears just two measures after the above example concludes:

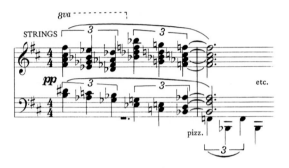

Those who can pick it out on the piano will see that the remarkably gentle, murmuring effect is caused by a long succession of chords of the same form (called major ninth chords), which slip by without causing a clear sense of tonality. This device was invented by Debussy and has been much imitated since, as in this once-famous song of the 1930s, Duke Ellington's *Sophisticated lady:*

Clouds might be said to fall into an A B A′ form. B is a new theme played by flutes and harp, and there is a suggestion of A returning at the end. But it is only the faintest suggestion. Debussy shrinks from clear formal outlines, and the musical form here seems much more fluid than that of A B A structures observed in other music. Mainly what we hear at the end, as the suggestion of A, is the English horn figure and the timpani roll—suggesting distant thunder clouds, perhaps. Did Debussy have the "Scene in the Fields" from Berlioz's *Fantastic Symphony* in mind when he wrote this conclusion? It might prove interesting to compare the two passages (see page 348).

FESTIVALS

The second of the Nocturnes, *Festivals,* is a more active piece, and in some ways a more conventional one. It has a clearer structure (A B C A') and a good healthy climax in the C section. This seems to represent a spectral parade heard from afar and then coming nearer and nearer until it is blaring in our ears. (But unlike the oxcart in Moussorgsky's "Bydlo"—see page 387—it does not go off down the road again.) The far-off parade is orchestrated unforgettably. Three muted trumpets play the march tune, while two harps join the timpani and pizzicato strings—all marked **ppp**—in beating out the meter.

The march tune itself is fascinating. Its rhythms are straightforward enough, but the harmonies cause a striking distortion of what would be "normal" march music. We spoke above of the distortion employed by early twentieth-century composers for effects of harshness or parody. Here distortion is being used for quite another effect—a fantastic and (we would have to say) highly romantic tone.

These marchers in the night are wearing mysterious costumes and carrying strange flares, it seems. Or else we are viewing them through some kind of tinted, scented fog. Probably everyone would agree that Debussy's distorted march music here is more beautiful, not less, than a "normal" Sousa march.

Near the end of *Festivals,* after the rushing, glittering first theme (A) has returned, the music slows down. A melancholy figure—brief, as usual—hovers in the oboe and other wind instruments, while the cellos and double basses rumble away quietly in the background. The mood recalls the ending of *Clouds,* though the musical material is not the same.

SIRENS

The third Nocturne, *Sirens,* returns to the wispy technique of *Clouds,* employed now for a much more sensual effect. These shadowy, melting, endlessly caressing sirens are Debussy's answer to the overheated blandishments pictured in so much late romantic music. Remember the ladies in Richard Strauss's *Don Juan,* for example (see page 384). (For a daytime siren by the impressionist painter Auguste Renoir, see page 418.)

The orchestra used to create the remarkable tone colors in the Nocturnes actually counts as a modest one, at least according to the standards of Strauss and Mahler. But in *Sirens* Debussy made one striking addition: female voices. The singers are provided with no words, only vowels—and not even these on occasions when they are directed to hum. Singing without words is called

vocalise

<u>vocalise</u> (rhymes with "ease"). It was an innovation that composers did not pick up again until the 1950s, though in a rather different spirit, as we shall see in the next chapter.

Again there is a suggestion of A B A' form, with two themes for the sirens in Debussy's typical aimless, winding style:

We may come to feel that, in among the watery shadows and half-lights of Debussy's music, a strange family resemblance links these two themes to the clarinet and English horn themes, respectively, of *Clouds.*

Expressionism

Debussy's reaction against the overemotionalism of late romantic music was shared by many other French composers and by foreigners in Paris such as Igor Stravinsky. Most of these composers also turned their backs on the delicate sensuousness of Debussy's style and evolved styles of their own that were hard or brittle, tough or dry, and in any case decidedly unromantic. In France, the most outspoken antiromantic composers of this time moved in the direction of simplicity and even triviality.

In Germany and Austria, however, composers pressed forward with music that was increasingly emotional and increasingly complex. More and more they found themselves exploiting extreme emotional states, ranging to hysteria, nightmare, even perversion and insanity. Perhaps this was their response to the state of the world, which they saw as more and more desperate, or perhaps this seemed the only way to go musically, once all the more usual emotional states had been exhausted. This movement, which had important precedents and parallels in literature and painting, is called expressionism.

expressionism

In the first decade of the twentieth century the works of Sigmund Freud began to emerge, with their revolutionary new analysis of the significance of dreams, the power of unconscious emotional drives, and the central role of sexuality. Freud's psychology was to become one of the main currents of modern thought, but at first it made its effect mainly in Germany and Austria. Directly or indirectly, German expressionist literature, art, and music came under the influence of Freud's ideas.

Arnold Schoenberg (1874–1951)

Arnold Schoenberg is the great paradoxical figure of twentieth-century music: to some, the great stumbling block. Though his works, with one or two exceptions, have never gained popular acceptance, he is regarded by musicians as unquestionably the most significant force and the most impressive personality in the music of our era. This position he earned first by the major innovations of his expressionist period, prior to World War I, and then by his development of the principle of twelve-tone music, or serialism, in the 1920s. This important principle is treated on pages 436–39.

Schoenberg was born in Vienna, the city of Johannes Brahms and Gustav Mahler (also of Sigmund Freud). He seems early to have acquired the somewhat messianic belief that he was destined to carry the great tradition of Bach, Beethoven, Brahms, and Wagner to its "logical" modern development. Listeners felt otherwise, and Schoenberg's revolutionary compositions of the 1900s were received with more hostility than any in the entire history of music. A man of unusual versatility, Schoenberg wrote the literary texts for some of his compositions, painted pictures in an expressionist style, and produced books of major importance on music theory.

Of all the great composers, Schoenberg was the first great teacher since Bach. Two of his students, as we shall see, were among the main composers of the early twentieth century; with Schoenberg, Alban Berg and Anton Webern are sometimes referred to as the "Second Viennese School." (The first consisted of Haydn, Mozart, Beethoven, and Schubert.) As a Jew, Schoenberg was forced to leave Germany, where he was then teaching, when the Nazis took over in 1933, and he spent his last years in Los Angeles, as a professor at the University of California (UCLA).

SCHOENBERG *Pierrot Lunaire* (1912)   SIDE S–2

The title of this celebrated and highly influential song cycle already presents a problem. Pierrot is the eternal figure of the sad clown—but why is he called "lunar"? In some of the strange poems that constitute this cycle, Pierrot is obsessed with the moon; in others, he "moons" in an inconsequential, melancholy way; in still others, he indeed seems lunatic. The poems are dotted with Freudian imagery. We hear vaguely about his amorous frustrations, his neurotic aspirations, his pranks and adventures. Some of the poems do not refer to him at all.

We have already mentioned Schoenberg's novel invention of *Sprechstimme* (speech-song) for the voice part of this song cycle (see page 409). Hardly less novel was his idea for the accompaniment. He has five instrumentalists play on eight instruments: piano, cello, violin sometimes switching to viola, clarinet switching to bass clarinet, and flute switching to piccolo (see page 63). They do not all play in all the songs. As a result, nearly every song has its unique accompaniment, ranging from a single flute in song No. 7 to all eight instruments in No. 21 (the players have to switch in the course of that single number). Schoenberg's dazzling variety of instrumental effects compensates for the inherent monotony of the *Sprechstimme.*

As is often the case in song cycles, there are transitions and thematic interrelations between many of the songs. The whole set is divided into three groups. The last group begins with No. 15, entitled *Homesickness*, a melancholy mood-picture scored for clarinet, violin, and piano along with the speaker-singer. The remaining instruments enter near the end in order to make a transition to the next two songs, satirical numbers introducing the figure of the bald Cassander, who seems to play the straight man in Pierrot's theatrical company. The piercing high notes of the piccolo depict Cassander's screams.

No. 18, *The Moonfleck,* continues the speedy tone of the last two songs and also the piccolo scoring. It begins, however, with a slower piano solo introduction, or transition from the previous number. Dense, highly dissonant, atonal, and alarmingly intense, this short passage breathes the spirit of the new music. It represents everything that Schoenberg was attacked for throughout his uncompromising career.

Impressionism and Postimpressionism

This is another impressionist picture: *Field of Poppies* by Claude Monet, one of the founders of impressionist painting.

Contrast this with a similar scene—a landscape with figures—by Vincent Van Gogh, the great "postimpressionist" painter, whose brooding, strong, disturbed, and increasingly unnaturalistic vision was an important precursor of early twentieth-century expressionism. The human beings in Monet fit in with nature as easily as do the poppies. In Van Gogh they are overwhelmed by nature. Van Gogh painted many versions of this scene, some of them darker and more boldly distorted than this one. Sometimes

two, three, or a dozen moons blaze in an inky sky pierced by menacing cypress trees.

We can perhaps take Van Gogh's *Evening Walk* as an illustration of act III, scene ii, of Alban Berg's opera *Wozzeck*—the moonlit murder scene (see page 430). The illustrative music of that scene oddly recalls the impressionistic music of Debussy. In examining these two landscapes, too, we can detect similarities of technique. Both Monet and Van Gogh used disconnected daubs of color with which to make their very different effects; both Debussy and Berg used disconnected fragments of melody and tone color.

The song itself is one of the shortest (nineteen measures) and fastest of the cycle, and one of the most fascinating. The piano, the string group, and the woodwind group have distinct motivic material each, treated contrapuntally. Simultaneous fugues and canons are at work, but what the listener perceives is a fantastic lacework of sound, as though there are a thousand flickering moon-flecks that Pierrot is trying frantically to brush off his tuxedo. Like much later music of the twentieth century, *The Moonfleck* uses extremely complex technical means to achieve a unique sonorous effect.

Einen weissen Fleck des hellen Mondes	With a white speck of the bright moon
Auf dem Rücken seines schwartzen Rockes,	On the shoulder of his black frock coat,
So spaziert Pierrot im lauen Abend,	Pierrot saunters off this languid evening
Aufzusuchen Glück und Abenteuer. . . .	To seek his fortune and look for adventure . . .

No. 19, *Serenade,* is set to a bizarre poem, but Schoenberg seems to take it quite seriously.

Mit groteskem Riesenbogen	With a giant bow grotesquely
Kratzt Pierrot auf seiner Bratsche,	Scrapes Pierrot on his viola—
Wie der Storch auf einem Beine,	Like a stork on one leg,
Knipft er trüb ein Pizzicato.	Sadly plucks a pizzicato.
Plötzlich naht Cassander—wütend	Suddenly here comes Cassander, fuming
Ob des nächtgen Virtuosen—	At this nighttime virtuoso,
Mit groteskem Riesenbogen	With a giant bow grotesquely
Kratzt Pierrot auf seiner Bratsche.	Scrapes Pierrot on his viola.
Von sich wirft er jetzt die Bratsche:	Now he puts aside the viola:
Mit der delicaten Linken	With his delicate left hand
Fasst den Kahlkopf er am Kragen—	Grasps the baldpate by the collar,
Träumend spielt er auf der Glatze	Dreamily plays upon his bald spot
Mit groteskem Riesenbogen.	With a giant bow grotesquely.

Pierrot's "scraping" is represented not by the viola, for some reason, but by the cello (and the cello does not play *pizzicato* when Pierrot does, in line 4). The long, expressionistic cello solo in this song is an example of the "sprung," distorted melodic style that Schoenberg developed. It begins with these widely spaced intervals:

This is profoundly unsingable and not easily apprehended as a melody. Nonetheless, the yearning, exaggeratedly romantic quality of the cello here is unforgettable.

At the end of this song the other instruments come in to prepare for No. 20, *Journey Home,* which has a haunting, restlessly moving quality. It suggests the rocking of Pierrot's boat:

Der Mondstrahl ist das Ruder,	The moonbeam serves as rudder,
Seerose dient also Boot:	Water lily as the boat
Drauf fährt Pierrot gen Süden . . .	On which Pierrot journeys south . . .

The last measure of this song refers ahead clearly to the main motive of the next one, which is the final song of the cycle.

No. 21, *O ancient scent,* is one of the simpler songs, and one of the simpler poems:

O alter Duft aus Märchenzeit,	O ancient scent from the days of fairy lore,
Berauschest wieder meine Sinne!	Intoxicate again my senses!
Ein närrisch Heer von Schelmerein	A foolish swarm of idle thoughts
Durchschwirrt die leichte Luft.	Pervades the gentle air.
* Ein glückhaft Wünschen macht mir froh*	A happy whim makes me aspire
Nach Freuden, die ich lang verachtet:	To joys that I have long neglected:
O alter Duft aus Märchenzeit,	O ancient scent from the days of fairy lore,
Berauschest wieder meine Sinne!	Intoxicate again my senses!
* All meinen Unmut gab ich preis;*	All my sorrow is dispelled;
Aus meinem sonnumrahmten Fenster	From my sun-encircled window
Beschau ich frei die liebe Welt	I gaze out freely on the lovely world
Und träum hinaus in selge Weiten . . .	And dream far beyond the fair horizon . . .
O alter Duft . . . aus Märchenzeit!	O ancient scent . . . from the days of fairy lore!

Romantic nostalgia, which we first encountered in Schubert, had been made into a specialty by Mahler; Schoenberg seems to strain that sentiment into something unbelievably—almost painfully—exquisite. The opening, for piano and *Sprechstimme* alone, is dissonant but bittersweet:

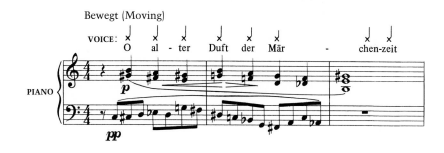

On page 413, we illustrated a passage from Richard Strauss using seven of the twelve notes of the chromatic scale simultaneously. Not simultaneously, but successively, all twelve are used by Schoenberg by the time he gets to beat 3 of measure 2 in the above passage: a good example of the increasing chromaticism of his style. (To be sure, this kind of thing was not entirely new, as can be seen from the second Mozart example on page 280. There, eleven of the twelve chromatic notes are used in the first five measures. Significantly, this example comes from a development section, where the composers of the First Viennese School always tended to shake up tonality.)

O ancient scent is the only one of the *Pierrot Lunaire* songs in which the same music comes back at the verbal refrains within the poem. (These refrains come at lines 7–8 and 13 in each poem.) At the central two-line refrain, the piano repeats its opening music an octave higher. At the final one-line refrain, the motive is played in a slight variation by the two string instruments, very beautifully:

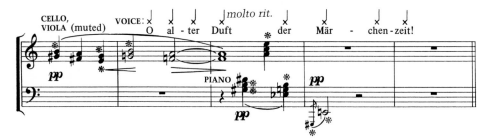

Despite the dissonant style, this passage has a clear sense of tonic centrality, as befits the concluding (cadential) page of a large composition. It is not a conventional cadence, of course, but it emphasizes the three notes of the tonic chord of E major, E–G♯–B, in a very deliberate way. They are marked with asterisks on the example.

We mentioned above that atonality is a relative concept. By Mozart's standards, this ending would seem thoroughly subversive of the kind of simple, unclouded functional tonality that existed in the eighteenth century. But, by the standards of the rest of *Pierrot Lunaire,* this ending is genuinely tonal, not atonal (despite the fact that the approximate notes indicated for the speaker-singer are not notes of the E major tonic chord at all). Compare the tonal feeling with, especially, the short piano transition introducing song No. 18. Schoenberg's song cycle about Pierrot and his neuroses ends perfectly at rest: as perfectly, at least, as the twentieth century knows how to rest.

ALBAN BERG (1885–1935) *Wozzeck*   Act III (1917–1919) SIDES 16, 17

Probably the best-known product of expressionist music is the opera *Wozzeck,* by Schoenberg's student Alban Berg. (The pronunciation is *Votseck,* with the first syllable rhyming with "lots.") *Wozzeck* is a work that sums up, if not all aspects of the early twentieth-century consciousness, at least one essential aspect of it. In this respect, *Wozzeck* occupies a position parallel to Wagner's *Tristan und Isolde* in the nineteenth century.

And between these two works the contrast could hardly be more complete. Set in the courtly Middle Ages of romantic fantasy, *Tristan und Isolde* shows how personal emotion unites the lovers in ecstasy and allows them to transcend the demands of society and, indeed, of life itself. Wagner's view of human aspirations and relationships was optimistic, indeed triumphant. *Wozzeck* is set in a slum. It shows the individual crushed by society into madness and catastrophe. Even human communication is an impossibility, to say nothing of love.

Berg's pessimism recalls that of another characteristic artist of the early twentieth century, Franz Kafka. Kafka's novels and stories show modern protagonists trapped by great impersonal systems they can neither influence nor understand. In *The Trial*, for instance, Joseph K. (he is even denied a real name) stands trial for a crime that is never revealed to him. He wanders through the novel as though in a nightmare, trying to discover the reason for his oppression. Neither his judge nor his lawyer nor his priest will enlighten him. Finally he is taken to the outskirts of town and stabbed in the heart, no wiser than before.

Joseph K. has turned out to be a recurring, all-but-mythical figure in the twentieth century. One version of him appears as the brainwashed "hero," Smith, in *1984,* George Orwell's ominous prediction of life in the future under Big Brother. A current comic (or tragicomic) version of him is the man who gets a wrong credit-card charge and is unable to communicate with the computers; they ignore his checks, cut off his credit, repossess his furniture, and cancel his auto insurance. Franz Wozzeck is an inarticulate and impoverished soldier, the lowest member of the military machine. He is troubled by visions and tormented for no apparent reason by his sadistic captain and by the regimental doctor, who uses him for scientific experiments. His mistress sleeps with his NCO, who beats up Wozzeck when he makes some objection. Finally Wozzeck murders his mistress, goes mad, and wanders into a lake. Passersby hear him drowning but make no effort to save him.

The third and last act of this opera, containing the final catastrophe, is divided into five scenes linked together without pause by orchestral interludes.

SCENE i: MARIE'S ROOM

Wozzeck's unfaithful mistress Marie is shown in a short scene of morning-after repentance. First she reads a few verses from the Bible, punctuated by cries of anguish, then she fondles her child and tells it a little story:

"Neither was guile found in his mouth." *Lord God, Lord God, do not look at me!*
"And the Pharisees brought unto him a woman taken in adultery. Jesus said unto her: Neither do I condemn thee, go, and sin no more." *Lord God! . . .*

Once there was a poor child and he had no father or mother—they were all dead—and there was no one in the world, and he was hungry and cried all day and all night. . . .

"And stood at his feet weeping, and began to wash his feet with tears, and kissed his feet, and anointed them with ointment." *Savior, if only I could annoint your feet!*

Savior, you had mercy on her—have mercy on me also!

Berg treats Marie's utterances in this scene in different vocal styles. When she is reading or narrating, she simply speaks, against a relatively gentle orchestral background, or else engages in "speech-song" (*Sprechstimme*) derived from Schoenberg's *Pierrot Lunaire.* On the other hand, her wailing cries of anguish are genuinely sung, mostly on high, intense notes that can hardly be said to coalesce into recognizable tunes.

This makes Marie seem psychologically very different from earlier operatic figures whom we have heard, such as Wotan or Aida. She is closest to Princess Amneris, but, if Amneris is distraught to the point of tantrum, Marie is truly hysterical. The orchestral background for her outcries is also characteristically intense and dissonant, and it does not fit in noticeably with her singing line. This establishes the general level of atonality that will be held through most of the act.

A blackout follows, and a short orchestral interlude runs from this scene into the next. The music surges up violently, with the trombones prominent. The audience has an opportunity to reflect in complete darkness upon Marie's misery and her desperate situation.

SCENE ii: A WOODLAND PATH BY A POND

Wozzeck takes Marie on a walk and speaks to her disconnectedly about their life together, her beauty, the darkness, and the blood-red moon they see rising. Her terror increases. In a sudden rage, he stabs her to death. Again, the words in this scene are sung in a dissociated style that sounds like neither recitative nor aria. Wozzeck's statements seem decidedly schizophrenic, ranging from tender one second to coarse and violent the next. The stabbing itself is very ugly, accompanied by a driving drumbeat.

What can we make of the orchestral music behind the singing? In its weirdly beautiful way, it is illustrating the nighttime scene: the black water of the pond, the shadows, the crickets, the frogs, the other woodland sounds. Berg has even learned something from the illustrative music of Debussy, but the effect of his scene is as different as night from day—nightmare from daydream. If a score by Debussy recalls an impressionist landscape by Monet, this one by Berg recalls an ominous, brooding landscape by Van Gogh (see page 425).

This scene also underlines the ambiguity of the term *atonality,* an ambiguity we stressed in the discussion above. Since neither the singing nor the orchestral music fits into conventional tonality, the effect may seem chaotic at first. Yet a single tonal center (the note B) is omnipresent in this scene. In its own way, the scene counts as more "tonal" than almost any other piece of music, in that it is chained to one central note. A really attentive listener should be able to detect the same note sounding in every single bar, in high or low octaves, played by one instrument or another.

The note B grows overpowering when the drum begins its beat. Marie's final shriek covers two octaves from soprano high B to low B, and then, in the blackout after the stabbing, the single note B is played by the whole orchestra in two gut-bursting crescendos. Don't turn down the phonograph if this famous passage hurts your ears—it is supposed to. (It is also hard on the stagehands, who are allowed just about twenty-one seconds to make the scene change.)

SCENE iii: AN INN

If Wozzeck seemed close to insanity during the murder, he now enters into pure nightmare. In a sordid dive of an inn he seeks consolation from Marg'ret, a friend (or perhaps one should say a colleague) of Marie's. Berg's idea of a honky-tonk piano opens the scene:

Here harmonic and rhythmic distortion of what might be a "normal" jazz piano is used for grotesque effect—an expressionist use of distortion, in contrast to Debussy's impressionist use of it in the march in *Festivals* (see page 421). Marg'ret gets up on the piano and sings a song, also distorted:

Suddenly she notices blood on Wozzeck's hands. It smells like human blood. In a horrible climax to the scene, all the people in the inn come out of the shadows and close in on Wozzeck to lynch him. But he escapes in the blackout, as the orchestral interlude surges frantically and furiously.

Berg contrived a very original musical form for this scene, a form that contributes directly to the dramatic effect he sought. The entire scene is built on a single short rhythm, repeated over and over again with only slight modifications—*but presented in many different tempos.* This twitching rhythm has been marked above the two previous musical examples, first at a fast tempo, then at a slow one. Perhaps its most obvious presentation comes when Marg'ret first notices the blood:

Even if the listener catches only a quarter or a tenth of the times this rhythm comes, the hypnotic effect of this rhythmic ostinato (see page 163) contributes powerfully to the sense of nightmare and fixation.

SCENE iv: BY THE POND

Wozzeck returns to the scene of the murder, and again the orchestra engages in nature illustration, making strange, macabre sounds, so different from those of Debussy. Wozzeck's mind has quite cracked. He shrieks out for the knife (*"Das Messer!"*), discovers the corpse (*"Mörder!"*), and sees once again the blood-red moon (*"Der Mond ist blütig."*). Finally he walks into the pond—which seems to him to be filled with blood—in order to wash himself and dispose of the murder weapon.

At this point, his two principal tormentors of acts I and II, the Captain and the Doctor, happen to walk by. They hear the vivid orchestral gurgles and understand that someone is drowning, but like people watching a mugging on a crowded New York street, they make no move to help. The Captain speaks the last words of the scene: "Come on, Doctor! Let's get out of here!" He uses plain speech again, not song, but it is speech that rises shrilly in terror: *"Kommen sie, Doktor! kommen sie schnell!"* Even the tormentors of this life, we realize, are driven by tormenting demons of their own.

So far, the orchestral interludes between the scenes have all been very brief. As a result the drama presses to its catastrophe with great urgency. Now, however, Berg writes a slow, lengthy interlude in which great waves of pity for Wozzeck well out from the orchestra into the darkened auditorium. Obviously Berg identified with Wozzeck, and he agonizes with him in a series of great orchestral climaxes. The almost unbearable emotionality of this interlude recalls the slow movement of Mahler's Fourth Symphony (see page 401), though the style is more atonal. By Berg's standards, however, the beginning and the end of this interlude are relatively tonal. If the score sounds crowded, that is because it finds place for all the many leitmotivs (see page 364) that have been running through the opera, in Wagnerian fashion, to symbolize persons and feelings.

As the interlude sobs to a close, there is a sudden whoosh of harp, celesta, and winds, synchronized with the stage lights flashing on again for the next scene. The sound was borrowed from Debussy's *Festivals.* Here it may remind us of movie technique, when the camera cuts suddenly to a new image.

SCENE v: EPILOGUE. OUTSIDE MARIE'S HOUSE. NEXT MORNING

The next scene is bright and clear, a sunlit morning, featuring high instruments from an orchestra reduced in size. They are playing some of the most ravishing sounds in the whole opera—but Berg is preparing to twist the knife in the wound. A group of children sing a ring-around-a-rosy game, whose melody is once again distorted:

Ringel, Ringel Rosenkranz, Rin - gel reih'n! Ringel, Ringel, Rosenkranz, Rin...
Ring around a rosy, a pocket full of posy...

The child of Marie and Wozzeck is also there, playing on a hobbyhorse; we hear his little switch and his giddap exclamations (*"Hop, hop! Hop, hop!"*). With a cruelty that is not uncommon in small children, the others come up and taunt him: "Hey you, your mother's dead!" He does not seem to understand. "Come on and see!" Hesitantly, he follows them off, as the curtain falls to quiet, sinister-sweet orchestral sounds.

The message is unmistakable. Just as the Captain shares the horror of Wozzeck's world, so also does the child. He is in for a shock as he goes out to the pond (though perhaps he has been prepared for it by the stories his mother had been telling him). His world, too, the daytime world of everyday children's games, is peopled by tormentors he cannot understand.

So ends an opera that many people consider one of the most gripping theater pieces of the century. Berg's skill at the musical depiction of insanity is really uncanny, but this very virtuosity may suggest some interesting questions. Was Wozzeck actually hounded and driven mad in an objective sense? For that matter, was Joseph K. actually accused, tried, and subjected to the fearful runaround described in *The Trial*? Or is each of these works perhaps a brilliant analysis of the paranoid personality, on a symbolic level? The age of Freud, an age fascinated by neurosis and psychosis, has found in Franz Kafka and Alban Berg artists who reflect its concerns.

ANTON WEBERN (1883–1945) Five Orchestra Pieces, Op. 10 (1913)   SIDE 16

Another expressionist composer who developed a highly individual "new language" was Anton Webern. He grew up in the world of late romanticism, surrounded by the grandiose musical structures of Strauss and Mahler—and his teacher Arnold Schoenberg composed some of the largest of all. Webern turned his music about-face, toward concentration, brevity, atomization, and quiet: quiet even unto silence. His compositions are almost all extremely brief. The Five Orchestra Pieces last 12, 14, 11, 6, and 32 measures, respectively! Webern's entire musical output has been recorded on four LP records.

His music is famous for its "atomized" melodic lines, lines shared among the different instruments, with one instrument often playing just one or two notes before another takes over. This breaks up the music into kaleidoscopic flashes—successive flashes and also simultaneous ones. With the beginning notes of the Five Orchestra Pieces, to take a famous example, it is tempting to write out the music with little spaces between instruments:

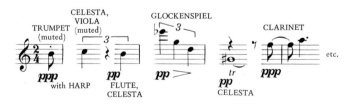

As this example suggests, with its muted trumpet, murmuring celesta, and near-silent clarinet, Webern explored the most exquisite and excruciating limits of musical delicacy. For the rich brocade of romanticism and the subtle silk of impressionism, Webern substituted a unique texture of glittering lace.

His music is thoroughly atonal; it is also athematic, lacking tunes, motives, and obvious repetitions. (If there are readers who have been growing weary of all the A B A diagrams in this book, they can now start listening to music without repetitions, music that never comes around again to a second A.) In place of tonality and motive, Webern achieves a remarkable quality by giving heightened significance to the individual notes, which he somehow turns into separate little sources of tremendous energy. The orchestration plays a big part in this effect by isolating the notes and pointing them up so sharply.

The fourth of the Five Orchestra Pieces is shown below—the whole of it, in a full-length line score:

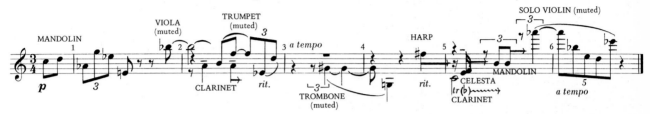

Webern's incessant **p, pp,** and **ppp** marks have been omitted from this score (elsewhere he also writes "scarcely audible," "fading," and "as light as possible"). While a strange, "sprung" melody is traced by the main instruments, other instruments enter with notes that are quietly repeated several times in various rhythms and then fade away entirely. These are indicated in the line score by arrows—the clarinet in measure 2, the harp in measure 4, the clarinet, celesta, and mandolin in measure 5. Meanwhile the main melody itself migrates from the mandolin to a single note in the viola, to the trumpet, down to the trombone, and then up very high in the violin.

Though the piece is written in $\frac{3}{4}$ time, the meter is scarcely apprehended. The complex rhythm is expressive and involuted. Each note seems to have been edged into place with a hushed sense of special urgency. And it has been well observed that in Webern's music, the rests (the silences) are as expressive and "pregnant" as the notes themselves. Listen hard to the rests in measures 1 and 4—and measure 6.

Everybody knows that to get the maximum dissonance from two notes on the piano, the two notes should be adjacent—B and C, for example, or C and C♯. An examination of the score above shows Webern constantly working with half steps, either simultaneously or successively, in one octave or another:

MEASURE	HALF STEPS
1	mandolin A♭ to G, and then E♭ to E♮
2	viola B♭ and clarinet A
	trumpet E♭ to D
2–3	clarinet A to trombone G♯
4	trombone G♯ to G♮
	trombone G to harp F♯
5	celesta E and F
	clarinet C and mandolin B
6	violin D to E♭

To hear all these would take sharp ears, certainly. But, even if they are not heard specifically, the constant dissonances help create the quiet, tense, edgy atmosphere that always seems to underlie Webern's music.

In later years, Webern followed Schoenberg in adopting serialism (see below). But his serial music sounds less like Schoenberg than like early, pre-serial music by Webern. Brevity and concentration remained his ideals.

There is some truth to the facetious remark that Webern was a composer who always quit while he was ahead. When his pieces end, we want more—or at least, we wonder why they ended quite as early as they did. Almost without realizing it, we find ourselves concentrating more intently on these tiny pieces than on longer ones by other composers. Not only is Webern working harder, infusing each note with unique energies, but the listener, in partnership, is listening more anxiously too.

What we hear is a curious blend of subdued yearning and pixieish imagination. Though at first the music may seem all charm, its strongly emotional nature soon makes itself felt (most strongly, perhaps, in the third of the Five Orchestra Pieces). But the expressionist vision has been remarkably distilled; it is as though passion is being viewed through the wrong end of a telescope. Like a Japanese haiku, Webern's music carries an intense whiff of suggestion; then thoughts and questions resonate in the ensuing void:

閑さや岩にしみ入る蟬の聲

Shizukasa ya iwa ni shimiiru semi no koe

The silence;
The voice of the cicadas
Penetrates the rocks.
—Basho

Serialism

serialism

Of all the advanced composers of this century, Arnold Schoenberg was the most keenly aware of the problem caused by ever-broadening dissonance and atonality. The problem, to put it simply, was the clear and present danger of chaos. In the 1920s Schoenberg made an impressive effort to impose a kind of order or control over the newly emancipated elements of music. This resulted in the *twelve-tone method*, later known as serialism.

As a basis for such control, Schoenberg felt he had to find a way of guaranteeing that the level of atonality and dissonance in his music would remain more or less constant. With this in mind, he went a step or two beyond Wagner's chromaticism (see page 415), the nineteenth-century technique that anticipated atonality. Wagner used all twelve notes of the chromatic scale very freely. Schoenberg used them even more freely, as we saw in the last song of *Pierrot Lunaire* (page 427). Finally he determined to use them all in a completely systematic manner.

Schoenberg chose a special arrangement, or ordering, of the twelve chromatic notes and then kept this fixed for the composition in question. Another composition would have a different arrangement. This ordering is called the *twelve-tone row* or *series;* hence the term *serialism.* Then, in principle, Schoenberg composed by writing the notes only in the order of the series—and before starting over again, he always went through the entire series of twelve without any backtracking. This guaranteed that no single note would become too prominent and thus receive any shade of tonal centrality.

Since for this purpose it makes no difference which way round the series goes, Schoenberg also composed with the series in certain different manipulations that still kept its essential character. Called *retrograde* (backward), *inversion* (upside down, or mirror image), and *retrograde inversion* (upside down and backward), they are illustrated below together with a basic series.

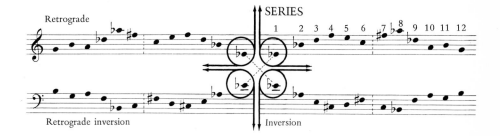

The series controls pitches, in a sense, but it does not say anything about rhythm, nor does it specify which octaves the various notes come in. Thus on page 438, the identical basic series, retrograde, inversion, and retrograde inversion can be written out with some notes an octave higher or lower.

Another important possibility is to *transpose* the series (and its retrograde, inversion, and retrograde inversion), that is, move it bodily up or down from one pitch level to another. For example, the "inversion" we have shown, beginning E♭ A♭ E♮, may be transposed down to D♭ G♭ D♮, or to A♭ D♭ A♮ (see page 438), etc. With all these extensions, it will be seen that the twelve-tone method leaves the composer plenty of flexibility.

It is hard to learn about serialism for the first time without finding the whole thing pretty strange. (But equally strange things were happening in other arts during the exact same period; consider our illustrations of paintings by Duchamp, Klee, and Kandinsky on pages 419 and 410–11.) Serialism may strike some people as a bold, ingenious, and highly imaginative attempt to open up new artistic horizons. It may strike others as arbitrary and crabbed, a force stifling music's true spontaneity. Listen at this point to the beginning of Schoenberg's Piano Concerto, Op. 42, written in 1942 (side 19). Does it sound imaginative or does it sound crabbed?

The series shown is one used in this concerto. The pianist's opening tune comes out of the series in a relatively simple way, as the music on the next pages shows. Phrase 1 of the tune follows the *series* itself, phrase 2 the *retrograde inversion* transposed, phrase 3 the *retrograde,* and phrase 4 the *inversion* transposed. There are a few "free" notes, marked with asterisks, and some note repetitions. You will see that the rhythm has nothing to do with the series.

The series notes are sometimes rhythmically very prominent, and at other times they go by almost without being noticed.

This is a clear example of twelve-tone writing. But it is such a simple one that it cannot be described as typical. In fact, for actual tunes to be made out of a twelve-tone series or for a series to be treated as a tune is exceptional. A series serves mainly as a source of motives and harmonies. The way in which the left-hand accompaniment is derived from the series shows a level of complexity that is more usual. Measures 7 and 8, for example, cover the entire series except for note 12, G, which appears in the right hand:

How does serialism impose a "new order" on the increasingly free and chaotic elements of music? The important thing about the series is not the twelve notes themselves but rather the intervals (see page 17) between them. When a twelve-tone series is used in inversion, retrograde, retrograde inversion, or transposition, the notes change from their original series locations. *But the intervals between adjacent pairs of notes all remain the same.*

The intervals in our series can be shown in a table (page 439). Every serial composition has its own series and hence its own special sound—its own "twelve-tonality," we might say—determined by the intervals and their ordering. In the Schoenberg Piano Concerto, the interval of the major third is prominent, while the half step and the tritone (six half steps) have been minimized. Throughout the work, then, certain melodic and harmonic patterns recur and stamp the music with a unique character.

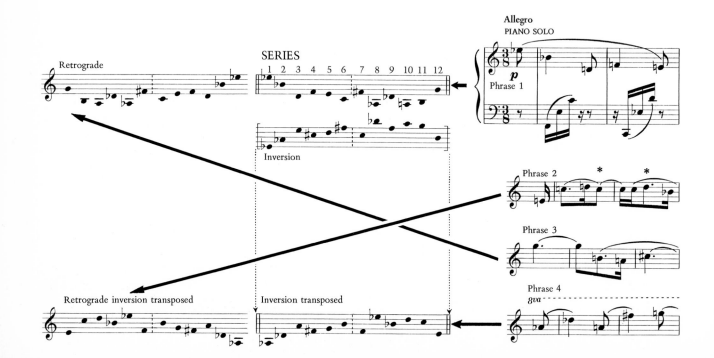

Indeed, serialism can be regarded as the end result of an important tendency of nineteenth-century music, namely, the tendency to seek strong means of unity within individual compositions. We have observed the "principle of thematic unity" in the music of Schumann, Berlioz, Wagner, and Mahler, and we have spoken of the various levels on which it operates: recurring themes, thematic transformation, and subtle or even subliminal similarities (see page 333). On its own rather different level, Schoenberg's serialism carried out the ideal of unity that the romantic composers were working toward.

INTERVALS IN THE SERIES OF SCHOENBERG'S PIANO CONCERTO

Name of Interval*	Number of Half steps in the Interval	Occurs between the Series Notes that are Numbered:	Number of Times the Interval Comes in the Series
Half step	1	4 and 5	1
Whole step	2	7 and 8; 10 and 11	2
Minor third	3	3 and 4	1
Major third	4	2 and 3; 5 and 6; 9 and 10; 11 and 12	4
Fourth	5	1 and 2; 8 and 9	2
Tritone	6	6 and 7	1

---

* All larger intervals reduce to one of the six listed here if the notes are shifted in the octaves until they are as close as possible.

© Arnold Newman

Stravinsky and Duchamp

A nostalgic photograph of two of the pioneers of early twentieth-century art, taken near the end of their lives: Igor Stravinsky (left), composer of *The Rite of Spring* (1913), and Marcel Duchamp, painter of the early cubist shocker *Nude Descending a Staircase* (1912) (see page 419). Duchamp, a tireless avant-gardist, even concocted a piece of music around this time that looked past Stravinsky to developments of our own era. His *Erratum musical* is a set of random notes drawn out of a hat, to be sung without any clues as to their time duration.

From the nineteenth century on, the various arts have grown together partly through increasing contacts among composers, painters, and writers. Stravinsky was associated with a long list of artistic figures of the twentieth century: the great ballet impresario Sergei Diaghilev, the choreographer George Balanchine, the painter Pablo Picasso, and the writers Jean Cocteau, André Gide, W. H. Auden, Evelyn Waugh, and Aldous Huxley.

The cast is international. Though Stravinsky was a Russian, he spent most of his life abroad, one of the first of a depressingly long list of twentieth-century artists who were driven from their homes by political regimes that they would not accept or that would not accept them. When the Russian Revolution broke out in 1917, Stravinsky stayed in Paris with his friends of the *Ballets Russes* and became a French citizen.

In 1939, when France was invaded by the Nazis, Stravinsky moved again and came to Los Angeles. The United States provided a haven for a remarkable number of European composers (as well as performers and musicologists): Stravinsky, Schoenberg, Bartók, Darius Milhaud, Paul Hindemith, Ernst Křenek, Kurt Weill, and others. This hospitality stimulated American musical life in a deeply significant way. In our own time, we have seen a similar enrichment of American ballet as a result of defections from Soviet Russia.

Igor Stravinsky (1882–1971)

One of the greatest of twentieth-century composers, Igor Stravinsky in his long career touched on many of the characteristic attitudes of his era and became a prisoner of none of them. His early work followed the romantic nationalism of Moussorgsky and other Russian composers. Young Stravinsky gravitated to Paris with a lively organization called the *Ballets Russes.* This Russian ballet company astonished the blasé Parisian public for many years with its exotic spectacles, combining the newest and most sensational in dance, music, folklore, scenery, and costume design. Famous and soon-to-be-famous artists worked for the *Ballets Russes:* Matisse, Chagall, Braque, Rouault, Picasso.

The first three scores that Stravinsky did for the *Ballets Russes* remain to this day his best-known pieces. Written from 1909 to 1913, they reveal an interesting progression toward more and more abstraction within the nationalist mold. The first of them, *The Firebird,* spins a romantic fairy tale about Prince Ivan Tsarevitch, the ogre Kastcheï, and the magical female Firebird. Its rich, half-oriental setting is matched by beautifully colored folk music and orchestral sound worthy of Debussy himself.

But the next ballet moves from the steppes to the urban marketplace. *Petrouchka,* the story of a carnival barker and his puppet, encouraged Stravinsky to put a hard, satirical, mechanical edge on his folk material. Finally, *The Rite of Spring* boldly and brutally evokes the fertility cults of prehistoric Asian tribes. Here Russian folk music, drastically simplified, is treated as the source of primitive rhythmic and sexual energy rather than picture-postcard charm.

STRAVINSKY *Le Sacre du Printemps* (The Rite of Spring) (1913)   SIDE 18

At its first performance, *The Rite of Spring* caused a near riot, the audience was so shocked at the dissonant sound in the orchestra pit and the suggestive choreography on the stage. Stravinsky employed an absolutely colossal orchestra, as though to show the world how well he could control the chief engine of musical romanticism. Compare this orchestra (page 442) with the Viennese and romantic orchestras tabulated on pages 248 and 330. Almost a symbol of prewar opulence in musical terms, the orchestra of *The Rite of Spring* was twice as large as anything Stravinsky cared to use again.

The Rite of Spring has no real story; Stravinsky even said that he preferred to think of the music as a concert piece. However, the score bears many inscriptions indicating that the ballet is to portray a number of fertility rites of various kinds, culminating in the ceremonial choice of a virgin for sacrifice. Apparently she is danced to death (in the concluding "Sacrificial Dance"). It is dubious anthropology but effective theater.

The first part or act of the ballet is entitled "Adoration of the Earth." The interior sections run into one another directly, but listeners usually have little difficulty determining when the new ones begin.

Introduction The famous opening theme is played by a bassoon at the very top—indeed, a little past the top—of its normal register. Early twentieth-century composers tended to stretch and strain at all the elements of music, including the ordinary capabilities of their instruments. The bleating bassoon is joined by odd hootings on other woodwind instruments, forming a highly dissonant contrapuntal web. The whole effect is indeed introductory, for what is played by the bassoon, followed by oboe, high clarinet (E♭ clarinet), and trumpet, sounds rather like a static series of preliminary fanfares.

AN EARLY TWENTIETH-CENTURY ORCHESTRA
(As in Stravinsky's *The Rite of Spring*)

Strings: first violins, second violins, violas, cellos, double basses, divided in many different ways

Woodwinds: 1 piccolo
3 flutes, 1 sometimes playing second piccolo
1 alto flute

4 oboes, 1 sometimes playing second English horn
1 English horn

1 high clarinet (E♭ clarinet)
3 clarinets, 1 sometimes playing second bass clarinet
1 bass clarinet

4 bassoons, 1 sometimes playing second double bassoon
1 double bassoon

Brass: 8 French horns, 2 sometimes playing tenor tubas

1 high trumpet (D trumpet)
4 trumpets
1 bass trumpet

3 trombones
2 bass tubas

Percussion: various timpani, bass drum
cymbals, gong, tambourine, triangle

Omens of Spring. Dance of the Adolescents   Probably this is where the original audience started to grow restive. The beginning of this dance is marked by heavy, harsh repetitions of a single dissonant chord in the strings, thirty-two times in all. Sforzatos (>) (see page 6) reinforced by short fat chords played by eight (!) French horns provide accents on the most unexpected beats:

1 2 3 4 5 6 7 8 9 1 2 1 2 3 4 5 6 1 2 3 1 2 3 4 1 2 3 4 5 1 2 3

The result is a contradiction of ordinary regular meter. Instead of eight standard measures in $\frac{2}{4}$ or $\frac{4}{8}$ meter containing four eighth-note beats each—8×4—which the notation would suggest, Stravinsky makes us hear 9 (or 4 + 5) + 2 + 6 + 3 + 4 + 5 + 3.

The exhilarating effect is heightened when lively new fragments are played against the repeating chords. Among these are the first of several fragments of made-up folk song:

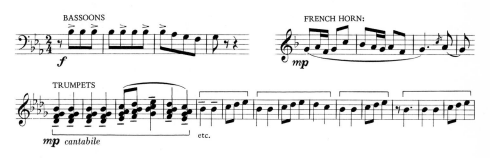

Stravinsky repeats these fragments over and over again at the same pitch but with slightly different rhythms and at slightly different lengths. This is Stravinsky's own variety of ostinato (see page 163); the technique is illustrated in the trumpet excerpt of the above example (the square brackets cover the repetitions). Like Debussy, Stravinsky tends to concentrate on small melodic fragments, but whereas Debussy usually abandons his fragments as soon as he decently can, Stravinsky keeps twisting and turning his, like a dog worrying a bone.

There are nearly 170 measures in this dance, and, in all but two of them, some instrument plays the four even eighth notes (♪ ♪ ♪ ♪) prominently. This kind of metrical insistence was unknown in conventional music. To understand the impact of *The Rite of Spring* in 1913, remember that at the time, few Europeans were used to the steady beat of jazz (let alone rock).

The Play of Abduction A whirlwind of brilliant rhythms, with much frantic work for the drums. This section ends with another good example of Stravinsky's rhythmic irregularity:

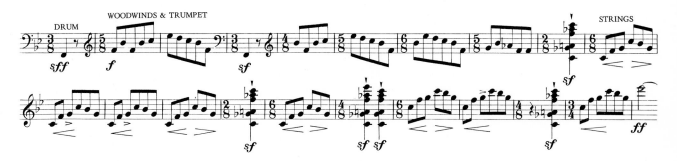

It is possible to hear this passage in a number of ways; something like the following jagged and highly complex metrical pattern emerges:

3 + 10 + 3 + 9 + 11 + 2 + 8 + 6 + 6 + 4 + 2 + 6 + 4 + 8 + 6 + 2 + 6

Round Dances of Spring   After a moment of respite, in an introduction featuring trills on the woodwind instruments, a slow, dragging dance is built out of the third folk song fragment of the "Dance of the Adolescents" (the trumpet fragment). The very strong downbeat makes the meter as hypnotic as that of any hard rock number—except for an occasional added or skipped beat, which always has a powerfully invigorating effect. This dance reaches a relentless climax with glissando (sliding) trombones, gong, and big drum. A sudden fast episode, and then the introduction returns to conclude the section. The introduction tune is played by a fascinating combination of high clarinet (Eb clarinet) and alto flute two octaves apart.

Games of the Rival Tribes   Another fast dance with two more folklike fragments treated in ostinato:

Procession of the Sage   We soon realize that ostinato is an essential feature of Stravinsky's style, the feature that contributes more than any other to its "primitive" quality. Here four tubas play a lumbering ostinato, during which we can imagine a huge masked shaman borne aloft by half of the dancers, while the others leap and gesture around them.

Adoration of the Earth. Dance of the Earth   "Adoration of the Earth" is performed briefly by the Sage, then everyone joins in the short and breathless "Dance of the Earth." The rhythmic irregularity is more exciting than ever, though in fact this entire dance is built over an ostinato repeated about thirty times:

First played by the double basses, this ostinato becomes more audible when the basses are joined by bass clarinets and bassoons.

   Notice that all the sections of *The Rite of Spring* end by simply stopping, without preparing for cadences in any special way. This is particularly apparent in the fast vehement sections, in which Stravinsky seems to lower his head and charge; the music usually gets louder and louder until it is turned off as though by a switch. This effect is striking in "The Dance of the Earth." We may indeed regard this as a "primitive" treatment of musical form.

   What is conspicuously absent from *The Rite of Spring* is emotionality. Tough, precise, and barbaric, this music is as far removed from Debussy's impressionism or Berg's expressionism as it is from the old-line romantic sentiment of Strauss or Mahler. In later pieces, Stravinsky abandoned the barbarism—and lost most of his audience. But the dry, precise quality remained, and so did the characteristic irregular rhythms. Throughout his life they provided Stravinsky with a powerful strategy of movement, a sense of springing, racing, fencing, propelling, all rolled into one—a quality of movement unlike that of any other composer. Rhythm was at the heart of Stravinsky's viable "new language" for music.

Twentieth-Century Nationalism

Stravinsky started his career in the Russian nationalist tradition of Moussorgsky and others, but soon moved off to a whole series of different new styles. After World War I he became the leading proponent of neoclassicism (see page 408); after World War II he adopted serialism. Some other composers of the twentieth century started out with nationalism and stayed with it. The evocation of folk music remained a central element of their style—perhaps *the* central element—whereas this was no longer the case with Stravinsky after the early 1920s.

These composers are generally counted among the twentieth-century conservatives (see page 408). Nationalism was a movement born of the nineteenth century, and there was undeniably something retrospective about continuing in this path fifty or more years later. However, all the new nationalists laced their music with twentieth-century style characteristics, such as high-level dissonance and complex, irregular rhythms, and a few of them were innovators in their own right. They developed their own musical languages combining the old and the new in various interesting ways.

Béla Bartók (1881–1945)

The Hungarian nationalist composer and folklorist Béla Bartók is a case in point. In the years around World War I, Bartók moved in the vanguard of musical experimentation along with Schoenberg and Stravinsky. He pioneered new methods for harmonic and formal organization, and evolved a distinctive rhythmic style, as vigorous as Stravinsky's but more earthy, more closely involved with the literal rhythms of folk dance. A famous "rhythm" piece by Bartók is the *Allegro Barbaro* for piano (1911). "Barbarously Fast": the title tells the story.

In the 1920s Bartók was attracted to neoclassicism, like Stravinsky and indeed nearly all other composers of the time. He wrote fugues and movements in sonata form (simple sonata form, at that). If he did not produce any actual symphonies, he did favor other old genres: he wrote six magnificent string quartets and a like number of concertos—for a modern composer, a considerable number and one that indicates a conservative orientation. Bartók also continued the tradition of romantic emotionality in his music (particularly in his late music, interestingly enough). He shunned neither romantic melody nor the characteristic harmonies that go with it.

Bartók in the Field

The composer Béla Bartók worked the rhythms of folk dance and the accents of folk song into all, or almost all, his music. In this he was an heir to the tradition of romantic nationalism; indeed, Bartók may be judged the most successful of all the nationalist composers. In his music the folk element always sounds deeply integral, never merely tacked on like an appliqué.

This is surely not unrelated to the fact that Bartók was also a professional folklorist. He published numerous pathbreaking studies on the music of his native Hungary and that of other countries. Nearly a quarter of his total music publications consists of sets of folk song arrangements and the like. Some nineteenth-century nationalists limited their contacts with "the folk" to what they could see from the windows of their well-heated Moscow apartments. Bartók actually got out into the field.

Composers of the baroque period worked and lived like skilled craftsmen. Romantic composers, who tended to regard themselves as geniuses, often thought they had something to tell the world as writers on philosophical and critical matters. It is perhaps fitting that the twentieth century should provide a major composer who was also a major research scholar—an ethnomusicologist.

That a major composer should have been deeply influenced by work in the social sciences is another sign of the times. Anthropology was one of the exciting new intellectual disciplines of the early twentieth century (and has been gaining importance ever since). Around the time Bartók was investigating folk music in the Balkans, the British folklorist Cecil Sharp was conducting his famous field studies of Anglo-American folk songs in Appalachia.

Our illustration shows Bartók busy at his research, having a back-country girl sing a song into a primitive recording device. This photograph was taken in 1908, when recordings were very new. It may make us smile, for, as far as these solemn peasants were concerned, the camera, too, must have been a new and doubtless awe-inspiring instrument. They are well scrubbed and decked out in their national costumes (the bashful girls on the right did not get to wear shoes because they were unmarried).

Back of all his music is the impressive harvest of Bartók's extensive field-work as an ethnomusicologist (see page 446). Even at its most complex and radical, the fabric of his music glitters with threads spun out of the rhythms of Hungarian folk dance and the accents of Hungarian folk song.

BARTÓK Music for Strings, Percussion, and Celesta (1936) SIDE 19

Though Bartók never produced an actual symphony, as we have said, his Music for Strings, Percussion, and Celesta is really a light-hearted symphony in four movements, written for an unusual orchestra. The strings are used in a particularly rich and imaginative way. The celesta is a small keyboard instrument in which the sound is produced by striking steel plates; it is most familiar from Tchaikovsky's *Dance of the Sugar-Plum Fairy* in his *Nutcracker Suite*. Bartók's "percussion" includes other melody instruments, the piano, harp, and xylophone—though by the way, we do not learn this all at once. He keeps surprising us by adding new resources of tone color. The celesta turns up for the first time halfway through the first movement, the piano and harp in the second, and the xylophone comes to the fore only in the third.

FIRST MOVEMENT

Bartók's first movement is a fugue. Nothing could show more dramatically his neoclassical inclinations than the use of this ancient form. In fact, Bartók was probably thinking of a specific "classical" model, a famous Beethoven quartet in which that composer had the unusual idea of opening a large composition with a slow, chromatic fugue.

But what counted as "chromatic" for Beethoven did not count as extreme for an early twentieth-century composer such as Bartók. His fugue subject is full of strange, hard-to-follow, un-Beethovenian intervals:

A typical fugue subject makes a forthright effect; this one sounds tentative, circuitous, and troubled. Notice that a number of passages in this subject are a half step lower than other passages—the end of phrase 2 compared to the end of phrase 1, the whole of phrase 4 compared to phrase 3 (though the rhythms are different). All these half steps give the movement its characteristic intensely chromatic sound.

Notice, too, how Bartók notates this fugue subject, using dotted bar lines to subdivide his $\frac{8}{8}$ ($\frac{2}{2}$) measures into 3 + 3 + 2 eighth notes, rather than the usual 4 + 4 or 2 + 2 + 2 + 2. In a faster tempo, these 3 + 3 + 2 rhythms are characteristic of much folk music, ranging from Bulgaria to Brazil. We shall meet them again before the Music for Strings, Percussion, and Celesta is over.

One by one the muted string instruments come in with the fugue subject, gradually getting louder until the mutes are removed and a powerful climax is underscored by percussion. Some entrances of the subject in stretto (see page

186) make it sound more troubled yet, even tortuous. After this the fugue quiets down and presents the subject in inversion (see page 210). Suddenly there is a magical tinkling blur of sound from the celesta, accompanying the last complete subject entry (inverted) very high on the violins.

When the celesta fades away, all that remains is a thinning group of string instruments playing phrase 1, very quietly, in both its regular and its inverted form. Eight times they start, always from the note A (as at the beginning of the movement); they seem to be searching or yearning for a resting point. In the cadence at the very end, which has become famous for its sense of simple, hushed relief, they find just that.

SECOND MOVEMENT

If we expect the pensive, rather solemn tone of the first movement to continue in the second, we are in for a surprise, perhaps a pleasant one. Bartók had his serious and his poetic side, but he also liked to entertain. The second movement shows (again) strong neoclassical leanings in its reliance on sonata form, but it also borrows liberally from folk music. In such situations, Bartók's spirits always seem to rise. He loved folk music too much to rein in his own infectious enjoyment.

This spirited movement would repay study in some detail, as an example of twentieth-century treatment of sonata form. Close study would show that in fact Bartók handles the form quite traditionally. (The cadence ending the exposition, for example, is marked off in such an exaggeratedly clear way—four fortissimo consonant chords in the second key, followed by drum beats—that we could almost suspect him of parody.) Here, however, we can take the time to mention only one or two of the movement's highlights, starting (naturally) with the first theme.

Bartók now divides his orchestra into two groups, each consisting of violins, violas, cellos, double basses, and a certain number of percussion instruments. These groups answer one another, a little like the choirs (some of them instrumental choirs) in the Venetian music of Giovanni Gabrieli around 1600. The first theme starts with a *pizzicato* (plucked) introductory passage in orchestra group 2, followed by the main tune in group 1, soon answered by group 2. This tune has the rollicking character of a folk dance, presumably a Hungarian one:

The short motive marked by a bracket on the example is used to make the bridge passage of the sonata form in a way that Haydn and Beethoven would have understood perfectly. The piano, which enters for the first time in this movement, is entrusted with the cadence theme ending the exposition, shortly before the clear cadence mentioned above.

The development section begins with orchestra group 2 and its introductory *pizzicato* material. Then follows a wonderful passage in which this group plays a figure derived from the introduction, five eighth notes long, over and over again, while group 1 and the piano punch out syncopated notes against it. The inspiration for this must have been Stravinsky's *Rite of Spring,* "The Dance of the Adolescents" (see page 442), but it is interesting to hear how differently it comes out in Bartók's hands:

THIRD MOVEMENT

In this slow (adagio) movement, Bartók deploys the full color resources of his string-and-percussion orchestra for the first time. He begins with a series of repeated-note clicks on the xylophone, speeding up and slowing down again—a remarkably brittle, almost inhuman sound. This is at once contrasted with rich, expressive phrases overlapping in the string instruments; they sound almost like human voices in lament. Dotted rhythms (see page 25) such as the following are another of Bartók's characteristic importations from Hungarian folk music:

At the point where the laments subside, and at some other points later, you may recognize phrases from the fugue subject of the first movement. But what you will probably remember most of all from the present movement are the unbelievably delicate sonorities that Bartók concocts out of celesta arpeggios, harp and piano glissandos (see page 353), high quiet tremolos in the strings, and a special sliding timpani sound for which he had a great fondness. Repeated xylophone notes end the movement as it began, sounding doubly dry and cryptic after the fantastic visions that the composer has summoned up in between.

FOURTH MOVEMENT

Discussing romantic music, we spoke a number of times of the composers' urge to establish thematic unity over the course of long compositions. Berlioz in a simple way, and Mahler in more subtle ways, unified their symphonies by bringing themes back from one movement to another. This was a romantic tradition that Bartók still adhered to. Although basically the fourth movement of the Music for Strings, Percussion, and Celesta sounds like a boisterous medley of folk dances, it also includes emphatic references to the thematic material of each of the three previous movements.

More strictly speaking, this movement is a very fast rondo built mostly out of folklike themes. Its form is A B A C B D A. The first theme, A, introduced by orchestra group 2 after a passage of excited strumming by group 1, races along in a "Bulgarian" rhythm:

What makes this unusually frenzied is that, while the actual tune in group 2 divides the $\frac{8}{8}$ $\left(\frac{2}{2}\right)$ measures into 2 + 3 + 3 eighth notes, group 1 continues its strumming in a different Bulgarian rhythm, 3 + 3 + 2.

The next theme, B, turns up very soon; it is a rather comical piano tune, at the end of which the piano recollects its striking Stravinskian passage from the development section of the second movement (see the first music example on page 449). The main theme of section C is simpler than any of the others, with an invigorating snare drum touch at the end of its phrases:

Then section D brings an impressive return of the fugue from the first movement. Many of the chromatic intervals of the original subject are now spread out and smoothed out; the original tortuous feeling has vanished. Compare the beginning of the new version of the subject, below, with the first phrase of the music example on page 447:

The two fugal "devices" used in the first movement also reappear, stretto and inversion (an especially attractive little passage is built on the free inversion shown to the right in the above example).

For a moment at the end of D, the lamenting sounds of the third movement are recalled, by the cellos. And Bartók is full of tricks in his concluding A section: an inverted version of the A theme, a quiet version of it with the rhythm all ironed out into even eighth notes (celesta and harp), and even an ecstatic, quite romantic version just before the end. This is the sort of movement that will leave listeners grinning with delight, if they haven't already cut loose and tried to dance their own trepak or czardas or hora to Bartók's whirling rhythms.

Charles Ives (1874–1954)

Why the United States produced no considerable composers in the nineteenth century, when we produced such painters as Mary Cassatt and Winslow Homer and such writers as Herman Melville and Emily Dickinson, is an interesting question. It was only in the 1920s and '30s that a sizable group of native composers emerged who could stand beside the composers of Europe. The output of our first major composer dates from around 1900 to 1920. He was Charles Ives, the son of a Civil War military bandmaster and music teacher of Danbury, Connecticut.

A great many of Ives's pieces have "American" subjects: *Lincoln, the Great Commoner,* the *Concord* Sonata for piano (*Concord, Mass., 1840–60*), *Some Southpaw Pitching,* and the *Holidays* Symphony in four movements that are called "Washington's Birthday," "Decoration Day," "The Fourth of July," and "Thanksgiving." Very often he employed fragments of American music: folk songs, popular songs by Stephen Foster, gospel hymns, ragtime—sometimes in great profusion. In the words of one historian of American music, Ives's music "emphatically declared that in its vernacular tradition American music had an artistically usable past."

Ives was our first important nationalist composer, then. But he was also a great deal more than that: a true American "original," a man with amazingly radical ideas about music, and an insatiable experimenter with musical materials. Working in isolation, Ives anticipated many of the most famous musical innovations of the early part of the twentieth century—and of the later part, too.

During his youth, the American musical climate was not at all friendly to modern trends. The main composers—men like Edward MacDowell (1861–1898) and Ives's own teacher at Yale, Horatio Parker (1863–1919)—wrote in a very dull traditional style. Partly for this reason, and partly out of inner conviction, when Ives got his bachelor's degree he did not enter the musical profession but instead went into insurance. He did music on weekends and in the evening, while pursuing a successful business career during the day. He never mixed with musicians and for years made little or no effort to get his innovative works performed or published.

All the while he was developing his unique mystical notions about music, notions that have been linked to nineteenth-century New England transcendentalism. To Ives, the actual sound of music seems to have counted less than the idea of music-making as a basic human activity. As a result, he believed that all kinds of music are equally valid, whether popular or sophisticated, whether simple or wildly dissonant, whether played in or out of tune. What mattered was people's communal joy in music-making. Believing also that every musical experiment has equal validity, Ives launched into visionary projects that no other composer of the time would have considered. He hated neatness and gentility; music for Ives had to have a grand Whitmanesque sweep.

We can sense these qualities even in some of his shorter works, such as the pair of linked orchestra pieces that he wrote around 1908 (they were not performed until the 1950s). *Central Park in the Dark in "The Good Old Summer Time"* purports to be a "slice of life" offering sounds of a hot New York evening: placid but highly dissonant night noises, interrupted by snatches of ragtime echoing from nearby saloons. "A Contemplation of Nothing Serious," Ives called this piece.

He called *The Unanswered Question* "A Contemplation of a Serious Matter" and provided it with an astonishing metaphysical program:

> The strings play **ppp** throughout, with no change in tempo. They represent "The Silences of the Druids" who know, see, and hear nothing. The trumpet intones "The Unanswered Question of Existence" and states it in the same tone of voice each time. But the hunt for the "Invisible Answer" undertaken by the flutes and other human beings [*i.e.*, clarinets and oboes *ad lib*] gradually becomes more active and louder. The "Fighting Answerers" . . . seem to realize a futility, and begin to mock "The Question"—the strife is over. . . . After they disappear, "The Question" is asked for the last time, and the "Silences" are heard beyond in "Undisturbed Solitude."

What is so novel here is the concept of three distinct levels of music that do not fit together in the least, in the terms of traditional polyphony. Ives even insisted that the strings, trumpet, and flutes, etc., sit well apart at different places on the stage. They each play streams of music in utterly different styles, without any fixed rhythmic or contrapuntal relationship. Yet this unusual dialogue between "Silences," "Questioner," and "Answerers" proves to be both coherent and strangely poignant. It provides a foretaste, perhaps, of our own age, an age marked by the quiet desperation of noncommunication.

Other Ives pieces used equally unheard-of ideas. In *Psalm 90* for chorus, organ, and bells, low C sounds continuously in the organ pedals for the whole length of the piece—nearly eleven minutes. Playing the *Concord* Sonata, the pianist has to use elbow as well as fingers, plus a special wooden block that holds down sixteen notes at once. The Second Symphony ends with a chord incorporating all twelve notes of the chromatic scale in several octaves (poor Richard Strauss! compare page 413). Ives wrote *Three Pieces* for two pianos tuned a quarter tone (half of a half step) apart, and several works in which certain elements can be played, or not played, or played in different ways, depending on the performer's choice.

These were indeed ideas born before their time. Small wonder that Ives's music never attained popularity during his lifetime and had to wait until after World War II, when the musical atmosphere for it had cleared. Indeed, it may make more sense to regard Ives as an isolated prophet of our newest music, rather than as another denizen of the musical world of Stravinsky, Schoenberg, Bartók, and Copland. The man exists, as it were, between chapters.

Aaron Copland (born 1900)

Aspiring young American composers around 1920 found more options open to them than the young Charles Ives did in 1898. The musical climate was much more favorable to new ideas, partly because the United States had been growing more aware of all things European, including European new music. This trend was greatly accelerated by the First World War.

American composers of the 1920s associated themselves with European modernism in a way that Ives never did. Our main composers of the period between the wars were Roger Sessions (born 1896), who is a New Englander, Roy Harris (1898–1979), a westerner, and Aaron Copland (born 1900), a New Yorker. Sessions studied with Ernest Bloch, a modernist Swiss composer who had settled in this country. After living for many years in Europe, Sessions came under the influence of Schoenberg's music. Harris and Copland both went abroad to study, in the Paris of Stravinsky and the other antiromantics.

In his role as an American nationalist composer, Copland journeyed all across the continent, and he also journeyed through time. His early success *Music for the Theater*, a very jazzy number, evoked New York in the Jazz Age. The ballets *Rodeo* and *Billy the Kid* are western in setting and include cowboy songs. *The Tender Land*, an opera about farm life in the corn belt, includes a big square dance scene and some country ballads. Copland wrote music for a movie version of *Our Town*, the well-known play by Thornton Wilder about a turn-of-the-century New England village. He wrote *A Lincoln Portrait*, for speaker and orchestra, and a fine song cycle to texts by Emily Dickinson, the nineteenth-century poet from Amherst, Massachusetts. Some of the songs include echoes of old hymns. *Appalachian Spring*, a ballet about Pennsylvania in the early 1800s, incorporates a melody sung by the Shakers, an extremist religious sect founded in the mid-eighteenth century.

COPLAND *Appalachian Spring* (1945)

This ballet was choreographed and danced by Martha Graham, the great lady of American modern dance. She conceived of "a pioneer celebration in spring around a newly built farmhouse in the Pennsylvania hills in the early part of the last century." From his ballet music, Copland arranged a concert piece (or suite) consisting of some seven sections, running directly into one another.

Section 1 is a very still, clear, static passage of a kind that Copland has made very much his own. It seems to catch the spirit of a vast silent landscape at dawn, perhaps, or just before dawn. In *section 2* "the bride-to-be and the young farmer-husband enact the emotions, joyful and apprehensive, their new domestic partnership invited." After a lively dance has begun, a new slower melody—something like a hymn—looms up in counterpoint, first in the wind instruments and then in the strings:

A slower version of this new figure, in a new rhythm and with hymnlike harmonies, forms the main substance of *section 3*.

The next two sections pick up the tempo: *section 4* evokes a whirling square dance and *section 5* is a danced sermon by a revivalist and his followers. Both sections include quiet statements of the hymn.

In *section 6* an agreeable Shaker tune, *A gift to be simple*, is played by a clarinet and followed by five variations. The variations are little more, really, than repetitions of the tune with new harmonies, in different keys, and in slightly different tempos.

Finally, after some music that the program says is "like a prayer," the hymn and the landscape music return once again (*section 7*). The ballet concludes very quietly. Perhaps the housewarming celebrations have gone on all night and we are now experiencing another clear gray dawn, a reminder of the many lonely dawns the pioneer couple will face together in the years to come.

CHAPTER 14 The Twentieth Century II

The Twentieth Century   II

We have seen that the early twentieth century witnessed a rapid evolution in all musical elements used by the romantics. There was a heady, urgent quality about musical developments in the years before World War I. It was almost as though composers felt that time was running out. Discussing the prewar musical scene, on page 409, we noted a characteristic quality of stretching and straining, a quality that seemed to affect all the individual elements of music. In the mid-twentieth century, after World War II, they snapped—and they snapped resoundingly.

Revolution, not expansion or evolution, animated the advanced musical circles of the 1950s. Not everybody participated in this revolution, of course; there were conservative (and even counter-revolutionary) composers in the 1950s, and there still are today. Nonetheless, after more than a quarter of a century no one can miss the deeply radical thrust of post-1950 music. We sense this in our bones as we listen to new music today, and we sense it in our heads as we try to think about it. For there are increasingly frequent occasions when none of the traditional terms and categories seems to apply anymore.

For example, in a really advanced composition of the 1950s, '60s, or '70s, there may be no melody, because (often) there is no fixed pitch. In music without any melody, the combination of melodic lines that makes up polyphony obviously cannot be experienced. Without melody and pitch, the whole question of dissonant and consonant harmony—which was endlessly discussed fifty years ago, which occupied the best minds among musicians, and which drove conservative listeners up the wall—has simply been bypassed.

Sometimes meter goes, too. It is not just made highly irregular, as in Stravinsky; it is eliminated altogether. When this happens, people begin experiencing rhythm in a new way. Rhythm is still present—whenever notes exist in time, rhythm exists too—but somehow it does not seem to count. This is a truly extraordinary outcome for music, which is (or was) preeminently the art of sound relationships in time.

Most extraordinary of all, perhaps, are new concepts in the general area of musical form. The idea of a meaningful progression from one part of a tune or piece to another part; the feeling of beginnings, middles, and ends; themes, repetitions, climaxes, developments, recapitulations, cadences—all these are thrown open to question. Some composers conceive of a kind of music in which there is no particular reason for any one sound to follow or precede another. They compose by fitting notes together in some random way or by having performers play things in a chance order.

In short, the "vocabulary for music" developed at the beginning of this book, which helps to a degree in following older music, seems now to be in the process of becoming obsolete in certain circles. We find we cannot use it and get results, any more than we can use English to communicate with one of those artificial intelligences that more and more are coming to control our existence. We need Fortran, Snobol, or whatever today's computer language is. Some kind of new vocabulary is sorely needed to talk about today's music, too.

Late Twentieth-Century Style

The two most emphatic tendencies in music during the years directly following World War II may strike us initially as contradictory in effect. The first demand of advanced composers was for new sound materials. The ordinary orchestra, even as expanded by Stravinsky and Bartók, seemed antiquated, used up; amazing new sonorities were investigated and put to use. At the same time, highly intellectual constructive tendencies came to the foreground, inspired by the serialism of Schoenberg (see page 436) but going far beyond it. Never before had such complex mathematical theories been advanced to explain or justify music, and never before had people been asked to puzzle over such abstruse musical analyses.

We might not expect a composer who is fascinated by sonority also to be preoccupied by construction; the first of these propensities seems sensuous in orientation, the second intellectual. Yet perhaps we can see how they go together. In discussing the baroque duality between emotionalism and systematic organization—between recitative and fugue—we remarked on the need composers have periodically felt for controls (see page 151). Especially when heady new means become available, composers need to systematize ways of dealing with them. Arnold Schoenberg's invention of the twelve-tone system, indeed, had been a "systematic" response to what some people called "the emancipation of dissonance" and of tonality (others called it a cutting adrift). Something of the same kind seems to have happened in the 1950s.

NEW SOUND MATERIALS

After the war, advanced composers began their search for new sonorities by attacking standard musical sources for unexpected new effects. Singers had to learn not only how to perform *Sprechstimme* (see page 409) and various kinds of *vocalise* (see page 421) but also how to lace their performances with hisses, grunts, clicks, and other "nonmusical" noises. Pianists were told to stand up, lean over the piano, and pluck at the strings or else strike them with rubber mallets.

Wired for Sound

This picture is also a sort of editorial on the current youth scene. The photographer has chosen his props unerringly: an electric guitar, a transistor radio, and a pair of sneakers.

One of the humorous things here is the way the photograph manages to downgrade today's music artifacts to the level of footwear. "Noise," as we have seen once before (page 368), is a familiar rallying cry of conservatives, and there is no doubt that today's electronics can get noisy. But neither humor nor anything else is going to make them go away. Electric guitars and electronic organs and pianos have tended more and more to take over popular music; they are easy to mass-produce, easy to play, and capable of achieving instant power as well as a great variety of musical effects. It is not likely that the trend will be reversed. And if the "horns" of jazz slang—trumpets, trombones, and saxophones—no longer play such a large role in popular music, some unexpected newcomers owe their acceptance to electronics: flutes, violins, cellos, even harpsichords. Without electronic amplification, these instruments play too quietly to hold their own.

As for the radio and the phonograph, their effects on young and old perhaps run even deeper than those of electronic instruments. We know so much more music nowadays, music of so many different kinds: classical and popular, medieval and electronic, Japanese and Indian. Just as a child of five has seen more on TV than his or her grandparents saw in a lifetime, so a youngster of fifteen has heard more music. Consequently, we take our music casually, cutting it off halfway through, raising and lowering the volume, mixing up all kinds of records on the changer, and setting up "music to read by."

Music lovers of the past either played music for themselves or went to concerts. A concert was an occasion. One could hear only what was on the program—in a fixed order—and, after paying one's money, one paid careful attention. Nearly everywhere today, the air seems to be saturated with music (polluted, it sometimes seems): transistors at the beach, eight-track stereos in cars, Muzak in supermarkets, "Adventures in Sound" on jetliners. Our attitude toward music and the whole listening experience has been determined accordingly, and so has the attitude of modern composers.

Composers also looked hard at the violin and other string instruments. Ordinarily, violin strings are bowed within the main part of their length, away from the *bridge,* the attachment that holds the strings up from the violin itself, and the *tailpiece,* the attachment that fastens down the ends of the strings. But a violinist can also obtain sounds by playing right on the bridge, right on the tailpiece, or at some point between them, where the strings are stretched tight and not tuned. You can also tap on the wood.

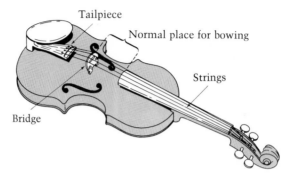

Such procedures begin to sound more like curiosities than really fruitful sources of new sound. If knocking or scraping sounds are wanted, why not invent special percussion devices rather than maul $13,000 Steinway pianos and $80,000 Stradivarius violins? A practical reason: because once performers have been hired, the presence of violins and pianos can be counted upon, which would not be true of newly invented percussion devices. A symbolic reason: because these procedures convey an attitude both contemptuous and innovative toward the very basis of traditional music-making. And a musical reason: because composers usually want swift alternation between these new sounds and the traditional ones produced by the same instruments.

However, when it comes to producing new sounds, the poor old musical instruments of yore are no match for the magnetic tape recorder, the electronic sound generator, and the various related machines that go with them. When composers got together with studio engineers and learned a little audio technology, they beheld a positively lunar landscape of sound spread out before them. Electronic music appeared to mark a giant step forward for musickind.

ELECTRONIC MUSIC

The electronic sound generator can *generate* sounds from scratch; the microphone and recording machine can *reproduce* them. The crucial technological advance was the development of magnetic tape, which made it very easy for the results of sound generation or reproduction to be stored, handled, copied—and doctored. Tapes can be subjected to all kinds of manipulation, both physical (cutting and splicing, speed change, tape loops) and electronic (echo chambers, filters, mixing).

Of course, electronic generators are just as likely to come up with "nonmusical" sounds—noises, without clear pitches—as "musical" ones, with clear pitches. Something of the almost endless range of possibilities is suggested below.

Reproduced Nonmusical Sounds (Noises): Traffic noises, amplified breathing, waterfalls—the sounds of life can be tape-recorded, stored, manipulated, and plugged into musical compositions at will. This is called musique concrète (concrete music)—an odd term, for it is hard to understand why a waterfall is more "concrete" than a woodwind instrument.

Reproduced Musical Sounds: A famous piece involving taped musical sounds is *Song of the Children* by the German composer Karlheinz Stockhausen, one of the most influential figures in postwar music. Stockhausen made a tape of a musical performance, of a hymn sung by a boy. He then used the tape in the composition again and again, after manipulating it in various ways. Sometimes the tape was cut up into half-second fragments separated by silences; sometimes it was superimposed upon itself (rerecorded, or dubbed), so that the effect is of a whole group of boys singing.

Electronically Generated Nonmusical Sounds (Noises): An endless variety of noises can be produced by generators. A familiar example is white noise, the hissing sound formed when every frequency of the audible spectrum is presented at the same intensity. (The color white is formed when every frequency of the visible spectrum is represented at the same intensity; "white" noise suggests the absence of tone "color.") Generators are also very good at producing sliding sounds, like sirens; the operator merely twists a dial.

Electronically Generated Musical Sounds: Machines can also produce musical sounds, a resource that was already put to use in an instrument of the 1920s called the theramin, and in the Hammond organ of the 1930s. Machines do this with deadly accuracy. Generators can be adjusted to provide any precise pitch, down to quarter tones and tenth tones in between our regular chromatic scale notes, if such refinements are wanted. Rhythms, too, can be controlled with a mathematical precision beyond the abilities of mere human beings.

Furthermore, as electronic apparatus became more and more sophisticated and computers came into play, all combinations of overtones (see page 15) were made instantly available. They are mixed in with the main pitch, and they influence the tone color. Composers of electronically generated music do not have to rely on a performer to be able to play the exact pitch, rhythm, or tone color that they have in their "mind's ear" or can calculate.

The one thing machines cannot do is duplicate human performance, with its subtle vagaries and tricks, its little inaccuracies of pitch and rhythm—its "personality," as we say. But of course, to duplicate human performance would be a futile exercise indeed. The whole point of working with electronic machines is that they suggest new sounds, new ways of connecting sound, whole new modes of sound experience that do not resemble standard music.

musique concrète

white noise

Does all this make electronic music "inhuman," then? No, for there is a human being behind it, and we can trace the play of mind and emotion in an electronic piece just as well, or almost as well, as in an older composition designed for performers. Perhaps one way in which the two kinds of music differ can be expressed as follows. Between the composer of older music and the audience stands the performer. The performer can have the effect of enriching, renewing, or popularizing (or bungling!) the human gesture made by the composer. Between the composer of electronic music and the audience stands a machine. The machine is either a neutral factor, or it may make the composer's gesture seem more distant.

Certainly electronic music is "cooler" and more impersonal than older music. Electric guitars are more impersonal than saxophones. Given the growing impersonality of every aspect of life in the twentieth century, this hardly comes as a surprise.

ON THE BOUNDARIES OF TIME

Time and rhythm mark the area in which modern music has made the most radical moves of all. Electronic devices can control rhythms of unprecedented complexity. But this is only one part of the story.

Earlier in the twentieth century, strange things had been done with time and rhythm by Anton Webern, composer of extremely brief pieces full of highly compressed, intense musical gestures (see page 434). These we might describe as short time segments of high "intensity." The post-1950s have seen, among other things, music of exactly the opposite character. In a representative composition by the American composer Terry Riley, *In C*, the instruments repeat little melodic figures that spell out only three extended harmonies, one at a time, each lasting for about fifteen to thirty minutes (according to an estimate by the composer). This we would call a very long time segment of very low density indeed.

With both Webern and Riley, we measure time—because we have no other way—in the same units: minutes and seconds. But one minute of Webern feels completely different from one minute of Riley. Like the difference in feeling between one minute at the end of a tied football game and one minute in the middle of an all-night run in a truck crossing South Dakota.

Webern was, in fact, one of the chief influences on advanced music of the 1950s. Composers were fascinated by his intense, seemingly disconnected notes, with their flickering colors and their highly complex rhythmic relationship. Rhythmic relationships were now made more and more complicated. Musicians knew how to divide up a measure or a beat into 3, 4, or even 5 equal spans, but when composers also wanted divisions into 7, 11, and 13 and wanted these divisions to sound at the same time as some of the others, performers were in deep trouble. Machines were the only reliable means for getting the desired results.

Composers also investigated the idea of treating rhythm according to serial principles. Twelve-tone series had been used by Webern directly after the concept was introduced by Schoenberg in the 1920s. The early serialists established a fixed order of the twelve different *pitches* of the chromatic scale and held to this order with various modifications (inversion, retrograde, etc.) throughout a piece. The new serialists of the 1950s set up a fixed pattern of twelve different *note lengths* and held to this pattern with various modifications (running backward, speeding up, etc.) throughout a piece. This was a peak of the new intellectualism in music.

rhythmic series   In the example below, showing such a <u>rhythmic series</u>—twelve notes of twelve different lengths—the numbers below the staffs indicate the number of thirty-second notes that are equivalent to the notes above them:

This excerpt comes from a two-piano piece called, perhaps appropriately, *Structures*; it was written by Pierre Boulez, another of the important composers in the period following World War II. (He is also an important conductor; from 1971 to 1977 he was director of the New York Philharmonic.) An interesting forecast of rhythmic serialization occurs in the Inn Scene from *Wozzeck*, by Webern's friend and fellow-Schoenberg-student Alban Berg (see page 431).

CHANCE MUSIC

chance music   The most sensational new trend in post-1950 music was <u>chance music</u>. (Another term is *aleatory music*, from *alea*, the Latin word for "dice.") Composers threw dice or consulted tables of random numbers to determine which instruments, which rhythms, which pitches, and how many should be introduced— or how far the dials on electronic apparatus should be turned. Between measures x and y of certain compositions, performers might be directed to play anything that came into their heads. Compositions were written out on separate sheets of paper, which the performers were told to throw in the air and play in whatever order they happened to come down.

    Chance music is even harder to understand than rhythmic serialization— harder to understand and harder to take. The same sort of outrage that used to be occasioned by dissonance was aroused all over again in response to chance music. But, in his own way, the chance composer is groping toward a new vision of time, just as the rhythmic serialist is, although in exactly the opposite spirit. Time for the chance composer is formless, cannot be grasped or molded, lacks directionality and any sense of priority, progression, sequence, or cause and effect. Sound simply exists, whenever it happens to be experienced. One sound does not lead us to expect another. It is there for its own sake, not as part of a tune, an A B A form, a serial pattern, or any kind of time organization.

Electronic Synthesizers

The march of technology: electronic music generators of the 1950s and the 1970s. (We may reflect with a sigh that the typical instruments of our time are considerably less easy on the eyes than those of the past: compare page 199 etc.) Below is part of the venerable and, in its time, path-breaking RCA Electronic Synthesizer, which covers the walls of a whole room in a building in New York.

It is said that RCA pioneered this instrument in the vague hope of making union musicians obsolete, and indeed some commercial radio station "breaks" were composed with it. During the 1950s, this formidable, sprawling machine had a de facto monopoly on the electronic music written in the United States. In an analogous way, European electronic music was centered at electronic studios located in radio stations, which are, in effect, state-controlled mass media outlets. Stockhausen's *Song of the Children* was composed at the famous studios of Radio Cologne, and John Cage's *Fontana Mix* (see page 478) at Radio Milan.

Below is an instrument of the 1970s. Produced in several different models, the Moog Synthesizer is easily portable, easy to use, and not unduly expensive.

Chance composers are really rejecting our whole goal-directed view of time—getting up at the alarm, ten minutes for breakfast, on schedule for the bus, punch a time clock, waste time till coffee break, and so on. Rather, their vision is "timeless," like the sense of suspended time in an oriental meditation or under drugs. (This doesn't mean we have to belong to the Hare Krishna movement or take drugs to appreciate their music, any more than we have to be eighteenth-century Lutherans to appreciate the church cantatas of Bach.) This radically new consciousness, a static sense of time that goes against our goal-directed culture, lies at the root of chance music.

THE OLD AND THE NEW

The radical tendencies that have been outlined above received their impetus in the 1950s and had a free run in the 1960s. Avant-garde music of this period was often criticized as esoteric, academic, and written with no regard—indeed, with positive contempt—for an ordinary audience. Such charges were not new. They had been leveled at the uncompromising Arnold Schoenberg and the other members of the Second Viennese School, and even at members of the First. "Too many notes, my dear Mozart," the Viennese Emperor Joseph II is supposed to have said to that composer, as much out of puzzlement as disapproval, probably. "Exactly as many as necessary, your majesty," Mozart replied. It was a tactless answer worthy of Schoenberg himelf. Postwar avant-gardists such as Stockhausen and Boulez were not noted for their tact, either.

In music, like so many other aspects of human behavior, the 1970s witnessed a general retrenchment. Younger composers showed remarkable resilience in adapting elements of complex serialism and chance music into their styles, but they also did not hesitate to apply more traditional procedures in the same compositions. And somewhat older, more conservative composers, who had had a hard time getting much of a hearing twenty years ago, emerged from the shadows with impressive portfolios of work. The work of these composers, too, presents a striking mixture of old and new stylistic features.

It is too early to speak with confidence about the next main direction that music will be taking. (This is true, incidentally, of popular music today as well as "classical.") The 1980s are not starting out as an age that feels very sure of itself, in music or in anything else. What seems clear is that many composers are taking a new, hard, practical look at their relation to an audience—any audience—and are subjecting the exciting new developments of the 1950s and '60s to a tempering process. There are signs of a new neoclassicism and a new neoromanticism. We are witnessing, perhaps, another episode in art's age-old adaptation of new possibilities to old certainties.

KARLHEINZ STOCKHAUSEN (BORN 1928) *Gesang der Jünglinge* (Song of the Children) (1956)

Song of the Children is one of the early classics of electronic music. No score exists, only a master tape and its duplicates. Composed and engineered in 1955–1956, when Stockhausen was only twenty-seven, *Song of the Children* was just about as revolutionary in impact as the *Fantastic Symphony*, produced by Berlioz at the same age. Since then, Stockhausen has taken a rather lonely path, producing one extraordinary composition after another, most of them extremely difficult to perform. He is still one of the most significant forces among advanced composers today.

The piece takes its name from a hymn or canticle from the Scriptures, sung by three children of Israel who are saved by an angel of the Lord after having been thrown into a "burning fiery furnace" by King Nebuchadnezzar of Babylon (Daniel 3). (Was Stockhausen also referring to the furnaces that, in his boyhood, had been used by Hitler to wipe out the Jews?) This canticle, known to Anglicans as the Benedicite, runs in part as follows:

Preiset [or sometimes *Jubelt*] *den Herrn,*
ihr Werke alle des Herrn;
lobt ihn und über alles erhebt ihn in Ewigkeit. . . .

O all ye works of the Lord, bless ye the Lord:
Praise Him and magnify Him for ever. . . .

Preiset den Herrn, Sonne und Mond;
preiset den Herrn, des Himmels Sterne.

O ye Sun and Moon, bless ye the Lord;
O ye Stars of Heaven, bless ye the Lord.

Preiset den Herrn, alle Regen und Tau;
preiset den Herrn, alle Winde.

O ye Showers and Dew, bless ye the Lord;
O ye Winds of God, bless ye the Lord.

Preiset den Herrn, Feuer und Sommersglut;
preiset den Herrn, Kälte und starrer Winter. . . .

O ye Fire and Heat of Summer, bless ye the Lord;
O ye Cold and icy Winter, bless ye the Lord. . . .

Sometimes these words can be heard, but more often they are obscured. Like Debussy in *Sirens* (see page 421), Stockhausen treats the voice not as a carrier of meaning but more as a source of pure sound. First he made a tape of a choirboy singing parts of the canticle and speaking other parts. Then he manipulated the tape in the studio—duplicating it, filtering it, cutting it up, running it at different speeds, and superimposing it upon itself until it sounded like a whole choir of different boys singing. From another copy of the original tape he snipped out pure vowels and also pure consonant noises. These, plus the manipulated tape and products of an electronic generator, constitute the "sound materials"—we no longer speak of notes or scales—for his piece.

The whole thing was then spliced together as a five-track stereo tape. In concert performances, the loudspeakers are strategically located at different corners of the hall; the directional sound creates an indescribable effect. Stockhausen also made a simplified two-track version for home phonograph records and binaural broadcasting. As if this were not complicated enough, pitch, rhythm, and many other musical elements were worked out according to strict serial principles, something the listener cannot actually expect to hear. It must have taken dogged patience and endless hours of work to put this piece together in those days, when tape and sound-producing technology was much less refined than it is today.

Yet, in spite of the complexity, the piece does not sound all that complicated. If we listen to it a number of times, we gradually come to hear a number of distinct sections with a sense of progression between them:

Introduction The music begins with a dramatic gesture, as clear an announcement or summons to the listener as the beginning of any Viennese symphony. Then the superimposed voices are introduced in a kind of speedy chatter, together with the hums, bloops, whistles, and bell-like tones that seem to be characteristic of electronically synthesized sounds.

First Section The voices come at different speeds, speaking as well as singing. Thanks to stereophonic sound, they also seem to come from different directions and distances. There are watery sounds, windy sounds, and ringing echo-chamber effects.

"Slow Movement" After a long-held vowel note, this section begins to treat the song as a series of separate words and syllables, broken off sharply with silences between them. One passage may remind us of a night scene with crickets clicking away; it may even remind us of the weirdly beautiful pond music in *Wozzeck* (see page 433). Indeed, to the extent that the sounds come together as chords in *Song of the Children,* the harmony may remind us of *Wozzeck* in general. Every once in a while, this "slow movement" is interrupted by exciting loud splashes. It concludes with a slowly broken word "Win---ter."

"Climax" Next is a long section in which the rhythm is picked up considerably by short bloops from the synthesizer. They are utterly jerky, and whether or not they are controlled by rhythmic serialization, they negate any sense of meter. The voices now tend to come as quiet sustained screams—some not so quiet.

Thanks to the machines, the rhythm gets very fast; it is hard to follow it exactly, but the rhythmic feeling is strangely stimulating. A final "solo" scream ends dramatically in a long low hum.

Conclusion The music grows slower and more sustained; it definitely seems to be winding down and preparing for a cadence, though there are still a number of spasms to come. When the final cadence arrives—a rush of notes after a brief rest—it paradoxically gives all the feeling of rest that could possibly be asked for in a piece of this description. An old-fashioned "Amen" cadence would hardly fit after this particular canticle!

Stockhausen could not have devised a more effective, even brutal, way of depersonalizing his singer than by cutting up the voice and subjecting it to all these scientific manipulations. Yet, through all the contortions, we come to really know this boy; we may even find it easier to relate to his disconnected song of praise than to some of the more ordinary hymns produced by past composers. The Sanctus of Bach's Mass in B Minor (see page 240) is a magnificent piece, but are his baroque angels really speaking for us, as they chant their triumphant "Holy, Holy, Holy" around the throne? Brilliant and visionary in technique, impersonal and tentative in its expression of faith, the *Song of the Children* makes its own cool authentic statement for the present age of technology.

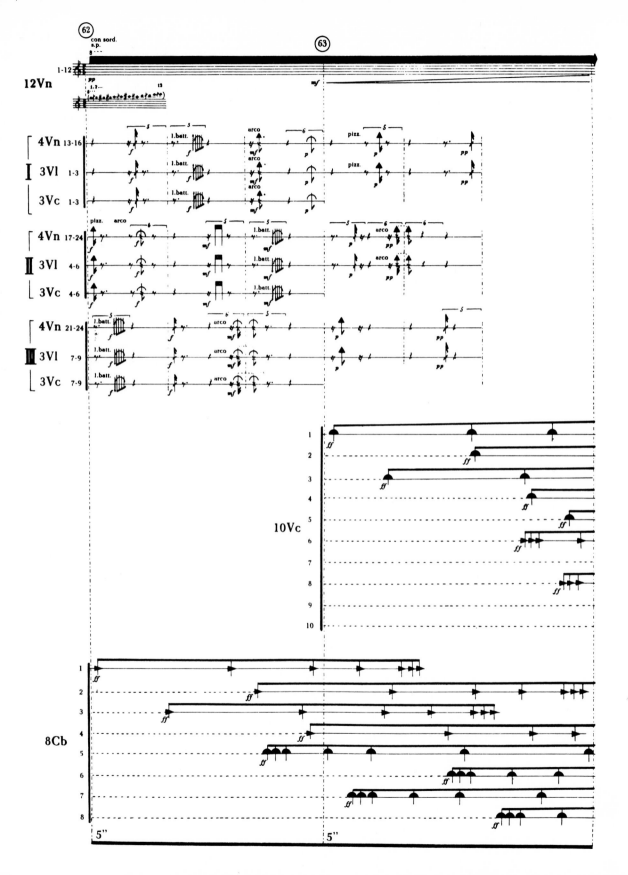

Musical Notation Today

The way people write things down depends on how they think. Systems of writing such as Egyptian picture script, or hieroglyphics, ordinary print, and punched computer input cards all reflect different styles of mental activity. Similarly, in music radically different styles call for radically different notation systems. With a little imagination, indeed, we can learn a good deal about music history simply by studying the history of musical notation as it has changed over the centuries.

For example, back on page 27 we saw that Gregorian chant notation specified the pitches, on a four-line staff, but it did not specify the lengths of the notes, the rhythm, or the meter. It did not need to, because this medieval church music was free in rhythm and had no concept of meter. Furthermore, the pitch range of the monks was modest enough so that four lines, covering an octave, were usually quite enough. Nobody dreamt of scores; the music was monophonic, involving one line only.

Then, from the baroque period to the middle of the twentieth century, musical notation remained essentially the same: pitch indicated by means of a five-line staff (or several staffs, when several instruments were to play) and rhythm and meter by means of whole note, half note, and quarter note signs and measure lines. But after 1950, when pitch and meter often went by the board, conventional notation proved to be hopeless.

Electronic composers often made no scores at all, only tapes. Other composers had to spawn a bewildering array of ad hoc notation systems, adapted to the individual composer or to an individual work.

To the left is a page of the score for Penderecki's *Threnody: To the Victims of Hiroshima*. Penderecki is still using a horizontal time scale (compare our elementary pitch/time graph on page 19), but instead of measures he marks off segments of time precisely in seconds (see the bottom of the score).

Pitch is rarely notated, since few exact pitches are heard in this piece. Instead Penderecki gets a great variety of new sounds by having violins and other string instruments play in thoroughly unconventional ways. For these, he had to make up a new notation, which is explained by the little table below, accompanying the score. (For violin terms, see page 460.) The thick line at the top is a graphic representation of the blurred, scratching-on-glass sound produced when ten violins play notes that are each a quarter tone apart between the high G and C. (This is spelled out on the small staff below the top.)

If you examine the cello and double bass parts (the latter marked *Cb*, for "contrabasso"), you will see something you will probably not hear: that this seemingly disorganized music is actually highly organized. There is one basic rhythm, consisting of seven pulses getting closer and closer, and this rhythm is staggered among the instruments, backward or forward. Compare Cb lines 1 and 5. This practice is related to rhythmic serialization, widely used in the 1950s (see page 463).

ABBREVIATIONS AND SYMBOLS

ordinario	**ord.**	highest note of the instrument (indefinite pitch)	▲	percussion effect: strike the upper sounding board of the violin with the nut or the finger-tips	
sul ponticello	**s. p.**				
sul tasto	**s. t.**				
col legno	**c. l.**				
legno battuto	**l. batt.**	play between bridge and tailpiece	↑	several irregular changes of bow	⊓ V
raised by 1/4 tone	⸸			molto vibrato	∿∿∿
raised by 3/4 tone	⸸	arpeggio on 4 strings behind the bridge	⋕	very slow vibrato with a 1/2 tone frequency difference produced by sliding the finger	∿∿
lowered by 1/4 tone	♭	play on tailpiece (arco)	✛		
lowered by 3/4 tone	ꝺ	play on bridge	✛	very rapid not rhythmicized tremolo	⨳

KRZYSZTOF PENDERECKI (BORN 1933) *Threnody: To the Victims of Hiroshima* (1960)

SIDE S–2

Something of the intensity and excitement of postwar developments in music is shown by their simultaneous adoption in places as different as the United States, Germany, Japan, and even Poland, behind what was then called the Iron Curtain. The new language for music went worldwide. In the 1950s people talked as though all countries in the Communist bloc followed the same policies, but this never made much sense as far as music was concerned. While the Soviet Union itself remained staunchly conservative and never let the new music in, Poland produced several interesting advanced composers. The best known is Krzysztof Penderecki.

The *Threnody* is written for a string orchestra that is sometimes divided into as many as fifty-two different parts. Penderecki is much interested in effects that can be obtained by new means of playing string instruments. Some of his special effects, and the new notation that he had to devise for them, are shown on page 468 (compare page 460). It is striking how much the strings can sound like electronic synthesizers—as though the faithful old dogs of symphonic music are striving mightily to learn new tricks.

Once again, *melody, harmony,* and *rhythm* are simply the wrong terms for talking about music of this kind. Penderecki deals in long patches of tone color, fascinating in themselves but connected to one another in relatively casual ways. The first patch consists of high, intense dissonances—real "space age" sounds. So many simultaneous different pitches are played in part of this opening patch of texture, including quarter tones between our normal chromatic notes, that the sound approaches white noise (see page 461).

Penderecki's second long patch consists of much blooping and skittering, with the strings sounding more like a shortwave radio or an electronic synthesizer than their ordinary selves. After about a minute, a pitch emerges and then dies away quietly. Patch 3 involves slow scooping sounds—like dense sirens—in the high, middle, and low registers, followed by steadier, harsher dissonant textures recalling those at the beginning of the piece. Patch 4, which is relatively short, begins with a series of definite notes that coalesce and swell up and down again into a single one, which lasts for a considerable time while wavering slightly. Patch 5 contains bloops again; perhaps here they feel like motives rather than flecks in the texture, for there is a real sense of climax about this lengthy passage. It culminates in (or, rather, explodes into) patch 6, a huge "chord" formed by all fifty-two instruments playing different pitches. They play all fifty-two of the quarter tones between the C below middle C and the C♯ above middle C (see page 471).

On pages 413–14 we discussed the relativity of the concepts of consonance and dissonance. A graph was used to help explain the idea. By now, the lines on the graph would have zoomed off the page; this wildly complex chord actually counts as a consonance, relative to the dissonances that precede it in *Threnody.* For on this sound the piece comes to rest, and in a sufficiently convincing fashion.

It is perhaps hard to see why any of the patches should go on for just the time they do rather than for a shorter or a longer time. Nonetheless, the piece

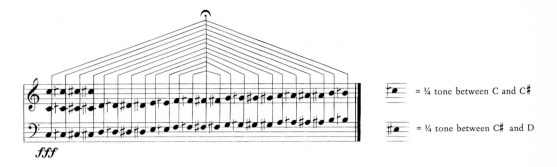

has a sense of form. As a climax, patch 5 is well placed just before the end, and patch 6 makes a good conclusion, as we have just said. Patch 1 sounds like a somewhat tentative version of patch 6; it balances patch 6 and therefore makes an appropriate beginning. So this piece has a beginning, a middle, and an end, which is what musical form has always been about.

As for Penderecki's title, to inquire about that is to ask all the old questions about program music that were raised on page 333. The piece hardly seems to express the grief, pity, or rage that might be expected in a threnody (a formal song of mourning). But perhaps that is the point: our age may be beyond pity and rage, beyond any feeling, when faced with an action such as the bombing of Hiroshima. Perhaps instead Penderecki has retreated into himself, preoccupied with "hearing the unhearable," just as the H-bomb strategists on both sides of the Iron Curtain are "thinking the unthinkable" as they project casualty figures in the hundreds of millions for World War III.

GEORGE CRUMB (BORN 1928) *Ancient Voices of Children* (1970)   SIDE 19

While Penderecki is exploiting new effects for a huge string orchestra—he also uses extraordinary new massed choral effects—other composers have been working at the opposite extreme, inventing chamber music sounds of equal novelty. Like Penderecki, the American composer George Crumb, who is a professor at the University of Pennsylvania, prefers not to work with electronic music. Instead he has devised new ways of playing an astonishing array of standard and nonstandard instruments.

Crumb is interested in delicate, echoing, resonating sounds, and like many other composers today, he is also much interested in oriental music. Thanks to such composers, Western music has for the first time employed large groups of percussion instruments with something of the subtlety known to the Far East. Harps, mandolins, specially treated pianos, and instruments of the "chimes" type such as vibraphones and marimbas create effects reminiscent of Indonesian gamelan orchestras (see page 55).

George Crumb has created his own unique new sound world—quiet, precise, vibrant, endlessly changing, a controlled musical kaleidoscope of fascinating elegance. In some other respects, his music is relatively conservative. Although his rhythms often become highly complex and although he likes to punctuate his pieces with vague, meditative silences, there is always a clear sense of direction in his music, a sense of beginning, evolving, and ending.

Thus all the songs in *Ancient Voices of Children* begin with the first lines of their poems and end with the last—which might be a ludicrously obvious thing to say about earlier songwriters, such as Schubert or Mahler, but no longer seems obvious today. In Stockhausen's *Song of the Children*, we have seen the text thoroughly chopped up and juggled around. The treatment of the text parallels that of the music in seeking to convey a whole new concept of temporal order.

Ancient Voices is a song cycle (see page 317) using verses by the great Spanish poet and playwright Federico García Lorca, who was murdered in 1936 during his country's Civil War. There is one main singer, a soprano, plus a boy soprano and seven instrumentalists. Besides a mandolin player, a harpist, a pianist, and an oboist, three percussionists manage some thirty different percussion instruments, including vibraphone, marimba, various gongs, cymbals, maracas, Tibetan prayer stones, and Japanese temple bells. Even the soprano and the mandolin player have to help out with the percussion, and in return the percussionists sometimes have to whisper or shout. In song No. 2, the mandolin player plays a musical saw with a violin bow. The pianist never uses a conventional piano, but instead plays either one that is amplified with contact microphones or else a little toy piano.

1. El niño busca su voz (The child is seeking his voice)   The cycle begins with a highly imaginative and arresting vocalise (see page 421), a fantastic cascade of cries, hums, warbles, musical coughs, and so on, for the soprano. A resonance effect (like an echo chamber, only more ghostly) is obtained by having her sing directionally into the piano, which is amplified and has the right pedal held down. Then she sings the first stanza of the poem, to a very "sprung" melody. The boy soprano, offstage, sings the second stanza, but his melody, though also "sprung," has a tantalizing faint air of Spanish folk song about it.

El niño busca su voz.	The child is seeking his voice.
(La tenía el rey de los grillos.)	(The king of crickets had it.)
En una gota de agua	In a drop of water
buscaba su voz el niño.	the child was seeking his voice.
No la quiero para hablar;	I do not want it for speaking with;
me haré con ella un anillo	I will make a ring with it
que llevará mi silencio	so that he will wear my silence
en su dedo pequeñito. . . .	on his little finger. . . .

There follows an instrumental interlude, *Dances of the Ancient Earth*, a solo for the oboe accompanied by oriental percussion sounds and karate shouts from the percussionists. The oboe keeps circling a few fixed notes, returning to them again and again. It may remind us of an Indian snake charmer's pipe.

2. Me he perdido muchas veces por el mar (I have lost myself in the sea many times)   The words of this short song are mostly whispered by the soprano through a cardboard tube, against the weird high sliding of the musical saw and the plunking of the amplified piano. Again, as in song No. 1, there is a haunting suggestion of folklike melody at the very end.

Me he perdido muchas veces por el mar
con el oído lleno de floras recíen cortadas,
con la lengua llena de amor y de agonía.
Muchas veces me he perdido por el mar,
como me pierdo en el corazón de algunos niños. . . .

I have lost myself in the sea many times
with my ear full of freshly cut flowers,
with my tongue full of love and agony.
I have lost myself in the sea many times
as I lose myself in the heart of certain children. . . .

3. *¿De dónde vienes, amor, mi niño?* (From where do you come, my love, my child?) No. 3 is a famous song from Lorca's great play *Yerma*. After another soprano vocalise, reminiscent of song No. 1, the three stanzas of the poem are performed in free strophic form over a steady bolero rhythm.

¿De dónde vienes, amor, mi niño?
De la cresta del duro frío.
¿Que necesitas, amor, mi niño?
La tibia tela de tu vestido.
  ¡Que se agiten las ramas al sol
  y salten las fuentes alrededor!
En el patio ladra el perro,
en los árboles canta el viento.
Los bueyes mugen al boyero
y la luna me riza los cabellos.

From where do you come, my love, my child?
From the ridge of hard frost.
What do you need, my love, my child?
The warm cloth of your dress.
  Let the branches ruffle in the sun
  and the fountains leap all around!
In the courtyard a dog barks,
in the trees the wind sings.
The oxen low to the oxherd
and the moon curls my hair.

¿Qué pides, niño, desde tan lejos?
Los blancos montes que hay en tu pecho.
  ¡Que se agiten las ramas . . .
Te diré, niño mió, que sí,
tronchada y rota soy para ti.
¡Cómo me duele esta cintura
donde tendrás primera cuna!

What do you ask for, my child, from so far away?
The white mountains of your breast.
  Let the branches ruffle . . .
I'll tell you, my child, yes,
I am torn and broken for you.
How painful is this waist
where you will have your first cradle!

¡Cuándo, mi niño, vas a venir?
Cuándo tu carne huela a jazmin.
  ¡Que se agiten las ramas . . .

When, my child, will you come?
When your flesh smells of jasmine flowers.
  Let the branches ruffle . . .

Crumb developed this unusual notation for this passage:

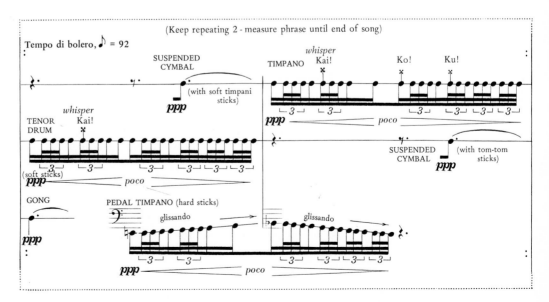

The driving bolero rhythm with its whispers or shouts, the wailing oboe, the growing stridency of the song and speech, the violent explosion at the end— this central song of the cycle is obviously the most powerful and gripping of them all.

4. *Todas las tardes en Granada* (Every afternoon in Granada) The steady underlying hum sounds electronic but is, in fact, obtained by two barely audible rolls on the marimba and a harmonica chord. The soprano sings, simply and (again) with a strange folklike air, two lines about the death of children:

Todas las tardes en Granada,	Every afternoon in Granada,
todas las tardes se muere un niño. . . .	every afternoon a child dies. . . .

There is no more text in this short song.

Then, most surprisingly, the toy piano quotes six measures by Johann Sebastian Bach, from a song about the acceptance of death, *Bist du bei mir* (If Thou abide with me). An "in" reference, no doubt, which not everybody will get, but there is poignancy enough in the symbolism of the toy piano—a child's toy—and in its pathetic tinkly sound. It is made to sound utterly dissonant in respect to the underlying hum, and it runs down like a clockwork toy without ever reaching the expected cadence note.

Another instrumental interlude, *Ghost Dance*, is a solo for mandolin. As played in a special way devised by Crumb, with a sliding glass rod, it sounds very much like a Japanese koto. The accompaniment consists only of maracas, South American gourd rattles.

5. *Se ha llenado de luces mi carazón de seda* (My heart of silk is filled with lights) Strong bell and vibraphone sounds punctuate the final song. The meandering, circling melody of the oboe recalls *Dances of the Ancient Earth.* At the very end of the piece, the boy, who has been offstage until now, is directed to walk slowly on stage, face the piano, and sing into it along with the soprano. They sing a vocalise that closely resembles the passage with which the cycle opened. Thus the piece ends with voices alone, as the whole impressive instrumental battery falls silent.

. . . Se ha llenado de luces mi corazón de seda,	. . . My heart of silk is filled with lights,
de campanas perdidas, de lirios y de abejas,	with lost bells, with lilies, and with bees,
y yo me ire muy lejos,	and I will go very far,
más allá de esas sierras, más allá de los mares,	farther than those hills, farther than the seas,
cerca de las estrellas, para perdirle a Cristo	close to the stars, to ask Christ the Lord
Señor que me devuelva mi alma antigua de niño. . . .	to give me back my ancient soul of a child. . . .

Lorca's beautiful poems tell of a child seeking his voice, but not for the purpose of speaking; they tell of the birth and death of children, and of adults' nostalgia for their "ancient voices of children." In song No. 3 the soprano spoke for the mother and the boy soprano spoke for the unborn child. At the end of the cycle, the boy has indeed found a voice, though not for speaking but for vocalise—a gesture of human communication below, or above, the level of speech.

With this occasional role-playing by the singers, the boy's "dramatic" entrance at the end, and the open invitation of the symmetrically placed dances (*Dances of the Ancient Earth*, bolero, and *Ghost Dance*), we shall probably respond eagerly to Crumb's suggestion on the score that *Ancient Voices* be performed in a theater version. Many of today's composers have experimented with "intermedia"—free-form combinations of music with dance, mime, speech, action, movies, light shows, whatever. Stockhausen has moved farther than Crumb in this direction, but the composer who has gone farthest of all is the one we next consider, John Cage.

John Cage (born 1912)

The most consistently radical figure of postwar music is a gentle, aging American named John Cage, the father of chance music (see page 463; Ives was the grandfather). Ever since the late 1930s, Cage has been asking questions that challenge all the assumptions on which traditional music rests. In words, and also in his compositions, he asks: Why should music be different from the sounds of life? Why "musical" sounds, rather than noises? For that matter, why any kind of sound at all, rather than silence? Why work out music according to melodies, climaxes, twelve-tone series, or anything else that gives the impression of one thing following another in a purposeful order? *Why not leave it to chance?* Why should a piece be the same the second time it is played? Why not play pieces—any pieces—simultaneously?

If we really start to think about them, these questions are so profoundly destructive of the music we know that perhaps it is just as well that Cage has always proceeded in a mild and humorous fashion. The simplest message that Cage has conveyed may be that we should open our ears to every possible kind of sound and every possible conjunction of sounds. Often, indeed, the actual sounds Cage produces are less successful than the "statement" he seems to be making *about* sounds, by means of the notions he develops for putting his pieces together.

Take *4' 33''*, one of Cage's most famous and provocative "works": it consists of four minutes and thirty-three seconds of silence (the piece has never been recorded—at least not intentionally). What Cage is saying is that silence is an entity, too, as well as sounds. When did you last really concentrate on silence? Try it. Was there *any* sound? And how would it feel to concentrate on silence for four minutes and thirty-three seconds, not three minutes or five?

Radio Music is performed by twiddling dials on eight radios according to a certain random plan, getting a mixture of talk, music, and silence, depending on what happens to be on the air at the moment. Cage may have been trying to recapture a not unfamiliar sound experience of modern life, the experience we get when we are out driving and keep punching buttons on the car radio in a random way, looking for a program we like. The sound is interrupted (again randomly) whenever the car goes under a steel bridge or passes a roaring truck. Many people would recognize the experience; few would think of it as organized music. Cage's "statement" is that music need not be organized, that all sound experience is equally interesting, equally music.

THE ARIA MAY BE SUNG IN WHOLE OR IN PART TO PROVIDE A PROGRAM OF A DETERMINED TIME-LENGTH, ALONE OR WITH THE <u>FONTANA MIX</u> OR WITH ANY PARTS OF THE <u>CONCERT</u>.

THE NOTATION REPRESENTS TIME HORIZONTALLY, PITCH VERTICALLY, ROUGHLY SUGGESTED RATHER THAN ACCURATELY DESCRIBED. THE MATERIAL, WHEN COMPOSED, WAS CONSIDERED SUFFICIENT FOR A TEN MINUTE PERFORMANCE (PAGE = 30 SECONDS); HOWEVER, A PAGE MAY BE PERFORMED IN A LONGER OR SHORTER TIME-PERIOD.

THE VOCAL LINES ARE DRAWN IN BLACK, WITH OR WITHOUT PARALLEL DOTTED LINES, OR IN ONE OR MORE OF 8 COLORS. THESE DIFFERENCES REPRESENT 10 STYLES OF SINGING. ANY 10 STYLES MAY BE USED AND ANY CORRESPONDANCE BETWEEN COLOR AND STYLE MAY BE ESTABLISHED. THE ONE USED BY MISS BERBERIAN IS: DARK BLUE = JAZZ; RED = CONTRALTO (AND CONTRALTO LYRIC); BLACK WITH PARALLEL DOTTED LINE = SPRECHSTIMME; BLACK = DRAMATIC; PURPLE = MARLENE DIETRICH; YELLOW = COLORATURA (AND COLORATURA LYRIC); GREEN = FOLK; ORANGE = ORIENTAL; LIGHT BLUE = BABY; BROWN = NASAL.

THE BLACK SQUARES ARE ANY NOISES ('UNMUSICAL' USE OF THE VOICE, AUXILIARY PERCUSSION, MECHANICAL OR ELECTRONIC DEVICES). THE ONES CHOSEN BY MISS BERBERIAN IN THE ORDER THEY APPEAR ARE: TSK, TSK; FOOTSTOMP; BIRD ROLL; SNAP, SNAP (FINGERS), CLAP; BARK (DOG); PAINED INHALATION; PEACEFUL EXHALATION; HOOT OF DISDAIN; TONGUE CLICK; EXCLAMATION OF DISGUST; OF ANGER; SCREAM (HAVING SEEN A MOUSE); UGH (AS SUGGESTING AN AMERICAN INDIAN); HA.HA (LAUGHTER); EXPRESSION OF SEXUAL PLEASURE.

THE TEXT EMPLOYS VOWELS AND CONSONANTS AND WORDS FROM 5 LANGUAGES: ARMENIAN, RUSSIAN, ITALIAN, FRENCH, AND ENGLISH.

ALL ASPECTS OF A PERFORMANCE (DYNAMICS, ETC.) WHICH ARE NOT NOTATED MAY BE FREELY DETERMINED BY THE SINGER.

FOR CATHY BERBERIAN

MILANO 1958

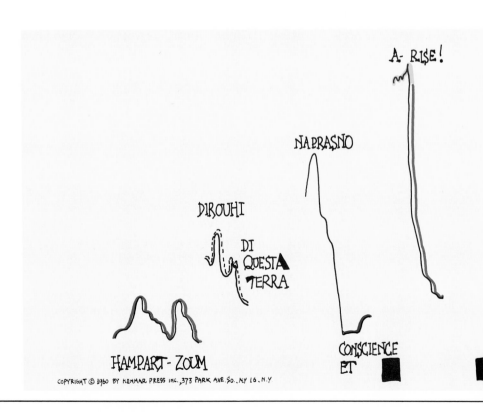

A Cage Score

John Cage is another modern composer, like Penderecki (see page 469), who invents all kinds of new notations for his music. The pretty score for *Aria* counts as "conservative" in that it still holds to general ideas of high and low pitch reading up and down and time reading from left to right. But nothing is specified exactly. Instead of clefs indicating the exact pitch level and measure lines marking the meter, Cage provides his own "key" in the long statement shown to the left.

Cage is also a very amusing lecturer and writer. His witty sayings have serious points behind them, or at least points that are serious to him. Here is one to think about: "When you get right down to it, a composer is simply someone who tells other people what to do. I find this an unattractive way of getting things done. . . ."

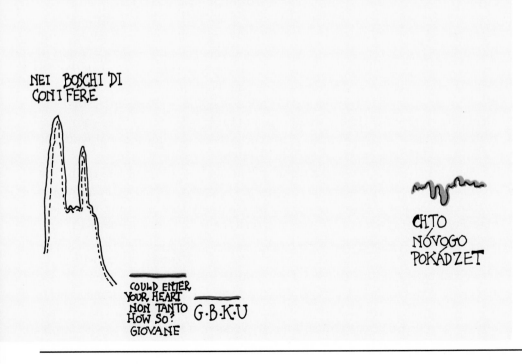

Aria is one of Cage's more conservative (!) pieces. It actually employs a score —a somewhat novel score, but one that is easy enough to grasp once the accompanying explanations have been digested (see pages 476–77). If you detect a note of put-on as you read these directions (and as you listen to the piece), you're probably not mistaken. One thing that Cage has worked tirelessly to oppose is the solemnity of traditional music-making.

Solemn or not, here is a table to show how the piece covers a range of composing techniques, from elements that are specified by the composer, to improvisation, performer choice, and chance:

Voice {	words	specified by composer
	pitch, rhythm	improvised by performer
	tone color	chosen by performer
Accompaniment		left to chance

Only with the words has Cage proceeded as a traditional composer would, by specifying them and specifying their order. (Since the words are nonsense, this does not make him all that traditional.) For pitch and rhythm, he gives neither notes nor measures but only very rough indications; these the singer follows in a general way, filling in the details according to her feeling of the moment. Here Cage is proceeding like a jazz composer, who writes out a tune with every expectation that the player will improvise around it.

In tone color, which is related to what Cage calls "style of singing," the performer chooses. She can pick any ten different tone colors or "styles" she likes, just so long as she sticks to them and changes from one to another as directed. (Again, this pattern of change is an element that is specified, but the piece would sound very different if someone chose dark blue to mean raga, black to mean growl, purple to mean Aretha Franklin, etc.) As for accompaniment, someone has to choose whether or not there is to be one. Cage goes so far as to suggest in a low-pressure way that one possible accompaniment would be an entirely different piece of his called *Fontana Mix*.

And if that hint is taken, the result will be random. *Fontana Mix* itself is an electronic and *musique concrète* (see page 461) piece composed according to chance procedures, procedures which we need not take the time to explain here. For however *Fontana Mix* is composed, the way it fits together with *Aria* is left entirely to chance anyhow.

A recording has been made of one version of the combination, with *Aria* performed by the brilliant singer for whom it was originally written, Cathy Berberian. (We give only a part of it on our record; Cage is one composer who will not mind if his compositions are abbreviated.) Obviously, dozens of other versions could also be performed. And any version, it seems safe to say, would turn up some sounds and some conjunctions of sounds that have never occurred to us before—as certainly happens with this one.

They never occurred to Cage, either; he did not "compose" them in the traditional sense of figuring them out in his ear ahead of time. Yet, without his complicated and whimsical array of chance, choice, and improvisation, these sounds would not have come into being. Some of them may strike us as arresting, others as dull and silly—though Cage would insist that each one is exactly as valid as the others. The totality has a reckless cuckoo quality that can come as a breath of fresh air in the stuffy atmosphere of much concert music.

Once again, the piece is making a statement. Perhaps it decodes like this: a woman singing in that highly artificial, singing-school style of voice production known as *contralto* is limiting her possibilities to a tiny (and solemn) fraction of those that exist in the sound universe. She can sing in ten styles, and, if she is Cathy Berberian, she can also sing in five languages. She can stomp and squeal and rattle, too. Berberian as she goes through life is going to get into many utterly unpredictable situations. Let her have an accompaniment—or not, as the case may be—that sometimes allows her to be heard and sometimes drowns her out, that makes her sound sometimes fascinating and sometimes silly. Life is unpredictable and full of surprises. Music should be, too. This is the philosophy represented by Cage and his music.

DANIEL LENTZ (BORN 1942) *Song(s) of the Sirens* (1975)   SIDE 20

Daniel Lentz, a Pennsylvanian, is a member of the generation that grew up on the music of Ives and Stockhausen. Of his compositions, one striking piece has been recorded that reflects many characteristic recent trends in musical composition. *Song(s) of the Sirens* takes its inspiration from the episode in Homer's *Odyssey* in which the ever-curious Ulysses has himself tied to a mast and rowed close to the sirens, after making his sailors plug up their ears and swear not to untie him. Ulysses thus becomes the only man ever to hear the sirens' song and not be seduced into a watery grave.

The slightly peculiar title of the piece refers to its construction. Basically it consists of a simple succession of ten sections, or "songs," as the composer calls them, each consisting of a few sounds only. They are designed so as to dovetail; when all ten "songs" are performed together, the eleventh long "song" emerges as the totality of the others.

The words are treated in the same way. Each "song" takes certain isolated phonemes, that is, the smallest basic units of sound in the language, from this beautiful poetic fragment of the *Odyssey:*

> Listen to our voices,
> Listen to the music which sounds from our lips, sweet as honey,
> Let the lovely tones touch your heart and the melodious song dissolve your
>   innocence:
> Listen, Ulysses.

The first "song" takes the phonemes LI from the first word, CE from the fourth, EN from the fifth, LI again from the thirteenth, and so on. (This one of the "songs" is called *Listen.*) Other "songs" extract other phonemes that form other words or phrases.

Action Painting

The American artist Jackson Pollock was called an "action painter" because he operated by standing over his huge canvases and flinging or dripping paint on them. Some viewers, needless to say, were incensed at being presented with random paint patterns. There is a certain analogy between action painting and chance music, though Pollock's *Wooden Horse,* shown here, dates from 1948, before even John Cage was launched on his career as a chance composer.

Pollock deliberately gave up full control over the exact appearance of his picture in certain areas in order to obtain qualities of force, spontaneity, excitement, and sheer vitality that painstaking draftsmanship could never match. Chance composers do something similar, and they do well if they get such stunning effects as Pollock's.

Notice the toy horse head of wood that Pollock glued to the side of his painting. If this technique, called *collage,* incensed people at the time less, it was only because they had gotten used to it from the works of Pablo Picasso and other famous painters during the period around World War I. Again there are analogies—and again they are not precise—between collage and certain techniques in post-1950 music. Consider *musique concrète,* the process of taping natural sounds, such as train noises or whale songs or waterfalls, and piping them into electronic compositions (see page 461).

Another analogy can be drawn between collage and the quotation of preexisting music in certain contemporary pieces, such as George Crumb's *Ancient Voices of Children,* with its toy-piano quotation of Bach's song *Bist du bei mir* (see page 474). Crumb also quotes from one of Mahler's symphonies in that work.

Jackson Pollock, The Wooden Horse   90 × 178 cm: Moderna Museet, Stockholm

The "songs" are performed successively, as we have said, but they are not performed alone. After the first, the second is heard together with a replay of a tape that has just been made of the first. After the second, the third is heard with an instant replay of the second plus the first, and so on. This results in a slow, fascinating process that might be described as accretion, until by the time of the eleventh "song," we at last understand the total text and hear the total melody. Half sung and half spoken, the phonemes now coalesce into words and sentences. Up to this point the accompaniment has been for piano and cello; now the clarinet enters for the first time to play the total melody.

How different the accretion of the "songs" in Lentz's composition feels from other kinds of time-processes that we have experienced in other music! It is not like music built out of matching and answering phrases, or developing motives, or even a theme followed by variations. Time stops for Ulysses as he strains to hear the sirens' mysterious insinuating song.

The integral use of electronic means, the atomization of the poem, the slow accretion process that risks monotony, even the faint whiff of linguistics, today's important new field of intellectual inquiry—all these mark *Song(s) of the Sirens* as a work very much of our time. On the other hand, there are traditional elements that would probably not have occurred in a composition of this sort written in the 1950s or '60s. Composers of the 1970s, as we remarked above (see page 465), tended to absorb all the new means of the postwar period into their personal vocabularies, but they also tended to return to more traditional aspects of music-making. The cello in Lentz's piece, though restricted to atomized fragments of melody, seems always to be seeking for its characteristic romantic voice. The whole is bathed in an impressionistic ebb and flow of watery piano arpeggios.

Song(s) of the Sirens draws together many of the threads that have been running through this book: or, to put it more fairly, we can use the piece to draw together many of those threads. To begin with, its first word, whose phonemes are repeated again and again throughout the eleven "songs," is one we have developed a special commitment to. Lentz's subject matter, furthermore, is the seductive power of music, which is why we are all here in the first place.

In a striking way, *Songs(s) of the Sirens* recalls two important early twentieth-century compositions that we examined in the preceding chapter. To compare it with Debussy's *Sirens* is to illuminate in a flash the change in sensibility that has occurred over the last seventy-five years. Debussy's sirens are a male fantasy—delicious but, in the last analysis, as childish as Renoir's picture (see page 418). Lentz's sirens are a mature threat.

Pierrot Lunaire, too, resonates in Lentz's composition, as it does in so many other chamber music works with voice that were composed in the second half of the century (see page 423). His instrumental combination—cello, piano, clarinet—is one of those that comes out of Schoenberg's multicolored, flexible instrumental group, and his singer, too, does not actually sing but rather engages in what could be described as a sort of *Sprechstimme*. Yet it is an entirely nonexpressionistic *Sprechstimme*, a reinterpretation of Schoenberg's enormously powerful idea of "speech-song" into contemporary American terms.

The monumentally simple cadence at the end of Lentz's piece—a sort of long melodious electronic rattle—is a new solution to what has become a perennial problem for composers of our time, how to end a composition persuasively and expressively. A cadence is like a frame, separating a work of art from ordinary existence—a painting from a plain wall, a piece of music from unarticulated time. Lentz's cadence owes a good deal to one we have heard before, at the end of Penderecki's *Threnody.*

Song(s) of the Sirens also pulls in an unexpected thread from a part of this book that is yet to come. In an intriguing transformation, Lentz catches the quality of American popular music of the 1960s and '70s in this work. The tone of voice, the simple harmonies, some of the atomized melodic fragments, the whole impassive repetition or accretion process—all these facets make the piece understandable in a way that few works of the 1950s were. It is unquestionably American, just as *Pierrot Lunaire* is inexorably Viennese and Debussy's *Sirens* eternally French. The relationship between popular and "classical" music will be treated in the two final chapters of this book. As we shall see, this relationship becomes especially interesting in twentieth-century America.

CHAPTER 15 | Popular Music   I

Popular Music   I

When we think of popular music, the first thing that comes to mind is music that belongs to here and now: disco, country, rock, maybe the latest hit, maybe our own personal favorites. In each of these cases, popular music means first of all music of the present, widely heard and easily accessible. If we take a little time, remembering back (let us say) to the early days of Elvis Presley, we can call up a picture of the sweep of this music over a period of twenty-five years or more. Still, even with this broader view, there doesn't seem much question about what popular music *is*. We also know what it is not. It is not, we would certainly agree, any of the music covered so far in this book.

In fact, no one would be very likely to use the term *popular music* instead of just *music* unless, subconsciously at least, he or she was contrasting it with some other kind. Let us not call this other kind "unpopular music"—because it is unquestionably popular with a respectable number of people—but rather *nonpopular,* music that is enjoyed by rather less than 100 percent of the population. Classical music, this is usually called (not a good name, but about the only one available).

What is the real basis for the distinction? Popular music is enjoyed by the great majority of people, we might think, whereas classical music appeals to special, favored groups. Highly educated people might form such a group, or the rich who have the leisure and opportunity to cultivate complicated tastes. It is a firm thesis in American folklore that the symphony and the opera exist as playgrounds for upper-crust snobs. To this day, opening night at the Metropolitan Opera is a caper for certain segments of New York society, and especially for society women. In the old comic strip "Bringing Up Father," Jiggs likes nothing better than a game of poker at the corner saloon, but his wife Maggie is always dragging him off to fancy teas, art shows, and concerts.

The trouble with this easy picture of popular and classical music is that when we really think about it seriously, it starts to disintegrate. The whole question of elites, to begin with, is a slippery one in today's society. There are many elites—the millionaire class, the wealthy, and then just the comfortably off. One prominent elite group that we are familiar with consists of young Americans who get to spend several of their postadolescent years at colleges; but they don't all go for classical music. Some rich people support the local symphony and the opera, if these exist in their communities, while others throw away the yearly appeals and spend their time and money on golf or politics. Similarly, there are many different audiences for popular music.

It is true that contemporary classical music—the music of Stockhausen, Crumb, Lentz, and the others discussed in chapter 14—is still largely directed to an intellectual and artistic elite. But this is no longer true of all earlier classical music. Egged on by the record companies, an impressive number of people in nearly all income groups now buy classical records; some classical recordings sell into the millions. True, this year many more people will listen to certain popular musicians, at concerts or by means of records and cassettes, than will listen to Beethoven. But if we look back to last year, and ten years ago, and if we look forward to next year, it is likely that over the long haul Beethoven will win more hearings than any popular composer, performer, or group of any era. In short, classical music includes some that is circulated and enjoyed at least as widely as some popular music.

TIME AND PLACE

As for popular music, it is worth asking the question: popular with whom? Think of China; it is easy to imagine that millions of Chinese people have their music, and also easy to imagine how different it must be from ours.

Or suppose we try going back in time. You sometimes catch a forty- or fifty-year-old movie musical on late night television. Though the music on the sound track does not resemble popular music today, you can readily understand that it was popular then.

If there was popular music fifty years ago, what about a hundred years ago? What about two hundred, five hundred years ago? We seem to have come a long way from our first snap association with disco, country, and rock.

It is perhaps surprising that there is no generally accepted definition of popular music; nevertheless, that is the case. Of course the word *popular* does mean "pleasing to many people." But the word also carries an idea of fun; it implies a certain lightness, an easy accessibility, a notion of something not to be taken too seriously. There is even something paradoxical in the notion that popular art needs to be studied. To be sure, a popular musician or artist may very well *deserve* to be taken seriously. The sad clown in the circus may be a mime of tremendous skill, an artist who projects a profound feeling of human haplessness and sorrow. The circus act is not designed to have the effect of a Shakespeare play, however, and neither the clown nor the circus manager expects the audience to be moved to tears.

We have been trying to suggest that popular music is not as straightforward a concept as it first appears. But if it cannot be precisely defined, it can usually be recognized. By looking for such signs as its distinction from nonpopular music, the breadth of its audience, its easy appeal, and its gratifying tone, we will be able to examine some of the manifestations of popular music through the ages.

The history of popular music, like the definition of the term, is bound up closely with that of nonpopular or elite music. We shall find, therefore, that most of the facts and concepts needed to understand this history are ones we have already introduced earlier in this book. So the following overview of past popular music can also serve as a sort of shadow review. We shall be interpreting the material a little differently, however, and filling in some new details. An important concept to introduce is that of folk music.

Folk Music

Folk music is one of the eternal components of Western music history. This is so because folk music flourishes most naturally in a rural environment, and until recently Europe and America were essentially rural societies.

So is the rest of the world to this day. The great mass of people live on the land, growing crops and cultivating herds, or, more likely, keeping just a few animals. Life centers around the struggle for food. Simple, anonymous music grows up in such societies, music that is not written down but rather passed on over the generations from father to son, from mother to daughter. The term *folk music* — folk music applies to music of this kind and, in a strict definition, only to music of this kind. Genuine folk music still existed in rural pockets of the United States up to and during the twentieth century.

Primitive societies use music in a wide variety of social contexts; recollections of such uses are still present in the music we all know. Songs are associated with rituals such as weddings, wakes, and birthdays (we still sing *Happy Birthday*). Songs celebrate the seasonal changes that count for so much in rural living (a Christmas carol such as *Deck the halls with boughs of holly* suggests by its words that originally it had less to do with Christianity than with a winter seasonal rite). Strongly metrical songs eased communal work such as spinning yarn and churning butter and cheese; powerful work songs emerged from the Southern chain gangs in the early part of this century. Shepherds and herders had music of their own, sometimes incorporating the cries or instrument calls they used to control their flocks. The American West in the nineteenth century could not exactly be called a primitive society, but the cowboys who sang *Git along, little dogies* were living under conditions of enforced primitivism. There were children's game songs, and, as one got older, courtship songs and the large, important category of folk dances, many of them also for courtship.

ballad — Another important type of folk music is the ballad. Ballads are songs that tell a story, rather than just expressing a sentiment. Instead of simply talking about love, as so many modern popular songs do, a ballad would tell how a great lady fell in love with a gypsy and rode away with him. Instead of talking about depression, as the blues do, a ballad would relate how a young man sickened and died as a result of being rejected:

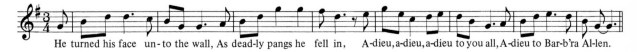

He turned his face un-to the wall, As dead-ly pangs he fell in,   A-dieu, a-dieu, a-dieu to you all, A-dieu to Bar-b'ra Al-len.

Narration of this kind required many stanzas—sometimes very many indeed —sung over and over again to the same tune (strophic form: see page 314).

While rural communities remained basically unchanged, folk ballads such as *The Raggle-taggle gypsies* and *Barbara Allen* were sung in much the same way from the late sixteenth century in England to the early twentieth century in Appalachia.

Folklorists have recovered some 200 versions of *Barbara Allen.* The most familiar version, shown above, has probably been housebroken; notice the tidy sequence in its third phrase. You may prefer the next version, in $\frac{5}{8}$ time, sung by an English folksinger in 1913:

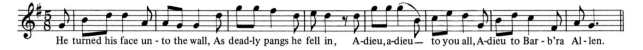

He turned his face un - to the wall, As dead-ly pangs he fell in, A-dieu, a-dieu— to you all, A-dieu to Bar - b'ra Al - len.

The Middle Ages and the Renaissance

Any attempt to indicate something about the history of popular music in medieval Europe at once runs into a great problem. We know so little about music at that period, except music of the Christian Church. The names of church music composers that have come down to us from the fourteenth century and earlier can be counted on the fingers of one hand; we certainly know of no composers of popular music. Before the troubadour songs of the twelfth century no secular music has survived at all. What we do know is that people all over the world have always had music. The peasants of the Middle Ages must have developed folk music.

Admittedly, we are groping in the dark as we seek for traces of this. Folk music in its natural state is never written down. The first English folk songs we have any record of, for example, come from the sixteenth century. But fair inferences, from several sources, can be made about earlier folk music. One can extrapolate back from the folk music that survives from somewhat later times. One can make comparisons with other, non-Western cultures that are analogous, still intact, and open to study by anthropologists. And one can make educated guesses on the basis of relics of presumed folk music embedded in the elite music of the time.

CROSSOVERS

crossover

The elite music of the Middle Ages and the Renaissance was first of all the music of the Church and then, after around 1100 A.D., that of the courts. We have discussed the great tradition of Gregorian chant, the development of polyphonic masses and motets, the troubadour songs, and their descendants the French chansons and Italian madrigals. From our present standpoint, the interesting thing is that, almost from the start, infiltrations of folk music can be detected in these elite traditions. Crossover is a term we shall use for folk elements that turn up in elite music, as well as for elite elements that turn up in folk music. First evident in the Middle Ages, crossovers are one of the great constants of popular and elite music up to the present day.

Tarlton and the Jig

The little man with the twinkle in his eye is Richard Tarlton, the greatest stage comedian, clown, stand-up comic, and court jester of Elizabethan England. It is thought that Shakespeare was influenced by him in creating the role of Bottom in *A Midsummer Night's Dream*, the irrepressible ham actor who wanders into fairyland to find himself with a donkey's head on his shoulders. Tarlton was famous for ad-libbing verses on subjects proposed by members of the audience, and he was the only person who could "undumpish" Queen Elizabeth when she was in one of her bad moods.

Tarlton also introduced or popularized an interesting kind of popular musical theater called the jig. The word *jig* usually means an Irish dance, ancestor of the gigue of the late baroque suite and distant ancestor of the banjo jig of the American minstrel show. But the theatrical jig was a little act that was danced, mimed, and sung to the words and music of a well-known ballad. The jig provides another example of the age-old alliance of music and the popular theater.

Tarlton would sing a ballad such as *Singing Simkin*, for example, probably playing every other verse or else simple ritornellos on his pipe and tabor (the small drum, also known as *tambourin*; we heard one in the pavane on side 2 of our record). Meanwhile he and other actors would caper their way through the story: the clown Simkin makes love to an old man's wife, hides in a chest when Bluster comes in on the same errand, tries to buy his way out of a difficult situation with a quart of sack (sherry), and ends up with a thrashing. Jigs were regularly performed after serious plays, even tragedies, so that the audience would leave the theater in good spirits.

Like many entertainment figures of later years, Tarlton went into the tavern business and opened two pubs in London. He came to a bad end, but his jokes were published and republished as *Tarlton's Jests*. Shakespeare is supposed to have had Tarlton in mind when he made Hamlet ruminate sadly on the skull of the jester Yorrick.

Among the medieval examples we have encountered are the tuneful hymns of the Gregorian chant tradition, the dancelike estampies for instruments, and perhaps also some aspects of that genial round *Sumer is icumen in.* Some, but not all aspects: it is unlikely that folk elements ever crossed over without at least some alteration. With the estampies, for example, we are of course fantastically lucky that they were written down at all—but that very fact suggests that in the form we have them they were no longer playable by any simple country fiddler. If there are folk dances in the background, as seems probable, it is also probable that their edges have been smoothed over by some enterprising composer of organa or motets.

It is not hard to see the reason for these crossovers. People have simple tastes before they develop more complicated ones, and an artist who makes an appeal to the familiar is always on strong ground. It would also be a mistake to imagine that all the members of the medieval courts had refined taste in the arts. Many barons must have ordered their jongleurs to sing and play simple folk music rather than elaborate polyphony. Many more of them must have preferred best of all the music of hunting horns.

Probably the most astonishing crossover of the whole Renaissance period was the use of the fifteenth-century song *L'homme armé* as the basis for polyphonic masses (see page 119). All the church composers of the day wrote masses based on this popular secular tune, which was probably not a folk song, but a recent song that had been composed in the style of one. The *L'homme armé* masses were not popular music, of course. Just the reverse: they were composed for a very small elite, that of other church musicians who could appreciate the ingenuity with which the tune was treated in each new version.

Folk elements are also evident in Renaissance chansons such as Josquin Des Prez's *Scaramella*—here some folk poetry crossed over, too—and *Petite camusette* (see page 117). The latter is especially interesting because chansons of this kind incorporate songs that we know belonged to the popular theater of the time. Here we have early evidence of another of the great constants in popular music, its natural association with popular entertainments of one kind or another. Plays, parades, carnivals, and in later centuries minstrel shows, vaudeville, and the movies, have always provided a fertile soil for the growth of popular music.

The Baroque Period

The link between popular music and the popular theater was strengthened by the invention of opera at the beginning of the baroque period. As we pointed out in discussing Monteverdi's *Orfeo,* the earliest operas, around 1600, were court entertainments, put on by princes (see page 167). But in 1638 the first public opera house opened, to be followed quickly by many others—in Venice, then in other towns in Italy, and finally in the rest of Europe. This in itself was a sign of significantly increasing urbanization. Opera became a popular art for the city dweller, analogous in some ways to the movies of later times. The fact that opera included an interesting story and marvelous stage effects as well as music made it all the more popular.

The analogy to the movies is not exact, for public opera still owed a good deal of its support to aristocrats, gentry, merchants, and bankers. Peasants who came to town on market days still found their entertainment in street theater and tavern diversions, not in the opera house. For the leisured urban classes, however, the opening of public opera theaters made a great difference. Instead of waiting for a neighboring prince to invite him to attend an opera, now a gentleman bought a subscription of his own. He would not want to criticize his host's entertainment—after all, it was put on by the prince's own court musicians—but he would not hesitate to make his tastes clear to the free-lance composers who wrote the public operas that he paid for directly. In short, with the popularization of opera, market conditions entered music more directly than ever before.

The contrast between Monteverdi's early court opera *Orfeo* and his late, public operas is indicative. Although *Orfeo* contains some agreeable tunes (we heard one, Orpheus's song to his lyre), the emphasis is on passionate recitative and choruses. In Monteverdi's late operas, more and more simple tunes occur. Soon opera in all countries depended more and more on simple tunes, and on displays of beautiful voices and virtuoso singing. This is what the opera public liked, and this is what the composers supplied.

The tunes were not folk songs, any more than the singers were folksingers. New tunes were composed for every new opera by sophisticated professionals. There was, however, a kind of massive crossover effect, in that composers to some extent imitated the folk music that they knew would be familiar to their audiences. They added something of their own, of course, and the best of them could be said to have led or set public taste, within certain limits. One way or another, what they were all working to create was a kind of urban popular music that would bring people back again and again to the box office.

The same composers wrote differently for nonopera audiences. Significantly, baroque musicians are the first who speak about the different styles in use for the music of their time. There was nothing popular about the Purcell Trio Sonata that we studied on pages 184–88, and Purcell did not mean it to be popular; this piece was addressed to other musicians and performers, principally. In Purcell's theater pieces, there is a much more insistent popular note. When we leave the theater after a performance of his opera *Dido and Aeneas,* we may be moved most of all by Dido's dying lament, but the music we will remember to hum is the Sailor's song or one of the other catchy light numbers.

Handel is an instructive case. We have seen how he could adopt a popular tone in his music for an unusual mass entertainment, the great fireworks display celebrating the end of the War of the Austrian Succession in 1749 (page 220). This was enjoyed by an enthusiastic audience of 12,000. But Handel could not quite maintain the same popular tone in his operas—and they failed. For this the responsibility falls mainly on a minor poet called John Gay and an unassuming, impudent work known as *The Beggar's Opera.*

The Enraged Musician

This is the title of a satirical engraving by the eighteenth-century artist William Hogarth, showing a classical musician frustrated by the music of London's streets. He covers his ears in despair as a boy beats a drum, a man grinds a knife, another blows a horn—he is a sow gelder—and a comely milkmaid sings out her street cry. Here is one that was used at the time:

Will ye have an-y milk, maids?

At the left a haggard ballad seller is singing her ballad, entitled *The Lady's Fall.* A street musician squawks away on a baroque oboe, whose nasal tone quality is certainly indicated in a graphic way.

Like the artists of certain comic strips today, Hogarth always meant his vivid, amusing pictures to convey serious (often moralistic) messages. We can take *The Enraged Musician* as a pointed commentary on the conflict between sophisticated and popular music, an issue that was on the minds of Hogarth's contemporaries as a result of the *Beggar's Opera* affair (see page 493). Inside, the little violinist has delicate features and an elegant wig; outside, everything is plain and earthy. It is not hard to see where the artist's sympathies lay. Perhaps, too, there is a reason why the violinist does not just slam down his window and shut out the noise. Perhaps Hogarth wanted to suggest that classical musicians must always listen, even if with half-covered ears, to the music of the people. Classical music must periodically renew itself and draw strength from popular sources.

Is it farfetched to read all this into a comic picture? Musical Londoners would have recognized the enraged musician as a certain Piero Castrucci, longtime leader of the local Italian opera orchestra. And the poster on his wall, whose details can hardly be made out at this reduction, is a playbill of the time announcing "The Sixty-Second Day: THE BEGGARS OPERA. Macheath by Mr WALKER, Polly by Miss FENTON . . ."

JOHN GAY AND JOHN PEPUSCH *The Beggar's Opera* (1728)

ballad opera

The Beggar's Opera is a spoken comedy interspersed with simple songs. Gay selected well-known songs of the day and wrote witty new verses for them to fit the dramatic situations; such a work is called a ballad opera. The sources of the songs are thoroughly diverse. Some are folk ballads such as *Greensleeves* and *Over the hills and far away,* known to everyone at the time, humble or highborn, in town or in country. There are also some theater songs by Purcell and even (adding insult to injury) a march from Handel's great hit, the opera *Rinaldo* (see page 224).

The story tells of the dashing highwayman Macheath and his "doxies," as he calls them, Polly, Lucy, Jenny, Suky Tawdry, Molly Brazen, and the rest, all drawn from London's lowlife. A pair of hypocritical rascals, Mr. and Mrs. Peachum, run a flourishing business in fencing and procuring, all shown with a considerable amount of vivid detail (in English slang, to "peach" means to inform or "sing"). *The Beggar's Opera* was a general satire on contemporary morals and a particular satire on the current prime minister, Sir Robert Walpole, and his wife and mistress.

It was also a devastating parody of Handelian opera. Audiences who had once applauded Handel, and had grown tired of him, flocked to *The Beggar's Opera.*

All of its seventy-odd songs are short, and most are very simple. See if you can sing the three examples given here. The first is Lucy's jealousy "aria":

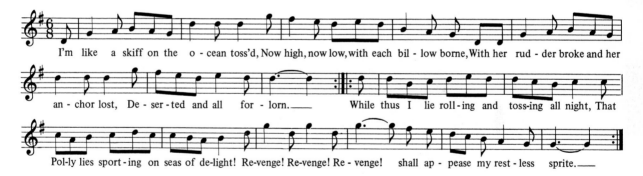

Sometimes the songs have attractive instrumental interludes, as this philosophical number by the gin-soaked Mrs. Trapes does:

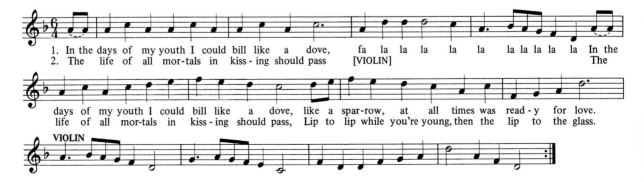

And sometimes they are divided among different characters, so as to reflect the stage action. This catfight between Lucy and Jenny in front of Macheath is an example:

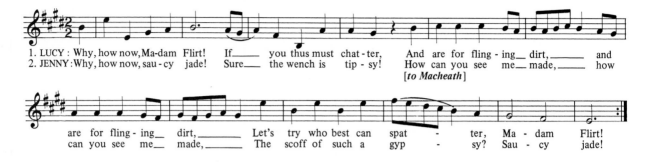

1. LUCY : Why, how now, Ma-dam Flirt! If_____ you thus must chat-ter, And are for fling - ing_ dirt,_____ and
2. JENNY:Why, how now, sau-cy jade! Sure_____ the wench is tip - sy! How can you see me_ made,_____ how
[to Macheath]

are for fling - ing_ dirt,_____ Let's try who best can spat - ter, Ma - dam Flirt!
can you see me_ made,_____ The scoff of such a gyp - sy? Sau - cy jade!

The orchestration of *The Beggar's Opera* was entrusted to John Pepusch, an immigrant German musician, like Handel himself. Pepusch also composed an overture for the occasion, a parody French overture (see page 180). Its second half contains an amusing fugue with Lucy's jealousy "aria" as subject.

The Viennese Period

The fluid approach toward popular and nonpopular composition that we have observed in baroque composers such as Monteverdi, Purcell, and Handel continued in the Viennese period. We have pointed out that a distinguishing characteristic of the new style was an emphasis on simple tunefulness, symbolized by the inclusion of a minuet—a simple dance, basically—in nearly every Viennese symphony and string quartet (see page 250). Originally a court dance, the minuet was now the most popular dance in ballrooms patronized by the middle classes. Whereas the main source of popular music in the baroque period was the theater, in the Viennese period the main inspiration was social dancing.

Besides the minuet, there were two other main social dances in the late eighteenth and early nineteenth centuries. The *contredanse,* in $\frac{2}{4}$ time, was descended distantly from the English country dance, a folk dance of the general variety of the square dance. The *Deutscher Tanz,* or German dance, in $\frac{3}{8}$ or $\frac{3}{4}$ time, was an ancestor of the *Ländler,* itself an ancestor of the waltz. The waltz became the most popular dance of the nineteenth century, a Viennese specialty from the time of Schubert on. It captivated the whole world and was imitated by every European and American composer of popular music.

Mozart, Haydn, and Beethoven wrote hundreds of these dances. They were commissioned by the dozen by Viennese ballrooms. One of Beethoven's contredanses crossed over with a vengeance to saturate the last movement of one of his most advanced and revolutionary works, the *Eroica* Symphony. Besides dances, Haydn and Beethoven also wrote hundreds of folk song arrangements, which sold briskly thanks to their names on the title pages. Schubert in his short lifetime wrote more than 400 minuets, ländlers, waltzes, and so on (for piano; Schubert did not score them for orchestra or dance band).

We have commented on Mozart's genius as an opera composer in combining vivid dramatic action with beautiful, instantly attractive melody (see page 266). Don Giovanni's seduction duet with Zerlina, "Là ci darem la mano," became one of the hit songs of the 1780s. Even Beethoven thought of writing some variations on it; years later, Chopin and Liszt actually did. There is also an amusing place in the act II finale of *Don Giovanni* that underscores the continuing popular aspect of opera in this period. Don Giovanni is shown at dinner, waited on by Leporello and entertained by a little stage band (a forerunner of Musak in our restaurants, perhaps). The musicians play songs from operas by Mozart's rivals, each identified by Leporello, who is stealing food behind his master's back. Finally they come to the favorite number from Mozart's own opera *The Marriage of Figaro*, which had been the great success of the previous season. The original audience must have roared, and audiences today still smile as Leporello makes a face and says he certainly knows *that* one, and then sings bits of it with his mouth full.

Romanticism

During the nineteenth century, rural folk music continued much as it always had (except that now musical peasants were sometimes greatly surprised by visits from city people wanting to write down their folk songs). But that was about all that stayed the same. If the baroque period saw the first major change in the history of popular music as a result of the invention of opera, the romantic period heralded a second, even greater change.

We can point to three factors that contributed to it. The first was demographic: the population explosion and the accelerating urbanization caused by the Industrial Revolution. It is estimated that between 1750 and 1800 the population of Europe went up by 25 percent, between 1800 and 1850 by 42 percent, and between 1850 and 1900 by another 50 percent. And while in 1750 the bulk of the population was rural, in 1900 the majority lived in towns. The urban audience for music, which was growing so spectacularly, also grew much more insistent about the kind of music it wanted.

A second factor that affected popular music deeply was a psychological one. This was the new attitude toward artistic creation that was promoted by romanticism. Artists no longer regarded themselves as craftsmen serving society, as Bach and the other baroque composers had done, but rather as free spirits writing for themselves, expressing their souls with a genius not granted to the common run of humanity. It was not the composer's job to write down to the public. The public had to work to keep up with the composer. Many people at the time deeply admired the music of Beethoven's last period while admitting they did not fully understand it: surely a first in the history of musical taste.

Composers in the main romantic tradition now began to make increasing demands on the listener, demands both intellectual and emotional. It was really Beethoven who started this, with his heroic aspirations and effusions in symphonies such as the *Eroica* and the Fifth. Schumann edited a magazine attacking the simple music of his time and demanding a more elevated tone from composers. When Wagner called his music "the Music of the Future," he was serving notice on "Listeners of the Present" that they would have to strain in order to understand his complicated message. Nineteenth-century symphonists wrote longer and longer symphonies that hypnotized listeners and drained them emotionally.

Not everybody chose to play in this particular ballgame. Many people with money to spend on music preferred to support composers who were ready to cater to simpler tastes, and who were able to bring a good deal of skill and talent to the task. A sharp distinction between "serious" and "light" music did not exist in the days of Handel or Mozart. It was a by-product of romanticism, of the attitudes and ambitions (and pretensions) of the romantic composers.

OPERETTA

This distinction even extended to opera. In the first half of the nineteenth century, opera continued to supply Europe with popular songs. Melodies by the main early romantic opera composers, mentioned on pages 354–55—Rossini, Donizetti, Bellini, and Weber—were known to all; melodies by Verdi, such as "La donna è mobile," are still known to all today. Wagner changed all that. He certainly wrote operas that in many ways are more impressive than any others, but he ruined opera as a popular art, at least outside of Italy. As operas grew more serious and even philosophical under his influence, a new type of light opera sprang up alongside of "grand opera," as it now began to be called, and siphoned off a good portion of its audience. Nineteenth-century light opera is

operetta   called operetta.

Operettas always have humorous—and very often frivolous—plots that come to a happy ending, and they always employ spoken dialogue in between the musical numbers, rather than recitative. Light, attractive tunes were the stock-in-trade of the new breed of operetta composers: Johann Strauss in Austria, Jacques Offenbach in France, Arthur Sullivan in England, and Victor Herbert in the United States (*Babes in Toyland*, 1903; *Naughty Marietta*, 1910—the titles alone give a good idea of the frivolousness of this genre). From here it is only one step to the musical comedy or "musical" of the 1920s.

Thus a split formed in musical life that is still with us today: on the one hand, popular composers writing for a popular audience; on the other hand, "serious," "classical," "elite," "nonpopular" composers—none of the terms is quite satisfactory—writing for an audience that was also rather more specialized than before. There *is* a satisfactory term for this new audience, however: we can now refer to it as the *concert audience*. These people were prepared (indeed, they liked) to sit still and listen to music for relatively long stretches of time. Except in church, where there was no choice, and in the opera house, where there was a lot to look at as well as listen to, this had not been the case before. The concert audience had a strong commitment to music—stronger,

Minstrel Shows

Popular music of all ages is associated with the popular theater—and most kinds of popular theater are inconceivable without music. In the 1840s a new kind of semitheatrical entertainment grew up in the northern cities of the United States, the minstrel show. Its basis was a stylized comic vision or parody of black life and character. This was served up as a sort of variety show consisting of songs, dances, instrumental numbers, jokes, and comic skits, performed by white men (never women) in blackface, using gawky gestures and the broadest of broad dialect accents.

Minstrel songs ranged from the raucous to the sentimental. Southern Negroes were supposed to joke about possums and blue tail flies, and northern Negroes were supposed to yearn nostalgically for the old plantation. But some diluted strains of genuine black folk music were carried over into these songs. The rhythmic features of ragtime and early jazz were foreshadowed by the main type of minstrel dance, the banjo jig. The banjo, the minstrel's favorite instrument, came from the plantations and ultimately from West Africa.

Our playbill shows what two bits would get you by way of entertainment in New York in 1859. Among other things advertised is a medley of "popular Ethiopian airs," a "Local Banjo Song," and the premiere of that most famous of all minstrel numbers, *Dixie*. Notice also the "Burlesque Italian Opera" with such characters as Mlle. Pickle Hominy, Count no-Count MacCaffery, and Signor Houlihan Stuffhisowni. Popular art often parodies the more elevated genres (such as Italian opera) that it has grown up in reaction to.

As for the parodying of supposed Negro traits, which is at the very heart of the minstrel show, that has been described (by whites) as "good-humored." Maybe so. But black Americans today are not likely to take a kind view of the minstrel tradition, even though it shows that the nation was already finding black musical sources more interesting and valuable than any others. It is a shaming fact about the American popular theater that many of its genres have been built squarely on exploitation. The minstrel show was one such genre; burlesque was another.

probably, than do many of its descendants who listen rather casually to classical records today.

We have spoken a number of times of the rise of concerts, from the eighteenth century on, and their effect on the consumption of music and types of music composed. The institutionalization of concerts in the nineteenth century is the third major factor that contributed to the popular music revolution of the time. It formalized the breach between popular and elite music in a decisive way.

THE NEW COMPOSERS OF POPULAR MUSIC

To examine representative members of the new class of popular music composers, we can do no better than start with the famous Strauss family of Vienna. (They are no relation to the Munich family of Richard Strauss, composer of symphonic poems: see page 383.) Johann Strauss, Sr., has been called the "Father of the Waltz"—misleadingly, for Schubert, among others, had already written excellent ones. Strauss began his career in the 1820s playing in Viennese dance bands, and soon formed a group of his own, consisting of three violins and double bass. A brilliant popular violinist, he mesmerized great crowds as he played his own compositions—waltzes mainly, but also other social dances of the day: polkas, galops, and quadrilles. He rose to the position of bandmaster to the Vienna militia regiment and also became conductor of the Viennese court balls.

Strauss tried unsuccessfully to stop his son, Johann, Jr., from becoming a musician, but the future "Waltz King" set up a band in competition with his father and eventually outstripped him in popularity. He toured as far as the United States, where he gave the first Woodstock-size popular concerts in this country—fourteen concerts in Boston for 100,000 people each. For this he got $100,000, in gold and in advance, plus all expenses. His brothers Josef and Eduard were also composers, but they seldom tried anything other than dance music; Johann Junior, however, branched out in the later part of his life to operettas. Not surprisingly, some of the best numbers in the Strauss operettas are written in waltz time.

In the United States, the most talented and beloved composer of popular music was Stephen Foster, who died in the last year of the Civil War, 1864. He was our first widely successful songwriter. Most of Foster's songs are sentimental numbers such as *I dream of Jeanie with the light brown hair* and *Beautiful dreamer.* Their lineage can be traced back to earlier English songs such as *Home, sweet home,* and beyond that to popular opera songs, and ultimately to folk songs. Foster also wrote minstrel songs (see page 497), among them *Oh! Susanna, De Camptown races,* and *The old folks at home. The old folks at home (Swanee River)* was popular indeed; it sold forty thousand copies of the sheet music in the first year of publication alone.

In England, Sir Arthur Sullivan presents a striking case of a composer who assiduously cultivated both popular and elite styles. He is remembered today for his unique series of operettas composed to librettos by the comic poet W. S. Gilbert, from 1875 to 1896. Gilbert poked dignified fun at various features of

Victorian society: the Royal Navy (*H.M.S. Pinafore*), the Houses of Parliament (*Iolanthe*), and fashionable young ladies' enthusiasm for refined poets such as Oscar Wilde (*Patience*). And Sullivan in his music poked fun at the serious musical theater of his time. He did this by imitating the style of Verdi and Wagner at moments in his operettas that were not serious in the least. Apart from "in" references of this kind, Sullivan's music is uncomplicated and tuneful, a perfect foil for the very clever and amusing (and frequently outrageous) rhymes of his collaborator.

Sullivan regarded himself primarily as a "serious" composer, however. He wrote a solemn grand opera on Sir Walter Scott's *Ivanhoe,* oratorios, string quartets, and so on. These are forgotten today, but they received ample recognition in the England of his own day. It is unlikely that he would have received a knighthood from Queen Victoria if he had done no more than contribute to the satirical "Gilbert and Sullivan operettas."

JOHANN STRAUSS, JR. (1825–1899) *Voices of Spring* (1883)   SIDE 20

Many of the famous Strauss waltzes, such as *The Beautiful Blue Danube* and *Tales from the Vienna Woods,* are substantial compositions in which a set of dances is preceded by an orchestral introduction, not in waltz time. Essentially the same arrangement is used for all Strauss waltzes, including some that amount to suites taken from his operettas, somewhat like Lully's seventeenth-century suite from an opera-ballet (see page 180). Whether derived from an operetta or composed independently, a Strauss waltz always consists of several distinct waltz numbers which are played consecutively, preceded by some kind of introduction and concluded by a coda.

Voices of Spring, a shorter piece than most, opens with just eight measures: a little flourish and then a vamp (see page 279). The first waltz, in A B A form, has an upward rushing figure which seems to have inspired the composition's title. Then follow two other waltzes, skillfully contrasted in melody, rhythm, and key—the modulations between them are quite obvious—so that although the waltz lilt keeps going throughout, the music always seems doubly fresh and interesting. After the third waltz, a coda brings back part of the first waltz, some new ideas, and the rushing figure to make a brilliant conclusion.

Discussing baroque dances, on page 180, we pointed out that they all have their own special rhythmic features. Besides being in triple meter, waltzes tend to have a slight subsidiary accent on the third beat: ONE two *three* ONE two *three,* etc. The second waltz number of *Voices of Spring* exaggerates this effect by putting a heavy accent on many of the "three" beats and skipping the "ones":

This is a striking (but, for waltzes, characteristic) example of *syncopation*—that is, displacement of a melody's main accents away from the normally accented beats of the meter (see page 8).

ROMANTIC NATIONALISM: A POSTSCRIPT

On pages 385–89 we examined the nationalist movement in nineteenth-century music. Many late romantic composers incorporated folk elements in their symphonies, operas, and program music pieces; sometimes actual folk songs were used as themes, at other times merely the melodic, harmonic, or rhythmic traits of a nation's folk music. Chopin absorbed the characteristic accents of Polish dances into his piano music; Moussorgsky depicted a self-consciously Russian picture gallery in music. Two of the most important early twentieth-century composers, Stravinsky and Bartók, relied heavily on their native folk music for the formation of their musical styles.

We can now see nationalism as another massive example of the crossover process, like many others in centuries before and after the nineteenth. Sophisticated music had often fortified itself by ingesting popular music, and would do so again. The main difference lay in the quasi-political aim behind nationalist music, that of promoting a sense of national identity by blending the music of the concert hall with that of the "folk."

One wonders what the "folk" themselves would have thought of all this, if they had been able to hear any nationalist music. They would have been amused or bemused, probably, if they had been able to view the whole matter without anger. Some of them were listening to a new, unmusical voice, that of Karl Marx, urging them to seek their sense of identity not in their nation but in their class. It was all very well for prosperous audiences and intellectuals to get a warm feeling by building musical bridges to the "folk," but the peasants and the factory workers had nowhere to go along those particular bridges.

One of the sturdiest warhorses of the nationalist movement (though it is probably time to let the poor nag out to pasture) is the *New World* Symphony by the Czech composer Antonin Dvořák, written during his extended stay in this country during the 1890s. The symphony was supposed to incorporate American Negro themes. What did Negroes think of this? Nothing, for few of them heard the piece, and those who did would scarcely have recognized themselves in it. Their *real* music, which they loved and treasured, and which was a part of them, had nothing to do with the concert hall. Years later, when social conditions had changed greatly, this love was turned into a source of national pride and identification. But the transformation was done by blacks, on black terms, and within the sphere of black popular music. In the United States in the 1960s, a new kind of nationalist music was initiated by the "folk" themselves.

CHAPTER 16 | Popular Music II

Popular Music II

The revolution in popular music was initiated by romanticism, as we have seen. It accelerated in the twentieth century at a dizzying pace. As "serious" concert music grew more and more esoteric, it grew less and less capable of filling the needs of the mass market for music. Popular music filled this need.

Around the turn of the twentieth century, furthermore, the demand for music began to expand very significantly. The poorer classes were becoming more affluent; indeed, class and financial barriers at last started to crumble in many countries. One by one, powerful new technologies were developed for the dissemination of music to the mass market: phonograph records from 1900 on, radio from the 1920s, sound movies from the 1930s, and ultimately television. It is no wonder that, in the twentieth century, popular music has grown so phenomenally in importance, variety, and artistic vitality.

And since social barriers crumbled fastest and technologies developed farthest in the United States, it is also no wonder that American popular music has assumed a dominant position in the world.

These were not the essential reasons, however. The most sophisticated technologies and marketing techniques known will not make people sing along and tap their feet to music they find stale and flabby. Our music gained its power from a unique amalgam of European and African or Afro-American sources. Without the infusion of elements from black music, American music would probably still be a pale imitation of European. Without its fusion with European music, Afro-American music might never have spread broadly to white America, let alone beyond our shores. But the amalgam proved an instant formula for international success. Today the telltale marks of American music have spread around the world.

They had already spread a long way by 1928, when a young German composer named Kurt Weill made a modern version of *The Beggar's Opera* by John Gay (see page 493) with music composed in his own brilliant and inimitable imitation of 1920s jazz. *Die Dreigroschenoper* (*The Threepenny Opera*—a more idiomatic translation might be *The Two-Bit Opera*) had a libretto by the great communist playwright Bertolt Brecht, who used it mainly not to satirize contemporary morals, as Gay had done, but rather to attack the capitalist system. So when Weill paid his ironic respects to the United States by adopting the accents of American jazz, he simply added to the bite. People were shocked by the combination of "sick" words and bland, sweet music in the operetta's theme song, "The ballad of Mack [for Macheath] the Knife." The piece later became a hit in a record by the great American jazz trumpeter and singer Louis Armstrong (see page 514).

The influence of American popular music abroad reached its peak in the 1960s, the era of rock. This was the heyday of an extraordinary and extraordinarily successful English rock group called the Beatles. The famous "Liverpool sound" of the Beatles, deeply influenced by American rock 'n' roll of the 1950s, came back to the United States from Britain and deeply influenced the course of popular music here.

In rock, like jazz, the characteristic marks of American popular music are rhythmic ones. Our popular music of the early 1900s did not sound very different from anyone else's as far as melody and harmony were concerned. But it was performed in a rhythmic style that was truly new, one that made a clear break with traditional concert music, and with earlier popular music too. This rhythmic style stems from American black music, and ultimately from Africa. We should discuss it first in general terms, before examining specific genres of American popular music.

THE RHYTHM OF AMERICAN POPULAR MUSIC

Since the nineteenth century, popular music in the United States has always been deeply involved with black folk music. Not only have American blacks evolved very vital genres of their own, but ideas from black music have also been taken over and modified by white musicians for the white mass audience. This happened in one way or another with minstrel music in the nineteenth century (see page 497), with ragtime and jazz in the early twentieth, and with rhythm and blues in the 1950s. The whole process can be regarded as enrichment or as a type of exploitation, depending on your point of view. It is also true that on another, perhaps deeper level, the process shows up an instinctive community of feeling among blacks and whites, a common national fund of musical response.

We should take a moment here to review the concepts of rhythm, meter, and accent introduced on pages 5–8. The new rhythmic style involved a special kind of *syncopation*. Syncopation, remember, is a term for the displacement of some of the main accents away from the normal metrical beats of the measure. In $\frac{4}{4}$ meter, for example, the normal accentuation is ONE two *three* four. Simple syncopation, sometimes called <u>metrical syncopation</u>, displaces the accent of the melody from the first and third beats to the second and fourth —one TWO three *four*.

metrical syncopation

Metrical syncopation occurs occasionally in all or almost all music. The Viennese waltz composers had learned how it could impart an irresistible lilt to popular dance music (see page 499). Black American music used a lot of syncopation of this simple kind, but that was just a beginning. It also developed syncopation of a more subtle kind, called <u>beat syncopation</u>. Here many of the accents are displaced *just a fraction of a beat* away from the normal metrical beat, or from some other clearly defined position in the measure.

beat syncopation

The process is not easy to describe and quite impossible to indicate accurately in musical notation. Equally impossible to specify is how the tone is controlled on instruments and on the voice so as to accentuate or even simulate beat syncopation. But the effect is immediately familiar to us. The melody picks up a lively yet easy drive, the basic regular meter seems to get a new springy quality, feet are set tapping and fingers begin snapping involuntarily. When this happens, the music is said to *swing.* And according to most people's rather loose definition, music that swings in this way means some kind of jazz.

jazz

That is *not* a strict definition of jazz (we will get to one on page 511), but this usage is so general that it would be pedantic to mount objections to it. In any case, the loose usage goes back to the earliest days of jazz. The 1920s were called the "Jazz Age" because all the popular music of the time was perceived to be "jazzy"—the musical comedy show tunes of George Gershwin as well as the New Orleans improvisations of Louis Armstrong. The "swinging" quality of American music unquestionably found its finest development in true jazz, but the quality is something we have to reckon with in discussing other genres of American popular music also.

Musical Comedy

Throughout the ages and throughout the world, the popular theater has always provided a fertile soil for the growth of popular music. America, once the Puritan spirit had subsided somewhat, proved no exception. Modern American popular music can be traced back to the thriving New York theatrical scene in the decades around 1900.

We have already mentioned the very successful operettas of Victor Herbert (see page 496). Some of their songs are still remembered, faintly, today: *Ah sweet mystery of life, I'm falling in love with someone,* and *Tramp, tramp, tramp.* Irish born and German trained, Herbert modeled his work on the European operetta tradition. Indeed, a suspiciously large number of the biggest Broadway successes in those days came from abroad. Gilbert and Sullivan operettas were the rage of the 1890s (to the exasperation of the authors, who had trouble collecting American royalties). In a later period, one of the most influential of all Broadway runs was *The Merry Widow (Die Lustige Witwe),* an excellent Viennese operetta in the Johann Strauss tradition by Franz Lehár. *The Merry Widow* is still frequently performed today; its famous waltz took New York by storm in 1907.

revue

Across the street from these relatively elevated entertainments, Broadway played host to a succession of revues whose stock-in-trade was music, but whose chief attraction was sex. A revue is a musical show without a coherent plot, which presents a series of different numbers—songs, dances, comedy acts, etc.—rather like a slightly organized vaudeville show. The frankly smutty burlesque shows were a type of revue, while uptown the Floradora Girls, the Gaity Girls, the Gibson Girls, and many others made their effect by undressing as far as was prudent or legal.

Song and Dance Man

Musicians like to talk about opera as though it were chiefly a matter of music, or at most music and drama, but from its beginnings around 1600 opera has always depended heavily on visual display also. In the seventeenth century, the designers of opera scenery—moving scenery, ingeniously constructed to yield amazing transformation scenes and the like—often got top billing, ahead of the composers and librettists. Nineteenth-century French audiences would not abide opera without ballet inserted. And American musical comedy was built not only on good songs and good jokes but also on dancing: by the inevitable chorus girls, and by lead actors who danced as well as sang.

Thus *Lady be Good,* the Gershwin show which introduced the songs *Lady be good, The man I love,* and *Fascinating rhythm,* owed much of its success to a young song and dance man called Fred Astaire, here shown with his sister Adele in a then-famous soft-shoe number from this musical. Praised by the ballet dancer Baryshnikov as one of the greatest dancers of all time, Astaire also sang in a pleasantly cracked voice and charmed three generations of Americans with his cool courteous good humor.

In the 1930s and '40s Astaire starred in a famous series of movie musicals. Audio amplification was good for his voice, and various spectacular studio effects put his dancing (and that of his partners Ginger Rogers, Cyd Charisse, and others) in a brilliant setting. Indeed, musicals were about the most popular and lucrative of Hollywood products in those years. For buffs, the greatest of all movie musicals is *Singin' in the Rain* (1952), featuring another song and dance man, Gene Kelly, also a distinguished choreographer. Our illustration from this film gives some sense of Kelly's extraordinary dynamism as a dancer.

In the 1940s, increasing sophistication marked all the elements of musical comedy—the staging and the dancing, as well as the plots and the music. A key work in this development was Richard Rodgers's *Oklahoma!* (1943) with a full-scale ballet by the American modern dance choreographer Agnes de Mille. So far from smothering the musical in culture, de Mille's ballet contributed significantly to its phenomenal success, lending new life to the stage genre at a time when it was under a serious threat from the movies.

BETWEEN THE WARS

It was only after World War I, however, that the American popular theater picked up its characteristic accent. It was a musical accent, and this came from jazz. True, musical comedies of the 1920s did not actually incorporate jazz as we shall define it and discuss it in the next section of this book; but Broadway audiences could not have cared less about strict definitions. The characteristic syncopation and swing of jazz were enough. Played by white theater bands and assimilated into the songs of the 1920s, this jazz accent was the one feature that contributed more than any other to the flourishing state of musical comedy in the years between the two World Wars.

It was a golden age of popular song. Among the songwriters were Jerome Kern (*Smoke gets in your eyes, All the things you are*), Irving Berlin (*Alexander's Ragtime Band, Easter parade, White Christmas*), George Gershwin (*Embraceable you, Summertime*), Richard Rodgers (*My heart stood still, Where or when*), and Cole Porter (*Begin the beguine, Night and day*). Each of us may not know each of these songs, but our heads are full of songs of this general kind, songs written in this period.

Most of them were written for musical comedies. Tin Pan Alley, as the song-writing and song-plugging industry was called, produced many songs outside the theater, too. But the theater provided composers with an extra fee and gave songs invaluable exposure and publicity, which was never quite equaled by sound recordings, the radio, and (after 1926) "talking pictures." Hearing a song sung in a real situation, by a "real" person—even though musical comedy plots were often artificial in the extreme—gives it a special vivid point and a special attractiveness.

In the 1920s, musical comedy plots were often topical but not often distinguished. Revues kept going, nuder than ever—the *Ziegfeld Follies of 1907, 1908,* on up to *1931,* the *Music Box Revues, Bare Facts of 1926, George White's Scandals,* and others. Some even had some fine tunes (George Gershwin's *Somebody loves me* in the 1924 *Scandals*). In the 1930s, the level of musical comedies improved to a considerable degree—and, significantly, revues dropped off in popularity. Gershwin's *Strike Up the Band* (1930) was a daring antiwar satire, and his *Of Thee I Sing* (1931) a hilarious parody of the American political system (still hilarious, for the system hasn't changed all that much). When Kurt Weill, the composer of *Die Dreigroschenoper* (see page 503), came to this country as a refugee from the Nazis, the times were ready for more sophisticated plots and music. Weill's *Lady in the Dark* (1941) took psychoanalysis as its subject. But this tendency toward greater sophistication waited for its fulfillment until after the second World War.

GEORGE GERSHWIN (1898–1937) *Fascinating Rhythm* (1924)   SIDE 20

We looked at tunes at an early stage of this book, when first discussing melody (see page 20). A good tune exhibits qualities of unity and variety, has a satisfying climax, balances its phrases in an elegant and delightful way, and so on. This is just as true of Gershwin's tunes as of those by Schubert or Verdi.

Popular songs consist of a *chorus*—the main song—preceded by a less important (and less memorable) *verse*. The verse is usually 8 or 16 measures long, the chorus almost invariably 32 measures, arranged in one of two forms.

The first form is A A', each letter referring to a 16-measure section. The second is a a b a (or some variant, such as a a' b a''), each letter referring to an 8-measure section.

Lady Be Good, one of Gershwin's first successful musical comedies, contained several great hits: the title number, *Lady be good* (in a a b a' form), *The man I love* (a a' b a'), and *Fascinating rhythm* (A A').

In *Fascinating rhythm* the verse is, as usual, not very memorable. But Gershwin skillfully makes it contrast with the chorus in order to make the latter seem all the more fresh when it comes. The verse is in the minor mode and employs dotted rhythms; the chorus is in the major and uses a motive consisting of undotted eighth notes.

It is Gershwin's highly ingenious deployment of this motive that gives the song its charm: the motive with its same notes is made to start at four different positions in the measure. This sets up an unconventional, irregular pattern of syncopations, as indicated by the sforzato (>) marks on line 2 of the score below (the marks have been put in parentheses because the singer doesn't have to sing louder on those notes; they automatically receive an accent on account of the repetition factor). Line 1 of the score shows a conventional phrase that Gershwin did *not* write, built out of the same motive. If you sing this through you will come to appreciate his own lively version all the more.

In the second part of the A section (measures 9–16), Gershwin stabilizes things with a new passage in a simpler rhythm, and the melody, freed from its intricate syncopation pattern, soars up to high F in measure 14. Notice the conventional jazz syncopation on the notes D in measure 10 and F in measure 14, shifting the accent back from the third beat. In measure 12, where the words are in parentheses, the music sounds parenthetical, too. Jazz players often improvise little interludes, called breaks, in between phrases. Gershwin's measure 12 is a vocal imitation of a jazz break.

breaks

The A' section begins like A, but the second part is compressed (measures 25–28). The feeling of climax on the high F in measure 27 is increased by the compression and by a fresh harmony. The compression also leaves room for yet another reference to the "fascinating rhythm." At last this seems to have stopped picking on our flapper—for in measure 30 the more conventional syncopation on the note C dissipates the teasing irregularity and allows for a satisfactory, solid cadence.

The dizzy words, by Gershwin's brother Ira, a very skillful writer of song lyrics, fit the music perfectly. *Fascinating rhythm* is a theme song for the Jazz Age, an age of skyscrapers, short skirts, and bootleg gin, fascinated by the new swinging sound of American popular music.

MUSICAL COMEDY AFTER WORLD WAR II

There are some eternal verities in the popular musical theater. Turn-of-the-century burlesque and the risqué revues of the 1920s found their counterparts in the sexually explicit revue *Oh! Calcutta,* which opened to gasps in 1969 and was still playing in New York ten years later. But while *Oh! Calcutta* is much dirtier than any of the *Ziegfeld Follies,* it is also much smarter and more sophisticated. In this it is typical of at least one tendency of postwar musical comedy.

Sophistication was evident in the staging of the musicals (see page 507), in their plots, and also in their music. Kurt Weill wrote *Lost in the Stars* about racism in South Africa as long ago as 1949. Leonard Bernstein, in *West Side Story* (1957), updated *Romeo and Juliet* into a contemporary love story. Bernstein's boy and girl belong not to great families locked in a vendetta, as they are in Shakespeare's play, but to rival teenage gangs from different ethnic groups in New York. For the rumble (street fight) between these gangs, Bernstein—who is also a classical composer, a symphony conductor, and an important writer on music—wrote a highly effective fugue. However, the musical adaptation of Shakespeare that had the greatest success was the resolutely sexist *Kiss Me, Kate,* Cole Porter's masterpiece of 1948 (from *The Taming of the Shrew*).

Naturally, there were efforts to write musicals using the new popular music of the 1950s and beyond, rock. The first of these, *Bye Bye Birdie* (1960), was about an Elvis Presley figure. Later came *Hair* (1968) and *Jesus Christ Superstar* (1971). Yet it is a striking fact that musical comedy in the 1970s stuck pretty much to songs in the old style—not rock, not jazz, but "jazzy" numbers that Gershwin and Cole Porter would have recognized, despite various new sophisticated features. This is evident in the songs of the latest Broadway nightingale, Stephen Sondheim, although his works cannot bear comparison with the best products of the golden age between the wars.

Jazz

Jazz is a remarkable performance style that grew up among black musicians around 1910 and that has gone through a series of more and more remarkable developments, decade by decade, until the present day. We shall trace just a few of these, through representative records of some of the greatest practitioners: New Orleans or Dixieland jazz of the 1920s (Louis Armstrong), big-band jazz of the 1930s (Duke Ellington), and bebop of the 1940s and 50s (Charlie Parker).

True jazz involves not only "swinging" syncopated rhythm, but also the idea of *improvisation.* Jazz soloists do not play a song the way they hear it or see it written down on paper. They always improvise *around* a song, adding brilliant high notes and elaborate runs, embellishing the main notes of the melody, and adding little interludes, called *breaks* (see page 509), of their own spontaneous invention. They perform, in fact, impromptu *variations* on the basic material. With its own modern American accent, jazz employs a much-used musical form that we have seen in various periods of the past (see pages 201, 283, 306, 398).

Jazz players sometimes—especially in recent times—vary a song so freely that the melody is disguised beyond recognition. However, the basic harmonies of the song are played in the background by instruments such as piano, organ, vibraphone, or guitar. These, together with a bass instrument, drums, and percussion, make up the so-called rhythm section of a jazz band. The harmonies it plays provide a framework that guides the other players in their flights of fancy and also helps the listeners to orient themselves.

rhythm section

Not only do jazz players develop imaginative personal improvisation styles, but they also often improvise simultaneously with other players. This requires both imagination and coordination; players have to develop a sort of second sense for what their partners are likely to do. The result is nonimitative polyphony (see page 38) of a particularly clear and exhilarating kind. This jazz polyphony has some affinities with baroque polyphony, in works such as Bach's *Brandenburg* Concertos. Baroque music, we remember, incorporates a good deal of improvisation of its own kind, and it is interesting to compare the role of the jazz rhythm section to that of the baroque continuo (see page 153).

Jazz is a special performance style, then; it is not a special kind of musical material. Jazz uses different kinds of material, and makes it into jazz by performing it *as* jazz. Some of it comes from popular songs, such as those associated with musical comedy, and some comes from an important type of black folk song called the *blues.* But neither *Fascinating rhythm* nor *St. Louis blues* is jazz—though, when played by jazz musicians, these titles become the titles of jazz numbers.

Jazz is very much a product of our century in its dependence on the recording industry. It would never have developed as it did without the dissemination of records, starting in the 1920s. This catapulted a local, New Orleans phenomenon into a nationwide experience. And it is in recordings, not in scores, that jazz has survived. Our national museum, the Smithsonian Institution in Washington, D.C., has issued an important six-record set called *The Smithsonian Collection of Classic Jazz,* which serves as a sort of permanent (though not exclusive) collection and survey of this art form from 1916 to 1966. (It can be found in any record library.) We shall refer to some of the Smithsonian records to supplement our necessarily brief coverage of jazz history in the following pages.

THE BLUES

Two important sources of jazz are *ragtime* and the *blues.* In ragtime, jazz found the basis for its own rhythmic style. In blues singing, jazz found an important source of material, and also aspects of melody and performance style that could be transferred from the vocal to an instrumental medium.

The blues is a special category of black folk song expressing misery in all its forms: loneliness, desertion, trouble, destitution, depression. Some of the most moving and powerful jazz records of the 1920s and '30s are improvisations on blues melodies. Simple in form and strong in emotional content, the blues continued to influence popular music strongly in the 1950s and '60s.

A typical blues melody consists of three four-measure phrases ("twelve-bar blues"), repeated again and again as the blues singer develops a thought by improvising more and more new (or half-new) stanzas. This is not too hard to do, since each stanza usually consists of only two rhyming lines (a couplet). Line 1 is repeated for phrase 2 of the music, as though the singer were so obsessed with misery there was nothing left to do but harp on its source. Line 2 of the poem arrives only with phrase 3 of the music.

However, the repetition of line 1 also has the effect of making us wait rather eagerly for line 2—for completion of the thought, and for the rhyme that seems to tie it all together. Not infrequently a glint of humor cuts through the gloom:

> You sprinkled hot-foot powder all around my do' [door].
> You sprinkled hot-foot powder all around my do'.
> It keep me with a ramblin' mind, Rider, every old place I go.

"Rider" means lover.

People first seem to mention the blues around 1900, but the genre must have been around for a long time before that. It was popularized by the black composer W. C. Handy, in his *Memphis blues* of 1912 and *St. Louis blues* of 1914. Note that *St. Louis blues* is as atypical as it is famous, consisting as it does of a twelve-bar blues tune ("Oh I hate to see"), followed by a tango ("St. Louis woman"), followed by another, different twelve-bar blues ("Got the St. Louis blues"). Evidently Handy was trying to make a folk genre more palatable to a sophisticated public—very successfully, as it turned out.

The blues has a distinctive scale and melodic style, evolved by black folksingers for their laments. They also worked out standard harmonic patterns for phrases 1, 2, and 3 as they accompanied themselves on a guitar or some other instrument. In *St. Louis blues* the typical melodic quality of the blues can be heard on the italicized words below:

> I hate to see de ev'nin' *sun* go down . . .

> *Got* de St. *Lou*is blues *jes* as blue *as* Ah can be . . .

The importance of the blues for jazz goes beyond that of providing material for players to improvise on. They also took certain aspects of blues melody into their instrumental style; indeed, a great deal of the power of jazz playing comes from its vocal quality, as though it were absorbing the vibrant, passionate accents of black singing. *Blue notes,* notes that deviate slightly from the normal pitch, become as characteristic of jazz as the swinging accents that deviate slightly from the normal metrical beat.

RAGTIME

Ragtime is a style of piano playing developed by black musicians who played in bars and honky-tonks in the last decades of the nineteenth century. The left hand plays strictly in time—indeed, it keeps going pretty relentlessly—but the right hand syncopates the rhythm in a crisp, cheerful way. A typical piano rag sounds like a rather lively, "jazzy" piano rendition of a march.

The most important name in ragtime is Scott Joplin (1868–1917). Joplin specialized in piano rags, though he also made several heartbreaking attempts to infiltrate the world of opera; the publication of his *Maple Leaf Rag* in 1899 popularized ragtime in a decisive way. Joplin made piano rolls of his compositions for the Pianola or player piano, and these have been transferred to disc recordings. You can hear him play *Maple Leaf* on Smithsonian side 1, band 1.

To modern ears, the reserved and even slightly stiff quality of Joplin's rags gives them a special kind of cool charm. However, piano ragtime did not develop significantly. Much more significant was the transfer of "ragging" rhythm to bands, especially in connection with a very popular dance called the cakewalk. We begin to meet with names like Will Marion Cook's American Syncopated Band and Dave Peyton's Symphonic Syncopaters. In World War I American soldiers in France stepped to the syncopated rhythms of the famous 369th Infantry Band of James Europe. One more step, and we are into jazz.

THE 1920s: NEW ORLEANS OR DIXIELAND JAZZ

New Orleans, like Vienna, is revered by musicians as the home of a major musical style, in this case jazz. New Orleans is where it all started. Jazz historians, who are a romantic lot, grow misty-eyed and honey-tongued about semilegendary New Orleans jazz pioneers such as the great cornet player Buddy Bolden, about the dance halls, funeral processions, and political rallies at which black bands were often featured, the riverboats that had bands to entertain people traveling up the Mississippi to Memphis and St. Louis, and the bawdy houses where jazz pianist "professors" plied their trade. New Orleans fathered the first impressive jazz band to make records in the early 1920s, King Oliver's Creole Jazz Band. Many of the great early jazz players grew up in this town, among them the trumpeter Louis Armstrong, the pianist Ferdinand (Jelly Roll) Morton, and the clarinetist Sidney Bechet.

Early jazz was played by quite small bands, made up of six to eight players, generally. These bands centered on the combination of a cornet or trumpet, a trombone, and a clarinet. The saxophone, later thought of as *the* jazz instrument, was not unknown, but it was still not common. The cornet was the leading instrument; if anything, New Orleans bands liked to add a second cornet.

Improvisation was at the heart of New Orleans jazz. A typical number would begin with a song, a march, or a blues played by the whole band. The instrumental parts might be written out, or, if the players did not read music, memorized; there might already be some improvised melodic ornamentation during this initial chorus, but probably not too much. Then each of the melody instruments in turn would improvise a chorus. They would be accompanied by the rhythm section, while the other players stood by or sometimes joined in, in a subsidiary way.

Finally the whole band would play another chorus together, with everyone improvising now so as to make a brilliant, exhilarating climax. It is in these improvised choruses, mainly, that we find the impressive examples of jazz polyphony mentioned above.

And of course the whole piece would "swing." Some players would swing better than others, maybe—and on early jazz records it is not uncommon to hear a rhythm section that does not swing as much as clunk or jiggle. But the Jazz Age was not called that for nothing. The new kind of rhythm swept all before it, and in the process it swept up nearly all of American popular music.

The sweep took place in two related ways. First, as we have said, the new sound was spread by the technology of 78 rpm recordings. This created an interest in and demand for jazz all around the country—so the New Orleans musicians started to travel. Chicago and New York were the next important jazz centers. Jazz historians prefer to keep the term *New Orleans* jazz for the original product; a more general term, *Dixieland,* is used for the versions of New Orleans jazz that evolved in the North during the 1920s. The Dixieland style has flourished among players and enthusiasts up to the present day, alongside more advanced jazz types.

Louis Armstrong (1900–1971)

The career of Louis Armstrong, greatest of the early jazz players, is a historian's dream, a microcosm of jazz history. Born in 1900 in New Orleans, he learned to play the cornet in the Colored Waifs' Home for Boys, where he had been placed for a juvenile infraction of the law. As a young man he played second cornet in King Oliver's Creole Jazz Band in Chicago, then first cornet in Fletcher Henderson's Band in New York, the pioneer among "big bands" (see page 516). Armstrong rapidly emerged as a more exciting and imaginative player than any of his colleagues. In the late 1920s he played in a famous series of records that did more than anything else to draw jazz to the serious attention of musicians all over the world.

In the 1930s, the ensuing popularity of jazz led to a great deal of commercialization, and the cheapening, stereotyping, and sentimentalization that always seem to result from this. Armstrong went right along, though often contributing moments of breathtaking beauty to records that are "listenable virtually only when Louis is playing," as one jazz critic has put it. Armstrong was still making hits with records like *Hello, Dolly* and *Mack the Knife* in the 1960s. In his youth, jazz was taboo even in many middle-class black households. At the end of his career, jazz was accepted everywhere, even in college music courses, and Louis Armstrong was lionized all over the world.

ARMSTRONG *Willie the Weeper* (1927)

In the late 1920s Armstrong made over a hundred records with various recording groups such as Louis Armstrong and His Hot Five or Hot Seven. (Incidentally, the early jazz numbers we hear are all about three minutes long, since that was the capacity of a ten-inch 78 rpm disc.) Based on a somewhat routine example of 1920s popular song, *Willie the weeper* is a typical and spirited example of New Orleans or Dixieland jazz.

After a couple of chords by way of introduction, the band launches into the simple, catchy melody. Armstrong plays it almost "straight," as in line 1 of the music example below. Underneath him the trombone marches along solidly, but the clarinet above (and around) is already full of interesting activity. The second time the tune is played, Armstrong cannot resist changing it a good deal. As shown by asterisks in line 2 of the example, only about 70 percent of the notes he plays are notes from the original melody—and what a free, soaring feeling is imparted to the unsuspecting *Willie the weeper* by the other 30 percent! As we listen, the popular song is turning into jazz.

Next the band plays the verse, which is not illustrated, and then come the first two solo improvisations on the chorus. We could call them variations on *Willie the weeper*, as in the theme and variation form. The clarinet chorus succeeds better than the trombone one, whose stiffness is highlighted by the prominent tuba part in the rhythm section. God did not create the tuba to swing.

This over, Armstrong improvises on the verse, followed by the pianist doing the same thing. (She was Lillian Harding Armstrong, Louis's wife and an active bandleader and songwriter in her own right.) It is the guitar's turn for a chorus next, followed by the trumpet. This time, only about 10 percent of Armstrong's notes stick to the melody—see line 3; he is beginning to create his own melody, in fact, a sequential one marked by square brackets on the example. The rinky-tink quality of the original tune is quite transcended by Armstrong's broadly scaled cadence, in the last four bars, and by his ecstatic high B♭ at the very end.

Finally, we have the splendid climactic chorus with all three soloists going at full tilt. We get caught up in the excitement, the precariousness, the sheer artistry of the group improvisation. The forceful voice of the trumpet presenting its variation, sounding like an elegant, joyful shout; the clarinet zooming up and down again in faster notes; the trombone underpinning the other instruments with marchlike support notes and sliding progressions—all these fit together miraculously over the basic chords and meter hammered out by the piano, guitar, and tuba of the rhythm section.

Not all of Armstrong's work was in the cheerful, enthusiastic vein of *Willie the weeper*. He could also provide superb matching accompaniments for Bessie Smith, the incomparable singer of the blues (listen to their *St. Louis blues* on Smithsonian side 1, band 4). And his famous *West End blues* shows how perfectly he could transfer the vocal blues genre to the instrumental field of jazz (Smithsonian side 3, band 9). Armstrong as both trumpeter and singer dominates this record, though it also features an important new pianist, Earl Hines, who was light years ahead of Mrs. Armstrong. Within the limited scope provided by the twelve-bar blues form, the depth of desolate feeling that Armstrong conveys and the height of his fantasy are overwhelming. Overwhelming, too, is the freely improvised introduction, a brilliant trumpet cadenza without any accompaniment whatsoever. *West End blues* is considered one of Armstrong's greatest records, one of the great jazz performances of all time.

THE 1930s: THE BIG BANDS

In the 1930s jazz rose in popularity and acceptance and reached larger and larger audiences, white as well as black. The most important developments occurred in jazz for bands consisting of ten to twenty players, called "big bands." Bands of this size had been introduced before, and the traditional small Dixieland groups did not die out altogether during the 1930s. Nonetheless big-band jazz, christened <u>swing</u>, gave its name to the era. Big-band jazz was the main type of popular music in the period from around 1930 to the beginning of World War II.

swing

Duke

It may be that the three most significant musicians the United States has produced are Charles Ives (see page 451), John Cage (see page 475), and Duke Ellington. Each of them was or is in some sense out of the mainstream: an old American tradition. Ellington, unlike Ives but not altogether unlike Cage, was not indifferent to popular success. He did fairly well, but he never hit the top of the charts, probably because behind his genial and commanding public manner, he was privately too fastidious about his art. He always went his own imperturbable way, keeping his big band in the 1960s and '70s, when such organizations were regarded as jazz dinosaurs.

His last phase as a composer found him writing lengthy religious pieces called Sacred Concerts for the Ellington Band, with a Swedish soprano, Alice Babs, who was not really a jazz singer at all.

Ellington's Sacred Concerts are inconceivable without Babs—but the same is also true of his earlier, more famous music and the musicians of his early band. Jazz buffs who talk about Ellington always talk about his individual soloists, or *sidemen,* as they are called: among them are Barney Bigard (clarinet), "Tricky Sam" Nanton (trombone), Johnny Hodges (alto saxophone), Cootie Williams (trumpet), and Harry Carney (bass clarinet) on *Saddest tale* (see page 519). Williams and Hodges are also the driving forces of *In a Mellotone.* There is more to this than mere name-dropping. These men were vital to Ellington's art in a way no singer or instrumentalist was or is to any classical music. We cannot conceive of his music being played by any other band: it would not be the same music. Ellington's enormously talented sidemen can be regarded as co-composers of his music, or better, perhaps, as its *material*—like the songs and blues that were transformed by the Ellington magic.

The characteristics of big-band jazz had been worked out in all essentials by black bandleaders of the 1920s. Fletcher Henderson and Don Redman were the most important of these early "arrangers"—they might just as well be called composers, for, besides the scoring, they devised introductions, modulations, interludes, everything in fact except the basic song or blues itself.

Fundamental to the big-band style was the division of the band into choirs. This is a term used for standard orchestras (see page 157), but whereas the symphony orchestra is said to have string, woodwind, and brass choirs, the choirs of the jazz band are brass and *reeds*—the latter including saxophones and clarinets. The saxophone now assumed its major importance in jazz. The choirs tended to cling together, playing closely knit chords. They engaged in interesting dialogues with the other choirs and with solo instruments, which could always be brought forward from the relative anonymity of the choirs into the limelight.

It is fair enough to draw an analogy between the big jazz bands and the symphony orchestra on the one hand, and to compare Dixieland jazz to chamber music on the other. Because of its dependence on improvisation and small band size, Dixieland jazz is more spontaneous and intimate. Because of its emphasis on "arrangements" and large band size, big-band jazz is more powerful, sophisticated, and impersonal.

What was the impact of this less intimate style on improvisation, which is so vital to the whole concept of jazz? Not to mince words, the impact was often disastrous, and fraught with danger even at best. Playing the middle notes of elegantly calculated chords in a choir is not improvising, and even when playing a solo against a choir, you have to be rather careful where you are going, with all that traffic. What tended to happen was that solos were written out in the *style* of improvisations, or, more likely, someone would improvise a solo and it would be memorized or written down and thus "frozen." Next time the player would play roughly the same thing. But only roughly: the best big bands still managed to leave a good deal of scope for individual spontaneity. Indeed, they fostered great new improvisers.

The best new band of the 1930s was Count Basie's Orchestra, and the greatest new talent was Basie's tenor saxophonist Lester Young. Basie himself was a delightful and innovative jazz pianist, and he gave Young more opportunities to shine than most big-band leaders accorded their soloists. The best white bands of the period were less distinguished than the best black ones; loud and swinging, they nonetheless lacked something in the way of verve and fire, and they indulged a fatal tendency toward slickness. But they were more successful. Benny Goodman, Tommy Dorsey, Artie Shaw, and Glenn Miller were household names in the 1930s, as familiar thanks to the radio as the names of Clark Gable, Fred Astaire, Greta Garbo, and Harpo Marx were thanks to the movies.

The elite white band was that of Benny Goodman, a musician of considerable vision. Goodman had the idea of drawing out of his big band satellite small groups—the Benny Goodman Trio, Quartet, Quintet, etc.—thus preserving something of the Dixieland tradition at a time when this was under a cloud (actually introducing it to most of his listeners, who had never heard it before). Goodman was the first major white leader to include some blacks in his band, and he managed to put on wildly successful jazz concerts at New York's Carnegie Hall. He always kept up a crossover interest in classical music, incidentally. One of the pieces he liked to play (and liked to record) is one we know, Mozart's Clarinet Quintet (see page 281).

The elite black band was that of Edward Kennedy (Duke) Ellington. Ellington's work stands in a class of its own, not only with respect to the 1930s big-band scene, but also with respect to jazz as a whole.

Duke Ellington (1899–1974)

Duke Ellington was born within fifteen months of Louis Armstrong, but into a very different black milieu. His father was a Washington, D.C., butler who occasionally worked at the White House. For a time the young Ellington considered a career as an artist, but he started playing in bands and soon organized his own.

Though Ellington was a good pianist, he did not have the rare pianistic ability of Count Basie or Armstrong's ideal partner Earl Hines, to name only two. What he did have was even rarer: a vision of how the work of other fine players could be melded into entire jazz compositions, compositions of unprecedented variety and imagination. Louis Armstrong was the greatest player in early jazz; Duke Ellington was the greatest composer.

It is no accident that the Ellington Band can easily claim the record for longevity in jazz history, and that some of its players stayed on for twenty or thirty years. (It started in 1923 and is still going, under Ellington's son Mercer.) Only by working with the same players over a long period could Ellington transform their individual powers into a totality that was more powerful still. His ear for tone color—for the fascinating new sonorities that could be derived from combinations of instruments played in the jazz manner—was as notable as his instinct for musical form. He was equally inventive and original with pieces that were melancholy and driving, simple and complex, short and long. Ellington was the first to write jazz compositions that were not based on songs at all but instead could be compared to jazz symphonies, or at least to jazz symphony movements.

ELLINGTON *Saddest Tale* (1934)   SIDE 20

Scored for fourteen instruments, this relatively early Ellington number is a big-band version of a twelve-bar blues—with a difference. We first hear an arresting, indescribably mournful clarinet solo, without any accompaniment (Ellington's tribute to Armstrong's *West End blues*). As this mounts up and up, it is greeted by the characteristic big-band sound of the saxophone and brass choirs playing this vigorous figure:

Suddenly there is a hush, and Duke Ellington mutters (he does not sing) the cryptic words "Saddest tale on land or sea/Is the tale they told when they told the truth on me." Then at once the first blues chorus is played in a decorated version by a muted trombone (muted brass was an Ellington specialty). The almost startlingly human quality of this muted instrument, with the suave, sliding saxophone choir behind it (or sometimes, it seems, in front of it), makes a soft, remote, melancholy, meditative texture of a kind that Ellington excelled in producing.

The actual blues tune is not heard until chorus 2, played by the low brass choir. How alive these instruments sound, even as a closely knit group. The melody is simple and repetitious, like most blues:

The alto sax keeps breaking in with beautiful rhapsodic solos; they *sound* improvised and must have been originally, even if they were pretty well "frozen" by the time this recording was made. Chorus 3 belongs to a muted trumpet; notice that this time the reed choir (saxes and clarinet) develops a rich countermelody of its own. The blues tune is transformed most radically in chorus 4, played by a bass clarinet.

Ellington's sense of musical form is shown by his treatment of one minor detail—his elegant little piano touches which come in between the choruses and set them off clearly from one another—and by one major one. This is a surprising return, after chorus 4, of the vigorous figure that originally greeted the clarinet introduction, together with the spoken words. We have seen A B A structures of this sort a hundred times in this book, but let us not get blasé about them. Why does this bright, affirmative gesture not sound incongruous at this bleak point in the piece? Do the nine repetitions of high B♭ now explain themselves as a development of the repetitions of F in measures 1, 3, and 10 of the blues? Furthermore, the fact that the blues have now given us some feeling of the "saddest tale" makes Duke's words seem even more cryptic the second time. What does he mean? Was that repetitious blues tune almost *too* sad? The originality and fascination of *Saddest tale* depends in large part on the questions it leaves in our mind.

Just as it would be unfair to judge Louis Armstrong solely by a brisk song like *Willie the weeper,* so it would be unfair to judge Duke Ellington solely by a slow blues. A faster number, *In a Mellotone* (Smithsonian side 7, band 1), accelerates in a remarkable way. Three clearly defined sections grow out of one another. After the introduction, section 1 provides an extended example of a big-band dialogue (saxes and muted brass choirs). In section 2, the dialogue shifts to a muted trumpet and the reed choir—but, instead of reconciling itself to a back position, the choir picks up everything the trumpet throws at it and tosses it right back, at an astonishing speed. Thus inspired, a solo sax in section 3 gets faster and faster, until after a break (see page 509) it is really going twice as fast as the rhythm section. Try counting an extra beat in this thrilling passage. But the ending is cool . . .

THE 1940s: BEBOP

Big-band jazz reached its apex in the late 1930s and early '40s. Duke Ellington made some of his finest records then, and Benny Goodman took Carnegie Hall by storm. Hotel ballrooms, roadhouses, and college proms echoed to the sounds of bands that were getting bigger and fancier all the time.

In this same period, however, a number of younger jazz players began to strike out on their own. Most of them played with big bands, and their hero was the somewhat older saxophonist with Count Basie's Orchestra, Lester Young. They would get together after hours to improvise at a Harlem night-club that has attained a certain celebrity in jazz history, called Minton's. There they worked out a radical new jazz style that came to be known as <u>bebop</u>. The most important of these figures were the pianist Thelonious Monk, the trumpeter John (Dizzy) Gillespie (both still playing today), and the saxophonist Charlie (Bird) Parker (1920–1955).

bebop

In many ways the new style went back to the simpler ideal of Dixieland jazz. Bebop was small-band jazz with the emphasis firmly back on improvisation, not "arrangement." The difference came in the orientation of this music around virtuoso "star" performers, by contrast with the democratic setup of the New Orleans tradition. We remember the fraternal spirit of Louis Armstrong's *Willie the weeper* and Duke Ellington's *Saddest song:* even the less talented brothers get to play their solos. But *West End blues,* which is practically a solo for Armstrong, in 1928 already indicated a trend that was to be accentuated by Ellington in the following years. (The title of one his best-known works, *Concerto for Cootie*—the trumpeter Cootie Williams—tells the story.) In the 1940s, the typical bebop number had only two soloists, plus rhythm section. Some of the greatest classic bebop records are Parker solos.

The point is that these men could handle sustained exposure. Their instrumental virtuosity was amazing, and they also developed a sense of melodic span that allowed their improvisations to maintain interest far longer than those of any earlier jazz players. They played infinitely more complex melodic lines, all kinds of irregular phrases, and increasingly esoteric harmonies. The melodies they were ostensibly improvising on were often abandoned completely. Only the harmonies were used as springboards for solo improvisations.

They played unbelievably fast. "That horn ain't supposed to sound that fast," an older sax player is supposed have said on first hearing Parker (though we have heard a forecast of this lightning playing by Ellington's sideman Johnny Hodges in *In a Mellotone*). And they played in a new hard, almost percussive style that gave the new jazz its name. Say the word *bebop* very fast and very loud and you will get a fair imitation of the way this music struck its first listeners.

Bird

Most pictures of musicians show them in action, playing or singing, or at least posing at their instruments. This picture shows jazz musicians engaged in another characteristic activity—listening to a playback, at a recording session. Charlie (Bird) Parker, whose life was generally turbulent, is here caught in a tranquil, serious, reflective moment. We can imagine him trying to weigh the sound on the speakers against the sound in his mind's ear.

Though Bird is completely wrapped up in his own thoughts, he dominates this picture the way he dominated jazz in his time. The other members of the combo look at him to see if he will okay the take or whether they will have to record it again.

Rejected takes (many are available today on special records) provide fascinating evidence about differences between one great jazz improvisation and another.

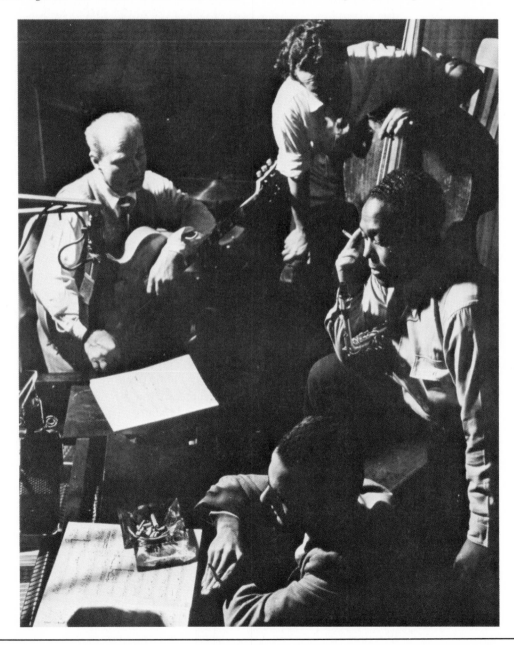

CHARLIE PARKER AND MILES DAVIS *Out of Nowhere* (1948)   SIDE 20

Our version of *Out of Nowhere* was recorded live in a New York nightclub, The Royal Roost, in 1948, so it gives an exact idea of what a bebop improvised number actually sounded like. Notice the informal opening—no arranged introduction, as in the Ellington and Armstrong numbers we have heard. Parker plays the attractive song fairly "straight" to begin with, but he inserts a sudden skittering passage just before the A' section (the song is in A A' form). This is a preview of things to come.

The trumpet solo by Miles Davis has the characteristic tense, bright bebop sound, some very rapid passage-work, and one or two piercing high notes. Then Parker's improvisation shows his impressive powers of melodic development. He works primarily with the opening motive of three eighth notes in the original song:

He had already expanded these three notes to many more, much shorter and faster ones, in his original presentation of the tune. Now he builds a whole series of phrases of different lengths, all starting with fast, increasingly elaborate runs derived from this basic rhythmic idea. The irregular, almost discontinuous-sounding rests between Parker's phrases have their own special fascination. You may recognize an Irish jig called *The Kerry Dancers,* which seems to have popped right into Parker's head in the middle of the solo as the outgrowth of a short figure that he had come to, and which he plays at a dizzying rate for just a moment, before inventing something else. Fantastically, it fits right in.

At the end of his solo the audience applauds, and the pianist has an interlude. The number ends with the A' section of *Out of Nowhere* played once again quite simply, except for the comical ending.

THE JAZZ PARADOX

Out of Nowhere is one of the more accessible bebop records. On others, including several of the Smithsonian selections, Parker takes off on complex, extended flights as though absorbed by a private vision. Like the bird of his nickname, he sometimes seems to dart faster than the eye can follow, hover, drop like a pellet, then swoop out of sight and lose himself like a speck in the sun. These wonderful improvisations by Parker will repay careful repeated listenings, just like the compositions by twentieth-century composers that may also elude our grasp at first. After Armstrong, he was the greatest musician that jazz has ever produced.

But the fact remains that his work requires careful, repeated listening. It requires concentration; it requires work. And this is a wondrous state for popular music to have come to. Popular music ordinarily goes for instant appeal.

The bebop musicians' attitude to their work was also disconcertingly different from that of the usual popular musician; they refused to regard themselves merely as performers who were out to please, but rather as artists with a mission. "'If you don't like it, don't listen,' was the attitude," according to the black writer LeRoi Jones, who is also a jazz authority. "These Negro musicians were thought of as 'weird' and 'deep,' the bebop glasses and goatees some wore seemed to complete the image."

This image was a romantic one, rooted in the nineteenth century. Romantic attitudes such as these had helped create the gulf between classical music and popular music in the first place. More tragically, the life of bebop's greatest genius, Charlie Parker, reads like the modern-day version of a persistent romantic myth, that of the artist who lives in torment, driven by the demon of his own creativity, and finding fulfillment only in his art. Parker was on drugs from the age of fifteen, and in later years could not control his immoderate drinking and eating; he would miss dates, make terrible scenes, and—too often—play poorly. Already a legend in his own lifetime, Parker died at the age of thirty-four, after a suicide attempt and a period of hospitalization in a California mental institution.

At the beginning of chapter 15, we remarked on the ambiguities latent in a satisfactory definition of "popular" music. Size of the audience cannot be the whole story. The great paradox of American popular music of our century is that its chief genre, jazz, has evolved from a popular to a nonpopular status. This started with the bebop movement and has continued with the increasingly innovative figures of the 1950s, '60s, and '70s.

When jazz began, its audience was relatively small, at least by today's standards—at a guess, a few hundred thousand people around New Orleans and the ports on the river route up the Mississippi. But for these people jazz was a genuinely popular art: it was simple, it was accessible, it was fun. Millions more thought so when jazz was filtered and diluted into show music and big-band swing. Modern jazz has a diminishing audience because it is no longer popular in this sense. For better or for worse, jazz has reached the status of high art. It has its devotees and coteries, its snobberies, and even its own musicology, just like contemporary avant-garde music. Indeed, there is a style called avant-garde jazz, which is a positive orgy of crossovers.

It would be a mistake to suggest that modern jazz is as esoteric as avant-garde classical music. But if you want to find the true popular music of the 1980s, look elsewhere.

Popular Music in the Electronic Age

There is a well-known saying attributed to the French statesman Georges Clemenceau that war is much too serious a matter to be left to the generals. In the 1950s it dawned on the captains of American industry that music was becoming much too lucrative a matter to be left to the musicians.

Since the Industrial Revolution in the late eighteenth century, capitalism has depended on ever-new technologies: railroads in the nineteenth century, the internal combustion engine in the early twentieth, and computer technology in our own time, to mention just a few representative examples. In the music industry, the technology in question was recording technology, at both of its ends. At what we might call the "output" end, the pressing and distribution of cheap LP records after 1950 increased the market astronomically. At the "input" end, refinements of amplification and recording techniques changed the creation of music itself and also its sociology in ways that were hardly less extreme.

"Input" Amplification made a huge difference to the tone color of popular music from the 1950s on. The blues, for example, had traditionally been accompanied by the singer playing a guitar. A guitar—an acoustic guitar—is basically a quiet instrument. Flamenco artists can play up quite a storm on it, but they can produce nothing like the percussive, violent, and very *loud* effects that are obtained on an electric guitar today as simply as turning on a light switch. The blues were transformed by the introduction of electrically amplified guitars. Out of this technology emerged the hard, driving, obsessive beat that was taken over as the main legacy from rhythm and blues to rock.

Powerful amplification allowed musicians to give pop music concerts of unprecedented size. (Not quite unprecedented, for Johann Strauss had conducted concerts for audiences of a hundred thousand in the 1870s—but Strauss conducted an orchestra of twenty thousand musicians. Imagine, today, hiring twenty thousand union musicians!) Here is another paradox: concerts had originally served to mark the breach between classical and popular music, but now popular music finds a major outlet in huge concerts put on at stadiums, racetracks, or just big fields (the famous Woodstock Concert of 1969, for example). There was a notorious mass concert given by the Rolling Stones at Altamount, during which a man was murdered and three others died, as cameras rolled to immortalize the event on a film called *Gimme Shelter.*

Most important of all, perhaps, new sophisticated recording techniques allowed for the packaging and doctoring of pop music performances in unusual ways. There is a direct analogy here with the use of electronic instruments and electronic sound effects in contemporary classical music, such as several pieces we examined in chapter 14: Stockhausen's *Song of the Children* (see page 465) and Lentz's *Song(s) of the Sirens* (see page 479). Like these classical works, rock numbers are sometimes conceived in the recording studio, with the process of recording entering actively into the shape and sound of the song that ultimately emerges. There is also a complicated process called *mixing,* in which the outputs of the instruments and singers are balanced electronically in such a way as to obtain the optimum sound. Each instrument is recorded separately on several different tracks, which are then combined or "mixed" to produce the single groove for your phonograph. Everything can be changed electronically: the dynamics, the balance, the echo, the tone quality (by adding and subtracting overtones), etc.

Carole and Joni

The composers shown here represent a new phenomenon in popular music. Until quite recently, women who wanted to make a name in popular music had to be singers, not composers or instrumentalists. Billie Holiday, Ella Fitzgerald, Aretha Franklin, and many others were and are marvelous artists, but they were allowed in primarily because they were sex objects, like woman opera singers and ballerinas.

Probably Carole King would never have got into songwriting if she had not started out collaborating with her husband. In the 1960s, her first big hit, *Will you love me tomorrow*, was sung by a female rhythm and blues group called the Shirelles. By this time, musical composition was no longer a simple matter of putting notes to paper; King would go to the studio and sing a demonstration record at the piano. This was then copied in every particular by the recording group. King proved adept at writing successful songs in all the styles current at the time: country and western (*Crying in the rain*), pop (*Halfway to paradise*), rhythm and blues (*Up on the roof*), and soul (*A natural woman,* an early hit of Aretha Franklin's).

After the breakup of her marriage in 1968, King started to compose her own kind of music, melodic soft rock, close in spirit to the old-time songs of Tin Pan Alley. Rock was still dominating popular music, and for a time she had little success composing against this trend. But in 1972, her album *Tapestry* sold eleven million copies, an industry record that had never been equaled.

Another composer who has moved through various popular styles is Joni Mitchell, shown at a jazz concert in Berkeley. She started with folk numbers, but developed more and more of an interest in jazz. She collaborated on an album with the important jazz bass player and composer Charles Mingus just before his death in 1979.

Women composers have come late to popular music, but they have not been exactly thick on the ground in classical music, either. Obviously this is not a matter of artistic talent—think of writers such as Virginia Woolf and Marianne Moore, artists such as Georgia O'Keeffe and Louise Nevelson—but a matter of social convention. While a number of names can be brought forward from the twentieth century, few can be found in earlier times. Clara Schumann, wife of the composer Robert Schumann, and Fanny Mendelssohn, sister of Felix, were both promising composers whose menfolk made it clear that their place was to be home- not music-makers. At the time of Monteverdi there was a very good composer-singer named Barbara Strozzi; a well-placed courtesan, she was therefore free from the restraints that kept respectable married women in more traditional feminine pursuits. Oddly, it is back in the age of chivalry that we hear of some woman troubadours and trouvères (see page 93), who may have written the music as well as the words to their songs, as King and Mitchell have today.

"Output" So much for the "input" side of electronic technology. On the "output" side, the whole ambience of today's popular music is controlled by the vision of the gold record, that is, the record that sells a million copies or more. Elvis Presley, who sold twenty-six million records in the first two years of his phenomenal success in the 1950s, made thirty-three gold records in his twenty-year career. But the fascinating fact about Presley's rise to fame is that it was manipulated by managers, record companies, and disc jockeys. Elvis did his thing, of course, and he did it very sexily; but his unusual combination of hillbilly music with rhythm and blues did not sell itself all at once. What catapulted Elvis and rock into the limelight was more like a committee decision. A southern promoter persuaded a music company executive to try pushing the Presley sound with northern deejays—and America's young womanhood did the rest.

The important thing about selling gold records is to keep selling them. It is not to anyone's advantage for a record to become a "classic," like Beethoven's Fifth Symphony, so that the audience is satisfied with it and listens to it over and over again instead of going out and buying new ones. Of course popular music keeps changing. There is built-in obsolescence in modern pop records, as there is in certain other products we are encouraged to purchase. As a consequence, the pop music of the last thirty years lacks a series of acknowledged masterpieces, comparable to the great Armstrong, Ellington, and Parker records of the past. The modern pop records that seem to have attained some longevity are those that have in some sense transcended the heavily commercial world from which they emerged. We shall look at one of the more famous of these records.

THE BEATLES *Abbey Road* (1969)

The Beatles were a group of four English rock musicians who started at the very bottom, playing dreary pubs in provincial Liverpool around 1960. In only a few years they became the greatest phenomenon in the history of American popular music. The adulation of their fans ("Beatlemania"), their huge concerts and delightful movies, their once-famous and endlessly discussed albums, the analyses of their work in highbrow literary magazines—all these belong as much to the sociology of the 1960s as to the history of music. Like the other great pop music successes, the Beatles were a creation of the music industry, starting with an astute manager who signed them up early on a contract giving him the largest cut of the five. But no manager could have spirited up the success of the Beatles unless he had a very good property on his hands.

Endowed with moderate musical talent, the Beatles were however blessed with an amazing ability to learn and to grow. After their initial success with rock numbers, they held their huge public with all kinds of new musical styles, experiments with popular and classical music elements, and endlessly intriguing song lyrics. They soon tired of giving concerts, which grew larger and larger and more and more perilous on account of the good-natured mayhem of their fans. During their last few years together as a group, they concentrated on highly structured records, employing all the technological resources that money (a great deal of money) could buy.

The title of their last gold record, *Abbey Road,* openly acknowledges the role of recording technology in modern popular music: Abbey Road is the address of the Beatles' recording studio in London. The song *You never give me your money* on side 2, moreover, with its mention of negotiations and the like, refers directly to the Beatles' current dispute over record royalties. Popular music lyrics had certainly come a long way from the June–moon–spoon days of Tin Pan Alley. Indeed, the extraordinarily varied (and often extraordinarily strange) song lyrics by the Beatles are an important factor in their artistic effect. Beatle John Lennon published a separate book of poetry, *In My Own Write.*

We mentioned earlier that the length (and thus to some extent the form) of jazz numbers was largely determined by the three minutes or so available on an old 78 rpm record side. LP records now have twenty minutes or more. The Beatles and other groups had the idea of making unified sides, with the songs arranged in a deliberate order of moods and with some interrelations among them. *Abbey Road* is, in effect, a popular music song cycle (see page 317).

The melody of *You never give me your money* turns up again in the second part of *Carry that weight,* and *Here comes the sun king* has a melodic outline very similar to *Here comes the sun,* despite the difference in tempo. The first and last songs of side 1 (*Come together* and *I want you*) and the next-to-last song of side 2 (*Carry that weight*) all end with the same technique—an ostinato figure repeated again and again and again, about a dozen times. (The very last song on side 2 is a tiny number called *The end.*) Seemingly endless ostinato repetitions were characteristic of both rock and some kinds of classical avant-garde music of the 1960s.

To be sure, by the time of *Abbey Road* the Beatles had gone far beyond rock. However, there are echoes of rock in many numbers, as well as of other styles. *The end* seems to parody the sort of music that used to surge up during the last moments of grandiose movies when those words would flash onto the screen. *Come together* evokes rock in a very interesting, quiet way, thanks largely to the imaginative and discreet use of percussion. The refrain "Come together right now over me," with its momentary electric guitar, appears three times with a striking modulation of a kind that became very common in 1960s rock. In stanza 3 of this song, the words "muddy water" hint at another musical evocation, for Muddy Waters is the name of a famous rhythm and blues singer.

As for the contribution of electronic technology to the songs, that is apparent everywhere. In *Come together,* as a result of the mixing process the voices sound pinched and distant, while the percussion which carries so much of the effect looms large in the foreground. Contrast this with the echo in the very next number, *Something;* here someone seems to be singing gently but resonantly right into your ear. The long ending of *I want you* is accompanied by an electronic hiss (white noise: see page 461) which very slowly gets louder and louder throughout the fifteen relentless appearances of the ostinato figure. A strange but very effective conclusion is provided to *You never give me your money* by the use of quiet outdoor sounds—an example of *musique concrète* (see page 461). More in fun—and thoroughly characteristic in this respect—are the gurgling water sounds introduced into *Octopus's garden.*

Will the music of the Beatles—or the Rolling Stones, Bob Dylan, Joni Mitchell, the Jefferson Airplane (Starship), the Eagles, the Bee Gees, and so many others—continue to be listened to (and bought) decades after it was recorded, as certain old jazz records still are?

That is a question that only the readers of this book will one day be able to answer. The authors are not so foolhardy as to try to predict the future course of American popular music. No one can guess whether it will derive new energy from the discotheque or the recording studio, from black sources or British, from bubblegum or Geritol, whether it will enter into a new primitive stage or a sophisticated one, whether it will go up or down. Even the music industry can slump, reorganize, or diversify. Only one thing is certain: between the writing of this book and the reading of it, the ever-changing, ever-vital face of popular music will have changed once again.

Biographies

Johann Sebastian Bach

1685–1750 German baroque composer

Bach was born in the same year as Handel, 1685. The Bach family produced so many musicians over a period of two centuries that, in their part of Germany, people are reported to have said "Bach" when they meant "musician" the way we might say "Rockefeller" to mean "millionaire." From the time of his first positions, as church organist in tiny mid-German towns, Bach seems to have been headstrong and stubborn. In his first important job, as a court musician at Weimar, he got into a dispute with the Duke of Weimar about quitting and was actually jailed briefly (typically industrious, he spent the time writing his *Little Organ Book,* a collection of chorale preludes). This was followed by another court position, at Cöthen, where he wrote much of his greatest chamber music.

In 1723 Bach was appointed cantor of St. Thomas' Church and Choir School in Leipzig, one of the main towns in what is now East Germany. This was the highest musical position in the Lutheran church, but it involved onerous chores and administrative restrictions which Bach was not the man to accept willingly. At first he composed a staggering amount of music for the Leipzig churches—hundreds of sacred cantatas. But then he quarreled with the authorities and, to their annoyance, spent more of his time in city music activities. Toward the end of his life Bach prepared a few of his finest pieces for publication and made careful manuscript collections and orderings of his works.

Bach married a cousin when he was about twenty; the couple had seven children before she died in 1720. A year later he married a young musician and they had another thirteen children. Of the twenty children, ten survived infancy and two became extremely important composers of the next generation: Carl Philip Emmanuel and Johann Christian (the youngest).

Bach was always widely admired as a brilliant organist, but from his middle years on he was considered impossibly "heavy" and old-fashioned as a composer. After his death his music attracted only a few connoisseurs (who included, however, Mozart and Beethoven) until it was rediscovered by the Romantics. For many musicians and listeners today, Bach is the greatest of all composers.

Chief works: *The Well-tempered Clavier,* consisting of forty-eight preludes and fugues for harpsichord; six Brandenburg Concertos; church cantatas, *Passion According to St. Matthew,* and Mass in B Minor; organ fugues and chorale preludes.

Béla Bartók

1881–1945 Hungarian twentieth-century composer

Bartók was born in Hungary, and it was soon evident that he was destined for a brilliant career as a pianist and composer. He wrote his first work for the piano when he was nine. Music was the avocation of his father, who was the principal of an agricultural school.

Few musicians have ever led as varied a career as Bartók. He was a prolific composer and a fine pianist. In conjunction with another important Hungarian composer, Zoltán Kodály, he undertook a large-scale investigation of Hungarian (and other) folk music, writing several standard books in the field of ethnomusicology (the scientific study of folk music and the music of non-Western cultures). Also with Kodály, he directed the Budapest Academy of Music, where the two men developed new ideas in music teaching. An outcome of this side of Bartók's career is his *Mikrokosmos,* a series of 153 graded piano pieces starting with the very easiest, which are well known to most piano students today. Bartók's compositions employ folk elements such as rhythms and melodic turns—though not actual folksongs—and he perhaps succeeded more than any other nationalist composer in making something truly individual out of such elements.

In 1940, after the outbreak of World War II, Bartók came to America, where he was not well known and where there was little enthusiasm for his works. He developed leukemia, and his last years were a desperate, poverty-ridden struggle to complete the Third Piano Concerto and the Concerto for Viola and Orchestra. Ironically, his important works earned a wide audience shortly after his death.

Chief works: Six string quartets; an orchestra piece, Music for Strings, Percussion, and Celesta; Second Violin Concerto and Third Piano Concerto; a fascinating Sonata for Two Pianos and Percussion.

Ludwig van Beethoven

1770–1827 Viennese composer

It must have been a miserable childhood. Beethoven's father, a minor musician at the court of Bonn in West Germany, tried unsuccessfully to push him as an infant prodigy like Mozart. A trip to Vienna to make musical contacts (with Mozart, among others) was cut short by the death of his mother. Still in his teens, he had to take over official control of his family because of his father's alcoholism.

Unlike Mozart, Beethoven was a slow developer, but by the age of twenty-two he had made enough of an impression to receive a sort of fellowship to study with Haydn in Vienna, then the musical capital of the world. In a few years he was widely acclaimed as a magnificent and powerful virtuoso pianist, frequently playing his own compositions. Too difficult a personality to study for long with anyone, he nevertheless remained in Vienna until his death.

After the age of thirty, he became progressively deaf, a devastating loss for a musician and one that kept him from making a living in the traditional way, by performing. He was supported, however, by the Viennese aristocracy, which was awed by his uncompromising character and his extraordinarily forceful and original music.

Beethoven, then, was probably the first musician to make a career solely from composing. Already in his lifetime, he was regarded as a great genius. His character contributed to this impression; an alarmingly brusque and forceful person, he suffered deeply and seemed to live for his art alone—his domestic life was chaotic and he was well known on the streets of Vienna as an eccentric. He had an immense need to receive and to give affection, but despite various love affairs, he never married. In his late years he adopted his orphan nephew, but his attitude was so protective and his love so smothering that the boy could not stand it and actually attempted suicide. The shock of this hastened Beethoven's death. Twenty thousand attended his funeral.

Taste has changed many times since Beethoven's lifetime, but his music has always reigned supreme with audiences and critics. The incredible originality and expressive power of his work never seem to fade.

Chief works: Nine symphonies, the most famous being the *Eroica* (No. 3), the Fifth, the Seventh, and the Ninth (*Choral* Symphony); sixteen string quartets; piano sonatas, including the *Pathétique,* the *Waldstein,* the *Appassionata,* and the late-period *Hammerklavier* Sonata; opera *Fidelio;* Mass in D (*Missa solemnis*).

Alban Berg

1885–1935   Austrian twentieth-century composer

Berg was a Viennese, a student of Schoenberg, and a dedicated member of Schoenberg's circle, "the Second Viennese School." Never in very good health, he nevertheless served in the Austrian army during World War I. After the war was over, he was able to turn his full attention to composition. In 1925, following the première of his opera *Wozzeck,* an event that shocked the Berlin audience, Berg found himself the object of attack and acclaim from all parts of Europe and the United States. He was to live for only ten more years; in that time all he wrote was a handful of works, but each had a special significance.

He was at work on the orchestration of his final opera *Lulu,* when the bites of an insect developed into an infection from which he died. His widow blocked access to his notes, but years later the orchestration of *Lulu* was completed according to his directions, and the complete *Lulu* was finally given its première in 1979.

Chief works: Operas *Wozzeck* and *Lulu;* a Violin Concerto; *Lyric Suite* for string quartet.

Hector Berlioz

1803–1869   French romantic composer

If the deaf Beethoven was the first great composer who made his living actually as a composer, and not as an instrumentalist or conductor, Berlioz was the first who was not an instrumentalist at all. His father, a country doctor, sent him to medical school in Paris. But as Berlioz told it, he was so horrified when he entered the dissecting room, where the rats were nibbling at the scraps, that he leaped out the window and went to the Paris Conservatory of Music instead. The anecdote is typical of his emotional and utterly romantic personality.

Berlioz had two unhappy marriages, the first to the Irish Shakespearean actress Harriet Smithson; she is immortalized as the *idée fixe* in the *Fantastic Symphony.*

In spite of suffering hugely all through his life, it was a triumph of his impetuous personality that Berlioz ultimately managed to get most of his enormous compositions performed and to gain a good measure of recognition in conservative Paris. He was obliged throughout his life to support himself with musical journalism, at which he was a master; his *Memoirs* is one of the most delightful books ever written about music. He also toured extensively as a conductor of his music, especially in Germany, where he was welcomed in modernist circles.

Chief works: *Fantastic Symphony* and other program symphonies entitled *Harold in Italy* and *Romeo and Juliet;* opera *The Trojans;* oratorios *The Damnation of Faust* and *The Childhood of Christ;* a Requiem Mass.

Johannes Brahms

1833–1897   German romantic composer

The son of an orchestra musician, Brahms was given piano lessons at an early age. By the time he was ten, he was studying with one of Hamburg's finest music teachers. Like most of the great composers, he was composing, as well as giving public recitals, while still in his teens. Typically, again, he early was forced to turn these talents into a means of livelihood, playing piano at dockside taverns and writing popular tunes.

A turning point in Brahms' life came at the age of twenty when he met Robert and Clara Schumann, who befriended and encouraged him and promoted his music. His style of composition was determined by his love and admiration for the Viennese "classic" composers, and it was in their city, Vienna, the city of his admired Haydn, Mozart, Beethoven, and Schubert, that he eventually settled and passed an uneventful bachelor existence, steadily turning out music. He had many close friends, especially Clara Schumann and an important violinist-composer named Joseph Joachim; he submitted his new music to them for searching criticism before releasing it. With Joachim, too, he issued a sophomoric manifesto in 1860 attacking the "modernist" music of Liszt and Wagner, and in turn he was himself attacked as a conservative.

Brahms was in his forties before his first symphony appeared, many years after its beginnings at his desk. It seems as though he hesitated to provoke comparison with Beethoven, whose symphonies constituted then, as now, a standard for the genre. Brahms went on to write three more symphonies, all harking back to forms used by Beethoven and even Bach, but thoroughly romantic in their expressive effect.

Brahms dabbled in musicology and enjoyed popular music, writing waltzes (Johann Strauss was a valued friend), delightful folksong arrangements, and the well-known *Hungarian Dances.*

Chief works: Four symphonies; much chamber music, including a fine Clarinet Quintet; piano music; songs; *A German Requiem.*

William Byrd

1543–1623   English Renaissance composer

After serving as organist at Lincoln Cathedral, Byrd was appointed a member of the Chapel Royal, which provided music for

Queen Elizabeth. Although Byrd was a Roman Catholic in Protestant England at a time when Catholics suffered from persecution, Byrd managed to keep the good opinion of the Queen. In fact, she gave him the monopoly of music printing in England for a period of years. Although he kept his position in the Chapel Royal, in middle age he retired from London life, and moved to the country where he could practice his religion in private. Widely respected in his lifetime, the teacher of many young composers (including Thomas Morley and Thomas Weelkes), he was regarded in his day as the "father of English music."

Chief works: Three Masses; motets; variations, pavanes, and galliards for harpsichord.

Frédéric François Chopin
1810–1849   French-Polish romantic composer

Chopin's father was a Frenchman who had emigrated to Poland and married a Polish lady. He ran a private school in Warsaw for young gentlemen, and in this atmosphere Frédéric acquired his lifelong taste for life in high society. Provided with the best teachers available, he became a remarkable pianist. A work for piano and orchestra which he published at the age of fifteen was already impressive enough to earn a rave review from Robert Schumann.

After twenty years in Warsaw, Chopin settled in Paris, where he found ready acceptance from society people and also from the literary and artistic figures of the time. He made his way as a highly fashionable piano teacher and by selling his piano music—he composed practically nothing else—to publishers. Chopin was a frail and delicate personality. Though he sometimes played in public, he really disliked the hurly-burly of concert life and preferred to perform for select audiences in great houses. The major event of his personal life was his ten-year romance with Madame Dudevant, a famous novelist and an early feminist, who wrote under the pen name George Sand. Sand sketched some scenes from their not-always-idyllic life together in one of her novels. After the affair broke up in 1847, Chopin's health declined with his spirits, and he died only a few years later at the age of thirty-nine of tuberculosis.

Chief works: Preludes, études, nocturnes, ballades, and other "miniatures" for piano.

Aaron Copland
1900–   American twentieth-century composer

The son of immigrants, Copland studied in New York and then in Paris, the center of musical experiment in the 1920s. At the same time that George Gershwin was struggling to make jazz more "classical" in his Piano Concerto, *Rhapsody in Blue,* and *An American in Paris,* Copland was working the other way around—injecting classical music with jazz in *his* Piano Concerto and *Music for the Theater.* (Copland and Gershwin both had the same piano teacher, the New York composer Rubin Goldmark.) Later Copland moved away from jazz but used other American sources in his compositions, such as the Shaker tune in *Appalachian Spring* and cowboy songs in the ballets *Billy the Kid* and *Rodeo.* In the 1940s he wrote some excellent movie scores—for *The Red Pony, Of Mice and Men,* and *Our Town.* After World War II, he began to work with serial techniques, but like most serial music these later compositions have not attained wide popularity. He

has written an opera for high schools, *The Second Hurricane,* and a fine music-appreciation textbook, *What to Listen for in Music.* Copland keeps out of the limelight, but he has accomplished a good deal of quiet work on behalf of American composers.

Chief works: Piano Variations, Piano Fantasy; Third Symphony; ballet *Appalachian Spring* (for the dancer Martha Graham).

Claude Debussy
1862–1918   French composer of the early twentieth century

One great composer, Debussy, was the product of a music school—the famous Paris Conservatory of Music, where he studied for ten years from the age of eleven. As a result of this training, Debussy's music was to be accepted by the musical establishment with an ease that was surprising in view of his theoretical innovations and the originality of his style. He was regarded as a radical in the composition classes, but not too radical to win the main prize (after several attempts), which earned him a three-year period of study in Rome. Later, Debussy traveled to Russia with Madame von Meck, Tchaikovsky's eccentric patron, who employed the young Frenchman to play in a trio at her home in Moscow. Debussy also visited Bayreuth, Germany, the home of the great Wagner festivals. At first fascinated by Wagner's "music dramas," Debussy eventually turned strongly against them and against most other German music as well.

Back in Paris, he settled into the city's café life, becoming a familiar, bearded figure in his broad-brimmed hat and flowing cape. In his early thirties he seems to have rather suddenly crystallized his musical style. It was at once very individual and very French, reflecting the influences of the French symbolist poets and the impressionist painters. One remarkable work after another was given its première, greeted with a flurry of controversy, and then generally accepted by the critics and the public.

For a short time he wrote music criticism, in which he expressed in pungent prose the anti-German attitudes that were already manifest in his music. Debussy died of cancer in Paris during World War I, actually during a bombardment of the city by his hated Germans.

Chief works: Orchestral works *Prelude to "The Afternoon of a Faun"* (a famous poem by the French symbolist poet Mallarmé), Nocturnes, *The Sea, Images, Games;* opera *Pelléas and Mélisande;* études and preludes for piano.

Josquin Des Prez
c. 1440–1521   Franco-Flemish Renaissance composer

He is thought to have learned his craft from a great master, the Flemish composer Johannes Ockeghem. Certainly he learned it to perfection. Martin Luther, who was something of a composer himself, is supposed to have said "other musicians do with notes what they can, Josquin what he likes"; what Josquin liked was to use his impressive musical technique in the service of a beauty and expressiveness that had not been heard before. It was a time when Italian Dukes and Popes were competing with each other to hire the best possible musicians, and the best had been trained in northern Europe. Josquin had his pick of positions. He changed from one employer to another a number of times, but he stayed longest with the Papal Chapel in Rome, and it was there that many of his most famous works were written.

Josquin's technical mastery and the originality and expressive richness of his music had a profound influence on younger composers. In his lifetime, he was considered the greatest composer of his age; he is now ranked as one of the greatest composers of all time.

Chief works: Masses, including two on *L'homme armé*; motets; chansons.

Guillaume Dufay
c.1400–1474   French Renaissance composer

He received his musical training at the Cathedral of Cambrai in North France, an important musical center of the time. He was a restless and ambitious young man, perpetually on the move, going back and forth between Cambrai and various posts in Italy: at the Papal Chapel in Rome, in Florence and Bologna, and several times with the Duke of Savoy. His travels culminated with a year at the University of Turin, where he studied jurisprudence and received a bachelor's degree. Then he returned to Cambrai and settled down to the enjoyment of a prominent position in the Church. The admiration in which he was held is expressed in the words of a fellow composer who called him "the moon of all music and the light of all singers."

Chief works: Masses, including the first based on *L'homme armé*; motets; chansons.

Edward Kennedy "Duke" Ellington
1899–1974   American jazz composer

Born into the stimulating atmosphere surrounding official Washington, the young Ellington acquired ambition and a taste for elegance, qualities which remained with him all his life. For a time he played in various jazz bands in New York. Then he organized his own band, which grew into his path-breaking Big Band of the nineteen-thirties. His 1932 song *It don't mean a thing if it ain't got that swing* gave the name "swing" to the Big Band Era. By 1943 he had developed jazz into a large-scale concert form, and he began to give annual concerts at New York's principal concert hall, Carnegie Hall.

Through its many metamorphoses, Ellington's band maintained its identity; each of its countless improvisations bore its leader's stamp. His music became famous in Europe in the early 1930s, and has had an international audience since that time.

Chief works: *Mood Indigo; Black and Tan Fantasy; Black, Brown, and Beige*; many songs.

Andrea Gabrieli
c.1510–1586   Italian Renaissance composer

Andrea Gabrieli was a member of a notable Venetian musical family. He was a pupil of the Flemish composer Adrian Willaert, who had settled in Venice and founded a Venetian school of composition. Andrea spent some years traveling and working in German courts. Then he returned to Venice, where he eventually became first organist of the great Cathedral of St. Mark. It happens that he was the first composer to write music in which he specifically designated the use of a wonderful new instrument: the vio-lin. Equally renowned as an organist, a composer, and a teacher, he had among his most important pupils his own nephew, Giovanni.

Chief works: Madrigals; motets; music for organ and various instrumental combinations.

Giovanni Gabrieli
c. 1555–1612   Italian late Renaissance composer

A nephew of Andrea Gabrieli, Giovanni studied composition with his uncle, and remained a devoted disciple; after Andrea's death, Giovanni published a collection of his uncle's works. When he was eighteen years old, he was recruited for the court of Munich by Roland de Lassus, who was the principal composer there. Four years later, he returned to Venice to become second organist at St. Mark's, under his uncle. Giovanni became an experimental, innovative composer, combining voices and instruments in ways that had never been done before. His sense of instrumental color was phenomenal, and he was one of the first composers to use harmony as a structural element. Through his pupils, who came from as far away as England, Germany, and Denmark, his innovations influenced the development of baroque music profoundly.

Chief works: *Symphoniae Sacrae* (Sacred Symphonies), a blanket term for instrumental canzonas, motets for many choirs and instruments, etc.

George Gershwin
1898–1937   American composer of popular music

Born to a poor immigrant family in Brooklyn, Gershwin did not have the opportunity to learn music till he was in his teens. But then he quickly gained skill as a pianist, and soon he was employed as a song writer for Tin Pan Alley. When he was nineteen, his song *Swanee* became a tremendous hit. For the rest of his short life, he was a highly popular composer, in Europe as well as the United States. Most of his work was written for Broadway, but in 1937 he went to Hollywood to embark on a further career as a film composer. But his life was cut short by a brain tumor; he was thirty-eight years old.

Chief works: Many favorite songs and show tunes; *Rhapsody in Blue* for piano and orchestra; opera *Porgy and Bess*.

George Frideric Handel
1685–1759   Anglo-German baroque composer

Handel was born in the same year as Bach, 1685. His father, an elderly and prosperous surgeon, distrusted music and wanted his son to become a lawyer. Handel actually studied law, but long before this his extraordinary musical talent had made his career a foregone conclusion. At twelve he was assistant organist at the cathedral in his hometown of Halle, composing a motet for the services every week; and by the time he was twenty he had made a sensation as an opera composer at Hamburg, the center of German opera at that time. Handel rapidly extended this success in Italy and England, where he finally settled in 1712 to become England's favorite resident composer for two generations. He wrote music for Queen Anne and Kings George I and George II, as well as for various members of the British aristocracy.

Handel was a big, vigorous man, hot-tempered but quick to make up. He ran a succession of opera companies presenting Italian opera in London—recruiting his singers in Europe, writing the music, and managing the finances—an exciting life, full of ups and downs, intrigue and activity. Ultimately Italian opera fell out of fashion, and the resourceful composer turned to writing oratorios, which were received even more enthusiastically. At the end of his life, when he had become blind, Handel still performed brilliantly on the organ and composed by dictating to a musically trained secretary. Though at times he had stood in danger of being thrown into a debtor's prison, Handel died a fairly rich man and was buried with great ceremony in Westminster Abbey.

Chief works: Operas; oratorios *Messiah, Israel in Egypt, Saul, Semele*; twelve concerti grossi for strings; *Water Music* and *Royal Fireworks Music.*

Joseph Haydn
1732–1809   Viennese composer

Haydn's career is a story of many years of hard work, steady development, and ultimate fame and fortune. He came from a musical, Austrian-village family, which sought sophisticated instruction for him. First the village schoolmaster and then a professional musician—who, though he maltreated the boy, also taught him extremely well—tutored the young Haydn. At the age of eight, he was sent to Vienna to be a choirboy in the great Cathedral of St. Stephen. After various musical jobs, he became assistant music director to Prince Esterházy and served the family faithfully for thirty years, until they retired him in 1790 with a handsome pension. His duties at the Esterházy Castle outside Vienna included performing two operas and two concerts every week.

Like Mozart, Haydn married the sister of the woman he actually loved, a mistake that might have been even more disastrous than Mozart's, for his wife was unpleasant and unkind. But Haydn soon separated from her.

After around 1765, his music slowly grew more and more popular and was widely published (it was mostly the publishers who provided the nicknames to so many of Haydn's symphonies and quartets). After he retired, he went on two triumphal tours of London, which occupied a position in the musical world like that of New York in later years. His last twelve symphonies were composed for concerts in London. Haydn scored his greatest success, however, back in Vienna with his oratorios *The Creation* and *The Seasons,* written when he was nearing seventy. At last, after producing an enormous quantity of symphonies, quartets, trios, operas, and Masses—works to which he invariably gave his best—Haydn's mind began to slip, and he could no longer compose.

Mozart, at twenty-five, was half Haydn's age when they met in 1781. Haydn readily acknowledged the younger man's genius and was deeply shaken when, eighteen years before his own death, Mozart died ravaged by debt and illness.

Haydn was a splendid person, basically simple and modest though quite aware of his worth, but also shrewd and worldly, and generous in his reports of others.

Chief works: Symphonies, especially the twelve *London* symphonies (which include *The Surprise, The Drum-Roll, The Clock,* and *The Military*); string quartets; oratorios *The Creation* and *The Seasons.*

Charles Ives
1874–1954   American twentieth-century composer

Today the most honored of American composers, Ives's long life was full of ironies and contradictions; one might say it was as unusual and dissonant as his music. Born in Connecticut, he was the son of a Civil War bandleader with an original turn of mind. From his father, young Charles learned to perform and compose, and also to experiment with sound: for example, Charles would sing a song in one key while his father played music in another key. At the age of twenty, he became a student at Yale University, where his training in composition was disciplined and conservative. Ives decided that he would never make a living writing the kind of music he wanted to write, and so upon graduation he entered the insurance business.

For the next twenty years, Ives led a double life. In public, he was a highly successful business man, founding his own insurance company. Privately, he composed one work after another, all of them too advanced and strange for the ears of musicians whom he tried to interest in his compositions. He had no public performances, and his work remained totally unknown.

Then in 1918, when he was forty-four, Ives suffered from a massive heart attack, which almost brought both of his careers to a complete halt. Yet he was to live on to the age of 80, and was to gain fame and recognition in his lifetime. When he had sufficiently recovered from the more acute stage of his illness, he began to print a few of his works at his own expense, and send them free to libraries and any musician who might be interested: first came his *Concord Sonata* for piano, and then his *114 Songs.* For years there was no public reaction, but this music was beginning to impress a number of young composers and performers. In 1939, a New York performance of the *Concord Sonata* produced a sensation. In 1947, Ives won the Pulitzer Prize for his Third Symphony. Now, in his old age, his remarkable life story caught the attention of the press. Famous at last, Ives's music began to be played and recorded and admired for its imaginative power and its daring.

Chief works: Second, Third, and Fourth Symphonies; *Concord Sonata; Three Places in New England* for orchestra; songs.

Roland de Lassus (Orlando di Lasso)
1532–1594   Netherlandish late Renaissance composer

He started as a choirboy, with such a beautiful voice that he was abducted three times by ambitious choirmasters. When he was twelve, his parents decided to let him enter service in Italy, and there he remained till he was in his twenties, working at a variety of musical jobs after his voice broke, and perfecting his skills as a composer. In 1556 he was offered a first-rate position at Munich, the seat of the Bavarian court; he was only twenty-four. For the remainder of his life he was based in Munich, though his post involved him in many journeys.

Lassus was married and had four sons (two of them became composers) and two daughters; he was widely admired for his genius, and liked for his pleasant personality: a highly successful career. But toward the end of his life, he suffered from periods of "melancholia," and in the year before his death, despite the solicitude of his family and his employer, he was too depressed to compose.

Chief works: Motets, including the *Penitential Psalms;* madrigals; chansons.

Franz Liszt

1811–1886   Hungarian romantic composer and pianist

No composer ever led a more glittering life. He learned music on the estate of Prince Esterházy, where Haydn had once served, and where Liszt's father worked as a steward. By the time he was eleven, he was giving his first concert in Vienna, and was well on his way to glory. His dashing looks and personality, his radical opinions, and his liaisons with noble women dazzled Europe as much as his incredible pianistic technique. In 1833 he met the Countess d'Agoult and went with her to Geneva, where they lived together for five years. She bore him three children, one of whom, Cosima, became notorious in her turn when she abandoned her husband for Richard Wagner.

After his relationship with the Countess came to an end, Liszt spent the next few years touring Europe, giving triumphant concerts from Portugal in the West to Turkey and Russia. Finally tiring of this life, he gave up his concert career to settle as a conductor at Weimar, with Princess Sayn-Wittgenstein. Under the Princess' influence, Liszt turned to religion. He became an abbé, a kind of secular priest. This position would have allowed him to marry, but the Princess was unable to get a divorce.

Liszt was a strong partisan of Wagner's music. His own compositions were radical works; his symphonic poems, like Wagner's music dramas, were written to be "Music of the Future." His works for piano demanded totally new techniques of performance. Though he spent most of his last years in Rome, he died in Bayreuth, where Wagner's music was being performed.

Chief works: *Les Préludes* and other symphonic poems; *Faust* and *Dante* Symphonies (program symphonies); Piano Sonata in B minor; piano versions of Schubert songs and opera medleys.

Jean-Baptiste Lully

1632–1687   French baroque composer

Lully was born in Italy, but he was brought to France as a child to work as a pageboy for a cousin of Louis XIV. Louis had become king when he was five years old. He was still a child when his admiration for Lully, a brilliant violinist at fifteen, prompted the boy king to hire the young composer for his own court. Prominent first as a musician and a dancer, Lully later developed the characteristic types of French baroque opera and ballet.

Lully turned out to be an exceedingly able courtier, retaining the king's favor all his life, and managing to amass a fortune. He died as the result of an accident. It was the practice at that time to conduct an orchestra by using a heavy cane as a baton; one day while conducting, Lully injured his foot with the baton, and the wound became fatally infected.

Chief works: Operas; ballets; opera-ballets, including many widely popular dances.

Guillaume de Machaut

c. 1300–1377   French medieval composer and poet

In the fourteenth century, a religious vocation did not necessarily express a deeply religious temperament. Guillaume became a priest as a very young man, and also earned a university degree in theology. But after this severe beginning, his life offered fame, a bit of adventure, and even a taste of notoriety. He traveled widely with his first employer, the reckless, blind King John of Bohemia,

witnessing twenty battles and a hundred tournaments. After John's death at the battle of Crécy, he was supported by a succession of royal patrons. In later years, he became Canon at the Cathedral of Rheims, a position that allowed him to devote himself to poetry and music. His love affair, when he was in his sixties, with an aristocratic admirer who was still in her teens became the subject of a book-length poem that was widely read.

Chief works: Mass of Notre Dame; chansons; isorhythmic motets.

Gustav Mahler

1860–1911   Viennese late romantic composer

Mahler's early life was not a happy one. Born in Bohemia to an abusive father, five of his brothers and sisters died of diphtheria, and others ended their lives in suicide or mental illness. Mahler began to play the piano at six, and at fifteen he entered the Vienna Conservatory of Music. Later, patrons encouraged and supported him in his rapid rise as a conductor.

Mahler was one of the great conductors of his time and also a very effective musical administrator. Ultimately he came to head such organizations as the Vienna Opera, the Metropolitan Opera in New York, and the New York Philharmonic. A dedicated and uncompromising musician, his disputes with the Philharmonic's Board of Directors discouraged him profoundly and are said to have contributed to his early death. Mahler carved out time for himself to compose only in the summers, so it isn't surprising that he produced fewer pieces (though they are very long pieces) than any other important composer. Ten symphonies, the last of them unfinished, and six song cycles for voice and orchestra are all he wrote.

He married a famous Viennese beauty, Alma Schindler, who after his death went on to marry the great architect Walter Gropius and then the novelist Franz Werfel—and then wrote fascinating memoirs of her life with the composer. Despite his eminent positions, Mahler's life was clouded by psychological turmoil, and he once consulted his Viennese contemporary, Dr. Sigmund Freud.

Chief works: Ten symphonies, several with chorus, of which the best-known are the Fourth and Fifth; song cycle *The Song of the Earth* for soloists and orchestra.

Claudio Monteverdi

1567–1743   Italian early Baroque composer

Monteverdi was born in the important musical town of Cremona, in northern Italy. He was already an accomplished composer when, at the age of twenty-three, he was offered a position by the Duke of Mantua, a town not far from Cremona. He soon became famous for his madrigals, but at the same time, because of his radical ideas about composition, he became the center of controversy.

In 1597, opera was invented in Florence; ten years later, Monteverdi wrote his first opera, *Orfeo*, for the Mantuan court. When the Duke of Mantua died in 1612, the new Duke fired Monteverdi, and he went home to Cremona almost as poor as when he had set out twenty-two years before. St. Mark's in Venice came to the rescue. He was offered a secure position as chapel master and he remained in Venice for the rest of his life. Opera, in the meantime, had become a highly popular art. The first public opera house in Venice opened in 1637, followed by many others, and Monteverdi once again began to compose operas.

Unluckily, only two of them remain. Of all the great composers, Monteverdi's works have suffered the most catastrophic losses. First, war took its toll: in 1630 Mantua was sacked and all the Monteverdi manuscripts that were stored there were destroyed. Then the work of the Venetian years was eroded by time and neglect. For two centuries Monteverdi's work was almost forgotten, and when at last musicians started searching for its traces, they found only a fraction left intact.

Chief works: Operas *Orfeo, The Coronation of Poppaea, The Return of Ulysses;* madrigals; Vespers of the Blessed Virgin Mary.

Modest Moussorgsky

1839–1881   Russian romantic composer

The high social class into which Moussorgsky was born dictated that he become an officer in the Russian Imperial Guard. He duly went to cadet school and joined a regiment after graduation, but he could not long ignore his deep-seated desire to become a composer. In the meantime, political-economic changes that were going on in Russia at the time caused the liquidation of his family estate. He was forced to work at a clerical job, while he struggled to master the technique of an art that he had come to late in life.

Moussorgsky never felt secure in his technique, and relied on his highly competent friend, the composer Nikolai Rimsky-Korsakov, to criticize his work. But his intense nationalism formed his vision of what he wanted his work to be—truly Russian music. Though he succeeded magnificently, he was filled with doubts, became alcoholic, suffered from seizures, and died in an army hospital at the age of 42.

Chief works: Opera *Boris Godunov; Pictures at an Exhibition* and *Night on Bald Mountain,* program pieces.

Wolfgang Amadeus Mozart

1756–1791   Viennese composer

Mozart was the son of a distinguished composer and writer on music, court musician to the Archbishop of Salzburg in Austria. Mozart's amazing musical ability was recognized early, and for ten years he toured all over Europe as a child prodigy. He played for the young Austrian princess Marie Antoinette, who was later to be Queen of France, at the age of six and composed his first professional opera for the Italian stage at fourteen. But Mozart grew up into the sort of person for whom nothing works out right. He felt he could not tolerate the servile life of a court musician, as his father had done, and so he left Salzburg for Vienna. He fell in love with a coloratura soprano, Aloysa Weber, but she turned him down and instead he married her disorganized sister Constanze.

When he tried to make a life for himself as an independent musician in Vienna, he had a dishearteningly difficult time, even though there were moments of success and though his genius was generally recognized. Haydn, who played in an amateur string quartet with Mozart, called him quite simply the greatest composer he had ever met. Mozart died at the age of thirty-five after ten years of struggle in Vienna, heavily in debt to his Freemason lodge brothers. Constanze had a breakdown and could not supervise the funeral, and Mozart was buried in an unmarked pauper's grave.

Of all the great composers, Mozart had perhaps the most extraordinary natural genius. His Viennese contemporaries thought his music was too serious, and the romantics thought it was too light. Today Mozart is generally ranked with Bach and Beethoven as the greatest of Western composers.

Chief works: Operas *The Marriage of Figaro, Don Giovanni, The Magic Flute;* symphonies, piano concertos, string quartets and quintets; a Requiem Mass (left unfinished at his death).

Giovanni Pierluigi da Palestrina

c. 1525–1594   Italian Renaissance composer

Though he is the greatest and best-known composer for the Roman Catholic Church, Palestrina was nevertheless a worldly man. He studied music in Rome and settled there, marrying well and raising a family. Employed as a musician in various Roman churches, his restrained, serene compositions quickly found official favor. In the midst of an active, productive life, he was suddenly battered by tragedy when an epidemic took the lives of his wife and two of his three sons. For a while, he thought about becoming a priest. In the end he consoled himself by marrying a rich widow, and ran her fur business while he continued a triumphant career as the leading composer of Catholic church music.

Chief works: Over a hundred Masses, including the *Pope Marcellus* Mass; motets.

Henry Purcell

1659–1695   English baroque composer

Born into a musical family, Purcell sang in the Chapel Royal as a boy, studying composition in the meantime with the well-known composer John Blow. He became organist at Westminster Abbey when he was twenty, and three years later was organist for the Chapel Royal as well. He married, had children, and enjoyed the esteem of his countrymen. He wrote songs, large choral works, and instrumental chamber music, but it was a chance invitation from a girls' school that produced his one opera. He was only thirty-six when he died. He was honored by being buried in Westminster Abbey, under the organ that he had played.

Chief works: Opera *Dido and Aeneas;* court ceremonial cantatas called odes; instrumental music.

Alessandro Scarlatti

1660–1725   Italian baroque composer

Sent by his musical Sicilian family to study in Rome, Scarlatti quickly launched a brilliant career as an opera composer. Queen Christina of Sweden, then in Rome, became the first of his royal patrons. The second was the King of Naples, who persuaded him to leave Rome for the Neapolitan court. At various times he wrote for Venice, for Rome, and for Naples: everywhere his fame and success were phenomenal. He was even awarded a knighthood, not a common honor for a musician in those days. His son Domenico became an important harpsichord composer, whose brilliant two-movement sonatas are better known today than any of his father's music.

Chief works: Over a hundred operas, including *Il Tigrane* and *La Griselda;* cantatas.

Arnold Schoenberg
1874–1951   Viennese twentieth-century composer

Largely self-taught in music, Schoenberg showed great originality not only as a composer, but also as a musical theorist. Nevertheless, for much of his lifetime he was obliged to eke out an existence with rather low-level musical jobs.

As a young man Schoenberg held the somewhat messianic belief that he was destined to carry the great tradition of Bach, Beethoven, Brahms, and Wagner through its "logical" modern development. Listeners felt otherwise, and Schoenberg's revolutionary compositions of the 1900s were received with more hostility than any in the entire history of music. At the same time, they attracted the sympathetic interest of Gustav Mahler and Richard Strauss and drew a coterie of brilliant young students to Schoenberg. A man of unusual versatility, Schoenberg wrote the literary texts for many of his compositions, painted pictures in an expressionist style, and produced very important books on musical theory.

Schoenberg's music had been growing progressively more and more atonal, but he was nearly fifty before he evolved the twelve-tone (or serial) system. For this, he was attacked even more. As a Jew, he was forced to leave Germany when the Nazis took over in 1933, and he spent his last years in Los Angeles. Schoenberg was a remarkable personality: proud, superstitious, suspicious to the point of paranoia. Of all the major composers, he was the first great teacher since Bach; among his students were Alban Berg and Anton Webern. At the end of his life he taught at UCLA.

Though his music has never won popular approval, Schoenberg is regarded by many musicians as far and away the most significant composer of the twentieth century.

Chief works: Four quartets; *Pierrot Lunaire* ("Moonstruck Pierrot"), a chamber-music piece with *Sprechstimme* singer; *Erwartung* ("Anticipation"), an expressionist "monodrama" for one singer and orchestra; the unfinished opera *Moses and Aaron*.

Franz Schubert
1797–1828   Composer of the late Viennese period

Schubert was probably the most unassuming of all the great composers. Born in Vienna, he learned music at home—there was a family string quartet—and at the choir school attached to the Imperial Court Chapel. He started pouring out music in his middle teens: songs, sonatas, symphonies, chamber music, an opera (never performed), and a mass. For a few years he taught at a school, alongside his father, but in later years he preferred to get along without a regular job, relying on what little he could bring in from a few private lessons and from selling music to publishers. Songs, part-songs (songs for several singers), waltzes, and piano four-hand music were most in demand, and Schubert turned these out with amazing facility.

He roomed at one time with a poet, Johann Mayrhofer, who supplied him with many gloomy song poems. Fortunately, a little cult of friends and admirers attached themselves to Schubert, promoting his music and helping him as best they could; there are accounts and pictures of various convivial trips and parties of the "Schubertianer," as they called themselves. Schubert died in a typhoid fever epidemic when he was only thirty-one. Works such as his two great symphonies were never performed during his life-

time, and a great deal of his music only came to light many years after his death.

Chief works: Songs, including the song cycles *The Fair Maid of the Mill, Die Winterreise, Swan Songs; Unfinished* Symphony and Symphony in C; sonatas and chamber music, including a great string quintet.

Robert Schumann
1810–1856   German romantic composer

Encouraged by his father, Robert Schumann began to study the piano when he was six. Unfortunately, his father died when the boy was in his teens and his mother disapproved of a musical career, insisting on law instead. Schumann finally persuaded her to his view and traveled to Liepzig, determined to become a piano virtuoso. He failed because of a finger paralysis which he is said to have induced in an effort to retrain his hands to a new pianistic style.

Besides his musical talent, Schumann had a great flair for literature, inherited from his father, who was a bookseller, writer, and editor. When he was only twenty-three, Schumann founded a magazine to compaign for a higher level of music; started writing regular music criticism of the highest quality, which encouraged such unknown composers as Chopin and (later) Brahms; and became a highly respected voice in the German music world. Before then, he had begun composing his highly original "miniatures" for piano—often providing them with half-programmatic titles of a literary nature such as *Carnaval, Novelettes, Butterflies,* and *Dances of the David League* (a make-believe society of young romantic spirits opposed to the Goliath of middle-class society and its conservative artistic tastes).

Schumann fell in love with Clara Wieck, the daughter of his music teacher. At sixteen, Clara was already on the way to becoming one of the great pianists of the century. Thanks to her father's fanatical opposition, the couple had to wait until she was twenty-one (minus one day) before getting married. A charming outcome of the marriage was that Schumann, whose early compositions were entirely for the piano, suddenly started to write love songs for his Clara; nearly 150 songs were composed in this "song year." He also turned to the composition of larger works, such as concertos and symphonies. Thereafter he assumed some important musical positions and did some touring with Clara, but began to develop tragic signs of insanity. In 1854, tormented by voices, hallucinations, and a loss of memory, he tried to drown himself in the Rhine and was committed to an asylum. He died two years later without regaining his sanity.

Chief works: Song cycles *A Woman's Life and Love, Poet's Love;* sets of "miniatures" for piano; piano *Fantasy* (a sort of free sonata); Piano Concerto; four symphonies.

Karlheinz Stockhausen
1928–   Present-day German composer

The end of World War II and the end of the Nazi regime meant that for the first time in a dozen years, German musicians mixed with foreigners and were exposed to the most modern trends in music, particularly the serialism of Schoenberg and Webern. Stockhausen was a student at this time—a time of amazing experiments and radical new ideas about music. Furthermore, the war had brought electronic technology to a stage where it could become a powerful tool for composers.

In 1947, Stockhausen entered Cologne's State Academy of Music to continue his study of the piano. After receiving his teacher's license *summa cum laude,* he played piano in the bars of Cologne, was an accompanist to a traveling magician, served as director of an amateur operetta theater, and held a number of non-musical odd jobs.

Stockhausen soon assumed leadership among the brilliant international group of composers who gathered in the 1950s at the avant-garde summer music school at Darmstadt, West Germany. Director of the electronic music studio at the Cologne Radio, he has also worked with chance music, "happenings," improvisation, and ideas derived from oriental music and philosophy. Many of his recent compositions—he has composed well over fifty works to date—have emerged from sessions of a special improvisational group with which he plays, using both conventional and electronic instruments. Like many present-day composers and artists, Stockhausen is a great theorizer, explainer, and propagandist, as well as a creator; he is a very impressive writer and lecturer about music.

Chief works: *Song of the Children* for five-track stereo tape; *Moments* for soprano, four choirs, and four orchestras; *Hymns* for electronically generated sounds and *musique concrète; Mantra* for two pianos.

Johann Strauss, Jr.

1825–1899   Austrian nineteenth-century composer of popular music

His father was the most popular composer and bandmaster in Vienna. At the age of nineteen, Johann Jr. formed his first band, performing his own music as well as his father's. With one triumph following another, he became the senior Strauss' successful rival—to the anger and frustration of the older man, though Johann Jr. had the secret support of his mother. After his father's death in 1849, Johann combined both orchestras and proceeded to a wildly popular career. During the American centennial of 1876, he gave a famous series of gigantic concerts in Boston and New York. Around this time he began to compose operettas; *Die Fledermaus* quickly became a great favorite. It has become a tradition in Vienna to perform it every New Year's Eve.

Chief works: Waltzes, including *The Beautiful Blue Danube,* and *Tales from the Vienna Woods;* operettas *Die Fledermaus* (The Bat), *Der Zigeunerbaron* (The Gypsy Baron).

Richard Strauss

1864–1949   German late romantic composer

Richard Strauss's father (not related to the famous Viennese Strauss family of waltz composers) was a well-known Munich orchestra player, his mother a wealthy beer heiress. Their son was a prodigy; at seventeen he saw his Symphony in D minor performed; and at the age of twenty-one he assumed the first of the many important conducting positions he was to hold in various German and Austrian towns. His earliest music was influenced by the conservative Brahms, but he turned to the style of Liszt and Wagner for his symphonic poems and operas. These were regarded as the most advanced and controversial music of the time in the years around 1900.

At thirty, he married the opera singer Pauline de Ahne; a scene (literally) from their continuously tempestuous private life forms the subject of his opera *Intermezzo* (Strauss had a predilection for such "autobiographical" compositions).

During most of World War II, Strauss remained in Switzerland. At first willing to accept the Nazis, he finally broke with them when they attempted to prevent him from collaborating on an opera with a Jewish author. Shortly after the worldwide observance of his eighty-fifth birthday, Strauss died at his beautiful villa in Garmisch in the Bavarian Alps.

Chief works: Symphonic poems *Don Juan, Till Eulenspiegel's Merry Pranks, Death and Transfiguration;* operas *Salome, Electra* and *Der Rosenkavalier* (The Cavalier of the Rose).

Igor Stravinsky

1882–1971   Russian international twentieth-century composer

The son of an important opera singer, Stravinsky studied law and did not turn seriously to music until he was nineteen. Then he studied with the great nationalist composer Rimsky-Korsakov, whose example served Stravinsky well in the famous (and still outstandingly popular) ballet scores he wrote for the *Ballets Russes,* a Russian ballet company centered in Paris. These brilliant, always sensational works were followed by others in a dazzling variety of styles, forms, and genres. One of the first composers, along with Debussy, to be interested in jazz, Stravinsky wrote *Piano Ragtime* in 1917 and *Ebony Concerto* for Woody Herman's swing band in 1946.

After the Russian Revolution in 1917, Stravinsky made his home in Paris, taking part in the celebrity-studded cultural life there. In 1939 he moved to Los Angeles. The end of World War II marked the start of a new, more classical, abstract, and formal style in Stravinsky's music. During the last twenty years of his life, Stravinsky had as his protégé the young American conductor and critic Robert Craft, who helped to manage his affairs, conducted and promoted his music, and introduced him to the music of Schoenberg and Webern. For a quarter of a century people had regarded Stravinsky (and he regarded himself) as the leading neoclassical composer in the French orbit, at the opposite pole from Schoenberg and the Viennese serialists. So he created yet another sensation when, in his seventies, he produced a remarkable final series of compositions employing serial technique.

Chief works: Ballet scores *Petroushka, The Rite of Spring, The Wedding, Orpheus, Agon;* the opera-oratorio *Oedipus the King; The Rake's Progress,* an opera in English; *Symphony of Psalms* for orchestra and chorus; *The Soldier's Tale,* an unusual chamber-music piece with narrator.

Piotr Ilyich Tchaikovsky

1840–1893   Russian late romantic composer

In nineteenth-century Russia, a serious musical education and a musical career were not accorded the social approval they received in Germany, France, or Italy. Many of the famous Russian composers began in other careers and only turned to music in their mature years, when driven by inner necessity. Once Tchaikovsky got started, after abandoning the civil service, he composed prolifically—six symphonies, eleven operas, symphonic poems, chamber music, songs, and some of the most famous of all ballet scores: *Swan Lake, Sleeping Beauty,* and *The Nutcracker.*

Though his pieces may sometimes sound "Russian" to us, he was not a devoted nationalist like Moussorgsky and other composers of the time.

Tchaikovsky was a depressive personality who more than once attempted suicide. The son of a mine inspector, he was an extremely delicate and hypersensitive child, completely dependent on his mother for emotional support. He developed into a highly neurotic, but very charming, adult whose central fear was that his dominant homosexual bent would be discovered and exposed. In an attempt to raise himself above suspicion through marriage, he selected an unstable young musician who had attached herself to him. The marriage was a fiasco; in a matter of weeks, Tchaikovsky fled and never saw the woman again, though she pursued him, trying to extort money.

For years Tchaikovsky was subsidized by a remarkable woman, Madame von Meck, whom, by mutual agreement, he never met. Nevertheless, they daily wrote intimate letters over the thirteen years of their friendship, which was terminated, without explanation, by Madame von Meck. Tchaikovsky was crushed by her rejection. Three years later he died of cholera after carelessly (or fatalistically, or purposely?) drinking unboiled water during an epidemic.

His music has been criticized as weak in form and sentimental in expression, but this has never affected its enormous popularity with concert audiences.

Chief works: Fourth, Fifth, and Sixth (*Pathétique*) Symphonies; operas *The Queen of Spades* and *Eugene Onegin*, based on works by the Russian romantic poet Alexander Pushkin.

Georg Philipp Telemann
1681–1767   German baroque composer

A contemporary of Bach, Telemann was a much more famous man at the time. He had been a student at Leipzig University, where he studied law and modern languages. Then, having decided on music as a career, he became a very skillful and unusually prolific composer, even for those prolific times. In 1721 he was made director of music for the city of Hamburg, a highly desirable post that Bach, too, had applied for. When a position as cantor at the Thomasschule in Leipzig opened up, Telemann once more was the first choice; only when he refused it was the Leipzig job offered to Bach. Telemann remained for the rest of his long life in Hamburg, then as now a major center of music and opera, composing expertly in all genres.

Chief works: Chamber music for very many instrumental combinations.

Giuseppe Verdi
1813–1901   Italian romantic composer

The son of a storekeeper in a tiny village in northern Italy, Verdi had a spotty education. He played church organ and conducted the band of the neighboring little town. In those days, the center of musical life in Italy was the famous opera house La Scala (The Ladder) in Milan. After several discouraging years in that city, Verdi scored a huge success with his Biblical opera *Nabucco* (*Nebuchadnezzar*) when he was twenty-nine years old. Thereafter, he composed successful operas for various opera houses in Italy

and in Paris, London, St. Petersburg (now Leningrad), and even Cairo.

Many of the operas had patriotic themes; Verdi was an ardent supporter of the *Risorgimento*, or Italian liberation movement, and was made an honorary deputy in the first Italian parliament. A dour character and a tough businessman, Verdi drove hard bargains with opera impresarios, bullied his librettists, and insisted on supervising the production of his new operas. When he had accumulated enough money, he retired to a fine country estate near his birthplace and spent his later years raising livestock and hunting.

His second marriage to the opera singer Giuseppina Strepponi, the star of *Nabucco*, who had befriended him in his youth—and was his mistress for many years—was a devoted one. When his wife died in 1897, Verdi was bereft. Disconsolate and declining, he moved into Milan's Grand Hotel; in 1901, at the age of eighty-eight, he suffered a fatal cerebral hemorrhage. By now a national institution, Verdi was mourned throughout Italy. Schools closed. Eulogies were delivered in a special session of the senate in Rome. Nearly 300,000 people saw the old man to his grave. His operas remain the most popular of all in the international repertory.

Chief works: Twenty-four operas, including *Rigoletto*, *La Traviata*, *Aida*, and two great Shakespeare operas composed after his retirement, *Otello* and *Falstaff*; a Requiem Mass.

Tomás Luis de Victoria
1548–1611   Spanish Renaissance composer

Victoria was a Spaniard of severely religious temperament. He moved to Rome when he was sixteen to study for the priesthood. For the first part of his life, he stayed in Italy, though much of his support came from the Spanish royal family. His beautiful music was written only for the Church; he absolutely refused to write secular music of any kind, though this was the great age of the Italian madrigal. Later in life, he returned to Spain to live out his years quietly in a religious community.

Chief works: Masses; motets; settings of Holy Week services and the Office of the Dead.

Antonio Vivaldi
1675–1741   Italian baroque composer

Vivaldi was a Venetian, the son of a violinist at St. Mark's Cathedral. In his lifetime the violin had been brought to a state of perfection; Antonio Stradivarius was making the instruments that are still the most valued in the world. It seems inevitable that Vivaldi should have become a violinist. He also became a priest, and his combined professions qualified him to become head music teacher at a well-known Venetian music school for orphan girls. His principal task seems to have been to provide concertos for his pupils to play. As he traveled around Europe—for the school was very liberal in giving him leaves of absence—he dutifully sent two new concertos a month back to Venice. His interests, however, had turned to writing operas, which were produced successfully in major European cities. Eventually Vivaldi decided to settle in Vienna, where he remained for life.

Chief works: Solo concertos and concerti grossi for a great variety of instruments.

Richard Wagner
1813–1883   German romantic composer

From his schooldays on, Wagner was a decided intellectual. His early interests, literature and music—Shakespeare and Beethoven were his idols—later expanded to include philosophy, politics, mythology, and religion. As a young man he worked as an opera conductor and started to develop his revolutionary ideal of a new kind of opera. This he finally formulated after being exiled from Germany (and from a job) as a result of his part in the revolution of 1848–1849. He wrote endless and often venomous articles and books expounding his ideas—ideas that were better known than his operas, for these were extremely difficult to stage.

Wagner's fortunes changed when he gained the support of the young, unstable, and finally mad King Ludwig II of Bavaria. Ludwig had Wagner's mature operas produced, at last. Wagner then promoted the building of a special opera house in Bayreuth, Germany, solely for his music dramas—lengthy, grandiose, slow-moving works based on myths, and characterized by high-flown poetry of his own, a powerful orchestral style, and the use of leitmotivs. To this day the opera house in Bayreuth is used only for the production of Wagner's operas.

A hypnotic personality, Wagner was able to spirit money out of many pockets and command the loyalty and affection of many distinguished men and women. He married his second wife Cosima (the daughter of the composer Franz Liszt) after breaking up her marriage to his friend, the conductor Hans von Bülow.

Half con man and half visionary, bad poet and very good musician, Wagner created a storm of controversy in his lifetime which has not entirely died down to this day. His ideas were very influential not only in music but also in other arts. Ultimately he was probably the most impressive and important of the romantic composers.

Chief works: Early operas, *Tannhäuser* and *Lohengrin*; mature operas, *Tristan and Isolde, The Mastersingers of Nuremberg, Parsifal,* and *The Nibelung's Ring,* which is a four-opera cycle consisting of *The Rhine Gold, The Valkyrie, Siegfried,* and *The Twilight of the Gods.*

Anton Webern
1883–1945   Austrian twentieth-century composer

A Viennese, like Schoenberg and Berg, Webern was the most scholarly member of the "Second Viennese School." He studied music history at the University of Vienna and received a Ph.D. with a dissertation on a fifteenth-century Netherlandish composer. He studied with Schoenberg, and in his own compositions used Schoenberg's method to exquisite effect.

Webern was a socialist; for a time he conducted the Viennese workers' orchestra and the workers' chorus in concerts. When the Nazis came to power, his music was banned as "Bolshevik," and he had to support himself as a proofreader, forbidden to teach, but giving secret lectures on music theory. In 1945, almost at the end of World War II, his son was killed in an air raid. Webern and his wife fled to the countryside near Salzburg. Rescue appeared at hand when the American occupying forces appeared, but one evening when Webern walked outside for a smoke, a nervous military policeman shot him to death.

Chief works: Five Pieces for Orchestra; Piano Variations; Concerto for Nine Instruments.

Thomas Weelkes
c.1575–1623   English Renaissance composer

Nothing is known about Weelkes' early life. The earliest record we have of him comes from the publication of his first book of madrigals in 1597. But his compositions attracted attention. He was a friend of the prominent composer Thomas Morley, who invited him to contribute to *The Triumphs of Oriana,* which Morley was editing. In 1602 Weelkes was granted a Bachelor of Music degree from Oxford University. Following this recognition, an appointment as organist at Chichester Cathedral gave him a permanent position though not, it seems, a very happy one, for the cathedral documents include complaints about his quarrelsomeness and his drinking. However, he wrote some of the finest church anthems of his time.

Chief works: Madrigals; anthems for the Anglican Church.

Chronological Charts

Pages 542–43 from 1250 to 1650
Pages 544–45 from 1600 to 2000

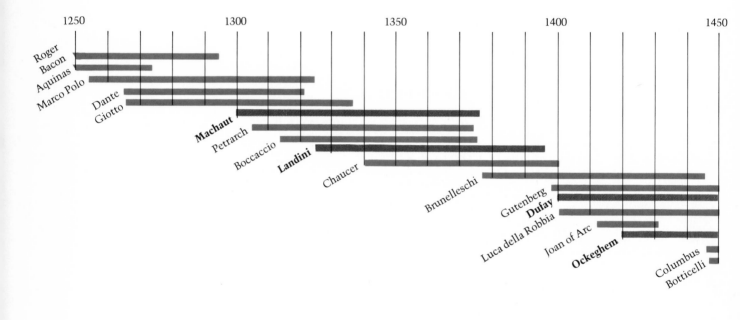

1250   1300   1350   1400   1450

Roger Bacon
Aquinas
Marco Polo
Dante
Giotto
Machaut
Petrarch
Boccaccio
Landini
Chaucer
Brunelleschi
Gutenberg
Dufay
Luca della Robbia
Joan of Arc
Ockeghem
Columbus
Botticelli

━━━━━━━━━━━━━ **Life span of major composers**

━━━━━━━━━━━━━ Other important historical and artistic figures

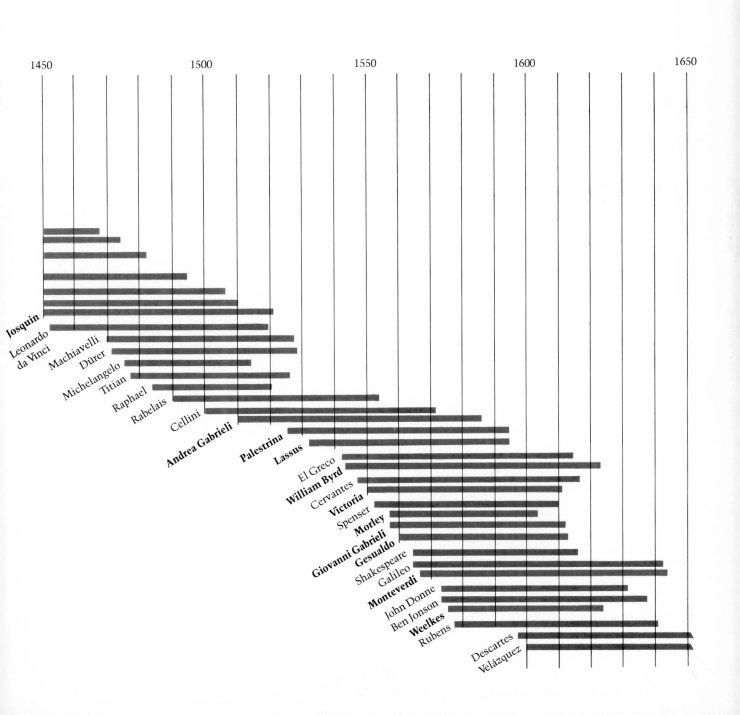

1450   1500   1550   1600   1650

Josquin
Leonardo
da Vinci
Machiavelli
Dürer
Michelangelo
Titian
Raphael
Rabelais
Cellini
Andrea Gabrieli
Palestrina
Lassus
El Greco
William Byrd
Cervantes
Victoria
Spenser
Morley
Giovanni Gabrieli
Gesualdo
Shakespeare
Galileo
Monteverdi
John Donne
Ben Jonson
Weelkes
Rubens
Descartes
Velázquez

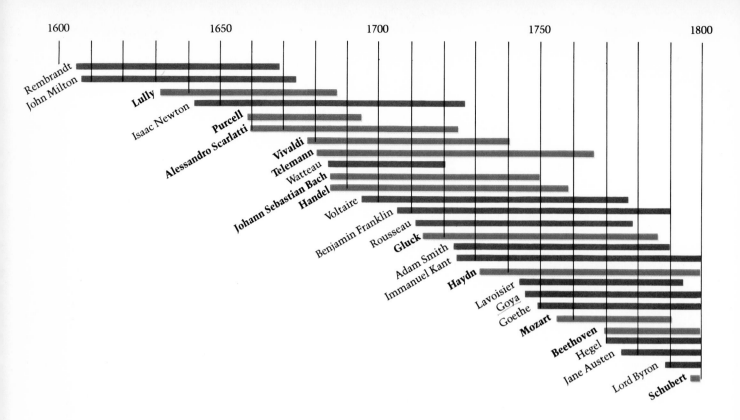

| | 1600 | | 1650 | | 1700 | | 1750 | | 1800 |

Rembrandt
John Milton
Lully
Isaac Newton
Purcell
Alessandro Scarlatti
Vivaldi
Telemann
Watteau
Johann Sebastian Bach
Handel
Voltaire
Benjamin Franklin
Rousseau
Gluck
Adam Smith
Immanuel Kant
Haydn
Lavoisier
Goya
Goethe
Mozart
Beethoven
Hegel
Jane Austen
Lord Byron
Schubert

━━━━━━━ **Life span of major composers**

━━━━━━━ Other important historical and artistic figures

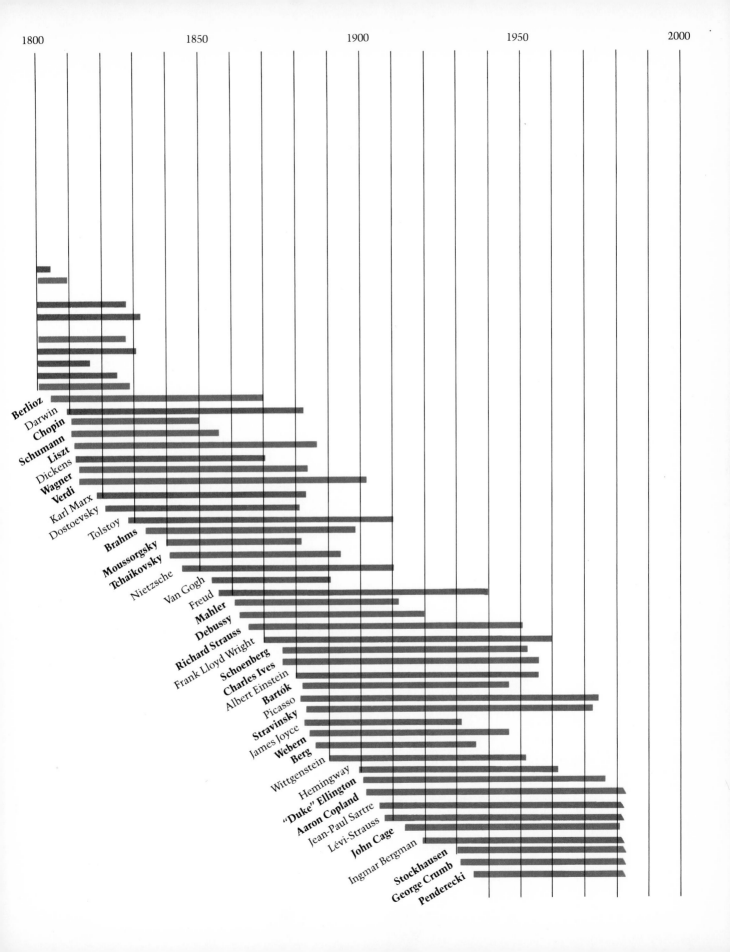

1800   1850   1900   1950   2000

Berlioz
Darwin
Chopin
Schumann
Liszt
Dickens
Wagner
Verdi
Karl Marx
Dostoevsky
Tolstoy
Brahms
Moussorgsky
Tchaikovsky
Nietzsche
Van Gogh
Freud
Mahler
Debussy
Richard Strauss
Frank Lloyd Wright
Schoenberg
Charles Ives
Albert Einstein
Bartók
Picasso
Stravinsky
James Joyce
Webern
Berg
Wittgenstein
Hemingway
"Duke" Ellington
Aaron Copland
Jean-Paul Sartre
Lévi-Strauss
John Cage
Ingmar Bergman
Stockhausen
George Crumb
Penderecki

Glossary of Musical Terms

The italicized words refer to other definitions in the glossary, which you can look up, if necessary. Page numbers refer to fuller explanations of important terms given in the text.

Absolute music: Music without extramusical associations; as opposed to *program music.*

A cappella: Choral music for voices alone, without instruments (*page 115*)

Accelerando: Getting faster

Accent: The stressing of a note—for example, by playing it somewhat louder than the surrounding notes (*page 5*)

Accidentals: In musical notation, signs indicating that a note is to be played *sharp, flat,* or *natural*

Acoustics: The science of sound; also, the technology of making concert halls disseminate sound well

Adagio: Slow tempo

Air, ayre: A simple song

Aleatory music: Same as *chance music*

Allegro, allegretto: Fast; moderately fast

Allemande: A baroque dance in moderately slow duple meter (*page 220*)

Alternatim setting: The practice of alternating newly composed stanzas with stanzas of Gregorian chant (*page 116*)

Alto, contralto: The low female voice

Andante: A fairly slow tempo, but not too slow

Andantino: A little faster than *andante*

Animato: Animated

Anthem: A relatively short choral composition for the Anglican or Protestant Churches (*page 143*)

Antiphony, antiphonal: A musical style in which two or more choirs and/or instrumental groups alternate with one another

Aria: A vocal number for solo singer and orchestra, generally in an opera, cantata, or oratorio (*page 166*)

Arioso: A singing style between recitative and aria (*page 176*)

Arpeggio: A chord with the notes played one after another in rapid succession, instead of simultaneously (from *arpa*, Italian for harp) (*page 302*)

Art song: A song consciously intended as a work of art; as opposed to a folksong or popular song

A tempo: At the original tempo

Atonality: The absence of any feeling of *tonality* (*page 414*)

Augmentation: The process of increasing the time values of all the notes in a theme at one of its later appearances, thus slowing it down. The most common form of augmentation doubles the time value of all the notes (*page 186*)

Avant garde: In the most advanced style

Bagatelle: "Trifle"; a name for a "miniature" piano piece, used by Beethoven and others

Ballad: A song or song-poem that tells a story, in several stanzas (*page 487*)

Ballade: A name for a "miniature" piano piece of a dramatic nature. Ballades sometimes suggest a *program* (*page 335*)

Ballad opera: Not really an opera, but a spoken play incorporating many popular and/or folk songs

Ballett: A type of Renaissance dance song, also called *fa-la* (*page 142*)

Bar: Same as *measure*

Barline: Same as measure line

Baritone: A type of adult male voice similar to the *bass,* but a little higher

Bass: (not spelled "BASE") (1) The low adult male voice; (2) the lowest vocal or instrumental line in a piece of music

Basso continuo: See *continuo* (*page 153*)

Basso ostinato: An *ostinato* in the bass

Beat: The regular pulse underlying most music; the lowest unit of *meter* (*page 6*)

Bebop: A modern jazz style of the 1940s, associated with Charlie ("Bird") Parker (*page 521*)

Bel canto: A style of singing that brings out the sensuous beauty of the voice

Bel canto opera: Term for early romantic opera (*page 355*), which featured *bel canto* singing

Binary form: A musical form having two different sections: AB form

Blue note: A note deliberately sung or played slightly off pitch, as in the *blues* (*page 513*)

Blues: A type of black folk music, used in jazz, rhythm-&-blues, and other forms of American popular music (*page 511*)

Break: In jazz, a brief solo improvisation between song phrases (*page 509*)

Bourrée: A baroque dance in fast duple meter (*page 181*)

Bridge: (1) In sonata form, the section of music which comes between the first theme and the second group, and which makes the modulation; also called "transition" (*page 257*); (2) a separable component of the violin, cello, etc., which holds the strings up from the main body of the instrument (*page 460*)

Cadence: The notes or chords (or the whole short passage) ending a section of music with a feeling of conclusiveness. The term "cadence" can be applied to phrases, sections of works, or complete works or movements (*page 22*)

Cadence theme: In sonata form, the final conclusive theme in the exposition; also called "closing theme" (*page 257*)

Cadenza: An improvised passage for the soloist in a concerto, or sometimes in other works. Concerto cadenzas usually come near the end of the first movement (*page 302*)

Canon: Strict imitative polyphony, with the identical melody appearing in each voice, but at staggered intervals (*page 118*)

Cantata: A composition in several movements for solo voice(s), instruments, and perhaps also chorus. Depending on the text, cantatas are categorized as *secular* or *church cantatas* (*pages 188, 231*)

Cantus firmus: A melody used as a basis for certain polyphonic pieces (*page 118*)

Canzona: An instrumental genre of the Renaissance

Chaconne: Similar to *passacaglia*

Chamber music: Music played by small groups, such as a string quartet or a piano trio (*page 184*)

Chance music: A type of contemporary music in which certain elements, such as the order of the notes or their pitches,

are not specified by the composer but are left to chance (*page 463*)

Chanson: French for song; a genre of French secular vocal music (*page 114*)

Chant: A way of reciting words to music, generally in *monophony* and generally for liturgical purposes, as in *Gregorian chant*

Choir: (1) A group of singers singing together, with more than one person singing each voice part; (2) a section of the orchestra comprising instruments of a certain type, such as the *string, woodwind,* or *brass choir*

Chorale: German for hymn; also used for a four-part *harmonization* of a German hymn, such as Bach composed in his Passions and many church cantatas (*page 233*)

Chorale prelude: An organ composition based on a *chorale* tune (*page 236*)

Chord: A grouping of pitches played and heard simultaneously (*page 39*)

Chorus: (1) Same as *choir*; (2) the main section of a modern popular song, as opposed to the *verse* (*page 508*)

Chromaticism: A musical style employing all or many of the twelve notes of the *chromatic scale* much of the time (*page 415*)

Chromatic scale: The set of twelve pitches represented by all the white and black notes on the piano, within one octave (*page 16*)

Church cantata: A *cantata* with religious words, often tied in directly to a particular church service, such as the Easter or Christmas service

Clef: In musical notation, a sign at the beginning of the *staff* indicating the pitches of the lines and spaces. The main clefs are the *treble clef* (𝄞) and the *bass clef* (𝄢) (*page 29*)

Closing theme: Same as *cadence theme*

Coda: The concluding section of a piece or a movement, after the main elements of the form have been presented. Codas are common in sonata form (*page 258*)

Coloratura: An ornate style of singing, with many notes for each syllable of the text

Compound meter: A meter in which the

main beats are subdivided into three, e.g., $\frac{6}{8}$ (ONE two three *four* five six), $\frac{6}{4}$, $\frac{9}{8}$, and $\frac{12}{8}$; as opposed to *simple meter* (*page 8*)

Con brio: Brilliantly, with spirit

Concertino: The solo group in a baroque *concerto grosso*

Concerto, solo concerto: A large composition for orchestra and solo instrument or small solo group (*page 298*)

Concerto grosso: The main baroque type of concerto, for a group of solo instruments and a small orchestra (*page 205*)

Concert overture: An early nineteenth-century term for a piece resembling an opera overture—but without any following opera. Often concert overtures amount to short pieces of orchestral program music

Con moto: Moving, with motion

Consonance: Intervals or chords that sound relatively stable and free of tension; as opposed to *dissonance* (*page 41*)

Continuo (basso continuo): (1) A set of chords continuously underlying the melody in a piece of baroque music; (2) the instrument(s) playing the continuo, usually cello plus harpsichord or organ (*page 153*)

Contralto, alto: The low female voice

Counterpoint, contrapuntal: (1) Polyphony; strictly speaking, the technique of writing polyphonic music; (2) the term "a counterpoint" is used for a melodic line that forms polyphony when played along with other lines; (3) "in counterpoint" means "forming polyphony" (*page 38*)

Countersubject: In a fugue, a subsidiary melodic line that appears regularly in counterpoint with the *subject* (*page 203*)

Courante: A baroque dance in moderately slow triple meter (*page 220*)

Crescendo: Getting louder

Cyclic form: A large form, such as a symphony, in which certain themes come back in various different movements (*page 333*)

Da capo: Literally, "from the beginning"; a direction to the performer to repeat music from the beginning of the piece up to a later point

Da capo aria: An aria in ABA form, i.e., one in which the A section is sung *da capo* at the end (*page 189*)

Decibel: The scientific unit of loudness

Declamation: The way words are set to music, in terms of rhythm, accent, etc. (*page 126*)

Design: A term sometimes used for the form or general plan of a piece of music

Development: (1) The process of expanding themes and motives into larger sections of music; (2) the second section of a sonata-form movement, which features the development process (*page 257*)

Diatonic scale: The set of seven pitches represented by the white notes of the piano, within one octave (*page 16*)

Dies irae: "Day of wrath": a section of the *Requiem Mass* (*page 84*)

Diminuendo: Getting softer

Diminution: The process of reducing the time values of all the notes in a theme at one of its later appearances, thus speeding it up. The most common kind of diminution halves the time values of all the notes

Discord: Sometimes used as a term for *dissonance*

Dissonance: Intervals or chords that sound relatively tense and unstable; in opposition to *consonance* (*page 41*)

Dominant: The fifth note of a diatonic scale, or the chord built on this note

Dotted note: In musical notation, a note followed by a dot has its normal duration increased by a half (*page 25*)

Dotted rhythm: A rhythm of long, dotted notes alternating with short ones (*page 25*)

Double-exposition form: A type of *sonata form* developed for use in concertos (*page 299*)

Double variation: A *variation* in which the repeated sections of the theme are varied in different ways (*page 307*)

Downbeat: A strong or accented *beat*

Duet, duo: A composition for two singers or instrumentalists

Duple meter: A meter consisting of one accented beat alternating with one unaccented beat: ONE two ONE two

Dynamics: The volume of sound, the loudness or softness of a musical passage (*page 11*)

Electronic music: Music in which some or all of the sounds are produced by electronic generators or other apparatus

Ensemble: A musical number in an opera, cantata, or oratorio that is sung by two or more people (*page 263*)

Episode: In a fugue, a passage that does not contain any complete entries of the fugue subject (*page 186*)

Espressivo: Expressively

Étude: A piece of music designed partly to aid technical study of a particular instrument (*page 330*)

Exposition: The first section of a sonata-form movement (*page 257*)

Expressionism: An early twentieth-century movement in art, music, and literature in Germany and Austria (*page 422*)

Fa-la: A type of Renaissance dance song, also called *ballett* (*page 142*)

Fantasia: (Usually) a piece of music in a free, improvisatory form

Fermata: A hold of indefinite length on a note; the sign for such a hold in musical notation

Figured bass: A system of notating the *continuo* chords in baroque music, by means of figures; sometimes also used to mean continuo

Finale: The last movement of a work; or the *ensemble* that concludes an act of an *opera buffa* or other opera (*page 267*)

Flat: In musical notation, a sign indicating that the note to which it is attached is to be played a semitone lower (♭). A double flat (♭♭) is sometimes used to indicate that a note is played two semitones lower (*page 30*)

Form: The "shape" of a piece of music (*page 48*)

Forte, fortissimo: Loud; very loud (*f, ff*)

French overture: A baroque type of overture to an opera, oratorio, or suite (*page 180*)

Frequency: In acoustics, the rate of vibration in a string, a column of air, or other sound-producing body

Fugato: A relatively short fugal passage within a piece of music

Fugue: A composition written systematically in imitative polyphony, usually with a single main theme, the *fugue subject* (*page 185*)

Functional harmony, functional tonality: From the baroque period on, the system whereby all chords have a specific interrelation and function for the total sense of centrality (*tonality*) (*page 156*)

Galliard: A lively, vigorous sixteenth-century dance (*page 144*)

Generator: An electronic apparatus that produces sounds for electronic music; also called *synthesizer*

Genre: A general category of music determined partly by the number and kind of instruments or voices involved, and partly by its form, style, or purpose. "Opera," "symphonic poem," and "sonata" are terms for genres (*page 52*)

Gigue, jig: A baroque dance in a lively compound meter; often fugal in style (*page 220*)

Glissando: Sliding from one note to another on an instrument such as a trombone or violin (*page 353*)

Grave: Slow; the characteristic tempo of the first section of a *French overture*

Gregorian chant: The type of *chant* used in the early Roman Catholic Church (*page 74*)

Ground bass: An *ostinato* in the bass (*page 163*)

Half step, half tone: The *interval* between any two successive notes of the chromatic scale; also called a *semitone*

Harmonize: To provide each note of a melody with a chord (*page 40*)

Harmony, harmonic: Having to do with chords, or the "vertical" aspect of musical texture (*page 40*). The term "harmonic" is sometimes used to mean *homophonic*

Hocket: The alternation of very short melodic phrases, or single notes, between two voices, used in late medieval polyphony (*page 101*)

Homophony, homophonic: A musical texture that involves only one melody of real interest, combined with chords or other subsidiary sounds (*page 39*)

Hymn: A simple religious song in several stanzas, for congregational singing in church (*page 76*)

Idée fixe: The term used by Berlioz for a recurring theme used in all the movements of one of his program symphonies (*page 345*)

Imitation, imitative counterpoint: A polyphonic musical texture in which the various melodic lines use approximately the same themes; as opposed to *nonimitative counterpoint* (*page 38*). See also *point of imitation*

Impressionism: A French artistic movement of the late nineteenth and early twentieth centuries (*page 416*)

Impromptu: A name for a "miniature" piano piece, of an improvisatory nature

Interval: The distance between two pitches, measured by the number of diatonic scale notes between them (*page 17*)

Introduction An introductory passage: the "slow introduction" before the exposition in a symphony, etc.; in an opera, the first number after the overture

Inversion: Reading or playing a melody or a twelve-tone series upside down, i.e., playing all its upward intervals downward and vice versa (*page 210*)

Isorhythm: In fourteenth-century music, the technique of repeating the identical rhythm for each section of a composition, while the pitches are altered (*page 99*)

Jazz: The most important type of twentieth-century popular music (*page 505*)

Jongleur: A medieval secular musician (*page 93*)

K. numbers: The numbers assigned to works by Mozart in the Koechel Catalogue; used instead of opus numbers to catalogue Mozart's works

Key: (1) A tonality, named after the main note in the tonality; (2) a lever pressed down with the finger to produce the sound on the piano, organ, etc. (*page 47*)

Key signature: Sharps or flats placed at the beginning of the staffs to indicate the key, or tonality

Largo, larghetto: Very slow; somewhat less slow than largo

Ledger lines: Short lines above or below the staff to accommodate pitches that go higher or lower

Legato: Playing in a smooth, connected manner; as opposed to *staccato*

Leitmotiv: "Leading motive" in Wagner's operas (*page 364*)

Lento: Very slow

Libretto: The complete book of words for an opera, oratorio, cantata, etc. (*page 224*)

Lied: German for song; often used as a term for *art song* (*page 314*)

Line: Used as a term to mean a melody, or melodic line

Madrigal: The main secular vocal form of the Renaissance (*page 136*)

Magnificat: The canticle of the Virgin Mary, often set to music for church use

Major mode: One of the modes of the diatonic scale, characterized by the interval between the first and third notes containing four semitones; as opposed to *minor mode* (*page 44*)

Manual: A keyboard of an organ or harpsichord, usually one of two or more on a single instrument

Mass: The main Roman Catholic service; or the music written for it. The musical Mass consists of five large sections: Kyrie, Gloria, Credo, Sanctus, and Agnus Dei (*page 118*)

Mazurka: A Polish dance in lively triple meter (*page 335*)

Measure (bar): In music, the unit of *meter*, above the level of the individual *beats.* Compositions are formed of equal time divisions, called measures, made up of several beats (*page 7*)

Measure line (barline): In musical notation, a vertical line through the staff(s) to mark the measure (*page 7*)

Melisma: A group of notes, either few in number or very extensive, sung to a single syllable (*page 80*)

Melody: The aspect of music having to do with the succession of pitches; also

applied ("a melody") to any particular succession of pitches (*page 20*)

Meter: A background of stressed and unstressed beats in a simple, regular, repeating pattern (*page 7*)

Metronome: The mechanical or electrical device that ticks out beats at all practicable tempos (*page 9*)

Metronome mark: A notation of tempo, indicating the number of notes per minute as ticked out by a metronome (*page 9*)

Mezzo: Medium (as in *mezzo forte* or *mezzo piano*—**mf, mp**)

Mezzo-soprano: "Halfway to soprano": a type of female voice between *contralto* and *soprano*

"Miniature": A term for a short, evocative composition for piano or for piano and voice, composed in the Romantic period (*page 332*)

Minor mode: One of the modes of the diatonic scale, characterized by the interval between the first and third notes containing three semitones; as opposed to *major* (*page 44*)

Minstrel show: A type of variety show popular in nineteenth-century America, performed in blackface (*page 497*)

Minuet: A popular seventeenth- and eighteenth-century dance in moderate triple meter (*page 179*); also a movement in a sonata, symphony, etc., based on this dance (*page 276*)

Modal harmony: The characteristically indefinite harmonic style of sixteenth-century music

Mode, modality: In music since the Renaissance, one of the two types of tonality: major mode or minor mode; also, in earlier times, one of several species of the diatonic scale (*page 44*)

Moderato: Moderate tempo

Modulation: Changing tonality within a piece (*page 47*)

Monophony: A musical texture involving a single melodic line and nothing else, as in Gregorian chant; as opposed to *polyphony* (*page 38*)

Motet: A sacred vocal composition (*page 115*)

Motive, motif: A short fragment of melody or rhythm used in constructing a long section of music (*page 22*)

Movement: A self-contained section of a larger piece, such as a symphony or concerto grosso (*page 184*)

Music-drama: Wagner's name for his distinctive type of opera (*page 364*)

Musicology: The scholarly study of music history and literature

Musique concrète: Music composed with natural sounds recorded electronically (*page 461*)

Mute: A device put on or in an instrument to muffle the tone

Nationalism: A nineteenth-century movement promoting music built on national folksongs and dances, or associated with national subjects (*page 385*)

Natural: In musical notation, a sign indicating that a sharp or flat previously attached to a note is to be removed (♮) (*page 31*)

Neoclassicism: A twentieth-century movement involving a return to the style and form of older music, particularly eighteenth-century music (*page 408*)

Nocturne: "Night piece": title for romantic "miniature" compositions for piano, etc.

Nonimitative polyphony, counterpoint: A polyphonic musical texture in which the melodic lines are essentially different from one another; as opposed to *imitation* (*page 38*)

Non troppo: Not too much (as in *allegro non troppo*, not too fast)

Note: (1) A sound of a certain definite pitch and duration; (2) the written sign for such a sound in musical notation; (3) a key pressed with the finger on a piano or organ

Octave: A pair of "duplicating" notes, eight notes apart on the diatonic scale (*page 13*)

Office services: The eight daily services, other than Mass, specified by the Roman Catholic Church (*page 71*)

Opera: A play set to music (*page 165*)

Opera buffa: Italian comic opera (*page 263*)

Opera seria: A term for the serious, heroic opera of the baroque period (*page 263*)

Operetta: A nineteenth-century type of light (often comic) opera, employing spoken dialogue in between musical numbers (*page 496*)

Opus: "Work"; opus numbers provide a means of cataloguing a composer's compositions (*see note on page 211*)

Oratorio: Long semi-dramatic piece on a religious subject for soloists, chorus, and orchestra (*page 228*)

Orchestration: The technique of writing for various instruments to produce an effective total orchestral sound

Ordinary of the Mass: The parts of the Mass that remain the same every day (*page 78*)

Organum: The earliest genre of medieval polyphonic music (*page 90*)

Ostinato: A motive, phrase, or theme repeated over and over again at the same pitch level (*page 163*)

Overtone: In acoustics, a secondary vibration in a sound-producing body, which contributes to the tone color; also called "partial" (*page 15*)

Overture: An orchestral piece at the start of an opera, oratorio, etc. (but see *concert overture*) (*page 180*)

Paraphrase: The modification and decoration of plainchant melodies in early Renaissance music (*page 111*)

Part: Used as a term for (1) a section of a piece; (2) one of the *voices* in contrapuntal music; (3) the written music for a single player in an orchestra, band, etc. (as opposed to the *score*)

Partial: Same as *overtone*

Passacaglia: A set of variations on a short theme in the bass (*page 201*)

Passion: A long, oratorio-like composition telling the story of Jesus's last days, according to one of the New Testament Gospels (*page 237*)

Pavane: A slow sixteenth-century court dance (*page 144*)

Pedal board: The keyboard of an organ that is played with the feet

Pedal point: In contrapuntal writing, a bass note held for a long time

Phrase: A section of a melody or a tune (*page 21*)

Piano, pianissimo: Soft; very soft (*p*, *pp*)

Piano trio: An instrumental group consisting of violin, cello, and piano; or a piece composed for this group; or the three players themselves (*page 280*)

Pitch: The quality of "highness" or "lowness" of sound; also applied ("a pitch") to any particular pitch level, such as middle C (*page 12*)

Più: More (as in *più forte*, louder)

Pizzicato: Playing a string instrument that is normally bowed by plucking the strings with the finger (*page 297*)

Plainsong: Liturgical *chant*, such as Gregorian chant (*page 74*)

Poco: Somewhat (as in *poco adagio* or *poco forte*, somewhat slow, somewhat loud)

Point of imitation: A short passage of imitative polyphony based on a single theme, or on two used together (*page 131*)

Polonaise: A Polish dance

Polyphony, polyphonic: Musical texture in which two or more melodic lines are played or sung simultaneously; as opposed to *homophony* or *monophony* (*page 38*)

Prelude: An introductory piece, leading to another, such as a fugue or an opera (however, Chopin's Preludes were not intended to lead to anything else)

Première: The first performance ever of a piece of music, opera, etc.

Presto, prestissimo: Very fast; very fast indeed

Program music: A piece of instrumental music associated with a story or other extra-musical idea (*page 333*)

Program symphony: A symphony with a program, as written by Berlioz (*page 345*)

Proper of the Mass: The parts of the Mass that vary from day to day, according to the season of the Church year (*page 78*)

Quarter tone: Half of a *semitone*. Quarter tones are occasionally used in twentieth-century music

Quartet: A piece for four singers or players; often used to mean *string quartet*

Quintet: A piece for five singers or players

Ragtime: A genre of American popular music around 1900, usually for piano, which led to *jazz* (*page 513*)

Range: Used in music to mean "pitch range," i.e., the total span from the lowest to the highest pitch in a piece, a part, or a passage

Recapitulation: The third section of a sonata-form movement (*page 257*)

Reciting formula: In Gregorian chant, a simple set of notes to which many different texts (such as psalms) can be chanted (*page 79*)

Recitative: A half-singing, half-reciting style of presenting words in opera, cantata, oratorio, etc., following speech accents and speech rhythms closely (*page 166*)

Reed: In certain wind instruments (oboe, clarinet), a small vibrating element made of cane or metal

Requiem Mass, Requiem: The special *Mass* celebrated when someone dies

Resolve: To proceed from *dissonant* harmony to *consonance*

Responsorial chant: A type of Gregorian chant in which soloists sing in alternation with the choir (*page 80*)

Rest: A momentary silence in music; in musical notation, a sign indicating momentary silence

Retransition: In sonata form, the passage leading from the end of the development section into the beginning of the recapitulation (*page 257*)

Retrograde: Reading or playing a melody or twelve-tone series backward and upside down

Rhythm: The aspect of music having to do with the duration of the notes in time; also applied ("a rhythm") to any particular durational pattern (*page 5*)

Rhythm-&-blues: A genre of black American popular music of the 1950s

Rhythmic series, rhythmic serialization: A fixed pattern of different note lengths held to throughout a piece; the technique

of composing with such a series (*page 463*)

Rhythm section: The section of a jazz band concerned mainly with bringing out the meter, or the beat: the drums, piano, string bass, guitar, etc.

Ricercar: An instrumental genre of the Renaissance

Ritardando: Slowing down the tempo

Ritenuto: Held back in tempo

Ritornello: The orchestral material at the beginning of a concerto grosso, etc., which always returns later in the piece (*page 206*)

Ritornello form: A baroque musical form based on recurrences of a *ritornello* (*page 206*)

Rondeau: A baroque form based on the regular return of a main theme; ancestor of the *rondo* (*page 181*)

Rondo: A musical form consisting of one main theme or tune alternating with other themes or sections (ABACA, ABACABA, etc.) (*page 277*)

Round: A simple type of sung *canon*, with all voices entering on the same note after the same time interval (*page 38*)

Row: Same as *series*

Rubato: "Robbed" time; the free treatment of meter in performance (*page 331*)

Sarabande: A baroque dance in slow triple meter, featuring an accent on the second beat (*page 220*)

Scale: A selection of ordered pitches which provides the pitch material for music (*page 13*)

Scherzo: A form developed by Beethoven from the *minuet* to use for movements in larger compositions; later sometimes used alone, as by Chopin (*page 297*)

Score: The full musical notation for a piece involving several or many performers (*page 32*)

Second group: In sonata form, the group of themes following the *bridge*, in the second key (*page 257*)

Semitone: Same as *half tone*

Sequence: In a melody, a series of fragments identical except for their placement at successively higher or lower pitch levels (*page 21*)

Serialism, serial: The technique of composing with a *series*, generally a twelve-tone series (but see also *rhythmic serialism*) (*page 436*)

Series: A fixed arrangement of pitches (or rhythms) held to throughout a serial composition (*page 437*)

Sforzato: An especially strong accent; the mark indicating this in musical notation (*sf* or >)

Sharp: In musical notation, a sign indicating that the note which it precedes is to be played a semitone higher (♯). A double sharp (x) is occasionally used to indicate that a note is played two semitones higher (*page 30*)

Simple meter: A meter in which the main beats are subdivided into two, such as $\frac{4}{4}$ (ONE two three four), and $\frac{4}{8}$; as opposed to *compound meter*

Singspiel: German for "singing play": a German comic opera with spoken dialogue interspersed with songs and other music

Slur: In musical notation, a curved line over a certain number of notes, indicating that they are to be played smoothly, or *legato* (*page 25*)

Sonata: A chamber-music piece in several movements, typically for three main instruments plus continuo in the baroque period, and for only one or two instruments in all periods since then (*pages 184, 304*)

Sonata form, sonata-allegro form: A form developed by the Viennese composers and used in almost all the first movements of their symphonies, sonatas, etc., as well as in some other movements (*page 256*)

Sonata-rondo form: A form combining elements of sonata form and rondo

Song cycle: A group of songs connected by a general idea or story, and sometimes also by musical unifying devices (*page 317*)

Sonority: A general term for sound quality, either of a momentary chord, or of a whole piece or style

Soprano: The high female (or boy's) voice

Sprechstimme: A vocal style developed by Schoenberg, in between singing and speaking (*page 409*)

Staccato: Played in a detached manner; as opposed to *legato*

Staff (or stave): In musical notation, the group of five horizontal lines on which music is written (*page 28*)

Stanza: In songs or ballads, one of several similar poetic units, which are usually sung to the same tune; also called *verse*

Stretto: In a fugue, overlapping entrances of the fugue subject in several voices simultaneously (*page 186*)

String quartet: An instrumental group consisting of two violins, viola, and cello; or a piece composed for this group; or the four players themselves (*page 280*)

Strophic form, strophic song: A song in several *stanzas*, with the same music sung for each stanza; as opposed to *through-composed song* (*page 314*)

Structure: A term often used to mean *form*

Sturm und Drang ("Storm and Stress"): A literary and artistic movement of the late eighteenth century (*page 291*)

Style: The combination of qualities that make a period of art, a composer, or an individual work of art distinctive (*page 53*)

Subdominant: The fourth note of a diatonic scale, or the chord built on this note

Subito: Suddenly (as in *subito forte* or *subito piano,* suddenly loud, suddenly soft)

Subject: The term for the principal theme of a *fugue* (*page 185*)

Suite: A piece consisting of a series of dances (*page 179*)

Swing: A type of big-band jazz of the late 1930s and 1940s (*page 516*)

Symphonic poem: A piece of orchestral program music in one long movement (*page 350*)

Symphony: A large orchestral piece in several movements (*page 271*)

Syncopation: The accenting of certain beats of the meter that are ordinarily unaccented (*page 8*)

Synthesizer: An electronic apparatus that generates sounds for electronic music; also called *generator*

Tempo: The speed of music, i.e., the rate at which the accented and unaccented beats of the meter follow one another (*page 9*)

Tenor: The high adult male voice

Tenor construction, tenor mass: In early Renaissance polyphony, a form based on the singing of a (usually slow) cantus firmus by one voice (usually the tenor) (*page 118*)

Ternary form: A three-part musical form in which the last section repeats the first: ABA form

Terraced dynamics: Two or more fixed, steady dynamic levels alternating during a piece of (baroque) music (*page 159*)

Texture: The blend of the various sounds and melodic lines occurring simultaneously in a piece of music (*page 37*)

Thematic transformation: A variation-like procedure applied to short themes in the various sections of Romantic symphonic poems and other works (*page 333*)

Theme: The basic subject matter of a piece of music. A theme can be a phrase, a short motive, a full tune, etc. (*page 23*)

Theme and variations: A form consisting of a tune (the theme) plus a number of *variations* on it (*pages 201, 283*)

Thorough bass: Same as *basso continuo* or *continuo*

Through-composed (*durchkomponiert*) song: A song with new music for each stanza of the poem; as opposed to *strophic song* (*page 314*)

Tie: In musical notation, a curved line joining two notes of the same pitch into a continuous sound (*page 25*)

Timbre: Another term for *tone color*

Time signature: In musical notation, the numbers on the staffs at the beginning of a piece which indicate the meter (*page 28*)

Toccata: A piece in free form designed partly to show off the instrument and the technique of the player (usually an organist or harpsichordist)

Tonality, tonal: The feeling of centrality of one note (and its chord) to a passage of music; as opposed to *atonality* (*page 43*)

Tone: A sound of a certain definite pitch and duration; same as *note* (1)

Tone color: The sonorous quality of a particular instrument, voice, or combination of instruments or voices (*page 11*)

Tone poem: Same as *symphonic poem*

Tonic (noun): In *tonal* music, the central-sounding note (*page 43*)

Transition: A passage whose function is to connect one section of a piece with another

Transpose: To move a whole piece, or a section of a piece, or a twelve-tone series, from one pitch level to another

Triad: The "common chord" of three notes, none of them adjacent in terms of the diatonic scale

Trill: Two adjacent notes played very rapidly in alternation

Trio: (1) A piece for three instruments or singers; (2) the second or B section of a minuet movement, scherzo, etc. (*pages 180, 276*)

Trio sonata: A baroque sonata for three main instruments plus the continuo chord instrument (*page 184*)

Triple meter: Meter consisting of one accented beat alternating with two unaccented beats: ONE two three ONE two three

Triplet: A group of three notes performed in the time normally taken by two (*page 25*)

Tritone: The *interval* consisting of six half steps

Trope: A short or extended segment of text added to or inserted into a Gregorian chant and set to music (*page 81*)

Troubadours, trouvères: Aristocratic poet-musicians of the middle ages (*page 93*)

Tune: A simple, easily singable melody that is coherent and complete (*page 20*)

Twelve-tone series: An ordering of all twelve notes of the chromatic scale, used in composing serial music (*page 437*)

Upbeat: A weak or unaccented beat leading to a *downbeat* (*page 179*)

Vamp: An accompaniment figure, usually improvised in popular music, preceding the first appearance of the theme (*page 279*)

Variation: A section of music which follows another section (the "theme") closely in certain respects—e.g., in phrase length and harmony—while varying other aspects of it (*page 201*)

Verismo: A realistic and sensational type of late Romantic Italian opera

Verse: (1) Another term for *stanza;* (2) the shorter, subsidiary section of a modern popular song, as opposed to the *chorus* (*page 508*)

Vivace, vivo: Lively

Vocalise: Singing without words (*page 421*)

Voice: (1) Throat sound; (2) a contrapuntal line—whether sung or played by instruments—in a polyphonic piece such as a fugue

Walking bass: In baroque music, a bass part that moves steadily in the same note values (*page 152*)

Waltz: A nineteenth-century dance in triple meter (*page 499*)

White noise: The sound containing every audible frequency at the same intensity (*page 461*)

Whole step, whole tone: The interval equal to two half tones (semitones) (*page 18*)

Whole-tone scale: A scale, used sometimes by Debussy, comprising only six notes to the octave, all at the interval of the whole tone (i.e., two semitones)

Word painting: Musical illustration of the meaning of a word or a short verbal phrase (*page 127*)

Illustration Acknowledgments

Page 2 Michael C. Hayman, Photo Researchers

Page 14 Gaffurio, *Theorica Musices,* Milan, 1492: Music Division, The New York Public Library at Lincoln Center; Astor, Lenox, and Tilden Foundations

Page 26 Gregorian Agnus Dei XI: MS Add. 3027E, fol. 212r, Cambridge University Library

Page 36 Llewellyn, Freelance Photographer's Guild

Page 45 Brian Brake, Rapho/Photo Researchers

Page 55 Photo Researchers

Page 57 United Nations Photo by Louis Falquet

Page 58 Loren McIntyre, Woodfin Camp

Page 59 Carl Frank, Photo Researchers

Page 60 Left: Thomas D. W. Friedmann, Photo Researchers; right: Marc and Evelyne Bernheim, Woodfin Camp

Page 61 Left: The Metropolitan Museum of Art, The Crosby Brown Collection of Musical Instruments, 1889; right: Marc and Evelyne Bernheim, Woodfin Camp

Pages 64,65 Violin, viola, cello, bass, and clarinet: Norlin Music, Inc. Trumpet, trombone, bass clarinet, french horn, tuba, oboe, and bassoon: Selmer Company, Elkhart, Indiana. English horn and contrabassoon: Susan E. Meyer. Piccolo and flute: W. T. Armstrong, division of Chicago Musical Instrument Company. Timpani and triangle: Ludwig Industries. Cymbal: copyright G. D. Hackett

Page 68 Kul Bhatia, Freelance Photographer's Guild

Page 72 From Walter Horn and Ernest Born, *The Plan of St. Gall,* University of California Press

Page 73 Stiftsbibliothek, St. Gallen

Page 82 Inge Morath, Magnum

Page 83 Yan, Rapho/Photo Researchers

Page 86 © Laura Pettibone

Page 88 St. Louis Post Dispatch/Black Star

Pages 94, 95 Universitätsbibliothek, Heidelberg

Page 98 Courtesy The Bancroft Library

Page 103 Stefan Lochner, *The Virgin in the Rose-bower,* Wallraf-Richartz-Museum, Cologne

Page 106 Fred Lyon, Rapho/Photo Researchers

Page 109 Luca della Robbia, Cantoria, 1431–1438, choirboys and drummers: Museo dell' Opera del Duomo, Florence, photographs Alinari/Editorial Photocolor Archives. Pashley Sarcophagus: reproduced by permission of the Syndics of the Fitzwilliam Museum, Cambridge

Page 122 Sibley Music Library, Eastman School of Music

Page 124 Bruce Tillinghast

Pages 128, 129 Raphael, 1483–1520, *Madonna of the Meadow:* Kunsthistorisches Museum, Vienna, photograph Peter Adelberg, New York; *Canigiani Holy Family:* Alte Pinakothek, Munich

Page 134 Cod. 18.744 der Musiksammlung der Österreichischen Nationalbibliothek, Vienna

Page 135 The Granger Collection

Page 140 By permission of Viscount De L'Isle, VC, KG, from his collection at Penshurst Place, Kent, England, photograph National Portrait Gallery, London

Page 148 Costa Manos, Magnum

Pages 154, 155 F. Berthoud, *Traité des horloges marines,* 1773

Page 161 Jerry Cooke, Photo Researchers

Page 168 Biblioteca Nazionale Centrale, Florence

Page 182 Kit harpsichord: Zuckerman Harpsichords, Inc.

Page 192 Copyright © Beth Bergman

Page 199 From Walter Haacke, *Orgeln in aller Welt,* Langewiesche-Köster (Verlag), Königstein im Taunus

Pages 208, 209 Nymphenburg: Dr. Max Hirmer, Hirmer Fotoarchiv; engraving by Mathias Diesel, 1722: from Luisa Hager, *Nymphenburg,* Hirmer Verlag, Munich

Page 217 Thomas Rowlandson, 1756–1827, *Old Vauxhall Gardens:* Victoria and Albert Museum, London

Pages 222, 223 Padre Andrea dal Pozzo, ceiling of the Church of Sant' Ignazio, Rome, 1685: SCALA/Editorial Photocolor Archives

Page 232 Private Collection

Page 244 Costa Manos, Magnum

Pages 252, 253 Jean-Antoine Houdon, statue of Voltaire, 1781, detail: photograph © H. H. Arnason, by permission of the Comédie Française; bust of Rousseau: photograph © H. H. Arnason, collection of Edmond Courty

Pages 268, 269 *An Opera Production at the Esterházy Castle* (artist unknown), 1775: Theatermuseum, Munich

Pages 274, 275 Stourhead Gardens: Edwin Smith; engraving by F. M. Piper, 1779: Reproduced by permission of the Trustees of The British Museum

Pages 286, 287 Jean-Antoine Houdon, bust of Benjamin Franklin, ca. 1786: photograph © H. H. Arnason, Boston Athenaeum; bust of Mme de Sérilly, 1782: photograph © H. H. Arnason, reproduced by permission of the Trustees of the Wallace Collection

Page 290 © 1979 Tom Copi

Pages 300, 301 *The Massacre in King Street, Boston, March 5, 1770,* engraving by Paul Revere: American Antiquarian Society; Francisco Goya, *The Third of May, 1808:* Museo del Prado, Madrid

Page 310 MS Mh 60: Beethovenhaus, Bonn

Page 316 Moritz von Schwind, *A Schubert Evening at Joseph R. von Spaun's:* Historiches Museum der Stadt Wien, Vienna

Page 320 Georges de La Tour, *The Hurdy-Gurdy Player:* Musée des Beaux-Arts, Nantes, Photographie Giraudon

Page 324 Jan Lukas, Rapho/Photo Researchers

Page 328 Gustave Doré, *King Arthur Looking at the Corpses of Two Brothers,* 1882: from Konrad Farner, *Gustave Doré,* Veb Verlag der Kunst, Dresden

Pages 338, 339 Eugène Delacroix, *Chopin,* 1857: Musée du Louvre, J. E. Bulloz; *Portrait of George Sand,* 1842: The Ordrupgaard Collection, Copenhagen

Page 344 J. H. Fuseli, *The Nightmare,* 1781: The Detroit Institute of Arts, gift of Mr. and Mrs. Bert L. Smokler and Mr. and Mrs. Lawrence A. Fleischman

Page 351 Josef Danhauser, *Franz Liszt and His Friends:* The Bettmann Archive

Page 360 Bruce Roberts, Rapho/Photo Researchers

Pages 362, 363 Neuschwanstein: photograph by Pierre Strinati, from *Les Châteaux Magiques de Louis II,* Editions Clarifontaine et Guilde du Livre, Lausanne; Festival Theater, Bayreuth: © Wilhelm Rauh

Page 368 "Field Marshal Berlioz": from Marc Pincherle, *An Illustrated History of Music,* Macmillan, New York (originally published in *Journal pour rire,* 1850)

Page 381 The Bettmann Archive

Page 389 Victor Hartmann, *The Great Gate of Kiev:* courtesy of Alfred Frankenstein

Page 396 Bill Brandt, *Halifax:* Rapho/Photo Researchers

Page 406 Eric Kroll, Taurus Photos

Page 411 Paul Klee, *Drawing with Fermata,* 1918: Paul Klee Foundation, Berner Kunstmuseum, Berne

Page 418 Auguste Renoir, *Nude Bather Standing,* 1888: private collection

Page 424 Claude Monet, *Field of Poppies,* 1873; Musée du Louvre, Service de Documentation Photographique de la Réunion des Musées Nationaux

Page 425 Vincent Van Gogh, *The Evening Walk,* 1889: Museu de Arte, São Paulo, Photographie Giraudon

Page 432 Jan Lenica, poster for *Wozzeck:* from *Quality,* edited by Louis Kronenburger, Atheneum, New York, 1969.

Page 456 Charles Moore, Black Star

Page 459 Burk Uzzle, Magnum

Page 464 Top: Mini Moog Synthesizer, Moog Music, Inc.; bottom: RCA Synthesizer, Columbia-Princeton Electronic Music Center, New York

Page 484 © 1977 Beryl Goldberg

Page 489 Harley MS 3885, fol. 19: Reproduced by permission of the British Library

Page 492 The Bettmann Archive

Page 497 Harvard Theatre Collection

Page 502 Tom Ebenhoh, Black Star

Page 506 Brown Brothers

Page 507 The Bettmann Archive

Page 517 Chester Higgins, Jr., Photo Researchers

Page 522 Joachim E. Berendt's Archives

Page 526 Doug Bruce, Camera 5

Page 527 © 1979 Tom Copi

Music Acknowledgments

Index